Following the Fairways

1987

Best wishes to John

Keith Williams

Ian MacDonald

KENSINGTON WEST PRODUCTIONS
LONDON
ENGLAND

Johnnie Ball. Champion

FOREWORD

During my lifetime I have seen a remarkable growth in the popularity of golf. This has inevitably led to a great increase in the number of golf courses. Personally I have been lucky enough to play on many courses, old and new, links by the sea, heathland and park courses inland. Like many golfers I have very happy memories of these visits and indeed of the hotels closely associated with the courses. Following the Fairways 1987 will remind me of them. I still share also the enjoyment of those who look forward to playing on a course for the first time. Again this book will inspire us all to such new visits and the map of golf courses will be especially valuable. Lastly, I have a non-golfing wife who has stoically borne her role as a golf widow for over 40 years. I welcome Fairways' suggestion of suitable visits for her.

For all these reasons I welcome the publication of Following the Fairways 1987 and wish it every success.

**The Rt. Hon. Viscount Whitelaw, C.H., M.C.
HOUSE OF LORDS**

ACKNOWLEDGEMENTS

It is with great pride that I come to acknowledge the many people who have helped in the compilation of this the first edition of 'Following the Fairways'. Pride because I could not possibly have hoped to have produced this book without the help of some of my very closest friends. While this may sound something akin to a cottage industry, this in a nutshell is what we are, whether the acorn will grow into the oak tree only time itself will tell. One thing that is certian is that if any acorns do grow it will be due entirely to the dedication, enthusiasm and kindness of some splendid people. From Jilly my Personal Assistant to Hil who always mangages to lift me at the right time. My Bank Manager – who adores his golf and also understands small businesses, I hope you enjoyed the Open. Other crucial people include the company's financial backers without whom the book or even bank manager could not have been possible. I hope this book sells well for your sake, but thanks for having the faith anyway. To produce this book takes a lot of help so to the people who wrote articles I offer sincere thanks and wish you well in 1987 on and off the golf course. Viscount Whitelaw – may I offer sincere thanks to you for writing such a pleasant foreword. I certainly wish you fortune in 1987 and especially to the Conservative Party if there is an election. There is little doubt, in my opinion that a small business in Britain is better off under Laissez Faire government. The actual production of this book is quite a palava – many thanks are therefore extended to people who hit almost impossible deadlines. From the map boys Dave and Ray to the typesetters Colin and Andy (the world's worst joke teller) amongst others. To our repro house and their representatives Peter, Jeremy and Michael – a really excellent job. Pages need to be made up and many thanks to Sharon for her help here. We thank I.M.G. for reproducing colour pages 104, 112, 136 and 236 and in advance I thank our printers, Wheatons I hope this isn't tempting fate too much!

Perhaps the people who deserve the most sympathy are the many typists who assisted so valliantly, Sue, Angie, Helen, Cath, Sarah and Maggie (special thanks to Maggie for being the most splendid temp one could possibly imagine) and also to Tim for his invaluable editing services. It goes without saying that the editor of this book has done an excellent job – not only a delight to work with, but a tremendous golfer – so he tells me. I wish him and his fiancee who has supported him so superbly an excellent 1987.

Finally, I would like to thank three other splendid females. M.A., S.H. and A.B. without whose support I might have given up a long time ago. Oh and one last thought, my thanks to you for buying this book. Without you the whole company would be in the rough. May I take this opportunity of wishing you some splendid golf while you are Following the Fairways.

4U

Published by:
Kensington West Productions
4 Comeragh Road, London W14 9HP

Edited by:
Nick Edmund

Printed and Bound in Great Britain by:
A. Wheaton and Co. Ltd. Exeter

Colour Reproduction by:
Savage Print and Production Services
Wells House, 77-79 Wells Street, London W1.

and

Columbia Offsett (U.K.) Ltd.
43 Lower Belgrave Street, London SW1.

Typesetting by:
Consort Art Graphics Ltd.
34-37 Bartholomew Close, London EC1.

Maps by:
Surtec Draughting Services
59 Kingston Avenue, Bedfont, Middlesex.

Formal Bits

Gleneagles Hotel

Auchterarder, Perthshire PH3 1NF Tel: 07646 2231. Telex: 76105

one of The Leading Hotels of the World

CONTENTS

CONTENTS
(continued)

Following the Fairway

Following the Fairways

* Royal Dornoch

* Nairn
Highland
Tulchan Lodge
Grampian
* Cruden Bay
* Royal Aberdeen
Raemoir House

* Montrose

Tayside & Central
Blairgowrie
Balcraig House
Gleneagles
Gleneagles
Cromlix House
* Carnoustie
* St. Andrews
Crail
Fife
Muirfield
Greywalls
* Dunbar

Lothian

Strathclyde
Chapeltown House
* Bamburgh Castle

Royal Troon
Prestwick
The Turnberry
Turnberry

Linden Hall

Dumfries & Galloway
& Borders

Durham,
Cleveland,
Tyne & Wear
&
Northumberland

Knockinaam Lodge

Silloth -On-
Solway
Cumbria
Michael's Nook

Jervaulx Hall
* Ganton

North Yorkshire
Middlethorpe Hall
* Fulford

Ireland

Kildwick Hall
Royal Lytham
and St. Annes
Lancashire
Moortown
Shaw Hill

Royal Birkdale

South & West
Yorkshire

Lincolnshire

Royal Liverpool
Bodysgallen Hall
Mere
Manchester
Grosvenor
Rookery Hall

Cheshire
& Gtr

& Humberside

Nottinghamshire
& Derbyshire
Riber Hall
* Woodhall Spa
* Sheringham

Gwynedd & Clwyd
Nefyn
Pale Hall
Royal
St. Davids
Hawkstone
Park
Warwicks,
Hereford
&
Worcs
Staffs
& West
Midlands
The Belfry
Northants &
Leics
The George
Congham Hall

Cambridgeshire, Suffolk
& Norfolk

1 The Berkshire
2 Sunningdale
3 Wentworth
4 Walton Heath
a Oakley Court
b Great Fosters

The Feathers
Grafton
& Manor
Shropshire
Ettington Park
Hambleton Hall
The Angel
Seckford Hall

Dyfed & Powys

Lygon Arms

Gliffaes

The
Greenway
Calcot Manor
Woburn *
Herts, Beds & Essex
Whitehall
Maison Talbooth

The Glamorgans
& Gwent
St. Pierre

Gloucestershire
Bucks & Oxon
Huntercombe
a
b
Greater
London

Moor Park

Royal Porthcawl
Ston Easton Park
Dorset
&
Wiltshire
Berkshire
1
2 3
4
Surrey
Royal St. Georges
Royal Cinque Ports

Burnham and Berrow
Saunton
Royal North Devon
Somerset & Avon
Chedington Court
Combe House
Gidleigh Park
Manor House
Hampshire
& the
Channel
Islands
Lainston House
Gravetye Manor
Liphook
East & West Sussex
Ferndown
Plumber Manor
Chewton Glen
West Sussex
Thakenham
Baillifscourt
Horsted Place
Kennel Holt
Eastwell Manor
Kent
Royal Ashdown Forest

Devon

Trevose
Treglos
Cornwall
Carlyon Bay
Carlyon Bay

Isle of
Purbeck

The maps and plans printed in
this publication have been designed
and produced by

Surtec Draughting Services

For further information about this
company and its services please
contact 59 Kingston Avenue,
Bedfont, Middlesex. Tel: 01-890 0326

GOLF GLORIOUS GOLF

Golf, glorious golf, a name for guile, greatness and graciousness among many other qualities. What other game so captures the total dedication of such a massive number of people? Well many may say several do, but let's think about it. It's we golfers who are the real gluttons we just can't get enough of it. It is for this reason and one other that we decided to produce 'Following the Fairways'. It helps if there are people who have a disposable income and what's more are well known for disposing of it, but it's also rather handy if those people enjoy a joke, play hard, work hard and when all is said and done have a splendid enthusiasm for the joie de golf. The pages and what they endeavour to include reflect your enthusiasm, but may not achieve your greatness. They endeavour to tickle your good humour and improve what we are sure you so enjoy, the habit of 'Following the Fairways'.

KENSINGTON WEST PRODUCTIONS

'Following the Fairways' is the second title to be produced by a small but flourishing British publishing house. The book's predecessor 'Travelling the Turf' sets the scene for horseracing enthusiasts and their less besotted friends 'Following the Fairways' endeavours to do the same for golfers and their less willing companions. The reason we selected golf was firstly, we found a title we liked, secondly we snared an editor to our taste, thirdly we were absolutely sick to death of people telling us to produce "a quality guide to golfcourses". This is the end product please do let us know your thoughts good and bad alike.

THE OPENING STROKES

The opening pen strokes are those of Viscount Whitelaw to whom we are most grateful. Our endeavours to cater for the 'golfing widow' were upper most in our minds and we very much hope that Lady Whitelaw enjoys Following the Fairways 1987 as much as her husband. The basic pattern of the book is to emphasise the golfing year, golfcourses in the country and some places of special appeal nearby. The following appraisal may serve as a guide to our completed issue.

A YEAR'S GOLF

Golf courses and sponsors are not exactly brilliant at finalising their arrangements and so the Year Planner is not as complete as it might otherwise be. However, we've done fairly well tracking down some of the various events that occur within the golfing year and we hope that this may be of some use to you. It had better be, it took a fair few phone calls!

A GOURMET'S GOLF

In order to dissect the country as well as possible we have split up the land into 36 areas, a handy two rounds. 35 are spread through Britain and Ireland acts as our eighteenth on the second circuit, what a splendid finishing hole to be sure. While catering is often excellent in the Clubhouses themselves, it may be that people will wish to try some of the simply splendid cuisine offered in restaurants nearby– especially if you are on a golfing tour or have some private business to discuss that can't be wound up on the isolated 7th green. We appreciate that a golfcourse like any other establishment has to make ends meet. We are therefore extremely grateful to them for courteously suggesting alternatives to their own menus. Indeed, at this time we offer our sincere thanks to the many Secretaries who helped us in our compilation, we wish you an excellent 1987 and naturally those who were unable to help we offer you our very best wishes for the forthcoming year. Our suggestions for alternative recreations are not as full as they might be largely because we believe that many golfers will be contented with their golf alone. If you do feel that there are restaurants, hotels, public houses or places of interest that should be noted please feel free to let us know – your assistance we feel sure will be invaluable in our updating and improvement.

Please note that we realise we have missed off some superb establishments, but this is often because in golfing terms they remain tragically isolated. We also acknowledge that some courses may have justified more of a mention, but it is extremely difficult to analyse – if you have strong opinions, here – once again do let us know. The maps we have had designed are simple, but effective and we very much hope that this leaves you with a clear understanding of where you may wish to play. We are particularly proud of our art collection – which will be added to as years go by – we are enormously grateful to the contributing galleries for the efficiency, kindness and courtesy they have shown in this compilation. We are also pleased with our fine collection of country house hotels. We think they look magnificent and we hope you are fortunate enough to spend time within them.

CHOICE GOLF

Choosing fifty-two golfcourses from the eighteen hundred or so course is somewhat tricky. We do not presume this to be the best 52, but if you played one a week in 1987, you'd be a far wiser more contented person than I. Glaring omissions, Rye and Brancaster spring to mind this is not through editorial incompetence, but because the courses did not wish to be included – we feel the book suffers as a result, but still offers what can only be described as choice golf. Others, Southerness and St. Mellion were supremely helpful and will as certain courses are changed in 1988 be included – variety is the spice.

BRITISH GOLF

The British love their golf and we are blessed with some magnificent courses. We have made a list of all the courses in a series of eighteen directories – every club in the country has been included and we very much hope these links will assist in your telephone reservations – so important these days. We have used some fairly outrageous names as titles – largely because this emphasises not merely the variety of the courses, but the remarkable landmarks that lie close to them.

GLORIOUS GOLF

Several articles have been specially written for us and we are most grateful to their authors who we wish the very best in 1987. It is clear that they love their golf and revel in its variety. In conclusion, we hope that this guide enables you to enjoy the glorious game more fully – we wish you the very best fortune both on and off the course – Following the Fairways 1987.

KENSINGTON WEST PRODUCTIONS
Julian West

Yawn, tweet, tweet, creek, clunk, key, door, dust, wipe, polish, hoover, coffee, biscuits, 'morning John', barman, push, pull, unlock, open, bang, shut, breeze, blind, schwp, sunlight, notice board, ring ring, buzz, scribble, score card, subscription, drawing pin, 'ouch', 'oh hello Mark', Secretary, punch, slap, gloves, clubs, clatter, yellow jumper, tees, balls, bounce, crack, crash, 'blast', professional.

Tweed suit, plus fours, big tummy, red face, flutter, game of bridge, television, the Open, table top, chair leg, comfortable, feet up, cards, back gammon, fruit machine, chick-ching, chick-ching, chick-ching, jackpot, irritation, orange juice, cold coffee, Mars bar, cigarette, 'hello sport', 'what's your tipple?', Captain.

Sausage roll, packet of crisps, whisky, water, soda, ginger, 'same again', a hearty sandwich, bank manager, lawyer, solicitor, accountant, sherry, ashtray, cigarette end, 'what', peanuts, bar billiards, golf bag, olives, ice, 'your round', pork scratchings, bottle of wine, 'let's have lunch', jacket and tie, heart attack, spillage, carpet stain, umbrella, loose change, cheque book, cheese roll, bar stool, beer mat, three lagers, two whiskies, snooker, bright jumper, 'must be going', cocktails.

'Just a half', President, local vet, club trophy, clock chimes, 'fore', crash, ' damn Professional', headache, annual dinner, 200 club, young Conservative, old conservative, pipe, cup of tea, game of bridge, five pound note, shortbread, Lady Captain, pert bottom, efficiency, smile, tweed skirt, pat, woof, a round of golf, flushed face, windswept hair, feel good, Captain, President, Secretary, Professional, gin and tonic, bloody mary, dry martini, lager, crisps, twiglets, 'my round', gray suit, perfume, cigar smoke, 'yes', oysters, cashmere, bucks fizz, charity box, phone, 'I'm on my way', pickled egg, Christmas raffle, large behind, limp, stutter, 'hic', scratch, 'evening, how are you?', 'how's your wife?', 'how's your father', chuckle, laugh, titter, 'no', five pound note, 'won't be long', touch of soda, 'evening Harry', M.P., silence, mmm.., red wine, campari, whisky, vodka, ice, 'ho ho ho', beltch, 'must be off now', yawn, 'wife'll kill me', whisky, 'oh hello darling', thwack, sore shin, brrm brrm, lock, key, zzzzzzz.

"The 17th Fairway, Prestwick".

JANUARY

MONDAY	TUESDAY	WEDNESDAY	THURSDAY	FRIDAY	SATURDAY	SUNDAY
			1	2	3	4
5	6	7 Presidents Putter (Rye)	8 Presidents Putter (Rye)	9 Presidents Putter (Rye)	10 Presidents Putter (Rye)	11 Presidents Putter (Rye)
12	13	14	15	16	17	18
19	20	21	22	23	24	25
26	27	28	29	30	31	

"Manor House, Moretonhampstead"

FEBRUARY

MONDAY	TUESDAY	WEDNESDAY	THURSDAY	FRIDAY	SATURDAY	SUNDAY
						1
2	3	4	5	6	7	8
9	10	11	12 Australian Masters (Huntingdale, Melbourne (Victoria))	13 Australian Masters (Huntingdale, Melbourne (Victoria))	14 Australian Masters (Huntingdale, Melbourne (Victoria))	15 Australian Masters (Huntingdale, Melbourne (Victoria))
16	17	18	19	20	21	22
23	24	25	26	27	28	

MARCH

"The Ladies Links" SOTHEBY'S

MONDAY	TUESDAY	WEDNESDAY	THURSDAY	FRIDAY	SATURDAY	SUNDAY
						1
2	3	4	5	6	7	8
9	10	11	12	13	14	15
16	17	18	19	20	21	22
23	24	25	26	27	28	29
30	31					

APRIL

"The Tee Shot, Westward Ho!" SOTHEBY'S

MONDAY	TUESDAY	WEDNESDAY	THURSDAY	FRIDAY	SATURDAY	SUNDAY
		1	2	3	4	5
6	7	8	9 U.S. Masters (Augusta) Halford Hewitt (Royal Cinque Ports)	10 U.S. Masters (Augusta) Halford Hewitt (Royal Cinque Ports)	11 U.S. Masters (Augusta) Halford Hewitt (Royal Cinque Ports)	12 U.S. Masters (Augusta) Halford Hewitt (Royal Cinque Ports)
13	14	15	16	17	18 Selborne Salver (Blackmoor)	19 Hampshire Hog (North Hants)
20	21	22	23	24	25	26
27	28	29 Ford Ladies Classic (Woburn)	30 Ford Ladies Classic (Woburn)			

"Moor Park"

MAY

MONDAY	TUESDAY	WEDNESDAY	THURSDAY	FRIDAY	SATURDAY	SUNDAY
				1 Ford Ladies Classic (Woburn)	2 Ford Ladies Classic (Woburn)	3
4	5	6	7	8	9	10
11	12	13	14	15	16	17
18	19	20	21	22	23	24
25	26	27 Walker Cup (Sunningdale)	28 Walker Cup (Sunningdale)	29	30	31

"Woburn"

JUNE

MONDAY	TUESDAY	WEDNESDAY	THURSDAY	FRIDAY	SATURDAY	SUNDAY
1 Amateur Championship (Prestwick)	2 Amateur Championship (Prestwick)	3 Amateur Championship (Prestwick)	4 Amateur Championship (Prestwick) Dunhill Masters (Woburn)	5 Amateur Championship (Prestwick) Dunhill Masters (Woburn)	6 Amateur Championship (Prestwick) Dunhill Masters (Woburn)	7 Dunhill Masters (Woburn)
8	9	10	11	12	13 Berkshire Trophy (Berkshire)	14 Berkshire Trophy (Berkshire)
15	16	17	18 U.S. Open (Olympic Club, San Francisco)	19 U.S. Open (Olympic Club, San Francisco)	20 U.S. Open (Olympic Club, San Francisco)	21 U.S. Open (Olympic Club, San Francisco)
22	23	24	25	26	27	28
29	30					

JULY

J.M. HENDERSON *"The Lighthouse Green"* SOTHEBY'S

MONDAY	TUESDAY	WEDNESDAY	THURSDAY	FRIDAY	SATURDAY	SUNDAY
		1	2	3	4	5
6	7	8	9	10	11	12
13	14	15	16 Open Championship (Muirfield)	17 Open Championship (Muirfield)	18 Open Championship (Muirfield)	19 Open Championship (Muirfield)
20	21	22	23	24	25 Welsh Amateur (Royal Porthcawl)	26 Welsh Amateur (Royal Porthcawl)
27 Welsh Amateur (Royal Porthcawl) Scottish Amateur (Nairn) English Amateur (Frilford Heath)	28 Welsh Amateur (Royal Porthcawl) Scottish Amateur (Nairn) English Amateur (Frilford Heath)	29 Welsh Amateur (Royal Porthcawl) Scottish Amateur (Nairn) English Amateur (Frilford Heath)	30 Welsh Amateur (Royal Porthcawl) Scottish Amateur (Nairn) English Amateur (Frilford Heath)	31 Welsh Amateur (Royal Porthcawl) Scottish Amateur (Nairn) English Amateur (Frilford Heath)		

AUGUST

AFTER CHARLES CROMBIE *"Putting For His Nose"* SOTHEBY'S

MONDAY	TUESDAY	WEDNESDAY	THURSDAY	FRIDAY	SATURDAY	SUNDAY
					1 Welsh Amateur (Royal Porthcawl) Scottish Amateur (Nairn) English Amateur (Frilford Heath)	2
3	4	5 Seniors Championship (Royal Cinque Ports)	6 Seniors Championship (Royal Cinque Ports)	7 Seniors Championship (Royal Cinque Ports) U.S. P.G.A. (P.G.A. National, West Palm Beach (Florida))	8 U.S. P.G.A. (P.G.A. National, West Palm Beach (Florida)) Irish Amateur Close Championship (Tramore)	9 U.S. P.G.A. (P.G.A. National, West Palm Beach (Florida)) Irish Amateur Close Championship (Tramore)
			U.S. P.G.A. (P.G.A. National, West Palm Beach (Florida))			
10 Irish Amateur Close Championship (Tramore) Boys Championship (Kilmarnock (Barassie))	11 Irish Amateur Close Championship (Tramore) Boys Championship (Kilmarnock (Barassie))	12 Irish Amateur Close Championship (Tramore) Boys Championship (Kilmarnock (Barassie))	13 Boys Championship (Kilmarnock (Barassie))	14 Boys Championship (Kilmarnock (Barassie))	15	16
17	18	19	20 Youths Championship (Notts.)	21 Youths Championship (Notts.)	22 Youths Championship (Notts.)	23
24	25	26	27	28 Amateur Challenge Trophy (Woburn)	29	30
31						

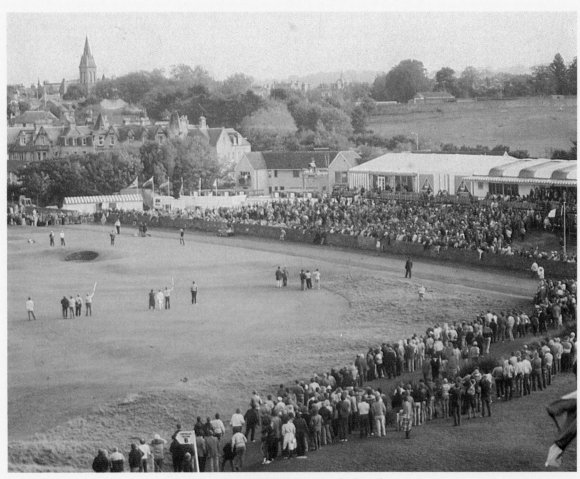

"The Dunhill World Cup, St. Andrews"

SEPTEMBER

MONDAY	TUESDAY	WEDNESDAY	THURSDAY	FRIDAY	SATURDAY	SUNDAY
	1	2	3	4	5	6
7	8	9 Home Internationals (Lahinch)	10 Home Internationals (Lahinch) European Open (Walton Heath)	11 Home Internationals (Lahinch) European Open (Walton Heath)	12 European Open (Walton Heath)	13 European Open (Walton Heath)
14	15	16	17	18	19	20
21	22	23	24	25 Ryder Cup (Muirfield Village (Ohio))	26 Ryder Cup (Muirfield Village (Ohio))	27 Ryder Cup (Muirfield Village (Ohio))
28	29	30				

"7th Hole, Wentworth, Burma Road"

OCTOBER

MONDAY	TUESDAY	WEDNESDAY	THURSDAY	FRIDAY	SATURDAY	SUNDAY
			1	2	3	4
5	6	7	8	9	10	11
12	13	14	15	16	17	18
19	20	21	22	23	24	25
26	27	28	29	30	31	

NOVEMBER

HARRY FURNISS *"He Only Goes Round With His Wife Now"* SOTHEBY'S

MONDAY	TUESDAY	WEDNESDAY	THURSDAY	FRIDAY	SATURDAY	SUNDAY
						1
2	3	4	5	6	7	8
9	10	11	12	13	14	15
16	17	18	19	20	21	22
23	24	25	26	27	28	29
31						

DECEMBER

CECIL ALDIN *"Sunningdale, The Fourth Green"* SOTHEBY'S

MONDAY	TUESDAY	WEDNESDAY	THURSDAY	FRIDAY	SATURDAY	SUNDAY
	1	2	3	4	5	6
7	8	9	10	11	12	13
14	15	16	17	18	19	20
21	22	23	24	25	26	27
28	29	30	31			

CORNWALL

P.H.P. "Golfer & Caddy" BURLINGTON GALLERY

TREGLOS HOTEL

The Treglos Hotel offers a totally relaxed and informal atmosphere, but at the same time promises good service amidst
pleasant surroundings. The country house offers 44 comfortable
bedrooms and most of these enjoy splendid views over Constantine Bay. The rooms have character as well as modern
comforts and these combine to make life easy.

One of the major attributes of the house is the excellent leisure
facilities. A charming indoor pool and jacuzzi are ideal for
relaxing after enjoying what must be the most appealing of the
hotel's attributes – Trevose Golf Course itself.

After a swim or a round of golf it is likely that you will wish to
enjoy some fully fledged cooking. The hotel is proud of its
excellent cuisine and its pleasantly informal dining room and
bars. Log fires and comfortable sofas make further leisure easy
and promising locations for conversation about today's golf or
perhaps more importantly tomorrow's round.

TREGLOS HOTEL
Constantine Bay,
Nr. Padstow,
Cornwall.
Tel: (0841) 520727

"Brandy for the Parson 'Baccy for the Clerk" – **Cornwall** is the land of the smuggler's cove. It is also the land of King Arthur and the Knights of the Round Table – a land of legends. To cross the Tamar is to enter foreign soil: for centuries the Cornish Celts had more in common with the Welsh and the French Bretons than the ever-invading Anglo-Saxons. Well, the Anglo-Saxons still invade but nowadays in a more peaceful manner: "grockles" they are called in Cornwall and they come in search of sun, sand and sea. But there is also a fairly recent addition, a sub-species commonly known as the "golfing-grockle" who comes to Cornwall to seek out some of the finest golfing country in the Kingdom.

If one commences an imaginary tour by crossing the Tamar at Plymouth, **St Mellion Golf and Country Club** has surely to be the first port of call. Located north of Saltash, off the **A388** St Mellion is the name presently on every Cornish golfer's lips – small wonder with **Jack Nicklaus** having described the new International course opened in 1986 as "potentially the world's greatest galleried golf course". In addition to this undoubted 'star of the future' St Mellion has a second 18 holes, which though less demanding is certainly worth a visit.

Heading westwards the wonderfully named **Looe Bin Down** Golf Club is situated on high ground to the north of Looe. An 18 hole moorland course it lies somewhat at the mercy of the elements and can get exceptionally windy.

Leaving, if you'll pardon the expression, the exposed Looe behind, St Austell is clearly the place to head for. There are two courses close to the town, **Carlyon Bay** (featured on a later page), and the **St Austell Golf Club**. The St Austell course is situated on the western edge of the town off the **A390**. Rather shorter than Carlyon Bay but with an ample spread of gorse and numerous bunkers, it possesses plenty of challenges and attractions of its own. The Club welcomes visitors although prior telephoning is essential.

Golfers should have little trouble getting a game at **Truro** Golf Club, again fairly short, but a pleasant parkland course which looks over Truro's impressive cathedral. Located west of the City it too can be reached via the **A390**. The cost of a day's golf here in 1986 was **£8** midweek, **£10** at weekends.

Falmouth with its famous harbour has, like St Austell, two courses close at hand, one in the grounds of **Budock Vean Hotel** and another, the **Falmouth Golf Club**, located south west of the town with views over Falmouth Bay.

Still heading down the coast, the course at **Mullion** is another of the short but sweet brigade. Seven miles south of Helston it can lay claim to being the most southerly on the British mainland. Nestling around the cliff edges overlooking some particularly inviting sands and with distant views towards St Michael's Mount, Mullion typifies the charm of Cornish holiday golf.

As well as having the most southerly golf course, Cornwall has, not surprisingly, the most westerly – the **Isles of Scilly Golf Club**, a nine hole course at Hugh Town on St Mary's. Always well-kept, visitors are welcome Mondays to Saturdays, fees in 1986 being **£7** per day.

Cornwall's northern coast is even more dramatic and rugged than that of the south. Waves pounding the jagged cliffs of Land's End is a familiar picture but much of the northern coast has a similar wildness. Occupying the more peaceful interludes are countless picturesque fishing villages, some glorious beaches and several spectacularly situated golf courses.

The **West Cornwall Golf Club** lies just beyond St Ives at Lelant. A beautiful and very natural links it was laid out almost a hundred years ago by the then Vicar of Lelant. One of the most popular courses in Cornwall it is probably a good idea to telephone the Club before setting off, but generally visitors (with handicaps) are welcome, fees being **£8**.

Passing numerous derelict tin and copper mines the inland course at **Tehidy Park** is soon reached. Located between Camborne and Portreath it presents a considerable contrast to the golf at Lelant: here we are amidst the pine trees, rhododendrons and bluebells – hopefully not right amidst them! Getting back to the coast **Perranporth** and **Newquay** look closer on the map than they are by road. Both are links courses offering outstanding sea views. Situated on higher ground a game at Perranporth in 1986 was priced at **£7** midweek, **£9** at weekends, while at Newquay (with its 100 bunkers) fees were **£9** during the week, **£12** at weekends.

St Enedoc (at Rock) and **Trevose** (Constantine Bay) are often considered as a pair, although they are in fact quite different. Trevose (also featured later) is the longer course but much more open and it doesn't possess the massive sandhills that are the feature of St Enedoc links. The 6th hole at the latter, has the famous **"Himalayas"** thought to be the highest sandhill on any course in Britain. Visitors to St Enedoc must possess proof of handicap, though there are no general restrictions on time of play. The fees are **£12** per day.

Getting close to the Devonshire border, final mentions go to the courses at Bude and Launceston both of which welcome visitors at all times. The **Bude and North Cornwall Golf Club**, like West Cornwall Golf Club, is approaching its centenary. Another links type course it is situated almost in the town centre and is known for its excellent greens. **Launceston's** undulating parkland course is similarly well-kept. Located on high ground it offers extensive views – to the west stretches Bodmin Moor, bogs and mystery, and to the east Dartmoor, bogs and even more mystery.

Bude and North Cornwall G.C.	(0288) 2006
Carlyon Bay G.C.	(072681) 4250
Falmouth G.C.	(0326) 40525
Isles of Scilly G.C.	(0720) 22050
Launceston G.C.	(0566) 3442
Looe Bin Down G.C.	(05034) 247
Mullion G.C.	(0326) 240685
Newquay G.C.	(0637) 874354
Perranporth G.C.	(0872) 573701
St Austell G.C.	(0726) 72649
St Enedoc G.C.	(020886) 3216
St Mellion G.& C.C.	(0579) 50101
Tehidy Park G.C.	(0209) 842208
Trevose G.& C.C.	(0841) 520208
Truro G.C.	(0872) 78684
West Cornwall G.C.	(0736) 753401

CORNWALL

Many moons ago when I was a lad we used to have the family hols in Cornwall. I wasn't a golfer then (and I'm not much of one now) but I have nothing but charmed memories of the quiet streams, the golden sands, the boisterous waves, the mackerel fishing and the delightful people. Clearly the holiday golfer must consider this outrageously excellent county high on his (or her) priority list. And having recently returned from the Highlands of Scotland, the point is made clearly. Golf is as popular in the county of Land's End as it is near John O'Groats. Honeymooners worried that two initially promising golf weeks may be missed should earmark Cornwall as the place to go – forget the Riviera.

Starting one's trip in North Cornwall one finds Bude, a pleasant seaside resort where the **Burn Court Hotel (0288) 2872** is as comfortable as any and has the advantage of overlooking the golf links, another popular spot for golfers is **The Camelot (0288) 2361**. In Morwenstow, a fine old pub **The Bush** is worth visiting – an excellent atmosphere and some simply breathtaking views from the clifftops. One mile north east of Bude, at Poughill, **Reeds (0288) 2841** is an outstanding place to stay and the food is first rate. If you're heading down the coast – a tremendous idea – then an early start for St Enedoc can be made from **Crackington Manor (08403) 397** at Crackington Haven. Closer still some first rate accommodation can be found at Port Isaac, a delightful fishing village, the **Castle Rock Hotel** has interesting food and is very good value (0208) 880300, while **The Port Gaverne Inn (0208) 880244** also offers tremendous food and a charming atmosphere. In Rock, the **St Enedoc Hotel (020886) 2311** for the two testing links courses nearby. Further afield in St Kew, the **St Kew Inn** is also a place to note.

In Constantine Bay near Padstow stands another relaxing hotel **The Treglos (0841) 520727** ideal for making the most of the nearby Trevose links. In Padstow itself a pleasant place to amble after a daunting day's golf and where better to reflect on one's game than over dinner overlooking the harbour at the aptly named **Seafood Restaurant (0841) 532485**. An inn of note is the **Old Custom House (0841) 532359**, a tremendous harbour setting. Returning to thoughts of food **Shipwrights** is also considered to be worth a visit between games.

Newquay, here, the crash of the Atlantic offers a surfing paradise but golfers also find it appealing. **The Atlantic Hotel (06373) 2244** is an ideal holiday spot while the **Hotel Bristol (06373) 5181** also has much to commend it. Connoisseurs of the public house might care to visit the Falcon at Mawgan. The North Cornwall coast has much to offer – golf in the morning, brousing in the early afternoon, golf mid-afternoon early evening, dinner, bed – ideal honeymoon, wouldn't you say? A busy place with all manner of tourist attractions is St Ives. Two hotels to note are **The Tregenna Castle (0736) 795** good leisure facilities and **The Garrick (0736) 796199** – ideal for the nearby cliffs and beaches as well as the golf course. Slightly further afield at Carbis Bay the **Boskerris Hotel (0736) 795295** is particularly friendly and provides comfortable accommodation

at reasonable prices.

In Mullion, the visitor will experience yet more splendid coastal scenery from the Lizard to Polurrion Cove, which the **Polurrion Hotel (0326) 24021** overlooks. Further up the coast in Manaccan, **The New Inn** offers a fine array of fish, lobster and oysters and the landlord is a keen golfer himself. Another warm welcome is most likely in Helford, a lovely area overlooking the estuary. The **Shipwrights Arms** offers excellent crab amongst other delights, including good beers. **The Riverside** is the place to go if you are really looking for quality cuisine – do look around and, if you can, try to stay in one of the six delightful bedrooms (032623) 443.

Falmouth, seagulls aplenty and a refreshing breeze: golf here is good. At **The Budock Vean (0326) 250288** golfers are offered superb food in luxurious surroundings. While other hotels to note are the **Crill House (0326) 312994** with its pitch and putt course, ideal for the family, not necessarily the honeymooners. **The Hotel St Michael's (0326) 312707** also has much to commend it. The opening words of 'The Wind in the Willows' were written at **The Greenbank (0326) 312440** and that can't be bad. **The Penmere Manor (0326) 314545** also has much to commend it. Further up the coast a whole host of excellent hotels gather – here are a few: in St Mawes and the Roseland peninsula, **The Idle Rocks (0326) 270771** offers reduced green fees at Truro golf course and a perfect setting. Grander but more expensive accommodation can be found in the excellent **Hotel Tresanton (0236) 270544**. On the way to St Austell, **The Pandora** is a charming thatched pub in Mylor Bridge, while **The Roseland Inn** offers good snacks and another most attractive setting. In Tregethan near St Austell itself **The Boscundle Manor (072681) 4996** is really first rate – food alone is worth the trip. Visitors who have decided that Truro is the place to stay may well have selected **The Carlton** as their hotel (0872) 72450. In Carlyon Bay another golfing gem is located, in this case the redoubtable **Carlyon Bay Hotel (072681) 2304**, ideal for families.

Our final stretch takes us along the coast to the area of Looe. In Fowey, two excellent restaurants can be considered, on the one hand **The Food for Thought (072 683) 2221** – splendid seafood, and on the other the restaurant **Cordon Bleu (0702 613) 2359**. Another hotel where the visitor can enjoy a little extra walking – on the cliffs as well as on the fairways, is at Talland-by-Looe, **The Talland Bay Hotel (0503) 72667** is a good base. **The Kitchen (0503) 72780** is an excellent restaurant in Polperro and In East Looe the **Elfford Court** is quiet and a pleasant place to stay (05036) 4769. Our last thought for Cornwall is appropriately near to St Mellion – where couples may have already reserved their honeymoon, **Tideford's** the place and the **Heskyn Mill (075538) 481** the restaurant. This is ideal for couples or batchelors, anybody actually,

What a place – the long weekend in August is coming up – and I'm off to Cornwall. I can't wait. Piskies, pasties, golf and I'm pleased to say no fiancée – I'm still a lad, you know.

Treglos Hotel
Constantine Bay,
Padstow, PL28 8JH
Tel: (0841) 520727
This personally run, country house hotel is situated conveniently close to the Trevose Golf and Country Club. Among its many excellent amenities the hotel has an indoor swimming pool although if it's golf you are seeking the hotel offers special tariffs to players.

The Carlyon Bay Hotel
Sea Road, Carlyon Bay,
St Austell, Cornwall
Tel: (072681) 2304
Cornwall's only 4 star establishment, The Carlyon Bay Hotel, amongst other things, offers free golf to residents on its own 18 hole championship course. Overlooking the expanse of Carlyon Bay itself, the hotel could not have been sited more perfectly and is one of Cornwall's most prestigious places to stay.

The Carlyon Bay Hotel

St. Austell, South Cornwall

AA ★★★★ RAC

THE RISE AND RISE OF ST. MELLION

St Mellion, the brainchild of farming brothers Martin and Hermon Bond, celebrated its 10th anniversary with the opening of their International Golf Course designed by the master golfer himself, Jack Nicklaus. The brothers first went into golf, when they developed 150 acres of land at St. Mellion and created a course set on rolling parkland with panoramic views over the Cornish Countryside – the course and Clubhouse were unashamedly based on the concept of the American Country Club. Within three years, their first golf course was chosen to be the venue of the 1979 Benson and Hedges International Open and more professional Tournaments were to follow when, in 1983 and 1984, the PGA European Tour brought the Tournament Players Championship and BBC Television to Cornwall – three major European Tournaments within five years had set the seal on St. Mellion being a regular tournament venue in the future.

To be recognised in both European and World Golf, the brothers were quick to realise that they must carry through their lifelong ambition and approach the greatest golfer in the history of the game, and the leading modern day golf architect Jack Nicklaus, to design their International course. This they did and initially they received a visit from the President of the Nicklaus Organisation to see if the proposed scheme of building an International Course was feasible at St. Mellion – it did not take the American visitor too long to realise that the approach was a very serious one and the two gentlemen behind the scheme were dedicated in their ambition and that the land in question was in a beautiful situation. The brothers flew to America for their very first meeting with Jack Nicklaus and returned with an agreement for Nicklaus to draw up plans for the new course – in Jack's words "potentially the world's greatest galleried golf course".

With Jack's design, Martin and Hermon built the golf course across three years and Jack flew in every few months to see that the work was progressing to his specification – during the construction period, more than 1.5m cubic metres of soil was moved to cut fairways through established land, vast spectator viewing areas were built throughout the course and beautiful lakes were created. The greens were laid to the American specification of a sand/peat mixture and a watering system built into the course covering tees, fairways and greens.

With the Nicklaus Course built and already open – a shade over 7,000 yards from the tournament tees - the brothers have amended their previous Championship Course to be a Resort Course of some 5,927 yards. Whilst the Nicklaus Course is already being played by the St. Mellion members and a great number of visitors this year, the "official opening" will be held in the Summer of 1987, when a big four exhibition match is to be staged and televised world wide – that will be a golfing occasion to witness. And what for the future – the Bond Brothers having developed potentially the finest golf course in Europe will now be seeking the most major of events and in their words "we would like to host the best events outside the Open Championship". Senior members of the PGA European Tour have already visited St. Mellion's new development and they use only one word to describe the golf course – fantastic. The brothers having achieved their dream are now happy to sit back (not for too long) for a year or so with a major tournament in their sights for 1988 and a regular each year thereafter.

With all that has happened at St. Mellion in ten short years, one would think that the Bond Brothers would be very satisfied with their achievements in golf alone, but that is only a part of an even more ambitious development programme. Whilst the Club has been running and golf courses being built and remodeled, a most luxurious Time-share village is also appearing – twelve lodges complete and a further thirty eight yet to be built on a beautiful shoulder of land over-looking the Resort Course. Wimpey Homes have the development rights to build and market the village – the whole project has an air of quality and quiet efficiency as the Timeshare Sales Office deal with a steady stream of buyers who seek the best in time owner-ship, golf and leisure at St. Mellion.

And the story does not finish there either, as the Brothers are now seeking planning permission for a certain number of freehold properties to be built in and around the golf courses – exclusive properties, just as one sees adjacent to the fairways of international golf resorts around the world.

Martin and Hermon Bond have achieved unbelievable success across their ten years at St. Mellion by leading with great vision and dedication – they are charming people but shrewed and successful business entrepreneurs too, and they were the first people in Britain to secure the services of Jack Nicklaus – that alone amply describes their persuasive powers and the fact that they mean business. St. Mellion is, without doubt, the most outstanding development in British golf this century and in private ownership.

Staring out of a window from inside an office in Central London, distracted by the rain cascading down, Carlyon Bay and the Cornish Riviera seem a million light years away. Thumbing through a glossy brochure I see a luxury 4-star Hotel and a Championship golf course stretching out along the cliff tops with views across the St Austell Bay and down to miles of golden sands. At least three distinct beaches are overlooked by the course – one of them frequented by naturists! – think I'll get a cup of coffee.....

Built in 1925 as a private enterprise, the course has been owned by the Hotel since 1929. In its early days the glorious setting attracted the **Duke of Windsor**, probably the keenest of all 'golfing Royals' while **Winston Churchill** too spent a few of his finest hours at CarlyonBay.

Considerable changes have occurred during the past decade or so. In 1978 golf architect **Hamilton Stutt** was commissioned to make alterations to various parts of the course and in the early '80's the Hotel came under new ownership. A greater emphasis has since been placed on the quality of the golf offered and the appointment of a Course Manager, **Mr Brian Summers**, was made with this view in mind.

Golfers visiting this part of the world are sure to receive a warm welcome at Carlyon Bay and there is no pre-requisite of providing a handicap certificate. The only restriction as such on times of play is that those wishing to tee-off between 8.30am and 12 noon must reserve their starting times at the pro-shop. **Nigel Sears** is the Club's professional, he may be contacted on **(072681) 4228**. The **green fees** for **1986** were set at **£8.50** for a full day's golf during the week, with **£10** payable at weekends and Bank Holidays. Also in 1986, Temporary Membership of the Club could be purchased for **£40**. Visitors may wish to note that the Club stages a number of open competitions throughout the year, details of which can be obtained by writing to Mr Summers at **The Carlyon Bay Hotel Golf Club, Carlyon Bay, St Austell, Cornwall**. Mr Summers can be reached by telephone on **(072681) 4250**.

The Cornish Riviera is not of course a million light years from London – it's about 250 miles away and with the now regular flights to nearby **St Mawgan Airport**, Carlyon Bay can be

reached in a very short time. For those travelling by more conventional methods, St Austell is the town to head for. The West Country is served by motorway as far as **Exeter (M5)** and thereafter the **A38** links Exeter with **Plymouth**. The A38 should in fact be followed to just beyond **Liskeard** from where the **A390** can be picked up. Carlyon Bay is well sign-posted from St Austell. From the West the **A390** approaches via **Truro** while those coming from the **Newquay** region should travel on the **A3058**. Finally St Austell railway station is only afew yards from the course.

From the back tees – always in play during the summer months – the course stretches to **6463** yards, par **72** (sss **71**) for the ladies, from the red tees, the course measures **5684** yards and is a par **75**. **Neil Coles** holds the course record at **65**. Carlyon Bay is the perfect length really for holiday golf: long enough to be challenging and with enough hazards to set you thinking, but hopefully not so difficult as to make the cliffs a tempting jettison point for clubs, trolleys etc. – besides, there are a number of disused mine shafts on the course – part of it having been built on old copper mine workings. But seriously golf at Carlyon Bay should always be an enjoyable experience and the course is maintained in excellent condition throughout the year. Furthermore, whatever the standard of your game the quality of the views can never be disputed. On a warm day with the sun reflecting off St Austell Bay this is truly an idyllic spot.

The most testing holes on the front nine are probably the **2nd** – a very long par 4 with the Paddington to Penzance railway line running along the left and the cliffs to the right – and the uphill **6th** where the green overlooks Polgaver naturist beach – always an excuse for three-putting! After the spectacular **10th** the holes move away from the cliff edges and turn back towards the Clubhouse.

Carlyon Bay possesses a first-class 19th with extensive facilities. A catering service is provided throughout the day and there is a Bar, Lounge and Dining Room – all of which again offer tremendous views.

.....Well, back in London the coffee's gone cold and I'm afraid the rain is still coming down in floods – but at least I know where I'm going for my 'hols this year!

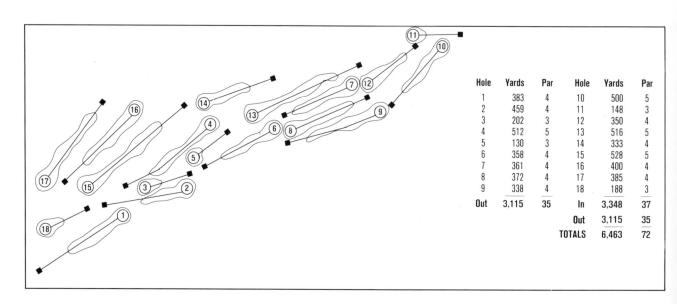

Hole	Yards	Par	Hole	Yards	Par
1	383	4	10	500	5
2	459	4	11	148	3
3	202	3	12	350	4
4	512	5	13	516	5
5	130	3	14	333	4
6	358	4	15	528	5
7	361	4	16	400	4
8	372	4	17	385	4
9	338	4	18	188	3
Out	3,115	35	In	3,348	37
			Out	3,115	35
			TOTALS	6,463	72

To some, mention of the north coast of Cornwall will invoke thoughts of golden sandy beaches and cool, inviting seas. For others it may conjure up images of romantic coves, wild, spectacular cliffs and incessant crashing waves. Either way the place has a certain magic, after all it was here that King Arthur is said to have met Merlin. Such is the setting of the Trevose Golf and Country Club.

Located near the quaint little fishing port of **Padstow**, Trevose is an ideal spot for a golfing holiday – or any kind of holiday come to that, but those who haven't made space in the boot for the golf clubs are missing out on something rather special. The Club boasts a splendid **18 hole Championship course** plus an adjacent **9 hole** short course.

A gentleman by the name of **Dr Williams** founded the Trevose Golf Club a little over sixty years ago. Today all administrative matters are in the capable hands of **Messrs P. Gammon** and **J.W.Duffy**. Both can be contacted by telephone on **(0841) 520208**. The Club's professional **Gary Allis**, can be reached on **(0841) 520261**. Not surprisingly the course (or courses) are at their busiest during the summer months, but whatever the time of year **visitors** looking for a game would be wise to make a quick telephone call before setting off. Visitors should find the Club very accommodating. Societies are also welcomed at Trevose, those organising should address written applications to the Secretary at **Trevose Golf and Country Club, Constantine Bay, Padstow, Cornwall**. Proof of handicap is required to play on the Championship course.

The **green fee** charged in **1986** varied according to the time of year with major reductions available to those wishing to obtain temporary membership of the Club. From November to mid-March a day's golf on the 18 hole course could be purchased for **£7.50**. From mid-March to the end of May, plus the month of October, the green fee was **£9.50** per day, whilst between June and September (inclusive) the same was priced at **£10.50**. The green fee for a day's golf on the 9 hole course was set at **£3** during the winter months with **£4.50** payable at all other times. **Junior** golfers could obtain **50% reductions** on all the above rates. Finally as an example of temporary membership, a fortnight's golf on the Championship course during the peak summer period could be obtained for **£58** per person in 1986.

Whereas the image of north Cornwall is perhaps a romantic one, the same could hardly be said of the actual journey to get there. Travelling to the West Country, however, is not the painful slog it once was. The roads have been improved and – whisper it quietly – they don't seem as congested as a few years ago. Presumably it's an indirect result of the growing annual pilgramage to Spain – Benidorm rather than Bude – Torremolinos instead of Torquay. Anyway, I am reliably informed that in addition to the improved roads there are now four flights daily from Heathrow to nearby **Newquay Airport** (six miles from the Golf Club). Motorists will normally head for **Bodmin** (via the **A30** from Exeter or **A38** from Plymouth). From Bodmin the **A389** should be taken towards Padstow. The Club is about four miles West of Padstow off the **B3276**. Finally those approaching from the St Austell area may find the B3274 helpful.

From the Championship tees the 18 hole course measures **6608 yards (par 70, sss72)**. The forward tees reduce the length by about 150 yards, while the ladies play over **5713** yards, **par 73**. The course can be described as a golf links though the visitor need not distress himself with fears of having to carry massive sandhills, and as a rule the rough is kept fairly short. The latter should ensure that the golfer spends more time admiring the scenery instead of searching for his golf ball. A word about the views: they are indeed tremendous, particularly those across **Booby's Bay**.

The wind at Trevose can often play a decisive role and prevent low scoring (no one, at least at the time of writing, has bettered 68). There are a great number of well-positioned bunkers and a stream meanders through much of the course. Trevose provides a good test for any standard of golfer.

The Clubhouse with its prime situation overlooking the course offers a whole range of first class facilities. There is a large comfortable Bar and a Dining Room which can cater for over a hundred people. Breakfast, lunches and dinners are served daily in the Dining Room and in addition light snacks can be obtained at all times. For children a separate games room is provided. Swimming and tennis are also all very much a part of the Country Club scene – what's more, there's even a trendy boutique!

There is an unmistakably relaxed, holiday flavour about Trevose. The atmosphere is perhaps best epitomised by the story of four lady Members involved in a foursome game: apparently when playing the short 16th they arrived at the green only to discover that they had been so busy chattering not one of them had remembered to tee off....so much for women 'drivers'!

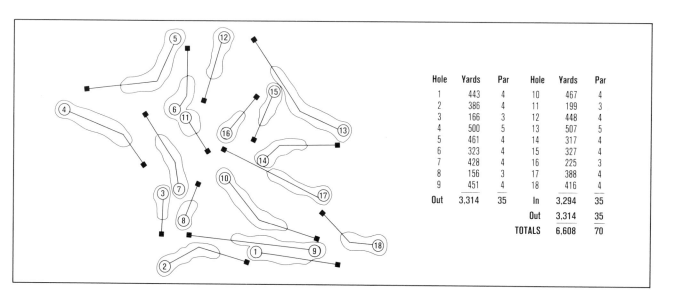

Hole	Yards	Par	Hole	Yards	Par
1	443	4	10	467	4
2	386	4	11	199	3
3	166	3	12	448	4
4	500	5	13	507	5
5	461	4	14	317	4
6	323	4	15	327	4
7	428	4	16	225	3
8	156	3	17	388	4
9	451	4	18	416	4
Out	3,314	35	In	3,294	35
			Out	3,314	35
			TOTALS	6,608	70

DEVON

SPY *"John Henry"* *BURLINGTON GALLERY*

Combe House
Hotel

...t amid the rolling fields and mature ...ods of East Devon, between Dartmoor ...d the Blackdown Hills, stands Combe ...ouse, the family seat of the Markers. ...ere has been a house standing on this ...e since Saxon times and much of the ...esent building dates from the late 16th ...d early 17th centuries. The house has ...ssed, usually by marriage, through ...ious families, the most notable of whom ...re the Putts and the Beaumonts.

...e conversion from family dwelling to ...untry house hotel has been undertaken ...h great care and the minimum of ...turbance to both the fabric and the ...nosphere of the house. Here we hope ...t you will relax amid the peace and ...iet of the countryside and will feel part ...a house party rather than an hotel ...est.

...e proprietors, John and Thérèse Boswell ...e both personally involved in the running ...the hotel and in the preparation of the ...od, bringing their personal touch to all ...ects of your stay.

...e cuisine is basically French in ...piration and with the very best of local ...n, meat and vegetables, some of which ...e produced from our own kitchen ...rdens, giving our restaurant a high ...utation locally as many Devonians come

out to eat at Combe. There are two dining rooms, each small and intimate enough for you to enjoy a romantic candle-light dinner, but yet large enough so you are not crowded.

The surrounding area is steeped in history and tradition and offers a variety of landscapes. Nearby is Dartmoor, rolling countryside, windswept and covered in gorse and heather. The valleys leading off the moor are by comparison lush with a patchwork of forest and fields and in one of the valleys is the former home of the most famous Devonian, Sir Francis Drake.

One may visit many stately homes and gardens in the area and also the Maritime Museum in Exeter. Should you wish to walk by the sea, then Sidmouth, a delightful Victorian seaside town, is but a few miles distant.

After visiting any of these, you may relax in front of a fire in the hall or sitting room and have a traditional Devon cream tea, or you may choose to walk around the hotel in the glorious parkland surrounding it. The choice is entirely yours.

We hope you will come and visit us and join in our friendly house party and enjoy the peaceful and relaxing atmosphere.

Combe House,
Gittisham, Near Honiton,
Devon EX14 0AD
Telephone: (0404) 2756

'Glorious Devon' they call it – beaches to the north, beaches to the south and Dartmoor in the middle. Well, amidst all the glory are some thirty golf courses the majority of which lie either directly on the coast or within a mile or so of it. The two most widely known and indeed the two Championship courses are both located to the north of the county: **Royal North Devon** (or **Westward Ho!** as it is commonly known) and **Saunton**. The greater number of courses, however, are on the southern coast, or to put it another way, whilst North Devon may have the cream, most of the tees are to be found in the south.

Firstly though, what about the 'middle'? The beautiful setting of the **Manor House Hotel Golf Course** at Moretonhampstead (see feature page) is known to many, however, it is not the sole course within Dartmoor, **Okehampton** lies on the edge of the National Park and is similarly surrounded by hills. Not surprisingly Okehampton is a moorland type course and whilst not overly long has a number of interesting holes. Visitors are welcome at all times, fees in 1986 being £6 Sunday to Friday, £7 on Saturdays. Well away from Dartmoor but still fairly centrally located is the parkland course at **Tiverton**. Easily reached from the **M5** (junction **27**) Tiverton also welcomes visitors throughout the week, however, pre-booking is essential. The cost of a day's golf in 1986 was priced at £**7.50** midweek, £**9** at weekends.

With its many Tudor buildings and impressive Cathedral **Exeter** makes for an attactive County Town. Golfwise the city has an 18 hole course at Countess Wear, south of the town off the **A377**. A fairly short parkland course it is renowned for its beautifully maintained greens. In 1986 the fees at Exeter Golf Club were £**10** per day.

To the east side of the River Exe and not too great a distance from Exeter are the courses at **Sidmouth** and Budleigh Salterton (**East Devon**). Both are on fairly high ground providing panoramic views out to sea. Sidmouth is perhaps more of a cliff top course with 'springy' turf while East Devon is of the downland variety with much heather and gorse. Green fees at Sidmouth are around the £**7** per day mark, East Devon being a little dearer.

To the east of the Exe Estuary the **Warren Golf Club** at Dawlish provides the only true links golf in South Devon. This is a much improved course with an interesting finishing hole that will have the wayward hitter threatening both the Members in the Clubhouse and/or quite possibly the passengers on a passing London to Penzance 125. Visitors are welcome at Dawlish seven days per week. A fairly near neighbour of "The Warren" is **Teignmouth Golf Club** (**B3192**). It may be near but Teignmouth offers a totally different challenge being situated some 900 feet above sea level on Haldon Moor. Teignmouth can become shrouded in fog during the winter (whereupon the members duly descended to "The Warren") but when all is clear it's a very pleasant course and most attractive too.

The three handiest courses for those staying in the Torbay area are probably **Churston, Torquay** and **Newton Abbot** (or **Stover**). **Churston**, located 3 miles from Paignton is a spectacular cliff top course at which visitors (with handicaps) are welcome at all times. Visitors are similarly welcome at Torquay Golf Club which is located just north of Torquay on the **A379**. Green fees in 1986 were £**8** midweek, £**9** at weekends. Stover lies a little to the north west of Newton Abbot off the **A382**. The abundant heather, woods and a meandering brook are likely to pose the most challenges here.

Heading further down the coast, the picturesque village of **Thurlestone** has one of the most popular courses in Devon. It is a quite superb cliff top course with several far-reaching views along the coast. Being so popular it is important to telephone in advance, fees are around the £**10** mark. **Bigbury** lies a short distance from Thurlestone. Approximately 300 yards shorter at around the 6,000 yards mark it is nevertheless equally attractive and looks across to Burgh Island, a favourite (or an ex-favourite) haunt of smugglers. Both Thurlestone and Bigbury can be reached from Plymouth via the **A379** or from the Torbay region via the **A381**.

Golfers in Plymouth have probably been noting with interest the recent developments at nearby St Mellion, just 'over the border' in Cornwall, however a little nearer to the great seafaring city visitors may care to note **Staddon Heights Golf Club** aat Plymstock, 5 miles south of the town centre. To the east of Plymouth, or towards the Moors if you prefer, is **Yelverton** lying midway between Plymouth and Tavistock on the **A386**. Yelverton is very much a moorland type course with heather, gorse and ponies providing the major hazards. Several long carries are required from the tee. The best times for a visit are weekdays and weekend afternoons, the fees in 1986 being £**7** midweek, £**9** at weekends.

North Devon can lay claim to having the oldest Golf Club in England, the Royal North Devon Club at Westward Ho! founded in 1864; it can also claim to have seen the lowest known score for 18 holes of golf. In 1936 the **Woolacombe Bay** professional recorded a 55 on his home course – 29 out and 26 back, including a hole in one at the last! As this took place on the 1st January one cannot help wondering quite what he did the night before! Unfortunately there is no longer a course at Woolacombe, however, there is one at nearby **Ilfracombe** (and has been for nearly 100 years). Situated several hundred feet above sea level it offers many outstanding views of the North Devon coastline. There is an interesting selection of par three holes, one of which measures a mere 81 yards. Visitors are always welcome at Ilfracombe – the cost of a day's golf in 1986 being £**8** in June, July and August and £**7** at all other times.

As for **Westward Ho!** and **Saunton**, both are featured on later pages, suffice it to say here that visitors to each can be guaranteed the warmest of welcomes.

Bigbury G.C.	(054881) 557
Churston G.C.	(0803) 842128
East Devon G.C.	(03954) 3370
Exeter G.& C.C.	(0392) 874023
Ilfracombe G.C.	(0271) 62176
Manor House Hotel G.& C.C.	(0647) 40355
Newton Abbot G.C.	(0626) 2460
Okehampton G.C.	(0837) 2113
Royal North Devon G.C.	(02372) 73817
Saunton G.C.	(0271) 812436
Sidmouth G.C.	(03955) 3451
Staddon Heights G.C.	(0752) 42475
Teignmouth G.C.	(06267) 4194
Thurlestone G.C.	(0548) 560405
Tiverton G.C.	(0884) 252187
Torquay G.C.	(0803) 37471
Warren G.C.	(0626) 862255
Yelverton G.C.	(0822) 852824

DEVON

Unlike Cornwall, there are courses inland in Devon. The game of bowls managed to grip Drake and the pursuit of golf has a similar attraction to many British citizens. A similar pull is made by the county of Devon itself. From its quiet coves to the wildness of Dartmoor from sailing at Salcombe to hang-gliding at Dawlish the county is brim full with super sports. Busy hotels for families, quiet inns, isolated pubs and splendid restaurants which come together to make this an ideal county to visit, golfer or otherwise. We start our tour in Tiverton, **Henderson's Restaurant**, to be precise **(0884) 254256** – excellent. The problem is where next? On the toss of the coin we opt for the south coast and Sidmouth.

On the way to the south coast many people may speed past Gittisham – a mistake, for **Combe House (0404) 2756** offers elegance and style that would befit the finest of holidays. In Sidmouth itself for grandness you should settle for **The Riviera (03955) 5201**. For convenience for Sidmouth's shops and excellent comforts at very good prices the **Torbay Hotel (03955) 3456** will appeal. For the family hols the **Westcliff (03955) 3252** merits attention. In Branscombe east of Sidmouth golfers will find the **Masons Arms (029780) 300** an attractive place to have dinner and stay if desired. In Dawlish Warren, the **Langstone Cliff Hotel (0626) 865155** leads to the course itself – what better reasons for visiting. Inland from East Devon's outstanding golf courses lies Lockwood, here **The Anchor** pulls a good pint in pleasant surroundings as well as serving good food. Returning to the coast one finds another pleasant establishment in the **Orestone House Hotel**, Maidencombe **(0803) 38099**, this is a handy place for Torquay without being too much in the middle of things. In Torquay itself – there are numerous fine hotels – the grandest is the **Imperial (0803) 24301**, which offers all manner of splendid facilities but charges for it! **The Palace Hotel (0803) 22271** is less costly but courtesy still prevails. Perhaps the best value to be found is at **Homers Hotel (0803) 213456** and its splendid restaurant, not one for young children though. A good place for dinner is **Remy's (0803) 223590**.

Another popular resort can be found in Brixham, **The Quayside Hotel (08045) 55751** is charming and the town retains a much quieter atmosphere than its neighbour across the bay. In Dartmouth two restaurants merit special comment. **The Cherub Dining Rooms (08043) 2571** adjoins the pub and the cuisine is excellent, seafood is a speciality. Cooking of the highest quality is also to be found at **The Carved Angel (08043) 2465** – food here is unsurpassed in the county but does not come cheap.

Travelling en route to Thurlestone not too lavish but excellent value cooking can be found in the **Church House** at Churchstow **(0548) 2237**. In Holberton lovers of the country mansion will not be disappointed by **Alston House Hotel (075530) 259**. And so the journey continues to Kingston, here **The Dolphin** has great character and is grand for an evening, unless you wish to leave for the excellent facilities offered at the **Thurlestone Hotel (0548) 560382**. Another pub to escape to is the **Pilchard** in Burgh Island – beware the tide!

Away from the coast Dartmoor beckons. The **Manor House Hotel (0647) 40355** has to be the first choice for superb golf acccompanies a fine mansion. Nearby, both to east and to west, golf abounds. In Exeter, **The White Hart (0392) 79897** appeals

– it serves well as an hotel, restaurant or merely a place to meet for a drink. Another extremely popular drinking haunt is the **Double Locks** while **The Rougemont (0392) 54982** is a good base in the City, while in Exeter one should note the excellent Maritime Museum – one of the best of its kind. A trip back to Moretonhampstead may result in a visit to **The White Hart (0647) 40406** – some accommodation while another splendid pub is found in North Bovey, the **Ring of Bells**.

In Ashburton, **The Holme Chase Hotel (03643) 471** has a gorgeous setting and a superior restaurant. Gelverton offers the **Moorland Links Hotel (0822) 852245** which takes its name from the nearby golfcourse and is particularly reliable. While in Miltoncombe nearby the **Who'd of thought of it** delights all comers.

Meanwhile in Lydford, **The Castle (082282) 242** is a pleasant place in which to eat or have a drink – possibly all three. Another place to stay in the village is the **Lydford House Hotel (082282) 347**, also excellent value. Perhaps the best place to stay in the area lies in Chagford a number of good hotels include **The Mill End (06473) 2282** and the extraordinarily beautiful **Gidleigh Park (06473) 2367**; both have good restaurants, Gidleigh Park's is outstanding.

Making our way to play the challenging North Devon courses three towns cross our minds. Milton Damerel for its outstanding hotel **The Woodford Bridge (040926) 481**, Hatherleigh for its handsome **George Hotel (0837) 810454** a splendid 15th century inn. Finally, the village of Winkleigh and its pub **The King's Arms**.

Reaching the north coast is a delight. Saunton awaits us after a day's golf a quick drive to Saunton Sands leads us to the hotel of that name **(0271) 89012** which is enormously popular with golfers. **The Preston House Hotel (0271) 890472** is also nearby and specialises in golfing holidays. A splendid good value place to have dinner, morning coffee or a light lunch is **Grays** in Northam **(02372) 76371** where some bedrooms are also available. Also in Northam **The Durrant House Hotel (02372) 72361** is first rate, good value with a dining room which is well worth visiting. At Fairy Cross, near Bideford, **The Portledge Hotel (02375) 262** is an inspired place for the peaceful minded. In Horns Cross **The Hoops Inn** is another most attractive dwelling: well priced accommodation and fine cooking makes this a strong recommendation after a busy day at Westward Ho!

In Bishops Tawton, near Barnstaple another splendid find is the **Downrew House Hotel (0271) 42497** where the food is excellent. Other local eating haunts include the **Lynwood House** in Barnstaple **(0271) 43695** and (good for sea food) **Otters (0271) 813 633** in Braunton. Returning Northwards and Croyde – a pub **The Thatched Barn** is popular, not the quietest place in the world though. In Ilfracombe, two hotels stand out **The Langleigh (0271) 62629** and **The Tracy House (0271) 63933**, comfortable, good food – ideal. But there are many more.

We end our trip in Combe Martin. **The Coulsworthy Country House (027188) 2463** is yet another one of these fabulous Devonshire hotels where civility, cuisine and comfort combine so well. As I finish my port in **Hendersons** I contemplate the delights ahead; no wonder so many people return to Devon – the character compels them.

Rocombe Country House Hotel
Lower Rocombe, Stoke in Teignhead
Shaldon, Newton Abbot
Tel: (0626) 873367
Quiet and relaxing 16th century 14 bedroom family run hotel. Set in open countryside, half way between Torquay and Teignmouth. All bedrooms en suite with colour TV and teamaking facilities, 6 course dinner, 5 course breakfast, sorry no children taken. Telephone for brochure and tarriff.

The Manor House Hotel
Moretonhampstead,
TQ13 8RE
Tel: (0647) 40355
The Manor House offers supreme comfort, outstanding character, attentive friendly service, 69 spacious bedrooms, every possible culinary delight, a testing eighteen hole golf course, outstanding fishing and riding facilities, as well as stupendous views over the Bovey Valley.

Dartmoor may seem an unlikely setting for one of Britain's finest golfing gems, but the Manor House Hotel course near Moretonhampstead is nothing less than that. Within howling distance of the Baskerville legends, it lies beneath a backdrop of granite tors and rolling hills.

Manor House itself is a vast and impressive Jacobean-style mansion, built between the Wars as a home for the **W. H. Smith family.** The golf course dominates the grounds of what is now a privately owned hotel and country club, indeed, immediately on entering the gates, the driveway will take you alongside the 13th and 14th fairways. However, it is only on reaching the mansion ('clubhouse' somehow doesn't seem appropriate) that the full beauty of the surroundings can be appreciated. From here the view out across the course is quite simply stunning, and the bracing moorland air should inject a sense of joie de vivre into even the most wretched of souls!

One gentleman who certainly isn't a wretched soul is **Mr Alan Egford.** As Golf Manager he effectively runs the administrative side of things and all correspondence relating to golfing matters should be addressed to him at **The Manor House Hotel Golf and Country Club, Moretonhampstead, Devon.** Mr Egford who is also a qualified PGA professional can be reached by telephone on **(0647) 40355.** In addition the Club has a resident PGA professional, **Richard Lewis,** who likewise can be contacted via the above telephone number.

Golfers wishing to visit the course are always made very welcome and are permitted to play on any day of the week. During the summer months it is essential to book a starting time and although at most times the course is pleasantly uncrowded, a quick telephone call to check for any tee reservations is always advisable – Manor House is not surprisingly a popular meeting place for golfing societies.

, In 1986 the **green fee** payable was **£8** per round or **£10** for a full day, with half-rates for juniors. Unless for some reason impossible, a day ticket is strongly recommended and if the prospect of 36 holes is a little daunting one could always consider the merits of hiring one of the electric-powered buggies that line up outside the pro-shop – who says Devon doesn't move with the times?

Whilst Moretonhampstead may look somewhat remote on the map, (the Hotel is 2 miles west of the town) the splendid scenery of these parts should make the journey a particularly pleasant one (assuming of course that one doesn't have the misfortune to get stuck behind a convoy of uncompromising farm vehicles and Sunday drivers). The **B3212** is the most direct as well as the most scenic route from **Exeter** – a distance of approximately 14 miles. The Club's entrance is immediately off this road and cannot be missed. Persons approaching from the **Plymouth** region may also find the **B3212** helpful, while those travelling from further west and from the Torbay area will probably need to use the **A30/A38.**

At **6016** yards the course in not overly long by modern standards – refreshingly so, some might say – nevertheless the par of **69** is a fairly strict one and there is only one five on the card. (From the ladies tees the course measures **5010** yards, par **70**).

To be frank though, length is really one of the last things the golfer should be concerned about when he comes to tackle this course – the sight from the elevated first tee should make this abundantly clear. The trout-filled **River Bovey** meanders its way through the centre of the course and is the dominant feature on the first seven holes. It takes a 'Sevvy' type to try and carry it on the **1st**, it runs immediately in front of the green on the dog-leg **2nd** and all the way along the right hand side of the narrow **3rd**. This tricky par three, with its overhanging trees to the left is surely one of the finest short holes in the country. At the back of the green, and circling round to the left, lie a profusion of rhododendrons and azaleas which in early summer burst into a kaleidoscope of colour: pinks and purples, yellows, reds, vivid blue and peach colours – as someone aptly remarked on seeing it, 'Augusta comes to Devon'!

The **4th** hole is the par five, and a genuine one at that with the river having to be carried from the tee, trouble all the way down the left and a raised green. The river crosses again in front of the **5th** green and reappears on the **7th**, where it twice cuts across the fairway. If you can reach the **8th** tee without having once gotten wet you're a better man than most! The 8th itself is fairly unspectacular but the **9th**, after a steep climb to the tee, gives you a chance to open the shoulders as you drive across a deep valley. Two fairly difficult par threes sandwich the **11th**, the longest par four on the course. The **13th** and **14th** are what television commentators might describe as 'potential birdie holes', but the closing stretch is quite tough, particularly the challenging **18th** with its acutely angled fairway and blind second. As you walk off the final green and sound the iron bell to signal 'all clear' you should be left in no doubt that you've played a very special golf course.

The Hotel acts as a rather grand 19th. An excellent and very full range of catering is offered with additional light snacks being available throughout the day. The balcony terrace, with its extensive views over the course and surrounding Hotel gardens is a must on a warm day .... imagine sitting out there on a bright and clear day in June, just a hint of breeze and a cool drink in your hand .... joie de vivre? I should say so!

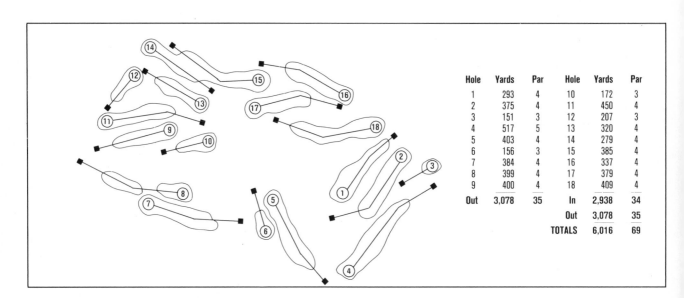

Hole	Yards	Par	Hole	Yards	Par
1	293	4	10	172	3
2	375	4	11	450	4
3	151	3	12	207	3
4	517	5	13	320	4
5	403	4	14	279	4
6	156	3	15	385	4
7	384	4	16	337	4
8	399	4	17	379	4
9	400	4	18	409	4
Out	3,078	35	In	2,938	34
			Out	3,078	35
			TOTALS	6,016	69

Gidleigh Park

Chagford, Devon ☎ Chagford (06473) 367/8/9 and 2225

To the best of my knowledge **Ben Crenshaw** has never visited Royal North Devon. If true more's the pity for here is a Club truly steeped in the history of the game. **Westward Ho!**, as it is commonly known, was the first English links course and being founded in **1864** the Royal North Devon Golf Club lays claim to being the oldest English Club still playing over its original land. Furthermore it boasts the oldest Ladies Golf Club in the world, the **Westward Ho! Ladies Golf Club** which was established in 1868.

Originally designed by **Tom Morris** and reconstructed by **Herbert Fowler** the 18 holes are situated on **Northam Burrows**. The Burrows is a vast, exposed and relatively flat area of common land which stretches along the coast a couple of miles north of Bideford between Westward Ho! and Appledore.

Several of Britain's historic courses, particularly those in Scotland, have fascinating ties with common land and associated local rights which have existed since 'time immemorial', but whilst the inhabitants of **St Andrews** no longer use their hallowed turf for practising archery upon, nor put their washing out to dry on the banks of the Swilcan Burn, the locals of Northam village still graze their sheep and horses on the Burrows. There can surely be no other Championship course in the world where you can have teed up on the first, taken a few steps backward to survey the drive ahead only to see a sheep wander up and peer inquisitively at your ball! One shouldn't get too alarmed though, the animals are well-versed in the etiquette of the game – they generally keep a respectful distance from the fairways and greens, they take care not to bleet when you putt and what's more they certainly won't contemplate stealing your golf ball as I'm told the crows do at Royal Aberdeen.

Seriously, golf at Westward Ho! is a rich experience and definitely one to be recommended, few Golf Clubs are prepared to go quite so far out of their way to accommodate visitors and to offer such a warm welcome. Indeed the Club stages several open competitions during the summer months. Presently responsible for continuing the tradition of friendliness is the Secretary **John Davies**, Mr Davies can be contacted via **The Royal North Devon Golf Club, Golf Links Road, WestwardHo! Bideford, Devon. Tel (027372) 73817.**

Persons considering a trip to the Club may find it advisable to telephone first in order to check if any tee reservations have been made. Fine weather can make the course particularly popular during the holiday season. **Societies** are also welcomed and bookings can be arranged with the Secretary. In 1986 a **green fee** of **£9** entitled the **visitor** to either a single round or a full day's golf. The same could be purchased at weekends for **£10**. For **juniors** the green fee was a mere **£3** – excellent value. Sets of clubs may be hired from the Club's professional, **Graham Johnston**. He can be reached by telephone on **(02372) 77598**.

The course can be approached from both East and West via the **A39**, although travellers from the West may be able to avoid the busy town of Bideford by joining the **B3236** near Abbotsham. Visitors travelling from the Dartmoor region should take the **A386** road which runs from Okehampton to Bideford whilst those from Exeter should follow the **A377** to Barnstaple, thereafter joining the A39 as above.

From the medal tees the course measures **6449** yards (the Championship course is some 200 yards longer) and is divided into two fairly equal halves. Westward Ho! has a traditional 'out and back' layout and there are some panoramic views across Bideford Bay, especially from the 6th tee where on a clear day the Isle of Lundy can be seen. In theory the links receives a degree of protection from the elements from a large bank of shingle which separates the Burrows from the beach. I say 'in theory' for this is surely one of Britain's most windswept courses. However, the wind is not the only factor that can make scoring extremely difficult. There are numerous ditches and hidden pot bunkers and then of course there are the **Great Sea Rushes**. To the uninitiated a word of caution – these giant marshland reeds, unique to Westward Ho!, can literally impale golf balls – so do as the sheep do – stay clear!

Westward Ho! is not only known for its golf course, it has literary fame as well. The village was founded a year before the Golf Club and was named after **Charles Kingsley's** adventure novel about Elizabethan seafarers. A decade or so later **Rudyard Kipling** attended the local college and remembered his days there in 'Stalky and Co'. There is no record to suggest that Mr Kipling was 'an exceedingly good' golfer but whilst he was studying, a young boy from Northam was out on the course caddying for sixpence a round. The boy was destined to become Open Champion on five occasions. **John H. Taylor** learnt his golf at Westward Ho! and his great affection for the Club remained throughout his long life. In 1957 the Club elected him their President.

In addition to a friendly and unpretentious atmosphere, the Clubhouse offers some excellent catering. It also houses the Club's own **museum**. It is most interesting and contains a great variety of golfing memorabilia, ranging from one of Tom Watson's gloves to some priceless art.

For the golfer who has confined himself to playing on gentle heathland fairways, sheltered from any wind by tall trees, a visit to Westward Ho! would probably create quite a shock to the system. But clearly, for those with even a moderate interest in the history of the game and of course who are not afraid of a stiff challenge, Westward Ho! is a golfing must.

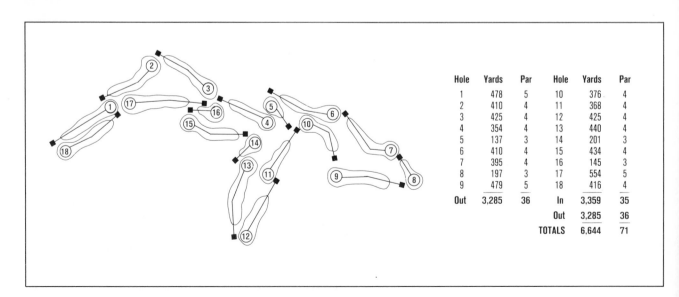

Hole	Yards	Par	Hole	Yards	Par
1	478	5	10	376	4
2	410	4	11	368	4
3	425	4	12	425	4
4	354	4	13	440	4
5	137	3	14	201	3
6	410	4	15	434	4
7	395	4	16	145	3
8	197	3	17	554	5
9	479	5	18	416	4
Out	3,285	36	In	3,359	35
			Out	3,285	36
			TOTALS	6,644	71

SAUNTON

At a time when the likes of **John H Taylor** and **Horace Hutchinson** were striding the windswept fairways on **Northam Burrows**, across the Taw Estuary on the **Braunton Burrows** other men were busy trapping rabbits. It took more than thirty years for matters to be put right.

Saunton Golf Club was founded in **1897**. In common with many great Clubs, Saunton's beginnings were rather modest. At first there were only nine holes and the original Clubhouse was a single room next to the local Post Office. Although the course was extended to 18 holes before the First World War (and a new Clubhouse acquired) it wasn't until after the War that Saunton's reputation really gained momentum. Chiefly responsible for this was golf architect **Herbert Fowler**, who having reshaped Westward Ho! performed a similar task at Saunton.

In **1932** the course was selected to stage the **British Ladies Championship** and this was followed by the **English Amateur Championship** of **1937**. Unfortunately the links didn't fare too well during the Second War as it was considered the perfect place for a Battle School and concrete and barbed wire covered the fairways. Reconstruction didn't begin until 1951, **C K Cotton** this time directing matters. Once restored the course quickly re-established itself as one of Britain's leading Championship links. In the early seventies a second 18 holes were added and today the two are known as the East (the former 'Old Course') and the West course.

In charge of all administrative matters at Saunton is the Club's secretary, **Mr V J Carlisle**. Mr Carlisle may be contacted by telephone on (0271) 812436. The Professional, **Mr J A McGhee** can be contacted on (0271) 812013. Other than being able to provide proof of handicap there are no general restrictions on visitors, however prior telephoning is strongly recommended. Golfing Societies are equally welcome at Saunton, those wishing to make written applications to the Club should address correspondence to the Secretary at **The Saunton Golf Club, Saunton, Braunton, Devon**.

The **green fees** for **1986** were set at £14 per day to play over the Championship **East Course** and £12 for a day's golf on the **West Course**. Juniors are offered a fifty per cent reduction on each.

Although on the map Saunton and Westward Ho! appear to be very neighbourly, travelling from one to another is in fact about a 20 mile trip via Barnstaple. The Club's precise location is off the **B3231** south of Saunton village. The **B3231** can be picked up at Braunton, with Braunton in turn being joined to **Ilfracombe** in the north and **Barnstaple** to the south by the A361. Those travelling from further afield should aim for Barnstaple. The town can be reached from **Exeter** by the A377 and from **Taunton** by the A61, while for those approaching from the north of Cornwall the **A39** is likely to prove of most assistance.

At **6703** yards, par **71** (s.s.s.73) from the Championship tees the **East Course** is nearly 400 yards longer than the **West** (6322 yards par 70). Both, however, provide a fairly stiff challenge with large sandhills being the dominant feature on each course.

The East Course could hardly be described as one of those that breaks you in gently: the first four holes all measure over 400 yards. Of the first twelve holes ten are par fours but perhaps the best on the course is the **16th** which demands a tee shot over a vast sandhill with a second needing to be carried over a deep bunker in front of the green. The course record on the East Course stands at a particularly high **70**.

Since its reopening in 1951 Saunton has hosted several important Championships, both professional and amateur. Twice the **English Open Amateur Stroke Play Championship** has been played on the East Course and in 1966 the **PGA Championship** was held at Saunton. Most recent was **The St Andrews Trophy** in 1984, when the British side defeated the Continent.

As for its 19th, the Clubhouse at Saunton has recently been completely refurbished and is most impressive. Full catering is offered throughout the week and in a similar vein to Westward Ho! the atmosphere is most relaxing and informal.

On more than one occasion I have read that if Saunton had a different geography it would be an Open Championship Course. Maybe I'm missing the point, but I've never fully appreciated the 'geography argument'. If it's a question of remoteness, surely North Devon is no more remote than certain parts of the east and west coasts of Scotland – especially now that a motorway runs as far as Exeter (one hour's drive away). Attendance figures? Such is the popularity of golf in modern times it seems most unlikely that the crowds wouldn't flock to the area. North Devon abounds with places to stay, and after all, what better place for a week's holiday in July? As for accommodating a tented village and finding sufficient parking space, well, dangle a carrot like the Open Championship and I bet the proverbial mountains could be moved. I suppose it's at this junction that I should declare an interest in as much as I am a biased Devonian! – Nevertheless I should still like to be enlightened. Who knows...... Saunton, Open Championship venue, 1993?

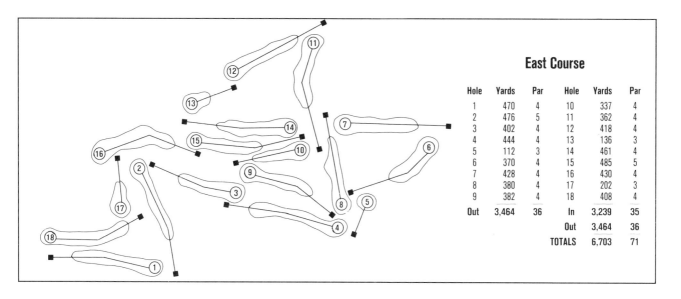

East Course

Hole	Yards	Par	Hole	Yards	Par
1	470	4	10	337	4
2	476	5	11	362	4
3	402	4	12	418	4
4	444	4	13	136	3
5	112	3	14	461	4
6	370	4	15	485	5
7	428	4	16	430	4
8	380	4	17	202	3
9	382	4	18	408	4
Out	3,464	36	In	3,239	35
			Out	3,464	36
			TOTALS	6,703	71

SOMERSET AND AVON

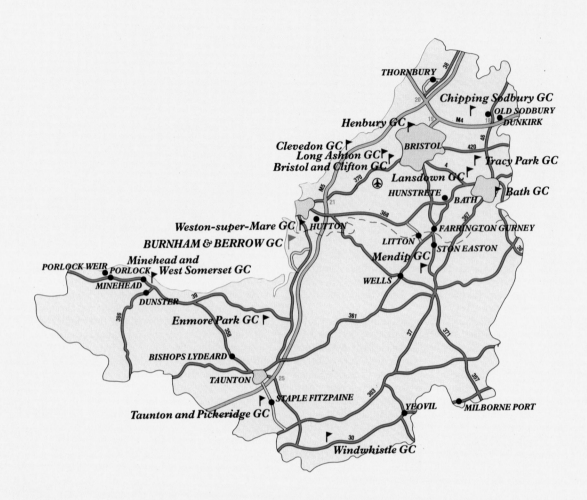

MICHAEL BROWN *"Preparing To Play"* BURLINGTON GALLERY

STON EASTON PARK

n Easton Park, in the village of Ston
ston, lies eleven miles south of the
orgian City of Bath and five miles north
Wells. This Grade I Palladian mansion
great distinction, contains some of the
st exceptional architectural and
corative features of its period to be
nd in the West Country.

e House, as seen today, was completed
1791 and still retains the core of an
lier Tudor house and its Queen Anne
litions within the present structure. For
r hundred years, Ston Easton Park was
home of the Hippisley family, one of
larger landowners of Somerset. More
ently, as the home of Peter and
ristine Smedley, the house has
dergone extensive restoration and now
vides a rare glimpse into the 'Upstairs,
wnstairs' world of the 18th century. The
use's survival is all the more remarkable
in 1957, the lead was stolen from the
f, causing much damage to the interior
a demolition order was sought to raze
house to the ground to salvage its
ber. Fortunately, a Preservation Order
s granted and, over the past twenty-five
rs, Ston Easton Park has gradually been
stated to its present grandeur.

the rooms 'Upstairs' have now been
nished with the finest antique furniture
provide a unique opportunity to enjoy
elegance and splendour of the
hteenth century in one of England's
st historic houses.

wnstairs' the basement contains the
ly kitchens, a fine 18th century linen
m, the old Servants' Hall, the Billiard
m and wine cellars—now re-stocked to
lude a fine selection of rare wines and
vintages.

e restaurant has been highly acclaimed
ernationally for its superb cuisine—fresh,
quality local produce is delivered daily
ensure the consistent excellence of the
d which is a subtle choice of English
French dishes. In 1982, Ston Easton
k was honoured to receive the Egon
nay Gold Plate Award for the Hotel of
Year.

Within forty minutes drive of Ston Easton
Park are some of the major tourist
attractions of the English countryside
—Bath, Wells, Stonehenge, Stourhead,
Wilton, Longleat, Castle Coombe, Lacock,
Avebury and Dyrham Park. Guides for
driving and walking tours can be arranged.

Ston Easton Park,
Chewton Mendip, Bath,
Somerset BA3 4DF
Telephone: (076 121) 631
Telex: 444738 (Avostl G)

The sporting image of Somerset, thanks largely to Messrs. **Richards** and **Botham** is one of leather striking willow rather than that of hickory striking gutta percha, while in the cities of Bristol and Bath shouts of "scrum down!" seem more at home than cries of "fore!".

However, those that golf frequently in these parts will know that both Somerset and the new-fangled county of Avon possess a number of challenging courses and the area as a whole has a greater variety than most to offer the visiting golfer: from traditional links golf at both Burnham and Weston to the rolling downland type courses of Long Ashton and Bath.

Burnham and Berrow (featured a few pages on) is without doubt the finest course in the area and the place where **J H Taylor** wielded his famous mashie to great effect. The two holiday towns of **Minehead** and **Weston-Super-Mare** house the region's other two links courses. The Minehead and West Somerset Golf Club has more than a hundred years of history – it therefore remembers the quieter days in the years 'Before Butlins'. A fairly flat and windy course, it is situated on the eastern side of the town. Visitors are welcome at all times, though during the peak season a quick telephone call to the Club is advisable. The same can be said of Weston – a slightly longer, well-maintained course, located just off the main **A370** Bristol road.

Moving further up the coast, the golf course at **Clevedon**, stares spectacularly out across the mouth of the Severn. But here the golf is played along the cliff tops and it cannot be described as a links. Always kept in good condition, Clevedon is certainly worth a visit. For 1987 the green fees have been set at **£9** per day during weekdays, with **£12** payable at weekends and on Bank Holidays. Societies are also welcome, but restricted to Mondays.

By travelling inland from Clevedon towards Bristol along the **B3128**, two of the city's best courses are reached before the famous Suspension Bridge. **Long Ashton** is actually immediately off the B3128, while to find **Bristol and Clifton** a left turn should be taken along the **B3129**. There is probably little to choose between the two, both being particularly attractive examples of downland golf. Visitors should be able to provide proof of handicap at both. To have a round at Long Ashton in 1987 it will cost **£12**, on weekdays and **£14** at weekends, while juniors can play on weekdays for **£5**. Societies are welcome to visit on Wednesdays.

Henbury's Golf Club is closer to the centre of Bristol, about three miles to the north to be precise, in the quiet suburb of Westbury-on-Trym. Henbury is a very mature parkland course with the abundance of trees making for some very attractive and challenging holes.

Anyone travelling from Bristol to Bath (or vice versa) is likely to pass within a few miles of the **Tracy Park** Golf and Country Club at Wick. If possible a detour is strongly recommended.

Tracy Park is a newish course, built in the mid-seventies around a 400-year old mansion which acts as a rather impressive Clubhouse. Quite a lengthy course, it welcomes visitors during weekdays, though a preliminary telephone call ought to be made.

Everybody, they say, falls in love with Bath – the Romans did, the Georgians did and the Americans think it's "cute". For visiting golfers, if the 'other half' should come under the spell, the City has two attractive propositions: **Bath** Golf Club and **Lansdown** Golf Club. The former, commonly known as **Sham Castle**, has an excellent situation high above the City and provides tremendous views over the surrounding countryside. In 1986 the fees to play at Bath were **£7.50** weekdays and **£9** at weekends. Societies can arrange to play on Wednesdays and Fridays. The fees at Lansdown are similarly priced. Here the course is on flatter ground adjacent to Bath Races. Visitors are welcome at all times, but as the course closes on racing days I cannot recommend an each-way double. A telephone call is again a good idea.

Taunton's Golf Course at Corfe, the **Taunton** and **Pickeridge** Golf Club is similarly near to the town's race track. Visitors (with handicaps) are welcome. Staying in central Somerset Enmore Park, south of Bridgwater, is a very pleasant medium-length affair, nestling around the foothills of the Quantocks. At both clubs, the green fees are quite moderately priced.

Moving from the Quantocks to the Mendips, the **Mendip Golf Club** at Gurney Slade offers possibly the most spectacular vistas of any course in the South West. From its 4th fairway, almost 1,000 feet above sea-level, on a clear day it is possible to sight the Cotswolds, the Welsh Mountains and the Purbeck Hills, Glastonbury Tor and Westbury's White Horse...need I go on? Mendip is an efficiently run Club that welcomes visitors at all times (societies particularly welcome on Thursdays and Fridays). The green fees for 1987 are **£7.50** for weekdays, **£10** at weekends with reduced rates for juniors.

Two final mentions go to the beautifully named pair of **Chipping Sodbury** (close to **Badminton**) and the **Windwhistle Golf and Squash Club** at Chard. The former Club now possesses two courses, one of which measures nigh on 7,000 yards. The latter is another course situated on high ground offering extensive views. Golfing families should also note that it is close to the famous **Cricket St Thomas Wildlife Park**. Weekday green fees were set at **£5** in 1986, with **£7.50** payable at weekends when starting times must be booked.

Rather like that colourful Somerset vicar, the **Reverend Pavey**, who in 1986 for a good cause played a hole on 18 different courses in the County, I am aware that we have zig-zagged our way across the region.....but then surely, having started our round at Burnham, it seems only appropriate that we should end up at Chard (apologies!).

Bath G.C.	(0225) 63834
Bristol and Clifton G.C.	(0272) 393474
Burnham and Berrow G.C.	(0278) 785760
Chipping Sodbury G.C.	(0454) 319042
Clevedon G.C.	(0272) 874057
Enmore Park G.C.	(027867) 481
Henbury G.C.	(0272) 500044
Lansdown G.C.	(0225) 22138
Long Ashton G.C.	(0272) 392316
Mendip G.C.	(0749) 840570
Minehead & W. Somerset G.C	(0643) 2057
Taunton & Pickeridge G.C.	(082342) 537
Tracy Park G.& C.C.	(027582) 2251
Wells G.C.	(0749) 75005
Weston-Super-Mare G.C.	(0934) 26968
Windwhistle G. & S.C.	(046030) 231

Even with the death of Beau Nash in 1761 Bath has remained one of the country's most stylish and uniformly loved towns – it offers so much. When the renowned Beau first visited Bath it was an "uncouth, dingy, rowdy place": as many people know this is far from the truth today. The Roman Baths, the Abbey, The Pump Rooms, a wealth of museums and galleries, the Royal Crescent and the Theatre Royal to name but a few. However, the region offers so much more: the open Somerset coastline, Exmoor, the Quantocks, a wealth of country houses: Longleat, Dyrham Park – the list goes on. What we need is a guide – a culinary caddy if you like. There is one man – a distant relative of Beau Nash – the flamboyant Beau Ned.

We catch up with the Nouveau Beau at **Popjoys (0225) 60494** his favourite restaurant in Bath, named after his ancestor's mistress who still frequents the place if rumour is to be believed. Spirits aside, or perhaps before dinner, complement a first class restaurant. However, as Ned is quick to point out, Bath is blessed with many. **The Hole in the Wall (0225) 25242** brings happy memories – a splendid dining room – and some delightful bedrooms. The **Clos du Roy (0225) 313774** – another favourite – offers excellent game and a superb wine list. Beau Ned, I should explain, is a somewhat tedious fellow. This was his cogent explanation of his favourite hotels. "**The Apsley House (0225) 336966** – superb, **The Priory (0225) 331922** – superb, the **Royal Crescent (0225) 319090** – superb."

You may be feeling a little aggrieved at our guide's selection – well, frankly, so am I – it's with great animosity that the fellow decided to leave Bath. "It's all here you fool", he snorts. A taxing day seems inevitable – so much so that a game of golf is in order – another mistake, Ned's closest thing to scratch was most ungainly. In contrast, however, we did hit a purple patch during the day, not on the Golf Course but at Ston Easton. **Ston Easton Park (076 121) 631** to be precise, a superbly luxurious country mansion thoroughly recommended in every way. That day we trudged remorselessly, so much so that I decided to lose the fellow. I left him in a bunker at the Mendip Golf Club and scurried up the fairway to the cries of "What about dinner! You promised to take me to Hunstrete House" (an outstanding hotel and restaurant **(07618) 578**). I had also considered another favourite at Hinton Charterhouse, on the A36 five miles south of Bath, specifically the **Homewood Park Hotel (022 122) 3771**, and its restaurant. Instead, I rushed to the car and consumed a much needed gin and tonic at Ye Old Kings Arms, Litton – a perfect place to escape the chaos. It was there that I decided to visit **The Old Parsonage, (0761) 52211**, an excellent restaurant in the village of Farrington Gurney, which also offers some pleasant accommodation.

Getting into my stride now, I considered the days ahead. I should visit Wells and inspect once again its delightful Cathedral and busy streets. Lunch at the **Ancient Gate House (0749)** 72029 will keep me going and after a round at Windwhistle a night at another Old Parsonage, this time in **Crewkerne, (0460) 73516**, delightfully personal. And what of Yeovil? Well, after a drink or two at **The Queen's Head, Milborne Port** – dinner at **Little Barwick House (0935) 23902**, sounds most appealing. I might even stay there if I don't find time to drive to my next port of call, Taunton.

Here lavish accommodation and excellent cuisine as well as friendly bars can be found in the **Castle (0823) 72671**, while the **County (0823) 87651**, offers more modest but a none the less equally welcoming place to stay.

Early next morning and a round at Taunton and Pickeridge is followed by that lovely old pub – the Greyhound, Staple Fitzpaine. A dilemma, do I travel straight to the coast or stay in Bishop's Lydeard and visit that excellent restaurant, **The Rose Cottage (0823) 432394?**

When I do arrive at Burnham and Berrow's first tee, I realise my schedule has waned somewhat – while my belly has done quite the opposite. Not to worry – after a splendid round a short visit to the **Luttrell Arms** in Dunster. I set sail to Porlock Weir and **The Anchor Hotel (0643) 862753**. After some drinks and a spirited walk contemplating the Bristol Channel and the distant Welsh coast, it's once again bedtime. **The Northfield Hotel (0643) 5155**, is the suggestion – not lavish but most welcoming for tired bods; an alternative is **Periton Park (0643) 5970** in Middlecombe. The next morning – up the coast, another dilemma, having played a round at Weston, should one stay at the **Grand Atlantic** in the town or visit Hutton and the **Hutton Court Hotel (0934) 814343**, nearby? With great remorse I opt for neither and head up the M5, by-passing Clevedon and the **Walton Park Hotel (0272) 874253**, also very pleasant. My student days spin past me as I reach the M4 and Bristol. Instead of trekking to the city centre and visiting the **Holiday Inn (0272) 294281**, particularly comfortable – or Clifton and its delightful restaurants, **(Michael 0272 276190)**, wine bars and pubs, a frolic on the terrace at **The Avon Gorge** – how that would bring back the memories. As I turn towards Old Sodbury, I see something terrible – Beau Ned – astride a steed. It's no good, he sees the car. Some hours later, bored out of my mind despite the pleasant setting of the **Cross Hands Hotel (0454) 313000**, my ears prick up – Ned has offered to take me to Thornbury and its outstanding hotel, **The Thornbury Castle (0545) 418511**. Even I can manage this awful fellow if this is my reward. By the time I reach the motor, I have changed my mind. I flee in haste avoiding the delights of Castle Combe and **The Manor House Hotel (0249) 782206**, and even Dunkirk's Bodkin House and Petty France – nothing, not even the wild ponies of Exmoor, would drag me back here.

Postscript: (Beau Ned was sadly killed endeavouring to overtake a lorry on the inside while still on his horse.)

Popjoy's Restaurant
Beau Nash's House, Sawclose,
Bath, BA1 1EU
Tel: (0225) 60494
An internationally famous restaurant in one of the most beautiful Georgian houses in Bath, next to the Theatre Royal. Very creative ideas in English and French food, friendly atmosphere and sensible prices. Booking essential. Open evenings only, Monday to Saturday.

The Old Vic
Theatre Royal, King Street,
Bristol, BS1 4ED
Tel: (0272) 277466
Established in 1946, the Theatre Royal, oldest working playhouse in the country. Built 1766, superb example of Georgian theatre. The company operates approximately 40 weeks in the year, presenting new plays, classical revivals and popular modern works.

OTHER PLEASURES PALE BESIDE IT

CALCOT MANOR

[Cal]cot Manor is set peacefully amid acres [of r]olling countryside near the historic town [of T]etbury, where the Parish Church bells [are] rung to celebrate Royal occasions.

[Th]e Cotswold Manor House dates back to [the] 15th Century and was until recently a [far]mhouse. Its beautiful stone barns and [stab]les include one of the oldest Tithe [Bar]ns in England, being founded in 1300 [by] the Cistercian Monks from Kingswood [Ab]bey. (In 1927 the stone slates and roof [tim]bers were sold to a Marievale town in [Cin]cinatti, and their Church now has the [Ca]lcot roof!). These buildings form a [qu]adrangle and the sight of the roofs [glis]tening in the morning sun or glowing at [du]sk can be quite breathtaking.

[Th]e conversion to a Country House Hotel [ha]s been done with great care not to [ch]ange the family atmosphere. The [Dr]awing Room offers peaceful relaxation [loo]king over the lawns and in Autumn and [wi]nter the log fires crackle and glow all [da]y! The perfect place to eat English

Muffins! Each of the bedrooms is individually designed with a co-ordinating bathroom and have every modern comfort and service needed to make you feel completely at home.

The Restaurant, decorated in soft greens and apricot is a perfect setting for Redmond Hayward's consistently delightful menus, that make maximum use of fresh and interesting produce.

Calcot is in the very heart of the South Cotswolds, perfectly situated between the many delights of Bath and the excellent shopping of Cheltenham. Close by is the Roman capital of Cirencester, Peter Scott's Wildfowl Trust and the perennial wonders of Westonbirt Arboretum. Indeed the region is among England's richest treasures for the simple pleasures of touring and discovery.

There is always a welcome at Calcot Manor and the Ball family enjoy sharing their home and pampering their guests.

Calcot Manor,
Near Tetbury,
Gloucestershire GL8 8YJ
Telephone: (066 689) 355

I wonder how many people have travelled along the M5 between Bristol and Exeter and wondered what lay beyond the great Iron Age fort that rises out of level ground, 'Like something from out of "Close Encounters",' midway between Weston and Bridgwater. Well, many golfers will know that a short distance behind the great hill lies one of England's finest links courses.

Burnham and Berrow appeared on the golfing map in 1891 and the first professional the Club engaged was no lesser man than **John H Taylor**. The great man was then in fact a lad of 19 although within 3 years he was to win the Open Championship at Sandwich – the first of his five victories. John Henry thought very highly of what, until quite recently, had been a "wild rabbit infested waste of sandhills" for he said it was here, at Burnham, that he was "given the splendid opportunity of developing my mashie play" (as the course) "necessitated very accurate approach play."

The present day visitor to the North Somerset club is most unlikely to confront a gathering of wild rabbits (at least of the animal variety) nor, one assumes, will he possess a mashie amongst his armoury, however, despite a number of alterations made over the years, the towering sandhills remain by far the course's most dominant feature.

Not surprisingly Burnham and Berrow is a popular course and whatever the time of year visitors would be wise to telephone the Club before setting off. **Mrs E.L.Slowman** is the new Secretary and she can be contacted on **(0278) 785760.** The Club's professional, **Noel Blake**, can be reached on **(0278) 784545.** Persons interested in organising a Society meeting are advised to write to the Secretary, the Club's full address being, **Burnham and Berrow Golf Club, St Christopher's Way, Burnham-on-Sea, Somerset.**

Green fees for 1986 were set at **£10** for weekdays with **£12** payable at weekends. For **juniors** the fees were half the above rates. Persons holidaying in the vicinity (Weston-Super-Mare is less than 10 miles away) might well consider the merits of a weekly ticket (**£55** in 1986) or a fortnightly ticket (**£85** in 1986). Furthermore in addition to the 18 hole Championship Course there is also an adjacent 9 hole course situated alongside the sea. Whilst probably not quite up to the standard of the full Championship course, at **3275** yards, par **36**, it certainly represents a fine challenge and the **green fee** of **£3** would appear to be excellent value. Golf clubs can be hired from the pro-shop and in summer it may be possible to find a caddy – hopefully one well acquainted with the best paths over and around the ginormous sandhills.

Approaching by car from both North and South the **M5** is the most direct route, leaving at exit 22. Thereafter one should follow the **B3140.** The course is situated about a mile north of Burnham-on-Sea and is well signposted.

It has been written that Burnham's setting is unspectacular: in a word "false". Whilst it may not be Gleneagles, Somerset is never dull. From many points on the course there are superb views across the Bristol Channel and the panorama from the 12th green is quite breathtaking.

Right from the first hole the premium on accuracy becomes apparent. Anything short of a straight tee shot will leave a blind, not to mention very awkward second. At one time the layout of the course necessitated the playing of several blind shots, however, today accurate driving will largely eliminate such difficulties although on a number of holes the base of the flagstick will not be visible when playing the approach shot. Burnham's 2nd is a good straight hole played from an elevated tee, whereas the 3rd at least from the back, is one of those 'bite-off-as-much-as-you-dare' holes with the fairway dog-legging sharply to the left towards a sunken punch-bowl green. From the 4th tee there is the first view of the Bristol Channel and distant Wales as the course moves nearer the sea. There are two par 3's on the front nine, the 5th and the 9th, the latter surely being one of the finest short holes to be found anywhere.

On reaching the turn anyone claiming to have mastered the large sandhills may well have to eat his words after playing the 10th: a minor mountain must be carried from the tee and there is a severe drop away to the right – be warned! If the front nine is perhaps the more interesting of the halves, the second nine is probably the more testing. The 12th and 13th require very precise second shots, both the short holes are exceptionally tricky and the 18th needs a couple of mighty big hits if it is to be reached in two. A good score at Burnham certainly has to be earned, but immensely satisfying if achieved.

Visitors should find the Clubhouse atmosphere pleasingly informal. The catering is of a high standard and is offered daily between the hours of 11 am and 6 pm. With prior notice both breakfast and dinner can be arranged. Burnham and Berrow is a friendly Club and well worth a visit. Clearly the message to all golfers who pass down the M5 oblivious as to what goes on beyond the 'great hump' is quite simply, come on over!

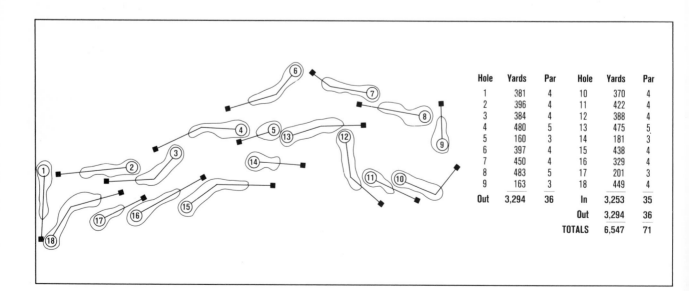

Hole	Yards	Par	Hole	Yards	Par
1	381	4	10	370	4
2	396	4	11	422	4
3	384	4	12	388	4
4	480	5	13	475	5
5	160	3	14	181	3
6	397	4	15	438	4
7	450	4	16	329	4
8	483	5	17	201	3
9	163	3	18	449	4
Out	**3,294**	**36**	**In**	**3,253**	**35**
			Out	**3,294**	**36**
			TOTALS	**6,547**	**71**

AVON

Bath G.C. (18)
Bath (0225) 63834

Bristol & Clifton G.C. (18)
Bristol (0272) 393474

Chipping Sodbury G.C. (18+9)
Chipping Sodbury (0454) 319042

Clevedon G.C. (18)
Clevedon (0272) 874057

Filton G.C. (18)
Bristol (0272) 694169

Fosseway G.C. (9)
Midsomer Norton (0761) 412214

Henbury G.C. (18)
Bristol (0272) 500044

Knowle G.C. (18)
Bristol (0272) 770660

Lansdown G.C. (18)
Bath (0225) 22138

Long Ashton G.C. (18)
Long Ashton (0272) 382316

Mangotsfield G.C. (18)
Bristol (0272) 565501

Mendip G.C. (18)
Gurney Slade, Bath
(0749) 840570

Saltford G.C. (18)
Saltford (02217) 3513

Shirehampton Park G.C. (18)
Shirehampton, Bristol
(0272) 822083

Tracey Park G. & C.C. (18+9)
Wick, Nr. Bristol (027582) 2251

Weston-Super-Mare G.C. (18)
Weston-Super-Mare (0934) 26968

Worlebury G.C. (18)
Weston-Super-Mare (934) 25789

CORNWALL

Bude & North
Cornwall G.C. (18)
Bude (0288) 2006

Budock Vean Hotel (9)
Falmouth (0326) 2500660

Carlyon Bay Hotel G.C. (18)
Carlyon Bay, St. Austell
(072681) 4250

Falmouth G.C. (18)
Falmouth (0326) 40525

Launceston G.C. (18)
Launceston (0566) 3442

Looe Bin Down G.C. (18)
Looe (05034) 247

Mullion G.C. (18)
Cury, Helston (0326) 240685

Newquay G.C. (18)
Newquay (0637) 874354

Perranporth G.C. (18)
Perranporth (0872) 573701

Praa Sands G.C. (9)
Penzance (0736) 763445

St. Austell G.C. (18)
St. Austell (0726) 72649

St. Enodoc G.C. (18)
Rock, Wadebridge (020886) 3216

St. Mellion G.C. (18+18)
Saltash (0579) 50101

Tehidy Park G.C. (18)
Camborne (0209) 842208

Trevose C.C. (18+9)
Constantine Bay, Padstow
(0841) 520208

Truro G.C. (18)
Treliske, Truro (0872) 78684

West Cornwall G.C. (18)
Lelant, St. Ives (0736) 753401

Whitsand Bay Hotel G.C. (18)
Crafthole, Torpoint (0503) 30418

DEVON

Axe Cliff G.C. (18)
Seaton (0297) 20219

Bigbury G.C. (18)
Bigbury on Sea, Kingsbridge
(054981) 557

Chulmleigh G.C. (18)
Chulmleigh (0766) 80519

Churston G.C. (18)
Churston, Brixham
(0803) 842128

Downes Crediton G.C. (18)
Hookway Crediton (03632) 3025

East Devon G.C. (18)
Budleigh Salterton (03954) 3370

Elfordleigh Hotel G & C.C. (9)
Plympton, Plymouth
(0752) 703824

Exeter G & C.C. (18)
Exeter (0392) 874139

Great Torrington G.C. (9)
Torrington (02372) 72792

Holsworthy G.C. (18)
Holsworthy (0409) 253177

Honiton G.C. (18)
Middlehills, Honiton
(0404) 44422

Ilfracombe G.C. (18)
Hele Bay, Ilfracombe
(0271) 62176

Manor House Hotel
G. & C.C. (18)
Moretonhampstead (0647) 40355

Newton Abbot (Stover) G.C. (18)
Newton Abbot (0626) 2460

Okehampton G.C. (18)
Okehampton (0837) 308

Royal North Devon G.C. (18)
Westward Ho! (02372) 73817

Saunton G.C. (18+18)
Saunton, Braunton (0271) 812436

Sidmouth G.C. (18)
Sidmouth (0395) 3451

Staddon Heights G.C. (18)
Plymstock, Plymouth
(0752) 42475

Tavistock G.C. (18)
Tavistock (0822) 2344

Teignmouth G.C. (18)
Teignmouth (06267) 4194

Thurlestone G.C. (18)
Thurlestone, Kingsbridge
(0548) 560405

Tiverton G.C. (18)
Tiverton (0884) 252187

Torquay G.C. (18)
Torquay (0803) 37471

Torrington G.C. (9)
Weare Trees, Torrington
(02372) 72792

Warren G.C. (18)
Dawlish (0626) 862255

Wrangaton G.C. (9)
Wrangaton, South Brent
(03647) 3229
(0803) 363688

Yelverton G.C. (18)
Yelverton (0822) 852824

DORSET

Ashley Wood G.C. (9)
Blandford (0258) 52253

Birdport & West
Dorset G.C. (18)
Birdport (0308) 22597

Broadstone G.C. (18)
Broadstone (0202) 692595

Came Down G.C. (18)
Dorchester (030 581) 3494

Christchurch G.C. (9)
Ilford, Christchurch
(0202) 874602

Ferndown G.C. (18+9)
Ferndown (0202) 874602

Highcliffe Castle G.C. (18)
Highcliffe-on-Sea, Caristchurch
(04252) 72210

Isle of Purbeck G.C. (18+9)
Studland (092944) 361

Knighton Heath G.C. (18)
Bournemouth (0202) 572633

Lakey Hill G.C. (18)
Hyde, Wareham (0929) 471776

Lyme Regis G.C. (18)
Lyme Regis (029 74) 2043

Meyrick Park G.C. (18)
Bournemouth (0202) 577375

Parkstone G.C. (18)
Parkstone, Poole (0202) 707138

Queens Park G.C. (18)
Bournemouth (0202) 34900

Sherborne G.C. (18)
Clatcombe, Sherborne
(0963) 814431

Wareham G.C. (9)
Wareham (0202) 690532

Weymouth G.C. (18)
Weymouth (0305) 773981

SOMERSET

Brean G.C. (14)
Burnham-on-Sea (027875) 467

Burnham & Berrow G.C.
(18+9)
Burnham-on-Sea (0278) 785760

Enmore Park G.C. (18)
Enmore, Bridgwater
(027867) 451

Kingweston G.C. (9)
Somerton (0458) 72081

Minehead & West
Somerset G.C. (18)
Minehead (0643) 2057

Taunton & Pickeridge G.C. (18)
Taunton (082342) 537

Tower Hill G.C. (9)
Bruton (074981) 3233

Vivary G.C. (18)
Taunton (0823) 71494

Vivary Park G.C. (18)
Taunton (0823) 3875

Wells G.C. (18)
Wells (0749) 75005

Windwhistle G.C. (12)
Cricket St. Thomas Chard
(046030) 231

Yeovil G.C. (18)
Yeovil (0935) 22965

WILTSHIRE

Brinkworth G.C. (9)
Brinkworth, Chippenham
(066 641) 392

Broome Manor G.C. (18+9)
Swindon (0793) 32403

Chippenham G.C. (18)
Chippenham (0249) 652040

High Post G.C. (18)
Great Burnford, Salisbury
(0722) 73356

Kingsdown G.C. (18)
Kingsdown, Corsham
(0225) 743472

Marlborough G.C. (18)
Marlborough (0672) 52147

North Wilts G.C. (18)
Bishops Cannings, Devizes
(038086) 627

RAF Upavon G.C. (9)
Upavon, Pewsey (0980) 630351

R.M.C.S. Shrivenham G.C. (9)
Shrivenham, Swindon
(0793) 78255

Salisbury & South Wilts G.C.
(18+9)
Netherhampton, Salisbury
(0722) 742645

Swindon G.C. (18)
Ogbourne St George,
Marlborough (067284) 327

Tidworth Garrison G.C. (18)
Tidworth (0980) 42301

West Wilts G.C. (18)
Warminster (0985) 213133

DORSET AND WILTSHIRE

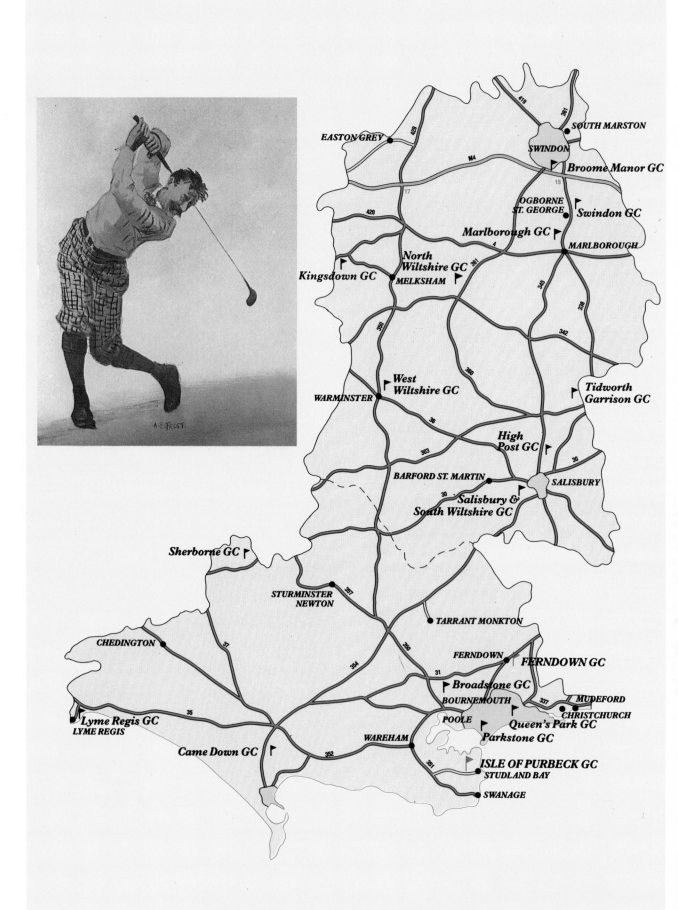

EASTON GREY
SOUTH MARSTON
SWINDON
Broome Manor GC
OGBORNE ST. GEORGE
Swindon GC
Marlborough GC
MARLBOROUGH
North Wiltshire GC
Kingsdown GC
MELKSHAM
West Wiltshire GC
WARMINSTER
Tidworth Garrison GC
High Post GC
BARFORD ST. MARTIN
SALISBURY
Salisbury & South Wiltshire GC
Sherborne GC
STURMINSTER NEWTON
TARRANT MONKTON
CHEDINGTON
FERNDOWN
FERNDOWN GC
Broadstone GC
BOURNEMOUTH
MUDEFORD
CHRISTCHURCH
Lyme Regis GC
LYME REGIS
POOLE
Queen's Park GC
Parkstone GC
Came Down GC
WAREHAM
ISLE OF PURBECK GC
STUDLAND BAY
SWANAGE

A.B. FROST   *"Good Form"*   ROSENSTIELS

Plumber Manor

...rounded by the home farm and in the ...1st of Hardy's Dorset, Plumber Manor ...been owned by the same family since ...17th century, The house was built by ...arles Brune in 1665. The painting of the ...ginal house hangs above the staircase ...i has been reproduced in Hutchins' ...story of Dorset' and numerous other ...torical accounts of the county. The ...use was partially destroyed by fire in the ...l 18th century and was more recently ...ernally reconstructed by the present ...ner's grandparents.

...1973 Richard, Alison and Brian ...deaux-Brune turned their home into a ...taurant with bedrooms, none of the ...ily atmosphere has been lost, family ...traits hang in the gallery and antique ...ces of furniture are in evidence ...oughout the house.

...1982 a stone barn, lying within the ...unds was converted into six spacious ...ms with views over the garden and ...velish stream.

...e restaurant is still a mainstay of the ...iness and Brian Prideaux-Brune the ...ef's talents have long since been ...ognised by all major guides.

...mber makes a perfect resting place for ...vellers going further west, but it is rather ...ideal centre for touring the marvellous ...spoilt countryside of Dorset, the ...turesque villages of Milton and Cerne ...bas, the Piddle valley and the small ...ist towns of Lyme Regis and ...botsbury. The historic splendours of ...ntacute, Stourhead, Wilton and ...merous National Trust properties are to ...visited.

...ere is a tennis court and a croquet lawn ...hin the grounds. Horseback riding and ...y pigeon shooting can be arranged ...arby and there are several golf courses ...hin easy reach.

...ase note that lunches are not served.

Plumber Manor,
Sturminister Newton,
Dorset DT10 2AF
Telephone: (0258) 72507

The heart of Wessex. Stonehenge, Avebury and The White Horse. Lyme Regis, Chesil Beach and Lulworth Cove. Two counties rich in history, once the most heavily populated corner of England, now one of the most peaceful and few would dispute one of the most pleasant.

There are twelve golf courses in **Wiltshire** and they are spread fairly evenly across the county. While none could be classed as genuine Championship material, the majority offer a particularly enjoyable day's golf amidst some exceptionally attractive surroundings. **Dorset** is quite different: golf wise the county is rather 'lopsided': it has a greater number of courses, but if the south eastern corner were suddenly to be removed (one wonders by what!!) the proverbial cupboard would be almost bare. The better golf courses in Dorset lie within a ten mile radius of the centre of Bournemouth. The town itself has no fewer than three Championship courses within a few miles – **Parkstone, Broadstone** and **Ferndown**, while just across Poole Harbour, the **Isle of Purbeck Golf Club** near Swanage boasts one of the most spectacular locations in Britain.

Beginning in the north of Wiltshire, Swindon is the county's largest town and there are two courses close at hand: **Broome Manor** and the **Swindon Golf Club**, both are situated south of the town. The latter at Ogbourne St George, despite its name, is in fact closer to Marlborough than Swindon. **Broome Manor**, (2 miles from junction **15** of the **M4**) is a public course and as such visitors can arrange a game seven days of the week. In addition to 27 holes of rolling parkland golf there is an excellent covered driving range. **Swindon Golf Club** (7 miles south of Swindon along the **A345**) is a downland type course, quite undulating with many extensive views. Visitors are welcome at Swindon between Mondays and Fridays and after 4pm on Sundays. Green fees range between **£6** and **£10**.

Marlborough Golf Club is a near neighbour of Swindon Golf Club, being situated to the north west of the town on the Marlborough Downs. Offering similarly wide ranging views (and similarly breezy!) it too welcomes visitors during the week. Weekends are naturally busier but it may still be possible to obtain a game. Fees in 1986 were around the **£6** to **£8** mark.

Over to the far west of the county and almost over the boundary in Avon is the heathland course at **Kingsdown**. It is the oldest Club in Wiltshire, being founded in 1880. Again visitors can play at most times, though prior telephoning is preferred at the weekend.

Dropping 'down the county' and returning to the Downs, West Wiltshire Golf Club lies midway between Warminster and Westbury off the **A350** (N.B. nearby Longleat House), while the other side of Salisbury Plain **Tidworth Garrison**, owned by the Army, is one to note if passing between Wiltshire and Hampshire. Fees at both are approximately £7 per day.

High Post is generally considered to be the leading course in the county. It is located to the north of Salisbury on the **A345** and is very close to Stonehenge. A downland course, measuring 6267 yards, there are no general restrictions on visiting golfers, the cost of a day's golf at High Post is priced at approximately **£8**.

A second in the Salisbury region is the **Salisbury and South Wilts Golf Club**. Pleasantly situated to the west of the county town at Netherhampton on the **A3094**, the course provides several magnificent views over Salisbury Cathedral. Once again visitors are welcome throughout the week, fees in 1986 were **£7** midweek, **£8** at weekends.

I knew I'd regret describing Dorset as "lopsided"! – **Sherborne** in the far north of the county is undoubtedly one of the prettiest inland courses to be found anywhere in Britain. Sherborne can be reached via the **B3145** and lies about one mile north of the town on the edge of the famous Blackmore Vale. Visitors are welcome although prior telephoning is recommended.

In the south west of the county **Lyme Regis**, famed for its fossils and more recently its French Lieutenant's Woman, has a fairly undulating 18 hole course which lies to the east of the town. Visitors are welcome here during weekdays and on most Sundays. The road between Lyme Regis and Weymouth provides dramatic views over Chesil Beach and passes through some of the most beautiful villages in England. The area north of Weymouth is Thomas Hardy country. Dorchester stands in the middle of it all and **Came Down Golf Club** is well worth noting when in these parts. (The course lies just south of the town off the **A354**).

The **Isle of Purbeck** has already been mentioned and is featured on a later page (as for that matter is **Ferndown**). But both **Parkstone** and **Broadstone** also fall into the 'must-be-visited' category for anyone staying in the Bournemouth area. Both are beautiful heathland courses with much heather and gorse and numerous pine trees. Visitors can play at either during the week (fees approximately **£11** to **£14**) and whilst it may also be possible to arrange a game at Parkstone at the weekend, prior telephoning is essential (indeed it is probably wise to do so at all times). As for their locations, Parkstone lies midway between Bournemouth and Poole on the **A35** and Broadstone is situated to the northwest of Bournemouth off the **B3074**.

Finally, one shouldn't forget the two public courses in Bournemouth: **Queens Park** and **Meyrick Park**. Each is of a particularly high standard, indeed the former is often considered to be the finest public course in England.

Broadstone G.C.	(0202) 692595
Broome Manor G.C.	(0739) 45761
Came Down G.C.	(030581) 3494
Ferndown G.C.	(0202) 874602
High Post G.C.	(0722) 73356
Isle of Purbeck G.C.	(092944) 361
Kingsdown G.C.	(0255) 743472
Lyme Regis G.C.	(02974) 2043
Marlborough G.C.	(0672) 52147
Parkstone G.C.	(0202) 707138
Queens Park G.C.	(0202) 34900
Salisbury & S. Wiltshire G.C.	(0722) 742645
Sherborne G.C.	(0963) 814431
Swindon G.C.	(067284) 327
Tidworth Garrison G.C.	(0980) 42301
West Wiltshire G.C.	(0985) 213133

DORSET AND WILTSHIRE

Dorset and Wiltshire, what a lovely pair, so to speak. They offer so much: Lyme Regis, Poole Harbour with its four tides, Abbotsbury and those splendid sub-tropical Gardens. The Purbeck Hills, Lullingstone and its silk farm, Shaftesbury with its splendid views overlooking Blackmoor Vale – gorgeous, Stourhead – quite superb, Broadlands, The Avebury Circle, Stonehenge. The Land of Dr Dolittle and Thomas Hardy has much to commend it. While its golf is not the country's finest – it's not bad at all and with its other attractions a visit is well worth while. Ideal for families, couples, the lot – in the words of the Americans – Go for it! (Thomas Hardy promptly turns in his grave.)

Where to start one's trip – well, Bournemouth is as good a place as any. Both the golf and the hotels are excellent and with everything the town has to offer, it is obviously the place for golfing parents to take their children. In Bournemouth itself – a holiday town – there are a number of hotels, a few of which stand out particularly. **The Carlton (0202) 22011** offers some good facilities and excellent service but is expensive and much the same can be said for **The Royal Bath (0202) 25555** which occupies a spectacular clifftop location, as does the **Highcliff (0202) 27702**, another well presented hotel with many amenities. Views overlooking Poole Bay can be found at the **Hotel Miramar**, a charming establishment. The list, of course could go on. The town offers such an infinite variety – but these hotels should do you well enough – now, where from here? Although price is important, quality is equally so and for this reason **Provence** in Southbourne is strongly recommended for its French cuisine (dinner only), while in the square, excellent seafood can be enjoyed at **Crusts (0202) 21430** where marvellous use is made of the local catch.

Poole also offers some delightful eating establishments. **Gullivers,** another of the French variety is particularly well thought of **(0202) 708810** while **The Mansion House (0202) 685666** has charming rooms and a good restaurant. Other places to note in this area of the world are numerous. For people wishing to get away from the sea and sand, or the water hazards and bunkers should visit Tarrant Monkton. Here a converted stables house makes for a really splendid little restaurant, **Langton's (025889) 225** and the local pub, **The Langton Arms**, is also tremendously well frequented.

After a first clear round of golf later, this time at Ferndown – you will wish to return to your hotel, in this case it may well be the **Dormy Hotel (0202) 872121**. This really is ideal for golfers and a new leisure complex gives the hotel added appeal. In Mudeford, **The Avonmouth ((0202) 483434** enjoys fine views of the estuary and is cheaper than its Bournemouth rivals while in nearby Christchurch another restaurant holds its head up high – **Splinters (0202) 483454**, a good French menu with yet more excellent fish.

No trip of the area is complete without contemplating the delights of Hardy. In Milton Abbas between Dorchester and Milford Forum, **The Milton Manor (0258) 880254** has a gorgeously tranquil setting in a model village situation – ideally relaxing and convenient for the Purbeck Hills, and significantly the Isle of Purbeck Golf Course. Studland Bay offers **The Knoll House Hotel (092944) 251**, a justifiably popular family hotel.

While in Swanage **The Pines (0929) 425211** and **The Grand (0929) 423353** both provide a happy hunting ground for golfers visiting the area.

Further down the coast and through the Purbeck Hills one finds Wareham, where **The Priory Hotel (09295) 2772**, a sixteenth century conversion, makes for an outstandingly tranquil situation. Having played a round in the morning (don't read that too quickly) at Cane Down and followed it by an afternoon's golf at Lyme Regis some thoughts arise – do we stay in Lyme Regis, dinosaurs and all (note the museum) or do we make tracks for Wiltshire and Salisbury. If you stay in Lyme Regis, then **The Mariners (02974) 2753** is the best bet, while seafood at a local pub, **The Pilot Boat** is well thought of. For those golfers looking for grander accommodation two thoughts spring immediately to mind. In Chedington, **Chedington Court (093589) 265** is excellent and in Sturminster Newton **Plumber Manor (0258) 72507** has pride of place; both have excellent restaurants and the welcome in the latter is a delight.

Salisbury has a fine cathedral, streets full of antique shops and the wonderfully situated **Rose and Crown Hotel (0722) 27908**; surely reason enough to travel here. The **Old Bell Inn** is another civilised place to stay **(0722) 27958**. A restaurant to note while in these parts is located in Barford St Martin its name – **Michel's** – a simply excellent place for dinner. Please forgive the omission of pubs in this piece, this is not because there are none. On the contrary when in the area merely find a charming village, and the pub generally awaits you. If one is playing the West Wiltshire, there is a clear piece of advice – Warminster, another delightful setting, **The Bishopstrow House (0985) 212312** offers supreme cooking and luxurious rooms while **The Old Bell (0985) 216611** is a fine old inn in which to stay. Restaurants also oblige – **Coopers (0985) 216911** is a perfect spot for some well imagined cooking. Elsewhere in East Street, **La Petite Cuisine Belge (0985) 215052** is also very good.

Travelling north along the **A350** one arrives at Melksham and the recommendation here is another inn, **The Kings Arms (0225) 707272** – good value. Nearby, in Beanacre **The Beechfield House (0225) 703700** stands out for its comfort, hospitality and restaurant. As the road diverges, where to now? To the north and Easton Grey, **Whatley Manor (06662) 2888** is a delight and also offers a good restaurant, while to the east Marlborough reveals for excellent food: **The Sun (0762) 52081** which provides some good value accommodation as well as a pleasant setting. In the direction of Swindon and Ogborne St George, **The Robin Hood Inn** is well thought of. Certainly Swindon may not appeal to some but it is the fastest growing town in the British Isles, business folk wishing to take in a round may also wish to stay at **Blunsdon House, Blunsdon (0793) 72170**, (north of the town off the A419) or at **The Wiltshire (0793) 28282** in the town itself. A particularly lively place can be found at South Marston, **The South Marston Hotel and Country Club (0793) 827777** – good for leisure facilities.

Leaving the land of Hardy with leisure on one's mind is ideal for the countryside offers so much: a wealth of beaches, although soon perhaps they'll be drilling for oil: Poor old Thomas! But this is Dorset not Dallas and for now it remains rich not in oil but in some outstanding places to stay.

---

1. The Manor Hotel
Dorchester
Tel: (0308) 897616
A charming 17th century manor house situated 500 yards from Chesil Beach. The Hotel enjoys panoramic views of the unspoilt Dorset coast from most of its bedrooms, excellent reputation for cuisine and service. Three real ales are available in the character cellar bar. Log fires among many other welcoming attributes make the Manor a tremendous place to stay.

2. Highcliff Hotel
West Cliff, Bournemouth
Tel: (0202) 27702
On Bournemouth's favoured West Cliff, the Highcliff Hotel, within easy reach of three of "Following the Fairway's" recommended golf courses, provides the visitor with some of the finest panoramic views in the south of England. Comfortably furnished and well appointed, the Highcliff is renowned for its fine cuisine, excellent facilities and friendly service.

Chedington Court

*Standing 700ft above sea level, on the Dorset Hills,
Chedington Court is just a stone's throw away from
the A356 Crewkerne to Dorchester road at
Winyard's Gap and commands magnificent views of
the Somerset, Devon and Dorset countryside.*

MANOR HOUSE HOTEL
CHIPPENHAM
WILTSHIRE
(0249) 782206

FERNDOWN

When it comes to beautifully manicured fairways and quick, ultra-true greens then the better American courses tend to be superior to their British counterparts. Ferndown is a definite exception. The fairways and greens are perhaps in the best kept condition in the whole of Britain. Someone deserves a mighty large pat on the back!

There are in fact two courses at Ferndown, the **Old** and the **New**. The Old Course was originally designed in **1912** by **Harold Hilton**, who was twice Open Champion before the turn of the century. The shorter New Course, which has nine holes but eighteen tees, has a much more recent history being designed in **1969 by J. Hamilton-Stutt** and opened two years later.

The Secretary at Ferndown is **Mr C.R. Johnson**, Tel. **(0202) 874602. Visitors** to the Club are welcome on any day provided prior permission is first obtained. **Societies** are limited to Mondays, Wednesdays and Fridays and written applications should be addressed to the Secretary at **Ferndown Golf Club, 119 Links Road, Ferndown, Wimborne, Dorset, BH22 8BU.** All visitors and Society members must be prepared to produce a handicap certificate or alternatively a letter of introduction from their home Club.

To play the Old Course the **green fee** charged in **1986** was **£16** – this sum was for a single round or for a full day's golf and applied seven days per week. The green fee for the New Course was **£7** in **1986** – again this was for a round or for the full day. **Doug Sewell**, the professional at Ferndown, can be reached on **(0202) 873825.** A former Walker Cup player and very fine professional, I once read that in an Alliance Meeting at Ferndown he played the course in 60 strokes – enough said! Ferndown has indeed been very fortunate with its professionals, Percy Allis served the Club for over 25 years.

Located approximately six miles north of Bournemouth, Ferndown is quite easily reached from all directions. Motoring from the West of England the **A35** from Dorchester, which near Bere Regis suddenly becomes the **A31** passes through Ferndown very close to the Golf Club. Approaching from the East, from London the **M3** runs to Southampton which in turn is linked to Ferndown (or Trickett's Cross to be precise) by the **A31**. The left fork should be taken at Trickett's Cross and this leads on to Golf Links Road, the course being immediately on the left. From the North the route is via Salisbury where the **A338** should be followed as far as Ringwood and thereafter the **A31** as with above. Finally anyone who happens to possess their own jet may wish to note that Bournemouth has a small airport at **Hurn**, very close to the Golf Club.

The Old Course at Ferndown measures **6442** yards from the back tees, par and standard scratch both being **71**. From the forward tees the length is reduced by a little over 200 yards. The layout is essentially one of two loops, an inner loop comprising holes one to eight and the outer containing the ninth to the eighteenth.

Its fairways are of the sandy heathland type and are gently undulating throughout. The rough consists mainly of heather and together with the many pines and firs gives the course a most attractive appearance. There are a considerable number of dog-leg holes necessitating much thought from the tee. The toughest holes on the course are possibly the **6th**, with its elevated green, the dog leg **9th** and the uphill **11th** – all fairly lengthy par fours from the back tees. One should also mention the **5th**, an excellent par 3, with the rhododendrons providing a splash of colour in the right season.

At **5,604** yards (**par 70**) the New Course is less demanding in terms of length but it too has its challenges and it is set in equally beautiful surroundings.

Ferndown's Clubhouse has a prime location grandly surveying the course from its elevated position. On a clear day there are views across the course to the Isle of Wight. The facilities are excellent with lunches being offered daily. Both breakfast and dinner can be arranged with prior notice. A jacket and tie should be worn in public rooms at all times.

In 1985 the Club played host to the **Women's English Amateur Championship** whilst the professionals and the television cameras have also recently visited Ferndown. The **Hennessy Cognac Cup**, a four man team competition, was played over the Old Course in 1982 and returned in 1984. On both occasions the event was a great success and the superb condition of the course not surprisingly proved a major talking point. The latter, together with the course's excellent location should ensure that Ferndown retains its considerable popularity.

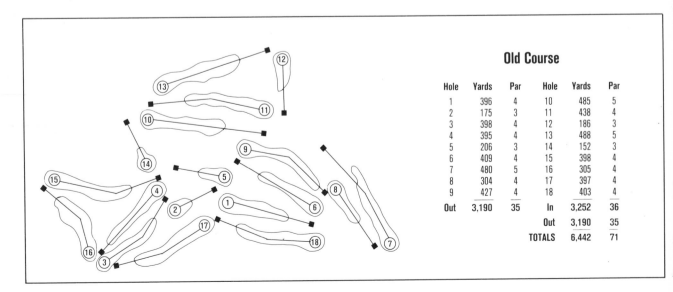

Old Course

Hole	Yards	Par	Hole	Yards	Par
1	396	4	10	485	5
2	175	3	11	438	4
3	398	4	12	186	3
4	395	4	13	488	5
5	206	3	14	152	3
6	409	4	15	398	4
7	480	5	16	305	4
8	304	4	17	397	4
9	427	4	18	403	4
Out	3,190	35	In	3,252	36
			Out	3,190	35
			TOTALS	6,442	71

THE ISLE OF PURBECK

Most people are a little suprised when they learn that the **Isle of Purbeck** Golf Club was founded as long ago as 1892 – a decade before Sunningdale and Walton Heath. They are probably even more surprised when they hear that Enid Blyton and her husband were once owners of the Club. Originally, only a 9 hole course there are now **27 holes** comprising the **18 hole Purbeck Course** and an adjacent, shorter **9 hole** course, **The Dene**. In 1966, a superb new Clubhouse was built using the local Purbeck stone and it was around this time that more and more people began to consider seriously the quality of the golf here as well as the sheer beauty of the Club's setting.

Today the Club is **owned** and **managed** by the **Robinson family. Mrs. Joan Robinson** is **Managing Director** and she can be contacted on **(0929) 44361**. All written communications should be addressed to her at **The Isle of Purbeck Golf Club, Swanage, Dorset, BH19 3AB**. The Club's **Professional** is **Tom Gates, telephone: (0929) 44354**.

Visitors to the Isle of Purbeck are welcome to play on both courses, although those wishing to play on the Purbeck course must possess a handicap. **Green fees** for 1986 were set at **£12** per day to play on the **Purbeck** course, with **£14** payable at **weekends** and **Bank Holidays**. It should be remembered that these sums were for a full day ticket as opposed to a single round fee. **Junior** golfers were asked to part with **£7** for a day on the **Purbeck** course. This same figure was the price of a day ticket to play over the **Dene** course, with a **£2** reduction for juniors and those teeing off after 4.30 p.m.

Swanage has become a very popular holiday centre and keen golfers perhaps should consider the merits of a short temporary membership of the Club. In 1986, a **week's** golf on the Purbeck course could be purchased for **£60, two weeks** for **£100, three** for **£120** and **four weeks** for **£135**. There are reductions for joint membership and for those wishing to limit their golf to the Dene course. Visitors may also wish to note that the Club stages a limited number of open competitions during the summer. Information concerning these can be obtained from Mrs. Robinson. Golfing Societies are encouraged to come to the Isle of Purbeck and those organising should find the Club very accommodating, indeed, Societies may book for up to two years ahead. What better place for an annual gathering?

Getting to the Isle of Purbeck may present the biggest headache. This is hardly the most accessible of Britain's golf clubs – not that the Club can be blamed for that! Anyway, the best routes are probably as follows: from the **West** the **A35** runs from Honiton through Dorchester and joins the **A351** at Lytchett Minster near Poole. The **A351** should be followed as far as **Corfe Castle** from which the **B3351** Studland road should be taken. The Club is situated just off this road. Travelling from the **North** the **A350** also joins the **A351** near Poole, whilst from the Bournemouth/Poole area a **car ferry** operates between **Sandbanks** and **Shell Bay** and avoids the drive around Poole Harbour.

Any of the aforementioned headaches should surely be dispelled on arrival at the Clubhouse. The south coast possesses a number of scenic courses, but one would be very pushed to find an equal to the magnificent views provided by the Isle of Purbeck. The view from the 5th on the Purbeck Course ("Agglestones") is particularly outstanding as you tee off from the top of an ancient Saxon burial mound. The Par 3 11th, "island", with its backdrop of pines and two tier green is also an exceptional hole.

For those who find the modern day monster courses somewhat tedious with the great emphasis they place on brute force (and ignorance?) the **Purbeck Course** should prove rather refreshing. From the **back tees** it measures **6,248 yards (par 71)** whilst from the **forward tees** the course is reduced to **5,823 yards (par 69)**. From the **Ladies Tees** the course measures **5,648, par being 73**.

The above distances may be a little deceptive for there is often a stiff breeze and besides, with its heather, gorse, stream and ditches the course has more than its fair share of natural hazards.

On returning to the Clubhouse, the golfer should find that a full range of catering is offered and that the food and service is of a high standard. Breakfast can be arranged and lunch, high teas and dinner are all offered daily. A **jacket and tie** should be worn for **dinner and Sunday Lunch**. Again, some splendid views are to be had from the Clubhouse.

When in South Dorset many visitors like to take in a spot of fossil hunting. Lyme Regis and Charmouth are within easy reach, however, golfers need not look beyond the four walls of the Clubhouse – it is full of old fossils. Lest I be accused of insulting the Members, I should quickly explain: when the Clubhouse was built several fossilised dinosaur footprints and some massive ammonites were incorporated into the interior walls. It therefore follows – and golf historians please note – that to a limited extent the Isle of Purbeck could be said to possess the oldest Clubhouse in the world!

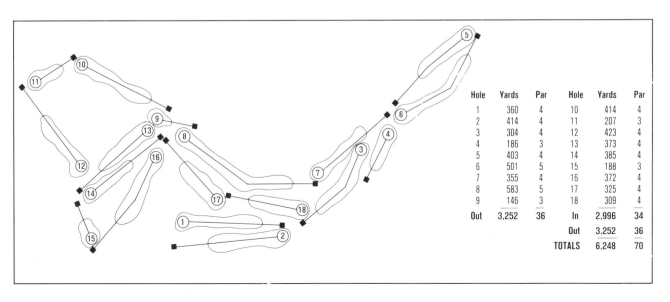

Hole	Yards	Par	Hole	Yards	Par
1	360	4	10	414	4
2	414	4	11	207	3
3	304	4	12	423	4
4	186	3	13	373	4
5	403	4	14	385	4
6	501	5	15	188	3
7	355	4	16	372	4
8	583	5	17	325	4
9	146	3	18	309	4
Out	3,252	36	In	2,996	34
			Out	3,252	36
			TOTALS	6,248	70

55

HAMPSHIRE AND THE CHANNEL ISLANDS

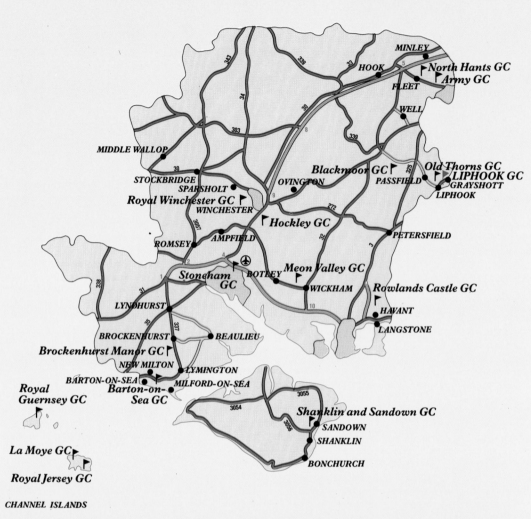

MINLEY

HOOK

North Hants GC

FLEET

Army GC

WELL

MIDDLE WALLOP

Blackmoor GC

Old Thorns GC

LIPHOOK GC

STOCKBRIDGE

OVINGTON

PASSFIELD

GRAYSHOTT

SPARSHOLT

LIPHOOK

Royal Winchester GC

WINCHESTER

Hockley GC

ROMSEY

AMPFIELD

PETERSFIELD

Stoneham GC

BOTLEY

Meon Valley GC

LYNDHURST

WICKHAM

Rowlands Castle GC

HAVANT

BROCKENHURST

BEAULIEU

LANGSTONE

Brockenhurst Manor GC

NEW MILTON

LYMINGTON

BARTON-ON-SEA

MILFORD-ON-SEA

Royal Guernsey GC

Barton-on-Sea GC

La Moye GC

Shanklin and Sandown GC

SANDOWN

Royal Jersey GC

SHANKLIN

BONCHURCH

CHANNEL ISLANDS

C.E. BROCK *"The Putt"* SOTHEBY'S

CHEWTON GLEN HOTEL

NEW MILTON · HAMPSHIRE BH25 6QS · ENGLAND
TELEPHONE · HIGHCLIFFE (04252) 5341
TELEX · 41456

HOW TO FIND US

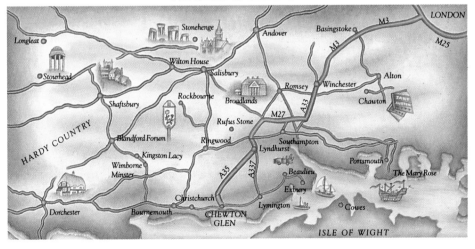

Even if the Isle of Wight and the Channel Islands were taken away from this region it would still score top marks, both for the quality of the golf and the quality of the accompanying scenery. With the New Forest to the south, the Downs to the north and Winchester Cathedral standing proudly in the middle, Hampshire is arguably the fairest of all English counties. And amongst all this finery stand the likes of **Liphook, North Hants, Blackmoor** and **Brockenhurst Manor** – four of the country's leading inland courses.

Three of those four mentioned above, Liphook, North Hants and Blackmoor lie towards the east of the county close to the boundary with Surrey. Not surprisingly they are staunch members of the 'heathland club' – silver birch and pine, fir, heather and a dash of gorse. **Liphook** is possibly the pick of the three, though it's a close thing, and both **North Hants** (at Fleet) and **Blackmoor** (off the **A325** at Bordon) annually stage major amateur events – North Hants the **Hampshire Hog** and Blackmoor the **Selborne Salver**. Each measures between 6,200 and 6,300 yards and is maintained in superb condition. Visitors looking for a game on any of the three should telephone the Club in question before making any firm plans. Certain restrictions apply, particularly at weekends. Green fees are around the **£12-15** mark.

The **Army Golf Club**, just north of Aldershot, is another fine and quite lengthy heathland type course with a reputation for separating the men from the boys. The final mention in this area goes to one of the country's newest recruits, the **Old Thorns Golf and Country Club**, situated south of Liphook. Old Thorns is owned by a large Japanese Company and in addition to a rapidly maturing Championship standard golf course (lakes and all) the famed Japanese hospitality offers French, English and Japanese restaurants, a heated swimming pool and even a Japanese masseur!

Winchester golfers, like those at Liphook, are doubly fortunate having two first class courses at hand: **Royal Winchester**, due to celebrate its centenary in 1988, and **Hockley** located two miles **south of the City on the A333**. Both are downland type courses where visitors should be able to arrange a game during the week, fees being approximately **£10**.

Getting closer to the south coast the **Rowlands Castle** parkland course occupies a peaceful setting. Visitors are welcome seven days a week though prior telephoning is advisable at the weekends. Fees in 1986 were **£9** midweek, **£11** on Saturdays and Sundays. The course can play fairly long, especially from the back markers (close to 6,700 yards). While we're on the subject of length, a hundred years ago the excellent links at **Hayling Island** is said to have measured **7,480 yards** – so much for the modern-day monster courses!

Midway between Portsmouth and Southampton (**M27** Junction 7) **Meon Valley Golf and Country Club** is similarly good for a visit on any day of the week. A fairly new parkland course, designed by **Hamilton Stutt**, it too has an attractive setting. Golfers (with handicaps) could enjoy a game in 1986 for **£11** during the week and for **£14** at weekends.

Stoneham is without doubt the pick of the courses in the Southampton area, 2 miles north of the town. The venue of the first Dunlop Masters tournament back in 1946 it is quite undulating with an ample sprinkling of gorse and heather which though appealing to look at is often the curse of the wayward hitter. Subject to Club competitions, visitors are welcome throughout the week, fees in 1986 being **£10** midweek, **£12** at weekends.

I'm afraid I know very little about William the Conqueror but I understand there are at least two things we should thank him for – one is the Domesday Book and the other is the New Forest, without doubt one of the most beautiful areas in Britain. **Brockenhurst Manor Golf Club** lies amidst the splendour, and several deer including a rare white buck frequent the surrounding woodlands. A superb heathland course, Brockenhurst welcomes visitors during the week and to a limited extent at weekends – telephoning again recommended. The cost of a day's golf in 1986 was **£14** on weekdays, **£18** at weekends, reduced if teeing off after 4 p.m. A short distance from the New Forest, **Barton-on-Sea**'s exposed cliff top course is well worth a visit if in the area. Not overly long but with enough challenges and some spectacular views across to the Isle of Wight and Christchurch Bay.

There are no fewer than seven golf courses on the Isle of Wight. Whilst **Shanklin and Sandown** is possibly the best known, an additional visit to one or two of the others is well worth considering. All courses welcome visitors and green fees tend to compare favourably with those on the mainland.

If the Isle of Wight is good for golf, the Channel Islands are even better. Not that there is a proliferation of courses but there are three **La Moye, Royal Jersey** and **Royal Guernsey** that are particularly outstanding. Unfortunately the German troops didn't share this opinion during the Islands' four year occupation: they demolished La Moye's Clubhouse and dug up the fairways at Royal Guernsey. Both have long since recovered and all three provide tremendous holiday golf. Visitors are welcome at Royal Guernsey Mondays, Tuesdays, Wednesdays and Fridays for a fee of **£8** per round, **£10** per day. The Jersey courses are a little more expensive but it may be possible to get a game at weekends. However, both being understandably popular prior telephoning is strongly recommended.

HAMPSHIRE AND CHANNEL ISLANDS

A jersey called Guernsey and a Guernsey called Jersey – "cows" you ask? Well, Cowes has a golf course but the Isle we call Wight has many more. The Channel Isles – a delightful haven for corporations and golfers is an ideal spot for holiday golf – and business if you have a corporation handy. Hampshire – from the New Forest to "Britain's Proudest Sight" – HMS Victory offers much to entice the golfer. Everybody needs a little time away, so why not Hampshire – its infinite variety not only sparks the imagination – it also fires the belly – with the batteries charged and the body brim full, where better place to be than on the Golf Course.

We start our holiday in a golfer's nightmare – Hook. However, the aptly named **Whitewater House (025672) 2436** should soon wash away the bad dreams! Pubs to ease your slumber include two first rate establishments. They are **The Crown and Cushion** in Minley and **The Chequers** in Well. Fleet dissects these two villages and **The Lismoyne Hotel (02514) 28555** is ideally located.

While on the subject of woods, we ought to talk about a small one – not a club – but a Forest, The New Forest – 90,000 acres of it – quite a big wood actually. In Passfield, **The Passfield Oak** does good food and some popular real ales. While in Grayshott – **The Woods (042873) 5555** return – this time in the form of an excellent little restaurant. Liphook lies close to the borders of Surrey and Sussex. The **Links Hotel** is reported to be comfortable and seafood is commended (very handy for the 9th and 10th tees). If you prefer curry then **Lal Quilla (0428) 722095** is recommended. Narrowly remaining within the Hampshire boundary we arrive at Petersfield, here **The White Horse** is a pub real ale chaps should not miss.

Two pubs later and the coast – they are **The Old House at Home** (superb name) in Havant and **The Royal Oak**, Langstone, both ideally situated for Rowlands Castle. Other establishments to sample in this area of Hampshire include the truly delightful **Old House Hotel (0329) 833049** in Wickham. Trekking northwards one comes to Botley, here **Cobbett's (04892) 2069** is a fine French restaurant.

In Ampfield, south of Winchester and Romsey also south of the cathedral town, two further establishments catch the eye. In the former **Potters Heron (04215) 66611** is comfortable and convenient for the A31 and **The Old White Horse (0794) 512431** is a welcoming inn located in Romsey's market place. In Winchester not too far from school and cathedral there are numerous restaurants, perhaps the best **The Old Chesil (0962) 53177**. Also in Winchester **The Wessex Hotel (0962) 61611** is by no means cheap but particularly comfortable. North west of Winchester is Sparsholt, where one finds one of those rare exquisite English Country House Hotels, **Lainston House (0962) 63588** – ideal for people who want true luxury. In Stockbridge, **The Game Larder (0264) 810414** is excellent and **The Sheriff House (0264) 810677** also offers outstanding food and for both, do book. In the splendidly named Middle Wallop, people coming from or returning to the west, should note Middle Wallop – more specifically – **Fifehead Manor (0264) 781565**, a delightful manor house with a good restaurant.

Meanwhile, I must point pub lovers in mid-Hampshire in the direction of Ovington where **The Bush** is excellent.

To the coast – not the hurry of Dorset's Bournemouth – a more sleepy air in Hampshire's coast prevails. In endeavouring to reach it you may come upon Lyndhurst – no bad thing – for here on the edge of the New Forest lies **The Parkhill House Hotel (042128) 2944** – an ideal spot, a good restaurant as well. Two Bs now, before you get offended, I refer to Beaulieu and Brockenhurst. In the former case **The Montagu Arms (0590) 612324** and its fine restaurant is ideal to hang up one's clubs and in the latter a number of places should be considered. Two include **Carey's Manor (0590) 23551** a great all rounder and **The Forest Park (0590) 22844** ideal. Further south on the A337 we arrive at Lymington. In another good hotel setting stands **The Passford House (0590) 682398** while among other things, **The Stanwell House (0590) 615174** is convenient for ferries leaving for the Isle of Wight,while **Limpets (0590) 75595** is a tasty restaurant in town. Further up the coast, westwards, one arrives in Barton-on-Sea where **The Red House Hotel (0425) 610119** is recommended. In New Milton, we arrive at the county's (quite probably the country's) finest country house hotel, **Chewton Glen (04252) 5341**, which is spectacular. (They're laying down a nine hole golf course in the grounds – marvellous!).

Across the water and the Isle of Wight – some good golf here with some really welcoming hotels. In Shanklin, **The Cliff Tops (0983) 863262** and **The Luccombe Hall (0983) 864590** stand out, though there are many more. Two pubs to visit include **The Fisherman's Cottage** – good food and a fine setting and **The Crab**, more seafood and a high street position on this occasion. Elsewhere on the island Cowes of course is busy and fun, especially during Cowes week itself, but for our purposes Bonchurch beckons where **The Peacock Vane (0983) 852019** is a delightful restaurant – with some rooms. Alternative accommodation can be tracked down in **The Winterbourne Hotel (0983) 852535**. In Sandown itself **The Broadway Park Hotel (0983) 402007** is an all in holiday makers dream.

And so to the delight of Guernsey and Jersey where moo cows welcome us as we triumphantly land preparing for business. In Guernsey St. Peter's Port offers a whole handful of excellent hotels – generally good value as well. **The St. Pierre Park (0481) 28282** is the most luxurious, but **The Old Government House (0481) 23787** is beautifully stylish, while **The Flying Dutchman (0481) 23787** has a good restaurant to match a friendly welcome.

In Jersey, another warm welcome where golfers really are spoilt for choice. What a finale to golf in the Channel Isles. In St. Brelade's Bay **Hotel L'Horizon (0534) 43101** is excellent but expensive, as is the superb **Atlantic (0534) 44101**. In St. Helier **The Grand Hotel (0534) 72255 and its restaurant are grand. In St. Peter Port The Mermaid (0534) 41255** is another great fun hotel. As we reflect on the sheer excellence of these Islands for holiday golf, we are dining at **Longueville Manor (0534) 2550**, St. Saviour's outstanding restaurant – we are prepared for a big bill – but we have earned it; the contract's in the bag – but far more importantly we both had birdies at the eighteenth.

Meon Valley Hotel
Golf and Country Club,
Shedfield, Southampton
Tel: (0329) 833455
Set in 145 acres of beautiful countryside, the Meon Valley has an 18 hole golf course in its grounds, designed by course architect J Hamilton Stutt. The hotel, though it is primarily geared towards golf, has other excellent sporting facilities. All in all this is an excellent spot for golfers and should not be missed.

Highcliff Hotel
West Cliff, Bournemouth
Tel: (0202) 27702
On Bournemouth's favoured West Cliff, the Highcliff Hotel, within easy reach of three of "Following the Fairway's" recommended golf courses, provides the visitor with some of the finest panoramic views in the south of England. Comfortably furnished and well appointed, the Highcliff is renowned for its fine cuisine, excellent facilities and friendly service.

Langrish House
Hotel and Restaurant

LAINSTON HOUSE HOTEL

Built in the late seventeenth century, set in sixty-three acres of grounds and overlooking some of England's loveliest downlands, this beautiful English Manor House has been discreetly restored to provide every luxury the discerning traveller could wish for. The hotel is approached by a curving drive of about half a mile, lined with lime trees. The walls of the octagonal kitchen garden, the well-house with its original horse wheel, the dovecote and ruins of the Norman Church are all of historic interest.

The thirty-two luxurious bedrooms, all with private bathrooms, have been individually designed and tastefully furnished. Drinks are served in the club-like atmosphere of the Cedar Room which is panelled with wood taken from a magnificent Cedar Tree which fell in the grounds long ago. The Restaurant is renowned for its high standards. The service is friendly and informal, the menu creative and interesting using the best of local produce. The individually cooked dishes are complemented by a thoughtfully compiled wine list.

The hotel is located off the A272 a mere two and a half miles from Winchester. It is convenient for Winchester and Hockley Golf Clubs and within easy reach of Broadlands, home of the late Earl Mountbatten, Wilton House, home of the Earl of Pembroke and, of course, Salisbury and Winchester Cathedrals.

LAINSTON HOUSE HOTEL
Sparsholt,
Winchester.
Tel: (0962) 63588.

The counties of Surrey and Berkshire don't have a monopoly of the outstanding heathland and heather type courses in England. There is Pulborough in West Sussex and Woodhall Spa in Lincolnshire and there is also Liphook, the pride and joy of Hampshire. Now the latter part of that sentence is troubling me somewhat – Liphook's quality is undeniable – it's the 'Hampshire bit'. As a town Liphook is undoubtedly situated in Hampshire, but a great part of the golf course lies over the border in Sussex. The 13th hole, appropriately named "Two Counties", has the golfer teeing off in Sussex and holing out in Hampshire. In exploring the quandary I telephoned the professional shop and on suggesting that the larger part lay in Hampshire I received the reply "debatable" and furthermore the remark "where I'm standing is Sussex"! Anyway it's a superb course wherever it is!

Liphook Golf Club was founded in **1922** and the course was designed by **A C Croome** and **Thomas Simpson**. The phrase, "natural golfing land" has become something of a golfers cliché, but hopefully it can be forgiven in this instance. Being sited on gently undulating terrain with a marvellous spread of silver birch and fir trees, heather and bracken, only the sand bunkers needed to be added and this was done with the most careful of planning. Striking a balance between being sufficiently testing yet not too severe requires a fine judgement – Messrs Croome and Simpson, if you'll pardon another expression, "got it right to a tee".

Persons wishing to explore the delights of Liphook must make prior arrangements with the Club's Secretary, **Commander J Ashton.** This can be through telephoning on (0428) 723785 or by addressing a written application to Commander Ashton care of **Liphook Golf Club, Wheatsheaf Enclosure, Liphook, Hants, GU30 7EH.** Generally visitors must be members of recognised Golf Clubs and be in possession of a handicap of 24 or less (29 or less for ladies). Subject to the above a game can normally be arranged between Mondays and Fridays and on Sundays after 1 pm. Golfing Societies are also received during the week, usually on Wednesdays, Thursdays and Fridays – written applications again to be addressed to the Secretary. In **1986** the **green fees** at Liphook were set at **£10** for a weekday round with **£16** payable for a full day's golf and **£20** at weekends and on Bank Holidays. Visitors and Societies should perhaps

also note that two ball matches (and foursomes) are preferred, indeed Societies are not permitted to play three balls or four balls. I should also add that Liphook's professional, **Ian Large** can be contacted on **(0428) 723271.**

Travelling to Liphook from London couldn't be more direct. The **A3** London to Portsmouth road passes right through the middle of the course! Those approaching from other directions may have a little more trouble. Coming from Birmingham and the North those in a hurry might choose to use a combination of the **M1, M25** and **A3**. The more scenic route is to travel via Oxford on the **A34** leaving at Newbury and thereafter taking the **A339** to Alton and the **B3004** to Liphook (well at least it avoids London!) Motoring from the South West, Winchester is probably the best place to head for. From Winchester the **A272** should be taken to Petersfield where the **A3** can be joined.

In the era of the 7,000 yard Championship course Liphook's modest **6,207** yards may not sound particularly daunting. Par, or bogey as seems to be preferred here, is a fairly tight **70** but primarily Liphook is a "thinking man's course" rather than a "hitting course". The bunkers are strategically placed and straying off the fairways can usually result in the dropping of a shot – such is the tangling nature of the heather.

Liphook is one of the few leading English courses that commences with a par 3 – Royal Lytham being another rare example. Measuring over 200 yards it is certainly a testing opener. The fourth hole is possibly the toughest on the front nine, after which the busy Portsmouth Road must be crossed. On the back nine, notable holes include the eleventh, a superb short hole with a narrow entrance to a green backed by fir trees and the thirteenth, the aforementioned "Two Counties", where a glorious downhill drive is followed by a second over a brook.

Liphook's Clubhouse stands on high ground, giving a perfect view of the first and the eighteenth. Within, lunches are served daily between 12 am – 2 pm and teas from 3.45 pm to 5.30 pm. Breakfasts and dinners are only available by special arrangement. A jacket and tie should be worn in the Clubhouse after 11 am with the exception of the small bar.

Notwithstanding the A3 and the railway line (which also cuts through the centre of the course!) Liphook exudes an air of genuine tranquillity and charm, the equal of which is difficult to find anywhere and one that once experienced is never forgotten.

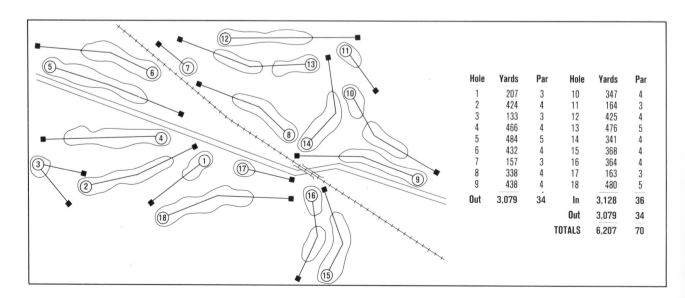

Hole	Yards	Par	Hole	Yards	Par
1	207	3	10	347	4
2	424	4	11	164	3
3	133	3	12	425	4
4	466	4	13	476	5
5	484	5	14	341	4
6	432	4	15	368	4
7	157	3	16	364	4
8	338	4	17	163	3
9	438	4	18	480	5
Out	**3,079**	**34**	**In**	**3,128**	**36**
			Out	**3,079**	**34**
			TOTALS	**6,207**	**70**

THE 2ND: GOREY TO BLOODY POINT

CHANNEL ISLANDS
Alderney G.C. (9)
Alderney (048182) 2835

L'Ancresse G.C. (18)
L'Ancresse, Guernsey
(0481) 23675

La Moye G.C. (18)
La Moye, St. Brelade,
Jersey (0534) 43401

Royal Guernsey G.C. (18)
L'Ancresse, Guernsey
(0481) 46523

Royal Jersey G.C. (18)
Gronville, Jersey (0534) 54416

EAST SUSSEX
Ashdown Forset Hotel (18)
Forest Row (034282) 2010

Cooden Beach G.C. (18)
Cooden (0959) 2040

Crowborough Beacon G.C. (18)
Crowborough (08926) 61511

Dale Hill G.C. (18)
Ticehurst, Wadhurst
(0580) 200112

Dyke G.C. (18)
Brighton (079156) 296

Eastbourne Downes G.C. (18)
Eastbourne (0323) 20827

East Brighton G.C. (18)
Roedean, Brighton (0273) 603989

Highwoods G.C. (18)
Bexhill-on-Sea (0424) 212625

Hill Barn G.C. (18)
Worthing (0903) 37301

Hollingbury Park G.C. (18)
Brighton (0273) 532010

Horam Park G.C. (9)
Horam (04353) 3477

Lewes G.C. (18)
Lewes (0273) 3074

Peacehaven G.C. (9)
Newhaven (0273) 512571

Piltdown G.C. (18)
Piltdown, Uckfield (082572) 2033

Pyecombe, G.C. (18)
Pyecombe, Brighton (07918) 4176

Royal Ashdown Forest G.C. (18)
Forest Row, East Grinstead,
(034282) 2018

Royal Eastbourne G.C. (18+9)
Eastbourne (0323) 29738

Rye G.C. (18+9)
Combes, Rye (0797) 225241

Seaford G.C. (18)
East Blatchington, Seaford
(0323) 892442

Seaford Head G.C. (18)
Seaford (0323) 894 843

Waterhall G.C. (18)
Brighton (0273) 601939

West Hove G.C. (18)
Hove (0273) 419738

Willingdon G.C. (18)
Eastbourne (0323) 638728

Worthing G.C. (18+18)
Worthing (0903) 60801

HAMPSHIRE
Alresford G.C. (9)
Alresford (096273) 3746

Alton G.C. (9)
Alton (0420) 82042

Army G.C. (18)
Aldershot (0252) 540636

Barton-on-Sea G.C. (18)
Barton-on-Sea (0425) 615308

Basingstoke G.C. (18)
Basingstoke (0256) 465990

Bishopswood G.C. (9)
Tadley, Basingstoke (07356) 5213

Blackmoor G.C. (18)
Bordon (04203) 2775

Boscombe Ladies G.C. (18)
Bournemouth (0202) 36198

Bramshaw G.C. (18+18)
Lyndhurst (0703) 813433

Bramshott Hill G.C. (18)
Dibden, Southampton
(0303) 845596

Brockenhurst Manor G.C. (18)
Brockenhurst (0590) 23332

Burley G.C. (9)
Burley, Ringwood (0425) 53706

Corhampton G.C. (18)
Droxford, Southampton
(0489) 877279

Dibden G.C. (18)
Dibden, Southampton
(0703) 845596

Dunwood Manor G.C. (18)
Romsey (0794) 40549

Fleming Park G.C. (18)
Eastleigh (0703) 612797

Gosport & Stokes Bay G.C. (9)
Haslar, Gosport (0705) 52794

Great Salterns G.C. (18)
Portsmouth (0705) 664549

Hartley Wintney G.C. (9)
Hartley Wintney (025126) 4211

Hayling G.C. (18)
Hayling Island (0705) 46446

Hockley G.C. (18)
Twyford, Winchester
(0962) 713165

Lee-on-Solent G.C. (18)
Lee-on-Solent (0705) 551170

Liphook G.C. (18)
Liphook (0428) 723785

Meon Valley G. & C.C. (18)
Shedfield, Southampton
(0329) 833455

New Forest G.C. (18)
Lyndhurst (042128) 2450

North Hants G.C. (18)
Fleet (0252) 616443

Old Thorns G.C. & Hotel (18)
Liphook (0428) 724555

Petersfield G.C. (18)
Petersfield (0730) 62386

Portsmouth G.C. (18)
Widley, Portsmouth (0705) 318640

Romsey G.C. (18)
Nursling, Southampton
(0703) 734637

Rowlands Castle G.C. (18)
Rowlands Castle (070541) 2784

Royal Winchester G.C. (18)
Winchester (0962) 52462

Southampton G.C. (18+9)
Bassett, Southampton
(0703) 768407

Southsea G.C. (18)
Portsmouth (0705) 812435

Southwick Park G.C. (18)
Southwick, Fareham
(0705) 380131

Southwood G.C. (9)
Farnborough (0252) 548700

Stoneham G.C. (18)
Bassett, Southampton
(0703) 769272

Tidworth Garrison G.C. (18)
Tidworth (0980) 42301

Tylney Park G.C. (18)
Rotherwick, Basingstoke
(025672) 2079

Waterlooville G.C. (18)
Cowplain, Portsmouth
(0705) 263388

North Foreland G.C. (18)
Broadstairs (0843) 62140

Poult Wood G.C. (18)
Tonbridge (0732) 351754

Prince's G.C. (18+9)
Sandwich (0304) 61200

Rochester & Cobham
Park G.C. (18)
Park Pale, Rochester
(047482) 3411

Royal Cinque Ports G.C. (18)
Deal (0304) 374007

Royal St. George's G.C. (18)
Sandwich (0304) 613090

Ruxley G.C. (18)
St. Pauls Cray, Orpington
(0689) 71490

St. Augustines G.C. (18)
Cliffsend, Ramsgate (0843) 590333

Sene Valley G.C. (18)
Sene, Folkstone (0303) 68513

Sheerness G.C. (18)
Sheerness (0795) 662585

Shooter's Hill G.C. (18)
London S.E. 18 (01) 854 6388

Shortlands G.C. (9)
Shorltands, Bromley (01) 460 8828

Shoreham G.C. (18)
Shoreham (09592) 2944

Sidcup G.C. (9)
Sidcup (01) 300 2150

Sittingbourne &
Milton Regis G.C. (18)
Newington, Sittingbourne
(0795) 842261

Sundridge Park G.C. (18+18)
Bromley (01) 460 0278

Tenterden G.C. (18)
Tenterden (05806) 3128

Tunbridge Wells G.C. (9)
Tunbridge Wells (0892) 36918

Walmer & Kingsdown G.C. (18)
Kingsdown, Deal (0304) 373256

Westgate & Birchington G.C. (18)
Westgate-on-Sea (0843) 31115

West Kent G.C. (18)
Farnborough (0689) 51323

West Malling G.C. (18)
Addington, Maidstone
(0732) 844785

Whitstable & Seasalter G.C. (18)
Whitstable (0227) 2733589

Wilderness G.C. (18)
Seal, Sevenoaks (0732) 61199

Woodlands Manor G.C. (18)
Woodlands, Sevenoaks
(09592) 3806

WEST SUSSEX
Bognor Regis G.C. (18)
Felpham, Bognor Regis
(0243) 821929

Copthorne G.C. (18)
Copthorne, Crawley (0342) 712508

Cottesmoore G.C. (18+18)
Crawley (0293) 28256

Cowdray Park G.C. (18)
Midhurst (073081) 3599

Effingham Park G.C. (9)
Copthorne (0342) 713011

Goodwood G.C. (18)
Goodwood, Chichester (0243) 774968

Ham Manor G.C. (18)
Angmering (09062) 783288

Haywards Heath G.C. (18)
Haywards Heath (0444) 414457

Littlehampton G.C. (18)
Littlehampton (0903) 717170

Mannings Heath G.C. (18)
Horsham (0403) 66217

Selsey G.C. (9)
Selsey, Chichester (0243) 602203

West Sussex G.C. (18)
Pulborough (07982) 2563

KENT
Aquarius G.C. (9)
Honor Oak, London (01) 693 1626

Ashford G.C. (18)
Ashford (0233) 22655

Barnehurst G.C. (9)
East Barnehurst (0322) 523746

Bearsted G.C. (18)
Bearsted, Maidstone (0622) 39198

Bexley Heath G.C. (9)
Bexley Heath (01) 303 6951

Braeside G.C. (18)
Beckenham (01) 650 2292

Bromley G.C. (9)
Bromley (01) 310 5434

Broome Park G. & C.C. (18)
Barham, Canterbury
(0227) 831701

Canterbury G.C. (18)
Canterbury (0227) 453532

Cherry Lodge G.C. (18)
Biggin Hill (0959) 72250

Chestfield G.C. (18)
Whitstable (022779) 2365

Chislehurst G.C. (18)
Chislehurst (01) 467 2782

Cobtree Manor G.C. (18)
Boxley, Maidstone (0622) 53276

Cranbrook G.C. (18)
Cranbrook (0580) 712833

Cray Valley G.C. (18+9)
St. Pauls Cray, Orpington
(0689) 37909

Darenth Valley G.C. (18)
Shoreham (09592) 2944

Dartford G.C. (18)
(0322) 26455

Deangate Ridge G.C. (18)
Hoo, Rochester (0634) 52495

Edenbridge G. & C.C. (18)
Edenbridge (0732) 856097

Eltham Warren G.C. (9)
Eltham (01) 850 4477

Faversham G.C. (18)
Faversham (079589) 561

Gillingham G.C. (18)
Gillingham (063) 53017

Hastings G.C. (18)
St. Leonards-on-Sea (0424) 52981

Hawkhurst G.C. (9)
Hawkhurst, Cranbrook
(05805) 2396

Herne Bay G.C. (18)
Eddington, Herne Bay
(0227) 373964

High Elms, G.C. (18)
Downe, Orpington (01) 462 2940

Kingsgate G.C. (18)
Thanet (0843) 62140

Knole Park G.C. (18)
Sevenoaks (0732) 452150

Lamberhurst G.C. (18)
Lamberhurst (0892) 890591

Langley Park G.C. (18)
Beckenham (01) 650 2090

Leeds Castle G.C. (9)
Nr. Maidstone (062 780) 467

Littlestone G.C. (18+9)
Littlestone, New Romsey
(0679) 63355

Lullingstone Park G.C. (18+9)
Chelsfield, Orpington (0959) 34542

Magpie Hall Lane G.C. (9)
Bromley (01) 462 7014

Mid Kent G.C. (18)
Gravesend (0474) 68035

EAST AND WEST SUSSEX

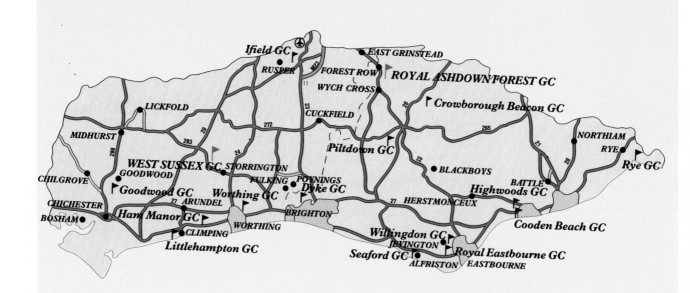

LAWSON WOOD   "Tongue Tied"   ROSENSTIELS

Horsted Place

...til recently the home of the late Lord ...pert Nevill, treasurer to Prince Philip, ...rsted Place has been host to many ...gant country weekend gatherings, with ...ests including the Queen and other ...mbers of the Royal Family. The 12th ...ntury Norman church in the nearby ...age of Little Horsted reserved a special ...w for the times when Royalty was in ...dence.

...might be expected in a house with such ...yal connections, the accommodation at ...rsted is regal in both style and ...pointments. Visitors are welcomed in the ...nd Gallery, stretching 90 feet across the ...ddle of the house and featuring family ...rtraits and period furnished conversation ...as. At the centre is the magnificent ...nd-carved oak staircase, designed by ...gustus Pugin for the Great Exhibition of ...50.

...rsted has 18 guest suites, all spacious ...n by international luxury hotel ...ndards. Most suites have two rooms; to ...e advantage of particularly attractive ...ndow arrangements or outstanding ...ws, others (including the Garden Suite ...oured by the Queen) consists of an ...ra large room, furnished to provide ...arate sleeping and sitting areas. All ...est suites have king-sized or twin beds, ...rth American style bathrooms, colour ...evision and direct-dial telephone service.

...floors are served by a commercial ...acity elevator and the entire house is ...essible to the handicapped.

...ests at Horsted can enjoy traditional ...untry estate living in the grand style. ...glish afternoon tea is served in the ...uble Drawing Room or on the South ...rrace with its beautiful views across the ...ssex Downs. Dining in the elegant Pugin ...ing Room is a gourmet blending of ...nch cuisine and the finest of British ...ats, fish and fresh vegetables ... with an ...ensive wine cellar to match. After ...nner, guests can relax in the Nevill ...rary, designed in antique rosewood and ...luding a secret door to the courtyard ...den—designed by Lord Snowdon as a ...to Lady Rupert Nevill.

Recreation at Horsted will appeal to all tastes ... tennis on the lighted all-weather court; swimming in the indoor, heated pool; strolling amid the 8-acre formal gardens designed by Sir Geoffrey Jellicoe, Britain's foremost landscape architect; croquet on the manicured lawn of the Hidden Garden set in a secluded grove of rhododendron trees. Golf, sailing, hunting and shooting are all available to Horsted guests as visiting members of area clubs.

Convenient to London for sightseeing, shopping or an evening of theatre, Horsted is located at the centre of England's most popular tourist region, minutes away from the most-visited historical sites, and scenic and tourist attractions.

Horsted Place,
Little Horsted, Uckfield,
East Sussex TN22 5TS
Telephone: (0825) 75581

Sussex, where the South Downs tumble gently towards spectacular chalk cliffs, as Tennyson wrote, "Green Sussex fading into blue". Here is the county of downland and weald, of dramatic rollercoasting cliffs, the Seven Sisters and Beachy Head.

Against such a background it is hardly surprising that a great number of the area's golf courses are outstandingly scenic. Tempting as it is to think of Sussex as one region, there are of course two counties, East and West, and between them they possess over forty courses. Golfers in these parts can count themselves pretty fortunate!

On a selective tour of some of the better courses in Sussex, there seems no more logical a place to commence than in the region's South West corner, and **Goodwood** – 'glorious Goodwood' to racegoers though the golf course is in a similarly idyllic spot, nestling in the southern foothills of the South Downs. Some four miles north of Chichester on the A286 it is in fact located just below the race course and has a magnificent 18th century clubhouse. The club welcomes visitors, particularly on weekdays. In 1986 the Green fees were 9 during the week and 12 at weekends. Before setting off a quick telephone call is recommended.

The course at **Littlehampton** lies about seven miles east of Bognor Regis off the A259. It is the nearest one gets to a links course in West Sussex. Always kept in first class condition, the club welcomes visitors on weekdays, though again it is wise to telephone before finalising any plans. Further along the A259 at Angmering is the friendly club of **Ham Manor**. A parkland course with an interesting layout of two distinct loops. Well worth visiting – there are no general restrictions on times visitors can play and furthermore the food there is quite outstanding! In 1986 Green fees were 9 weekdays 13 at weekends.

As a town, **Worthing** is somewhat overshadowed by neighbouring Brighton (though apparently it inspired Oscar Wilde) overshadowed or not; it has one of the leading clubs in Sussex. The venue for the 1987 Sussex Amateur Championship, Worthing has two eighteen hole courses, the Lower and the Upper. Both are exceptionally fine tests of golf. Visitors are welcome although prior arrangement with the Secretary is essential. Fees for 1986 were £10 for weekdays, £14 at weekends.

Moving into East Sussex and the town of Brighton, probably the best course in the area, and there are a number to choose from, is **The Dyke Golf Club** located five miles north of the town centre. One of the more difficult courses in Sussex, it is on fairly high ground and provides some splendid views. Visitors should first telephone but are generally welcome. Greens fees for 1986 were £10 for weekdays and £12 at weekends.

Leaving Britain's most famous resort behind, but still following the A259, one soon arrives at Seaford. **The Seaford Golf Club** at East Bletchington is due to celebrate its centenary in 1987. A fair sprinkling of gorse and hawthorn are the feature of this interesting downland course. Also worth noting is the dormy house adjacent to the course where you can stay. Visitors are able to play after 9.30am on weekdays and after 1.00pm at weekends. Green fees for 1987 are 15.

Passing near to Beachy Head we arrive at Eastbourne where there are two fine courses – **Royal Eastbourne** and **Willingdon**. The former is another due to celebrate its centenary in 1987. It is situated very close to the town centre with the enviable address of Paradise Drive. Fees in 1986 were £9 weekdays, £10 at weekends. Willingdon, north of the town off the A22, is quite a hilly course and very tough. Its interesting design has been likened to an oyster shell with the Clubhouse as the pearl. Willingdon accepts visitors during the week. Both Clubs advise telephoning in advance. In the area around Bexhill, both **Cooden Beach** and **Highwoods** are well established courses. For visitors wishing to play the former some prior arrangement with the Secretary is essential. At Highwoods there are no general restrictions, but players should be able to provide proof of handicap.

The majority of the leading courses in Sussex are located either on the coast or within a few miles of it – hardly surprising considering this is where the major towns are situated, however, inland there are a handfull of exceptionally attractive courses particularly worth visiting. **Piltdown**, 2 miles to the west of Uckfield, is certainly one of these. Piltdown is a heathland course with a beautiful setting and, in common with Royal Ashdown Forest, has no bunkers – though there are certainly enough natural hazards to set the golfer thinking. The best days for a game here are Mondays, Wednesdays and Fridays. Green fees for 1986 depended on the seasons – £8 in Winter and £11 in Summer, with reductions after 4 pm.

Towards the north of the area, Royal Ashdown Forest (see feature page) and **Crowborough Beacon** are again two wonderfully scenic courses where the heather and gorse run riot. The golf club at Crowborough is a mile South of town off the A26. The Club welcomes visitors during the week, though there are restrictions at weekends. Green fees were priced at £12.50 in 1986.

Returning to West Sussex **The Ifield Golf and Country Club** near Crawley is recommended for a weekday visit while in the heart of West Sussex is Pulborough, or more accurately **The West Sussex Golf Club**. It too is featured on a later page – suffice it to say here that its reputation extends far beyond the bounds of East and West Sussex.

Cooden Beach G.C.	(0959) 2040
Crowborough Beacon G.C.	(08926) 61511
Dyke G.C.	(079156) 296
Goodwood G.C.	(0243) 774968
Ham Manor G.C.	(09062) 783288
Highwoods G.C.	(0424) 212625
Ifield G. &.C.C.	(0293) 0222
Littlehampton G.C.	(0903) 717170
Piltdown G.C.	(082572) 2033
Royal Ashdown Forest G.C.	(034282) 2018
Royal Eastbourne G.C.	(0323) 29738
Rye G.C.	(0797) 225241
Seaford G.C.	(0323) 892442
West Sussex G.C.	(07982) 2563
Willingdon G.C.	(0323) 638728
Worthing G.C.	(0903) 60801

The situation in Sussex is superb. The golf is glorious as is the countryside all around while at no time can you claim to be isolated – except perhaps when you visit the gorse at Ashdown Forest. West Sussex is as charming an area as one could find – the golf course of the same name is delightful and reflects the quality of some splendid country house hotels. While in Rye the golfer must visit with a packed wallet in order to seduce a member in a local drinking haunt and thus secure that elusive thing – a round of golf at Rye – a more spectacular day could not be wished for.

The Sussex area is blessed with some exceptional hotels. In Gravetye, near East Grinstead, **the Gravetye Manor (0342) 810567** is simply excellent. The creeper clad Elizabethan mansion offers beautiful rooms and a restaurant of the very highest quality – an ideal point to celebrate after a good round at Royal Ashdown Forest. Another hotel in East Grinstead is **The Felbridge (0342) 26992** which offers excellent cuisine, facilities and a pleasant atmosphere. In Ashdown Forest itself – more precisely at Forest Row lies the aptly named Ashdown Forest Hotel in a tremendous environment and it has a restaurant with an excellent reputation. If you are fortunate enough to play at Rye, then if you are not local you may choose to stay in a charming inn in Northiam – **The Hayes Arms (07974) 3142**. If you are hoping for an early start then in Rye itself, **The Mermaid Inn** is an historic establishment standing in a steep cobbled street. After a frustrating day at Rye one may wish to sympathise with another loser – poor old Harold. His heart now lies buried in Battle beneath a stone where formerly the church altar stood. While there, a good place to relax and regain spirits is the extremely elegant **Netherfield Place (04246) 4455**. From the solace of Battle to the bustle of Brighton and Eastbourne one is troubled with where to stay – there are simply hundreds of hotels. In Brighton **The Old Ship Hotel (0273) 29001** offers very pleasant accommodation, while **The Lansdowne (0323) 25174** has numerous facilities and is excellent value. Out of the town and into the village of Alriston to be precise **Deans Place Hotel** is the place, thoroughly recommended.

West Sussex is renowned for its excellent hotels and where better place to start than Arundel, where **the Norfolk Arms (0903) 882101**, a Georgian Coaching Inn has welcomed travellers for over two hundred years and the tradition continues today. South of Arundel, lies Climping, here **Bailiffscourt (0903) 723511** a 13th century replica offers superb comforts and an excellent restaurant.

Midhurst – **The Spread Eagle** another landmark – is an excellent base while exploring the delights of the area – the restaurant also offers an ideal post golfing meeting place before cuddling up in a four poster in one of the quaint bedrooms. Return south, Chichester offers a variety of attractions including numerous antique shops and the excellent **Festival Theatre (0243) 781312**. **The Dolphin and Anchor (0243) 785121** opposite the cathedral near the Market Cross is most welcoming (note

fine bar snacks). **Clinch's (0243) 789915** is also a friendly place to stay, the restaurant is good and breakfast ideal before a day in the South Downs.

A theatre of the open air variety can be found at Bosham as can **The Millstream Hotel – (0243) 573234** – excellent. Golfers at Goodwood should note the glorious **Goodwood Park Hotel (0243) 775537** where excellent weekend rates include an excursion to **Goodwood House**. A different atmosphere totally but great value just the same can be found at **The Chatsworth, Worthing (0903) 36103**. In Storrington a pinnacle of Sussex emerges – **Little Thakeham (09066) 4416** is quite delightful – a really all round success – and that really is rare in England nowadays – sadly. Nearby, another peach can be tasted **Abingworth Hall (07983) 3636** – and more relevant its restaurant – inspired. Before one leaves these hotels of Sussex, one should make mention of Little Horsted and its hotel and restaurant **Horsted Place (0825) 75581** easy to miss, but a blunder to do so.

Without doubt several splendid hotels have been omitted, but such is life. In order to fit in more restaurants, please forgive this somewhat hasty appraisal. **Le Francais (0273) 680716** at Brighton is busy while **Byron's (0323) 20171** at Eastbourne is fishy – and good. In Rusper, **Ghyll Manor (029384) 571** provides, while in Rye **Simmons (0797) 222026** stands by. Returning to Alfriston, we see **Moonrakers (0323) 870472** – try a Hot Sussex Smokie! In Herstmonceux, **The Sundial (0323) 832217** is French, whilst **Jevington's Monk is Hungry (03212) 2178** and outstanding. In Chichester, **Little London (0243) 784899** is fine and **Rassell's (0243) 782146** is noted for house wine. In Midhurst try **Mida**, in Pulbrough plump for **Stane Street Hollow**, while in Poynings **Au Petit Normand (079156) 346** should answer your prayers. But for a finale to end this array, try **Manley's (09066) 2331** in Storrington today – (if you can get a table!)

No trip to Sussex is complete without a visit to one of their country houses, castles or pubs. **The White Horse Inn** in Chilgrove has an excellent restaurant, while **The Shepherd and Dog** in Fulking and the **Lickfold Inn** at Lickfold are also worthwhile. Aside from the antiques of Chichester – Arundel, (an excellent castle to see here) and Petworth – which offers the superb **Petworth House**. There is a summer of unsurpassed opera at **Glyndebourne**. In contrast, a totally flamboyant place to spend time is Brighton. The streets in the old town offer several bargains while **The Grand Pavilion** is as striking as ever. Returning to the subject of castles, then **Bodiam** in East Sussex is majestic. Any other thoughts for the player who had troubles in the groping gorse at Ashdown? Well, Blackboys, the pub of the same name is superb while **The Roebuck** in Wych Cross is nearer if you're really desperate. But perhaps the best plan is to return to Alfriston. **The Smugglers** and **The Star** are great value. Sussex, in short, is a true delight on and off the golfcourse.

Gravetye Manor
Gravetye, Nr East Grinstead, RH19 4LJ
Tel: (0342) 810567
Internationally renowned, the hotel firmly preserves an atmosphere of quiet hospitality. The restaurant is rated among the finest in Britain. Fine cooking and an overwhelming gentle atmosphere make a meal memorable. The grounds are a further delight.

Eastwell Manor Hotel and Restaurant
Eastwell Park, TN25 4HR
Tel: (0233) 35751
With a royal history and patronage, Eastwell Manor has elegant bedrooms and luxurious bathrooms. In the restaurant meals of unsurpassed quality are served. Set in 62 acres of undulating parkland in the heart of the Kentish Downs, Eastwell Manor is most peaceful.

Baillifscourt,
Climping,
Nr. Littlehampton,
West Sussex.

Little Thakeham

le Thakeham is one of Sir Edwin
:yen's finest examples of a private
nor House with strong architectural
ificance of the period. Tim and Pauline
:tliff have converted Little Thakeham
) a luxurious country house hotel. The
iversion has been beautifully contrived
h the minimum alterations necessary to
vide 20th Century standards of comfort
1 the atmosphere of the grand manor
ise has been retained with antique
iishings, the Minstrels Gallery and large
en log fires.

e magnificent six acres of gardens were
ated by Gertrude Jekyll, foremost of
den designers of the last century. They
lude paved walks, rose pergola and
nerous specimen trees and shrubs. The
ated swimming pool, grass tennis court
1 croquet lawn all prove very popular in
summer months.

e restaurant has a fine reputation for
ditional English and French Cuisine
pared from local produce. Specialities
lude Southdown Lamb, Selsey Lobsters
1 fresh home grown produce from local
rseries. The comprehensive wine list
orporates Loires and Rhones at very
sonable prices as well as the famous
at French Chateaux wines.

e house is situated on the South Downs
1 commands beautiful views over acres
orchard and farmland. There are many
al facilities and for those interested in
r heritage there are the famous country
uses:—Goodwood, Petworth, Parham
rk and Arundel Castle. All this within 50
es of London and most convenient for
twick Airport.

for country lovers, jaded town dwellers
1 all who appreciate good food and
ie, this Edwardian Manor House is
nething very special and, if you should
h to experience the peace and
nquillity of this English countryside, Tim
1 Pauline Ractliff welcome you to their
me.

Little Thakeham,
Merrywood Lane,
Storrington, West Sussex
Telephone: (09066) 4416

In **1988 Royal Ashdown Forest** will celebrate its centenary. It was on Christmas Eve nearly a hundred years ago that the **Reverend A.T. Scott** teed up his ball and struck the very first shot. The course has changed very little over the years, a fact which speaks volumes for the original layout. The Club acquired the title 'Royal' during Queen Victoria's reign and long before the turn of the century had established itself as one of the finest tests of golf in southern England.

The charm of Royal Ashdown Forest lies in its setting, and of course the name gives it away. Deeply secluded in a forest of pine and silver birch it is difficult to believe that the frantic chaos, commonly called Greater London, is little more than half an hour's drive away.

Many great players have been associated with Royal Ashdown Forest over the years. The **Cantelupe Club,** the artisan club connected to Royal Ashdown, included **Abe Mitchell and Alf Padgham** (Open Champion of 1936) among it's ranks and several celebrated amateurs have improved their technique on this most challenging course.

Casual visitors are welcomed at Royal Ashdown – rather more so, it must be said, than at some of the south-east's leading courses. A recognized club handicap is, however, a requirement and it is normally advisable to telephone the Club before finalising any plans. Not suprisingly the course is very popular in the summer months.

The Club **Secretary is Mr. K.P.A. Mathews,** who can be contacted via the **Royal Ashdown Forest Golf Club, Forest Row, East Sussex. Tel. (034282) 2018.** Those wishing to organise a Society meeting should write to Mr. Mathews at the above address. Societies can normally be accommodated during the week, **Tuesday** being an exception. The **green fees** for **1986** were set at **£12.50** for weekdays with **£15** payable at weekends and on Bank Holidays. Visitors should note that singles and foursomes are generally preferred. **Hector Padgham** is the **professional** at Royal Ashdown and it is he who is responsible for the course record being an alarmingly low **62.** Mr. Padgham can be reached on **(034282) 2247.**

The Club is located within Ashdown Forest, approximately 4 miles south of East Grinstead. Motoring from **London and the North** the A22 is by far the most direct route. This can be joined from the **M25** at **Junction 6.** The A22 should be followed for some 4 miles beyond East Grinstead as far as Forest Row. There

one should take the **B2110** Hartfield road turning left after a quarter of a mile on to Chapel Lane where the Club can be found. Approaching from the **South** the A22 can be joined from a number of roads north of Eastbourne.

The generally held view is that Royal Ashdown Forest is a particularly difficult course. Whilst not overly long (the course measures **6,4039yards** from the **medal tees**) on several of the holes a fairly lengthy tee shot will be required in order to find the safety of the fairway. The ever present stream and the considerable scattering of gorse and heather create a multitude of problems for the wayward golfer – and as if they are not enough, on several of the holes the fairway is narrow and the forest will gratefully accept the product of a slice or a hook. So the message is hit it hard and hit it straight!

Despite the variety of hazards of all the country's leading courses Royal Ashdown Forest must surely be unique in its not possessing a single bunker. **Bernard Darwin** is doubtless not the only golfer who failed to discover this fact until the conclusion of his game, as he put it, "It is only at the end of a round that we realise with a pleasurable shock that there is not a single hideous rampart or so much as a pot bunker". The Club was prevented long ago by the Forestry Commission, or the then equivalent, from creating bunkers and their absence now forms part of the character of the course.

The undulating nature of the landscape produces some truly magnificent views over the Forest and whatever be the standard of his game the visitor who does not relish a return to Royal Ashdown must be a very rare kettle of fish.

The Clubhouse offers a very high standard of catering. A light lunch, such as a ploughman's, can be obtained whilst a full four course meal can also be arranged. During the months of November and December a full English breakfast is available – a welcome facility which many clubs would do well to copy: golfers are hungry animals and some are more than quick to claim that the missed three footer is a result of a missed breakfast!

Whether or not the Members decide in their centenary year to invite the local Reverend to come along to the course on Christmas Eve and perform the necessary ritual, Royal Ashdown Forest can confidently look forward to an interesting second century.

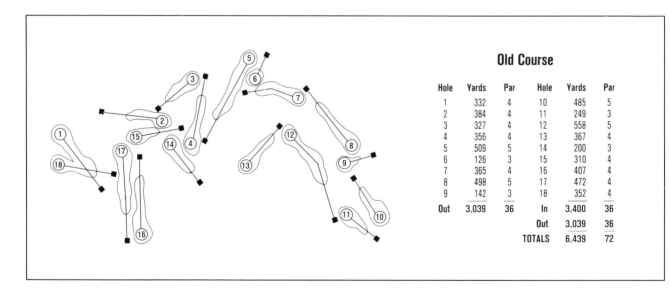

Old Course

Hole	Yards	Par	Hole	Yards	Par
1	332	4	10	485	5
2	384	4	11	249	3
3	327	4	12	558	5
4	356	4	13	367	4
5	509	5	14	200	3
6	126	3	15	310	4
7	365	4	16	407	4
8	498	5	17	472	4
9	142	3	18	352	4
Out	3,039	36	In	3,400	36
			Out	3,039	36
			TOTALS	6,439	72

WEST SUSSEX (PULBOROUGH)

In the opinion of many **West Sussex**, or **Pulborough** as it is commonly known, is quite simply the most beautiful course in England. The setting is the South Downs and seclusion is total. **Commander George Hillyard** founded the Club in **1930** having conceived the idea it is said as he looked out of his bathroom window one day while taking his morning shave! (His house overlooks the present layout). The course was designed by **Sir Guy Campbell** and **Major C. K. Hutchison** and was opened for play in October 1930.

In a similar vein to Woodhall Spa in Lincolnshire, Pulborough has often been described as something of an oasis, the surrounding countryside being predominatly meadow and marshland with the course lying on sandy soil and heather running throughout. Heather naturally adds charm to any golfcourse but it is perhaps the magnificent spread of pines, oaks and silver birch that are most striking at Pulborough.

Mr G. R. Martindale is the present Club Secretary, he may be contacted via the **West Sussex Golf Club, Pulborough, West Sussex**, telephone (07982) 2563. **Visitors** are most welcome although it should be noted that three ball and four ball matches are not generally permitted – singles and foursomes being preferred. The only general restrictions on times visitors can play are before 9.30 am (throughout the week) and on Tuesdays. **Golfing Societies** are also welcome, the usual Society days being Wednesdays and Thursdays.

The **green fees** for 1986 were set at **£12.50** for a single round during the week with **£15** for a day ticket and **£15** for a round at the weekend with **£20** securing a full day's golf. One final introduction: **Geoffrey Gledhill** is the Club's professional, he may be reached by telephone on **(07982) 2426.**

While Pulborough, as it is, may enjoy a gloriously peaceful setting situated right in the heart of the glorious Sussex countryside, it could hardly be described as remote and it is easily accessible from all directions. The Club's precise location is about 2 miles south of Pulborough just off the **A283** road to **Storrington**. The **A283** links Pulborough to the outskirts of Brighton on the southcoast and to **Milford** (near **Guildford**) to the north. For those approaching from westerly directions the **A272** from **Winchester** is likely to prove of most assistance, it joining the **A283** at **Petworth** approximately five miles from Pulborough. Motoring from the **London** area the quickest route is probably to take the **M23** towards Gatwick joining the **A264** at **Crawley** and travelling through **Horsham**. The **A264** merges into the **A29** near **Billingshurst** which in turn joins with Pulborough.

One of the features of Pulborough is its conspicuous absence of a par five beyond the first hole – a hole which in any event becomes a four when played from the tees of the day. At 6156 yards, sss **70**, the par of **68** is a difficult one to match. With none of the par fours being overly short there aren't any really obvious 'birdie opportunities'. Perhaps the best known hole on the course is the par three **6th**; measuring 220 yards it requires an exceptionally accurate tee shot across water to a green that has an out-of-bounds to the right and tall trees directly behind it. **Henry Longhurst**, a great admirer of Pulborough, very aptly said of the 6th "If ever there was an all or nothing hole, this is it." Immediately after the potential disaster of the 6th, the **7th** requires a long uphill drive to carry over some thick heather and scrub not to mention an enormous sand bunker. The **13th** and **15th** are two more superb holes and the round finishes with a pair of testing par fours.

As for its nineteenth West Sussex has a very comfortable Clubhouse offering full catering facilities including two bars. A jacket and tie should be worn in all public rooms.

Henry Longhurst is only one of a number of celebrated admirers of Pulborough and **Bobby Locke**, four times Open Champion considers it his favourite English course. While no major men's tournament has been played over the course (somewhat surprisingly) the Club has hosted both the **English Ladies Amateur Championship, Vanessa Marvin** winning in **1978** and more recently the **1986 British Ladies Championship**, won by New Zealander **Marnie Maguire.**

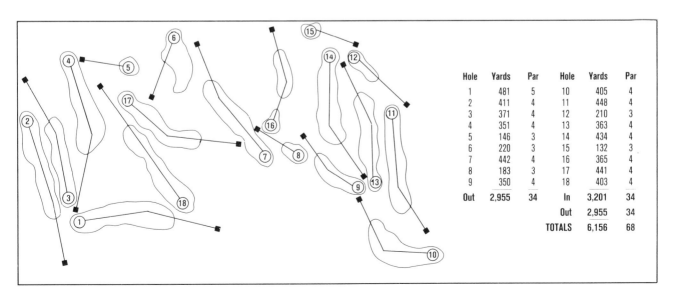

Hole	Yards	Par	Hole	Yards	Par
1	481	5	10	405	4
2	411	4	11	448	4
3	371	4	12	210	3
4	351	4	13	363	4
5	146	3	14	434	4
6	220	3	15	132	3
7	442	4	16	365	4
8	183	3	17	441	4
9	350	4	18	403	4
Out	2,955	34	In	3,201	34
			Out	2,955	34
			TOTALS	6,156	68

KENT

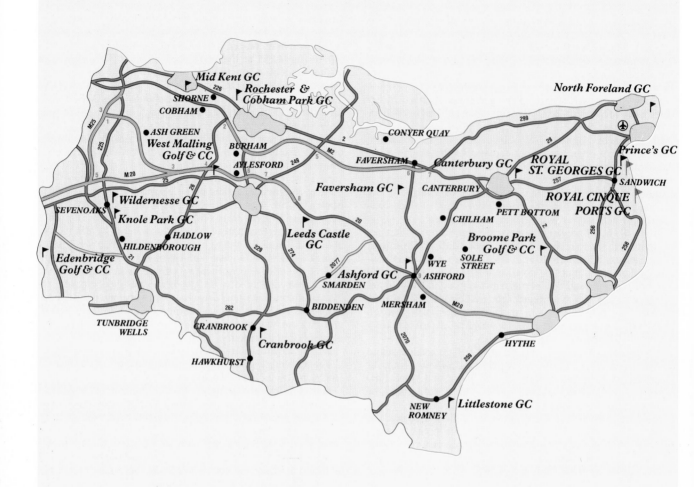

JULIAN BARROW *"Royal St. Georges"* **BURLINGTON GALLERY**

astwell Manor,
astwell Park,
hford,
ent.

From the mysterious and desolate lands of Romney Marsh to the famous White Cliffs of Dover. From the rich orchards of the Garden of England to the outskirts of Greater London. A county of great contrast. From the windswept links of Sandwich and Deal to the secluded Parks of Belmont and Knole, a county of great contrast.

Kent's reputation as one of the country's greatest golfing counties has been built around a three mile stretch of land lying midway between St Margaret's Bay and Pegwell Bay. Within this short distance lie three Open Championship courses: **Princes** (1932), **Royal Cinque Ports** (1909 and 1920) and **Royal St Georges** (too numerous to list!). Kent has two other fine links courses, namely **Littlestone** and **North Foreland** but the golfer who sticks hard to the coast will be missing out on some of the most enjoyable golf Southern England has to offer.

In common with each of the counties that border Greater London many of Kent's courses are gradually finding themselves more in London than in Kent. When the Blackheath golfers left their Common and set up base at Eltham they were doubtless surrounded by the green fields of Kent. Charles Darwin's village of Orpington is now feeling the pinch but happily the **West Kent Golf Club** provides a most pleasant retreat.

Enough grousing! The ancient town of Sevenoaks is categorically in Kent and a very fortunate place too with **Wildernesse Golf Club** to the north and **Knole Park** to the south. The former is arguably the finest inland course in the county, narrow fairways and thickly wooded, it is also one of the toughest. **Knole Park** is one of several Kentish courses that enjoy stately surroundings, being laid out in the handsome Deer Park of Lord Sackville. At both courses visitors should be able to arrange a game during the week, however, restrictions apply at weekends and as both are popular, prior telephoning is preferable.

To the north of the county, both **Mid Kent's** downland course at Gravesend and **Rochester and Cobham Park** are handy for those travelling along the **A2**. Further along this road is the attractive town of Faversham and south of the town off the **A251** is Belmont Park, the estate of Lord Harris and the home of **Faversham Golf Club**. Here golf is played in the most tranquil of settings, particularly delightful in autumn when the fairways abound with countless strolling pheasants. Visitors are welcome during the week, fees in 1986 being **£8** per round, **£12** per day.

Leaving behind the pheasants of Faversham, for those who have made the pilgrimage to Canterbury, **Canterbury Golf Club**, situated to the east of the cathedral town along the **A27** is well worth a visit. A much improved parkland course and one of the best in the county, a game is usually possible in midweek, the cost of a round in 1986 being **£8.50** with **£13** entitling a full day's golf.

South of Canterbury (via the **A2** and **A260**) at Barham is the **Broom Park Golf and Country Club**. A third course set in the grounds of a famous country home – this time a beautiful 300 year old mansion, the former home of Lord Kitchener. Visitors are usually received between Mondays and Saturdays, fees being approximately **£15** per day. A very pleasant parkland course and quite lengthy too, measuring some 6,600 yards.

Ashford is pretty much in the middle of the county, and another strongly worth noting. A heathland type course, which in itself is fairly unique to Kent and where except before 11.30 am on Saturdays and Sundays, golf can be enjoyed throughout the week (**£9** Mondays to Fridays, **£12** at weekends).

Similarly unrestricted is the course at **Cranbrook** on the **A229**, apparently the last course **Bing Crosby** played in England. In 1986 a day's golf over the parkland course was priced at **£11** per day midweek, **£14** per day at weekends. Having back-tracked towards London, a word also for **Edenbridge Golf and Country Club** where a game is usually possible seven days a week and where one's skills can be sharpened up on a driving range.

Situated on the edge of the flatlands of Romney Marsh, **Littlestone** enjoys a somewhat remote setting. A splendid links and an Open Championship qualifying course, which doesn't deserve to be overshadowed by Kent's more illustrious trio further along the coast. Visitors are welcome at Littlestone although prior arrangement with the secretary is essential. In 1986 the green fees were **15** per day.

North of the Sandwich is the **North Foreland** links at Broadstairs, also an Open Qualifying course and where visitors are welcome at most times, telephoning recommended, while to the south of Deal is **Walmer and Kingsdown,** a downland course providing views to Holland and France (clear day plus exec ellent vision essential!). Apart from weekend mornings, vistors are welcome on any day of the week, the fees in 1986 being **£10** per day midweek, **£12** at weekends.

Perhaps not surprisingly where there is one great golf links there is often another nearby. Troon, Turnberry and Prestwick in Ayrshire, Birkdale, Lytham and Hoylake in Lancashire. Of Kent's famous three, St. Georges and Royal Cinque Ports are featured ahead but Princes too has its admirers and it goes without saying that those wishing to admire any one of the three should contact the particular Club before setting off.

KENT

Kent, the Garden of England – where the village greens are busy with the country life, but there are of course other greens where the local dogs are not so welcome, they are naturally the golfcourse greens for which the county is so very famous. Kent however is made up of contrasts – oh how it blows on the coast – whereas the inland region stillremains calm. The county's principal courses are near the sea, but many of the better hotels lie far from the East Kent shore. What then to recommend while a-golfing in Kent? One could start with a round of castles complemented by golf, Leeds, Rochester and Hever to name but three. The latter has a tremendous maze – ideal for losing the wife for a day or two – or a hubby for that matter. Knole is an extraordinaryly impressive country house while Broadstairs is where Charles Dickens penned 'Bleak House'. Let us award a word to this noted author "Kent, Sir– everybody knows Kent – apples, cherries, hops and women" – marvellous.

As we set off to Sandwich with our fruit, women and clubs, that eternal problem which can only be resolved by planning. The best bet is to play the better known courses in the middle of the week and the excellent inland courses at the week-ends. (Unless of course you are a Member when you will no doubt play whenever you wish and take not a blind bit of notice of this piece) ..... or will you? Sandwich itself offers **The Bell Hotel** confortable and convenient (0304) 613388, its quayside setting is pleasant and handy for **The Fisherman's Wharf Restaurant** (0304) 613636 while two pubs to note are the **Kings Arms (0304) 617330** and the **Fleur-de-Lis (0304) 611131**. In Deal, **The Bell Hotel (0304) 375555** is another popular golfing haunt. St. Margarets Bay, located on National Trust land is worth a look and the **Cliffe Tavern (0304) 852749** nearby is a good place to wet one's whistle and stay if you wish.

While Sandwich and Deal are convenient Canterbury is easy to reach and a delight when one does so. The streets are loaded with interesting shops and the Cathedral is delightful. Any pilgrimage to St. Georges should take in Canterbury. The leading hotel which also houses a commendable restaurant is **The County (0227) 66266**. There are eating places a-plenty in Canterbury; two superb examples include **Waterfields (0227) 450276** with its French and English provincial cooking and the **Restaurant Seventy Four (0227) 67411** which offers nouvelle style cuisine.

If you decide to head south towards Littlestone, then a pub crawl is seriously on the cards. Kent is riddled with them – what a delight. In the splendidly named Pett Bottom **The Duck Inn** is the first to consider; a **White Horse** is our next companion – set in a delightful village ideal for Chilham Castle. Next tavern on the agenda (hic) is the cosy **Compasses** at Sole Street. Moving on to Wye a real classic here – **The Wife of Bath (0233) 812450** not a pub, but a restaurant – first rate. Not a pub or a restaurant now but a manor house – **Eastwell Manor (0233) 35751** a true delight – the best in Kent.

Awakening from one's slumber and having breakfasted well, another decision – South or West. The South offers Mersham and the quite excellent **Stone Green Hall Hotel and Restaurant (023372) 418** well worth visiting. Hythe, handy for Littlestone offers the **Hythe Imperial (0303) 67441** – keen on golfing holidays as is the **Stade Court Hotel (0303) 682623** also in Hythe. Along with other ports this offers the ideal opportunity to play some of North France's courses and at the same time stock up the cellar!

In New Romney itself **The Blue Dolphins** appeal. Avoiding the temptations of Rye we approach Hawkhurst and **Osborne House (05805) 3265** as excellent place to have dinner. If you wish to stay locally then the **Tudor Arms (05805) 2312** has a beautiful Weald setting. In nearby Cranbrook, another Kent favourite, **The Kennel Holt Hotel (0580) 712032** is a charming place to stay and/or to have dinner. Another good eating place in the area is in Biddenden, **The Three Chimneys (0580) 291472** an excellent pub restaurant, while a restaurant proper **Ye Maydes (0580) 291306** is also good. We end our trip of South Kent in **The Bell** near Smarden, a pleasant pub with goodvalue accommodation **(023377) 283**.

Another day and another area – North Kent – in Shorne, the **Inn on the Lake (047482) 3333** is a most satisfactory place to stay. An alternative for pub lovers is the Dickensian **Leather Bottle (0474) 814327** in Cobham where perfectly adequate bedrooms are good value. More expensive accommodation is located near Ash Green in the alarmingly named village of Fawkham, the hotel **The Brandshatch Place (0474) 872239** offers tremendous comfort and a very good restaurant. Two pubs to note in the area are the **Golden Eagle** in Durham and the particularly pleasant and aptly named **Little Gem** in Aylesford.

Another splattering of places to frequent can be found near to Sevenoaks, **The Royal Oak Hotel (0732) 451109** is comfortable and offers particularly good bar snacks and makes an ideal base. From Sevenoaks several restaurants are in close proximity – they are **La Cremaillere** in Hadlow (0732) 851489 (French cooking), the **Gate Inn** in Hildenborough (0732) 832103 (good seaford) and the delightful **Thackeray's House** in Tunbridge Wells (0892) 37558 – outstanding. If you are short of a place to stay in Tunbridge Wells **The Royal Wells Inn (0892) 23414** is particularly comfortable and good value.

To assess the journey we return to Faversham and a restaurant named **Reads (0795) 535344** more fine French cooking – it's enormously popular in Kent. An additional popular occupation is the game of golf– if you're a visitor to the area or have lived there all your life it might be a good idea to discover some of these places where one can combine the words fore and fare so happily.

Hotel Imperial
Princess Parade, Hythe CT21 6AE
Tel: (0303) 67411
Sea views at the front and gardens at the back add to the attraction of this Victorian Hotel. Modern bathrooms, 83 interesting bedrooms, pleasant reception rooms and bars. Facilities for exercise are good, including swimming, tennis, golf, snooker, keep fit and table tennis.

Eastwell Manor Hotel and Restaurant
Eastwell Park, TN25 4HR
Tel: (0233) 35751
With a royal history and patronage, Eastwell Manor has elegant bedrooms and luxurious bathrooms. In the restaurant meals of unsurpassed quality are served. Set in 62 acres of undulating parkland in the heart of the Kentish Downs, Eastwell Manor is most peaceful.

My perfect round of golf must start and finish in the month of May! – Hot sun (on this particular day!), larks chirping and the cuckoo giving background accompaniment.

HOLE 1 (478 YARDS) 8TH HOLE AT ROYAL WEST NORFOLK

Starting at the Royal West Norfolk Golf Club, Brancaster, and playing the 8th hole as our 1st – very intimidating. The tide is particularly high and the drive requires a 170 to 180 yard carry over the sea to an island Fairway, just one degree right of the marker post and you are sunk – sea water and tangle. I follow my perfect drive with a superb 5 wood carrying another 160 yards across yet more ocean to a Fairway leaving a pitching wedge to the Green. As is more usual than not I chip to 5 feet and hole for a birdie 4 – not a disappointing start! This is almost my favourite golf course, one gains such inspiration from the remoteness, the marshes on one side, the sea and the sand dunes on the other.

HOLE 2 (371 YARDS) 12TH HOLE OLD COURSE WALTON HEATH

This is a not too long Dog-Leg Right – down wind a 3 wood is enough followed by a punched 9 iron and 2 putts. The painter of the original picture – Julian Barrow – was nearly decapitated by a socket from the 6th hole while he was seated at his easel! Another point of interest is that this hole is famed because Henry Cotton drove the Green playing in a 4 ball before the last war. Near to London there is no lovelier Heath, and you can see Kingswood Church spire in the distance – used by James Braid as a feature for lining up his drive when playing from the 16th tee, Old Course.

HOLE 3 (156 YARDS) 6TH HOLE AT ROYAL ST GEORGES

I choose the Maiden as our first short hole, so named for obvious reasons if you study the topography, and not too closely either! This hole was originally a blind spot but now played downwind is only an 8 iron, although into a prevailing South Westerly as much as a 1 or 2 iron. There are bunkers short, left, far and right and to find the green is a sheer relief – to take 3 putts over the undulations spoils it all – I made it in 2 putts for my 3 and was much relieved. This is a glorious setting with Pegwell Bay and Ramsgate behind, and was of course the location of eleven Open Championships, including that of 1985.

HOLE 4 (361 YARDS) 3RD HOLE AT ROYAL WORLINGTON

To me one of the most exacting of drives and 4 par holes is the 3rd/12th at 9 Hole Royal Worlington – Henry Longhurst described this as the finest 9 hole course in the world, many would agree. The drive has minimum margin for error – any semblance of a slice is likely to be lost in deep hay, bushes or trees and a pull or hook is equally severely punished by a ditch and very long grass. The Fairway is shaped as a hogs back, so the ball will bound off towards either side if given the slightest inclination. However, having bisected the Fairway on this windless day a fine 7 iron finds the centre of the fast firm Green, followed by 2 putts which gives me a safe but satisfying par 4. The village of Mildenhall is down the road, and we find ourselves amidst glorious pine trees and heathland on the edge of the Breckland Country.

HOLE 5 (452 YARDS) 15TH HOLE BERKSHIRE BLUE COURSE

I now return to the South of London and the 16th hole of the Berkshire Blue Course. This is a long and difficult par 4 dog leg. I manage, as is somewhat unusual, to drive over the left-hand bunker which leaves me with a 5 wood to the elevated Green. On the left is a mass of broom, deep yellow flowers, and also gorse – to the right are pine trees and birch trees, and approximately sixty yards short of the Green is a stream some six feet wide which trickles across the Fairway with fresh rain water and carrying the odd golf ball. I failed to make the Green, although I clear the stream, and finish on the upslope. One is now surrounded by huge Scots pines (Pinus Sylvestris) – a few flies hover but a firm chip four feet past and a curly putt arriving by the side door confirm a rickety par 4.

HOLE 6 (440 YARDS) RISK AND HOPE 14TH HOLE AT TURNBERRY AILSA COURSE

Turnberry, the scene of the 1986 Open Championship, a superb links, although not entirely natural as this was constructed by the original company which owned the famous Railway Hotel. We find Ailsa Craig lurking like a monster some 1-2 miles from the coast and the Isle of Arran in the middle distance. I choose to play the 14th hole par 4. This hole is not by the sea, but to my mind is the perfect par 4 straight and level, thick rough either side for the drive, bunkered short left of the Green and to the right. Even on a calm day the second shot demands a long iron, and if one gets home in 2 it's a rewarding experience, followed by two putts and a par 4 giving maximum satisfaction.

HOLE 7 (476 YARDS) TWO COUNTIES, 13TH HOLE AT LIPHOOK

I am not now returning to the Surrey/Hampshire border to get away from Scotland, and to that country we will be returning. However, the par 4 13th at Liphook has a lovely drive downhill. The hole is divided by a brook over which one has to hit a medium to long iron to an elevated Green well bunkered left and right. Although I was too far in 2 I chipped back and holed for the inevitable par 4!

HOLE 8 (200 YARDS) THE ALPS, 12TH HOLE AT ROYAL LIVERPOOL (HOYLAKE)

Short holes need to be somewhat intimidating, and an outstanding hole in this respect must be the par 3 12th at Royal Liverpool. One is more likely to be taking at least a 4 wood. There is a dip and also a bunker to the right, and thick rough beyond, and to the left a sharp fall towards the Dee Estuary and North Wales. One hits over a valley and has to be critically accurate. I suppose I was fortunate to hit the kind of shot you never feel, which came up two feet short of the hole and gave me my second birdie of the round.

HOLE 9 (441 YARDS) 13TH HOLE AT WENTWORTH WEST COURSE

To complete the outward nine holes I think a long and testing par 4 is required, and I have chosen the 13th at Wentworth, known as the "Burma Road" due to the rough's affinity to the Burmese jungle. On this dog leg to the left it is essential to set one's drive up right of centre, otherwise one is blocked by tall pines to the left and if we are too far to the right the Fairway falls away to rough and trees. It is a calm and glorious May day, and I fire a three iron to the back of the Green, followed by two downhill putts, which is always satisfying. I find myself out in 33 and quite pleased to be several holes ahead!

HOLE 10 (396 YARDS) 15TH HOLE AT MUIRFIELD

Muirfield is to many people the perfect golf links. The first nine holes are laid out clockwise, and the inward nine go anti-clockwise inside the early holes. This maximises the variety of different wind directions. I chose to play the par 4 15th drive, over large bunkers onto a Fairway bunkered either side. Having reached the prepared surface on a calm day one is faced with a marvellous 3 or 4 iron over more bunkers to a Green set slightly in a hollow. It is most rewarding to hit the Green and stay there, and equally so to make a par 4. This lovely place is located overlooking the Firth of Forth with views towards the Fife coast. The Course is surrounded by stone walls with pine trees and sea-holly growing in abundance.

HOLE 11 (461 YARDS) 17TH HOLE OLD COURSE ST. ANDREWS

The Old Course at St. Andrews must surely feature, and one is spoilt for choice. I choose the 17th Road hole for sheer intimidation, and an all-or-nothing par 4. To play this hole correctly one drives over the old railway sheds, now reinstated I think. This area is out of bounds together with the grounds of the Hotel and Country Club. Needless to say there is thick rough and hidden bunkers if you go left. I hit the perfect drive over the corner just right of centre, with a slight draw. Only on this line does one have a chance to find the Green in 2, and any shot to the left is blocked by a severe Greenside bunker from which it took a famous Japanese professional some five or six shots to extricate his ball in the 1978 Open. I play a little defensively to avoid going through the Green on to the road, or possibly over a stone wall. I settle for a 5 which is one over par.

HOLE 12 (218 YARDS) WITCHES BOWSTAR, THE QUEEN'S COURSE GLENEAGLES

This par 3 on the Queen's Course Gleneagles is a gem – often a full 3 iron to a two tier Green. Water to the right and bunkers to the left and right, it is most satisfying to hit the top tier so long as the pin is not placed on the bottom, otherwise there is much golf remaining! I managed a par 3.

HOLE 13 (542 YARDS) 17TH HOLE AT MUIRFIELD

I return to Muirfield for our second par 5 – really fine par 5 holes are few and far between, but here the drive has to be rifle straight. Gaping bunkers loom to the left, and in all probability one has to play out sideways – they have a grabbing habit at Muirfield. There is thick rough to the right, so having hit the perfect drive one is positioned to follow with a pefect second over humps, hollows and more bunkers and achieving the long carry to safety. An applied approach shot is necessary to a Green surrounded by high sand dunes. I was relieved to leave this Green with a par 5.

HOLE 14 (432 YARDS) 15TH HOLE AT WOBURN DUKES COURSE

A relatively new Course and a part of the Duke of Bedford's estate. In fact there are two Courses, the Dukes and the Duchess, both carved out of huge pine forests. This 15th hole is a classic par 4 requiring an accurate drive right of centre, which sets up a marvellous 4 iron shot over a ravine. If one fails punishment is unforgiving. I putted far too strongly but holed a 7 footer to make a par 4.

HOLE 15 (423 YARDS) 12TH HOLE AT SUNNINGDALE OLD COURSE

The second nine at Sunningdale is in my opinion far superior to the earlier holes, and the 12th is a splendid par 4. Having hit a longish drive bisecting the Fairway, with thick heather on either side, one is faced with a really well struck 5 iron or more to hit a raised Green. If one is short the ball finishes in deep heather and gorse, so there is a great premium to be up. Left and right are very tricky chip shots should one stray. I enjoyed my 5 iron and 2 putts for a par 4.

HOLE 16 (210 YARDS) 10TH HOLE AT SWINLEY FOREST

This is a beautiful long iron shot to an undulating Green with bunkers left and right, and punishing heather to the left and beyond. It is a most satisfying hole to play well and a 2 is fairly elusive. I settle for my 3. This course is very secluded and has only about 250 members. As far as I know there has never been a Club competition. The golf is delightfully informal and the Clubhouse is built as if it were a private house.

HOLE 17 (362 YARDS) 10TH HOLE AT ROYAL CINQUE PORTS

A typical links situation, this dog leg with a fiery Fairway can be a drive and chip in the height of the summer with a following wind, and conversely 2 woods into a North easterly force 6. It is so easy to run off this sloping Green, and although disappointing to lip the hole for a 3 I cannot complain about my 4.

HOLE 18 (458 YARDS) 18TH HOLE AT ROYAL ST. GEORGE'S

Finally I return to Royal St. George's, where I feel the 18th is one of the finest tests at this stage of a round. For perfection it is wise to be left of centre, although there is always a danger of running off the Fairway. On this particular day I take out my 4 iron and fire the ball over the cross bunkers, and it just makes the ridge at the front of the Green. There are several dangers here, such as a deep pot bunker to the right, and out of bounds too far and what is known as Duncans' Hollow to the left. (So named as the great George Duncan needed two shots to tie the Open in 1922 but regretfully for him took one too many.) My par 4 completes a most satisfying round over what I think most peole would agree are a lovely combination of holes. Obviously one could select another eighteen, or even many combinations, and achieve an equally interesting Course. A score of 69 is most satisfying, and I would dearly like to achieve such a score in reality!

Thank you for bearing with me, but at least we have not had to hunt for balls in the rough!

ANGUS LLOYD

ROYAL CINQUE PORTS, DEAL

In the year 55B.C. **Julius Caesar** landed on the coast near Deal. In 1920 an American invader by the name of **Walter Hagen** came to Deal to play in his first Open Championship. Both came, both saw, but neither conquered. In fact both returned from whence they came tails firmly between legs – small wonder Deal is often considered the toughest of all England's Championship links!

The Royal Cinque Ports Golf Club was founded in February 1892 by **Major General J.M.Graham** whilst at lunch in Deal's Black Horse Hotel. The 18 hole course was opened in 1895 and has required very few alterations during its distinguished history. Today the gentleman responsible for the efficient organisation of the Club is the Secretary, **Mr N.S.Phillips**. Mr Phillips may be contacted at the **Royal Cinque Ports Golf Club, Golf Road, Deal, Kent. Tel (0304) 374007. Andrew Reynolds** is the professional. He can be reached on **(0304) 374170**.

Visitors with official handicaps are welcome to play the famous links although prior booking with the Secretary is essential. As with a number of the more traditional Clubs, three and four ball matches have no standing on the course, indeed they are only permitted by arrangement with the Secretary.

In **1986** a **green fee** of **£16** entitled the visitor to a full day's golf. Persons arriving after 1 pm could obtain a **25%** reduction. Weekend bookings are possible, if a little difficult, in 1986 the weekend green fees were set at **£20** per day and **£16** per round. The Club also offers a twilight green fee where there is a **50%** reduction for those teeing off after **5pm**. An early start in winter with a later start in summer would appear to be the best bets.

The golf course is situated approximately one mile north of the town. Probably the best route from **London** is to travel on the **A2/M2** as far as **Canterbury**. There one should pick up the **A257 Sandwich** road and thereafter the **A258** which takes you to **Deal**. From the South the **A258** runs from **Dover**. Also worth noting is the Deal Railway Station which is on the northern side of the town, near the pier.

Very often it is Mother Nature who can provide the greatest challenge at Deal. Strong winds billowing in from the sea, capable of changing direction several times during a round can turn what appear to be modest holes into monsters. The course measures **6409** yards from the medal tees (**par 70**) with the Championship tees extending the course to some **6744** yards

(**par 72**). The corresponding distances for the ladies are **5190** yards and **5675** yards (par being **74**). The outward nine is generally considered the easier half (**Michael Bonallack** turned in 31 during his record amateur score of 65 – a record which has stood for 23 years). Certainly the back nine is longer and Deal is renowned for its tough finish, the 16th perhaps being the most difficult hole on the course. The fairways are humpy and hillocky and well bunkered. The rough is often thick and many of the greens stand on natural plateaux. On a clear day there are some magnificent views across the course towards the English Channel and to the distant white cliffs beyond Pegwell Bay.

Two Open Championships have been held at Deal, in **1909** and in **1920**. The 1909 Championship was won by the Englishman **John H Taylor**, his fourth victory in the event. The 1920 Open has already been referred to – the luckless Hagen in fact finished fifty third in a field of fifty four. Also entitled to feel somewhat peeved that year was **Abe Mitchell** who allowed **George Duncan** to come from thirteen strokes behind him to snatch victory. Plans to stage a third Championship at Deal in 1949 had to be abandoned when extensive flooding led to a temporary closure of the course.

The Royal Cinque Ports Club has also twice been selected to host the **Amateur Championship**, firstly in **1923** and secondly during its centenary year in **1982**. One of the annual highlights on the Club's calendar is the **Halford Hewitt Challenge Cup**, an 'Old Boys' competition played for in April. In 1987 the Seniors Open returns to Deal.

The Members of Royal Cinque Ports are doubly fortunate. Blessed with such a fine course, they also possess an excellent Clubhouse. The facilities are first class and both the early starter and our 'twilight golfer' will be glad to find that hot and cold snacks are normally available at all times. With prior notice both breakfast and dinner can be arranged. For those just wanting a quick drink in between rounds (a stiff one may be in order!) a 'spikes bar' is provided.

It would not of course be fair, either to the Romans or Mr Hagen, to leave Deal without recording that both did eventually achieve their ambitions. The Romans returned a century later and conquered the Brits, and as for Walter, he didn't have to wait quite so long, in 1922 he won the first of four Open Championships, none of which though, alas, was at Deal.

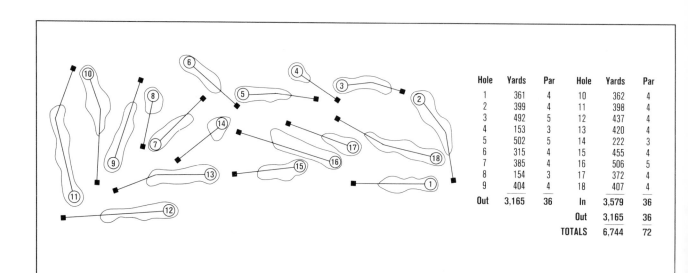

Hole	Yards	Par	Hole	Yards	Par
1	361	4	10	362	4
2	399	4	11	398	4
3	492	5	12	437	4
4	153	3	13	420	4
5	502	5	14	222	3
6	315	4	15	455	4
7	385	4	16	506	5
8	154	3	17	372	4
9	404	4	18	407	4
Out	**3,165**	**36**	**In**	**3,579**	**36**
			Out	3,165	36
			TOTALS	**6,744**	**72**

ROYAL ST GEORGES

I come to write this piece on a particularly Black Monday – June as well. England's cricketers have just received a second routing from the Indians and yesterday was even worse – the Argentinians put us out of the World Cup. The flag of St George hangs at half mast. Still, life must go on and thoughts drift towards St Georges, Royal St Georges, the patron saint of English golf.

The Club was founded in **1887**, rather ironically by two Scottish gentlemen, **Dr Laidlaw Purves** and **Henry Lamb** after what can only be described as a rather eccentric venture. Like all good Scotsmen they had been bitten by the 'bug', however, both were presently living in Victorian London which meant that their golf was more or less confined to the various commons where the game was played alongside every conceivable activity imaginable. To them golf was meant to be played on a links by the sea. Hence we find the pair at Bournemouth setting off in an easterly direction looking for a suitable sight. Having reached the eastern shore of Kent they had drawn the proverbial blank, then with patience no doubt wearing thin, "land ahoy" Doctor Purves sights a vast stretch of duneland at Sandwich. The story is that he "spied the land with a golfer's eye" from the tower of St Clement's Church. Quite what he was doing at the top of the tower is irrelevant – **St Georges** had been located. Within seven short years the Open Championship had 'come south' and St Georges was the first English venue.

One hundred years on **Captain R J Hitchen RN** is the Secretary at St Georges, he can be contacted by telephone on **(0304) 613090**. All written communications should be directed to the Secretary at **The Royal St Georges Golf Club, Sandwich, Kent CT13 9PB**. Golfers wishing to visit the course must make prior arrangements with the Secretary. As a general guide visitors are welcome between Mondays and Fridays and gentlemen must possess official handicaps of 18 or less, ladies 15 or less. Other points to note are that the 1st tee is reserved daily for Members until 9.45am and between 1.15pm and 2.15pm, however, the 10th tee is usually free in the early mornings. St Georges is essentially a singles and foursomes Club and three ball and four ball matches are only permissible with the agreement of the Secretary.

The **green fees** as set on 1st March 1986 are **£18** per round, **£25** per day. During the months of December, January and February the **£18** fee is applicable for a full day's golf. Should there be a wish to hire golf clubs arrangements can be made with the professional, **Cyril Whiting**, telephone **(0304) 617380**. Finally the services of a caddie can be booked via the Caddiemaster on **(0304) 617380** – a week's warning is preferable.

Travelling to Sandwich should be relatively straightforward. The town is linked to Canterbury to the west by the **A257**, a distance of approximately 15 miles and to **Deal**, 6 miles south east of Sandwich by the **A258**. Motoring from London, the most direct route is to head for Canterbury using a combination of the **A2** and **M2** and thereafter following the **A257** as above. For those coming from the south coast **Ashford** should be aimed for. **Ashford** is joined to Canterbury by the **A28**. Sandwich can also be reached by train.

Since its first Open of **1894**, won by **John H Taylor**, the Championship has been held at Sandwich on ten further occasions, most recently of course in 1985 when **Sandy Lyle** became the first British winner for sixteen years. The visitor will not have to tackle the course from the Championship tees but he'll still have to confront the many dunes and the awkward stances that St Georges is so famous for. And then of course there is the ever present wind.

St George's has seen many great happenings: **Walter Hagen** winning the Championship in **1922** and then promptly handing his winnings straight to his caddie; **Henry Cotton's** opening 67-65 in the **1934** Championship and then the **Harry Bradshaw** 'broken bottle' episode of 1949. After a gap of 32 years the Open returned to St Georges in 1981 when the American Bill Rogers won.

Having done battle with the elements the golfer will find the Clubhouse welcoming. Excellent lunches are served daily and both breakfasts and dinners can be obtained with prior arrangement. A jacket and tie should be worn in all public rooms.

While one must admit that some British teams have lost their edge and we avid sports fans tend to get a little demoralized – my, that Ryder Cup victory seems so long ago! But worry not fellow countrymen we have at least one consolation – for while our top professionals fail to show their class no one will doubt the sporting amphitheatres of Britain – Wimbledon, Lords, Wembley, Ascot, the list goes on and so of course does the game – all games are meant for playing – and in Britain we are blessed with ample arenas in which to play – Sandwich is as fine an example as any – the flag of St Georges flutters fully.

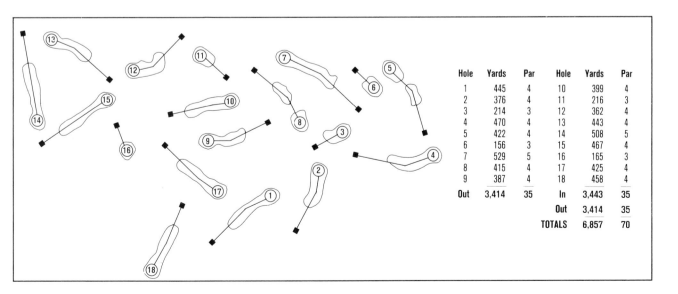

Hole	Yards	Par	Hole	Yards	Par
1	445	4	10	399	4
2	376	4	11	216	3
3	214	3	12	362	4
4	470	4	13	443	4
5	422	4	14	508	5
6	156	3	15	467	4
7	529	5	16	165	3
8	415	4	17	425	4
9	387	4	18	458	4
Out	**3,414**	**35**	**In**	**3,443**	**35**
			Out	**3,414**	**35**
			TOTALS	**6,857**	**70**

SURREY

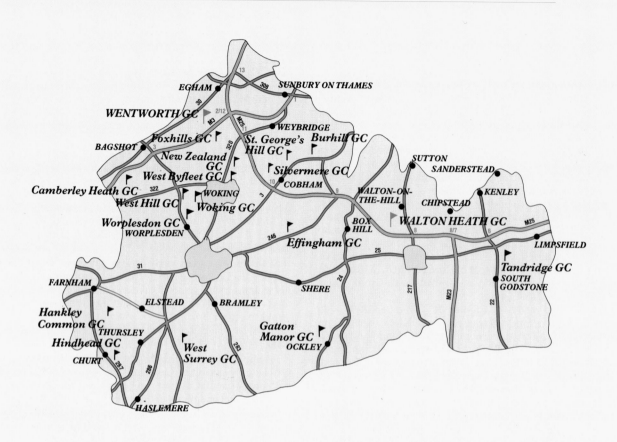

Map labels:

EGHAM · 13 · 308 · SUNBURY ON THAMES
WENTWORTH GC · 30 · 2/12 · M3 · M25
BAGSHOT · Foxhills GC · 3 · 320 · WEYBRIDGE · St. George's Hill GC · Burhill GC · SUTTON · SANDERSTEAD
New Zealand GC · West Byfleet GC · Silvermere GC · COBHAM · WALTON-ON-THE-HILL · CHIPSTEAD · KENLEY
Camberley Heath GC · 322 · WOKING · 10 · 9 · WALTON HEATH GC · M25
West Hill GC · Woking GC · 3 · BOX HILL · 8 · 8/7 · 6 · LIMPSFIELD
Worplesdon GC · WORPLESDEN · 246 · Effingham GC · 25 · Tandridge GC
31 · SHERE · 24 · 217 · M23 · 22 · SOUTH GODSTONE
FARNHAM
Hankley Common GC · ELSTEAD · BRAMLEY · Gatton Manor GC · OCKLEY
THURSLEY · West Surrey GC · 283
Hindhead GC · CHURT · 287 · 286 · 233
HASLEMERE

JULIAN BARROW   "Walton Heath"   BURLINGTON GALLERY

Gravetye Manor
Near East Grinstead, West Sussex, RH19 4LJ, England.
Telephone Sharpthorne (STD 0342) 810567
Telex 957239

When Providence distributed land best suited for building golf courses it wasn't done in the most democratic of spirits. Suggesting the top dozen or so courses in a county like Cumbria is a fairly straightforward task – there aren't many more than a dozen or so to choose from. Recommending a similar number in Hampshire is, as the Americans would say, "a different ball game", there being a number of very fine courses. Attempting the same in Surrey is nigh on impossible for in golfing terms no other county in England is so well-endowed.

Though very different in appearance it is probably safe to suggest that **Walton Heath** and **Wentworth** are the county's two leading courses. (Sunningdale of course being just over the border in Berkshire) But Walton and Wentworth (both featured on later pages) are only two of Surrey's famous "W Club" – there's also **Worplesdon** and **Woking, West Hill, West Surrey** and **West Byfleet.**

Located off the **A32** to the west of Woking, Worplesdon, West Hill and Woking Golf Clubs lie practically next door to one another, indeed it might be possible to devise a few dramatic "cross-course" holes – though in view of the value of some of the properties that would have to be driven over it's perhaps not such a good idea! **West Hill** is generally considered the most difficult of the three, the fairways at times being frighteningly narrow, **Worplesdon** with its superb greens is probably the most widely known (largely due to its famous annual foursomes event), while **Woking**, founded almost a century ago, perhaps possesses the greatest charm. Whatever their particular merits all three are outstanding examples of the natural heathland and heather type course. Visitors are welcome at each during the week although prior telephoning is essential and proof of handicap is normally required. A full day's golf on any of the three can be enjoyed for around the **£15-£20** mark.

Slightly closer to the capital and very much in the heart of stockbroker-belt country is a second trio of courses centred around Weybridge: **St George's Hill, New Zealand** and **West Byfleet.** Once again heathland type courses where golf is played amidst heavily wooded surroundings, the combination of pines, silver birch and purple heather making for particular attractive settings. **St George's Hill** is in fact one of the more undulating courses in Surrey and calls for several spectacular shots. It need hardly be said that all three courses are very popular and one shouldn't consider arranging a game without first telephoning the Club in question.

Golf in Surrey isn't of course all heathland and heather. Just a short drive from Weybridge is the delightful parkland course at **Burhill**, situated some 2 miles south of Walton-on-Thames.

Burhill's Clubhouse is a particulaly grand affair, at one time it was the home of the Dowager Duchess of Wellington. Much less grand but to some of equal interest is the "Dick Turpin" cottage sited on the course and reputed to have been used by the infamous highwayman. Green fees at Burhill for 1986 were priced at **£12** per round, **£18** per day. Also worth noting is a nearby public course, **Silvermere**, located midway between Byfleet and Cobham off the **A245**. It should be possible to arrange a game here on any day of the week, the cost of a round in 1986 being **£5** during the week, **£6.50** at weekends.

Generally speaking golf in southern England and golf in America have precious little in common, however, the **Foxhills** Club at Ottershaw (off the **A320**) can make a genuine claim to have married the two successfully. A Jacobean-styled manor house run on American country club lines including an outstanding range of leisure facilities it has two Championship length heathland type courses. Not surprisingly Foxhills is a popular haunt for golfing societies, but it is normally possible for individual visitors to play either (or both) courses during the week. Fees in 1986 were **10** for a single round, **14** for a full day's golf.

The country club scene may not of course appeal to all types and excellent golf in a more sedate atmosphere can be enjoyed at **Gatton Manor** situated in Ockley near Dorking. The 18 hole course was opened in 1969 and from its back tees can be stretched to 6906 yards. The course has a very scenic layout running through woods and alongside lakes. With the exception of Sunday mornings visitors are welcome throughout the week for a fee of **£10** midweek, **£12** at weekends.

The rich heathland seam runs the breadth of the county and over to the west practically straddling the three counties of Surrey, Berkshire and Hampshire lies the superb **Camberley Heath** course, while down in the south west corner there is yet another outstanding trio of clubs: **Hindhead, West Surrey** and **Hankley Common.** West Surrey, perhaps more of a heather/parkland mix, is one of the few leading courses in the county where visitors can play at weekends, however, prior telephoning is again to be recommended. **Hankley Common** was for many years a favourite of the South African **Bobby Locke**, four times Open Champion who once owned a house adjacent to the course. Hankley Common is widely known for its fire of ten years ago and its spectacular 18th hole – one of the greatest closing holes in golf. A vast gulley which seems to possess magnetic powers looms in front of the green. Visitors are welcome to test their skills during the week, prior contact with the secretary being essential.

Burhill G.C.	(0932) 227345
Camberley Heath G.C.	(0276) 23257
Foxhills G.C.	(093287) 2050
Gatton Manor G.C.	(0306) 79555
Hankley Common G.C.	(025125) 2493
Hindhead G.C.	(042873) 4614
New Zealand G.C.	(0932) 342891
St. Georges Hill G.C.	(0932) 47758
Silvermere G.C.	(0932) 6007
Walton Heath G.C.	(073781) 2380
Wentworth G.C.	(09904) 2201
West Byfleet G.C.	(09323) 43433
West Hill G.C.	(04862) 4365
West Surrey G.C.	(04868) 21275
Woking G.C.	(04862) 60053
Worplesdon G.C.	(04862) 2277

SURREY

I'm not sure but I think there would be more hotels in Surrey if it wasn't for the fact that there are so many damned golfcourses. The county's literally littered with them. Litter is hardly the correct word, for without much doubt this county is what can only be described as an abundance of tremendous golfcourses. Surrey certainly has the well-to-do air about it – pleasant houses – commuter belt – but as you look up at the stars from your recently mown lawn you ask yourself what it's all about. You might be in the middle of Beirut or deepest Africa trapped in no man's land, starving and freezing. But you are in Surrey and as you kick your heels and stride towards the house – you are contented – not because of your lot but because tomorrow you are playing golf – at Walton Heath – one of the best.

Surrey is also home to some other great establishment names of sport, Epsom and Wimbledon spring to mind. The area also has within its midst some gorgeous parklands: Richmond and Bushy; and Hampton Court is one of several superb houses to visit while visiting the county. The Gardens at Wisley and Kew are also splendid attractions. To those who think that Surrey has little to offer but rows of houses may be delighted to hear that the county offers a huge range of charming villages after one has broken through the commuter belt chain.

The journey commences in Kenley just fifteen miles from Piccadilly Circus but in the country all the same. The pub, here is the **Wattenden Arms**, a splendid place for lunch and a friendly local in the evening – ideal for getting acquainted with a member from Walton Heath although given the prestige of this club – and some of its members you may think that a slightly more lavish evening should be thought of, these are the suggestions, in Sutton. **Partner's 23, 01 644 77433** is a really excellent establishment, friendly service combine with some splendid food. Ideally situated for Walton Heath itself in Walton-on-the-Hill is the **Ebeneezer Cottage (073 781) 31663** a restaurant which offers some excellent house specialities.

If you fail to get a game at Walton Heath then Sanderstead is the home of the **Selsdon Park 01 657 8811** which has an enormous array of leisure facilities – including a golf course. As with many golfing hotels your visit will not be cheap.

Returning to restaurants – of which there are so many in Surrey – one visits Chipstead, where **Dene Farm (073 75) 52661** with its gorgeous country setting, offers an imaginative menu backed up by a good wine list. In Box Hill, near Dorking, a popular place for travellers and tourists to stay is the **Burford Bridge Hotel (0306) 884561**, a convenient location coupled with a warm atmosphere. South of the M25 in West Surrey one finds two other restaurants or more. In Limpsfield **The Old Lodge (08833) 2996** is a splendid place for dinner – set priced menus are the order of the day and the cooking (French) is spectacularly good. Meanwhile, in South Godstone another restaurant to note – French again I'm delighted to report. The name, **La Bonne Auberge**. It is as well to remember that while the quality of these restaurants is unquestioned the prices are once again fairly high – but such is life in Surrey. However good value food of various kinds can be found in many of the pubs in the area one such example is **The White Horse** in Shere.

It is in the south of the county that one finds some of the best scenery and in Ockley one also finds **The Kings Arms (0306) 711224** and lest you lust there for your pints of ale may I warn you that this is a restaurant. If a boozer is what you are seeking then look no further than **Oakwoodhill** near to Ockley for here the **Punch Bowl** is an ideal country pub. Some good whiskies to try – ideal for a post-round round at Walton Heath. In Bramley, **The Bramley Grange Hotel (0483) 893434** is an ideal base from which to tour the county. Close to the Sussex borders lies Haslemere and another fine hotel, a timbered farmhouse on this occasion. **The Lythe Hill Hotel (0428) 51251** where bedrooms in the original house have great character. People who have still not found a restaurant to visit must surely do so here for **Morels (0438) 51462** offers some simply splendid dishes here in an excellent atmosphere. In Churt, another hotel of some distinction **The Frensham Pond Hotel (025125) 3175**. The restaurant has fine views over the pond itself and also has a good reputation. This is a must for golfers who like the old water sports although is there such an animal I ask myself? In Thursley, a welcoming pub is the **The Three Horseshoes**, ideal for a visit before travelling on to Elstead where among other things **Emmerichs's (0252) 702323** not far from France – this time a Swiss menu is available.

In Farnham, a former coaching inn, **The Bush (0252) 715237** is an excellent place to stay while just outside Farnham on the A31 towards Alton lies the **The Trevena House Hotel (0252) 716908**. The splendid exterior reveals within its interior a pleasant hotel which is good value for these parts.

Returning north towards London one finds an area that hides some truly superb golfcourses. In Worplesdon, near Guildford the ancient capital of Surrey, lies Worplesdon Place – this is another splendid base – which is also good value. Woking is an area beseiged by outstanding golfcourses. If you are fortunate enough to be playing there – **The Wheatsheaf Hotel (04862) 73047** is a good spot to collect one's thoughts, another well thought of hotel is the **Mayford Manor (04862) 66166**. In Weybridge the **Ship Thistle Hotel (0932) 48364** is a a more expensive but exceedingly well appointed town centre hotel; another Weybridge hotel that is well worth considering is the **Oatlands Park (0932) 47242**. In Cobham **The Ladbroke Seven Hills Hotel** carries a good reputation, while **The Cricketers** on Downside Common, Cobham is a sporting little pub. The restaurants in this particular area are in abundance. In Weybridge **Casa Romana (0932) 43470** is good (Italian). While East Molesey's offerings include **The Lantern 01 979 1531** and **Vecchia Roma 01 979 5490** (Italian).

Elsewhere is the county – Camberley to be precise **Tithas (0276) 23279** is an excellent Indian restaurant. It is near to Camberley, in Bagshot that one finds Pennyhill Park a distinguished Country House hotel that has managed to squeeze its way between the golfcourses – Wentworth is a jewel close by. We end our Surrey saunter in Egham, not at the **Runnymede Hotel (0784) 36171** which is excellent nor at the simply gorgeous hotel, **Great Fosters (0784) 33822**. Not even at the splendid French restaurant **La Bonne Franquette (0784) 33206**. No we end it in a lay-by – things look bad – extremely bad – missed lunch at the superb **Castle, Sunbury-on-Thames (09327) 83647**, but what is worse it looks as if we won't see the tees in time for nightfall – at a time like this you might just as well be in the middle of Beirut!

Selsdon Park Hotel
Addington Road, Sanderstead,
South Croydon, Surrey CR2 8TA
Tel: 01 657 8811
The Selsdon Park is Britain's largest proprietor-owned hotel, 150 bedrooms set in 200 acres of parkland with its own 18 hole golf course, tennis, riding, swimming, snooker, new tropical leisure complex with an indoor swimming pool, squash, and mini gym.

La Bonne Franquette
5 High Street,
Egham,
Surrey
Tel: (0784) 39494
Enjoy lunch or dinner at one of the country's top restaurants. A la cartè always available. 'Fixed price' luncheon £12.50 inc. 'Menu inclusive' evenings – 5 courses including selected wines £20 inc. All prices include service and VAT.

GREAT · FOSTERS
England's *most distinguished* country hotel

Great Fosters was once a Royal hunting lodge in the heart of Windsor Forest and for nearly four centuries the stately Elizabethan home of many notable families. Great Fosters to-day is no ordinary hotel. It is a very English institution – a place of great charm and tradition – and a scheduled Grade I Historic Monument. For over half a century it has entertained a galaxy of important and discriminating guests from the film star world, from high society and from big business. Great Fosters maintains the atmosphere and splendour of the past and is renowned worldwide as England's *most distinguished* country hotel.

With all the old atmosphere retained
Great Fosters is rich in antique furniture, ornate plaster ceilings and oak panelling. It has a rare oakwell staircase and some fine Jacobean chimney pieces with log fires on winter evenings. In giving the hotel high standards of comfort, the character of the 16th century house has been wonderfully preserved.

Bedrooms of character
The suites and bedrooms are sumptuously furnished and in keeping with the period of the house. The most important have tapestries and antiques, all have great character. All rooms have private bath or shower en suite, are centrally heated and equipped with colour T.V., radio and telephone. The greatest care has been taken to keep fire precautions up to date and ensure the safety of guests.

Magnificent setting for private parties
The 15th century Tithe Barn is a magnificent setting for banquets, private parties, dances and receptions. Every Saturday there is a dinner and dance to which non-residents are welcome.

The hotel has very high standards of food and service and a well chosen wine list.

The most romantic garden
The house is set in 17 acres of the most romantic garden. Its mullioned windows look out upon sculptured yews surrounded by a Saxon 'homestead' moat. A Japanese bridge across this moat leads to a sunken rose garden.

The Conference Centre is purpose built
Purpose built within the old coach house and stables, the conference centre, with its water garden, is well designed, fully equipped and up to date.

Great Fosters is the ideal centre and highly accessible
Only *7 miles* from Heathrow Airport, less than *20 miles* from London's West End by road and *35 minutes* by train to Waterloo, the hotel is on Stroude Road between Egham and Virginia Water and signposted from both directions. It is easy to get to from the M25, M3, M4, M1 and A1.

Surrounded by many famous places, Great Fosters is the ideal centre for any holiday from overseas.

The House from the Drive

Recommended ★★★★ and [CD] Scheduled Historic Monument

It is autumn. A reddish-gold leaf scurries across the 18th green. The huge gallery is silent. Fully fifty yards away, to the right of the fairway close to the trees and in the rough is the defending champion, Severiano Ballesteros. He is one down to the legendary Arnold Palmer and he needs a miracle. The blade flashes, and a ball flies towards the green. It pitches, it rolls, and it drops....the eagle has landed.

A stunningly beautiful place, Wentworth is set in the heart of the famous Surrey heathland belt. The name first appeared on the golfing map in the mid nineteen twenties when **Harry Colt** was commissioned to design two eighteen hole courses. The **East Course** was first to open in 1924, with the **West Course** following two years later. Before the War it was the East Course that captured the limelight by staging the Club's first important events: in 1926 an unofficial match between British and American teams and in 1932 the first ever playing of the **Curtis Cup**. In the period since 1945 the longer West Course has grabbed most of the glory. In the 1950's came the **Ryder Cup** and the **World Cup** and in the 60's, the **World Matchplay Championship**.

The administration of the Club is presently in the very capable hands of the Secretary, **Colonel Beard** and his staff. Colonel Beard may be contacted via the **Wentworth Golf Club, Virginia Water, Surrey. Tel. (09904) 2201**. It is essential for persons wishing to **visit** Wentworth that they pre-book a starting time with the Secretary. Unless accompanied by a Member, visitors are limited to playing during weekdays and must be in possession of a current handicap. Also well-worth noting is that from Fridays to Mondays inclusive a system of course allocation is operated. One of the courses is designated for two balls or foursomes with the other for three ball or four ball matches. Society days at Wentworth are Tuesdays, Wednesdays and Thursdays.

In **1986** a **green fee** of **£28** entitled the visitor to a full day's golf. It is usual for the green fee to be half the normal rate during the winter months. The Club has excellent practice facilities and both electric trolleys and sets of clubs can be hired from the professional shop. **Bernard Gallacher**, the Scottish Ryder Cup player, is the professional at Wentworth. He can be reached on **(09904) 3353**.

Travelling to Wentworth ought not to present too many difficulties, the area being well served by major roads. The entrance to the Wentworth Estate is on the main **A30** road, some two miles west of Staines. The **M3, M4** and **M25** all pass close to the course making access easy from any direction. Finally **Heathrow Airport** is no more than twenty minutes drive away.

Wentworth's West Course, or **'Burma Road'** as it has become commonly known, is one of Britain's longest (and most difficult)

inland courses. From the back tees it stretches to a formidable **6,945** yards with a par of **72**, while from the forward yellow tees it is still a very testing **6675** yards. Even from the ladies tees the Course measures a shade over **6000** yards! The East Course is considerably shorter it being **6176** yards from the back markers, however, the par is a tough **68** with five of the par fours measuring over 420 yards. Apart from their length the two courses differ slightly in general appearance, as the Club's redoubtable Secretary puts it, "The West Course is mainly wooded with some heather while the East Course is mainly heather with some woods."!

In terms of staging major championships while **Royal Birkdale** can probably claim to have established itself as England's most fashionable links course, so the West Course at Wentworth can claim to be the inland equivalent. Indeed the television cameras have visited the Burma Road so often of late that Wentworth is arguably Britain's best known course. Certainly the opening holes and the closing stretch have become familiar to millions.

In 1986 the **Whyte and Mackay** sponsored **P.G.A.** Championship was held at Wentworth for the third successive year and in a repeat of 1985 produced a dramatic play-off, victory in this instance going to the Australian, **Rodger Davis**.

Few, however, would dispute that the word 'Wentworth' instantly invokes thoughts of early Autumn – Wentworth in all its glory – the setting of course for the World Matchplay Championship. First held in 1964, when matchplay events were few and far between, the Championship immediately caught the imagination of the public. People to this day talk of **Gary Player's** incredible comeback against **Tony Lema** in the semi-final of 1965 when he was seven down with seventeen to play. The South African won that year as he did on four further occasions. There was also **Isac Aoki's** hole in one at the 2nd during the 1979 Championship – his reward for four seconds of work being a £55,000 luxury summer house! In more recent years **Severiano Ballesteros** has come to dominate the event winning four times between 1981 and 1985.

It is perhaps not too surprising that 'El Gran Senor' should feel so at home at Wentworth – the elegant Clubhouse was once the home of a Spanish Countess. The more mortal golfer may wish to note that beyond the castle-like exterior some excellent catering is provided. Although breakfasts are not offered, dinners can be arranged for parties of 25 or more. In fact Wentworth's 19th (or should one say 37th?) provides an admirable compliment to the quality of the golf – and that is saving something!

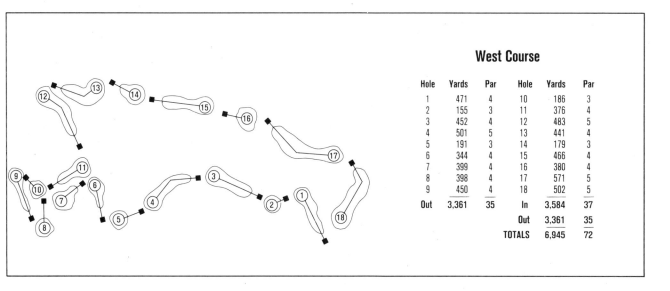

West Course

Hole	Yards	Par	Hole	Yards	Par
1	471	4	10	186	3
2	155	3	11	376	4
3	452	4	12	483	5
4	501	5	13	441	4
5	191	3	14	179	3
6	344	4	15	466	4
7	399	4	16	380	4
8	398	4	17	571	5
9	450	4	18	502	5
Out	3,361	35	In	3,584	37
			Out	3,361	35
			TOTALS	6,945	72

Gavrillo Princip may have pulled the trigger that ignited the Great War but our history books tell us that tension in Europe had sometime earlier reached boiling point. In their Palaces in St. Petersburg and Berlin the Czar and the Kaiser pondered the strength of their armies. Meanwhile the great statesmen of Britain were engaged in battles of a different nature......

All square as they reach the 18th green on the Old Course at Walton Heath, **Churchill** turns to **Lloyd-George** and says, "Now then, I will putt you for the Premiership".

Herbert Fowler once said, "God builds golf links and the less man meddles the better for all concerned." Herbert Fowler designed Walton Heath. However, before the opening of the Old Course in **May 1904**, a little meddling was called for. The glorious heathland through which the emerald fairways were cut was once covered, or nearly covered, in thick heather in parts as much as two feet thick (the Members will tell you it still is!). While many of Britain's leading Clubs took several years to establish their reputations, that of Walton Heath was assured months before the first stroke was even played; in **January 1904 James Braid** agreed to become Walton's first professional. Braid initially signed a seven year contract, his performances in the next seven Open Championships were: **2nd, 1st, 1st, 5th, 1st, 2nd and 1st**, after which he became the first ever golfer to win five Opens. Hardly surprisingly his contract was extended and so indeed began an association with the Club that was to last for nearly fifty years.

In the years immediately before the First War, Walton Heath Members included no fewer than 24 M.Ps (including Winston Churchill and Lloyd George) and 21 Members of the Lords. Another famous Walton golfer was **W.G. Grace** (who it is said achieved as many hundreds on the Heath as he did at the Oval). After the War a more 'Royal Flavour' dominated with the **Prince of Wales** becoming an Honorary Member in **1921** and **Captain** in **1935**.

Time to leap forward to the present and introduce the Club's Secretary, Wing Commander W.E. McCrea is the very helpful gentleman in question. He may be contacted at **The Walton Heath Golf Club, Tadworth, Surrey (073781) 2380**. Subject to prior arrangement with the Secretary, golfers are welcome to visit Walton Heath between Mondays and Fridays. Proof of both Club Membership and an official handicap is required. The Green fees for 1986 were set at **£20** for a full day's golf, with a reduced rate of **£15** available if teeing off after 11.30am. For juniors the fees were half the above rates. Golfing with societies are equally welcome, pre-booking being essential. The hire of golf clubs and the arranging of a caddy can be done through the Club's professional, **Ken MacPherson**. He may be reached by telephone on **(073781) 2152**.

Located south of London, motoring to the Club is assisted greatly by the **M25**. Those aproaching on this motorway are best leaving at exit **8** turning south on to the **A217**. The A217 should be followed for approximately 2 miles after which a left turn should be taken on to the **B2032**. The Golf Club is situated a mile or so along this road. Travelling from further afield, the M25 is linked to the **M23** to the South, the **M20** to the East and to the North and West by the **M3, M4** and **M1**.

There are of course two great courses at Walton Heath, the **Old** and the **New** (the latter first appearing as nine holes in 1907 but later extended to the full 18). Lying adjacent to one another each possesses the same classical heathland characteristics – heather, bracken, gorse, pines and silver birch. The Old Course is slightly longer than the New, their respective distances being **6813** yards (par **73**) and **6659** yards (par **72**). From the ladies tees the lengths of the two are **5957** yards (par **74**) and **6005** yards (par **74**). The finishing three holes on the Old are thought by many to be the finest on any course. The **16th** is a very mild dog-leg to a raised green which slopes from left to right, with the right side of the green heavily guarded by bunkers. The par three **17th** has sand traps practically encircling the green creating a near island effect and the **18th** requires a testing second to carry an enormous cross bunker.

Over the years Walton Heath has played host to many important tournaments. The major amateur championships have included the English Amateur and both the Ladies English Amateur and the Ladies British Open Amateur Championships. Among the professional events, twenty-two of the **PGA Match Play Championships** were staged at Walton Heath and in recent years **The Ryder Cup** of **1981** and two **European Open Championships**. In 1987 the **European Open** returns to Walton Heath.

Walton Heath has a fine Clubhouse with an exellent restaurant and lounge. A jacket and tie should be worn in all public rooms after 11am. Lunches are served between 12pm and 2.30pm and both breakfast and dinners (minimum number 24) can be arranged with prior notice.

Understandably wherever you turn in the Clubhouse you are likely to see a reminder of the long association with James Braid. One small note sent to him from the Prince of Wales conveys a message all golfers can appreciate. It relates how the Prince came to the 18th requiring a four for a 79. After explaining how his second finished just through the green he then tells how, "with the chance of breaking 80, I couldn't stand the nerve-strain and fluffed the chip and took two putts..." How the mighty fall!

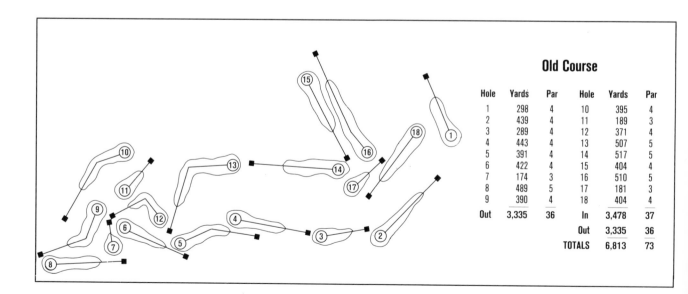

Old Course

Hole	Yards	Par	Hole	Yards	Par
1	298	4	10	395	4
2	439	4	11	189	3
3	289	4	12	371	4
4	443	4	13	507	5
5	391	4	14	517	5
6	422	4	15	404	4
7	174	3	16	510	5
8	489	5	17	181	3
9	390	4	18	404	4
Out	3,335	36	In	3,478	37
			Out	3,335	36
			TOTALS	6,813	73

BERKSHIRE
Berkshire (18+18)
Ascot (0990) 21496

Calcot Park G.C. (18)
Calcot Nr. Reading (0734) 27124

Datchet G.C. 9)
Datchet (0753) 43887

Downshire G.C. (18)
Wokingham (0344) 424066

East Berkshire G.C. (18)
Crowthorne (0344) 772041

Eton College G.C. (9)
Windsor (0753) 55299

Goring & Streatley G.C. (18)
Streatley-on-Thames
(0491) 873229

Hawthorn Hill G.C. (18)
Maidenhead (0628) 75588

Hurst G.C. (9)
Hurst, Reading (0734) 345143

Lavender Park G.C.
Centre G.C. (9)
Ascot (0344) 884074

Maidenhead G.C. (18)
Maidenhead (0628) 24693

Newbury & Crookham G.C. (18)
Newbury (0635) 40035

Reading G.C. (18)
Emmer Green, Reading
(0734) 472909

Royal Ascot G.C. (18)
Ascot (0990) 25175

Sonning G.C. (18)
Sonning-on-Thames (0734) 69332

Sunningdale G.C. (18+18)
Sunningdale, Ascot (0990) 21681

Sunningdale Ladies G.C. (18)
Sunningdale, Ascot (0990) 20507

Swinley Forest G.C. (18)
South Ascot (0990) 20197

Temple G.C. (18)
Hurley, Maidenhead
(062 882) 4795

West Berkshire G.C. (18)
Chaddleworth, Newbury
(04882) 574

Wexham Park G.C. (18)
Wexham, Slough (028 16) 24615

Winter Hill G.C. (18)
Cookham, Maidenhead
(062 85) 27613

BUCKINGHAMSHIRE
Abbey Hill G.C. (18)
Stony Stratford, Milton Keynes
(0908) 542513

Beaconsfield G.C. (18)
Beaconsfield (04946) 6546

Buckingham G.C. (18)
Buckingham (0280) 815566

Burnham Beeches G.C. (18)
Burnham (06286) 61448

Chesham & Key Hill G.C. (9)
Chesham (0494) 784541

Chilton Forest G.C. (9)
Halton, Aylesbury (0296) 630899

Denham G.C. (18)
Denham (0895) 832801

Ellesborough G.C. (18)
Butlers Cross, Aylesbury
(0296) 622114

Farnham Park G.C. (18)
Stoke Poges (06286) 61521

Flackwell Heath G.C. (18)
Flackwell Heath, High Wycombe
(062 85) 20929

Gerrards Cross G.C. (18)
Gerrards Cross (0753) 883263

Harewood Downs G.C. (18)
Chalfont St. Giles (02404) 2184

Iver G.C. (9)
Iver (0753) 655615

Little Chalfont G.C. (9)
Little Chalfont, Amersham
(02404) 4877

Stoke Poges G.C. (18)
Stoke Poges (0973) 26385

Weston Turville G.C. (18)
Weston Turville, Aylesbury
(0296) 24084

Weston Turville, Aylesbury
(0296) 24084
Whiteleaf G.C. (9)

Whiteleaf, Aylesbury
(08444) 3094
Windmill Hill G.C. (18)
Bletchley, Milton Keynes
(0908) 648149

Woburn G. & C.C. (18+18)
Bow Brickhill, Milton Keynes
(0908) 70756

OXFORDSHIRE
Badgemore Park G.C. (18)
Henley-on-Thames
(0491) 572206

Burford G.C. (18)
Burford (099382) 2583

Cheswell Edge G.C. (18)
Chacombe, Banbury
(0295) 711591

Chesterton G.C. (18)
Bicester (0869) 241204

Chipping Norton G.C. (9)
Frilford Heath G.C. (18+18)
Frilford Heath, Abingdon
(0865) 90428

Henley G.C. (18)
Harpsden, Henley-on-Thames
(0491) 575742

Huntercombe G.C. (18)
Nuffield, Henley-on-Thames
(0491) 641207

North Oxford G.C. (18)
Oxford (0865) 54924

R.A.F. Benson G.C. (9)
Benson (0491) 35536

Southfield G.C. (18)
Oxford (0865) 242158

Tadmarton Heath G.C. (18)
Wiggington, Banbury
(0608) 737278

SURREY
Addington G.C. (18)
Croydon (01) 777 6057

Addington Court G.C.
(18+18+9)
Addington, Croydon
(01) 657 0281

Addington Palace G.C. (18)
Addington, Croydon
(01) 654 3061

Banstead Downes G.C. (18)
Belmont Sutton (01) 642 2284

Barrow Hills G.C.
Longcross, Chertsey
(0932) 48117

Betchworth Park G.C. (18)
Dorking (0306) 882052

Bramley G.C. (18)
Bramley, Guildford
(0483) 892696

Burhill G.C. (18)
Walton-on-Thames
(0932) 227345

Camberley Heath G.C. (18)
Camberley (0276) 232571

Chessington G.C. (9)
Chessington (01) 391 0948

Chipstead G.C. (18)
Coulsdon (07375) 55781

Coombe Hill G.C. (18)
Kingston Hill (01) 942 2284

Coombe Wood G.C. (18)
Kingston Hill (01) 942 0388

Coulsdon Comb G.C. (18)
Coulsdon (01) 660 0468

Croham Hurst G.C. (18)
Croydon (01) 657 2075

Crondall G.C. (9)
Crondall, Farnham
(0252) 850880

Cuddington G.C. (18)
Benstead (01) 393 0952

Dorking G.C. (9)
Dorking (0306) 886917

Drifer G.C. (18)
East Horsley (04865) 4641

Dulwich & Sydenham
Hill G.C. (18)
London SE21 (01) 693 3961

Effingham G.C. (18)
Effingham (0372) 52203

Epsom G.C. (18)
Epsom (037 27) 21666

Farnham G.C. (18)
Farnham (025 18) 2109

Farnham Park G.C. (9)
Farnham (0252) 715216

Foxhills G.C. (18+18)
Ottershaw (039 287) 2050

Gatton Manor Hotel & G.C. (18)
Ockley, Dorking (030 679) 555

Goal Farm G.C. (9)
Pirbright (048 62) 3183

Guildford G.C. (18)
Merrow, Guildford (0483) 63941

Hankley Common G.C. (18)
Tilford, Farnham (025 125) 2493

Hindhead G.C. (18)
Hindhead (042 873) 4614

Hoebridge G. Centre (18+18)
Old Woking (04862) 22611

Home Park G.C. (18)
Hampton Wick (01) 977 2423

Kingswood G.C. (18)
Kingswood, Tadworth
(0737) 832188

Lakeham G.C. (18)
Chertsey (09328) 64211

Leatherhead G.C. (18)
Leatherhead (037 284) 3966

Limpsfield Chart G.C. (9)
Limpsfield (0959) 61380

London Scottish G.C. (18)
Wimbledon (01) 789 7517

Malden G.C. (18)
New Malden (01) 942 0654

Mitcham G.C. (18)
Mitcham Junction (01) 648 4197

Moore Place G.C. (9)
Esher (0932) 220575

New Zealand G.C. (18)
Weybridge (093 23) 42891

North Downs G.C. (18+18)
Woldingham (088 385) 2057

Oaks Sports Centre (18+9)
Carshalton (01) 643 8363

Purley Downs G.C. (18)
Purley (01) 657 8347

Puttenham G.C. (18)
Puttenham, Guildford
(0483) 810498

Redhill & Reigate G.C. (18)
Redhill (073 72) 44626

Reigate Heath G.C. (9)
Reigate (073 72) 45530

Richmond G.C. (18)
Sudbrook Park, Richmond
(01) 040 435

Richmond Park G.C. (18)
Richmond Park (01) 876 3205

R.A.C. C.C. (18)
Epsom (03722) 76311

Royal Mid-Surrey G.C. (18+18)
Richmond (01) 940 1894

Royal Wimbledon G.C. (18)
Wimbledon (01) 946 2125

St. George's Hill G.C. (18+9)
Weybridge (0932) 47758

Sandown Park G.C. (9)
Esher (0372) 63340

Sandown Park C.C. (9+9)
Esher (0372) 63340

Selsdon Park Hotel G.C. (18)
Sanderstead (01) 657 3127

Shillinglee Park G.C.(9)
Chiddingfield, Godalming
(0428) 53237

Shirley Park G.C. (18)
Croydon (01) 654 1143

Silvermere G.C. (18)
Cobham (0932) 6007

Surbiton G.C. (18)
Chessington (01) 398 6619

Tandridge G.C. (18)
Oxted (088 33) 2273

Thames Ditton & Esher G.C. (9)
Esher (01) 751 3076

Tyrrells Wood G.C. (18)
Leatherhead (0372) 376025

Walton Heath G.C. (18+18)
Tadworth (073 781) 2380

Wentworth W.G.C. (18+18+9)
Virginia Water (099 04) 2201

West Byfleet G.C. (18)
West Byleet (093 23) 43433

West Hill G.C. (18)
Brookwood, Woking
(048 62) 4365

West Surrey G.C. (18)
Eaton Green, Godalming
(048 68) 21275

Wimbledon Common G.C. (18)
Wimbledon Common
(01) 946 7571

Wimbledon Park G.C. (18)
London SW19 (01) 946 1250

Windlemere G.C.(9)
Woking (09905) 8727

Woking G.C. (18)
Woking (048 62) 60053

Woodcote Park G.C. (18)
Coulsdon (01) 668 2788

Worplesdon G.C. (18)
Woking (048 62) 2277

BERKSHIRE

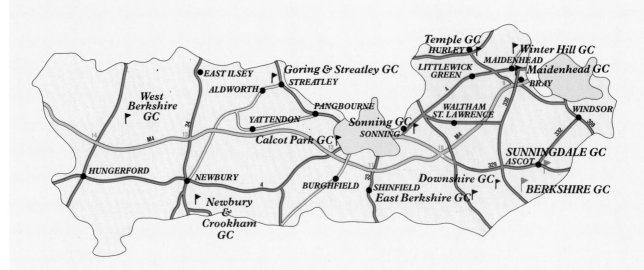

JULIAN BARROW   *"The Berkshire"*   BURLINGTON GALLERY

OAKLEY COURT

Oakley Court is a luxury hotel situated on the banks of the River Thames, 3 miles from Windsor town centre. The Victorian Mansion was built in 1859 in the Gothic style and 5 million pounds was spent on renovation and restoration to its original splendour. There are 90 bedrooms including 18 suites and four poster rooms. All rooms are beautifully furnished and include all the items to make your stay relaxed. The Mansion's interior has been faithfully restored capturing all the atmosphere of its Victorian hey-day. The Library, Bar and Dining Room are rich with oak panelling and open log fires, creating a warm welcome for guests.

The landscaped gardens offer mature oaks and firs and the lawns slope down to greet the River Thames. There is a 9 hole pitch and putt course and a croquet lawn within the grounds.

The Oak Leaf Room Restaurant offers a table d'hote lunch and dinner and a 6 course Menu Gourmand as well as an A La Carte Menu. During the summer light lunches are served on the terrace overlooking the river.

There are numerous attractions in the Windsor area. **Windsor Castle, The Windsor Great Park and Safari Park, Eton, Oxford and Blenheim Palace at Woodstock**. The hotel is conveniently situated for London and Heathrow Airport and for seasonal events such as Royal Ascot, Henley Regatta, Wimbledon Tennis and the Suntory Golf Championship at Wentworth.

OAKLEY COURT
Windsor Road,
Nr. Windsor,
Berkshire.
Tel: (0628) 74141

Berkshire – or should one say 'Royal Berkshire' is often described as being cigar-shaped. Now whilst this may not say much for the present day talents of cigar-makers it does serve as a fairly rough description in as much as the County is indeed peculiarly long and thin. When it comes to surveying the County's twenty or so golf courses it is tempting to adopt another cigar analogy in that one end could be said to glow rather more brightly than the other.

To the east of the County there is the famous heathland belt and it is here that the twin pearls of **Sunningdale** and **The Berkshire** are to be found. Both Clubs possess two 18 hole courses which can stand comparison with anything that golf can offer. (Each is in fact featured a few pages ahead). **Swinley Forest** is the other outstanding heathland course in the area but as we were courteously informed, visitors are only permitted to play as guests of Members and so the stranger must look further afield for his game.

Still in heather and pine country is the very attractive **East Berkshire** course at Crowthorne. It is possible for visitors to get a game here during the week although a handicap certificate or letter of introduction from a Golf Club is required. A quick telephone call is also advised before finalising any plans. In close proximity is the popular **Downshire** public course. A game can be arranged for any day of the week but booking in advance is essential. Golfing Societies can also be organised but these are restricted to weekdays. **Green fees** in 1986 were very reasonably priced at **£4.50** for a summer round, with **£3** payable during the winter months. Reduced rates are offered to juniors and over 65's.

Towards the north east of the County, heading towards Buckinghamshire, there are a number of attractive courses. **Maidenhead Golf Club** is conveniently placed for a visit. It is a parkland course close to the town centre with particularly good greens. Before arranging a game there it is again probably best to give the Club a call first. To the north and west of Maidenhead the River Thames forms the boundary with Buckinghamshire. A particularly scenic area where the Berkshire Downs meet the Chiltern Hills. The delightful Burnham Beeches Club is of course 'over the border' (and well worth visiting if in the area) but still within the 'Royal County' are three excellent tests of golf – **Temple, Winter Hill** and **Sonning**.

Temple's fine course can be viewed from the main **A23** Maidenhead to Henley Road. It has an interesting layout with many fine trees and lush fairways. Designed by Willie Park early this century, it was for a number of years the home of Henry Cotton. The course is always maintained in first class condition and the Club welcomes visitors who are able to provide proof of handicap on weekdays. Thursday mornings should be avoided as Lady Members have reserved tees. A game at Temple could be obtained for **£14** in 1986, with reductions for juniors and those teeing off after 2.30 pm. **Winter Hill** is on fairly high ground – apparently its name derives from the particularly chilling winds that sweep across in winter (I have no explanation for nearby 'Crazies Hill'!) From the course there are some spectacular views over the Thames – definitely worth a visit. So for that matter is **Sonning**, situated further towards Reading, south of the **A4**. Visitors here are welcome between Mondays and Fridays but must accompany Members at weekends.

On the western edge of Reading, **Calcot Park** poses many interesting challenges, it can also boast Guinness Book of Records fame in that one sterling fellow sprinted round the course in a motorised cart in just over 24 minutes – a more leisurely round is recommended!

Further to the west of Reading, along the **A329** are the boating villages of Goring and Streatley. **Goring and Streatley Golf Club** is located just beyond Streatley off the **A417**. It is a pretty tough course, perhaps more accurately described as moorland than parkland and where visitors should be able to get a game during the week.

Newbury is of course better known for its racing than its golf, but the **Newbury and Crookham Golf Club** close to Greenham Common (not too close!) is one of the oldest Clubs in Berkshire and is again strongly recommended. Visitors providing proof of handicap are welcome to play on weekdays, the **green fees** being **£10** in 1986. The course is quite hilly and well-wooded, though not overly long.

Before leaving Berkshire it is worth noting one of the county's most recent additions, **West Berkshire**, situated just south of the village of Chaddleworth. It is a splendid downland course, but not exactly one for the weak-kneed – it stretches to around the 7000 yard mark with one par five measuring well over 600 yards!

BERKSHIRE

Windsor and Eton, Ascot and Newbury, The Berkshire and Sunningdale. The Castle, the Safari Park, the School, the racecourses and last but quite definitely not least the golf-courses. Berkshire is made up of some gorgeous winding lanes but the A4 and the M4 dissect it. It has some beautiful countryside within it. The style of Royal Ascot is forgotten when one hears the bar chat in a busy local hidden in the Downs or the Chilterns. But perhaps the greatest appeal for Berkshire's visting golfer is the fact that London is so close and yet if needs be far away. Not only the capital of England but the capitals of the world are within easy access when one considers the proximity of Heathrow. On an international note let the boys of Berkshire make one more recommendation. Tourists who visit Britain may think that this island is made up of one small town – London. The real Britain, however, lies hidden in counties such as Berkshire – there is no better place to meet the British than in the country – why not on the golfcourse – if you can get a game!

If you do decide not to stay on Park Lane then here are some ideas that may go a long way to satisfying the luxury that you would expect. (We are also going to recommend some things you certainly will not find – a country pub for example.) Many people have heard of the Roux Brothers – to some extent their flagship is **Le Gavroche 01 730 2820** in London's busy West 1, their fame spreads further and certainly to Bray **(0628) 20691** the **Waterside Inn** which is quite probably the country's finest restaurant which sits happily in Berkshire's countryside. Fearing that you may have to camp out – due to the fact that London is some way off perhaps we ought to clear this one up as well. Near Windsor, off the A308 towards Maidenhead there is a hotel deserving of the high accounts it receives. It is, of course, **Oakley Court (0628) 74141** its outstandingly comfortable rooms are complemented by splendid grounds and a delightful dining room, **The Oak Leaf**.

Elsewhere in Windsor other good accommodation can be found. **Wrens Old House 07538 61354** named after the famous Sir Christopher is excellent; there are an array of things to see in Windsor and naturally the Castle stands out, numerous pubs and some quaint restaurants are also worth visiting. In nearby Eton antiques are the order of the day, a good wine bar in the High Street is ideal for lunch. In Ascot a number of good establishments can be found, **The Thatched Tavern (0990) 20874** is an excellent place to have lunch or dinner while **The Berystede Hotel (0990) 23311** is a satisfactory place to stay. A good local pub is the **Slug and Lettuce** in Winkfield Row – a good atmosphere and a charming restaurant.

Another fine hotel for the primary Berkshire courses is located in Bagshot **The Pennyhill Park (0276) 71774**. Returning North of the M4 and the Thames Valley one arrives in Maidenhead, here **Fredrick's Hotel (0628) 35934** has an outstanding reputation for comfort, its restaurant is also highly acclaimed. Nearby, and Boulters Lock an idyllic part of the Thames. **The Boulters Lock Inn (0628) 21291**, standing on Boulters Island, is a gorgeous place to stay. If you are dining in Maidenhead then **Shoppenhangers Manor (0628) 23444** is a splendid French restaurant located in a charming English Manor. West of Maidenhead, Littlewick Green and the **Warrener Restaurant (062882) 2803** charming setting for a fine restaurant. North of here, in Hurley, one finds yet another gem, one of those that should make our visitors from across the water squeal with delight this time **Ye Olde Bell (062882) 5881** a Norman Inn – they'll love it, so do many British, so book for the restaurant. Meandering further down the Thames other excellent hotels include **The White Hart at Sonning (0734) 692277** which has a charming Elizabethan courtyard while also in Sonning **The French Horn (0734) 692204** is a super restaurant. In Streatley, further up the Thames, **The Swan Hotel (0491) 873737** is another fine hotel with a splendid riverside setting. The restaurant here is extremely well thought of. In case our American friends are beginning to doubt the existence of pubs – then a visit to **The Bell** at Aldworth should do the trick. Another nearby local is the **Crown and Horns** at East Ilsley – tremendous. Another town with a good hotel and restaurant combination is Pangbourne on this occasion it is the **Copper Inn (07357) 2244**.

Heading south again **The Royal Oak (0635) 201325** at Yattendon awaits, this is a true delight – a simple bar for a quiet drink, a restaurant which serves excellent food, bar snacks if required and on top of this first class accommodation – a real help for people who are difficult to please. Near Newbury, in Kintbury, **The Elcot Park Hotel (0488) 58100** is splendid while further down the A4 one finds another antique seekers paradise, Hungerford. **The Bear (0488) 82512** offers excellent accommodation and a terrific restaurant while The John O'Gaunt is a favourite pub – ideal for bar snacks and a civilised chat and pint. They say all roads lead to London and so perhaps we should return.

But before we do we should note the excellent restaurant hidden in Burghfield – **Knights Farm (0734) 52366** – tremendous wines complement a fine menu. In Shinfield – another pointer to Berkshire's pull is the resiting of **Chez Nico (0734) 883763**. A name popular to London now settled in the civilised Berkshire countryside – marvellous move.

As the tarmac at Heathrow greets our guests from the world over one other establishment of note should be pointed out – it is Cliveden. The house of the Astor family for so many years it is now a delightful country house hotel. Imagine how the friendly Japanese would click merrily and our American friends would say "oh my, just wait 'til Babs sees this". We certainly have it in Britain and a fair share of it nestles in the glorious county of Berkshire. On seeing Windsor Castle one dear Yank was heard to say "by the airport – what a crazy place to build a castle". While we welcome tourists to our shores we must educate them – no visit is complete with a mere inspection of London.

The Waterside Inn
Ferry Road, Bray,
Maidenhead, Berkshire, SL6 2AT
Tel: (0628) 20691/22941
One of the country's leading eating establishments, ideally set on a beautiful stretch of the Thames where swans and willows abound. The restaurant, which seats 70, is open from Tuesday dinner to Sunday lunch in winter, and Tuesday to Sunday dinner in summer – booking essential.

Berystede Hotel
Bagshot Road,
Ascot,
Berkshire SL5 9JH
Tel: (0990) 23311
Nine acres of pine-encircled landscaped gardens surround this country house hotel, convenient for Berkshire's famous golf courses, Windsor Castle and Runnymede, Thameside site of the Magna Carta and the John F Kennedy memorials.

Who keeps looking forward to keep you looking ahead?

THE BERKSHIRE

The residents of Ascot must number among the luckiest folk in England – at least those who are into horseracing and golf, for right on their doorsteps lies the cream of each. They have of course three golfing pearls close at hand, Sunningdale, Wentworth and The Berkshire, the youngest of the illustrious trio.

The two **eighteen hole** courses of **The Berkshire, the 'Red' and the 'Blue'** were designed in 1928 by **Herbert Folwer** – a master among golf architects whose other great works include Walton Heath and Saunton. They occupy some **400 acres** of Crown Land over which Queen Anne's carriage used to pass en route to the hunting in Swinley Forest.

Today, both courses give the appearance of having been hewn out of a dense forest, rather in the way that the Duke and Duchess courses were created at Woburn. This, in fact, was not the case, much clearing of the forest occurred during the First World War when the land was used for military purposes and much of the present thick woodland is of comparatively recent origin.

The Berkshire has been described as being primarily a Member's Club, this largely through the conspicuous absence of any big-time professional golf tournament. Perhaps the Club does not wish to have its tranquillity stirred or its rough trampled over by hordes of excited spectators, but this does not imply that the club closes its doors to the outside world, or makes visitors unwelcome. Indeed, the Berkshire is a busy and popular Club with a great number of Societies choosing to return year after year. For individual visitors, no less than Societies, booking with the **Secretary** is essential and **Major P.D. Clarke** is the gentleman in question. He can be contacted at the **Berkshire Golf Club, Swinley Road, Ascot, Berkshire. Tel. (0990) 21496**. It should be emphasised that unless otherwise invited **visitors** are only permitted to play the course during **weekdays. Green Fees** for **1986** were set at **£13** for a single round with **£20.50** payable for a **day ticket**, thus securing a game on both courses – something to be strongly recommended. If

clubs need to be hired the **professional, Mr. K.A. MacDonald** can assist – some prewarning is advisable. Mr. MacDonald can be contacted on **(0990) 22351**.

The Berkshire can be reached easily from London. It lies just off the A332 road between Ascot and Bagshot. The **A332** can be joined from Windsor to the north and Guildford to the south, whilst motoring from Reading and the **West** the M4 should be left at **junction 10** and the **A329** followed to Ascot.

The two courses are of fairly similar length – the **Red** slightly longer measuring **6,356 yards** to the **Blue's 6,258 yards**, although the latter's **par** is one fewer at **71**. The Red course is perhaps the better known of the two, to some extent due to its comprising an unusual **six par threes, six par fours and six par fives**. In any event, most people probably agree that there is little to chose between the two, both in terms of beauty and in degree of difficultly.

The Berkshire is famed for its glorious tree-lined fairways. There is a splendid mix of mature pines, chestnuts and silver birch and both courses are kept in the most superb condition. Much of the rough consists of heather and the Berkshire provides a stern test for the wayward hitter.

The Club may have avoided professional tournaments, but it does play host to a number of important amateur events. The Berkshire Trophy is one of the annual highlights on the amateur calendar and before turning professional **Messrs. Faldo and Lyle** were both winners. It is an open event limited to 3 handicap players. A major ladies amateur open, the **Astor Salver** is also played at the Berkshire, it has a handicap limit of 7.

As for its 19th the Club possesses one of the country's largest and grandest Clubhouses, furthermore, it has a reputation for providing the most stupendous roast lunches. A gentleman by the name of **Sam** is responsible for these veritable feasts. Well now, 18 holes on the Blue, one of 'Sam's specials' and then 18 on the Red – what better way to spend a day?

Red Course

Hole	Yards	Par	Hole	Yards	Par
1	518	5	10	187	3
2	146	3	11	338	4
3	481	5	12	328	4
4	394	4	13	484	5
5	182	3	14	436	4
6	353	4	15	477	5
7	201	3	16	221	3
8	427	4	17	529	5
9	477	5	18	177	3
Out	3,179	36	In	3,177	36
			Out	3,179	36
			TOTALS	6,356	72

Blue Course

Hole	Yards	Par	Hole	Yards	Par
1	217	3	10	200	3
2	340	4	11	478	5
3	477	5	12	360	4
4	152	3	13	159	3
5	316	4	14	365	4
6	481	5	15	406	4
7	363	4	16	452	4
8	405	4	17	375	4
9	310	4	18	402	4
Out	3,061	36	In	3,197	35
			Out	3,061	36
			TOTALS	6,258	71

On seeing the spectacularly beautiful 18th hole at **Killarney** during one of his visits to Ireland the late **Henry Longhurst** declared, "What a lovely place to die". Now whilst one rarely wishes to dwell on the subject of 'meeting our maker', golfers have been known to indulge in a considerable amount of speculation as to the type of course they might find on the arrival of such an occasion. There is a story of one heated discussion which involved, quite per chance, an Englishman, a Scotsman and an American. The latter argued with great conviction that a large number of the holes would, "as sure as hell", resemble **Augusta**, the Scotsman vehemently insisted that even the most minute deviation from the **Old Course** at **St Andrews** would constitute an act of heresy and as for the Englishman, he naturally had no doubts whatsoever that he could stroll through the Pearly Gates and meet a second **Sunningdale**.

Well perhaps the heavenly blend is a mixture of all three but in any event the gentleman in charge of the terrestrial Sunningdale is the Secretary, **Keith Almond**. Mr Almond may be contacted on **(0990) 21681**. **Keith Maxwell** is the Club's resident professional and he can be reached on **(0990) 20128**.

As with neighbouring Wentworth and The Berkshire there are two eighteen hole courses, the **'Old'**, designed in 1900 by **Willie Park** and the **'New'** which was constructed by **Harry Colt** in 1922. Both are splendid, and many would say the leading, examples of the famous Berkshire – Surrey heathland type course. The holes wind their way through glorious forests of conifer and pine with heather and gorse bordering each fairway. All around there are splashes of silver sand.

With its great reputation and close proximity to the capital, Sunningdale is not suprisingly very popular. Unless accompanied by a Member **visitors** are restricted to weekdays and must make prior arrangement with the Secretary. A letter of introduction is also required. All written communications should be addressed to Mr Almond at **The Sunningdale Golf Club, Ridgemount Road, Sunningdale, Berkshire**. In **1986** the **green fee** was set at **£29**. This entitled the visitor to a full days golf, enabling a round over both courses. Sets of clubs can be hired from the professional shop should the need arise. Persons keen to organise a **Society** meeting are also advised to approach Mr Almond via the above address. A handicap limit of 20 normally applies and the Society days are Tuesdays, Wednesdays and Thursdays.

Sunningdale is situated just off the **A30**, about 28 miles West of **London**. Motoring from the South and West the **M3**, (leaving at junction 3) and the **M4** (junction 10) may be of assistance,

while from the North both the **A332** and the **A330** pass through nearby **Ascot**. The Club's precise location is some 300 yards from Sunningdale Railway Station.

When golfers talk of Sunningdale, invariably it is the Old Course they have in mind, this despite the fact that a large number of people consider the New to be its equal. The former has acquired such pre-eminence largely as a result of the many major professional and amateur tournaments that have been staged there. However the Old Course is perhaps best known for a single round of golf played by the legendary **Bobby Jones**. In qualifying for the 1926 Open Championship, which he in fact went on to win, the great man put together what has often been described as the finest 18 holes of golf ever seen. Jones' record 66 comprised twelve fours and six threes – 33 for the front nine and 33 for the back nine. More remarkably Jones played only 33 shots from tee to green and took 33 putts – as Bernard Darwin put it, "incredible and indecent".

In more recent years Sunningdale has repeatedly been selected to host the prestigious **Panasonic European Open**. During the 1970's the finest lady golfers assembled for the Colgate sponsored **European WPGA Championship** and in 1987 the **Walker Cup** is to be played at Sunningdale.

At **6341** yards (**par 70**) the Old Course is more than three hundred yards shorter than the New (**6676 yards, par 70**). The respective distances from the Ladies tees are **5825** yards and **5840** yards (both being par **74**). It seems somehow wrong to single out individual holes, each course possessing its own wealth of variety and charm. The views from the 5th and 10th tees on the Old Course are, however, particularly outstanding and the 18th on the same provides a spectacular closing hole as it gently dog-legs towards the green and the giant spreading oak tree, so much the symbol of Sunningdale.

Behind the famous oak tree is the Sunningdale Clubhouse. With the exception of Mondays, lunches are served daily and there are three bars. Breakfasts can be made available as can dinners to golfing parties of forty or more provided prior arrangement is made. A jacket and tie should be worn in the Dining Room.

Sunningdale's glorious setting has been described as both 'heavenly' and 'hauntingly beautiful', certainly the golfer privileged to stroll up the final fairway on a summer's evening as the sun begins its leisurely dip can be forgiven if he amends the words of Henry Longhurst and declares "What a lovely place to be alive!"

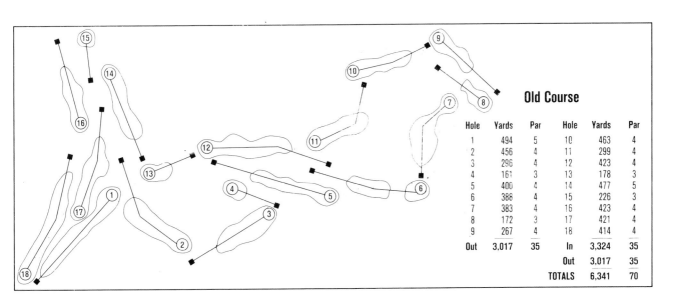

Old Course

Hole	Yards	Par	Hole	Yards	Par
1	494	5	10	463	4
2	456	4	11	299	4
3	296	4	12	423	4
4	161	3	13	178	3
5	400	4	14	477	5
6	388	4	15	226	3
7	383	4	16	423	4
8	172	3	17	421	4
9	267	4	18	414	4
Out	**3,017**	**35**	**In**	**3,324**	**35**
			Out	**3,017**	**35**
			TOTALS	**6,341**	**70**

GREATER LONDON

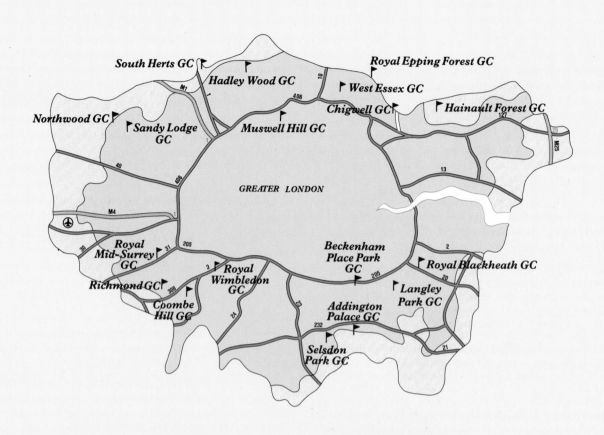

South Herts GC

Royal Epping Forest GC

Hadley Wood GC

West Essex GC

Chigwell GC

Northwood GC

Sandy Lodge GC

Muswell Hill GC

Hainault Forest GC

GREATER LONDON

Royal Mid-Surrey GC

Beckenham Place Park GC

Royal Blackheath GC

Richmond GC

Royal Wimbledon GC

Langley Park GC

Coombe Hill GC

Addington Palace GC

Selsdon Park GC

AFTER L.F. ABBOTT "Blackheath" *BURLINGTON GALLERY*

MR JOHN BALL JNR
WATERCOLOUR
BY "LIB"
SIGNED
SIGHT 12¼ × 7¼ INCHES

THIS FINE AND RARE
WATERCOLOUR IS THE
ORIGINAL FROM WHICH
THE FAMOUS VANITY FAIR
PRINT WAS MADE.

TINKLER'S GILL, 12TH HOLE, QUEENS COURSE, GLENEAGLES
OIL PAINTING
BY ARTHUR WEAVER
SIGNED AND DATED 1979
INSCRIBED WITH TITLE ON LABEL ON REVERSE
CANVAS 23¼ × 35¼ INCHES

Records suggest that golf was first played in England in **1608**, the venue was **Blackheath Common** in London but the participants were Scottish not English. **James I** (James VI of Scotland) and his courtiers are generally credited with bringing the game south of the border. The exact date that the English caught "the bug" is unclear, certainly in the 18th Century it was still pretty much an alien pastime – in his first English dictionary compiled in 1755 **Dr Samuel Johnson** described golf as, "a game played with a ball and a club or bat".

During its formative years golf in London was largely confined to the public commons such as those at Blackheath, Clapham, Chingford and Tooting Bec, the golfers having to share their rather crudely laid-out courses with "nursemaids, dogs, horses and stubborn old ladies and gentlemen".

Not surprisingly when the first Golf Clubs started to form the tendency was to retreat from the public stage. The **Royal Blackheath Golf Club**, fittingly enough the first English Club to be founded (it dates from 1787) eventually moved from the common and now plays on a private course at Eltham. Golf is no longer played (or at least shouldn't be!) on the commons at Clapham and Tooting Bec. However, golf does survive on those at Wimbledon and Chingford, the latter being the home of **Royal Epping Forest** and where golfers are still required to wear red coats in order that they are distinguishable from other users of the common.

Well, enough of the history, if by chance you are visiting the capital and have the opportunity to exercise your swing where should you head for? To be frank, although Greater London has a large number of courses very few are of a particularly high standard and the wisest move may be to look beyond the City Limits: to the south and west lies the magnificent heathland belt of Surrey and Berkshire with the delights of **Walton Heath**, and **Sunningdale**, while to the north, reachable by tube plus a short walk, is **Moor Park**.

The majority of "London Clubs" are for obvious reasons set in deepest suburbia and with many it is often far from clear as to whether they fall within Greater London or not. In anyone's book **Muswell Hill** is in London, which for present purposes is just as well because it's an excellent course. Measuring close to 6,500 yards, and quite undulating, it represents a fairly stiff test. Visitors can normally arrange a game here between Mondays and Fridays, green fees in 1986 being **£10** per round, **£13** per day. The course is located at Wood Green close to the North Circular. Elsewhere in North London, **Hadley Wood**, near Barnet with its elegant Clubhouse is also well worth a weekday visit. A beautiful course with tree-lined fairways, fees in 1986 were **£12** per round, **£18** per day. Close by are **South Herts** and **Sandy Lodge** (at Totteridge and Northwood respectively). Both are excellent courses, the former can boast having had both **Henry Cotton** and **Dai Rees** as its professional while the latter could be said to be "Sandy by name and sandy by nature", it being about as close to an inland links as you can get.

Over towards Essex, **Royal Epping Forest** has been mentioned (prior telephoning is recommended), also within Epping Forest itself, **West Essex** is a fine parkland course (where again visitors are welcomed on weekdays) and there are two excellent public courses at **Hainault Forest** (a particularly friendly club, where visitors can play seven days a week).

Those looking for a game in south west London might consider looking in the Wimbledon area where there are several clubs. **Royal Wimbledon** is just about the best course in London but golfers should definitely telephone the Club before making any fixed plans. It may be easier to arrange a game (at least during the week) at the **London Scottish Club**, located two miles from Wimbledon railway station. A little further out at Richmond, games can be enjoyed at **Royal Mid Surrey** (on weekdays) and at **Richmond Golf Club** with its superb Georgian Clubhouse.

For anyone in the Croydon area there is Addington Palace, a very fine parkland course located midway between the **A232** and **A212** roads and there is also the Selsdon Park Hotel course – of championship standard it comprises some 6,400 yards of superb rolling parkland. A game should be possible here on any day of the week though a preliminary telephone call is recommended. The fees for a round in 1986 were **£10** during the week, with **£15** payable on Saturdays, **£17** on Sundays.

The best course towards the south east of London is probably **Langley Park**, a heavily wooded course which often plays quite long. It is located close to Wickham West station along the **A214**, and the Club receives visitors on weekdays, **£15** being the cost of a day's golf in 1986. Finally a public course worth noting in these parts is **Beckenham Park Palace**, set in the grounds of a former stately home. The course is situated to the north of Bromley off the **A222**. The green fees in 1986 were a modest **£3.80** midweek, **£5** at weekends.

Addington Palace G.C.	01 654 3061
Beckenham Palace Park G.C.	01 650 0704
Hadley Wood G.C.	01 449 4328
Hainault Forest G.C.	01 500 2097
Langley Park G.C.	01 650 2090
London Scottish G.C.	01 788 0135
Muswell Hill G.C.	01 888 1764
Richmond G.C.	01 940 1463
Royal Blackheath G.C.	01 850 1795
Royal Epping Forest G.C.	01 529 6407
Royal Mid Surrey G.C.	01 940 4847
Royal Wimbledon G.C.	01 946 2125
Sandy Lodge G.C.	(09274) 25429
Selsdon Park Hotel G.C.	01 657 8811
South Herts G.C.	01 445 0117
West Essex G.C.	01 529 7558

Are the streets of London paved with gold? No they are made predominantly out of concrete slabs. Another vital question. Are the parks of London filled with golfcourses – well this is slightly tricky – yes if you go to Richmond but no if you are stuck with the likes of Hyde Park. Do businessmen and women (sorry girls nearly forgot you again) play golf – yes of course they do. Problem – London has lots of business going on and limited resources to golfcourses. Answer go to office six o'clock – business breakfast – game of golf – lunch meeting, late afternoon golf. Evening placate partner by a trip to the theatre and the business of the evening. Result – a tremendous day shattered tomorrow. The better answer is not to work in the city, however, for the thousands who do this piece is dedicated to you.

Driving into the centre of London perhaps towards the fountains of Trafalgar Square or the Serpentine one finds a delightful array of hotels. Many of which are located within a good iron's shot from each other. The following is a small appraisal of some of London's very best hotels. In Park Lane, **The Inn on the Park 01 499 0888** is quite excellent and its restaurant, **The Four Seasons** is outstanding. Luxury of the highest order is also offered in the **The Dorchester 01 629 8888** as it proudly overlooks Hyde Park (alas no golf). **The Grill Room** and **The Terrace** are both restaurants of distinction, the Walton Heath and Wentworth of the culinary circuit. The international class the **Ritz 01 493 8181** one can quite simply sniff the style. Nearby, **Browns 01 493 6020** is contrastingly English and justifiably proud of it. These two hotels are both convenient for the delightful shops of Bond Street and Piccadilly. If you have a minute – pop into the Burlington Gallery in Burlington Gardens – very helpful if you want to know a little about golf.

The Savoy group is one of the most bullishly proud and prestigious companies to be found. This totally laudable atitude is reflected in their hotels. **The Savoy 01 836 4343**, note the delightful settings of its restaurants **The Grill Room** and **The River Restaurant. The Connaught** quite magnificent personal service – but particularly low profile – one of the best restaurants in town where the class is almost tangible. Another member of the group on this occasion **Claridges 01 629 8860** particularly traditional but extremely popular among the lunching fraternity of the city's businessmen. Of course there are many other superb hotels and I certainly deserve no medals for picking out these rather obvious bastions of luxury. However, two establishments which command a little more thought are **Whites Hotel 01 262 2711** – a pleasant situation overlooking Kensington Gardens and **The Alexander 01 581 1591**.

No prizes are awarded for hotel orginality still less perhaps for the restaurant selection. **The Roux Brothers Le Gavroche 01 408 0881** is simply outstanding in every way. **Rue St. Jacques** also offers outrageously good French cooking. A little different but no less brilliant food is offered in the Hungarian **Gay Hussar 01 437 0973**. Another restaurant which will give as much pleasure as a hole in one is **La Tante Claire 01 352 6045** – marvellous. Lovers of seafood might try **Le Suquet 01 581 1785** or **La Croisette 01 373 3694** both excellent.

Not quite so expensive as London's top restaurants but outstanding all the same are **Gavvers 01 730 5983** excellent French cooking, **Polyannas 01 228 0316** for people south of the river – delightful atmosphere, **Simpson's 01 836 9112** particularly English in character and cuisine, **Hilaire 01 584 8993** particularly popular and finally **Leith's 01 229 4481** perhaps the priciest of the quintet but excellent just the same.

It is difficult to even hint at what London has to offer but it certainly boasts as rich a life as any – from Dickens to Gandhi, people have been impressed by its sheer motion. Naturally, its theatres are noted throughout the world, its galleries and musuems are a delight and if people are journeying to London with their non-golfing loved ones you need never have any conscience about leaving them while you delight in your own fascination – the game of golf.

From Cockney barrow boy to bowler hatted gent from standard salesmen to the Lord Mayor himself the city is a delight of variations. Compare Brixton with shall we say Green Park. The life of England is often best judged by its pubs. This generalisation is perhaps less true in the city. However, these four are all tremendous in their own way. One Scotsman decided to buy property near the area with no regard for his investment – the pub was all – its name **The Ship** off Wandsworth Bridge. **The Grenadier** in Wilton Row, SW1 (pleasant restaurant for lunch 01 235 3074) has a tremendous Mews location. **The Flask** in Highgate Village is popular amongst North London drinkers while **The Prospect of Whitby** is a splendid place if you like sheer exuberance. (But may the Lord forgive me there are many more.)

For people not wishing to stay in Central London these hotels may be of some help. In Hadley Wood, **The West Lodge Park 01 440 8311** is a superb 19th century mansion – good golfcourses can be found in this area of South Hertfordshire. A galleried hall is one of the features of **The Grims Dyke 01 954 4227** the former home of W.S. Gilbert this hotel is located in Harrow Weald. Another hotel handy for a motorway, this time the M11, is the **Woodford Moat House** in Woodford Green, The Epping Forest is nearby and glorious. Moving eastwards and the **Bromley Court Hotel, Bromley 01 464 5011** good restaurants here – notably the Chinese. Good Chinese restaurants can also be found in Limehouse notably **Chinatown 01 987 2330** and **Good Friends 01 987 5541**. South of the river and Wimbledon with its lovely village, here the aptly named **Village Restaurant 01 947 6477** is excellent. In Enfield, **The Royal Chance** is a totally satisfactory establishment in which to curl up one's tootsies.

There are many pubs to recommend and again there just isn't time – to point out the delights of London completely – well this is a golf book after all. Well O.K. just a small tip – try Richmond – all manner of pubs and eating placs. A good hotel **The Richmond Gate 01 940 0061** and last but not least **Lichfield's 01 940 5236** a really excellent if expensive restaurant – an ideal stop off point if leaving or entering London before of after golf or business. Well that covers about one per cent of what London offers. If you can enjoy any of the above you will have had a good time – I hope your golf is of equal quality and or character.

Grims Dyke Hotel and Restaurant
Old Redding, Harrow Weald, Nr Stanmore,
Middlesex HA3 6SH
Tel: 01 954 4227
A delightful Country House Hotel and Restaurant with ten acres of private gardens set among two hundred acres of woodlands. The Grims Dyke Golf Club is adjacent to the Hotel's grounds and Moor Park is a short drive away. The Music Room Restaurant offers fine English cuisine for lunch and dinner.

Richmond Gate Hotel
Richmond Hill,
Richmond,
Surrey,
Tel: 01 940 0061
The Hotel stands at the top of Richmond Hill and lies conveniently close to Richmond Golf Club. Continually setting high standards, it is the obvious choice when involved with golf, tennis at nearby Wimbledon or rugby at Twickenham.

HERTFORDSHIRE, BEDFORDSHIRE AND ESSEX

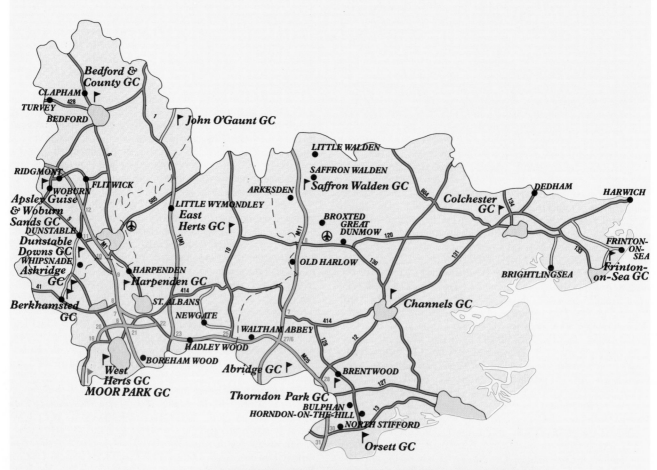

A.B. FROST "Temper" *ROSENSTIELS*

Maison Talbooth

t in the heart of the Dedham Vale,
ison Talbooth Hotel and its nearby
erside restaurant, Le Talbooth, is but
ty miles away from the bustle of
ndon. John Constable, one of England's
st famous painters, recreated the East
glian skies, lush riverside pastures and
minating village churches—the very view
u enjoy from the hotel.

ison Talbooth, in its 15th year, is a
arming Victorian house quietly tucked
o a hill overlooking a landscape that
vnspeople and travellers dream about.
droom suites, named after well loved
itish poets, are individually decorated
h bold colour schemes to complement
luxurious drapes and period furniture.
acious bathrooms, some with circular
iken baths, are a special pleasure with
ge fluffy towels, bath oils and many
er homelike comforts provided. The
awing room, complete with log fire,
ctorian picture collection and grand
ino, leads through french doors into the
o acres of garden and croquet lawn.

eakfast and other light snacks are
ovided at the hotel but house guests
ist be sure to sample the delights of Le
lbooth, ¾ of a mile down the road. This
cient timber framed house, once a 'Toll-
oth' for horse-drawn river traffic, is
iowned to be one of the finest
taurants in the country. Specialising in
ditional English and French cooking,
ly fresh local ingredients can produce
ch dish with its distinctive forthright
vour, complemented by a fine wine
lar.

well as countless places of local interest,
wmarket, Cambridge, the ports of
lixstowe and Harwich are all under an
ur's drive away. One could choose to go
ing, play squash, hire one of the hotel's
ling yachts or just take a rowing boat
wn the River Stour to see Constable's
ned Flatford Mill, Willy Lott's Cottage
d the golden fields that inspired his
iywain painting.

Maison Talbooth,
Dedham, Colchester,
Essex CO7 6HN
Telephone: (0206) 322367
Telex: 987083 LETAL BG

Unfortunately, for all too many, the first and often lasting impression of a place can be determined by the great blue ribbons that now stretch the length and breadth of the country – Britain's ever expanding motorway network. The **M1** (not to mention the **M25**) cuts through the heart of **Hertfordshire** and slices off the left ear of **Bedfordshire**. Between London and Luton it is a fearsome animal at the best of times and passing beyond these two counties can often draw a sigh of relief. The greater expanse of **Essex** fairs a little better escaping with a few nasty scratches, but in all three counties the deeper realms are not as often explored as they might, except needless to say by those who live there.

The golfing breed is a little more fortunate than most, in every county in Britain he, and she, can visit golf courses that are tucked away in the most secluded and tranquil of settings and Hertfordshire, Bedfordshire and Essex are certainly not exceptions to the rule.

A glance at the map tells you that **Ashridge** in Hertfordshire isn't all that great a distance from London and the **M1** but it occupies a particularly peaceful spot and the approach road which runs alongside **Berkhamsted Golf Club** passes through some glorious countryside – the kind that once covered much of this part of the world. Both are delightful heathland/parkland courses. **Berkhamsted** is best known for its conspicuous absence of bunkers, though like Royal Ashdown Forest in Sussex has more than enough hazards to test any golfer, while **Ashridge** is perhaps most famed for its long association with **Henry Cotton**, for many years the Club's professional. Both courses are decidedly worth a visit though at each prior arrangement with the Secretary is essential.

Remaining in Hertfordshire, **Harpenden** on the other side of the **M1** has two fine courses, **Harpenden** and **Harpenden Common**, the former at Hammonds End being perhaps the pick of the two and **East Herts** near Buntingford, is also worth noting, if travelling along the **A10**. The greater concentration of courses, however, perhaps not surprisingly, is in the area just north of London. **Moor Park**, featured a few pages on, is the most widely known though nearby **Porters Park** (in the quiet of Radlett) and **West Herts** (on the edge of Watford, yet similarly peaceful) also strongly merit attention. Both Porters Park and West Herts receive visitors during the week, fees being around

the **£10** mark.

Bedfordshire is much less endowed in terms of numbers of courses but in **John O'Gaunt** and **Dunstable Downs** it has two of the finest courses in Southern England. The former, located at Sandy was the venue for the 1986 English County Finals. A parkland course, the Club welcomes visitors throughout the week; a day's golf in 1986 being priced at **£12** midweek, **£15** at weekends. John O'Gaunt has an additional 18 holes, the **Carthagena** course, which though some 500 yards shorter at just under 6,000 yards is kept in similarly superb condition.

The **Dunstable Downs** course is laid out on high ground, offering remarkably extensive views – both Surrey to the south and Warwickshire to the north west can be sighted. A downland type course, visitors are received Mondays to Fridays at a cost in 1986 of **£8** per round, **£11** per day.

Elsewhere in the county **Aspley Guise and Woburn Sands** (the more famous Woburn Golf and Country Club lies over the border in Buckinghamshire), is another that provides far reaching views and at which a game can be enjoyed seven days of the week (**£10** per day in 1986). Also of note is the **Bedford and County Golf Club**, just north of the county town off the **A6**.

Although one of England's largest counties, Essex possesses a relatively small number of top class courses, however, within that category fall **Thorndon Park** (2 miles South of Brentford) and **Orsett** (2 miles East of Grays and in the wonderfully named area of Mucking and Fobbing). Each can be reached via the **A128**. Thorndon Park, as its name suggests, is a parkland type course whereas Orsett is much more of the heathland variety with sandy subsoil. Both welcome visitors during the week, a game again being priced at around **£10**.

In a similar vein to Hertfordshire a number of the county's better courses are being gradually swallowed up by Greater London, the fine parkland course at **Abridge** being one of them, it now lying the "wrong side" of the M25 (as does the famous course of **Epping Forest**).

Further afield both **Colchester** (the oldest town in England) and **Saffron Walden** have courses set in very pretty surroundings and for lovers of seaside golf there is a pleasant (though windy!) course at **Frinton-on-Sea**. Finally, for those visiting Chelmsford the **Channels Golf Club** with its superb Elizabethan Clubhouse can be recommended.

Abridge G.C.	(04028) 388
Aspley Guise and Woburn Sands G.C.	(0905) 583596
Ashridge G.C.	(044284) 2244
Bedford and County G.C.	(0234) 52617
Berkhamsted G.C.	(04427) 3730
Channels G.C.	(0245) 440005
Colchester G.C.	(0206) 852946
Dunstable Downs G.C.	(0582) 604472
East Herts G.C.	(0920) 821923
Frinton-On-Sea G.C.	(02556) 4216
Harpenden G.C.	(05827) 2580
John O'Gaunt G.C.	(0767) 260360
Moor Park G.C.	(0923) 773146
Orsett G.C.	(0375) 891 352
Porters Park G.C.	(09276) 4127
Saffron Walden G.C.	(0799) 22689
Thorndon Park G.C.	(0277) 810345
West Herts G.C.	(0923) 24264

You can't beat a good woman – unless of course this is what you both happen to enjoy. One place to find out is Great Dunmow for it is here that the great Flitch Trials take place. In case you did not know this is a basic check on the suitability of man and woman and of course vice versa. On the golf course the lady golfer is as tirelessly dedicated as her male member and the thought of Flitch Trials taking place for various players would amuse. One point to note here is that both editors of this book are male – in case the females feel hard done by– I hereby dedicate this piece to the lady golfer.

There are, however, problems for our female friends, the dedication has a price – they pay, now where shall we start? Essex, to be precise Dedham, to be exact **Le Talbooth (0206) 323150**. This is a monument to good food, an ideal place to celebrate. Close by, also in Dedham, **The Maison Talbooth (0206) 322367** offers stylish accommodation. This delightful village with its views of the Stour also offers the **Dedham Vale Hotel (0206) 322273** and its first class restaurant. The area is also convenient for many Suffolk courses. Resisting the temptation to venture further up the Stour and discover the delights of Constable's country we arrive at the coast and Harwich – heading directly for **The Pier (0255) 503363**, here as you may suspect the seafood is the speciality of the house. Golfers taking in the course at Frinton may wish to sample a local hotel, **The Frinton Lodge (02556) 4391**. Two others also merit a mention, they are **Greenings (02556) 77379** and the **Rock Hotel (02556) 5173**. The area remains quiet and its sandy beaches and its golfcourse appeal.

Further up the coast in Brightlingsea a restaurant and a pub should be pointed out. **Jacobes (020630) 2113** is the restaurant while the **Cherry Tree** is the pub. A busy schedule may include a round of golf and an evening at the **South Lodge (0245) 64564**.

Brentford·is our next port of call – where the **Brentwood Moat House (0277) 225252** is a really good example of this chain of hotels. Another one is locally situated in North Stifford, **The Stifford Moat House (0375) 71451**. In Bulphan, **Ye Olde Plough House (0375) 891592** is convenient for the motorway network, but don't worry it's not a bad setting at all. An excellent pub to recommend in the area is situated at Horndon-on-the-Hill, **The Bell**.

Remaining in Essex and following the M25 to Waltham Abbey, the burial place of King Harold also the home of a charming restaurant **Blunks (0992) 712352**.

Crossing the border we find the delights of Hertfordshire. The county is particularly convenient for London, but some good establishments do lie outside the central London ring. In Newgate Street, **The Ponsbourne Hotel (0707) 875221** has good leisure facilities. In Hadley Wood, **The West Lodge Park** is an elegant mansion house **01-440 8311**, while Boreham Wood carries a restaurant to note **Signor Batti's**.

The best bet if you are playing the delightful Moor Park is the **Grims Dyke Hotel 01-954 4227** in Harrow Weald. St. Albans and Harpenden where the traffic races through is littered with good pubs off the busy high streets. St. Albans offers its superb Cathedral and the delightful **St. Michaels Manor (0727) 64444** which lies in its shadow, while Harpenden's **Moat House (05827) 64111** is expensive, but extremely well thought of. From West Herts to East Herts and Little Wymondley, **The Redcoats Farmhouse (0488) 729500** – cosy.

Close to the border with Bedfordshire lies Berkhamsted, **The Swan Inn** is a great little place to stay so convenient for the delights of Ashridge and South Bedfordshire. In Whipsnade, the Zoo is excellent while the downs nearby are a good place to get rid of some energy. Hit a golf ball from the pinnacle of the Dunstable Downs and see how far it slices (second thoughts, better not you may wing a hang glider). In Dunstable's town centre **The Old Palace Lodge (0582) 62201** is well worth a visit.

In Woburn – some excellent hotels can be found as well as the delightful house and game reserve. The **Paris House (052525) 692** is an outstandingly good restaurant while the **The Bedford Arms** is a welcoming Georgian coaching inn **The Black Horse** and **The Bell** are good pubs to visit while if your appetite is large after a days golf visit **Crispins (052525) 516** – good value. Outside the town itself in Flitwick, the 17th Century **Flitwick Manor (0525) 712242** is very good and the restaurant is also excellent. En route to the county town the **Rose & Crown** in Ridgmont serves a good pint and bar snacks. In Bedford itself we once again call upon the services of the Moat House group – **The Bedford Moat House (0234) 55131** a functional modern type of hotel. For grander accommodation **The Woodlands Manor** in Clapham offers a delightful hotel with a good restaurant. Finally, in the corner of Bedfordshire Turvey offers two restaurants, **The Three Fyshes (023064) 264** and **Laws (023064) 213** some accommodation is available in the latter.

Returning to Essex and Arkesden where the thatched pub the **Axe & Compasses** provides good food and a cheerful hostelry. Saffron Walden and the **Saffron Hotel (0799) 22676** nothing grand, but extremely comfortable with a well thought of restaurant. Another Walden this time a Little one, north of Saffron, in the quiet village lies **The Crown** – good bar food. Another Essex hotel handy for a motorway, this time the M11 is **The Green Man (0279) 442521** in Old Harlow– opposite the village green the hotel totally belies the proximity of the nearby autoroute. Not that close to the golfcourses, but well worth a trip is **The Whitehall Hotel (0279) 850603** in Broxted where the restaurant is excellent.

So where to now ladies? Return to the Talbooth? Not a bit of it, no there's only one place Great Dunmow and the Flitch Trials. **The Saracens Head Hotel (0371) 3901** acts as our base and as my lady friend takes me to **The Starr (0371) 4321** for dinner. We have played a round together, had dinner, drank well but as we look into each others eyes – that eternal question looms ever large – are we compatible? As the Flitch Trial approaches I contemplate: excellent – I ponder, a beautiful woman for certain, intelligent – yes, generous – undoubtedly, I certainly love her. So what's the problem? Well it happened on the golf course – She beat me and that at the end of the day just won't do.

Woburn Abbey
Woburn
Probably Britain's most famous stately home, Woburn Abbey is the ancestral home of the Dukes of Bedford and has been open to the public since 1955. Some 300 acres of the surrounding woodland have been given over to a superb Wild Animal Kingdom. Situated just off the M1 in Bedfordshire.

Pontlands Park Country Hotel and Restaurant
West Hannisfield Road, Great Baddow,
Tel: (0245) 76444
A luxurious hotel with an adjoining health and leisure complex on the outskirts of Chelmsford. Everything from dance studios to jacuzzi can be found in this sport orientated establishment close to many of Essex's golf courses.

NICK FALDO

Born Welwyn Garden City, Herts, 18.7.57.
Ht: 6'3" Wt: 13st 7lb. Turned Pro: 1976. Nick's
three victories in the PGA Championship, between
1978 and 1981, established him as one of Britain's
top golfers. He went on to win five European
events in 1983 to top the Order of Merit then
captured the Sea Pines Heritage Classic on the US
PGA Tour. His results suffered in 1985, whilst he
was moving through a swing change, but he
produced an encouraging performance on this
course with two closing 69s taking him into a
share of third place. Nick finished a
creditable third in this year's New
Orleans Open and is surely
on the brink of a major
comeback.

WHITEHALL

[..]e lovely old manor house sits on a [hill]side overlooking the delightful rolling [cou]ntryside of N.W. Essex. Set in a [bea]utiful walled garden with swimming [poo]l and tennis court, it exudes an [atm]osphere of bygone days.

[Bro]xted itself appears in the Domesday [Boo]k, and the earliest reference to the [ma]nor is in 1151 when Alured de [Man]daville gave it to the hospital of St. [Joh]n of Jerusalem. This gift was confirmed [by] King John (died 1216) and Hubert, [Arc]hbishop of Canterbury and was [par]ticularly significant in that it enabled the [Ord]er to establish a preceptory in Essex. In [154]1 King Henry VIII granted the property [to] one George Harper, a shadowy figure [wh]o had obviously been of some service to [the] King. Two years later in 1543 Harper [con]veyed it to Sir Thomas Audley, then [Lor]d Chancellor of England. The estate [eve]ntually passed to the Countess of [Wa]rwick, a noted society hostess of the [Ed]wardian era, who often entertained King [Ed]ward VII.

[Fro]m the moment one enters the cheerful [rec]eption hall, with its roaring log fire and [co]mfortable sofas, one feels immediately [the] friendly atmosphere and the light and [airy] decor that is the hallmark of Whitehall.

[Eac]h of the bedrooms has a character all [its] own and each has been decorated in [bea]utiful pastel shades, and along with [the]ir en-suite bathrooms offer the utmost in [co]mfort.

[Th]e vaulted timbered dining room offers a [spe]ctacular setting for superb cuisine, [wh]ich is rapidly gaining the reputation for [bei]ng amongst the finest in the country.

[Wh]itehall is but an hour's drive from [Lo]ndon and is located close to the [his]torical town of Cambridge, where [visi]tors can spend many days enthralled by [the] architecture and history. The [sur]rounding area is filled with many [del]ightful Tudor towns and villages like [Bro]xted, Saffron Walden and [Fin]chingfield. Real gems of the English [cou]ntryside.

[Th]e most enduring memory a visitor to the [old] manor house must take away is the [frie]ndly atmosphere allied to the exquisite [de]cor and cuisine.

Whitehall,
Church End, Broxted,
Essex CM6 2BZ
Telephone: (0279) 850603

I don't suppose many would dispute that the Clubhouse at St Andrews is the best known 'nineteenth in the world'. However, for the title of 'most magnificent' or 'most grand' it is doubtful whether **Moor Park** can have any serious rivals. The **Moor Park Mansion** dates from the **13th century**, in its illustrious history it has been the home of earls, dukes, cardinals, archbishops and even a queen – **Catherine of Aragon** living there in the 16th century. During the last war the Mansion was requisitioned becoming first the headquarters of the Territorial Army, then of the A.T.S. and later of the American 2nd Airborne Corps and it was from within Moor Park that preparations were made for the invasion of **Arnhem** in **1944**.

Golf first came to Moor Park in **1923**, **Lord Ebury** founding the Golf Club just four years after the estate had been purchased by Lord Leverhulme. **Harry Colt** was called in to design three golf courses, two of which remain with the Club, **The High** and **The West** courses, the third now being a public course (**Rickmansworth**) although it is in fact maintained by the Moor Park Club.

The Club's current **Secretary** is **Mr J E Linaker**, he may be contacted by telephone on (**0923**) **773146**. The professional, **Mr E R Whitehead** can also be contacted via this number. **Visitors** are welcome at Moor Park between Mondays and Fridays although it is essential to telephone the Club in advance in order to book a starting time and visitors should note that proof of handicap is required. The only general restrictions during the week are on Tuesday and Thursday mornings, when both courses are reserved for members between 8.30am and 10am. Moor Park is extremely popular with Golfing Societies and up to 65 players can normally be catered for. Those organising must make prior arrangements with the Club, written applications to be addressed to **The Secretary, Moor Park Golf Club, Rickmansworth, Herts WD3 1QN**. In 1986 the **green fee** for a full day's golf was priced at **£18**, this entitling a round over both courses.

Situated on the north western outskirts of Greater London, Moor Park is very accessible from all parts of the country. Its precise location is off the **A404** Northwood to Rickmansworth road. Those travelling from afar should find the new **M25** of great assistance with junctions **17** or **18** probably being the best points of exit. As for **rail stations**, Moor Park is the nearest at a distance of approximately three-quarters of a mile from the Golf Club (a good uphill walk mind you!). Rickmansworth is also less than two miles away.

The major Championships staged at Moor Park are all played over the **High Course**. Measuring **6713** yards (par **72**, s.s.s. **72**) it is some 900 yards longer than the **West Courses**, though this at 5815 yards (par **69**, s.s.s. **68**) is certainly no 'pushover'. Both courses, it need hardly be said, are kept in superb condition.

The **High Course** begins with a fairly straightforward, slightly uphill first but the second which dog-legs to the right, is one of the toughest 'fours' of the round. Towards the middle of the front nine a sliced tee shot will send a ball into some particularly pleasant properties whose gardens border the fairways (attempting to retrieve your ball is not to be recommended!). The back nine contains three excellent short holes including the 12th (surrounded by willows and surely one of the best par threes in the country) and rather unusually the 18th.

Within two years of the Club being founded Moor Park played host to the **1925 PGA Matchplay Championship**, won by Archie Compston. Several professional tournaments have been played since, most recently **The Evening Standard Four Star Pro-Celebrity Tournament in 1986**. One of the major amateur events, the **Carris Trophy**, is staged annually at Moor Park; limited to junior golfers, winners in the past have included **Sandy Lyle** and **Ken Brown**.

Perhaps the best known game of golf at Moor Park took place back in 1928. A 72 hole challenge match was played between the American **Walter Hagen**, the leading professional of the day, and the aforementioned **Archie Compston**, one of Britain's finest players. With only one hole completed of the final round the match was all over, Hagen having been defeated **18** up with **17** to play – the greatest margin of victory ever recorded. Ironically a few weeks later Hagen won his third Open Championship at **Sandwich**, finishing three strokes ahead of Compston.

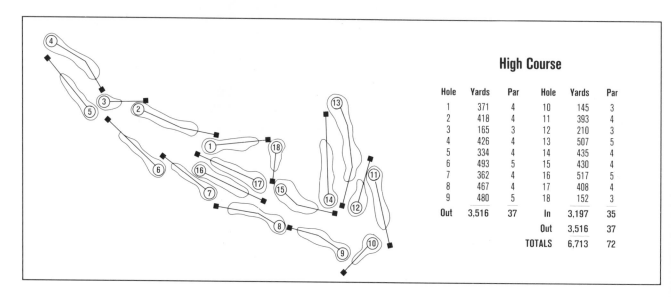

High Course

Hole	Yards	Par	Hole	Yards	Par
1	371	4	10	145	3
2	418	4	11	393	4
3	165	3	12	210	3
4	426	4	13	507	5
5	334	4	14	435	4
6	493	5	15	430	4
7	362	4	16	517	5
8	467	4	17	408	4
9	480	5	18	152	3
Out	3,516	37	In	3,197	35
			Out	3,516	37
			TOTALS	6,713	72

BEDFORDSHIRE

Aspley Guise &
Woburn Sands G.C. (18)
Milton Keynes (0905) 583596

Bedford & Country G.C. (18)
Bedford (0234) 52617

Bedfordshire G.C. (18)
Bedford (0234) 53241

Caintoe Wood G & C.C. (18)
Shefferd, Beds (0525) 60800

Dunstable Downs G.C. (18)
Dunstable (0582) 604472

John O'Gaunt G.C. (18)
Biggleswade (0767) 260360

Leighton Buzzard G.C. (18)
Leighton Buzzard (0525) 373811

Mill Brook G.C. (18)
Ampthill (0525) 404683

Mawsbury G.C. (18)
Bedford (0234) 771042

South Beds G.C. (18+9)
Luton (0582) 591500

Stockwood Park G.C. (18)
Luton (0582) 413704

Tilsworth G.C. (9)
Leighton Buzzard
(0325) 210721/2

Wyboston Lakes G.C. (18)
Huntingdon (0480) 219200

ESSEX

Abridge G & C.C. (18)
Stapleford (04028) 388

Ballards Gore G.C. (18)
Rochford (03706) 8717

Basildon G.C. (18)
Basildon (0268) 3297

Belfours Pk G.C. (18)
Southend-on-Sea (0702) 525345

Bellus Park Municipal G.C. (18)
South Ockendon (0708) 854260

Bentley G & C.C. (18)
Brentwood (0277) 73179

Birch Grove G.C. (9)
Colchester (020634) 276

Bayce Hill G.C. (18)
South Benfleet (03745) 3625

Braintree G.C. (18)
Braintree (0376) 24117

Brentwood G.C. (18)
Brentwood (0277) 218714

Bunsay Downs G.C. (9)
Maldon (024541) 2648

Burnham-on-Crouch (9)
Maldon (0621) 782242

Canons Brook G.C. (18)
Harlow (0279) 21482

Channels G.C. (18)
Chelmsford (0245) 440005

Chelmsford G.C. (18)
Chelmsford (0245) 50555

Chigwell G.C. (18)
Chigwell (01) 500 2059

Chingford G.C. (18)
Chingford (01) 529 2107 or
(01) 529 5708

Clacton G.C. (18)
Clacton-on-Sea (0255) 424331

Colchester G.C. (18)
Colchester (0206) 852946

Forrester Park G.C. (9)
Maldon (0621) 891406

Frinton G.C. (18+9)
Frinton (02556) 4216

Hainault Forest G.C. (18+18)
Hainault (01) 500 2097

Hartswood G.C. Play Over
Brentwood Public Course
Brentwood (0277) 217128

Harwich & Dovercourt G.C. (9)
Harwich (02555) 3616

Havering G.C. (18)
Romford (0708) 22942

Ilford G.C. (18)
Ilford (01) 5545174

Maldon G.C. (9)
Maldon (0621) 53212

Manifold G.C. (18)
Maldon (0621) 860410

Maylands G.C. (18)
Ingrebourne, Romford
(04023) 42055

Orsett G.C. (18)
Grays Thurrock (0375) 891352

Pipps Hill G.C. (9)
Basildon (0268) 27278

Risebridge G.C. (18)
Romford (0277) 27376

Rochford Hundred G.C. (18)
Rochford, Southend
(0702) 544302

Romford G.C. (18)
Romford (0277) 40007

Royal Epping Forest G.C. (18)
Chingford (01) 529 6407

Saffron Walden G.C. (18)
Saffron Walden (0799) 22689

Skips, G.C. (18)
Ingrebourne (04023) 48234

Theydon Bois G.C. (18)
Theydon Bois (0378) 2279

Thorndon Pk G.C. (18)
Brentwood (0277) 811666

Thorpe Hill G.C. (18)
Southend-on-Sea (0702) 582050

Three Rivers G & C.C. (18+9)
Maldon, Chelmsford
(0621) 828631

Upminster G.C. (18)
Upminster (86) 20249

Wanstead G.C. (18)
London (01) 989 0604

Warley Park G.C.(18+9)
Brentwood (0277) 224891

Warren G.C. (18)
Danbury, Maldon (024541) 3198

Westcliff G.C. (18+9)
Purleigh (0621) 828631

West Essex G.C. (18+18)
Chingford 01 529 4637

Woodford G.C. (9)
Woodford (01) 504 0553

HERTFORDSHIRE

Aldenham G & C.C. (18)
Radlett, Watford (09276) 7775

Arkley G.C. (9)
Barnett (01) 449 0394

Ashridge G.C. (18)
Little Gaddesden, Berkhamsted
(044284) 2244

Batchwood Hall G.C. (18)
St. Albans (0727) 3349

Berkhamsted G.C. (18)
Berkahmsted (04427) 3730

Bishops Stortford G.C. (18)
Bishops Stortford (0279) 54027

Boxmoor G.C. (9)
Hemel Hempstead (0442) 42434

Brickendon Grange G.C. (18)
Bayford Hertford (099286) 228

Brookman's Park G.C. (18)
Potters Bar, Hatfield
(0707) 52487

Bushey G.C. (9)
Bushey (01) 960 2283

Bushey Hall G.C. (18)
Bushey, Watford (0923) 25802

Chadwell Springs G.C. (9)

Cheshunt Park G.C. (18)
Waltham Cross, Cheshunt
(0992) 24009

Chorleywood G.C. (9)
Chorleywood (09278) 2009

Dyrham Park C.C.
Barnet (01) 440 3361

East Herts G.C. (18)
Ware (0920) 821923

Hadley Wood G.C. (18)
Barnet (01) 449 4486

Harpenden G.C. (18)
Harpenden (05827) 2580

Harpenden Common G.C. (18)
Harpenden (05827) 2856

Hartsbourne C.C. (18+9)
Bushey Heath (01) 950 1113

Elstree G.C. (18)
Elstree (01) 953 6115

Knebworth G.C. (18)
Stevenage (0438) 812752

Letchworth G.C. (18)
Letchworth (0462) 683203

Little Hay G.C. (18)
Hemel Hempstead (0442) 833798

Mid Herts G.C. (18)
Wheathamsted (058283) 3118

Moor Park G.C. (18+18)
Rickmansworth (0923) 773146

Old Ford Manor G.C. (18)
Barnet (01) 449 2266

Panshanger G.C. (18)
Welwyn Garden City
(0707) 33350

Potters Bar G.C. (18)
Radlett (09276) 4127

Potters Bar G.C. (18)
Potters Bar (0707) 52020

Redbourn G.C.(18+9)
Redbourn (058205) 3493

Rickmansworth G.C. (18)
Rickmansworth (0923) 773163

Sandy Lodge G.C. (18)
Northwood (65) 25429

South Herts G.C. (18+9)
London (01) 445 0117

Stevenage G.C. (18)
Stevenage (0438) 88424

Verulam G.C. (18)
St. Albans (0727) 53327

Welwyn Garden City G.C. (18)
Welwyn Garden City
(0707) 322722

West Herts G.C. (18)
Watford (0923) 24264

Whipsnade Park G.C. (18)
Little Goddesden (044284) 2330

GREATER LONDON

Ashford Manor G.C. (18)
Ashford (07842) 52049

Beckenham Place
Park G.C. (18)
Beckenham (01) 650 2292

Bush Hill Park G.C. (18)
Winchmore Hill N21

Crews Hill G.C. (18)
Enfield (01) 363 0787

Dulwich &
Sydenham G.C. (18)
Dulwich (01) 693 1221

Ealing G.C. (18)
Greenford (01) 997 2595

Enfield G.C. (18)
Enfield (01) 363 3970

Finchley G.C. (18)
Finchley NW7 (01) 346 2436

Fulwell G.C. (18)
Hampton Hill (01) 977 3188

Greenford G.C. (9)
Greenford (01) 578 3949

Grim's Dyke G.C. (18)
Pinner (01) 428 4093

Hampstead G.C. (9)
London N2 (01) 455 0203

Harefield Place G.C. (18)
Uxbridge (0895) 31169

Haste Hill G.C. (18)
Northwood (01) 866 3175

Hendon G.C. (18)
Hendon NW7
(01) 346 8990

Highgate G.C. (18)
Highgate NW6
(01) 340 1906

Hillington G.C. (9)
Uxbridge (0895) 39810

Holiday G.C. (9)
West Drayton
(0895) 444232

Hounslow Heath G.C. (18)
Hounslow (01) 570 5271

Langley Park G.C. (18)
Beckenham (01) 650 2090

Leaside G.C. (9)
Edmonton N9 (01) 803 3611

London Scottish G.C.
Wimbledon (01) 788 0135

Mill Hill G.C. (18)
Mill Hill NW7
(01) 959 2282

Muswell Hill G.C. (18)
Wood Green N22
(01) 888 1764

North Middlesex G.C. (18)
London N20 (01) 445 1732

Northwood G.C. (18)
Northwood (65) 21384

Perrivale Park G.C. (9)
Greenford (01) 803 3611

Picketts Lock G.C.
London N9 (01) 803 4756

Pinner Hill G.C. (18)
Pinner Hill (01) 866 0963

Richmond G.C. (18)
Richmond (01) 940 24351

Richmond Park G.C. (18)
Richmond Park
(01) 876 3205

Roehampton G.C. (18)
London SW15 (01) 876 3858

Royal Blackheath G.C. (18)
Eltham (01) 850 17975

Ruislip G.C. (18)
Ruislip (Ruislip) 38835

South Herts G.C. (18)
Totteridge (01) 445 0117

Stanmore G.C. (18)
Stanmore (01) 954 4661

Sudbury G.C. (18)
Wembley (01) 902 3713

Trentpark G.C. (18)
Southgate NW14
(01) 366 7432

Twickenham G.C. (9)
Twickenham (01) 979 3450

West Middlesex G.C. (18)
Southall (01) 574 3450

White Webbs G.C. (18)
Enfield (01) 363 4454

Wyke Green G.C. (18)
Isleworth (01) 847 0685

BUCKINGHAMSHIRE AND OXFORDSHIRE

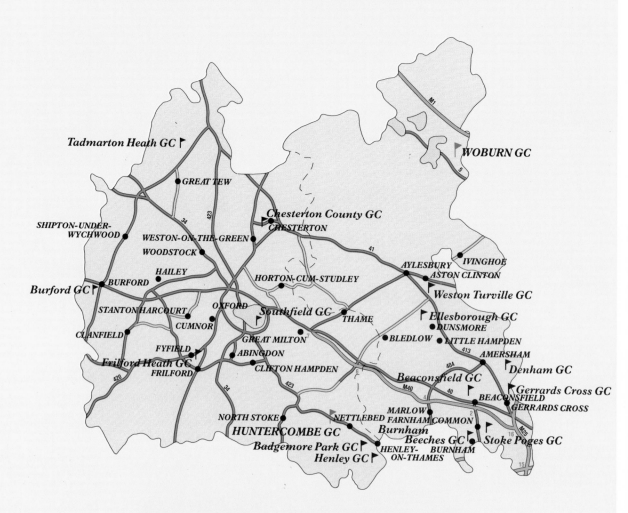

Tadmarton Heath GC
WOBURN GC
GREAT TEW
Chesterton County GC
CHESTERTON
SHIPTON-UNDER-WYCHWOOD
WESTON-ON-THE-GREEN
WOODSTOCK
AYLESBURY
IVINGHOE
ASTON CLINTON
HAILEY
HORTON-CUM-STUDLEY
Weston Turville GC
Burford GC
BURFORD
STANTON HARCOURT
OXFORD
Southfield GG
THAME
Ellesborough GC
DUNSMORE
CUMNOR
GREAT MILTON
BLEDLOW
LITTLE HAMPDEN
CLANFIELD
ABINGDON
AMERSHAM
FYFIELD
Denham GC
Frilford Heath GC
CLIFTON HAMPDEN
Beaconsfield GC
FRILFORD
Gerrards Cross GC
BEACONSFIELD
GERRARDS CROSS
NORTH STOKE
NETTLEBED
MARLOW
FARNHAM COMMON
HUNTERCOMBE GC
Burnham
Beeches GC
Stoke Poges GC
Badgemore Park GC
HENLEY-
BURNHAM
Henley GC
ON-THAMES

A.B. FROST   *"By Sheer Strength"*   ROSENSTIELS

The Lygon Arms with its quite outstanding frontage nestles in the delightful Cotswold village of Broadway. For some 400 years the inn has played host to the many visitors who flock to this quiet country setting. The gabled and mullioned windows peep out from the ivy that surrounds them and hide what can only be described as a splendid interior.

The restaurant is situated in a huge dining room so renowned in the Cotswolds. The cooking makes excellent use of local produce as well as fine ingredients from further afield, salmon for instance. Not only lunch and dinner but also tea can be enjoyed in the inn – a naturally popular idea for people without quite so much time on their hands.

The bedrooms are all charmingly decorated if you are able to stay a while, the character and charm does not, however, exclude those comforts that we clearly expect in the modern day world.

Whether you are going to the theatre at Stratford, enjoying a sporting occasion in Gloucestershire or merely taking in the villages of the Cotswolds the Lygon Arms is a landmark to quality hospitality.

THE LYGON ARMS
High Street,
Broadway.
Tel: (0386) 852255

Buckinghamshire and Oxfordshire – two very English counties, don't you think? From Burnham Beeches to Banbury Cross, the region extends from the edge of the Chilterns to the edge of the Cotswolds and occupies a very prosperous part of southern Britain. Both counties are essentially rural, that is of course, once you've escaped the grasping claws of Greater London.

The three best known courses in Buckinghamshire are probably **Woburn, Burnham Beeches** and **Stoke Poges** – whether they are the best three is inevitably open to dispute. Few, however, I suspect, would disagree that the outstanding trio in Oxfordshire are **Huntercombe** and the two 'heaths', **Tadmarton Heath** and **Frilford Heath**. Before I get lynched by the inhabitants of Henley, Oxford and Bicester it should be said that both counties, whilst not possessing a vast number of courses have more than enough to interest the would-be visiting golfer.

Taking Buckinghamshire first, **Woburn** stands rather alone in the far north of the county. Within a short distance of Milton Keynes, it is particularly convenient when the business meeting finishes early. It is equally convenient after a morning exploring Woburn Abbey and the famous Safari Park.

Leaving Woburn which is featured on a later page and heading 'down' the county, **Ellesborough** is another with rather stately surroundings being sited on part of the property of Chequers. Quite a hilly course and rather testing, there are some commanding views across the Buckinghamshire countryside. The Club welcomes visitors during the week, though prior tele—phoning is recommended. Elsewhere in the centre of the county, there is a fairly lengthy parkland course at **Weston Turville**, 2 1/2 miles south of Aylesbury. Visitors should be able to get a game here most days of the week.

It is in southern Buckinghamshire where most of the county's better courses are to be found. **Stoke Poges** has staged many leading amateur events, not at all surprisingly, this being one of the finest parkland courses in the south of England. Several lengthy par fours are a feature of the 6700 yard layout. The Club receives visitors at weekends, once again prior telephoning is a good idea.

Denham is a near neighbour of Stoke Poges lying some 3 miles north of Uxbridge, and as the Club handbook will tell you "half an hour's drive from Marble Arch". Denham enjoys an exceptionally tranquil setting, deeply secluded amidst some glorious countryside. The Clubhouse is a most unusual building having being built around a 16th century tithe barn. The course itself is slightly undulating and of medium length. The Club welcomes visitors between Mondays and Thursdays though

handicaps of 24 or less are required.

In equally beautiful surroundings is the Burnham Beeches Club, situated approximately 4 miles west of Slough. Always immaculately kept, it has some prodigiously difficult rough and staying on the fairways is to be strongly recommended. Again, visitors should be able to arrange a game during the week. Others of note in southern Buckinghamshire include **Beaconsfield** and **Gerrards Cross**, both are within fairly easy access of the capital.

The cost of a game on any of the above courses tends to range between £10-15, and it is probably advisable for the visitor to bring proof of handicap with him.

Heading into Oxfordshire, **Huntercombe** with its views across the Oxford Plain is also featured on a later page. Fairly nearby there are two courses at Henley, the more established **Henley Golf Club** and **Badgemore Park**, a fairly new course but one that has settled down quickly. Both are of the parkland type with many attractive trees. Visitors should be able to get a game on either between Mondays and Fridays, fees being around the **£10** mark.

Frilford Heath situated to the west of Abingdon on the **A338**, is due to stage the **English Amateur Championship** in **1987**, a fact which, of course, speaks volumes for the quality of the golf here. There are two 18-hole courses, the **Red** and the **Green**. Both are heathland types with gorse, heather and many pines and silver birch. Both are also renowned for their large greens. Visitors are welcome during the week, though being a fairly busy course a quick telephone call before finalising plans is advisable.

Southfield Golf Course lies about a mile south-east of the centre of Oxford along the **B480**. The home of Oxford University, it is a fairly challenging course, though not overly long. Visitors are welcome weekdays, fees in 1986 being **£9** per day.

Further north in the county there is the **Chesterton County Golf Club** at Bicester, a flattish parkland course, where the fees in 1986 were 7 weekdays, **£9** at weekends with reductions after 4 p.m. There is also a much improved course at **Burford**. However, the best in the north of the county is clearly **Tadmarton Heath**. At less than 6000 yards in length, it is fairly short by modern standards, but the narrow fairways and a great spread of gorse can make it a very difficult test. It also has a wonderfully remote setting. Golf can be enjoyed here between Mondays and Fridays, though telephoning is once again recommended.

Badgemore Park G.C.	(0491) 572206
Beaconsfield G.C.	(04946) 6545
Burford G.C.	(099382) 2583
Burnham Beeches G.C.	(06286) 61448
Chesterton County G.C.	(0869) 241204
Denham G.C.	(0895) 832801
Ellesborough G.C.	(0296) 622114
Frilford Heath G.C.	(0865) 390428
Gerrards Cross G.C.	(0753) 883263
Henley G.C.	(0491) 575742
Huntercombe G.C.	(0491) 641207
Southfield G.C.	(0865) 242158
Stoke Poges G.C.	(0973) 26385
Tadmarton Heath G.C.	(0608) 737278
Weston Turville G.C.	(0296) 24084
Woburn G. & C.C.	(0908) 70756

BUCKINGHAMSHIRE AND OXFORDSHIRE

Oxford "The Dreaming City" with its narrow passageways and ancient colleges. Then the Chilterns with tiny villages and some outstanding country pubs and in total contrast to a thatched bar stands Blenheim Palace, near Woodstock. The area also kisses the Cotswolds at Burford. And through these delightful settings some uncaring motorways have ripped through the country, but the convenience this has created opens up the possibility of this scrumptious menu. Breakfast in the Chilterns followed by golf at Burnham Beeches, luncheon on the Thames and golf at Huntercombe, dinner in the Cotswolds – golf at Tadmarton Heath (P.S. I think you'd have to move pretty sharpish – not doing the golfcourses and restaurants justice or yourself much good!) Take your time instead and enjoy some really leisurely golf.

We begin our visit in North Bucks to one of the country's most gorgeous golfcourses, Woburn. While the golfcourse falls in Bucks the town stands in Beds and the Lions presumably amble from county to county (The house is superb and really ought to be fully inspected). In Woburn Park itself – **The Paris House** (052525) **692** is thoroughly recommended, expensive for sure but outstanding just the same. An hotel to sample is the **Bedford Arms** (052525) **441** a particularly welcoming coaching inn.

The south of the county is littered with fine courses: a few thoughts to try while playing them. In Ivinghoe, **The King's Head** (0296) **668264** is a splendid restaurant, good English and French food in a 17th Century posting inn. A number of very comfortable hotels in the area where the dining is also well up to scratch include **The Bell** (0296) **89835** in Aylesbury's market place, **The Bellhouse Hotel** (0753) **887211** on the A40 outside the pleasant town of Beaconsfield, **The Burnham Beeches Hotel** (06286) **3333** a former hunting lodge, ideal for the golf course and breakfast beforehand if required. Two other hotels deserve a slightly stronger recommendation. They are the **Compleat Angler** (06284) **4444** which enjoys such a superb riverside setting, while further north in Aston Clinton **The Bell** (0296) **630252** is as charming an eating place as you are likely to find. Dinner here is a delight and the wine list is as comprehensive as Jack Nicklaus' golf (there is no greater compliment). If these hotel settings are not for you and you merely want a pint and a snack after a game then the following may be of interest: **The Rising Sun** in Little Hampden – superb snacks and beer, **The Fox** at Dunsmore – handy for meetings at nearby Chequers! In Amersham, **The King's Arms** is really cheerful and is a fine building, while in Bladlow, **The Lions at Bladlow** also offers excellent food. One final thought before we leave the area is to be found at Farnham Common where **Oscar's** (02814) **6211** is an informal restaurant ideal for dinner.

So into Oxfordshire, where the Thames offers Henley and the town in turn provides **The Red Lion** (0491) **571261** another commendable hotel. A brief return to Bucks and Remenham across the Bridge from Henley, a splendid pub here **The Little Angel**. Further afield, in Nettlebed lies the **White Hart** (0491) **641245** a pleasing pub with some good value bedrooms. The **Springs Hotel**, North Stoke (0491) **36687** is handy for Huntercombe and provides excellent accommodation and a first class restaurant – **The Fourways**, not The Fairways, in Wallingford

nearby, a number of delights come to mind but two in this delightful town (good shopping) are **The Shillingford Bridge Hotel** (086732) **8567** and **Brown and Boswell** a first rate restaurant (0491) **34078**.

On to Frilford, an excellent golf course, blessed by the close proximity of the **White Hart**, Fyfield, and its excellent bar snacks and restaurant. What else, well Frilford offers **Noah's Ark** (0865) **391470** – an excellent Italian restaurant which hides in a 16th century inn. Abingdon, another pleasant town where the **Upper Reaches Hotel** (0235) **22311** has a joyful situation beside the Thames. Nearby **The Barley Mow** (086730) **7847** has some accommodation if required. Next stop, another pleasant town Thame – and here a restaurant, **Thatchers** (084421) **2146**. A beamed cottage complements what can only be described as outstanding cuisine. While on the subject of good food a word in your ear – five actually – **Le Manoir Aux Quat' Saisons** (08446) **8881** probably the country's finest restaurant. Rooms are gorgeous and the whole setting is stimulating – magnificent. It's a difficult one to follow so let's go to Oxford where tradition holds sway. **The Randolph** (0865) **247481** in the centre of town is a monument to hospitality – while **Brown's** is a great fun brasserie (0865) **511995**. Other good dining haunts include **The Cherwell Boat House** (0865) **52746** and on a worthwhile sequitor to Le Manoir **Le Petit Blanc** (0865) **53540**, another classic restaurant. There are numerous shops (note the covered market), museums and pubs in the university town and a day in Oxford goes quickly past. Outside the town in Cumnor **The Bear and Ragged Staff** serves good food while a little further afield in Stanton Harcourt **The Harcourt Arms** (0865) **882192** has a tremendous atmosphere, a good restaurant, a good pint and excellent accommodation. Another fine restaurant within striking distance of Frilford is **The Plough** at Clanfield (036781) **222** – nouvelle cuisine accompanies excellent accommodation.

Making way to the Cotswolds Burford has much to delight, **The Inn For All Seasons** (04514) **324** is ideal while **The Lamb** is a delightful Cotswold inn (099382) **3155** comfortable accommodation. A good aleing pub is to be found in Hailey, **The King William IV**. Hotels in this area are really excellent. In Woodstock, **The Bear Hotel** (0993) **811511** an enormously popular and distinguished coaching inn; and **The Feathers** (0993) **812291** with its splendid restaurant is equally appealing and rather cheaper. Another noted hotel is the **Weston Manor** (0869) **50621**, at Weston-on-the-Green – ideal for Chesterton Golf Club, as is Chesterton itself and more specifically its superb restaurant – **Woods** (0869) **241444**. Less convenient but great fun is **The Shaven Crown Hotel** (0993) **830330** a delightful fourteenth century inn where excellent food complements some appealing bedrooms.

We end our excursion in Great Tew, **The Falkland Arms** (060883) **653**, a pub in a gorgeous village setting, so befitting the area in general where the food is good and the limited accommodation is cosy. As we sup our pints and sip our gin and tonics and slurp our orange juice – we have happy memories. We have seen some delightful country houses, Hughendon Manor, Disraeli's house – to name but one and we have enjoyed our golf. As the sun goes down and the pub gets busy – we still have plenty of time, no rush for breakfast at Burnham tomorrow.

Compleat Angler Hotel
Marlow Bridge, Bucks, S17 1RG
Tel (06284) 4444
In riverside gardens on the Berkshire banks of the Thames facing Georgian Marlow and close to the 150-year-old suspension bridge, the Compleat Angler has been welcoming guests for over 300 years. An ideal situation for the area's many golf courses.

Red Lion Hotel
Henley on Thames
Tel: (0491) 572161
Occupying a superb position overlooking the river Thames, this 16th century hotel is a must when playing in this part of Oxfordshire. With first class bedrooms and magnificent cuisine in the Riverside Restaurant, the Red Lion makes a stay in this delightful regatta town all the more pleasurable.

SEVERIANO BALLESTEROS

Born Pedrena, Spain, 9.4.57. Ht: 6'0". Wt: 12st 9lb.
Turned Pro: 1974. Seve followed his first important
win, in the Dutch Open in 1976, by three years later
taking the British Open at Royal Lytham and St
Annes. A star had been born – another Open win at St
Andrews in 1984 and two US Masters triumphs
confirmed that – and without a doubt the Spaniard
injected the kind of spice and vitality into the game
which nobody had done since Arnold Palmer.

True, of course, Seve has had his controversial
moments, and his current altercation with the US PGA
is a frustrating affair for all concerned, but there is no
doubt whatsoever that Ballesteros determination and
desire have taken him to the top of his profession.

THE PARLIAMENTARY HANDICAP

Formal Parliamentary golf started in 1891. A match between the two sides of the House was impossible owing to the weakness of the Liberals and it was decided to have a handicap tournament. Inspired by J P Croal, later editor of The Scotsman, who considered that golf "was the ideal pastime to sustain the health and distract the mind of the sedentary legislator", the tournament was played on the course on Tooting Bec Common. Lord Newton later described this course as "a confined area intersected by numerous roads frequented by perambulator-wheeling nursemaids and also by loafers and tramps. The hazards consisted largely of street lamps – one of which I broke several times myself – and of forbidding gorse clumps whole recesses, for various reasons, were best left unexplored."

Thirty-two players took part, including 20 Members of the Commons and 1 Peer. A number of ladies were seen hovering about the greens and "teeing grounds"; the tournament had evidently attracted considerable public attention. The tournament was won by H B St John, a House of Lords Clerk and the then heir to the Bolingbroke Viscountcy. The LCC banned further golf on Tooting Bec Common in 1892, the parliamentary handicap being the last golf played there, so a move was made in 1893 to Furzedown, south of Tooting Bec Common. In 1893 and 1896 T W Legh MP, later raised to the peerage as Lord Newton, won; fifty years later, in his memoirs, he recalled that "the general standard of play was very low" and he also recorded that his success had been "charitably ascribed by my friends to the fact that at that time I was a member of the handicapping committee."

Arthur Balfour, Prime Minister from 1902 to 1905, won three victories in 1894, 1897 and 1910 – the last time aged 62. Balfour was a very keen golfer; in the Badminton Library volume he coined the fine phrase "Care may sit behind the horseman; she never presumes to walk with the caddie". The participation of such a major political figure did much to stimulate public interest in the competition.

"When Mr Balfour was playing, therefore, the crowd soon grew into a respectable size by the addition of wondering nurse-maids with their noisy charges, of phlegmatic brewers' draymen who had left their horses standing at the roadside in order to watch Mr Balfour's play on the putting green, and of squabbling, bare-legged boys with cricket bats and wickets, or with primitive fishing rods from the nearest ponds. They all wanted to see Mr Balfour play "this weird pastime brought from Scotland". (Golf Monthly, 1911)

In 1900 it had been decided to play the tournament in rotation at the great seaside courses – Rye, Deal, Littlestone and the two courses at Sandwich. Pre-War winners included Bonar Law in 1907. Lloyd George played in 1911 and lost in the first round: an observer drily noted that "his style is not orthodox".

The first Handicap after the War in 1920 was won by the remarkable all-rounder F S Jackson, MP for Howdenshire, cricket captain of England and Yorkshire, and later Governor of Bengal. Golf Illustrated (June 18 1920) gave an amusing account of play at Sandwich. Apparently at least two Members completely missed the ball on the first tee: this prompted the correspondent to claim that in a long experience of Parliamentary handicaps he had not seen this before, and he suggested that the House of Commons should appoint its own professional and devote a Westminster Committee Room to indoor practice.

The 1930's was notable for the public interest aroused mainly because of the participation of the Prince of Wales, Lady Astor, Sir John Simon and other distinguished figures of the age. From 1931, the handicap was played regularly at Walton Heath, a course much favoured by leading parliamentarians. It was on the green there that Churchill offered to putt Lloyd George for the Premiership.

In 1932 the Prince of Wales reached the semi-final, where he was narrowly beaten by 1 hole by Lord Balfour. The Prince of Wales reached the final in 1933, losing at Coombe Hill to George Lambert, later Viscount Lambert. But the main attention focused on the semi-final on 5 July between Lady Astor (20) and the Prince (12) at Walton Heath. An immense crowd gathered to watch, which apparently disturbed the Prince. He won however 2/1 having been 2 down at the turn. Lady Astor had been informed by her daughter of her engagement on the morning of the match. The 1950 winner was Selwyn Lloyd, then a relatively junior backbench MP, but eventually to become Speaker. He is the only Speaker to have won – so far. The 1959 handicap deserves a special mention because the winner, PB "Laddie" Lucas, has left a fine description of it in his book "Sport of Princes" (1980). The following extract, by kind permission of the publishers, Stanley Paul, is the best published explanation of the Handicap's peculiar charm.

"In the weeks which ran up to the affair I was surprised to find myself slipping off for a round here, finding time for an hour's practice there. As with all my other preoccupations in those years, I had been able to play but little golf, this was a curious departure. After all that had gone before, it was, to be truthful, faintly absurd.

But I knew quite well why I was doing it. I secretly wanted to win the thing like the very devil....I wanted to add the name of a mere golfer to the winners' roll which contained some of the best-known Parliamentarians of the times. Two Prime Ministers were there. Arthur Balfour was three times a winner, and Bonar Law; an embryo Speaker of the House of Commons; secretaries of state and lesser ministers of the Crown; peers of the realm; Members of the Lower House who, in their day, had become familiar to readers of the British Press; and then a police constable whose friendly figure had been a part of the Westminster scene.

Dammit, I thought, if an England cricket captain can get his name on the roll of honour, why not a Walker Cup counterpart to keep him company? It was certainly a variously assorted bunch. The urge to be among the alumni was considerable.

Tradition, alone, was the spur.....

As we set off round the Old Course, waterproofs, scarves, towels and all, leaning with our umbrellas against the side wind, I could hardly credit the feeling. Years had passed since I had last gone out on a golf course, resolved to try on every shot, insisting on the caddy keeping the clubs dry under the hood, and endeavouring to play a tactical forward-thinking game. Fancy, I thought, after all this time, being driven on again like this. I really wondered whether I was still quite right in the head.

As I drove back to London with the spoils – such as they were – in my pocket, I mocked at my elation.

Childish ecstasy was understandable, but this was the Parliamentary Handicap. How could the nectar of victory still taste so sweet?

Tradition in golf is a strangely intoxicating thing.

In 1976, the Handicap was won by one of the Society's most distinguished golfing Members, Willie Whitelaw (now Viscount Whitelaw), Captain of the Royal and Ancient in 1970. In 1982 Stanley Clinton Davis became the first Labour Member to win. He won again in 1983 and returned in 1984 as a former Member and holder of the trophy to win an unprecendented third consecutive victory. The two most recent winners have been Michael Morris MP and Sir Anthony Grant MP.

SIR ROBERT SPEED
DAVID NATZLER

In all probability there are more dog legs on the course at **Huntercombe** than on any other in the British Isles. I do not however refer to an abundance of right-angled and left-angled holes, but rather to the canine breed. It is difficult to play a round at Huntercombe without coming across one of our four legged friends. Collies, labradors and gun-dogs all proudly parade the fairways, canine caddies you might say, or the wondrous hounds of Huntercombe.

Few Golf Clubs can have enjoyed as colourful a history as this charming Oxfordshire Club. Situated almost 700 feet above sea level on the edge of the Chilterns and overlooking the Oxford Plain, Huntercombe was founded in **1901. Young Willie Park** the son of the first Open Championship winner, both designed and opened the course. Park's creation met with the instant approval. **Walter Travis** the great American amateur golfer said of Huntercombe "it is easily the best laid out links that I have ever played over anywhere," while another commented "the turf on the putting greens is so excellent and the ball runs so truly that the golfer who cannot putt or learn the art of putting at Huntercombe had better resign himself to the fate of never being able to putt at all."

In the early years of the century three rather old Daimler motor cars were used to ferry Members to and from the local station and later a thirty seater bus was acquired for the same purpose. The course itself passed through various owners – at first a property company, then an insurance company (the Norwich Union) later **Viscount Nuffield** before finally becoming a Members Club in **1963**.

Approaching a quarter of a century later the Secretary at Huntercombe is **Mr. J.P. Bromley** he may be contacted by telephone on **(0491) 641207**. All written correspondence should be addressed to the Secretary at **Huntercombe Golf Club, Nuffield, Henley-on-Thames, Oxfordshire, RG9 5SL. John Draycott** is the Club's professional and he can be reached on **(0491) 641241**.

Visitors are welcome at Huntercombe throughout the week, the only general restrictions being before 10.30 am at weekends and on Bank Holidays. The cost of a day's golf in 1986 was priced at **£12.50** between Mondays and Fridays with **£17.50** payable at weekends. Golfing Societies are also welcome, the usual society days being Tuesdays and Thursdays. It should be added that three ball and four ball matches are discouraged with singles and foursomes strongly preferred.

The Golf Club is located approximately 7 miles from **Henley-on-Thames** and **12 miles** from **Reading** off the A423. Travelling from **London** the best route is to take the **M4** westbound leaving at exit **8** and thereafter following the Henley Road (which is in fact the **A423**). Approaching from the Midlands and the north of England the **A423** can be picked up at Oxford while those coming from the south and west of the country should head for Reading, the **A4** and **M4** assisting from the west and the **A33** helping from the south.

Huntercombe might be described as both downland and woodland in nature. When first there were very few trees making the course quite exposed and being on fairly high ground it could get rather breezy. However, many mature trees now provide shelter with a considerable spread of heather and gorse and a wide variety of wild flowers. Huntercombe is an exceptionally attractive course. From the men's tees it stretches to **6223** yards par **70** while the ladies course measures 5672 yards, par **72**. With the exception of a slope on the 3rd hole the course is very flat, making for easy walking. Sand bunkers are few and far between though there are several grass pots and hollows. If there is one feature of the course that particularly stands out it is probably the superb greens which are always true and generally quite fast.

The 19th at Huntercombe is a splendid building built in the mid 1960s and views over much of the course can be enjoyed from the terrace. In addition to bar snacks which are available throughout the day lunches can be prepared with prior notice and dinners may also be arranged for societies if required.

With its quiet situation on the edge of the Chilterns, Huntercombe is a delightful retreat from the nearby confusion. The mood at Huntercombe is of the nature that A J Balfour described when he said: "Give me my books, my golf clubs and leisure and I would ask for nothing more".

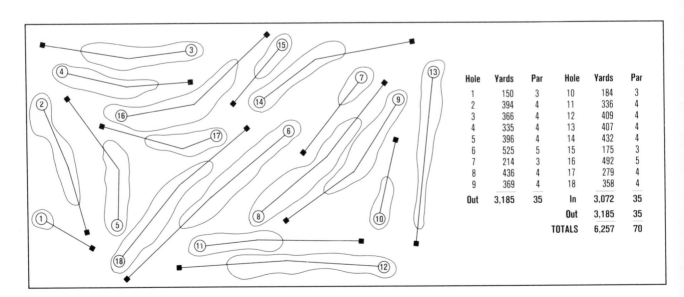

Hole	Yards	Par	Hole	Yards	Par
1	150	3	10	184	3
2	394	4	11	336	4
3	366	4	12	409	4
4	335	4	13	407	4
5	396	4	14	432	4
6	525	5	15	175	3
7	214	3	16	492	5
8	436	4	17	279	4
9	369	4	18	358	4
Out	3,185	35	In	3,072	35
			Out	3,185	35
			TOTALS	6,257	70

WOBURN

A magnificent Stately Home housing one of the finest art collections in the world, the largest wildlife safari park in Europe and two of the finest inland golf courses in Britain – quite a place Woburn!

The Stately Home is of course **Woburn Abbey** which since the reign of Henry VIII has been the home of the Dukes of Bedford, while the Wildlife Park and the golf courses lie within the grounds of the great estate.

In a game that prides itself on its antiquity **The Woburn Golf and Country Club** might be described as a remarkably precocious youngster. It was founded as recently as 1976 and its two courses, aptly named the **Duke's** and **Duchess**, were not opened until 1977 and 1979 respectively. In such a short period of time Woburn has acquired an enviable reputation.

In charge of all golfing matters at Woburn is **Alex Hay** whose Celtic tones are well-known to millions of television viewers. Mr. Hay acts as both Managing Director and resident professional. In the former capacity he may be contacted on **(0908) 70756** and when donning his golf professional hat Mr Hay can be reached by telephone on **(0908) 647987.**

Visitors, Societies and Company Days are all welcome at Woburn, although **prior booking** is essential. In addition visitors must be Members of recognised golf clubs and be able to provide proof of handicap. All written enquiries should be addressed to the **Managing Director, Woburn Golf and Country Club, Bow Brickhill, Milton Keynes, MK17 9LJ.**

Having booked a game, travelling to Woburn ought not to present too many problems. The Club is located approximately 45 miles from London and 73 miles from Birmingham and is well-served by major roads. Both the **M1** (junction **13**) and the **A5** pass close by. For those using British Rail, **Bletchley Station**, some 4 miles away has good connections from both London and **Birmingham. Luton and Heathrow Airports** are also within fairly easy reach. The town of Woburn and the Abbey are both actually within the county of Bedfordshire while the Golf and Country Club lies a short distance over the boundary in Buckinghamshire.

Fifteen years ago if someone had suggested that a Championship Course (never mind two) could have been built on the Woburn Estate, the famous lions would probably not have been the only ones to roar. The present site was then a dense forest, with giant trees and bracken restricting vision beyond a few yards (in fact today to gain a picture of how the whole scene looked one has only to take a few paces off any of the fairways – even Robin Hood would have been unimpressed).

Golf architect **Charles Lawrie** was called in and plans were drawn up. The bulldozers soon arrived and from amidst the pines and the chestnuts great avenues were carved. The fairways flourished on the sandy subsoil and within two years of opening The Duke's Course was considered fit to stage a major professional tournament. It proved a popular decision and a succession of sponsors decided to follow suit. Following its opening the Duchess matured with equal rapidity and Woburn soon possessed two precious gems.

The tournaments held at Woburn have included four **Masters Championships, the Hitachi Ladies British Open (1984)** and, in each year since 1982, **The Ford Ladies Classic.** Under the sponsorship of Dunhill, Woburn has become something of a home for the British Masters event – **Lee Trevino** and **Severiano Ballesteros** winning in 1985 and 1986. What is it they say about great courses producing great champions?

From the back markers (or tiger tees?) the Duke's course stretches to **6883** yards (par **72**), while the Duchess measures **6616** (par **71**). The corresponding distances for the ladies being **6065** yards (par **75**) and **5831** yards (par **74**).

From their forward tees both courses are considerably reduced in length and straight hitting rather than sheet distance ought to be the chief priority – as enchanting as they may be, the woods should be avoided at all cost.

Set approximately 500 feet above sea level both courses provide commanding views across rural Buckinghamshire and when the gorse and the great spread of rhododendrons are in full bloom Woburn is nothing short of 'paradis terrestre'.

As one might expect from a modern Golf and Country Club the facilities at Woburn are excellent. The Clubhouse offers a full complement of catering, though dinners must be pre-arranged. For the sporty types there is tennis, squash and an open-air heated swimming pool. The majority of golfers, however, will probably head for one of the two Bars.... and toast the Duke and the Duchess.

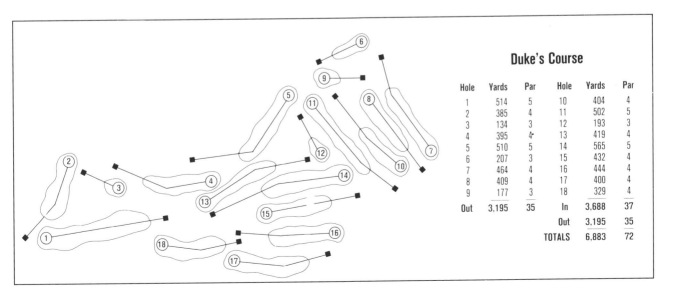

Duke's Course

Hole	Yards	Par	Hole	Yards	Par
1	514	5	10	404	4
2	385	4	11	502	5
3	134	3	12	193	3
4	395	4	13	419	4
5	510	5	14	565	5
6	207	3	15	432	4
7	464	4	16	444	4
8	409	4	17	400	4
9	177	3	18	329	4
Out	3,195	35	In	3,688	37
			Out	3,195	35
			TOTALS	6,883	72

GLOUCESTERSHIRE

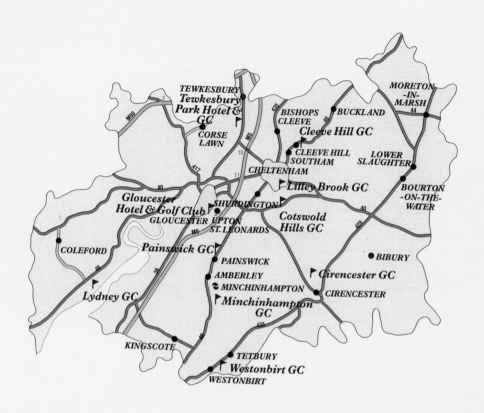

C.E. BROCK *"The Drive"* SOTHEBY'S

THE GREENWAY

Greenway, built in 1584 as a private
nor House by the Lawrence family,
althy wool merchants, was the original
se on the Shurdington Estate.

house takes its name from the historic
00 year old walkway which runs beside
hotel up onto the Cotswolds. This
kway, the Green Way, was the original
vers' road through the lowlands which
e then marsh and forest inhabited by
animals.

ated only 2½ miles from the lovely
orgian spa town of Cheltenham, The
eenway is the perfect base for exploring
of the most charming areas of Britain.
wns and villages whose very names
jure up the aura of mellow Cotswold
he, such as the Slaughters, Moreton-in-
rsh, Bourton-on-the-Water, Chipping
mden, Stow-on-the-Wold and
nswick.

nheim Palace, Stratford-on-Avon,
adway, Suddeley Castle, Slimbridge
dfowl Trust under the direction of Sir
er Scott, the Norman abbey at
vkesbury, the Saxon church at
erhurst and the magnificent cathedral at
oucester, the Roman corinium of
encester and the dreaming spires of
ford, are some of the places of interest
t can fill one's days and yet all are an
r's drive or less from The Greenway.

urn at the end of your explorations and
ve through the gentle parkland to the
nt door of The Greenway, where you
find a warmth of welcome and the
nquil atmosphere of a real home, for
t is what The Greenway offers. Ground
or rooms that are elegant and spacious,
truly comfortable, with roaring log fires
winter and access to the formal gardens
summer. Upstairs the twelve bedrooms
individually decorated and furnished
h fine antiques, yet each with the pre-
uisites of the twentieth century, namely
hrooms en suite, direct-dial telephones,
our televisions, and views through the
ne mullioned windows over the gardens
parkland to the Cotswold Hills
ond.

panelled dining room overlooking the
ken lily pond, where romantic candlelit
ing is the order of the day, features a

small but highly individual menu offering
unusual but well balanced dishes with an
international appeal.

An excellent and comprehensive wine list
complements the food, add to this the
personal attention you will receive from
Tony and Maryan Elliott who are the
resident owners and their well trained and
extremely friendly team of staff, and you
will understand why The Greenway should
be your home in the Cotswolds.

The Greenway,
Shurdington, Cheltenham,
Gloucestershire GL51 5UG
Telephone: (0242) 862352
Telex: 437216

GLOUCESTERSHIRE

Gloucestershire, the County of Grace, is also a county of magnetic charm and great beauty. The Cotswolds dominate Gloucestershire, its wonderfully named towns and villages of Stow-on-the-Wold, Moreton-in-Marsh, Upper Slaughter and Lower Slaughter providing a haven for tourists.

However, turning to more serious subjects, I trust that when Doctor Foster went to Gloucester he wasn't a golfer. The county has very few courses and Gloucester itself didn't possess one at all until as recently as 1976. Neighbouring Cheltenham has been a little more fortunate but granted one or two exceptions, the quality of the golf in this part of the world doesn't exactly match up to the undeniable quality of the scenery.

The county's two best known courses are probably **Cotswold Hills** and **Lilley Brook**, located to the north and south of Cheltenham respectively. Both offer commanding views of the Gloucestershire countryside, especially perhaps Lilley Brook, one of southern England's most undulating courses. Each is well worth a visit – generally possible on all days of the week although prior telephoning is advisable. A weekday game at Lilley Brook can be enjoyed for **£6** (**£7.50** for a day ticket) and for **£10** at weekends. Cotswold Hills' fees are similarly priced.

Cleeve Hill is Cheltenham's third 18 hole course. Situated on high ground to the north of the town it can be rather cold in winter. One anonymous person said that when visiting Cheltenham he enjoyed a game at Lilley Brook in the summer as half of him was mountain goat and at Cleeve Hill in the winter because the other half of him was eskimo!

In a relatively short period of time the **Gloucester Hotel** course has acquired a considerable reputation. Located close to the **M5**, only a mile from the Roman town at Robinswood Hill, the course is set amidst some truly delightful surroundings. The facilities are quite excellent and a game can be arranged on any day of the week. The Green fees are **£6** midweek, **£8** at weekends.

Further north along the **M5** (junction 9) lies the market town of Tewkesbury, famed for its Norman Abbey and its Roses Battle of 1471. Situated actually on the site of the Battle is the **Tewkesbury Park Hotel** and accompanying golf course. Another newish creation designed by Frank Pennick, it too has gained a speedy reputation. The attractive parkland layout has been centred around an 18th Centry country house, quite undulating with trees and water providing the major hazards. Visitors with handicaps are made most welcome, though starting times must be pre-booked. The cost of a day's golf at Tewkesbury is **£10** during the week, with **£12** payable at weekends.

Elsewhere in the county there are two courses at **Minchinhampton**, South East of Stroud, one of which measures a lengthy 6,675 yards. Much less testing (though it mightn't sound like it) is **Painswick**, a little to the north of Stroud off the **A46**. Two 9 holers of note are the underrated **Westonbirt** course at Tetbury (**A433**) where golf can be enjoyed seven days a week for a modest fee, and **Lydney**, though visitors here are restricted at weekends. Lydney is in the south west corner of the county and visitors to these parts should perhaps consider travelling an extra 15 miles or so along the **A48** to Chepstow to sample the delights of the **St Pierre Golf and Country Club**.

GLOUCESTERSHIRE

By all accounts the Cotswold heathland of Gloucestershire isn't quite up to scratch when it comes to the small matter of golf. Although reading between the lines it appears that a number of clubs are endeavouring to put this matter straight. However, while Gloucester golfers twiddle their thumbs and dream of St Andrews one matter ought to be made perfectly clear: every golfer worth his or her salt should visit Gloucestershire not for the golf necessarily but to emphasise to his frustrated friends or peeved partners that a golfing holiday can offer so much more in the way of tremendous places to stay and all manner of other ideas to embark upon. The plan is merely part of a larger plot: a long weekend will suffice – little golf played and then the partner may fall for the oldest trick in the book "Come on darling, you remember that weekend in Glocuestershire – Fife will be just the same – the two weeks will fly by". It may work, here are a few ideas.

The Gloucestershire hotels are outstanding. A mixture of beautiful manor houses and welcoming inns should cater for all tastes. There are only four bedrooms at **Corse Lawn Hotel (045278) 479**, Corse Lawn, but they are good value and it might be an idea to organise a group to take the place over. One thing is certain if you choose to have lunch or dinner here you will enjoy the fayre of the very highest quality. Another 18th century building this time a manor house, is the **Tewkesbury Park Hotel (0684) 295405** comfortable accommodation complements a good days golf. Another establishement which has a quite excellent restaurant and a small number of rooms is the **Cleeveway House (024267) 2585** in Bishops Cleeve. As the name sugests the **Malvern View Hotel (024267) 2017** at Cleeve Hill is nearby – good value accommodation and once again the restaurant is an excellent place to have dinner (note home made sorbets). The Cheltenham area has many fine hotels, but perhaps the best known is the **Queen's Hotel (0242) 514724**. Two hotels in the surrounding hills are the **Hotel De La Bere (0242) 37771** in Southam and the simply splendid **Greenway (0242) 862352** which lies in Shurdington. This hotel offers an excellent welcome: a first class menu and gorgeous grounds. It could be the ideal point to close the Fife fortnight! Where next, well, a trip to Bibury never comes a miss. The Tudor **Bibury Court (028574) 337** is steeped in history and is worth a visit on this score alone, (note also the excellent snack lunches and a la carte evening menus).

Another fine place to stay though slightly more expensive is the **Swan Hotel (028574) 204** a pleasant 17th century coaching inn. A market town is our next suggestion, Cirencester to be precise. The **Stratton House Hotel (0285) 61761** is a manor house in delightful grounds while in contrast to the black and white exterior of the **Fleece Hotel (0285) 68507** hides a charming inn. The restaurant in the Fleece is also well thought of. Returning to the Cotswolds some veritable treats lie in wait. In Lower Slaughter **The Lords of the Manor Hotel (0451) 20243** with its outstanding grounds, excellent restaurant and bars is first rate while Moreton-in-Marsh offers (among others) a

welcoming hotel of a similar name, aptly, **The Manor House (0608) 50501** where one of the four-poster bedrooms is ideal for popping the question – (again) – "What about Fife Couchie?" (a slightly slimy approach rarely succeeds!)

Golfers taking in the course at Lydney may wish to visit the **Speech House (0594) 22607** at Coleford – an inn which nestles cosily in the Forest of Dean. Painswick players should not forget the **Painswick Hotel (0452) 812160**, convenient, friendly and an above average restaurant. Other hotels nearby include the spectacular **Burleigh Court (0453) 883804** (this is handy for the nearby courses as well as boasting its own miniature course for early risers). In Amberley, to the north **The Amberley Inn** with its fine views over the Woodchester Valley has great character. If one wishes to visit the county town of Gloucester **The Gloucester Hotel (0452) 25653** is satisfactory. However, the **Tara Hotel (0452) 674112** in Upton St. Leonards may prove a better choice and the restaurant is also good. One may also wish to visit Tetbury: **The Snooty Fox (0666) 52436** is stylish and dominant in the Market Place while the **Hare and Hounds** at Westonbirt nearby is handy for the short golf course (ideal for a round before dinner). Also near Tetbury, at Calcot, **The Calcot Manor** has a tremendous setting and its welcome is friendly which is typical of this area.

We have decided only to pinpoint a number of pubs and restaurants in the area for the principal reason that the county is riddled with them! However, some establishments must be noted. **The Rose Tree**, at Bourton-on-the-Water (0451) 20635 offers a splendid English restaurant with French cuisine. Another tremendous French restaurant can be found in **La Ciboulette (0242) 573449** on Cheltenham's Suffolk Road. Splendid pub food can be enjoyed at the **Hunters Hall** Kingscote– which is strongly recommended. Another 'local' of interest is the **Dog at Over** situated just west of the city of Gloucester. Other worthwhile houses include the **Royal Oak** at Painswick, **The Yew Tree** at Chaceley Stoke and the **New Inn** at North Nibley.

The Cotswold towns are riddled with craft and antique shops as well as delightful walks and pleasant views. Badminton House and the 12th Century Berkeley Castle are splendid, the Cathedral at Gloucester is quite outstanding and Sudely Castle is well worth visiting – the Cirencester market is worth a look. Near Tewkesbury with its historic streets and Inns (note the Royal Hopp Pole) lies bloody meadow. This messy mead is not the result of some skirmish between the above mentioned loved ones.

Indeed, a major transformation has developed – you ought to know about it; it's Fife you see it's been dropped, yes the two weeks totally forgotten. Why? well, it's Gloucestershire you see – not only was it easy to get a game, but the hotels and dining rooms are outstanding. A cottage has been purchased and it's the Cotswolds not the Ochils that have won the day!

Buckland Manor Hotel and Restaurant
Buckland,
Nr Broadway, WR12 7LY
Tel: (0386) 852626
A delightful Manor House between Cheltenham and Stratford-on-Avon with comfortable bedrooms, some with four-poster suites. Interestingly furnished with antiques. The excellent restaurant prides itself on fresh Vale of Evesham or the hotel's own produce.

Tewkesbury Park Hotel Golf and Country Club
Lincoln Green Lane, Tewkesbury
Tel: (0684) 295405
Similar to its sister Golf and Country Clubs in Hants and Wales, Tewkesbury Park offers everything a golfer could ever want. It is, however, a place for all the family with many excellent amenities on the premises. The Club is of historical interest also – it has been built on the site of the fifteenth century Roses Battle of Tewkesbury.

THE GLAMORGANS AND GWENT

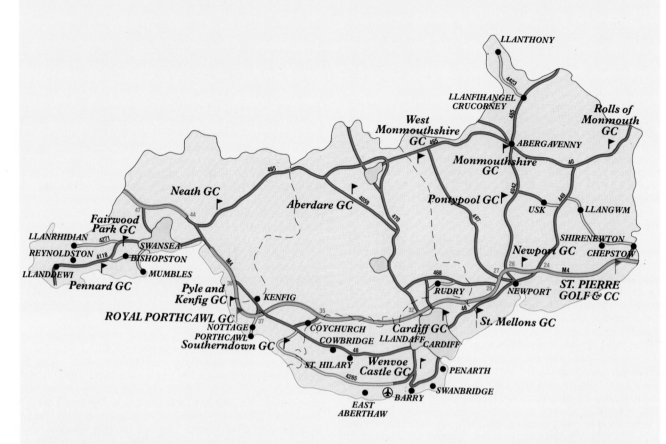

HARRY ROUNTREE   *"It's A One"*   *BURLINGTON GALLERY*

LLWYNDERW

e wild highlands of central Wales
ained their medieval roads until a few
ars ago. Recently, one of Europe's most
ccessful new road systems has been
veloped, and the hauntingly beautiful
idscape, with its rare birds and flowers
ce gazed on only by the little Welsh
ountain sheep and a few intrepid
ikers, lies open before the motorist of
e 'eighties. So far these splendid roads
main almost empty of traffic, skirting
ge lakes and climbing craggy moorland
dernesses, most enticing to the painter,
e walker, the salmon and sea trout
ierman, the photographer, the bird
itcher (the extremely rare red kite) and
e naturalist, to say nothing of its intense
raction for the tourist. Llwynderw is the
ly new (1969) hotel in this vast area to
ovide first quality food and comfort. With
own spring water—its peat fires and
in bread, Llwynderw lies 1,000 feet
ove sea level, protected by ancient
eches and oaks, and on a mountain
rent, no house in sight.

wynderw is especially recommended as a
ice of relaxation (comprehensive library)
reassemble energies in the midst of a
uelling tour of the U.K., lying as it does
tween Chester and the Cotswolds or
th. A two- or three-night stay would also
able visits to the world-famous Bodnant
rdens, Caernarvon, Conwy, Beaumaris
d Harlech castles and the amazing slate
nes of Blaenau Ffestiniog—or to the
uth and west, Caerphilly castle, one of
e finest in Europe; the South Wales
dustrial area museums; or to Pembroke
th its long, preserved coastal walk and
e glorious pilgrimage shrine of Saint
avids.

wynderw is a small Georgian house
796) on earlier foundations. A visit to it
strictly for the connoisseur who will enjoy
many unique features, and an utter lack
unfortunate hotel commercializations.
le proprietor cannot say he is always
ailable as some nights he likes to cook
Velsh mountain mutton—a very rare
ticle now), but usually he is all too
xious to meet the great variety of
teresting guests who have followed the
ide book advice "well worth a detour".

Llwynderw Hotel,
Abergwesyn,
Llanwrtyd Wells,
Powys LD5 3TW
Telephone: (05913) 238

Balls in South Wales are often large, oval-shaped and made of leather. However, those belonging to the much smaller dimpled breed – usually white, though these days sometimes shocking yellow – are to be found in some particularly pleasant spots, and in a great variety of places between the Wye Valley and the Gower Peninsular.

For present purposes South Wales comprises Gwent and the three Glamorgans – this may alarm the good people of Llanelli but the whole of Dyfed and Powys has been labelled 'Mid Wales' (if you look at a golf course map of central Wales perhaps you will appreciate why!)

For many travellers their first sample of golf in South Wales will be the impressive **St Pierre Golf and Country Club** at Chepstow (see feature page). Unfortunately far too great a number make St Pierre their one and only stop. Further up the Wye Valley both **Monmouthshire** and **The Rolls of Monmouth** offer an outstanding game in delightful sourroundings. Bounded by the River Usk the Monmouthshire Golf Club lies half a mile west of Abergavenny at Llanfoist. The Club will soon celebrate one hundred years of golf – quite an achievement when one considers its unusual beginnings. Laid out on ground formerly used for polo and later for horseracing, golf was started here in 1892, as the Club handbook tells you, "the result of a bet as to whether such a venture could be run successfully at Abergavenny"! Clearly the golfers backed a winner. Visitors are welcome to play the course during the week at a cost of **£8**, proof of handicap being required. Societies are also catered for on Mondays and Fridays. Golf at 'The Rolls' is played around a spectacular mansion house, the Hendre, country seat of the Rolls family since 1767. A new Club founded in 1982, it provides quite a tough test, but an immensely enjoyable one. The course is located some 3 miles west of Monmouth on the **B4233**.

Other courses of note in Gwent include **West Monmouthshire**, up in the hills on the edge of the Brecon Beacons at Nant-y-glo, **Pontypool** (not one for the out-of-condition-types) and the **Newport Golf Club** at Rogerstone – a fine downland course very close to the **M4** (junction **27**) and where a preliminary telephone call is recommended.

Golfers in Cardiff (or Caerdydd) are quite fortunate having a number of well-established courses close at hand. Not surprisingly they tend to be busier than the majority of Welsh courses and therefore before setting off it is probably wise to contact the particular Club in question. The **Cardiff Golf Club** is a superior parkland course situated some 3 miles from the city centre at Cyncoed. Visitors must accompany Members at weekends, but a game can be enjoyed there on weekdays, the cost of a

game being **£9**. Societies are welcome on Thursdays. **St Mellons**, north east of the City within easy access of the **M4**, is another popular parkland course. Quite challenging, with several interesting holes, and well worth a visit. To the south of Cardiff, **Wenvoe Castle** one of the more hilly courses in South Glamorgan, should be good for a game during midweek, as should the **Glamorganshire** course, located to the west of Penarth.

Before heading off to the glorious coastal strip around Porthcawl a course certainly deserving a mention is **Aberdare** – and not merely because the professional goes by the impressive name of Mr A Palmer! Aberdare is an excellent woodland course, the finest in 'the Valleys' and where golf can be enjoyed for the modest fee of **£6** during the week, **£7** at weekends.

One would have to travel many a mile to find a course the equal of **Royal Porthcawl** (also featured later this chapter) but its near neighbour to the east, **Southerndown** gets closer than most. Situated on high ground it is an outstandingly scenic downland course measuring a little over **6600** yards (par **70**).

Visitors are welcome between Mondays and Saturdays, the green fees in 1986 being **£8** on weekdays with **£12.50** payable on Saturdays. Even closer to Porthcawl is the fine links of **Pyle and Kenfig** on more than one occasion venue of the Welsh Amateur Stroke Play Championship. Fairly testing, being open to the elements, visitors are able to play on weekdays at a cost of **£9**.

Beyond Pyle and Kenfig the M4 heads into West Glamorgan passing through Port Talbot towards Swansea. Midway between the two towns golfers should have no trouble getting a game at the mountainous **Neath** Golf Club, located north west of the town centre at Cadoxton. Beyond Swansea is the beautifully secluded Gower Peninsular. If you're visiting these parts two courses that can be strongly recommended are **Fairwood Park** and **Pennard**. The former, situated close to Swansea Airport, is a second course over which racehorses once galloped. A recent change of ownership has seen a rapid improvement in both the course and the facilities offered. Visitors are received at all times and Societies can nearly always be accommodated. In 1986 the cost of a weekday round was **£7** with **£10** payable at weekends and Bank Holidays. Several long par fours are the feature of this attractive course. From Pannard's cliff-top course there are some splendid views out across the Bristol Channel. Again visitors can play on any day of the week, fees here being **£8** Mondays to Fridays, **£9** at weekends.

Beyond the Gower, still along the coast is Carmarthen Bay. But by now we have crossed the boundary into Dyfed and must imagine ourselves in Mid-Wales.

Aberdare G.C.	(0685) 871188
Cardiff G.C.	(0222) 7533320
Fairwood Park G.C.	(0792) 203648
Glamorganshire G.C.	(0222) 707048
Monmouthshire G.C.	(0873) 2606
Neath G.C.	(0639) 3615
Newport G.C.	(0633) 892643
Pennard G.C.	(044128) 3131
Pontypool G.C.	(04955) 3655
Pyle and Kenfig G.C.	(0656) 713093
Rolls of Monmouth G.C.	(0660) 5353
St Mellons G.C.	(0633) 680401
St Pierre G. & C.C.	(02912) 5261
Southerndown G.C.	(0656) 880476
West Monmouthshire G.C.	(0495) 310233

THE GLAMORGANS & GWENT

The slogan 'made in Wales' endeavours to attract an abundance of new businesses and naturally boost the local economy. The Welsh Development Board knows the success of this slogan – not me. But what about this for another slogan, boyyos – 'Played in Wales'! Certainly, golf is of a good standard and if you desire to take the girl friend/boyfriend, mistress/lover or husband/wife with you, then another Welsh jingle shoots to mind. It would be wrong to give the impression of an area of sumptuous country houses and wonderful inns, but nevertheless there are a number of good hotels which ought to be mentioned.

In Chepstow itself two hotels immediately spring to mind. On the one hand, **St Pierre (02912) 5261**, and on the other, **The Castle View Inn (02912) 70349**. The former, a 14th century mansion, offers excellent golf facilities as well as a range of other leisure pursuits, while the latter is cheaper and is more homely and comfortable. If you do opt for the golf, then a bar snack at the Castle View and a stroll around the old town is worthwhile. Perhaps the best hotel in Gwent is found near Newport – **The Celtic Manor (0633) 413000** (exit junction 24 off the M4). While the hotel is expensive by Welsh standards, it offers style and comfort which are far from prevalent in the region – note the patio restaurant. Another unmistakably Welsh town, Pontypool, is served by Usk, specifically **The Glen-yr-Afon (02913) 2302** – a quiet unassuming hotel which makes for a comfortable stay. In the valleys, beautiful countryside is guaranteed. This is especially so in the Abergavenny area. **The Crowfield Hotel (0873) 5048** is situated two miles north east and is a splendid base to take in the delights of the Brecon Beacons. If after a day out at the Rolls of Monmouth you have the energy, you will certainly find inspiration in a drive north to Llanthony. Your aim is **The Abbey Hotel (087382) 487**. The food here is excellent, the setting spectacular and the catch is, this is no secret, so do book early.

Crossing the border from Gwent to Glamorgan, one arrives at the capital – Cardiff. If you have been seduced into business in Wales, then Cardiff may be your port of call. Perhaps the best two hotels are the Victorian style of the **Park Hotel (0222) 383471** or the far more modern but comfortable **Stakis Inn on the Avenue (0222) 732520**. Outside the city in Cowbridge, **The Bear Hotel (0656) 860621**, former coaching inn, or the **Coed-y-Mwstwr Hotel at Coychurch (0656) 860621** are handy for an overnight call while en route to the delights of Porthcawl or Southerndown. In Porthcawl, the **Fairways (065671) 2085** is aptly named and a particularly suitable place to visit. While in Nottage, **The Rose and Crown (065671) 4849** is an excellent pub which has some rooms and is ideally situated 2 miles from junction 37 off the M4. Further west in the superbly named Mumbles Stands, the **Norton House Hotel (0792) 404891** – most comfortable and excellent breakfasts – crucial for a good round at Pennard. Another likely port of call for Welsh visiting

businessmen is Swansea. The **Dragon Hotel (0792) 51074** is first class and the outstandingly beautiful Gower Peninsula offers an inspired contrast to the busy streets of the city. Still further west, we come to Reynoldston, where the **Fairyhill Country House (0792) 390139** is a friendly and well recommended place to stay and which also offers excellent cuisine.

With a day's golf and much Welsh air inhaled, some thoughts on liquid refreshment and nutrition would not go amiss. In Glamorgan, **The Drangway** in Swansea is very popular – note the Pembrokeshire oysters. A tremendous pub in Mid-Glamorgan is the **Prince of Wales** in Kenfig – excellent character where great value bar food is available. In Bishopston another popular haunt can be located, namely the **Joiners Arms**. Returning to Cardiff, **Gibsons (0222) 41264** in Romilly Crescent is very well thought of, while the **Blas-Ar-Cymru (0222) 382132** offers a delightful taste of Wales. Outside Cardiff, in Llandaff is **La Chaumiere (0222) 555319**. Another restaurant that merits a mention is found in Penarth, **The Caprice (0222) 702424** – excellent sea food accompanies fine views over the Bristol Channel. Also in Penarth **The Captain's Wife** (public house) is recommended – so to speak. Two pubs to the north and south of Cardiff are the **Maenllwyd** at Rudry and the beautifully thatched **Bush at St Hilary**. Still further south, the **Blue Anchor** in East Aberthan is delightful despite being near an industrial area. Not liking to leave on an industrial note, let us return to the Gower and Llanrhidian. Here, **Welcome to Town** beckons, a simple but friendly local.

From the Gower to Gwent and Llandewi Skirrid here the **Walnut Tree (0873) 2797** holds the pride of place – an excellent restaurant and possibly the best wine list in the region. Pubs in the area are generally blessed with splendid country views, **The Bridge Inn (02915) 249** is busy as a result of some excellent food and a good atmosphere. Do book a table (and you can stay if needs be). Quality is one thing, age another – the oldest pub in Wales is the **Skirmish**, in Llanfihangel Crucorney – (don't get lost for goodness' sake – imagine asking directions!). Returning Chepstow way, **The Tredegar Arms** in Shirenewton is well worth visiting.

I certainly hope it is clear that South Wales offers a lot – whether it's the place to set up a business is quite another matter. If golfers have thoughts of matters other than golf – unlikely, I would think – then the Brecon Beacons, the rivers and the countryside are generally beautiful. A particularly lovely area is the Magram Country Park which boasts, among other things, the largest orangery in Britain. The borders are riddled with interesting castles, Caerleon, Chepstow and Monmouth are all beautiful. If golfing partners are at a loss – fear not, take a few extra quid and just watch how far your money goes. It really is worthwhile. Businesses, note well!

St Pierre Hotel, Golf and Country Club
St Pierre Park, Chepstow
Tel: (02912) 5261
Only two miles from Exit 22 of the M4, St Pierre has so much to offer everyone. As well as two Championship golf courses in its grounds, it has everything from a jacuzzi to a bowling green. The Restaurant overlooks the 18th green.

Park Hotel
Park Place, Cardiff
Tel: (0222) 383471
An impressive, well managed, late Victorian hotel in the middle of Cardiff. With 108 attractively decorated bedrooms and an excellent restaurant, the Park Place claims to be Cardiff's premier hotel are well founded.

GOLF WORLD

Europe's Best Selling Golf Magazine

OPEN CHAMPIONSHIP PREVIEW
What chance another Turnberry shoot-out?

Complete 21-page guide to this year's championship

PLUS
My memorable shots in the majors – a new Jack Nicklaus series

The changing fortunes of Langer and Faldo

Win a set of Dunlop 'Deltic' clubs

THE 5TH: FANT-Y-GARY TO LLANFAIRYNGHORNWY

CLWYD
Abergele & Pensarn G.C. (18)
Abergele (0745) 824034

Bryn Morfydd G.C. (18)
Denbigh (074571) 313

Denbigh G.C. (18)
Denbigh (074571) 4159

Flint G.C. (9)
Flint (03526) 2327

Hawarden G.C. (9)
Hawarden, Deeside
(0244) 531447

Holywell G.C. (9)
Holywell (0352) 710040

Mold G.C. (18)
Mold (0352) 740318

Old Colwyn G.C. (9)
Colwyn Bay (0492) 515581

Old Padeswood G.C. (18)
Buckley, Nr Mold (0244) 547401

Padeswood & Buckley G.C. (18)
Buckley, Nr Mold (0244) 542537

Prestatyn G.C. (18)
Prestatyn (07456) 4320/88353

Rhuddlan G.C. (18)
Rhuddlan, Rhyl (0745) 590217

Rhyl G.C. (9)
Rhyl (0745) 53171

Ruthin-Pwllglas G.C. (9)
Ruthin (08242) 2296

St Melyd G.C. (18)
Prestatyn (07456) 4405

Vale of Llangollen G.C. (18)
Llangollen (0978) 860050

Wrexham G.C. (18)
Wrexham (0978) 364268/261033

DYFED
Aberystwyth G.C. (18)
Aberystwyth (0970) 615104

Ashburnham G.C. (18)
Burry Port (05546) 2269

Borth & Ynyslas G.C. (18)
Borth (097081) 202

Cardigan G.C. (18)
Cardigan (0239) 612035

Carmarthen G.C. (18)
Carmarthen (0267) 87214

Glynhir G.C. (18)
Llandybie, Nr Ammanford
(0269) 850571

Haverfordwest G.C. (18)
Haverfordwest (0437) 3565

Lampeter G.C. (9)
Llangybi, Lampeter (057045) 286

Milford Haven G.C. (18)
Milford Haven (06462) 2368

Newport (Pem) G.C. (9)
Newport (0239) 820244

St. Davids City G.C. (9)
St. Davids (0437) 721620

South Pembrokeshire G.C. (9)
Pembroke (0646) 683817

Tenby G.C. (18)
Tenby (0834) 2787

GWENT
Blackwood G.C. (9)
Blackwood (0495) 223152

Caerleon G.C. (9)
Caerleon (0633) 420342

Greenmeadow G.C. (9)
Cwmbran (06353) 69321

Llanwern G.C. (18+9)
Llanwern (0633) 412380

Monmouth G.C. (9)
Monmouth (0600) 2212

Monmouthshire G.C. (18)
Abergavenny (0873) 2606

Newport G.C. (18)
Newport (0633) 892643

Pontnewydd G.C. (10)
Cwmbran (06333) 2170

Pontypool G.C. (18)
Pontypool (04955) 3655

The Rolls of
Monmouth G.C. (18)
Monmouth (0600) 5353

St. Mellons, G.C. (18)
Castleton, Cardiff (0633) 680401

St Pierre G. & C.C. (18+18)
Chepstow (02912) 5261

Tredegar Park G.C. (18)
Newport (0633) 895219

Tredegar & Rhymney G.C. (9)
Rhymney (0685) 840743

West Monmouthsire G.C. (18)
Brynmawr (0495) 310233

GWYNEDD
Aberdovey G.C. (18)
Aberdovey (065472) 210

Abersoch G.C. (9)
Abersoch (075881) 2622

Bala G.C. (10)
Bala (0678) 520359

Betws-y-Coed G.C. (9)
Betws-y-Coed (06902) 556

Caernarfon G.C. (18)
Caernarfon (0286) 3783

Conway (Caernarvonshire)
G.C. (18)
Conway (049263) 3400

Criccieth G.C. (18)
Criccieth (076671) 2154

Dolgellau G.C. (9)
Dolgellau (0341) 422603

Ffeshiniog G.C. (9)
Blaenau, Ffestiniog (076681) 615

Llandudno G.C.
(Maesdu) G.C. (18)
Llandudno (0492) 76450

Llandudno (N. Wales) G.C. (18)
Llandudno (0492) 75325

Llanfairfechan G.C. (9)
Llanfairfechan (0248) 680144

Llangefni G.C. (9)
Llangefni (0248) 722193

Nefyn & District G.C. (18)
Nefyn (0758) 720966

Penmaenmawr G.C. (9)
Penmaenmawr (0492) 623330

Portmadog G.C. (18)
Portmadog (0766) 2037

Pwllheli G.C. (18)
Pwllheli (0758) 612520

Rhos-on-Sea
Residential G.C. (18)
Llandudno (0492) 49641

Royal St. Davids G.C. (18)
Harlech (0766) 780203

St. Deiniol G.C. (18)
Bangor (0248) 353098

ISLE OF ANGLESEY
Anglesey G.C. (18)
Rhosneiger (0407) 810219

Baron Hill G.C. (9)
Beaumaris (0248) 810231

Bull Bay G.C. (18)
Amlwch (0407) 830960

Holyhead G.C. (18)
Holyhead (0407) 3279

MID GLAMORGAN
Aberdare G.C. (18)
Aberdare (0685) 871188

Bargoed G.C. (18)
Bargoed (0443) 830143

Bryn Meadows G. & C.C. (18)
Blackwood (0495) 225590/227276

Caerphilly G.C. (14)
Caerphilly (0222) 883481

Creigiau G.C. (18)
Pentyrch (0222) 890263

Llantrisant & Pontyclin G.C. (12)
Llantrisant (0443) 222148

Maesteg G.C. (18)
Maesteg (0656) 732037

Merthyr Tydfid G.C. (9)
Merthyr Tydfid (0685) 3308

Mountain Ash G.C. (18)
Mountain Ash (0443) 472265

Pontypridd G.C. (18)
Pontypridd (0443) 402359

Pyle & Kenfig G.C. (18)
Porthcawl (065671) 3093

Rhondda G.C. (18)
Tonypandy (0443) 433204

Royal Porthcawl G.C. (18)
Porthcawl (065671) 2251

Southerndown G.C. (18)
Southerndown (0656) 880476

Whitehall G.C. (9)
Aberaynon (0443) 740245

POWYS
Brecon G.C. (9)
Brecon (0874) 2004

Builth Wells G.C. (9)
Builth Wells (0982) 553296

Cradoc G.C. (18)
Brecon (0874) 3658

Knighton G.C. (9)
Knighton (0547) 528646

Llandrindod Wells G.C. (18)
Llandrindod Wells (0597) 2059

Machynlleth G.C. (9)
Machynlleth (0654) 2000

Newtown G.C. (9)
Newtown (0686) 25844

Old Rectory C.C. (9)
Crickhowell (0873) 810373

St. Giles G.C. (9)
Newtown (0656) 25650

St. Idloes G.C. (9)
Llanidloes (05512) 2559

Welshpool G.C. (18)
Castle Caereinion (093883) 249

SOUTH GLAMORGAN
Brynhill G.C. (18)
Barry (0446) 735061

Cardiff G.C. (18)
Cardiff (0222) 753067

Dinas Powis G.C. (18)
Dinas Powis (0222) 512157

Glamorganshire G.C. (18)
Penarth (0222) 707048

Llanishen G.C. (18)
Lisvare, Nr Cardiff
(0222) 752205

Radyl G.C. (18)
Radyl (0222) 842442

RAF St. Athan G.C. (9)
St. Athan (0446) 751043

Wenvoe Castle G.C. (18)
Cardiff (0222) 591094

Whitchurch (Cardiff) G.C. (18)
Cardiff (0222) 620125

WEST GLAMORGAN
Clyne G.C. (18)
Swansea (0792) 401989

Fairwood Park G. & C.C. (18)
Swansea (0792) 203648

Glynneath G.C. (9)
Glynneath (0639) 720452

Inco G.C. (13)
Clydach (0792) 844216

Langland Bay G.C. (18)
Langland Bay (0792) 66023

Morriston G.C. (18)
Swansea (0792) 71079

Neath G.C. (18)
Neath (0639) 3615

Palleg G.C. (9)
Glantawe (0639) 842193

Pennard G.C. (18)
Southgate, Nr Swansea
(044128) 3131

Pontardawe G.C. (18)
Swansea (0792) 863118

Swansea Bay G.C. (18)
S/Lewes (0792) 812198/814153

One of the first jokes that an English Schoolboy learns is "how do you get two whales in a mini?" (Answer) – "Cross the Severn Bridge". For golfers the act of crossing the famous bridge usually means one thing – **The St Pierre Golf and Country Club** at **Chepstow**.

St. Pierre has only been in existence for 25 years. **Mr Bill Graham** founded the Club in **1961** with the **Ken Cotton** designed **Old Course** being opened the following May. The first thing to strike one at St. Pierre is the setting: quite simply magnificent. The golf course occupies land that was originally a deer park and it has an abundance of mature trees. There is also a lake covering eleven acres situated in the heart of the course. Whilst the 'Old' Course is understandably St. Pierre's 'pride and joy', there are of course 36 holes, with a second eighteen, the **New Course** opened in **1975**.

Mr Terry Cleary is the **Golf Secretary** at St. Pierre, he may be contacted by telephone on (02912) 5261. All written correspondence should be addressed to **The Secretary, St. Pierre Golf and Country Club, St. Pierre Park, Chepstow, Gwent NP6 6YA**. The Club's professional, **Renton Doig**, can also be contacted via the above telephone number.

Visitors wishing to arrange a game at St. Pierre must book starting times in advance. Other than proof of handicap there are no general restrictions on times of play. The **green fees** as set in April 1986 are as follows: £14.50 for a round over the **Old Course** during the week, £17.50 at the weekend, with £10 and £12 payable for a game on the New Course at similar periods. For those wishing to play a round over both courses the fees are £19 Mondays to Friday, £21 at the weekend. For junior golfers a single round on the Old Course is priced at £8 with £6 purchasing a game on the New. Both courses are extremely popular with Golfing Societies and prior arrangements can be made with the Secretary. Societies are normally received during the week.

Travelling to St. Pierre ought to present few problems. The Golf Club is located to the South of Chepstow off the **A48**. The M4 links Chepstow to **Cardiff** and **Swansea** in the west and to **London** and **Bristol** in the east. The **M4** should be left at exit 22, the **A446** then taken into Chepstow where the **A48** can be joined and followed to St. Pierre. The best route for those approaching from **Birmingham** and the north of England is probably to travel south on the **M5** leaving at exit **8**, thereafter picking up the **M50** to **Ross-on-Wye**. From Ross-on-Wye a combination of the **A40** and **A466** provides a pleasant drive through the Wye Valley to Chepstow.

The Old and the New Course differ quite considerably in length. The Old is the Championship Course and from the back tees it measures 6700 yards,(par 71). The forward tees reduced the length to 6285 yards, while for the ladies it measures 5718 yards, (par 73). The respective distances for the New course are 5762 yards (par 68), 5593 yards and 5214 yards (par 70). Despite being a relatively young course St. Pierre has staged a number of major professional events, notably the **Dunlop Masters** and the **Silk Cut Masters**. Winners have included **Bernhard Langer, Tony Jacklin** and **Greg Norman**, who on his way to victory in 1982 drove the 362 yard tenth with a 3 wood. In **1980** the **Curtis Cup** was held at St. Pierre. The 18th hole on the Old Course is one of the most famous finishing holes in golf – a par **3** measuring **237** yards, it requires a brave tee shot across the edge of the lake, with large trees lining the left hand side of the fairway. Behind the green is the beautiful St. Pierre Hotel.

The Hotel is in fact a former 14th century country mansion and it serves the golfer as a particularly impressive 19th. In addition to an excellent restaurant which offers breakfasts, lunches and dinners, there are four bars. Celebrating at the end of a round is always to be recommended – particularly if the 18th hole has been tackled successfully. Share a thought though for a person by the name of Arwyn Griffiths who came to the 18th needing a three for a gross 63. A few minutes later he walked off the green having taken eleven strokes – even he celebrated though, for he still won the competition!

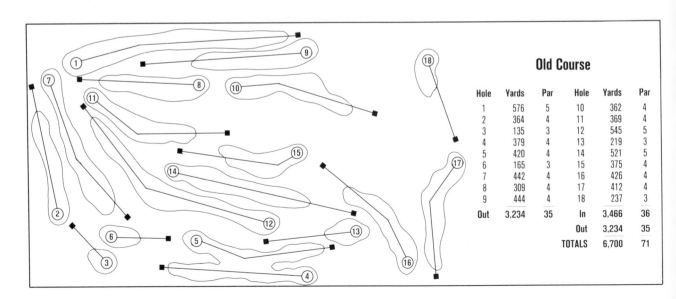

Old Course

Hole	Yards	Par	Hole	Yards	Par
1	576	5	10	362	4
2	364	4	11	369	4
3	135	3	12	545	5
4	379	4	13	219	3
5	420	4	14	521	5
6	165	3	15	375	4
7	442	4	16	426	4
8	309	4	17	412	4
9	444	4	18	237	3
Out	3,234	35	In	3,466	36
			Out	3,234	35
			TOTALS	6,700	71

ROYAL PORTHCAWL

By common consent **Royal Porthcawl** is not only the finest course in Wales, it is one of the greatest Championship links in the British Isles. Like many famous Clubs Porthcawl's beginnings were rather humble. The Club was founded in June **1891** and the following year a nine hole course was laid out on a patch of common land known as **Lock's Common**, consent having been given by the local parish vestry. Having to share the 'course' with amongst other things cattle soon frustrated the Members and a second nine holes were sought. These they found on the present site closer to the shore. By **1898** Locks Common was abandoned altogether and the 'favoured' second nine holes were extended to a full eighteen. Once settled the Club prospered and in 1909 patronage was bestowed upon the Club. Royal Porthcawl had well and truly arrived.

The Members were extremely fortunate in finding this new home for today Royal Porthcawl is not only considered to be one of Britain's finest golfing challenges but also one of its most beautifully situated. Every hole on the course provides a sight of the sea, and from many points there are spectacular views across the Bristol Channel to the distant hills of Somerset and North Devon.

Presently presiding over the Royal domain is the Club's helpful Secretary, **Squadron Leader D W Samuel**; he may be contacted by telephone **(065671) 2251**. The professional **Graham Poor** can be reached on **(065671) 6984**. Golfers wishing to visit Royal Porthcawl can expect a warm welcome. Subject to possessing a Golf Club handicap there are no general restrictions, however, being an understandably popular Club prior telephoning is advisable. Those wishing to organise Golfing Society Meetings should either telephone or preferably address a written application to the Secretary at **The Royal Porthcawl Golf Club, Porthcawl, Mid Glamorgan, Wales**. Tuesdays and Thursdays are the usual Society days.

The **green fees** at Royal Porthcawl for 1986 were set at **£12** per day during the week with **£14** payable at weekends. A rather novel and most encouraging policy is adopted towards junior golfers. Junior Members of the Club can introduce an 'outside' junior during the week for a green fee of **£1**.

The course is situated approximately 15 miles east of Swansea and about 20 miles west of Cardiff. The **M4** makes travelling to Porthcawl fairly straightforward. Approaching from either east or west the motorway should be left at **junction 37**; thereafter the **A4229** can be followed into Porthcawl. The course's precise location is towards the northern end of the town.

In the opening paragraph Porthcawl was described as a 'links'. This isn't perhaps entirely accurate for although much of the course is certainly of a links nature, certain parts are more strictly downland and heathland in character. Certainly there aren't the massive sandhills that feature so prominently on the great Championship links of Lancashire, and which are indeed to be found at neighbouring **Pyle and Kenfig**. The absence of sandhills means there is no real protection from the elements on stormy days and when the winds blow fiercely Porthcawl can be as tough a challenge as one is likely to meet.

From its Championship tees the course stretches to **6605** yards (par **72** sss**74**) while from the medal tees it measures **6409** yards (par **72**) with the ladies playing over **5682** yards (par **75**). Good scores at Porthcawl (the course record stands at **65**) are likely to be fashioned on the first ten holes; from the tough par 3 11th inwards there are some very difficult holes. The second shot from the fairway on the dog-leg 13th is one not to be hurried, the views out across the course are quite breathtaking. The 15th and 16th are two quite lengthy par fours and the round ends with a glorious downhill finishing hole.

Royal Porthcawl has staged the **Amateur Championship** four times since the last War and it returns once more in 1988. In 1987 the **Welsh Amateur Championship** will be held at Porthcawl.

As for its 19th Porthcawl has a splendid Clubhouse. There is an informal Men's Bar where spikes may be worn, a mixed lounge (jacket and tie after 7 p.m.) and a Dining Room (jacket and tie at all times). Both lunches and dinners can be arranged with prior notice, and light snacks are offered at all times excepting Sundays.

One final thought for those wishing to explore the delights of Royal Porthcawl, I beg you to consider carefully before deciding to visit late on a November's afternoon: as the light fades and a mist starts to descend upon the links the ghost of the Maid of Sker walks the 17th fairway – you have been warned!

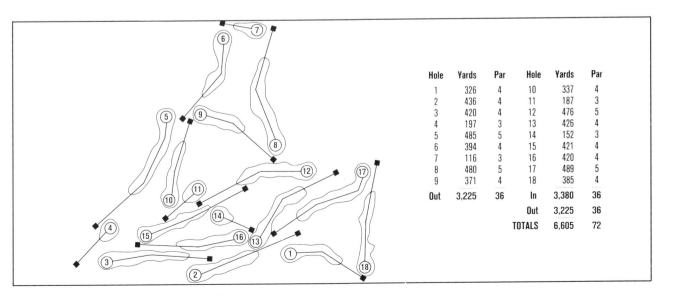

Hole	Yards	Par	Hole	Yards	Par
1	326	4	10	337	4
2	436	4	11	187	3
3	420	4	12	476	5
4	197	4	13	426	4
5	485	5	14	152	3
6	394	4	15	421	4
7	116	3	16	420	4
8	480	5	17	489	5
9	371	4	18	385	4
Out	3,225	36	In	3,380	36
			Out	3,225	36
			TOTALS	6,605	72

DYFED AND POWYS

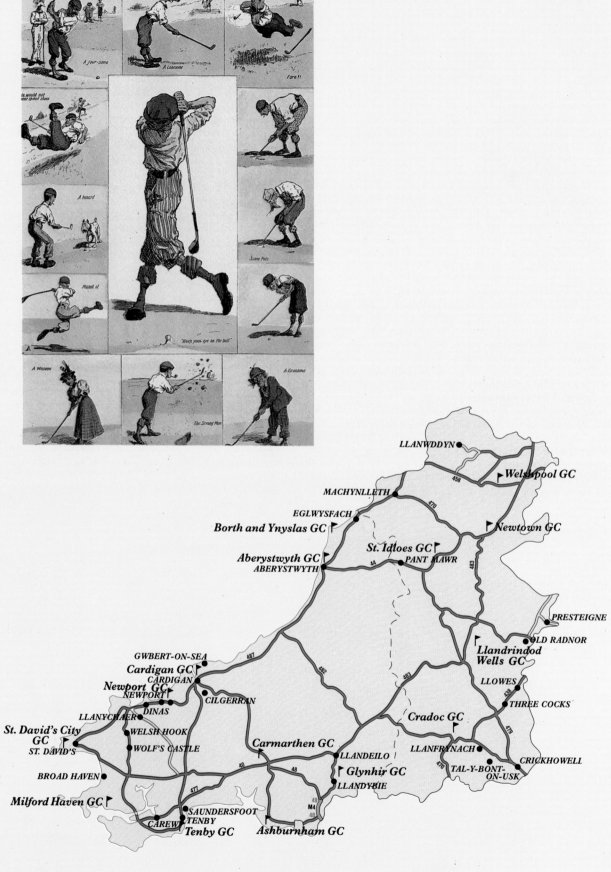

LLANWDDYN

Welshpool GC

MACHYNLLETH

EGLWYSFACH

Borth and Ynyslas GC

St. Idloes GC

Newtown GC

Aberystwyth GC
ABERYSTWYTH

PANT MAWR

PRESTEIGNE

OLD RADNOR

Llandrindod
Wells GC

GWBERT-ON-SEA

Cardigan GC
CARDIGAN

Newport
GC
NEWPORT

LLOWES

THREE COCKS

CILGERRAN

LLANYCHAER

DINAS

Cradoc GC

St. David's City
GC
ST. DAVID'S

WELSH HOOK

WOLF'S CASTLE

Carmarthen GC

LLANFRYNACH

CRICKHOWELL

LLANDEILO

BROAD HAVEN

Glynhir GC

TAL-Y-BONT-
ON-USK

LLANDYBIE

Milford Haven GC

SAUNDERSFOOT

49
M4
48

CAREW

TENBY

Tenby GC

Ashburnham GC

A.B. FROST "*Golfing Incidents*" ROSENSTIELS

GLIFFAES

A thoroughly charming Victorian country house hotel, Gliffaes
boasts fine gardens and parkland within its 29 acres. Breakfast is
served from a sideboard, lunch from a basket. Dinner is table
d'hote. In fact, country house standards of the old order are
carefully maintained by rsident owners all of the Brabner family
who have held sway here since 1948. There are 19 bedrooms all
with their own bathing facilities; the more lavish having a good
private bathroom. External facilities include fishing for salmon
and trout in the part of the Usk which the hotel overlooks,
tennis, bowls, putting and croquet, childen are welcome. The
hotel is justly proud of its in house cooking and remains open
from the middle of March to the end of the year.

GLIFFAES
Crickhowell,
Powys, Wales.
Tel: (0874) 730371

For every person in New Zealand there are 23.8 sheep. Regrettably I don't have the figures for Dyfed and Powys but I suspect they're fairly similar. The 'bad news' is that the lack of human beings is unfortunately reflected by a low number of top class golf courses (unlike in New Zealand it should be said). However, the 'good news' is that even during the summer months most of the courses remain relatively uncrowded and the green fees tend to be cheaper than in most parts of Britain.

The two Championship courses in this area lie on Dyfed's southern coast, some 30 miles apart. Both **Ashburnham** and **Tenby** were founded before the turn of the century and each has staged more than one **Welsh Amateur Championship** Ashburnham in fact being a regular venue.

Located one mile west of Burry Port, Ashburnham's links is fairly close to industrial South Wales which I suppose extends as far as Llanelli, or at least to where the **M4** from London fizzles out. The course measures 7,000 yards from the Championship tees and 6,696 yards from the medal tees – certainly not a course for the inexperienced. Connoisseurs of the game, however, should find it an excellent challenge and for a fee of **£10** per day during the week and **£10** per round, **£12** per day at weekends the Club offers a warm welcome to visitors.

There are more glorious sandy beaches around **Tenby** than one could care to count. There is a story of one five year old boy who raced on to one of these golden stretches arms aloft shouting, "This is the sixth beach I've been on today!" Anyway as well as being a haven for the bucket and spade it is also a wonderful place for a round of golf. Tenby is a true links course with natural sand hazards. A day's golf here in 1986 could be enjoyed for **£7.50** during the week and for **£8.50** at weekends.

Moving westwards along the Dyfed coast the next 18 holes are to be found at **Milford Haven**, a medium-length parkland course to the west of the town. In days of old the former whaling town may well have been a 'haven' but the present day 'landscape in oils' isn't everyone's cup of tea. More attractive is **St. Davids** with its beautiful Cathedral making it the smallest city in Britain. Unfortunately for golfing visitors there is only a modest 9 hole course. 20 miles away at **Newport**, although again only a 9 holer, there is a very fine golf course, and one which offers some tremendous sea views. The Club welcomes visitors at all times.

Leaving 'Little England beyond Wales' and heading still further up the coast, the University town of **Aberystwyth** has an 18 hole course that looks out over Cardigan Bay. More impressive though is **Borth and Ynyslas,** one of the oldest Clubs in Wales. Borth is a superbly-maintained seaside links. A road, the **B4353,** runs right alongside much of the course and is often peppered by golf balls. Taking out insurance before playing Borth is to be recommended.

Inland there is precious little to speak of in Dyfed. Though there is a fairly testing hilltop course at Carmarthen, one which is decidedly better in summer than in winter and an attractive parkland course at Glynhir, near the foothills of the Black Mountain Range. The latter is a particularly friendly Club situated close to the Glynhir Mansion where the first news of Wellington's victory at Waterloo is reputed to have been received by carrier pigeon (must have been a pretty sharp pigeon)!

The golf courses in Powys are few and far between, but those that there are tend to be set amidst some splendid scenery. There is an 18 hole course at **Welshpool** up in the hills near the English border and two interesting 9 hole courses at Newtown (**St Giles**) and at Llanidloes (**St Idloes**) in the quiet of the Cambrian Mountains. The two best courses are probably **Cradoc** and **Llandrindod Wells**. Cradoc is quite a challenging course some 2 miles west of Brecon with views towards the famous Brecon Beacons. Llandrindod is a course good enough to have staged the Welsh Professional Championship. It is an outstandingly pretty moorland course sited on a plateau approximately 1,000 feet above sea level. The Club makes visitors very welcome and the **£5** green fee (**£6** at weekends) represents money well spent.

DYFED & POWYS

"There grew pied wind-flowers and violets,
Daisies, those pearled Arcturi of the earth,
The constellated flower that never sets;
Faint oxslips; tender bluebells, at whose birth
The sod scarce heaved."

This is the sort of inspiration one feels when sitting in the solitude of Dyfed and Powys. Indeed the great poet is not the only one to have been inspired by this place. It is an area of striking variety. On the one hand, the coast line is gorgeously open and boasts some splendid beaches, while in Dyfed, mountains are the dominant feature. In order to get the most from your visit to South Wales it might be an idea to visit some of the following. It would be nigh on impossible to tackle all of them, for on the one hand they are scattered far apart and on the other they provide a curious mixture of hospitality.

If you happen to be journeying from England then one of the best places in which to start your visit is without doubt Crickhowell. **The Bear Hotel (0873) 810408** is particularly friendly and has an interesting history, while **Gliffaes (0874) 730371** is a superb country mansion which proudly overlooks the river Usk – an ideal place to rest or have dinner. Another excellent base from which to explore Mid-Wales is located in **Three Cocks Hotel (04974) 215** in the aptly named Three Cocks. The calm is almost tangible here and this is a splendid place to unwind before an important day's golf. Remaining in the southern part of the region, though in neighbouring Dyfed, The Mill in **Llandybie (0269) 850672**, is really pleasant and the golf course is a mere 400 yards away. Tenby is on the coast and is a well-known holiday area; two of its best hotels are **The Imperial (0834) 3737**, and in nearby Milton, the **Milton Manor** – most friendly **(06467) 398**. Another local favourite is the **St. Brides Hotel, Saundersfoot (0834) 812304** which enjoys superb views of Carmarthen Bay and its restaurant makes the best use of locally captured lobster. Another good hotel which also offers excellent sea food can be found in Broadhaven, **The Druidstone Hotel (043783) 221**. Crab here is the order of the day. Continuing one's trek along the coast one arrives in St David's. A number of excellent hotels can be found here, among them the **St Non's Hotel (0437) 720239** – most comfortable and the **Warpool Court (0437) 720300** – good food. If one should strangely become tired of the coast, try the welcoming Wolf's Castle at **Wolf's Castle (043 787) 225** (pleasant restaurant also). Perhaps the place for golfers who have played somewhat waywardly is the village of Welsh Hook. **Stone Hall (0348) 840212** is the establishment – a small number of bedrooms and an excellent restaurant carries a first rate recommendation.

In Gwbert-on-Sea, near Cardigan, the **Cliff Hotel** is a comfortable place to stay at, while the **Rhyd-y-Wen (0239) 612742** is a particularly worthwhile place to endeavour to find, some rooms are available and the restaurant is excellent.

Further round the coast to Chancery, near Aberystwyth, and the **Conrah Country Hotel (0970) 617941** has an excellent hillside setting and pleasant bedrooms. Before one returns to Powys, the 16th century **Ynyshir Hall (065474) 209** is worth inspecting – a beautiful bird sanctuary is an added attraction, the hotel can be found in Eglwysfach.

Back in Powys and Machynlleth, the **Wynnstay** is a convenient base for exploring. Further North in LLanwddyn a shooting Lodge named **Lake Vyrnwy (069 173) 244** is a pleasant place to stay and the restaurant is also recommended. If you have had a tiring round at St Idloes then the aptly named Pant Mawr offers the cosy **Glansevern Arms (05515) 240**. If Welshpool is your selected course, then the **Royal Oak (0938) 2217** offers a bed for the night while in nearby Newtown the **Bear Hotel (0686) 26964** provides the ideal atmosphere for a pre-match kip. Returning south and to Dyfed, the **Cawdor Arms (0558) 823500** at Llandeilo is promisingly peaceful – and has breathtaking scenes of the river Towy. If this leaves you uninspired I'm afraid today's round must have been quite appalling. Perhaps the answer is to have a few 'swifties' or a good nosh.

Good food is certainly obtainable in Crickhowell, not merely at Gliffaes but also at the **Nantyffin Cider Mill (0873) 810775** – good food complemented by a first class wine list. **The Star** at Tal-y-Bont on Usk is an ideal place for a snack and a drink as is **The Harp (054421) 655** at Old Radnor – you can stay and many people do. (If an hotel is more to your liking then the **Radnorshire Arms (0544) 267406** at Presteigne could be the answer). Another local with a lively reputation for food can be found at Llanfrynach – **The White Swan**.

Dyfed also has its fair share of fayre. **The Swan** at Broadhaven has an idyllic location and a good restaurant. Other establishments to consider include the contradictory **Sailors Safety** and the **Ship Aground** at Dinas. The **Golden Lion** at Newport and the **Black Lion** and the **Halfway Inn** at Aberystwyth. The latter named establishment is apparently the only pub in the world where you pour your own ale from casks on your side of the bar – the landlord did not explain whether the ale was on the house. If you are still hungry then the very best solution is to visit **The Pantry (0239) 820420**. Failing the Pantry, try The Kitchen – **The Castle Kitchen (0239) 615055**, an informal but well-run restaurant. I have one last thought on the restaurants in the area and that's Cobblers, but before you take offence, try out **The Cobblers, (0269) 850540** – a friendly restaurant making the best of some delightfully fresh produce.

Still uninspired – well, there's only one thing for it – give up golf. You've become a bore, old boy! But what about the old girl! Well, she's had a wonderful time sniffing out some superb antique shops and visiting numerous castles hidden in the Welsh countryside. Welshpool was particularly impressive by all accounts. The children enjoyed the beaches and The Vale of Rheid's railway trip and slept soundly every night. And you – you old grump – didn't have an inspired time. Before you next play, read a little Shelley – it might inspire your swing!

St Brides Hotel
St Brides Hill, Saundersfoot,
Tel: (0834) 812304
A truly excellent hotel, enjoying panoramic views of the harbour and Carmarthen Bay. The hotel, amongst other things, offers golfing packages as well as a wide variety of 'Mini Weekend' and 'Midi Week' breaks throughout the year, ideal for a golfing vacation in Wales.

Lake Vyrnwy Hotel
Llanwddyn, via Oswestry
Tel: (069173) 244
If you are not Welsh then you may have trouble in pronouncing this hotel's name but trouble is the last thing you will have when staying at Lake Vyrnwy. The view from the hotel is superb and its cuisine is excellent. The hotel has the sole fishing rights on the lake and extensive shooting rights.

HEREFORD & WORCESTER AND SHROPSHIRE

Hill Valley GC

WHITCHURCH

495

OSWESTRY

HAWKSTONE PARK GC

483 53 41

Llanymynech GC

LLANYBLOOWEL *Oswestry GC* 49 WESTON UNDER REDCASTLE

5

458

Shifnal GC

SHREWSBURY

Shrewsbury GC 7 5 4 M54 SHIFNAL

Bridgnorth GC

458 *Patshull Park GC*

Church Stretton GC CARDINGTON CLAVERLEY

CHURCH STRETTON BRIDGNORTH

442

Ludlow GC BELBROUGHTON

LUDLOW HOPTON 448 BROMSGROVE

WAFERS 4

449 M5 38

ABBERLEY 5

441

Kington GC WORCESTER 6 422

44 44

KINGTON *Worcester GC* 7

4112 WEOBLEY

Herefordshire GC MALVERN WELLS

4103 GREAT MALVERN

TILLINGTON COLWALL *Worcestershire* *Broadway GC*

HEREFORD 438 *GC* 435

WOOLHOPE BROADWAY

49 ROSS-ON-WYE *Ross-on-*

WILTON *Wye GC*

SYMONDS YAT WEST

A.B. FROST "Brassy Lie" ROSENSTIELS

...ce the residence of William the ...nqueror's nephew, Grafton has a long ...d distinguished history. The present ...nor was built in 1567 but records show ...t the Manor of Grafton predates this by ...east 600 years.

...was Sir John Talbot, Earl of Shrewsbury, ...o commissioned the present building ...d it remained the family seat until 1710, ...en the Manor was severely damaged by ... The house was rebuilt over the next ...years to its original form, the addition ...he ornate ceiling and impressive Coat ...Arms over the fireplace in the Great ...lour perhaps illustrating that every cloud ...s indeed have a silver lining.

...1980, the Manor opened to the public ...the first time as a country house ...taurant. This concept, under the ...sonal direction of the Morris family who ...ve lived at Grafton since 1945, has now ...wn into a small, stylish country house ...el. Set in 26 acres of glorious ...rcestershire countryside, the Manor ...ers a peaceful home in the Heart of ...gland.

...the rooms have been individually ...corated under the personal supervision ...he proprietors and all feature period ...niture and open fires, as well as ensuite ...hrooms, colour television, trouser-press ...d direct-dial telephone.

...e grounds are a major feature at ...afton, the six acres of beautiful gardens ...viding the ideal setting for a relaxing ...-dinner stroll. The large formal herb ...den provides essential raw materials for ...restaurant kitchens, as does the 16th ...tury fish stew. There is also a ...corative water garden and a 15th ...tury private chapel.

...addition to the excellent coarse fishing in ...own two acre lake, there are two ...arby 18-hole golf courses for the more ...ergetically inclined. The internationally ...owned Avoncroft Museum of Buildings ...lose to the hotel and Worcester ...thedral or Stratford with the Royal ...akespeare Theatre are both less than ...ty minutes drive away. The Royal ...rcester Porcelain works and the Royal ...erley Crystal factory both provide an ...eresting and different day trip.

...afton, where the Morris family will ...lcome you to their home, is the ideal ...tel for your visit to the Heart of England.

Grafton Manor,
Grafton Lane, Bromsgrove,
Worcestershire B61 7HA
Telephone:(0527) 31525

Until the powers-that-be interfered with the old county boundaries it used to be said that from the summit of Worcestershire Beacon, the highest point of the Malverns, you could sight fifteen different counties. People obviously had excellent vision in those days but in any event on a clear day the Malverns certainly provide commanding views over much of Hereford and Worcester and across to neighbouring Shropshire.

Bordering the Principality, the region is arguably the most peaceful in England. It is an area of rich pastures and cider orchards, of small market towns rather than crowded cities and encompasses not only the **Malverns** but the beautiful **Wye Valley** and **Vale of Evesham**. Truly a green and pleasant land.

In terms of golf courses the area is a little thin on the ground. However, it is one that has seen much recent development and a growing number of Clubs are gaining considerable reputations – **The Hill Valley Golf and Country Club** is a prime example. Designed in the mid-70's by **Dave Thomas** and **Peter Alliss** it is based on American Country Clublines with a Clubhouse that provides first class facilities and a course where water affects several of the holes. It is located about a mile north of **Whitchurch** not far from the Shropshire/Cheshire border. Green fees for 1987 are **£7.50** during weekdays and **£11** at weekends.

Moving further south in Shropshire, **Hawkstone Park** thanks to the exploits of **Sandy Lyle** now needs no introduction (and besides is featured a few pages on).

Two of the county's more undulating courses are **Oswestry** and **Llanymynech**. Both lie to the west of the **A5** and close to the Welsh border. A unique feature of the latter is that on the fourth hole you stand on the tee in Wales and drive into England (always good for the ego). It is also the Club where **Ian Woosnam** another of Britain's Ryder Cup players improved his game.

For a weekday fee of **£8**, **£10** at weekends, visitors are welcomed at the **Shrewsbury** Golf Club. Located some five miles south of the County Town off the **A49**, it is a newish but interesting course with a railway track running through the middle. Travelling a little further down the **A49** into southern Shropshire, **Church Stretton**, set amidst the Long Mynd Hills, is well worth a visit. Not the longest course in Britain, but one that offers quite outstanding views.

Shifnal, to the east of Telford is a fairly popular place for Societies – not all that surprising really: the course is set in a glorious park with an old manor house acting as an impressive 19th. The Society days are Tuesdays, Wednesdays and Fridays but individual visitors are welcome at all times, fees being **£7.50** per day.

Bridgnorth is one of the oldest and longest courses in the county and is known for its excellent greens, as is **Ludlow**. Ludlow itself is one of those sleepy towns miles from anywhere, but if you want to get away from it all and are happy to enjoy a flutter on the nags as well as a game of golf it's the tops – the course takes you around the race track (or is it vice versa?)

Before leaving Shropshire, **Patshull Park** certainly deserves a mention – though it's not all that clear whether the course belongs to this county or not. Despite being much closer to the country's industrial heart it is none-the-less a most tranquil spot. It is under the same ownership as Hawkstone Park and possesses similar luxurious facilities. The golf course is a new creation, designed by **John Jacobs** and a very popular place for Societies and Company Days.

Heading into Hereford and Worcester, a number of delightfully scenic courses are again to be found though many are quite hidden away. To the North West of Hereford **Kington** and **Herefordshire** Golf Club are two typical examples. The latter is located off the **A480**. Visitors are welcome though a telephone call is advisable. Green fees for 1986 were set at **£6** for weekdays, **£7** for weekends. Kington is further towards Wales and is reputed to be the highest course in either country. Well worth a visit and where poor golf can always be blamed on the rarefied atmosphere.

The **Worcester Golf and Country Club** is situated only a mile or so from the centre of the beautiful Cathedral City, off the **A4103**. Visitors are welcome to play this parkland course during weekdays, though must accompany Members at weekends.

The oldest course in the county, and quite possibly the finest, is aptly named **The Worcestershire Golf Club**. It is located two miles south of Great Malvern close to the **A449/B4209** junctions. Visitors are able to play during weekdays and at weekends after 10am. The green fees payable in 1986 were **£9.50** (weekdays) and **£11.50** (weekends) with cheaper rates for juniors. From the course there are extensive views towards the Malverns, the Severn Valley and the Cotswolds.

About 15 miles further down the **A449** from Malvern is the **Ross-on-Wye Golf Club**. It is set in the heart of the glorious Wye Valley but surprisingly only one mile from the **M50** (junction 4).

Last but not least, **Broadway Golf Club**. Last in as much as strictly speaking we have now crossed the border into Gloucestershire – the course being a mile and a half or so from "the loveliest village in England". Those wishing to visit are advised to telephone before setting off. The fees for 1986 were **£10** during weekdays, **£12** at weekends, with considerable reductions for juniors. True to form there are again some marvellous views – this time looking out across the splendid Vale of Evesham.

HEREFORD & WORCESTER, SHROPSHIRE

A hush descends as you ponder your first swing in Worcestershire. Apple and cherry trees are in blossom and in the distance a herd of white faced Herefords appraise your stance. You're fortunate for several hundred years ago the air was thick with the clatter of sword against sword but now there is peace. Crack. Straight down the fairway – the echo resounds and then dies: you're on your way. While the heart of England may not be the centre point of golf in the British Isles there are without doubt some of the country's most established drinking and eating establishments as well as some first rate hotels and inns. The neighbouring counties' entertainment appeals for their beautiful walks, hunting and shooting are all popular in this area. The hotel restaurants are particularly good and there should be no excuse for poor play– comfort, quiet and excellent local produce will combine to make an excellent visit.

In order to maximise your drive, the following hotels are thoroughly recommended, for differing reasons. In Broadway **The Lygon Arms (0386) 852255** with its outstanding frontage is excellent as is its restaurant, accommodation and cooking (note the puddings) can be found in the **Collin House Hotel (0386) 858354**, Broadway. If you wish to explore the county towns then Worcester's **Giffard Hotel (0905) 27155** is an excellent starting place, no hotel enjoys such fine views of the Cathedral. If Hereford should be your particular choice then the **Green Dragon Hotel (0432) 272506** is charming – four poster lovers, note well. Finally, in Shrewsbury the **Prince Rupert Hotel (0743) 52461** is good value and the oak beams and sloping floors add charm. One hotel to contemplate while visiting Shropshire is the Stretton Hall Hotel (0694) 723224 at Church Stretton which is good value and comfortable without being grand. Perhaps the obvious choice for people who wish to eat, sleep, drink as well as play golf is the **Hawkstone Park Hotel (093924) 611**, Weston under Redcastle. Returning south one may contemplate the excellent **Park House Hotel** in Shifnal (0952) **460128** where great attention to detail is made– consider sherry and fruit in your bedroom before an evening in the splendid Idsall Rooms, the hotel's restaurant. In Oswestry, the **Wynnstay (0691) 655261** is a pleasant Georgian coaching inn. However, perhaps the best of all in accommodation and cooking in Shropshire can be found in the former capital of the West Marches, Ludlow – the hotel is **The Feathers (0584) 5261** and it is excellent. One last thought for Shropshire is the **Terrick Hall Hotel**, Whitchurch, convenient after an afternoon at Hill Valley.

Returning South into the Malvern Hills, three excellent stop offs should be made if at all possible. Firstly, the **Colwall Park Hotel (0684) 40206** which is great value and offers a good menu riddled with local produce, secondly the **Foley Arms (06845) 3397**, Great Malvern – a charming nineteenth century coaching inn and finally the **Cottage in the Wood (06845) 3487**, Malvern Wells – another excellent place to have dinner after a day's golf. If one delights in water settings the **Wye Rapids Hotel** at Symonds Yat is ideal. The **Pengethley Hotel (098987) 211** four miles north of Ross-on-Wye is also splendid while the Walford House Hotel (0989) 63829 is tremendous value and houses a really good restaurant (note fish starters). No trip round this area is complete without considering the **Red Lion Inn, (05445) 220/419**, Weobley – a pleasant building which hides an immensely cheerful welcome.

If you want to stay in the vicinity then for goodness' sake don't miss some of the area's excellent restaurants. The **Bell Inn** at Belbroughton and the Grafton Manor (0527) 31525/37247 in Bromsgrove are excellent. Penrho's Court in Kington is convenient for the golf course and the ragout of monkfish is outstanding. A tremendous place to have dinner where some accommodation is also available is **Walmer Lodge, Malvern (06845) 4139**. Meanwhile in nearby Malvern Wells the **Croque-en-Bouche (06845) 65612** offers the area's leading menus – simply outstanding in every way. Finally, in Wilton the **Orles Barn** is well thought of. The restaurants in Shropshire are less distinguished, but the **Haywain** in Bridgnorth (0746) **780404** offers five course menus which may interupt a free flowing swing the next day.

There are numerous country pubs to be found and **The Butchers Arms** at Woolhope is great fun – note the good value accommodation. Meanwhile, **The Bell** at Tillington is ideal for a pint and a snack before, after or during a round (of golf). In Shropshire **The Howard Arms** is good fun while the **Royal Oak** in Cardington is also a friendly establishment. If you stay here – a splendid breakfast will be an ideal forerunner to the day's golf. **The Crown** at Hopton Wafers offers excellent home cooking and a good drop of ale while to the West **The Horseshoe** at Llanyblodwel has a splendid setting and is ideal for the golf course.

The underlying pre-occupation of visitors to these parts is walking. One can amble through the Forest of Dean, the Malvern Hills, the Cotswolds and the rolling Welsh border country. It may be that golfers are the world's best walkers and if one is short of the odd golf course, why not just grab a club and let fly into the hills. Market towns abound and excellent local meals and fruit can be purchased. Worcester is home of the Royal Worcester Porcelain Works – which is worth a visit, while in contrast Ironbridge serves as a unique monument to the industrial revolution. Theatres at Great Malvern and Worcester (0905) 27322 are splendid and the half-timbered streets of Shrewsbury houses some excellent shops. Attingham Park west of Shropshire's county town is open between April and October and is well worth a visit. Hereford's Museum of Cider is a fitting monument to this drink tha engenders so much red into the smiles of the welcoming locals. Lower Broadheath houses the birthplace of Edward Elgar and the pomp of his music is a fitting tribute to this quiet but quite beautiful area of Britain. The walking golfer will do well to visit here to play and partake of some of these pleasures. Thomas Parr (Old Parr) was a Ludlow lad who died at the age of 152. (He would have lived longer if he'd stayed in these parts but Charles I had him taken to London and that killed him.)

The Feathers
Bull Ring,
Ludlow, SY8 1AA
Tel: (0584) 5261
Renowned for its Jacobean facade, the hotel is a focal point of one of England's most beautiful and historic towns. The Feathers itself is renowned for its hospitality and the quality of its fresh country food. In short, an ideal place to stay when golfing in Shropshire.

Grafton Manor
Grafton Lane, Bromsgrove,
Worcs., B61 7HA
Tel: (0527) 31525/37247
A stylish hotel provides the ideal place for a visit to the heart of England. Imaginative menus complemented by a fine wine list served in the elegant dining room. Luxuriously styled bedrooms retain the grace of years gone by. Surrounded by countryside yet only minutes from the M5.

SANDY LYLE

Born Shrewsbury, 9.2.58.
Ht: 6′1″. Wt: 13st 5lb. Turned
Pro: 1977. "When Tony
(Jacklin) won in 1969
at Royal Lytham and St Annes I was in the grandstand
next to the 18th green. He threw the ball high into the air
in his moment of triumph and I was only a few feet away
from catching it. I thought then how nice it would be to
some day emulate Tony."

Sandy, of course, did emulate Jacklin when he won the
Open Championship, the most prestigious prize on offer
to any British player, at Royal St George's last July. That
victory elevated Lyle to superstar status.

Sandy is now a truly international player with significant
wins in Japan, Hawaii and more recently the USA where in
April he captured the Greensboro Open and finished a
creditable 11th in the US Masters the following week.

Having finished 1985 atop the European money list
with record earnings of £162,552 Sandy is currently
ranked in the top half dozen players in the world on the
Sony Rankings.

THE FEATHERS

It is surely impossible to explore the history of Ludlow and the beautiful surrounding countryside without stumbling across the famous Feathers Hotel.

It seems that the name originates from as long ago as 1616 when Prince Charles (son of James I) visited Ludlow Castle. At that time Ludlow was the seat of the Lord President of Wales and the Council of the Marches. Indeed, the 17th century was probably the most prosperous period in Ludlow's history.

In 1870, the Feathers was bought by Robert Edwards for the grand sum of £1,950. Whilst old brochures from the 1920's show how a dinner for two, including champagne, could cost less than £1.00!

The 'Royal' flavour of the Inn is continued to the present day and the principal apartments include the Richard III Restaurant, James I Lounge, Edward IV Writing Room and the Prince Charles Banqueting Suite.

With its magnificently half-timbered frontage and richly decorated interior, the Feathers is one of the most elegant and relaxing Inns in Britain.

The Feathers Hotel,
Ludlow,
Shropshire.
(0584) 5261

The three members of the Great Triumvirate who dominated golf at the turn of the century; **Harry Vardon, James Braid** and **John H Taylor**, each left his mark on the game in an immeasurable number of ways; each also became uniquely associated with a particular Golf Club, so much so that it is often difficult to dissociate one from the other. It is almost impossible to talk of Ganton without mentioning Harry Vardon; it is almost impossible to talk of Walton Heath without mentioning James Braid and it probably is impossible to talk of Westward Ho! without mentioning John H Taylor. And so it has become with **Hawkstone Park** and **Sandy Lyle**. The 1985 Open Champion not only learnt his game at Hawkstone Park, he practically grew up there with his father Alex as the Club's Professional.

Hawkstone Park is, of course, much more than the 'birth-place' of Sandy Lyle. There are two 18 hole courses, the **Hawkstone** and the **Weston** and they are set in the beautiful grounds of the Hawkstone Park Hotel (described in a guide book of 1824 as "more like the seat of a nobleman than an Hotel").

The hotel runs the golf courses and although there are no general restrictions on visitors, starting times must be pre-booked: this can be done either by telephoning the Hotel on **(093924) 611** or by contacting the professional shop on **(093924) 209**. Parties of twelve or more are deemed to be golfing societies, subject again to making prior arrangements. They are equally welcome and written applications may be made in writing to the **Banqueting Manager, Hawkstone Park Hotel, Weston-under-Redcastle, Nr Shrewsbury SY4 5UY**.

Green fees for 1986 to play on the Hawkstone course were priced at **£12.50** per day during the week, and **£15** at weekends, while the fees for the shorter Weston course were **£9** midweek,

£10 at weekends. On paying the green fee, the above sums in addition to entitling a day's golf will also purchase a voucher worth £2.50, (whatever you do don't lose it – it comes in very handy at the end of the day!) One brief introduction – **Keith Williams** is the Hawkstone professional (Alex Lyle having recently retired).

It has been said that one of the reasons for Hawkstone Park enjoying such a delightfully peaceful setting is that it is 'miles from anywhere' – not strictly true: it is only seven miles south of **Whitchurch**, or if you prefer, 12 miles north of **Shrewsbury**. The **A49** is the best route when approaching from either of these towns. Shrewsbury itself is linked to the West Midlands essentially by way of the **M54** and the **A5**, while those motoring from the north may find the **M6** of assistance.

At **6465** yards (par **72**) from the medal tees the Hawkstone course is 1,000 yards longer than the Weston (**5368** yards, par **66**), both courses, however, are maintained in superb condition and if possible a round over both should be attempted. In need hardly be added that Sandy Lyle holds the Hawkstone course record at **67**, achieved while still an amateur.

I earlier begged the visitor not to lose his £2.50 voucher. The 19th hole is where it can be put to good use. An alternative (or in addition to the Hotel with its restaurant and bars – jacket and tie required) Hawkstone Park also possesses its own pub! – The Hawkstone Arms. **Real** Ales are served and there is the most novel of menus. You may care to consider the 'Cheese Divot', a particularly tasty offering and then there is the 'Woosnam Wedge' (the favourite of many), however, the last word must surely go to Sandy Lyle and with this in mind, the 'Sandy Lyle Sirloin Burger Steak' gets my vote . . . Bon Appétit!

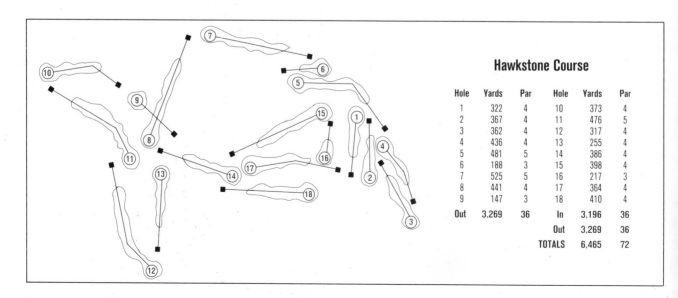

Hawkstone Course

Hole	Yards	Par	Hole	Yards	Par
1	322	4	10	373	4
2	367	4	11	476	5
3	362	4	12	317	4
4	436	4	13	255	4
5	481	5	14	386	4
6	188	3	15	398	4
7	525	5	16	217	3
8	441	4	17	364	4
9	147	3	18	410	4
Out	3,269	36	In	3,196	36
			Out	3,269	36
			TOTALS	6,465	72

THE 6TH: NORTH NIBLEY TO SPOONLEY

GLOUCESTERSHIRE
Broadway G.C. (18)
Broadway (0386) 853561

Cirencester G.C. (18)
Cirencester (0285) 3939

Cleeve Cloud G.C. (18)
Bishops Cleeve, Cheltenham
(024267) 2025

Cleeve Hill G.C. (18)
Bishops Cleeve (024267) 2025

Coleford G.C. (18)
Dean, Coleford (0594) 33689

Cotswold Hills G.C. (18)
Cheltenham (0242) 522421

Gloucestershire Hotel (18+9)
Gloucester (0452) 411331

Lilley Brook G.C. (18)
Cheltenham (0242) 526785

Lydney G.C. (9)
Dean (0594) 42614

Minchinhampton G.C. (18)
Nailsworth, Stroud
(045383) 3866

Painswick G.C. (18)
Painswick (0452) 812180

Stinchcombe Hill G.C. (18)
Dunsley, Stroud (0453) 2015

Tewkesbury G.C. (18)
Tewkesbury (0684) 295405

Westonbirt G.C. (9)
Tetbury (0666) 242

HEREFORDSHIRE
Belmont G.C. (18)
Belmont, Hereford (043274) 445

Herefordshire G.C. (18)
Hereford (0432) 760662

Leominster G.C. (9)
Leominster (0568) 2863

Ross-on-Wye G.C. (18)
Gorsley Ross-on-Wye
(098982) 267

SHROPSHIRE
Bridgnorth G.C. (18)
Bridgnorth (04762) 3315

Church Stretton G.C.
Church Stretton (0694) 722281

Hawkstone Park G.C. (18+18)
Leer Brockhurst, Shrewsbury
(093924) 611

Hill Valley G. & C.C. (18)
Whitchurch (0948) 3584

Kington G.C. (18)
Kington (0544) 230340

Lilleshall Hall G.C. (18)
Telford (0952) 603840

Llanymynech G.C. (18)
Llanymynech, nr Oswestry
(0691) 830542

Ludlow G.C. (18)
Bromfield (058477) 285

Market Drayton G.C. (13)
Market Drayton (0630) 2266

Meole Brace G.C. (9)
Shrewsbury (0743) 64050

Oswestry G.C. (18)
Queens Head (0691) 88221

Shifnal G.C. (18)
Shifnal, Telford
(0952) 460467/460330

Shrewsbury G.C. (18)
Bayston Hill, Shrewsbury
(074372) 2976

Telford Hotel G & C.C. (18)
Telford (0952) 585642

Wrekin G.C. (18)
Telford (0952) 44032

WORCESTERSHIRE
Blackwell G.C. (18)
Blackwell, Bromsgrove
(021) 445 1781

Brand Hall G.C. (18)
Warley (021) 552 7475

Broadway G.C. (18)
Broadway (0386) 853561

Churchill and Blakedown (9)

Kidderminster (0562) 700200

Cocks Moor Woods G.C. (18)
Kings Heath Birmingham
(021) 444 2062

Droitwich G.C. (18)
Droitwich (0905) 770129

Dudley G.C. (18)
Dudley (0384) 53719

Evesham G.C. (9)
Evesham (0386) 860395

Fulford Heath G.C. (18)
Wythall, Birmingham
(0564) 822806/824758

Gay Hill G.C. (18)
Birmingham (021) 430 6523

Habbersley G.C. (9)
Kidderminser (0562) 745756

Hagley G.C. (18)
Stourbridge (562) 883701

Halesowen G.C. (18)
Halesowen, Birmingham
(021) 550 1041

Kidderminster G.C. (18)
(0562) 2303

Kings Norton G.C. (18+9)
Alvechurch (0564) 826789

Lickey Hills G.C. (18)
Birmingham (021) 453 3159

Little Lakes G.C. (9)
Bewdley (0299) 266385

Moseley G.C. (18)
Kingsheath, Birmingham
(021) 444 2115

North Worcesteshire G.C. (18)
Birmingham (021) 475 1026

Pitcheroak G.C. (9)
Redditch (0527) 41054

Rose Hill G.C. (18) Play Over
Lickey Hills)
Birmingham (021) 453 3159

Stourbridge G.C. (18)
Stourbridge (0384) 393062

Tolladine G.C. (9)
Worcester (0908) 21074

Warley G.C. (9)
Birmingham (021) 429 2440

Worcester G. & C.C. (18)
Worcester (0905) 422555

Worcestershire G.C. (18)
Malvern (06845) 5992

WARWICKSHIRE, STAFFORDSHIRE AND THE WEST MIDLANDS

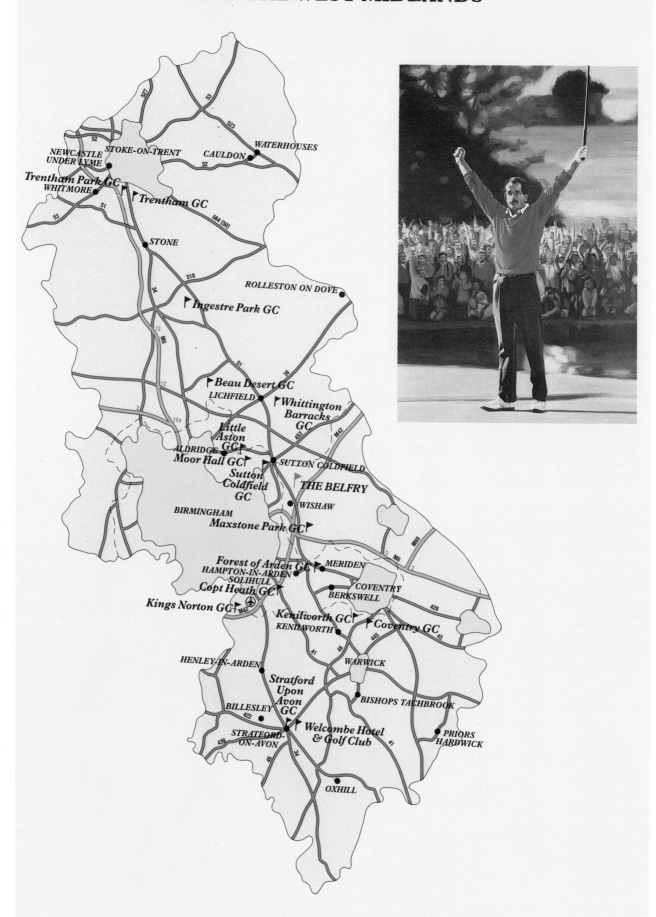

NEWCASTLE UNDER LYME
STOKE-ON-TRENT
CAULDON
WATERHOUSES
Trentham Park GC
WHITMORE
Trentham GC
STONE
ROLLESTON ON DOVE
Ingestre Park GC
Beau Desert GC
LICHFIELD
Whittington Barracks GC
Little Aston GC
ALDRIDGE
Moor Hall GC
SUTTON COLDFIELD
Sutton Coldfield GC
THE BELFRY
WISHAW
BIRMINGHAM
Maxstone Park GC
Forest of Arden GC
MERIDEN
HAMPTON-IN-ARDEN
SOLIHULL
COVENTRY
Copt Heath GC
BERKSWELL
Kings Norton GC
Kenilworth GC
Coventry GC
KENILWORTH
HENLEY-IN-ARDEN
WARWICK
Stratford Upon Avon GC
BISHOPS TACHBROOK
BILLESLEY
STRATFORD-ON-AVON
Welcombe Hotel & Golf Club
PRIORS HARDWICK
OXHILL

P. ADAMS   *"Sam Torrance"*   *P. ADAMS*

ETTINGTON PARK

ETTINGTON PARK,
Alderminster,
Stratford-Upon-Avon,
Warwickshire.
Tel: (0789) 740740

WARWICKSHIRE, STAFFS, & WESTMIDLANDS

Golfers in the City of London have often been known to get frustrated at having to travel many a mile for a decent game of golf. In 1919 one obviously disgusted individual teed up at **Piccadilly Circus** and proceeded to play along **The Strand**, through **Fleet Street** and **Ludgate Hill** firing his last shot at the **Royal Exchange**. Such behaviour is, as far as I'm aware, unknown in **Birmingham** – the **Bull Ring** and the **N.E.C.** in their admittedly shorter existence, have never been peppered with golf balls, this I suspect may be because the needs of its golfing citizens have been properly attended to.

Within a sensible distance (i.e. easy access) of the town centre lie the likes of **The Belfry** and **Little Aston** to the North, **Copt Heath** and **Kings Norton** to the South, with **Sandwell Park** and **Maxstone Park** on either flank. Golfers to the North of Birmingham are indeed particularly fortunate for in addition to The Belfry and Little Aston there is also **Sutton Coldfield** and **Moor Hall**. With the exception of Sutton Coldfield, which is a heathland course, the above are all tree-lined parkland types and provide pleasant retreats from the noise and confusion of England's second largest City.

Despite its relative youth, **The Belfry** (featured on a following page) has become the area's best known golfing attraction thanks largely of course to the European **Ryder Cup** victory there in **1985**. However, **Little Aston** has long been regarded as one of Britain's finest inland courses and has staged numerous major events – both amateur and professional. At Little Aston, as indeed at all of the Birmingham Clubs mentioned, visitors are welcome between Mondays and Fridays though restrictions normally apply at weekends (The Belfry being a notable exception). Green fees tend to range between **£10** and **£13** for a day's golf and at each Club prior telephoning is recommended.

Like Birmingham, the City of Coventry has been removed from Warwickshire and now bears the West Midlands label. **Coventry Golf Club** enjoys a decidely peaceful setting at Finham Park, 2 miles south of the City along the **A444**. To the north west of Coventry at Meriden, the **Forest of Arden Golf and Country Club** offers a pretty stern test, its course measuring close to 7,000 yards. Both welcome visitors in midweek, fees being approximately **£12** per day.

Birmingham and Coventry removed, Warwickshire has been left with only a handful of courses. The county's two most popular towns (tourist wise) are unquestionably **Stratford** and **Warwick**. Whilst Warwick has only a 9 hole course located inside its race track, Shakespeare-spotters who've sneaked the clubs into the boot will be well rewarded. There are two fine 18 hole courses in Stratford, **Stratford Golf Club** and the **Welcombe Hotel Golf Course**. The latter might be said to be particularly welcoming in that visitors can play seven days a week (telephoning advisable at weekends). Fees for a day's golf in 1986 were **£10** during the week, **£12** at weekends. A word also for Kenilworth often described as being at the very centre of England.

Kenilworth Golf Club, just north of the town has a well established and pleasantly undulating parkland course. The Club is one of many due for centenary celebrations in 1987.

Staffordshire certainly doesn't suffer from a shortage of golf courses, indeed in **Whittington Barracks** and **Beau Desert** it has two of the finest (and most attractive) inland courses in the country. The former, located near Lichfield off the **A51**, is a heathland type course with fine views towards the three spires of Lichfield Cathedral. Quite a testing course, visitors should be able to arrange a game between Mondays and Fridays. **Beau Desert Golf Club** near Hazel Slade occupies an unlikely setting in the middle of **Cannock Chase**. Surrounded by fir trees and spruces it is indeed quite a haven. Perhaps a mixture of heathland and woodland, and less testing than Whittington barracks, it is nonetheless equally enjoyable. A day's golf on either course (weekdays only at Whittington Barracks) should set the visitor back between **£10** and **£12**. Both can be very popular and prior telephoning is recommended.

From the heart of Cannock Chase to the heart of the Potteries, there are a number of courses in and around Stoke-on-Trent. **Trentham** and **Trentham Park**, near neighbours to the south of the City, are both well worth a visit particularly perhaps the latter where visitors are welcome throughout the week, fees for 1986 being **£9** midweek, **£11** at weekends.

Finally, in the centre of the county, one of Staffordshire's most recent additions, **Ingestre Park**, is also worth noting and is only a short drive from Stafford along the **A51**. Set in the delightful grounds of Ingestre Hall, the former home of the Earl of Shrewsbury, visitors are welcome between Mondays and Fridays.

Beau Desert G.C.	(05438) 2626
Copt Heath G.C.	(05645) 2650
Coventry G.C.	(0203) 414152
Forest of Arden G. & C.C.	(0676) 22118
Ingestre Park G. & C.C.	(0889) 270061
Kenilworth G.C.	(0926) 54296
Kings Norton G.C.	(0564) 826706
Little Aston G.C.	(021) 353 2066
Maxstone Park G.C.	(0675) 62158
Moor Hall G.C.	(021) 308 6130
Sandwell Park G.C.	(021) 553 4637
Stratford-Upon-Avon G.C.	(0789) 297296
Sutton Coldfield G.C.	(021) 353 2014
The Belfry	(0675) 70301
Trentham G.C.	(0782) 658109
Trentham Park G.C.	(0782) 658800
Welcombe Hotel G.C.	(0789) 295252
Whittington Barracks G.C.	(0543) 4332212

WARWICKSHIRE, STAFFORDSHIRE, AND THE WEST MIDLANDS

One of the delights of editing a title that spans the whole of Britain is that one appreciates the striking variety the country has to offer. As a Formula 3 race is prepared in Birmingham so the curtain comes down at the outstanding Royal Shakespeare Theatre (0789) 295623. There is enormous variety in the world's golf courses, none more so than in Britain. A similar annunciation of delight can be found in the hotels that lie within these shores. Golf is a game enjoyed for business and pleasure and that being so it welcomes a huge range of personalities. One day more on the greens will inevitably follow that disastrous round the day before. But as the sun sets behind the clubhouse the delights of the night and that famous nineteenth hole await you.

One of the most convenient courses at which to play and do pretty much every activity under the sun is **The Belfry (0675) 70301**: nouvelle cuisine, English Fayre, an ivy-clad country manor house and all manner of golfing activities. However, like many of the golf and country clubs demand remains huge and prices are reflected accordingly. Some alternatives you may wish to try in this area are **The Moor Hall Hotel 021-308 3751**, located in the golf course grounds, while the lakeside setting of **Penns Hall 021-351 3111** is an alternative for people not requiring to be a mere chip shot from their beloved fairways every minute of the day and night. Naturally hotels are ideal for other fine golfcourses but alternative hotels to note include **The Fairlawns (0922) 55122**. Aldridge slightly less value than some. And for slightly finer architecture – the spectacular Coventry Cathedral. Outside Coventry and another striking building, this time the Castle of Kenilworth. If you are choosing to stay here then **The Clarendon House (0926) 57668** is an ideal choice. Restaurants abound in the town. The **Restaurant Bosquet** is outstanding **(0926) 52463** while **Romano's (0926) 57473** is a particularly welcoming Italian establishment. Another hotel to consider in the Midlands is the **Manor Hotel, Meriden (0676) 22735**, convenient for the **A43** and the Exhibition Centre. Solihull is surrounded by good golf and has Birmingham on its doorstep, **The George Hotel 021-704 1241** is a modernised coaching inn that is a perfectly adequate place in which to stay. **Liaison** is a pleasant spot to have dinner **021-743 3993**. Another suburb of Birmingham on this occasion Edgbaston provides the restaurant **Sloans 021-455 6697**. Two pleasant and popular pubs to track down when visiting these parts include **The Bear** at Berkwell and another beast on this occasion **The White Lion** in Hampton-in-Arden.

Returning to the mediaeval scene another castle to visit is the simply outstanding Warwick monument. A restaurant to note in the town is **Randolph's (0926) 491292** – delightful. While **The Westgate (0926) 492362** and its restaurant is also well thought of. It is in this area of the region that hotels really flourish which is hardly surprising given the popularity of Shakespeare's Stratford. Here **The Welcombe Hotel (0789) 295252** offers a fine mansion house and restaurant as well as a golfcourse. The gem of the area is without doubt the Ettington Park Hotel

(0789) 740740 – quite majestic, its restaurant is building up an outstanding reputation. In Billesley, **Billesley Manor (0789) 763737** west of Stratford is also outstanding, only pitch and putt on this occasion! A restaurant in the town to note is **Hill's (0789) 293563**. At a totally different end of the market pub food is good at both the **Butcher's Arms** in Prior Hardwick and **The Pheasant** in Oxhill.

People who are doing business in Birmingham, as an increasing number of people seem to be doing, must expect to stay in a modern city-type hotel. **The Albany 021-643 8171** is well thought of, while close to the National Exhibition Centre **The Metropole and Warwick (021) 780 4242** is also good. Perhaps the best word for Birmingham's restaurants is cosmopolitan, a huge range can be sampled, The Albany restaurant **The Four Seasons** is as good as most.

From the city of Birmingham to Lichfield where the Cathedral is glorious. A restaurant is also worth considering. **Thrales (0543) 255091, The Angel Croft (05432) 58737** is a pleasant hotel to note. There is some glorious countryside to be seen in Staffordshire which by the same token is sprinkled with some fairly ordinary towns! The Potteries at Stoke are, however, worth noting – the hotel to note in this traditionally railway town is **The North Stafford (0782) 48501**. Overall, however, the area is not blessed with good hotels, the best plan is to visit Stone where **The Crown Hotel (0785) 813535** is most comfortable and where **Stone House (0785) 815531** is also recommended. **The Star** is a friendly local also in Stone, while in Whitmore **The Mainwaring Arms** does good bar food. The county's greatest delights lie on its west side. In Waterhouses, **The Old Beams (053 86) 254** is a really excellent restaurant while in nearby Cauldon **The Yew Tree** is a splendid public house. Next to the brewing town of Burton one finds Tuthney, here **The Old Dog and Partridge (0283) 813030** is a good inn in which to stay. Leaving the best until last one must consider **The Brookhouse Inn (0283) 814188**, in the delightful Rollestone-on-Dove – an intriguingly converted farmhouse, outstanding but not sadly cheap, as one would expect.

Returning to the Metropolis on this occasion Coventry, once again a whole range of seventeenth century designs. The best if you happen to be on the expense account is the **De Vere (0203) 51851**, particularly comfortable and convenient. Worthwhile restaurants can also be located in Henley-in-Arden, **The Beaudesert (05642) 2675** and in Bishops Tachbrook, **The Mallory Court (0926) 30214** is quite marvellous. There are also some superb bedrooms if you are looking for a quality establishment in which to stay.

It is somewhat unfair to compare Stoke with Stratford – the conclusions are somewhat obvious. But in many fine excursions around Britain's golfcourses it is the variety that makes the occasion – this is certainly true of one's golf and it might just as well be the same for the rest of one's preoccupations.

The Royal Shakespeare Theatre
Waterside,
Stratford-upon-Avon
Tel: (0789) 295623
A 1400 seat theatre where visitors may enjoy outstanding Shakespearian drama. A resident internationally renowned Company performing works of Shakespeare from March to January – 5 different plays each year in repertoire. Joint Artistic Directors Trevor Nunn and Terry Hands.

The Belfry Hotel
Wishaw, Sutton Coldfield,
North Warwickshire, B76 9PR
Tel: (0675) 70301
High quality golf is matched by the hotel itself. French restaurant, snack in the Buttery, luxurious en-suite bedrooms and a whole range of sporting and leisure facilities. It is one of Britain's finest golfing hotels enhanced by a quiet professionalism that ensures a perfect stay.

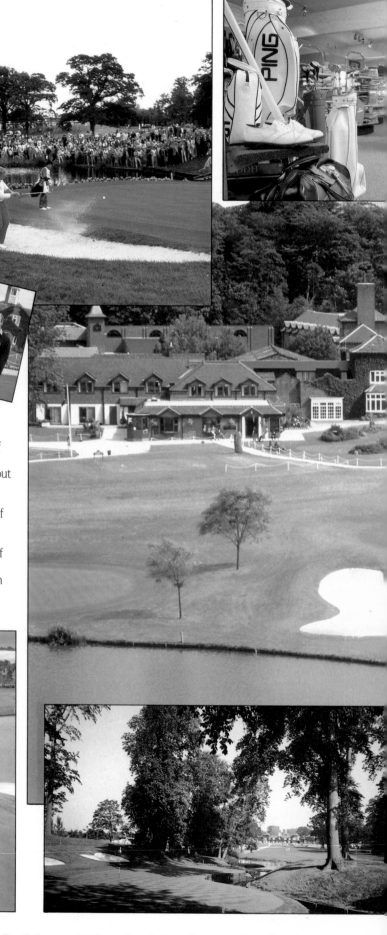

T HE BELFRY is, of course, synonymous with golf. Venue for some of the world's leading tournaments, such as the Hennessy Cognac Cup, State Express Classic, Lawrence Batley International and, of course, scene of the glorious European victory in the 1985 Ryder Cup, it's naturally a mecca for golfers everywhere, and no wonder.

Two 18 hole courses, The Brabazon, par 73 now internationally renowned as one of the foremost tests of golf in the world.

Then there's The Derby, par 70, providing a pleasant, but enjoyable round of golf.

In addition there is a floodlit driving range, open from 7am – 10pm, a spacious golf shop displaying high quality golf clothing and equipment, plus a comfortable Spike Bar.

All in all the golfer's dream, but one where you can make the dreams come true as you follow in the footsteps of the great names of golf – Player, Marsh, Trevino's U.S. team and not forgetting Tony Jacklin's victorious European team in the Ryder Cup.

But there's so much more to The Belfry than just golf.

The setting for example, it's quite idylic, 370 acres of parkland where you could be miles from anywhere. Yet you are literally only half a mile from the motorway, right at the heart of England.

The hotel itself — 4 star luxury in the very best country house tradition, with 168 supremely comfortable bedrooms, each with its own en-suite bathroom, colour t.v., radio, direct dial telephone, hospitality tray and in-house movies.

Then there's the award winning Restaurant, as well as the Garden Room Carvery, both offering fine food and wine with unsurpassed service.

But there's more . . .
The Belfry boasts one of the finest sports and leisure clubs in Britain —

It's the perfect aprés-golf scene, with squash and tennis courts, swimming pool, spa bath, steam room, solariums and saunas, trimnasium and 4-table snooker room — in fact, something for everyone, even its own cafe and bar where you can simply relax and enjoy delicious meals, snacks and drinks.

The newest and most exciting addition to The Belfry is 'Bel Air', a fabulous nite-spot with three bars including a conservatory cocktail bar, overlooking the famous Ballesteros 10th hole, traditional beamed bar and winebar adjoining our Pasta Restaurant 'Spaghetti Junction', plus Rustic Barbecue Terrace.

Here you can dance and drink the night away without even leaving the hotel grounds.

To adopt lawyers' jargon, it is 'beyond any reasonable doubt' that the game of golf was invented in Scotland. A handful of golfing pioneers brought the game south and today with the exception of a few notable areas in the north, where to live is to golf, the sport is almost as popular south of the border.

One cannot help wondering quite what those early pioneers would have made of the 'Belfry project'..... "American-style target gowff".... "and what d'ya mean man-made mounds and lakes!"....."more than 7,000 yards did ya say?".... "Too many whiskies m'friend, you must be out o'your wee mind!"

The 'Belfry project' involved not only a plan to build a Championship course on American lines where in due course the **Ryder Cup** could be staged, but also the siting of a new headquarters for the P.G.A. **Peter Allis** and **Dave Thomas** were given the task of designing the show piece and a very great task it was for the land they were given was flat, uninteresting and comprised one small lake, a stream and numerous acres of potato fields.

Well, the boys didn't hang about: earth mountains were moved, the potatoes disappeared and hundreds of trees were planted – the end result in fact produced two 18 hole courses, opened in June 1977. The feature course was named the **Brabazon**, after Lord Brabazon a former President of the P.G.A. and the shorter, easier course the **Derby**.

Right from its outset the Belfry became the centre of great controversy and some stinging criticism was levelled at the Brabazon. In particular many claimed that the place was still flat and uninteresting and that a sluggers paradise had been created. Some cruelly suggested that by far the best hole on the course was the nineteenth and although some did accept the **10th** to be a good hole, they quickly added that the reason for its have been so often photographed was that it was the only good hole. So what happens?....

In September 1985 the Great Britain and Europe team comes to the Belfry and amidst scenes of near hysteria gives the American side a mighty good walloping to win the Ryder Cup for the first time in nearly thirty years...and, yes you've guessed it..."what a marvellous course!"

A unique feature of the Belfry is that it is a Club without any Members. Both courses open their doors to the general public at all times all the year round. Not surprisingly the Brabazon is particularly busy and before setting off it is best to telephone and book a starting time. The Administration Manager, **Mrs Butler** and the Professional, **Peter McGovern** run the show efficiently. They can be contacted on **(0675) 70301**. Persons wishing to make a written enquiry should address a letter to the Administration Manager at **The Belfry, Lichfield Road, Wishaw, Sutton Coldfield, West Midlands.**

In **1986** the **green fees** payable for a round on the Brabazon course were **£13** for weekdays and **£15** for weekends. This contrasted with **£7.50** for a weekday round on the Derby course and **£9.50** payable at weekends. For the fitter among us intent on tackling the pair in a day a weekday ticket cost **£18.50** with **£22.50** payable at weekends. For the less fit (or lazy?!) petrol driven caddy carts may be hired from the professional shop at £10 per round, £15 per day. Half sets of clubs can also be hired at £5 per round.

Situated close to the country's industrial heart there is surely no golfing complex in Britain better served by communication networks. The Belfry is one mile from the **M42** (junction 9), five miles from the **M6** (junction 4), nine miles from Birmingham city centre and less than ten minutes from Birmingham International Airport and the N.E.C. Railway Station. The exact positioning of the Golf Club is at the apex of the **A446** and **A4091** Lichfield-Tamworth roads.

The bulk of the criticism directed at the Brabazon tended to centre on the condition of its fairways and the generally barren appearance, but surely such criticism can be levelled at any new course? In any event the 1985 Ryder Cup clearly showed that great strides had been made and those responsible deserve much praise. Will we ever forget the scenes on the giant 18th green as **Sam Torrance** after a massive drive across the lake and a bold second, steered home his birdie putt to defeat **Andy North** and make victory certain?

Apart from the sheer length of the Brabazon course the many water hazards are likely to present the greatest challenge. One can only speculate as to how many thousands have attempted to emulate Messrs. **Ballesteros, Norman** and a handful of others by driving over the lake at the par 4 10th onto the green. What is clear though is that the majority of those thousands have failed. Of course should you decide to flex the muscles and fail then whatever you do don't put on your snorkel and flippers and go wading into the lake – or at least if you do, make sure that it's your ball you fish out!

In addition to being a luxury four-star hotel with a full complement of facilities, the **Belfry Hotel** has public bars and restaurants open to the general public. If after a meal and a few drinks you're still not satisfied with your golf there's a final opportunity to put things right on the impressive floodlit covered driving range.

Mention has been made of how this American-styled extravaganza was created out of a field of potatoes, well interestingly the American legend Sam Snead on first viewing **St Andrews** declared that it "looked like the kind of real estate you couldn't give away".... obviously the message is clear – let's plough the old place up, fill the Road Hole Bunker with water, plant a few trees, create a lake out of the Valley of Sin......

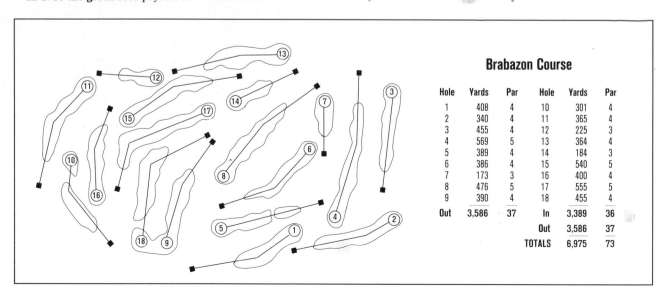

Brabazon Course

Hole	Yards	Par	Hole	Yards	Par
1	408	4	10	301	4
2	340	4	11	365	4
3	455	4	12	225	3
4	569	5	13	364	4
5	389	4	14	184	3
6	386	4	15	540	5
7	173	3	16	400	4
8	476	5	17	555	5
9	390	4	18	455	4
Out	3,586	37	In	3,389	36
			Out	3,586	37
			TOTALS	6,975	73

STAFFORDSHIRE

Alsager G & C.C. (18)
Alsager, Stoke on Trent
(09363) 5700

Beau Desert G.C. (18)
Hednesford, Cannock
(05438) 2626

Blackhill Wood G.C. (18)
Wombourne, Nr Dudley
(0902) 892279

Bloxwich G.C. (18)
Bloxwich (0922) 405724

Branston G.C. (18)
Burton-on-Trent (0283) 45207

Brocton Hall G.C. (18)
Brocton, Stafford (0785) 662627

Calderfields G.C. (18)
Walsall (0922) 32243

Dartmouth G.C. (9)
W. Bromwich (021) 5882131

Drayton Pk G.C. (18)
Tamworth (0827) 61451

Druids Heath G.C. (18)
Aldridge (0922) 55595

Enville G.C. (18+18)
Stourbridge (0384) 872551

Great Barr G.C. (18)
Birmingham (021) 357 1232

Greenway Hall G.C. (18)
Stoke on Trent (0782) 503158

Himley Hall G.C. (9)
Wombourne Dudley
(0902) 895207

Ingestre Park G.C. (18)
Weston, Stafford (0889) 270061

Lakeside G. & C.C. (18)
Barlaston (078139) 3242

Leek G.C. (18)
Leek (0538) 385889

Little Aston G.C. (18)
Streetley, Sutton Coldfield
(021) 353 2066

Newcastle Under Lyme G.C. (18)
Newcastle (0782) 616583

Newcastle Municipal G.C. (18)
Newcastle (0782) 627596

Onneley G.C. (9)
Crewe, Cheshire (0782) 750577

Oxley Park G.C. (18)
Wolverhampton (0902) 20506

Patshull Pk G.C. (18)
Pattingham (0902) 700100

Penn G.C. (18)
Wolverhampton (0902) 341142

Sandwell Pk G.C. (18)
W. Bromwich (021) 553 4637

S. Staffs G.C. (18)
Wolverhampton (0902) 751065

Stafford Castle G.C. (9)
Stafford (0785) 3821

Stone G.C. (9)
Stone (785) 813103

Tamworth Municipal G.C. (18)
Tamworth (0827) 53850

Trentham G.C.
Stoke-on-Trent (0782) 658109

Trentham Pk G.C. (18)
Stoke-on-Trent (0782) 658806

Uttoxeter G.C. (9)
Uttoxeter (08893) 4844

Walsall G.C. (18)
Walsall (0922) 22710

Westwood G.C. (9)
Leek (0538) 383060

Whittington Barracks G.C. (18)
Whittington, Lichfield
(0543) 4332212

Wolstanton G.C. (18)
Newcastle (0782) 616995

WARWICKSHIRE

Atherstone G.C. (18)
Atherstone (08277) 3110

The Belfry (18+18)
Wishaw, (0675) 70301

Boldmere G.C. (18)
Birmingham (021) 354 2324

City of Coventry (Brandon
Wood) G.C. (18)
Walston, Coventry (0203) 3141

Copt Heath G.C. (18)
Knowle, Solihull (05645) 2650

Coventry G.C. (18)
Coventry (0203) 414152

Coventry Hearsall G.C. (18)
Coventry (0203) 713470

Edgbaston G.C. (18)
Birmingham (021) 454 1736

Forest of Arden G & C.C. (18+9)
Meriden, Coventry (0676) 22118

Grange G.C. (9)
Coventry (0203) 451465

Handsworth G.C. (18)
Birmingham (021) 554 0599

Harborne G.C. (18)
Birmingham (021) 427 1728

Harborne G.C. (18)
Birmingham (021) 427 1204

Hilltop G.C. (18)
Birmingham (0221) 554 4463

Hilltop & Marwood
Farm G.C. (18)
Birmingham (021) 554 4463

Kenilworth G.C. (18)
Kenilworth (0926) 54296

Ladbrook Park G.C. (18)
Tamworth in Arden, Solihull
(05644) 2264

Leamington & County
G.C. (18)
Leamington Spa (0926) 20298

Maxstoke Park G.C. (18)
Coleshill, Birmingham
(0675) 62158

Moor Hall G.C. (18)
Sutton Coldfield (021) 308 0103

Newbold Comyn G.C. (18)
Leamington Spa (0926) 21156

North Warwickshire G.C. (9)
Meriden, Coventry (0676) 22259

Nuneateon G.C. (18)
Nuneaton (0682/0203) 347810

Olton G.C. (18)
Solihull (021) 705 1083

Purley Chase G.C. (18)
Chapel End, Nuneaton
(0203) 393118

Pype Hayes G.C. (18)
Sutton Coldfield (021) 351 1014

Robin Hood G.C. (18)
Solihull (021) 706 0159

Rugby G.C. (18)
Rugby (0788) 2306

Shirley G.C. (18)
Solihull (021) 744 6001

Sphinx G.C. (9)
Coventry (0203) 458890

Stratford-on-Avon G.C. (18)
Stratford-on-Avon (0789) 297 296

Sutton Coldfield G.C. (18)
Sutton Coldfield (021) 353 2014

Walmley (Wylde Green)
G.C. (18)
Sutton Coldfield (021) 373 0029

Warwick G.C. (9)
Warwick (0926) 494316

Welcombe Hotel & G.C. (18)
Stratford-on-Avon (0789) 295252

NORTHAMPTONSHIRE AND LEICESTERSHIRE

HARRY ROUNTREE   "Bulldog Breed"   *BURLINGTON GALLERY*

HAMBLETON HALL

Hambleton Hall,
Oakham,
Leicestershire.

Centrally located, yet two of the quieter counties of the Midlands – one or two towns excepted, that is! Both, though, have known disquiet in the past: two of the bloodiest and most historic battles fought on English soil occurred in these parts – **The Battle of Bosworth Field** in **1485**, just to the west of Leicester and **The Battle of Naseby** in **1645**, some 3 miles north of Cold Ashby in Northamptonshire. However, let us not stray from the burning question … over which soil should the modern-day golfer do battle?

I don't suppose many would dispute that **Luffenham Heath** and **Northamptonshire County** are the leading courses in their respective counties, but whilst not being exactly renowned for their golf each has a fairly even spread of courses stretching from one corner of the shire to the other.

Starting in **Leicestershire, Luffenham Heath** lies over to the very far east of the county within what was formerly **Rutland** and very close to the border with Lincolnshire. It is without question one of the most attractive heathland courses in England and being a conservation area something of a haven for numerous species of wildlife. Measuring 6,254 yards from the back tees (par 70) it isn't the longest of courses but then, thankfully, golf isn't always a question of how far you can belt the ball! Visitors are welcome at Luffenham Heath, green fees in 1986 being **£10.50** weekdays and **£16** at weekends. However, prior arrangement with the secretary is essential.

The town of Leicester is well served by golf courses and there are no fewer than three 18 hole municipal courses within four miles of the centre of Leicester, **Western Park** perhaps being the best of these. **Leicestershire Golf Club** is situated just 2 miles from the city centre along the **A6**. An undulating parkland with a stream running through it, it is always maintained in excellent condition. Visitors should be able to get a game here most days of the week, fees being around the **£12** mark.

Rothley Park Golf Club, adjacent to 13th century Rothley Court, is one of the county's more picturesque parkland courses and is within easy access of Leicester, lying some 7 miles to the north of the county town off the **A6**. Those looking for a game would probably do well to contact the Secretary in advance, Wednesdays, Thursdays and Fridays normally being the best days for a visit. In 1986 a day's golf at Rothley was priced at **£9** midweek, **£12** at weekends.

Looking further afield in the north of the county the ancient town of **Melton Mowbray** has a fine nine hole course sited on high ground to the north east of the town off the **A607**, and Loughborough possesses an 18 hole heathland type course, (**Longcliffe**) which is heavily wooded with a particularly testing front nine. In the south of the county **Market Harborough's** nine hole course offers extensive views across the surrounding countryside.

To the north west of Leicester is Charnwood Forest, one of the Midland's most pleasant retreats, an area where heath and woodland confront rocky crags and granite outcrops. The village of **Woodhouse Eaves** lies on the eastern edge of the 'Forest' and has two extremely pleasant nine hole courses at hand, **Lingdale** and **Charnwood Forest**. Though they are less than two miles apart they offer quite different challenges. Lingdale (**B5330**) has a parkland setting with a trout stream flowing through it, while Charnwood Forest (**B591**) is a heathland type course – no bunkers but several outcrops of granite around which one must navigate. Visitors can normally play either course throughout the week though a quick call at weekends is recommended. Fees are approximately **£8** a day.

Hinckley is linked to the centre of Leicester by the **A47**. Hinckley's golf course is a fairly new creation, built over the original nine hole Burbage Common layout. Several lakes and much gorse have to be confronted making this potentially the toughest in the county. Visitors can look for a game in midweek (Tuesdays excepted), **£10** securing a day's golf in 1986.

Before leaving Leicester, **Willesley Park Golf Club** at Ashby-de-la-Zouch is strongly worth noting. The golf course lies south of the town on the **A453**. A fine parkland/heathland course and for about **£10** good for a game at all times other than Saturday and Sunday mornings before 9.30 a.m.

The **Northamptonshire County** course is situated some five miles north of Northampton at Church Brampton, and indeed is often referred to locally as 'Church Brampton'. Famed for its many testing par fours it is a splendid heather and gorse type with a fair few undulations in its 6,500 yards. Rather like Liphook in Hampshire a railway line bisects the course. The venue in the past of the British Youths Championship visitors are welcome on most days, though being the most popular course in the county it can get a little busy and arrangements are best made in advance.

Elsewhere in the county **Wellingborough** is a fairly lengthy course measuring close to 6,600 yards. Two miles east of the town it is set around the former Harrowden Hall. Quite hilly again with several lakes and mature trees visitors can play during the week, the cost of a day's golf being **£12** in 1986. **Kettering's** course is very close to the town centre. One of the oldest Clubs in the county, now approaching its centenary, it is another that welcomes visitors midweek (**£9** in 1986).

Staverton Park at Daventry and **Woodlands** close to Towcester are two of the newer courses in the county worth noting, as certainly is **Cold Ashby** located to the far north of the county (close to Naseby) with superb views across the Northamptonshire Uplands. Not a terribly long course but with several streams and ponds to be tackled (or avoided). A friendly Club, Cold Ashby (or as they like to call it 'Warm Ashby') welcomes visitors seven days a week. The fees in 1986 were **£7.50** per day during the week, **£9** per day at weekends.

Charnwood Forest G.C.	(0509) 890259
Cold Ashby G.C.	(0604) 740548
Hinckley G.C.	(0455) 615124
Kettering G.C.	(0536) 511104
Leicestershire G.C.	(0780) 720205
Lingdale G.C.	(0509) 890035
Longcliffe G.C.	(0509) 239129
Luffenham Heath G.C.	(0780) 720205
Market Harborough G.C.	(0858) 63684
Melton Mowbray G.C.	(0664) 62118
Northamptonshire G.C.	(0604) 842170
Rothley Park G.C.	(0533) 302809
Staverton G.C.	(0327) 705911
Wellingborough G.C.	(0933) 677234
Willesley Park G.C.	(0530) 414596
Woodlands G.C.	(032) 736291

LEICESTERSHIRE AND NORTHANTS

The Battles of Bosworth Field, Naseby and many others – the castles of Belvoir and Rockingham and several more. The hunting horn shrieks, the shotguns blaze – it's a wonder anyone gets any sleep. They call them quiet rural retreats – not a bit of it – if it's not a civil war it's the Quorn. Is there any place where a man or woman can have some peace – why of course – the golfcourse. I do not know whether the likes of Spalding or Slazenger have equipped their golf bags with a shot gun support, but it might be an idea. What would the Secretary say when a partridge plummeted on to the eighteenth green, certainly one four lettered word beginning with F.... (Fore). The countryside in Leicestershire and Northamptonshire is excellent; one good hunting friend rates it the best he knows. Amid these green fields lie some fairly worthwhile stop off points for the golfer, but one would be misled if one presumed that the area as a whole boasted excellent accommodation.

To start at a pinnacle – go near Oakham to **Hambleton Hall** (0572) 56991. The hotel is expensive but outstanding. Room rates are reduced between November and April in the middle of the week if you stay 3 nights or more. The splendid Luffenham Heath is nearby while courses at Stoke Rochford and Burghley Park are also convenient. If you cannot stay well you should visit the restaurant – simply outstanding. Next, well it's a difficult one to follow, but in total contrast in Oakham's pleasant Market Square is the **The George** (0572) 56971 – an inn which offers good beers, snacks and some comfortable accommodation. Note that this is Ruddles Country – some excellent country pubs lie in wait. **The King's Arms** in Wing is a good example and there's a nearby maze in which to discard the children before a round of golf or a pint of County. Another good pub is the **Cavalier** at Collyweston – famous for its stone. **The Boot and Shoe**, South Luffenham (0780) 720177 is also a comfortable pub in which to stay or merely have a pie n' pint. Moving west through the countryside one reaches Uppingham, here the **Falcon Hotel** (0572) 823535 is fairly popular for a bar snack, its restaurant and more obviously for its comfortable bedrooms. In Market Harborough perhaps the best place to stay is the **Three Swans Inn** (0858) 66644. And so to another public school town – my favourite – Oundle. Here the **Talbot** (0832) 73621 is ideal for a night's sleep before playing in the county and another thought is to try **Tyrrell's** (0832) 72347 – splendid food with an excellent atmosphere. Other good food can be found in nearby Fotheringhay at **The Falcon** an excellent pub with imaginative food. Note also the church tower at night – is it Mary Queen of Scots shadow on the church spire when it's lit up at night? (This is my own personal theory developed after one hell of a bash at The Falcon – it may therefore be a little dubious!) Further afield, one finds a **Black Horse** in Nassington, once again excellent bar snacks are available as well as a very good pint – thoroughly recommended.

And so to Northampton. If you are staying in the town, **The Moat House Hotel** (0604) 22441 is modern, but comfortable and handy for the centre, while the **Westone Moat House** (0604) 406262 is a mansion with modern additions. The towns of Wellingborough and Kettering are both particularly busy, but are surrounded by some splendid countryside. Perhaps the best bet for some accommodation in the area is **The Hind** in Wellingborough (0933) 222827. South of Northampton in Horton **The Horton Inn** (0258) 840252 is recommended for its comfortable bedrooms and excellent restaurant. Another establishment to note is the **French Partridge** (0604) 870033 for essentially French food. In Long Buckby, **The Buckby Lion** is a good pub while people wishing to stay near Woodlands may wish to try the **Crossroads** (0327) 40354 at Weedon or **The Saracens Head** (0327) 50414 at Towcester– both are particularly welcoming. Returning to the Leicestershire border some pubs should be sampled while en route – they are the **Pytchley** (dam huntsman again!) and **the Elizabethan**, Welford.

Leicestershire, Husbands Bosworth, the **Fernie Lodge** (0858) 880551 – yet another hunt not the bugle horn here though, rather an elegant Georgian dining room where dining is excellent. Further north in the charming village of East Langton one finds **The Bell Inn** (085884) 567 where excellent food and a varied menu are offered. With so many good courses near Leicester it would be wrong to overlook it. However it is not the country's most attractive city but it does have its good points. The **Haymarket Theatre** offers a variety of productions while the Art Gallery includes works by English sporting artists and if you have business in town the **Grand Hotel** (0533) 531161 will prove the best selection. Outside the town at Quorn, the **Quorn Country Hotel** (0509) 415050 offers style in a particularly English environment. Also convenient for the county town and Rothley Park Golfcourse is **Rothley Court, Rothley** (0533) 374141, with fine food, a history to delight the humblest thinker and elegant surroundings. This hotel is thoroughly worthwhile. A hotel with a Roman past can be found at Hinckley **The Hinckley Island** (0455) 631122, where another promising restaurant adds weight to the reasons for visiting.

How about a pork pie or some Stilton – well if that's what you're after Melton Mowbray is the answer to your prayers: A small hotel a mile from Melton's town centre, **The Sysonby Knoll** (0664) 63563. It is here that the local hunt meets – a good opportunity to get even – it's only a thought! In the town itself **The George** (0664) 62112 is a charming inn which has comfortable bedrooms and pleasing bars.

When considering clubs to the north west of the county it is the tummy that rumbles. In Sileby, **The Old School House** (050981) 3941 has a strong reputation as does the charming **Cottage in the Woods, Woodhouse Eaves** (0509) 890318. Further afield, but equally appealing is the **Restaurant Roger Burdell** (0509) 231813. The **Kings Head** (0509) 233222 is a residential option and the Bar is popular. We end our journey round these parts in Old Dalby – why, well why not? **The Crown** offers excellent food and a range of fine ales – well worth a visit.

It's a funny thing, but even with the sound of the horn and the hounds I think we will play good golf – and if we don't it's pleasant to know that such delights exist in an area which many people haven't yet had the fortune to discover.

Hambleton Hall Hotel and Restaurant
Hambleton,
Oakham,
LE15 8TH
Tel: (0572) 56991
The outstanding small country hotel and restaurant of its region. In a spectacular position with wonderful views over Rutland Water. A high class small restaurant with a stylish and comfortable interior designed by Nina Campbell.

The Bell Inn
Main Street, East Langton,
Leicestershire, LE16 7TW
Tel: (085884) 567
The Bell stands in a charming village set in the lovely Leicestershire countryside. The attractive pub offers a daily-changing menu. Tables should be booked in the evenings. Equally good for ale and snacks. Situated to the north of Market Harborough.

CAMBRIDGESHIRE, SUFFOLK AND NORFOLK

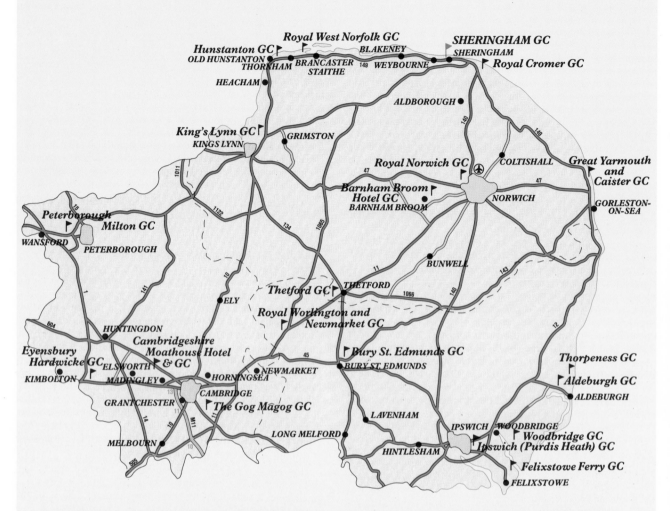

Royal West Norfolk GC
SHERINGHAM GC
Hunstanton GC
BLAKENEY
SHERINGHAM
OLD HUNSTANTON
Royal Cromer GC
THORNHAM
BRANCASTER
149 WEYBOURNE
STAITHE
HEACHAM
ALDBOROUGH
140
149
King's Lynn GC
GRIMSTON
KINGS LYNN
1011
Royal Norwich GC
COLTISHALL
Great Yarmouth and Caister GC
1122
47
Barnham Broom Hotel GC
NORWICH
47
Peterborough
134
BARNHAM BROOM
GORLESTON-ON-SEA
Milton GC
1085
WANSFORD
PETERBOROUGH
BUNWELL
143
10
11
141
Thetford GC THETFORD
140
604
ELY
1066
12
1
Royal Worlington and Newmarket GC
Eyensbury
Cambridgeshire Moathouse Hotel & GC
45
Bury St. Edmunds GC
Thorpeness GC
Hardwicke GC
ELSWORTH
BURY ST. EDMUNDS
Aldeburgh GC
KIMBOLTON
MADINGLEY
HORNINGSEA
NEWMARKET
ALDEBURGH
GRANTCHESTER
CAMBRIDGE
LAVENHAM
IPSWICH WOODBRIDGE
14
The Gog Magog GC
Woodbridge GC
10
M11
Ipswich (Purdis Heath) GC
MELBOURN
LONG MELFORD
HINTLESHAM
Felixstowe Ferry GC
505
FELIXSTOWE

JULIAN BARROW   "Brancaster"   BURLINGTON GALLERY

Congham Hall
COUNTRY HOUSE HOTEL

elcome to peaceful West Norfolk. As you
rn off the King's Lynn to Fakenham road
wards the village of Grimston and
ongham Hall, the peace and quiet of the
orfolk countryside unfolds before you.
cres of farmland, natural woodlands and
dgerows stretch as far as the eye can see.
et in forty acres of beautiful parkland, yet
ly six miles from King's Lynn, Congham
all offers its guests complete relaxation.
ith its paddocks, orchards and country
rdens, visitors can unwind and enjoy
eir holiday—or quietly deal with their
siness meeting—in an atmosphere of
arm and tranquillity.

orfolk is the holiday area for the
nnoisseur with its miles of quiet beaches
d unhurried countryside. There are
cellent golf courses nearby and the
cecourses at Fakenham and Newmarket
e within easy reach. There is much to
e in the vicinity; the Queen's Royal
tate at Sandringham, National Trust
operties, stately homes and bird
nctuaries. Congham Hall has its own
imming pool, tennis court, cricket pitch
d stabling.

you are staying for business reasons you
ll find your requirements are understood
d catered for; from the superb
oardroom with its peaceful views across
e lawns to a quiet business lunch

followed by a stroll in the grounds. There
is ample room for cars, or the chairman's
helicopter, and you are within easy access
of the business centres of Norfolk or
Norwich airport.

In the hotel you will find everything you
would expect from an elegant Georgian
Manor House run by its owners. As
experienced hoteliers who bring with them
a reputation for friendly, thoughtful and
efficient service, their pride and enthusiasm
for this lovely house will be evident to all
their guests.

Ten bedrooms, comfortably furnished in
period style, all with bathrooms en suite,
offer a selection of double, twin or single
accommodation, with a four poster suite
for that special occasion. There is a Jacuzzi
Spa bath for guests, and each room has a
telephone, colour TV, radio and writing
facilities.

The restaurant is attractively decorated in
the Georgian manner and under the
individual care of Mr John McGeever, a
talented British chef with an especial
enthusiasm for the finest English and
Nouvelle cuisine. His menus feature fresh
local produce and vegetables, fruits and
herbs from our own gardens.

Congham Hall,
Grimston, Kings Lynn,
Norfolk PE32 1AH
Telephone: (0485) 600250
Telex: 81508 CHOTEL

The three counties of East Anglia stretch from 'Constable Country' in the south, through the Fens and the Broads to the tip of the Wash. For golfers this means it stretches from Felixstowe Ferry, through Thetford to Hunstanton. There are numerous other combinations capable of whetting the golfing appetite for East Anglia is one of the game's richest regions. It is also a corner of Britain where golf has long been a popular pastime. Of the twenty Golf Clubs in Suffolk, half were founded in the 19th century and **Felixstowe Ferry Golf Club** which dates from 1880 is the fifth oldest Club in England. Given its location close to the boundary with Essex it is as good a place as any to begin a golfing tour of East Anglia.

The course lies a mile north east of Felixstowe and is a classic test of traditional links golf. This part of Suffolk is fairly remote and at times it could easily be imagined that one was playing a Scottish links, the greens are first class and the wind is often a major factor. Visitors are welcomed at all times except before 10.30 pm at weekends, green fees are **£8** midweek and **£12** at weekends.

The **Ipswich Golf Club** at Purdis Heath is possibly East Anglia's finest parkland course, always well-maintained, the fairways wind their way between large ponds and are bordered by an attractive assortment of hardwood trees. **Woodbridge** is a near neighbour of Purdis Heath and similarly mature in nature, though more undulating and of the heather and gorse variety as opposed to parkland. An exceptionally attractive course, it welcomes visitors on weekdays at **£11** per round, **£15** per day.

Thorpeness and **Aldeburgh** lie fairly adjacent to one another on the Suffolk coast. Ideal centres for holiday golf, both are again of the heather and gorse type. The town of Aldeburgh is of course famed for its annual music festival and Benjamin Britten once lived next to the 14th fairway. Thorpeness is a most scenic course where on the 18th green an unusual water tower ('The House in the Clouds') and a restored windmill provide a unique background. In 1986, green fees were **£9** midweek, **£11** weekends.

Over to the west of Suffolk, are **Bury St Edmunds** and **Royal Worlington**. The former is due to stage the County's Amateur Championship in 1987. Royal Worlington (near Mildenhall) is often called the 'finest 9 holes in the world', not surprisingly it is very popular and visitors must contact the Club before making any arrangements.

Stepping over the county boundary into Cambridgeshire and the 'land of the Fens' the golf courses tend to be rather flat. One great exception to the rule is the wonderfully named **Gog Magog Golf Club**. Situated on hilly ground south east of Cambridge it is a superb test of golf. Four miles north west of the City the **Cambridgeshire Moat House Hotel** welcomes golfers seven days a week. From the back tees the course can play fairly long and has a lake and several ditches. Green fees in 1986 were **£8.50** during the week, **£12.50** at weekends. A preliminary telephone call is again essential. Before heading into Norfolk, **Peterborough Milton** certainly deserves noting. A fairly flat course but a very good test with many well positioned trees and bunkers. The cost of a game in 1986 was **£11.50** midweek, **£15** at weekends.

It is doubtful whether any county can surpass Norfolk's great range of outstanding courses. There are the magnificent links at **Hunstanton** and **Brancaster**, some terrifically scenic golf along the cliffs at **Sheringham** and **Royal Cromer**, and a number of superb inland courses of which **Thetford** and **Kings Lynn** stand out. The title of 'Oldest Club in Norfolk' though goes to **Great Yarmouth and Caister**, founded in 1882. A seaside links, located north of Great Yarmouth close to the old Roman town of Caister-on-Sea.

Cromer, 25 miles north along the **A149** is famed for its crabs – the town, not the golf course I hasten to add – and also for its 150 year old lighthouse. The 14th at **Royal Cromer**, the 'Lighthouse Hole' was played by Tony Jacklin during his '18 holes at 18 different courses helicopter round'. Several elevated tees and a generous spread of gorse make for an interesting round. In 1986 a day's golf could be enjoyed for **£9** during the week, **£11** at weekends. **Sheringham** is only five miles further along the coast and is Norfolk's other great cliff top course – (it is featured a few pages on). **Brancaster (Royal West Norfolk)** 'a living museum amid the salt marshes' is a popular links and one should contact the Club before making any arrangements. The Championship links at **Hunstanton** has also acquired a considerable reputation. Golf here is played among the sandhills and when the winds blow it can play exceptionally difficult. Many claim the lightning fast greens to be the best in the country.

Switching inland, Norwich has a fine combination of the old and the new – **Royal Norwich** and **Barnham Broom**. The former is located close to the **A1067** Fakenham Road and welcomes visitors with handicaps. Seven miles west of Norwich, Barnham Broom Hotel and Country Club has facilities to rival The Belfry, and in a similar vein a course where water (the River Yare) provides the major hazard. Thetford, some 28 miles from Norwich, is a beautiful heathland course, arguably the finest inland course in East Anglia, set amid glorious oaks, firs and silver birch. It is also home for a variety of wildlife including golden pheasants, red deer and Chinese Water-Deer (whatever they may be!). Visitors are welcomed at all times in 1986 weekday fees were **£9**, with **£12** at weekends. Having begun at Felixstowe Ferry, East Anglia's oldest course, it is perhaps appropriate to end at **King's Lynn** one of the region's newest courses and close to The Wash and the boundary with Lincolnshire. Designed by Peter Alliss and Dave Thomas it is heavily wooded and a very demanding test of golf – 73 being the course record! Visitors (with handicaps) are welcome on weekdays, excepting Tuesdays, **£11** being the cost of a day's golf in 1986.

Aldeburgh G.C.	(072 885) 2890	King's Lynn G.C.	(055 387) 654
Barnham Broom G.C.	(0603) 545 393	Peterborough Milton G.C.	(073 121) 489
Bury St. Edmunds G.C.	(0284) 5979	Royal Cromer G.C.	(0263) 512884
Cambridgeshire Moat House Hotel G.C.	(0954) 80555	Royal Norwich G.C.	(0603) 45712
Felixstowe Ferry G.C.	(0394) 286834	Royal Worlington & Newmarket G.C.	(0638) 712216
Gog Magog G.C.	(0223) 247626	Sheringham G.C.	(0263) 823488
Great Yarmouth & Caister G.C.	(0493) 720421	Thetford G.C.	(0842) 2169
Hunstanton G.C.	(04853) 2811	Thorpeness G.C.	(0728 85) 2176
Ipswich G.C.	(0473) 78941	Woodbridge G.C.	(0394) 2038

'Tis said they speak a little slow in Norfolk – well why not – there's no hurry! Yes Norfolk the home of the 'good old boy'; the Fens and the Broads also boast some of Britain's best loved golf courses. The wild coastline commands beautiful views while further inland the Broads which smother Norfolk have their quite mystical appeal. The sheer magnificence of Sandringham and the quite delightful halls at Blickling and Holkham add further grace to the area. In contrast the market towns of Bury St Edmunds, Lavenham and Long Melford display an array of shops and churches while Cambridge stands superbly with its quite magnificent colleges, being threatened by streams of wild punters on the Cam and the razzmatazz of May Balls.

With the day behind you – incidentally congratulations on a simply marvellous round – the thought emerges – where now? Well of course the Club House always has that appeal but what else? Well, here are some thoughts.

In Sheringham itself there are two hotels to consider, **The Beacon (0263) 822019** and **The Beaumaris (0263) 822370**. Neither are grand but both are restful – ideal for golfers after a hard day's sport. Those of you who are not keen on putting their feet up should note Weybourne, where **Gasche's (026370) 220** is a splendid Swiss restaurant in a delightful setting. An hotel to note here is **The Malkins (026370) 275**, another perfect base. Blakeney, offers a glorious coastline and this golfing homeland also has two hotels to note. One **The Blakeney (0263) 740797** and the other **The Manor Hotel (0263) 740376**, both have pleasant settings and once again act as ideal pads for golfers. Further down the coast a pub with a restaurant can be found namely **The Jolly Sailors (0485) 210314** at Brancaster Staithe. Following the coastline westwards one arrives at Thornham where **The Lifeboat (048526) 236** offers a variety of bar food and if you like pub accommodation, then bedrooms are also available. In Old Hunstanton, another fine golf club is complemented by a further hotel duo: **The Lodge Hotel (04853) 2896** lies adjacent to the links itself, while **The Strange Arms and Golf Links Hotel (04853) 34411** speaks for itself. The thought of spending a week in this delightful part of the world with these splendid courses and civilised hotels must surely appeal to many golfers.

En route to Kings Lynn one passes Heacham, where rests as homely a country hotel as you will find – **The Holly Lodge (0485) 70790**. In Kings Lynn itself, **The Duke's Head Hotel (0553) 774996** overlooks the market place and is pleasant. Elsewhere in Kings Lynn **The Riverside Rooms (0553) 773134** enjoys a pleasant situation and the food is good. For a combination of excellent food and accommodation a short journey out of Kings Lynn is required to Grimston where the delights of **Congham Hall (0485) 600250** await you.

Jumping counties we arrive in the cathedral city of Peterborough which boasts a massive shopping centre and a quite awful one-way system. On the outskirts of the city **The Moat House (0733) 260000** is convenient for the golf course. People who would prefer a less modern hotel should try **The Haycock**

(0780) 782223$ at Wansford – really excellent for snacks and restaurant – ideal. In Huntingdon, The Old Bridge (0480) 53681 is good and has a fine restaurant – while in Kimbolton **La Côte d'Or** is an ideal place to have dinner. Towards Cambridge, at Elsworth, **Meadow Farm (09547) 413** is a grand little restaurant, and in Madingley – **The Three Horseshoes** has good bar snacks and serves a grand pint. Outside Cambridge in Grantchester **The Green Man** is another splendid pub. Enter Cambridge and the delights of the University town await you. In a nutshell **The Garden House Hotel (0223) 63421** and outside the nutshell the particularly luxurious **Post House Hotel (022023) 7000**, at Impington. If you want a good restaurant – then **Jean Louis (0223) 315232** is thoroughly recommended. On the way to Ely, another fine cathedral, one finds Horningsea – here **The Plough and Fleece** is recommended. In Ely itself, the thoroughly British **Old Fire Engine (0353) 2582** makes excellent use of local ingredients, while **The Peking Duck (0353) 2948** is also well thought of.

Some distance to the East in Thetford, **The Bell Hotel (0842) 4455** is charming and in Bury St Edmunds, **The Angel (0284) 3926** is an ever improving hotel – now first rate. South of Bury lies the delightful town of Lavenham, where **The Swan (0787) 247477** is an excellent stopping-off point in a gorgeous town. In Long Melford – **The Bull** offers cosy accommodation within its fifteenth century frame; and in Hintlesham, **The Hintlesham Hall (047387) 268** is a glorious country house with an extremely fine restaurant.

If you are staying in Ipswich it may be that you will have selected **The Marlborough (0473) 57677** – good value and comfort – an ideal combination. However, it may be that you have decided to stay outside Ipswich, Woodbridge perhaps. Here, **The Melton Grange (03943) 4147** has great appeal while **Seckford Hall (03943) 5678** is simply outstanding. Another recommended establishment near Woodbridge, in Orford is **The Butley-Orford Oysterage (03945) 277** specialising in, you've guessed it, lobster – superb! Another, **Marlborough Hotel (0394) 285621**, this time in Felixstowe is also commendable and more good food can be found at **André's (0394) 270199** also in Felixstowe.

Wallop! – just in case you're nodding off, we're heading towards Norwich, another splendid country town. **The Maids Head (0603) 28821** is probably the best of a pretty good bunch. Restaurants also abound – **Greens Seafood (0603) 623733** and **Marco's (0603) 24044** are ideal for lunch or dinner before or after a round of golf.

East of Norwich is Coltishall – where things happen. For Yarmouth – such a pleasant seaside town – stay in Gorleston – (apologies Yarmouth) – **The Cliff Hotel (0493) 662179**.

To end our trip we visit Aldborough – **The Old Red Lion (0263) 761451** or is it Aldeburgh – **The Uplands Hotel (072885) 2420** or **The Cross Keys** perhaps. Who knows, they're all most pleasing and that when you've double bogied the eighteenth is all that counts.

Congham Hall Country House Hotel
Nr Grimston, Norfolk
Tel: (0485) 600250
An elegant Georgian manor house run with pride and enthusiasm by its owners. 10 bedrooms with excellent facilities and an outstanding restaurant catering for residents and non-residents serves breakfast, lunch and dinner. A perfect country setting.

Gasche's
Weybourne,
Norfolk
Tel: (026370) 220
Open from Tuesday lunch to Sunday lunch. A very popular Swiss restaurant which serves traditional dishes – it is vital to book. The restaurant is in an old Norfolk flint building on the A149 approximately 3 miles northeast of Holt.

It is said that Queen Elizabeth the First once held a Court at Seckford Hall. This may well be, for one of the Seckford Family held the high office of "Master of the Court Requests" to Her Majesty. Since 1672, when the last of this powerful Suffolk family died, the hall has known various fortunes, but happily has lost none of the Tudor splendour which the Seckford family knew so well. Indeed, the very walls whisper of the pomp and intrigue that was England in Tudor days.
Seckford Hall is furnished throughout as a private house rather than an hotel. The furnishings, though not exclusively Tudor, are mostly period pieces, many inherited from Windsor Castle.

The twenty-four guest bedrooms ensure absolute comfort with private bathrooms, individual colour schemes, modern central heating, colour TV's, deep-pile carpeting – in fact everything to the standard expected at Seckford Hall. The Restaurant is very popular with local diners. Personally supervised by the owners, there is a superb à la Carte Menu, a well-trained, pleasant staff and the cuisine is excellent, materially helped by the fresh vegetables, meat and fruit from local farms. Specialities include Norfolk Duckling, Orford Smoked Salmon, Lobsters and Soles from the coast nearby.

Six golf courses are within easy reach the nearest being at Woodbridge, with championship courses at Aldeburgh and Ipswich. Other 18 hole courses include Thorpeness, Felixstowe and Rushmere whilst there are two picturesque 9 hole courses at Newbourne and Easton. A golf Practice Driving range is located at Bucklesham, near Ipswich.

Seckford Hall

HOTEL AND RESTAURANT

*** AA   *** RAC

WOODBRIDGE, SUFFOLK, IP13 6NU
TEL: WOODBRIDGE (0394) 385678 TELEX 987446

SHERINGHAM

I suppose one could whimsically remark that here we have a Club fit for British heroes – no, not necessarily of the Sandy Lyle species, but both **Robert Falcon Scott** and **Douglas Bader** were one time members at Sheringham. Well, an interesting thought perhaps, but here alas is probably not the place to delve into the subjects of snowshoes and spitfires.

Sheringham's splendid clifftop course is in one of the more remote parts of Britain, tucked away on Norfolk's northern coast, staring out across the bleak North Sea. When Sheringham Golf Club was formed in December **1891** the Members had only 9 holes at their disposal on which to pursue their favourite pastime, however, before the turn of the century a further 9 holes were added and the course quickly came to be regarded as one of the finest in the East of England. In recognition of its growing stature Sheringham was selected to host the English Ladies Championship in 1920 – indeed more of which a little later.

Today, **visitors** are welcome at Sheringham although they are required, as seems to be the norm these days, to be in possession of a Club handicap. It is probably advisable to make a quick telephone call to the Secretary **Mr M J Garrett** to check whether any tee reservations have been made. Mr M Garrett may be contacted on **(0263) 823488**).

Green fees for 1986 were set at **£10** for weekdays with **£12** payable at weekends and Bank Holidays. For **juniors** there is a 50% reduction which in fact applies to all and sundry after 4.30pm. **Societies** are also encouraged although not at weekends between the months of April and October. Written applications should be addressed to the Secretary, **Sheringham Golf Club, Weybourne Road, Sheringham, Norfolk**.

Anyone approaching Sheringham is likely to be travelling on the **A149**, or at least ought to be as the course is situated about a half mile west of the town just off this road. Coming directly from Norwich one should take the **A140** before joining the **A149** at Cromer. For those travelling from the West the **A148** links Kings Lynn with Sheringham. A level crossing heralds the entrance to the Club, however, a warning to all drivers eager and excited at the prospect of hauling the clubs out of the boot – the crossing is unattended!

The professional at Sheringham is **Malcolm Leeder** (17 times Norfolk Professional Champion no less), he can be reached on **(0263) 822980**. Before stepping out onto the first tee it might be advisable to step into his well stocked pro-shop and top up on the supply of golf balls – not forgetting that this is very much a cliff top course! Golf clubs may be hired from the professional should the need arise.

So, having got to the first tee what are we confronted by? In short, from the back tees, **6430** yards of challenging, varied and at times most spectacular golf. The par for the men is **70** with a standard scratch of **71** while for the ladies the course measures **5807** yards, par **73**. The course has been laid out on a strip of land sandwiched between the cliffs on the one side and the North Norfolk Steam Railway line on the other. Throughout the turf is of that springy seaside nature and although in places the fairways are quite generous it would be prudent to stay upon them. There is an abundant scatter of gorse and heather and whereas the sea can beckon on some of the front nine holes so the railway line becomes very much a feature on the home stretch.

The opening two holes, a short four followed by a par five, may well provide a solid start and dare I suggest for the mightier among us the chance of beginning three, four? The next five holes run close to the cliff edges and are possibly the most enjoyable of the round, certainly the views here are tremendous. Particularly breathtaking is the panoramic view from the 5th looking out across the north Norfolk coastline – certainly not a hole to be hurried. On the next seven holes the gorse becomes the most likely devil to wreck a promising card, perhaps the most testing holes here being the 10th and 12th. Sheringham has a fine finish and with the railway line acting as a continuous boundary on the right this is not the time to suddenly develop a slice. Mention must be made of the 17th, a hole made famous by the great **Joyce Wethered**, now Lady Heathcote-Amery, when winning the first of five consecutive English Ladies Championships in 1920. Playing in the final against her great rival, **Miss Cecil Leitch**, Miss Wethered was faced with a crucial putt on the 17th green. Just as she was preparing to strike the ball the 4.20 train from Sheringham thundered past. She continued her stroke and after making a fine putt was not surprisingly questioned as to whether the train had put her off. Apparently back came the reply "What train?"!

The Ladies Championship returned to Sheringham in 1950 and the Club is due to stage the same once again in 1991, the year it celebrates its centenary.

As for its 19th, Sheringham has a pleasant Clubhouse with full catering offered seven days per week. **Visitors** wishing to take advantage of the above should not forget the jacket and tie, though during the summer there is no general requirement as such before 7.00pm.

Many 'city golfers' appear to gain a new lease of life when they escape to the coast and inject some of that invigorating sea air. Whether it's the ozone or whatever, a visit to Sheringham can certainly work wonders, and who knows, with a bit of that fresh air inside you and those marvellous cliff top views life's major worries may seem a little less pressing.

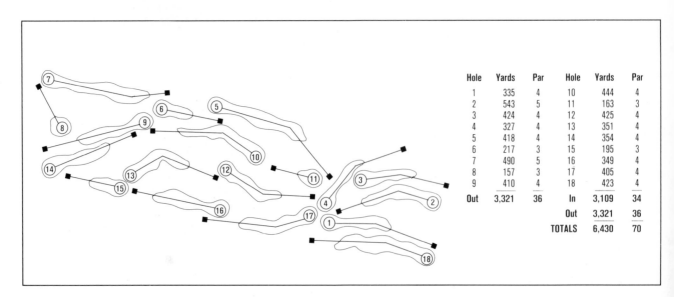

Hole	Yards	Par	Hole	Yards	Par
1	335	4	10	444	4
2	543	5	11	163	3
3	424	4	12	425	4
4	327	4	13	351	4
5	418	4	14	354	4
6	217	3	15	195	3
7	490	5	16	349	4
8	157	3	17	405	4
9	410	4	18	423	4
Out	3,321	36	In	3,109	34
			Out	3,321	36
			TOTALS	6,430	70

THE 8TH: SHINGLE STREET TO SNETTISHAM

CAMBRIDGESHIRE
Cambridge Moat House
Hotel G.C. (18)

Crafts Hill, Cambridge
(0954) 80555

Ely City G.C. (18)
Ely (0353) 2751

Eynesbury Hardwick G.C. (18)
St. Neots (0480) 215153

Girton G.C. (18)
Girton, Cambridge (0223) 276169

The Gog Magog G.C. (18+9)
Cambridge (0223) 247626

Links (Newmarket) G.C. (18)
Newmarket (0638) 662708

March G.C. (9)
March, Knights End
(03542) 2364

Ramsey G.C. (18)
Ramsey (0487) 813573

Royston G.C. (18)
Royston (0763) 42177

St. Ives (Hunts) G.C. (9)
St. Ives (0480) 64459

St. Neots G.C. (18)
Huntingdon (0480) 74311

NORFOLK
Barnham Broom
Hotel G & C.C. (18)
Norwich (0603) 545393

Dereham G.C. (9)
Dereham (0362) 3122

Eaton G.C. (18)
Norwich (0603) 52881

Fakenham G.C. (9)
Fakenham (0328) 2867

Feltwell G.C. (9)
Feltwell (0842) 828795

Great Yarmouth &
Caister G.C. (18)
Gt Yarmouth (0493) 720421

Hunstanton G.C. (18)
Hunstanton (04853) 2811

King's Lynn G.C. (18)
Castle Rising (055387) 656

Links Country Park
Hotel & G.C. (9)
West Runton (26375) 691

Mundesley G.C. (9)
Mundesley (0263) 720279

Norwich Golf Centre G.C. (9)
Bawburgh, Norwich
(0603) 746390

Royal Cromer G.C. (18)
Cromer (0263) 512884

Royal Norwich G.C. (18)
Norwich (0603) 45712

Royal West Norfolk G.C. (18)
Brancaster (0485) 210223

Ryston Park G.C. (19)
Downham (0366) 382133

Sheringham G.C. (18)
Sheringham (0263) 823488

Sprawston Park G.C. (18)
Norwich (0603) 410657

Swaffham G.C. (9)
Swaffham (0760) 21611

Thetford G.C. (18)
Thetford (0842) 2258

SUFFOLK
Aldeburgh G.C. (18+9)
Aldeburgh (072885) 2408

Beccles G.C. (9)
Beccles, Suffolk (0502) 712244

Bungay & Waveney G.C. (18)
Bungay (0986) 2337

Bury St. Edmunds G.C. (18)
Bury St. Edmunds (0284) 5979

Diss G.C. (18)
Diss (0379) 2847

Felixstowe Ferry G.C. (18)
Felixstowe (03942) 86834

Flempton G.C. (9)
Culford, Bury St. Edmunds
(028484) 291

Fornham Park G.C. (18)
Bury St. Edmunds (0284) 63426

Gorleston G.C. (18)
Gt. Yarmouth (0493) 661082

Haverhill G.C. (9)
Haverhill (0440) 61951

Ipswich (18+9)

Newton Green G.C. (9)
Sudbury (0787) 77501

Rookery Park G.C. (18)
Lowestoft (0502) 60380

Royal Worlington &
Newmarket G.C. (9)
Mildenhall (0638) 712216

Rushmere G.C. (18)
Ipswich (0473) 77109

Southwold G.C. (9)
Southwold (0502) 723234

Stoke by Nayland G.C. (18+18)
Nayland, Colchester
(0206) 262836

Stowmarket G.C. (18)
Rattleden (04493) 392

Thorpeness G.C. (18)
Aldeburgh (072885) 2176

Woodbridge G.C. (18)
Woodbridge (03943) 2038

LINCOLNSHIRE AND HUMBERSIDE

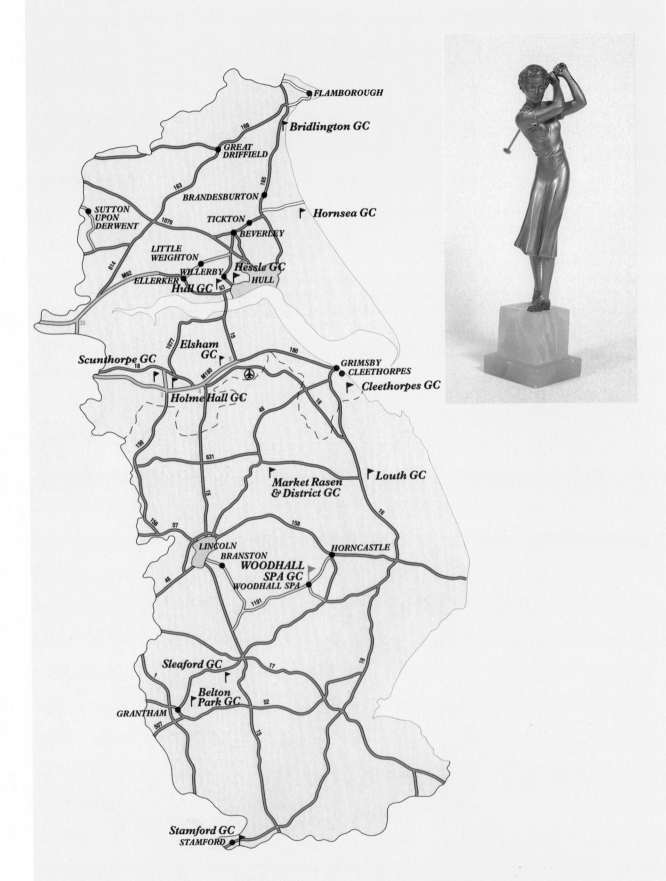

FLAMBOROUGH

Bridlington GC

GREAT DRIFFIELD

BRANDESBURTON

SUTTON UPON DERWENT

TICKTON

Hornsea GC

BEVERLEY

LITTLE WEIGHTON

WILLERBY

Hessle GC

ELLERKER

Hull GC

HULL

Elsham GC

Scunthorpe GC

GRIMSBY CLEETHORPES

Cleethorpes GC

Holme Hall GC

Louth GC

Market Rasen & District GC

LINCOLN

BRANSTON

HORNCASTLE

WOODHALL SPA GC

WOODHALL SPA

Sleaford GC

Belton Park GC

GRANTHAM

Stamford GC

STAMFORD

"Joyce Wethered"   BURLINGTON GALLERY

Anyone who has had the fortune, or dare I say misfortune, to have studied English Contract Law will know that legal writers have spilt countless gallons of ink scribbling about some hypothetical person who offers another £50 if he will walk from London to York – strange people lawyers! Well, just for the fun of it, let us have a hypothetical golfer who sets off from London, clubs on his back, and heads for York (equally strange people golfers!).

Having trekked through Hertfordshire, Bedfordshire and Cambridgeshire he reaches **Lincolnshire** and decides it's about time he swung a club. Problem, **Woodhall Spa** apart, Lincolnshire and Humberside are not exactly renowned for their golf courses. Indeed Woodhall Spa is often referred to as a "golfing oasis" and along a fairly lengthy stretch of coast between **The Wash** and **Flamborough Head** it might be said that there is something approaching a drought. Rich farming country it would seem rarely partners rich golfing country.

Back to our travelling friend, having looked around the pretty town of Stamford, after a sumptuous night at the George, he decided to sneak over the border into Leicestershire and enjoy a round at Luffenham Heath (shame on him!). Returning to southern Lincolnshire, Spalding he avoided (it being the busy carnival week) but interesting games were had at **Belton Park**, 2 miles north of Grantham (where there are 27 holes) and at **Sleaford**, a James Braid designed course where visitors are welcome seven days a week (1986 fees being **£7.50** midweek, **£10** at weekends).

Now many people would walk a long way to play a game at **Woodhall Spa**, located right in the centre of the county and widely considered to be one of the finest inland courses in Britain (see feature page). Nearly 20 miles away the county town of **Lincoln** with its magnificent cathedral has two or three courses close at hand. Here our friend chose to play the 18 hole course at **Southcliffe and Canwick** and, still feeling fit, a further round at the **Lincoln Golf Club** northwest of the city at Torksey (prior telephoning is recommended here).

I have to report that at this point, having covered threequarters of his journey a dramatic diversion was made and instead of continuing northwards towards York our golfer decided to head for **Market Rasen** (such is the lure of the East!), which although better known for its horse racing has a particularly fine woodland-type golf course where visitors are welcome between Mondays and Fridays, green fees being **£7** in 1986. After crossing the Lincolnshire Wolds **Louth** was soon reached. **Louth Golf Club** has a most tranquil setting in a local beauty spot, the Hubbards Hills. Without doubt one of the best courses in the county a game was priced at **£8** in 1986 with **£10** payable for a full day's golf.

Taking in some of the bracing sea air a game was next enjoyed at **Cleethorpes**, just south of Grimsby. Striding towards Scunthorpe 18 holes were slipped in at **Elsham** (Tony Jacklin's old haunt and good for a game during the week at **£6.50**). **Scunthorpe Golf Club's** parkland course was also enjoyed but perhaps the most testing 18 holes in these parts are to be found at **Holme Hall**, just south of the town at Bottesford. Holme Hall is a championship length parkland course noted for its superb greens. Visitors are welcome during the week, a day's golf costing **£7** in 1986.

The large rugby-conscious town of Kingston-upon-Hull lies north of the famous Humber Bridge (all 1,542 yards of it). It has two good courses, one of which is at **Hessle** just over the Bridge. Hessle is a fairly newish creation, designed by Peter Alliss and Dave Thomas. Measuring over 6,600 yards visitors should be able to arrange a game most days of the week. **Hull Golf Club**, 5 miles west of the town at Kirk Ella, is a more established course and welcomes visitors on weekdays.

Looking around Humberside our friend considered pottering up to **Hornsea** for a game – an excellent parkland-come-moorland course – but felt it was high time he made tracks for York.

Well, the outskirts of York are in sight … it's at this point that lawyers start arguing as to what the position would be regarding the £50 should the wicked 'offeror' say "I've changed my mind". Golfers of course wouldn't think of such things. York is duly reached, the £50 handed over and by way of celebration 18 holes are enjoyed at Fulford.

Belton Park G.C.	(0476) 633355
Cleethorpes G.C.	(0472) 814382
Elsham G.C.	(0652) 688382
Hessle G.C.	(0482) 650171
Holme Hall G.C.	(0724) 862078
Hornsea G.C.	(04012) 2020
Hull G.C.	(0482) 658919
Lincoln G.C.	(042771) 210
Louth G.C.	(0507) 603681
Market Rasen & District G.C.	(0673) 842416
Scunthorpe G.C.	(0724) 866561
Sleaford G.C.	(052 98) 326
Southcliffe and Canwick G.C.	(0522) 22166
Woodhall Spa G.C.	(0526) 52511

Ridiculous, there's some lout strolling round Lincoln with his golf clubs – a disgrace, walk to York – damn fool. Oh well, bugger the idiot "Jones, get me the Daimler and take the roof down, I feel like a little air." Some of the thoughts and words of General Crowsworthy a direct sort of fellow. The story he's cottoned onto is this chappie who's walking around Lincolnshire so in the words of local lad made good, Alf Tennyson, he says "Lead and I follow".

Well the General's Daimler's off into the early spring morning and here we have one happyman for he's off to play at his favourite Club, Woodhall Spa. While the minority of the Golfing Society of which he is president stayed at the Hall – the hoy polloy as the General puts it stayed elsewhere. Some tried the **Dower House Hotel (0526) 52588** and commented on the cosy atmosphere, while others preferred the **Golf Hotel (0526) 53535** for its convenience to the beloved golfcourse, while others had no complaints about the accommodation in **The Abbey Lodge (0526) 52538** or The Petwood (0526) 52411. The consensus is that while none had claims to be the Savoy they all were comfortable and friendly. One lone fellow, for reasons best known to himself, (though a blonde from Peterborough was suspected) went to Stamford. "So far," you cry. Well, in his book and this one, no distance is too far to go to **The George (0780) 55171** at Stamford– excellent, marries beautifully with a simply charming restaurant – a must if you're golfing in the area. Stamford is also riddled with excellent shops and Burghley House – which has to be one of the grandest Elizabethan houses in existence.

Another member of the party – the Conservative Party – decided to make his annual pilgrimage to Grantham **The George (0476) 63286** to be precise. Not that it stops here – for while the hotel is good it is **Premier's (0476) 77855**: our man loves the Downing Street atmosphere – better than it sounds and the food is excellent. Although there are a number of inns in Stamford for convenience sake most people selected Woodhall Spa.

It is perhaps in Lincoln that this jolly gathering should have met, not only are the hotels good but there are some delightful restaurants. The City also boasts a magnificent cathedral and a splendid castle and an interesting history. Part of the story can be traced to the Jews' House– the oldest house in Europe. It is here that you will find an excellent patisserie and a first class restaurant in **Whites (0522) 24851**. Another splendid eating place is **Harvey's Cathedral Restaurant (0522) 21886**. Simpler food and a great pub can be found in the **Wig and Mitre (0522) 35190** a delightful fourteenth century place – ideal for breakfast. Two hotels to note are **The White Hart (0522) 26222** in Lincoln, good views of the Cathedral – but quite pricey. Better value – especially for week-end breaks can be found just outside Lincoln, in Branston **The Moor Lodge Hotel (0522) 791366**. The hotel also offers some good cooking and thus makes for a particularly reasonable place to stay. After a splendid day's golf, the General heads for home, via Horncastle – he doesn't stay,

though he has done before at **Magpie's (065 82) 7004** – a chirpy restaurant with a splendid and interesting menu.

Another super dawn, the General breaks wind as usual and once again the plan of the day is golf this time at Louth. The morning flew past but another 18 beckons, this time at Cleethorpes. Then it happens – out of the fish and chip shop – **Mr Chips (0507) 603756**, one of the finest in the country, comes a man with golf clubs – most extraordinary. Leaning over, the General quizzes "you're not that chump walking around ..." After a crisp discourse the General with Chump sets off to the coast. After an amusing nine holes a certain rapport has developed, this is what occurs. "Fancy dinner, old boy?" – before an answer is given off they go to the General's favourite. Not stopping at Cleethorpes or Grimsby where **The Kingsway (0472) 601122** and the **Humber Royal Crest (0472) 50295** are both good. As the car heads northwards Market Rasen and the **Limes Hotel (0673) 842357** are ignored. **The Royal (0724) 868181** in Scunthorpe is also overlookd and even Hull with its delightful port, its very characterful hotel, **The Waterfront (0482) 227222**, its fine restaurant – **Cerutti's (0482) 28501** (splendid seafood) and its popular pub – **The Olde White Harte**, the General has his mind made up. But where's he going – not north, a sin. Beverley with its 13th century minster and fine hotel **The Beverley Arms** is ignored (0482) 869241 – not even a pit-stop at that excellent pub **The White Horse**, Brandesburton, **The Dacre Arms** and in Sutton-Upon-Derwent **The St. Vincent Arms** are left trailing. As conversation builds the General recites his old favourite which goes on a little: it takes in not only the **Tickton Grange** at Tickton, **(0401) 43666** most friendly, but also a favourite of the General's, the splendid **Bell** at Great Driffield (0377) 46661– thoroughly recommended. The story, however, centres around a head, Flamborough Head. Here the **Timoneer Country Manor (0262) 850219** – near another welcoming establishment is ideal for viewing the delightful rock scenery of the nearby coast. Having built up a decent hunger **Copperfields (0262) 850495** is recommended or if you prefer a bar snack, then **The Royal Dog and Duck** is the answer.

As the Daimler rolls on the General makes another mistake **The Willerby Manor** and its fine restaurant **(0482) 652616** are passed by. **The Black Horse** at Ellerker is so tempting but the foot is against the boards. What do we have in store?

The Spalding bulbs have flourished, the pottery at Hornsea is its glorious self – (excellent low priced seconds). The Houses of Wilberforce and Amy Johnson (Sewerby Hall) beckon but lie forgotten by the General – no culture.

At last we have two happy men – Why? Well York has arrived – no walk to York – a drive in a Daimler, but where for dinner, well without question – as the receptionist smiles, we are at **Middlethorpe Hall (0904) 641241** – his favourite. The moral of the story – well, there are several, here are two; buy your fish at Mr Chips and don't walk to York, take the Daimler.

White Hart Hotel
Bailgate, Lincoln LN1 3AR
Tel: (0522) 26222
Between Lincoln's hilltop cathedral and Norman castle, near the Newport Arch, unspoilt Bailgate's Roman gateway, the hotel is over 250 years old replacing a 14th century inn. The Lincolnshire Wolds are a short drive away, as, of course, are the county's golf courses.

The Golf Hotel
The Broadway, Woodhall Spa
Lincolnshire
Tel: (0526) 52588
There is direct access to the Championship golf course from the hotel. Set in extensive grounds, the Golf Hotel, as its name suggests, is the ideal place to stay when playing at Woodhall Spa or visiting other areas of Lincolnshire.

Invariably, those of distinguished character are impeccably dressed.

To us, how a bottle of Laurent-Perrier Champagne looks is almost as important as how it tastes. Or, put another way, what is outside must be an absolute reflection of what is inside. (And inside this bottle is our pink champagne, Cuvée Rosé Brut, renowned the world over for its finesse, delicate colour and fruity bouquet.)

Consequently, each and every bottle is individually finished and 'dressed' by hand, by craftsmen. So while each bottle Laurent-Perrier Champagne may for ye lie maturing in a dark cellar, it will neve the light of day unless it's properly dresse

Laurent-Perrier. The Champagne of champagnes.

During the last decade the growth of golf throughout Britain has scaled new heights with each passing year as more and more people become smitten with its addictive qualities. It was Tony Jacklin who initially sparked this explosion of interest with his victories in the Open Championship and the United States Open some 17 years ago and further fuel has been added by the emergence of Severiano Ballesteros as one of the most exciting players the game has ever seen. The historic events of the last Ryder Cup will provide new impetus to interest in the game and with increased television coverage of the world's major tournaments, golf is poised for another up-surge.

Many of those people who will be drawn to the charm of golf will be youngsters – girls and boys who witness the achievements of today's stars and feel that they too would like to experience the allure of the game with dreams, perhaps, of emulating some of the modern-day heroes and heroines. In a great many cases, these dreams are frustrated at the outset. If the parents of a child do not play golf then all the questions a child may have about starting golf can go unanswered. He or she may enquire about the game from school teachers but unless one of them is a golfer, it is unlikely that this approach will bear any fruit so the seeds of interest are soon stifled and the child turns to other games which are included in the school curriculum.

It is this gap in the education of young, potential golfers that the Golf Foundation fills. Founded in 1952, the Golf Foundation's original motives of promoting the development of junior golf throughout the country still hold good today and in the space of 34 years, thousands of junior golfers have benefited from its work. From this number have emerged some famous names such as Bernard Gallacher, Brian Barnes, Peter Oosterhuis, Michelle Walker and, more recently, Paul Way, Michael McLean and Ronan Rafferty, all of whom received instruction and assistance under the Golf Foundation Coaching Scheme.

This Scheme forms the basis of the Golf Foundation's work whereby it subsidises instruction by qualified members of the PGA to students of schools, universities and other places of higher education and to junior members of golf clubs who are in full-time education. This enables schools which do not have golf as part of their sports' programme to take advantage of giving their pupils an introduction to the game and a solid grounding in its techniques.

But the work of the Foundation does not begin and end there. The Foundation realised that young people's intitial interest in the game must be sustained. Thus, over the years the Golf Foundation has expanded its field of operations to cover the development of a junior golfer right through to the adult ranks.

This area includes the awarding of vouchers for individual tuition to promising girls and boys; the sponsoring of Open Coaching Centres during school holidays: the encouragement of school competitive golf and the assistance of the formation of the Schools' Golf Association: the operation of a film and visual aids service: the promotion of an eclectic competition for club juniors and the operation of a Merit Award Scheme whereby juniors can have their progress rewarded as their aptitude develops.

The Golf Foundation also organises and promotes two important tournaments for youngsters. The Golf Foundation Under-15 Championship fills an important gap in the junior calendar by providing competition in this age group and many of the competitors produce scores which would not shame a competent adult player. The Golf Foundation Schools' Team Championship represents a major contribution to junior golf, attracting as it does, over 1,000 schools throughout the country. The entries are divided into the four Home Countries and from various qualifying rounds and national finals, the respective winners from England, Ireland, Scotland and Wales go forward to the international final which involves schools from Sweden, Denmark, West Germany, India, France and Canada.

The implementation of these activities and the running of the Coaching Scheme requires a great deal of money and the Golf Foundation relies heavily on club golfers for a large part of its income. Organisations within the game and companies also assist in providing funds so that the work of the Golf Foundation can continue and expand.

At present, the future of British golf looks bright but in order to maintain that progress, more and more youngsters must be given the opportunity to learn about and play golf. The junior golfers of today are the club golfers of tomorrow and it is the Golf Foundation which strives to maintain that continuity.

For further information about the Golf Foundation and its work, please contact: The Golf Foundation, 78 Third Avenue, Bush Hill Park, Enfield EN1 1BX. Tel: 01-367 4404.

It has been said that if fifty years ago the golf course at **Woodhall Spa** had been disturbed from its pleasant Lincolnshire surroundings, picked up and carried two hundred miles or so and then dropped (gently!) into the heart of Surrey it would have staged as many major professional tournaments as any inland course in the British Isles. A bold statement perhaps but there are many who feel that whilst Woodhall Spa may have one or two equals, it has no betters.

Woodhall Spa Golf Club was founded in **1905**. The course itself was originally laid out by **Harry Vardon** although substantial alterations to the course were made firstly by **Harry Colt** and later by **Colonel Hotchkin**.

As one of the country's greatest (and most beautiful) heathland courses Woodhall Spa is understandably extremely popular and visitors looking for a game must make prior arrangements with the Club's Secretary. (This applies to individual visitors and Golfing Societies alike). **Mr S R Sharp** is the gentleman in question, he may be contacted via **The Woodhall Spa Golf Club, Woodhall Spa, Lincolnshire**, telephone **(0526) 52511**. The Club's professional, **Peter Fixter** can be reached on **(0526) 53229**.

The **Green fees** at Woodhall Spa for 1986 were set at **£9** per round during the week with **£12** payable for a full day's golf and **£10** per round at weekends, **£13** for a full day. Reduced rates are normally available to junior golfers.

Glancing at the map Woodhall Spa looks fairly close to Lincoln. By road the distance is, in fact, at least twenty miles. Those approaching from the Cathedral city should take the **B1188** towards **Sleaford**, taking a left fork onto the **B1189** towards the village of **Martin**. At Martin the **B1191** road should be picked up and followed to Woodhall Spa, the Club being directly off this road. Those travelling from further north will probably need to use a combination of Motorways before joining the **A15** – this road linking Lincoln to the **M180** (juntion **4**). Persons motoring from the south may have to do even more map-reading! Anyway the following is hopefully of assistance:

the **A1** is likely to be a starting point; it should be left just north of **Colsterworth** and the **B6403** taken towards **Ancaster** and **R A F Cranwell**. Just beyond R A F Cranwell the **A15** can be joined. A right fork should be taken towards **Ashby de la Launde** on to the **B1191**. The **B1191** takes us to Martin – remember Martin? The **B1191** runs from Martin to Woodhall Spa.

The journey across Lincolnshire will have taken the traveller alongside many miles of flat agricultural land – hardly golfing country. Suddenly all changes as Woodhall Spa looms on the horizon like a mirage. Often described as the golfing oasis, Woodhall Spa has all the characteristics of the great heathland courses of Surrey and Berkshire – sandy subsoil, heather running riot and glorious tree lined fairways.

The course measures a lengthy **6866** yards, par **73** (from the ladies tees, **5771** yards par **73**). It is arguably most renowned for its vast cavernous bunkers and while it is almost impossible to select individual holes perhaps those that particularly stand out are to be found towards the middle of the round, between the **9th** and the **13th**. A plaque beside the **12th** tee records how in March 1982 two Members halved the hole in one.

Although none of the major professional tournaments have visited Woodhall Spa numerous major amateur events have; these have included: the **Youths Amateur Championship, the English Amateur Championship,** and the **English Ladies Amateur Championship**.

Woodhall Spa boasts a wonderfully intimate Clubhouse. The atmosphere is friendly and informal and a full complement of catering is offered throughout the week, hot meals being available at all times. I referred earlier to the often alarmingly deep bunkers; apparently a competitor in the **1974 English Amateur Championship** in his endeavours to find the entrance to the Club drove his car straight into a particularly huge bunker beside the 4th green.....one wonders whether this might have had a little to do with the aforementioned friendly atmosphere to be found at the 19th!

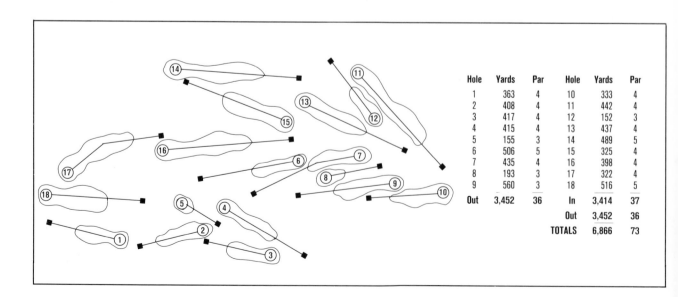

Hole	Yards	Par	Hole	Yards	Par
1	363	4	10	333	4
2	408	4	11	442	4
3	417	4	12	152	3
4	415	4	13	437	4
5	155	3	14	489	5
6	506	5	15	325	4
7	435	4	16	398	4
8	193	3	17	322	4
9	560	3	18	516	5
Out	3,452	36	In	3,414	37
			Out	3,452	36
			TOTALS	6,866	73

THE 9TH: PIDDINGTON TO SPRIDLINGTON

DERBYSHIRE
Alfreton G.C. (9)
Alfreton (0773) 832070

Allestree Park G.C. (18)
Derby (0332) 550616

Ashbourne G.C. (9)
Ashbourne (0335) 42078

Bakewell G.C. (9)
Bakewell (062981) 2307

Breadsall Priory G.C. (18)
Derby (0332) 832235

Burton-on-Trent G.C. (18)
Burton-on-Trent (0283) 68708

Buxton & High Peak G.C. (18)
Buxton (0298) 3453

Cavendish G.C. (18)
Buxton (0298) 3494

Chapel-en-le-Frith G.C. (18)
Chapel-en-le-Frith (0298) 812118

Chesterfield G.C. (18)
Chesterfield (0246) 79256

Chesterfield Municipal G.C. (18)
Chesterfield (0246) 73887

Chevin G.C. (18)
Derby (0332) 766323

Craythorne Golf Centre (18)
Burton (0283) 64329

Derby G.C. (18)
Derby (0332) 766323

Erewash Valley G.C. (18)
Ickeston (0602) 323258

Glossop & District G.C. (11)
Glossop (04574) 3117

Ickeston G.C. (9)
Ickeston (0602) 320304

Kedleston Park G.C. (18)
Derby (0332) 840634

Matlock G.C. (18)
Matlock (0629) 2191

Mickleover G.C. (18)
Derby (0332) 513339

New Mills G.C. (9)
New Mills (0663) 43485

Ormonde Fields G.C. (18)
Ripley (0773) 42987

Pastures G.C. (9)
Mickleover (0332) 513921

Renishaw Park G.C. (18)
Renishaw, Nr Sheffield
(0246) 432044

Stanedge G.C. (9)
Chesterfield (0246) 566156

Tapton Park G.C. (18)
Chesterfield (0246) 73887

LEICESTERSHIRE
Birstall G.C. (18)
Leicester (0533) 674450

Charnwood Forest G.C. (9)
Woodhouse Eaves,
Loughborough (0509) 890259

Cosby G.C. (18)
Leicester (0533) 864759

Glen Gorse G.C. (18)
Leicester (0533) 712226/714159

Hinckley G.C. (18)
Hinckley (0455) 615124

Humberstone Heights G.C. (18)
Leicester (0533) 761905

Kibworth G.C. (18)
Kibworth (053753) 2301

Kirby Muxloe G.C. (18)
Leicester (0533) 393107

Leicestershire G.C. (18)
Leicester (0533) 736035

Lingdale G.C. (9)
Woodhouse Eaves,
Loughborough (0509) 890035

Longcliffe G.C. (18)
Loughborough (0509) 216321

Luffenham Heath G.C. (18)
Stamford (0780) 720205

Lutterworth G.C. (15)
Lutterworth (04555) 2532

Market Harborough G.C. (9)
Market Harborough (0858) 63684

Melton Mowbray G.C. (9)
Melton Mowbray (0664) 62118

Oadby G.C. (18)
Leicester (0533) 700326/700215

RAF North Luffenham G.C. (9)
Stamford (0780) 720041 Ex 470

Rothley Park G.C. (18)
Leicester (0533) 302019

Scraptoft G.C. (18)
Leicester (0533) 419000

Ullesthorpe Court G.C. (18)
Leive (0455) 209021

Western Park G.C. (18)
Leicester (0533) 872339/876158

Whetstone G.C. (9)
Leicester (0533) 862399

Willesley Park G.C. (18)
Ashby de-la-Zouch (0530) 414596

LINCOLNSHIRE
Belton Park G.C. (27)
Grantham (0476) 63355

Blankney G.C. (18)
Merheringham (0526) 20263

Boston G.C. (18)
Boston (0205) 62306

Burghley Park G.C. (18)
Stamford (0780) 53789

Carholme G.C. (18)
Lincoln (0522) 23725

Cleethorpes G.C. (18)
Cleethorpes (0472) 814060

Elsham G.C. (18)
Barnetby (0652) 688382

Grimsby G.C. (18)
Grimsby (0472) 42823

Holme Hall G.C. (18)
Scunthorpe (0724) 840909

Immingham G.C. (18)
Immingham, Grimsby
(0469) 75298

Kingsway G.C. (9)
Scunthorpe (0724) 840945

Lincoln G.C. (18)
Torksey (042771) 210

Market Rasen &
District G.C. (18)
Market Rasen (0673) 842416

Normaby Hall G.C. (18)
Scunthorpe (0724) 720226

North Shore G.C. (18)
Skegness (0754) 3298

RAF Waddington G.C. (18)
Lincoln (0522) 720771

Sandilands G.C. (18)
Sutton-on-Sea, Marblethorpe
(0521) 41432

Scunthorpe G.C. (18)
Scunthorpe (0724) 866561

Seacroft G.C. (18)
Skegness (0754) 3020

Sleaford G.C. (18)
South Rauceby (05298) 273

Southcliffe & Canwick G.C. (18)
Lincoln (0522) 22166

Spalding G.C. (18)
Surfleet (077585) 234

Stoke Rochford G.C. (18)
Great Ponton (047683) 275

Sutton Bridge G.C. (9)
Holbeach (0406) 350323

Thonock G.C. (18)
Gainsborough (0427) 3088

Woodhall Spa G.C. (18)
Woodhall Spa (0526) 52511

NORTHAMPTONSHIRE
Cherwell Edge G.C. (18)
Banbury (0295) 711591

Cold Ashby G.C. (18)
Northampton (0604) 740548

Daventry & District G.C. (9)
Daventry (0327) 702829

Delapre G.C. (18)
Northampton (0604) 64036/63957

Kettering G.C. (18)
Kettering (0536) 512074

Kingsthorpe G.C. (18)
Northampton (0604) 711173

Northampton G.C. (18)
Northampton (0604) 711054

Northamptonshire
County G.C. (18)
Northampton (0604) 842170

Oundle G.C. (18)
Oundle (0832) 73267

Peteroborough Milton G.C. (18)
Castor (075121) 204

Priors Hall G.C. (18)
Corby (0536) 60756

Rushden & District G.C. (9)
Rushden, Wellingborough
(0933) 312581

Staverton Park G.C. (18)
Daventry (0327) 705911

Thorpe Wood G.C. (18)
Peterborough (0733) 267701

Wellingborough G.C. (18)
Wellingborough (0933) 673022

Woodlands G.C. (18)
Towcester (0327) 36291

NOTTINGHAMSHIRE
Beeston Fields G.C. (18)
Nottingham (0602) 257062

Bulwell Forest G.C. (18)
Nottingham (0602) 278008

Chilwell Manor (18+18)
Nottingham (0602) 257050

Coxmoor G.C. (18)
Mansfield (0623) 559878

Kilton Forset G.C. (18)
Worksop (0909) 472488

Mapperley G.C. (18)
Mapperley, Nottingham
(0602) 265611

Newark G.C. (18)
Fenton, Claypole (063684) 241

Nottingham City G.C. (18)
Nottingham (0602) 278021

Notts G.C. (18)
Mansfield (0623) 753225

Oxton G.C. (18)
Nottingham (0602) 653545

Radcliffe on Trent G.C. (18)
Radcliffe (06073) 3125

Retford G.C. (9)
Retford (0777) 703733

Rushcliffe G.C. (18)
East Leake (050982) 2209

Sherwood Forset G.C. (18)
Mansfield (0602) 23327

Stanton-on-the-Wolds G.C. (18)
Plumtree (060237) 2044

Wollaton Park G.C. (18)
Nottingham (0602) 787574

Woodhouse G.C. (9)
Mansfield (0623) 23521

Worksop G.C. (18)
Worksop (0909) 472696

NOTTINGHAMSHIRE AND DERBYSHIRE

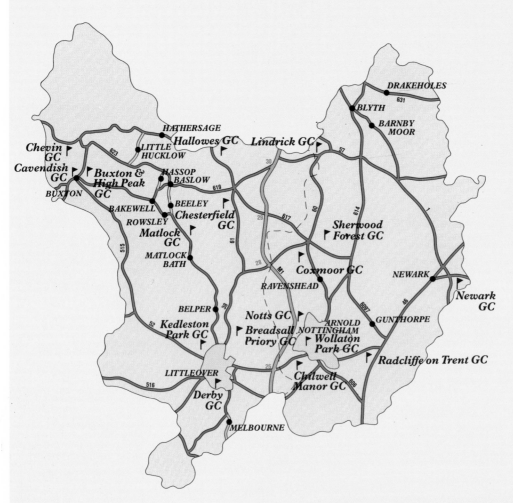

DRAKEHOLES
631
BLYTH
BARNBY MOOR

HATHERSAGE
Hallowes GC   Lindrick GC
Chevin GC   LITTLE HUCKLOW
57
Cavendish GC   HASSOP
Buxton & High Peak GC   BASLOW   30
BUXTON   619
BAKEWELL   BEELEY   614
ROWSLEY   Chesterfield GC   617   60
Matlock GC   29   Sherwood Forest GC
MATLOCK BATH   61   28
M1   Coxmoor GC   NEWARK
RAVENSHEAD   Newark GC
BELPER   38   Notts GC   ARNOLD   GUNTHORPE
52   Kedleston Park GC   Breadsall Priory GC   NOTTINGHAM
Wollaton Park GC   Radcliffe on Trent GC
LITTLEOVER   25   Chilwell Manor GC   606
516   Derby GC
MELBOURNE

515
823
515
6097
46

A.B. FROST   "*Good Show*"   ROSENSTIELS

Riber Hall

n the borders of the Peak District
ational Park, in the peaceful backwater of
ber village, lies Riber Hall, an elegant
izabethan Manor House, set in its own
ounds, with a delightful Old English
alled garden and orchard.

e Hall itself was built in the 1400's by
e Riberghs of Riber, passing by marriage
the Robothams and then to the Wolleys,
ho lived there for seven generations, until
68. The latest addition to the Hall was
1661. Restoration from near derelict
ondition commenced in 1970 and such is
e quality of this Manor House, that it is
ow a listed building, starred in its class.

ex and Gill Biggin and their family have
stefully refurbished Riber Hall and their
re and attention is strongly reflected in
e highly personalised service and the
laxed and friendly atmosphere.

e twelve half-timbered bedrooms are
ely furnished with period furniture; the
ıtstanding feature being the antique four-
oster beds. In addition to this, some of
e bathrooms are equipped with whirl-
ool baths. The decor of the dining rooms
so reflects the different periods in the
story of Riber Hall and they are
hanced by the fine carved oak furniture
d fireplaces.

idely acknowledged as an outstanding
staurant, Riber Hall is renowned for
xcellent cuisine and fine wines. Using the
est fresh produce, the Chef has created
superb à la carte menu.

tuated only twenty minutes from the M1
otorway, ¾ of an hour from East
idlands airport and 1½ hours from
anchester airport, Riber Hall is
nveniently located for easy access to
me of the finest Stately Homes in
orthern England, in particular,
hatsworth House, Haddon Hall,
edleston Hall, Sudbury Hall and
ardwick Hall.

et in the foothills of the Pennines, Riber
all truly enjoys peace, quiet and
clusion, with extensive views and
eautiful walks. Here, 'excellence is
andard'.

Riber Hall,
Matlock,
Derbyshire DE4 5JU
Telephone: (0629) 2795

Having earlier referred to the map of Berkshire as being "cigar-shaped" I'm afraid I cannot resist describing the combination of Derbyshire and Nottinghamshire as "heart-shaped". Given their geography it doesn't seem too inappropriate though I don't suppose the people of Nottinghamshire are all that happy being told that they inhabit the left ventricle of England, nor the Derbyshire folk that they live in the right ventricle – just put it down to the way some minds work!

Heart-shaped or otherwise between them the two counties possess a number of very fine golf courses. While those of Nottinghamshire are perhaps more widely known, especially **Lindrick** and the **Notts Golf Club**, Derbyshire too has plenty to interest the visiting golfer.

Taking **Nottinghamshire** first, **Lindrick** lies some 4 miles west of Worksop along the A57 very close to the South Yorkshire border. Originally known as the **Sheffield and District Club** Lindrick is soon to celebrate its centenary. However, it wasn't really until 1957 that the magnificent heathland course gained its rightful acclaim, the year it staged the **Ryder Cup**. Doubtless assisted by a rare home victory the event proved a major success and the Club was rewarded by hosting the **Curtis Cup** three years later. Today visitors are welcome at Lindrick, although prior telephoning is essential. The cost of a game in 1986 was priced at **£14, £17** securing a full day's golf. Whilst Lindrick enjoys a fairly remote setting the majority of Nottinghamshire's courses are situated in the south of the county, centred around Nottingham itself. The **Notts Golf Club** at Holinwell stands comparison with any of the heather and gorse courses of southern England and at 7000 yards from the Championship tees is longer than most. It was here that **Sandy Lyle**, as a 17 year old, won his first major title, the 1975 Brabazon Trophy. The Club limits visitors to weekdays and again no firm plans should be made without first contacting the club.

Apart from this rather splendid "Nottingham gorse affair" those visiting the county town should strongly consider the merits of **Wollaton Park**, an atttractive course set amidst the deer park of a stately home, close to the centre of Nottingham. Slightly further afield but well worth noting are the parkland courses at **Chilwell Manor** (**A6005**) and **Radcliffe on Trent** (**A52** East of the town).

Two of the county's finest courses lie fairly close to one another near the centre of Nottinghamshire, **Coxmoor** and **Sherwood Forest**. The former is a moorland type course situated just south of Mansfield at Sutton-in-Ashfield. The Sherwood Forest course is more of a heathland type, well wooded, (as one might expect given its name) with much tangling heather. Measuring over 6,700 yards it is quite a test too. Visitors (with handicaps) are welcome at Sherwood Forest, green fees in 1986 were **£12** during the week, **£15** at weekends.

Finally for anyone heading out towards the border with Lincolnshire **Newark Golf Club**, four miles east of the town off the **A17**, should be good for a game most days of the week. Reasonably flat and quite secluded golf here is a little less testing

than at some of the county's bigger Clubs.

Not wishing to be unkind but Derby the town isn't one of earth's more inspiring places – nor for that matter are most of the Midland's industrial sprawls but **Derbyshire** the county is a different matter altogether. **The Peak District** is without question one of the most scenic regions in Britain and commencing only a short distance north of Derby, it covers the greater part of the county – the Pennine Way of course starts in Derbyshire.

As well as being the beginning of all things beautiful the area just north of Derby is where three of the county's leading golf courses are to be found: **Kedleston Park, Breadsall Priory** and **Chevin**. Located approximately 4 miles from Derby off the **A111** (and well signposted) **Kedleston's** golf course occupies a beautiful situation on the Kedleston Park estate. For many years considered to be the leading course in Derbyshire, it measures 6636 yards from the back tees (par 72) and has a variety of challenging holes. Eyeing the course from across a lake is the impressive Kedleston Hall, historic house of Lord Scarsdale. Visitors are welcome during the week, the cost of a game in 1986 being **£12**, though it is probably just as well to give the Club a quick call before setting off.

I'm not sure what the 13th century monks would have made of the **Breadsall Priory Golf and Country Club**, 3 miles north east of Derby off the **A61**, but for us heathens of the 20th century it provides an ideal setting for one of the most enjoyable games in the Midlands. Golfwise Breadsall Priory has only been on the map since 1976 but the undulating parkland course with its imported Cumberland turf greens has matured rapidly and at **£9** a round during the week is well worth a visit.

Chevin lies slightly further north off the **A6** at Duffield, it is an interesting layout, the first ten holes are a steady climb towards a spectacular vantage point after which holes eleven to eighteen gently bring you down to earth (or at least to Duffield!).

Moving "up" the county, the picturesque town of **Matlock** has a fairly short but pleasant course situated north of the town on the Chesterfield road, and if heading in that direction **Chesterfield's** course at Walton is also worth a visit.

The town of Buxton lies in the heart of the Peak District and is for many people their idea of the perfect town. This may have something to do with the fact that some of the finest pubs in England are located round about, but it is also helped by the fact that there are two excellent golf courses either side of the town – **Buxton and High Peak** and **Cavendish**. Of similar length it is difficult to say which is the better, in any event both welcome visitors seven days a week at greens that should leave a few pennies for celebrating nearby.

Having done my bit for the Buxton tourist board I shall end by noting a course in the far north of the county, the **Hallowes** Golf Club, close to the steel city of Sheffield. I'm not too certain whether it falls in Derbyshire or South Yorkshire, like Lindrick it's a bit debatable – either way it's an enjoyable moorland course, and a game should be possible there during the week.

Buxton and High Peak G.C.	(0298) 3453
Breadsall Priory G.C.	(0332) 832235
Cavendish G.C.	(0298) 3494
Chesterfield G.C.	(0246) 79256
Chevin G.C.	(0332) 766323
Chilwell Manor G.C.	(0602) 257050
Coxmoor G.C.	(0623) 559878
Hallowes G.C.	(0246) 413734
Kedlestone Park G.C.	(0332) 840035
Lindrick G.C.	(0909) 475282
Matlock G.C.	(0629) 2191
Newark G.C.	(063 684) 241
Notts G.C.	(0623) 753225
Radcliffe-on-Trent G.C.	(06373) 3125
Sherwood Forest G.C.	(0623) 26689
Wollaton Park G.C.	(0602) 787574

The theory of taking from the rich and giving to the poor has been about since brave Robin and his merry men started clobbering all-comers as they trotted merrily through Sherwood. Now this principle is equally applicable to the golf course. The Handicap takes from the Rich – the good player, you for instance, and gives to the poor – the idiot, me for example. (Note, the subtle flattery is a disguised thank-you for purchasing this here tome.) A similar theory cannot so easily be applied to our hotels, restaurants, etc. Suffice it to say that most are happy to take from rich and poor alike! This of course is not fair, largely because there are some splendid establishments in the area and most, by today's standards, are exceptionally good value.

As one takes the final putt at Lindrick, having played simply majestically – celebrations come to mind. Perhaps you should return to make merry in Nottingham or tuck into some tasty venison at Southwell's **Saracen's Head (0636) 812701**. The news locally is not too good and the nearest establishment of any merit is **Ye Olde Bell Hotel at Barnby Moor (0717) 705121** – a pleasant enough coaching inn. There are two pubs in the area that may appeal. The **Angel at Blyth (090976) 213**, a welcoming pub which serves a good range of bar meals and some accommodation is available if things get out of hand; or alternatively, try **The Griff Inn** at Drakeholes. Another popular local, this time south of Lindrick near to Coxmoor and Sherwood Forest Golf Club is the appropriately named Little John at Ravenshead. Traditionalists may feel that this pub is a little modern for their liking.

Lord Byron's home, Newstead Abbey, is also in Ravenshead and can be viewed between Easter and September. Moving still further South East to Newark with its twelfth century castle and cobbled market square, **The Clinton Arms (0636) 72299**, a Georgian listed building boasts Gladstone and Lord Byron amongst its former guests, and is still a welcoming hotel. The Old King's Arms offers fine beer and good value bar snacks.

Instead of travelling south our friend on his birdie putt may wish to travel West – into the Peak District and sample delights that Nottinghamshire simply does not offer. South of Matlock, **Riber Hall (0629) 2795** is an impressively luxurious Elizabethan Manor House with an excellent restaurant and wines to match. Another splendid Peak District hotel is found on the Chatsworth Estate in Barlow, The Cavendish. This hotel also boasts and offers friendly accommodation and good food (especially cold lunches). The village also lays claim to being the birthplace of one John Little. In the West of the county Buxton offers **The Buckingham Hotel (0298) 79414** as well as the summer repertory season which could be taken in, with the nearby trio of

recommended clubs. For people who love their pubs, **The Bull i' th' Thorn** situated on the A515 is well worthwhile. Before we leave the Peaks a stop off at Matlock Bath: the **New Bath Hotel (0629) 3275**, overlooks the Derwent and is comfortable.

South Derbyshire in comparison to its noble Peaks is somewhat bleak and Derby itself does not appeal. With the sad departure of Restaurant 524 from the Derbyshire Restaurant Scene, one may wish to visit Belper. A somewhat unobtrusive high street hides a first class French eating place in **Remy's (077 382) 2246**, a good restaurant. Another beautiful area to visit is the countryside which surrounds Bakewell. In the town itself **Fisher's Restaurant (062981) 2687** is all stone and the beams and the atmosphere accompany some exquisite cooking. Another impressive country residence can be found in Hassop – **Hassop Hall (062987) 488** – a genuinely luxurious establishment. When one considers elegance and style one can already notice the attractions of the area – but all this class is shamed when compared with the delights of Chatsworth; the house, its works of art and furniture within are simply breathtaking. Chatsworth is open to the public from April to October and lies north east of Bakewell.

The Peaks, as one would imagine, hide some gorgeous settings for pubs. The Old Bulls Head, Little Mucklow, is a quiet spot to have lunch while the Devonshire Arms in Beeley is near Chatsworth and, equally important, offers some fine beers and lunches. In Hathersage, The George is a most satisfactory pub and in the same lovely village, the Hathersage Inn is a most satisfactory place to stay. South of Derby in Melbourne, the John Thompson run by a landlord of the same name, is an excellent public house.

Returning Nottingham way in the direction of Breadsall Priory, the hotel of the same name – **(0332) 832235** could well be the answer to our contemplative competition on the eighteenth. A relaxing stay and a round before business in Nottingham. In Nottingham itself the Modern Hotels, **The Albany (0602) 570131** and **The Royal (0602) 414444** are geared for excellent accommodation if you wish to stay in the centre. An alternative, i'n Sandiacre, is **The Post House (0602) 397800**, good location for an overnight visit (close to exit 25 of the M1). North of Nottingham in Arnold, **The Bestwood Lodge** is more reasonable but less stylish than its downtown competitors. A final thought for the area lies in Gunthorpe, where good food is available at **Mr Toad's (0602) 663409**, an unlicensed bistro.

Other points to note in the area include Belvoir Castle, Thoresby Hall and Hardwick Hall. There are numerous antique shops in the Peaks and Bakewell is famous for its tarts. On that rather dubious note let us return to the eighteenth green.

The Royal Hotel
Wollaton Street, Nottingham
Tel: (0602) 414444
An architecturally impressive contemporary hotel with palm trees and glass roof; set in the heart of Nottingham. It possesses a marble staircase, penthouse bar and amazing city views. Its modernity includes sport and entertainment facilities and full amenities in the bedrooms.

Olde Trip to Jerusalem
Brewhouse Yard, Castle Road,
Nottingham
Tel: (0602) 473171
A vintage public house dating from 1189 with impressive ancient rock facade. Possesses a variety of rooms including a suitably named Snug. Free house with real ale, cider, Old Brewery bitter. Ancient weapons are on view.

CHESHIRE AND GREATER MANCHESTER

SPY *"James Braid"* BURLINGTON GALLERY

ROOKERY HALL

...sed on a hill, near the historic town of ...twich, overlooking the green Cheshire ...ns stands Rookery Hall. Built by ...iam Hilton Cooke about 200 years ..., the Hall was purchased by Baron ...iam Von Schroder in 1867. The Baron ...nged a traditional Georgian Mansion ... a fine Victorian Manor House which is ... a Grade II listed building.

... lovely setting of the Hall amidst 28 ...es of gardens and wooded parkland, ...ging the banks of the River Weaver, ...ures complete tranquility and the ...osphere of a bygone age. Internally, ... beautifully proportioned reception ...ms are notable for the elegance of the ...on, the splendid oak main staircase, ... the wood panelling throughout the ...l. Most memorable is the highly ...shed mahogany and walnut panelling ...he dining room and the superb plaster ...ing.

... personal warm welcome from Audrey ... Peter Marks and the general ...bience, with experienced and friendly ... reminds guests of country house ...ertaining in days gone by. The spacious ...eymoon suite, with its genuine ...liam IV four poster bed and the ...urious coach house rooms with French ...dows opening on to the lakeside ...den, all add to the feeling of peace in a

country setting. Naturally, every bedroom has a private bathroom.

To dine by candlelight in the splendid Victorian dining room is an outstanding experience, with Brierly crystal glass and fine Aynsley china gracing the tables. Only the freshest produce is used in the preparation of the six course a la carte menu which changes with the seasons. The wine list is outstanding, offering a large selection of fine Burgundy, great Bordeaux and vintage Port.

Tennis, croquet, putting, clay pidgeon shooting, coarse fishing in the River Weaver and a helicopter pad are all within the grounds. Riding, golf and squash are available nearby.

Rookery Hall is ideally situated being fifteen minutes from the M6 motorway, thirty minutes from Manchester International Airport and ten minutes from Crewe Station. The great cities of Manchester and Liverpool are only forty-five minutes drive away.

There are many fine museums, country houses and gardens to be visited in the area. Chester is only thirty minutes away and Stoke-on-Trent, where the majority of fine English china is manufactured, is a similar distance and tours can be arranged around such famous factories as Royal Doulton, Minton and Wedgewood. Finally, North Wales and the Peak District are within easy driving for a day tour in wonderful countryside.

Rookery Hall,
Worleston, Near Nantwich,
Cheshire CW5 6DQ
Telephone: (0270) 626866
Telex: 367169

Two rather contrasting counties you could say – Cheshire, so much rural, famed for its plain and Greater Manchester, so much industrial, famed for its rain. The latter belief, as Mancunians will quickly inform you, is pure mythology and the only time rain is guaranteed is during the five days of an Old Trafford Test Match.

The golf too differs markedly: while the Manchester courses are essentially parkland in character, a number of the better courses in Cheshire are of the sandy-heathland variety – not too dissimilar in fact to the Surrey-Berkshire courses. The Cheshire sandbelt commences just a short distance south of the ill-defined Greater Manchester border and encompasses such gems as the **Mere Golf and Country Club, Delamere Forest** and **Sandiway**. (Though Mere is perhaps more a parkland/heathland mix).

Designed by James Braid, Mere is perhaps the leading course in Cheshire and is highlighted on a later page. Delamere, a creation of Herbert Fowler, architect of The Berkshire and Walton Heath, is an excellent heather and gorse affair and runs Mere pretty close. It is located about a mile from the **A566** Manchester to Chester Road, immediately off the **B5152**. The words "temporary green" do not exist at Delamere Forest (something winter-golfers might wish to bear in mind) nor apparently does the word 'par' – the old fashioned term 'bogey' being preferred as a more realistic yardstick of a hole's difficulty – at least for the non-pro.

The visitor is always welcome but is advised to ring the Club before setting off as Delamere is a popular meeting place for Societies. For visitors three and four ball matches are restricted to weekdays and a green fee of £10 was charged in 1986 (half price for juniors).

A little closer to Manchester, Bramhall with its impressive Tudor mansion and attractive gardens has two fine courses, **Bramhall** and **Bramhall Park** and visitors are welcome at both. Prosperous **Prestbury**, home of the rich and famous (and where on Sunday mornings dog-walking seems a way of life!) and **Wilmslow** possess extremely well-kept courses. The casual visitor is welcome at Prestbury on Mondays, Tuesday afternoons, Wednesdays and Fridays. Thursday is Society day and at weekends visitors must accompany Members. In 1986 the green fee at Prestbury was priced at £11.

For many years **Wilmslow** played host to the **Greater Manchester Open**. Like at Prestbury the rough is normally kept fairly short and it has one of those par three holes where you stand on the tee and look so far down to the flagstick that vertigo becomes a major concern. Again a green fee of £11 was charged in 1986 (£14 at weekends). Visitors are welcome at all times though individuals may wish to check for Society reservations on Tuesdays and Thursdays.

Situated at the end of a very leafy lane in Altrincham is the impressive **Dunham Forest Golf and Country Club**. Despite being no more than two miles from the **M56** (junction £7) it has an incredibly tranquil setting. The mature tree-lined fairways are a sheer delight to play on. It is surely one of the area's most beautiful courses. The green fees for 1987 have been fixed at **£11**, with a 50% reduction available to those teeing off after 5 pm. The tees are reserved daily between 12.45 and 1.45 pm for Members but visitors can play at all other times excepting Tuesday mornings and Wednesdays before 5 pm. Sets of clubs can be hired from the professional.

Moving into 'Lowry Country' the **Stockport Golf Club** at Offerton is a good test but for those looking for a particularly scenic course a trip further east towards the Derbyshire Peaks will be well rewarded. **Chapel-en-le-Frith** is a friendly Club and welcomes visitors seven days per week. The green fees are fairly cheap too: **£6** during weekdays, **£7** at weekends (for juniors, **£2** and **£4** respectively.)

To the far west of Cheshire is the fascinating Roman city of **Chester**. The pick of the courses in these parts is probably **Eaton**. It is a fairly new parkland course located some 2 miles south of the city on the **A483**. Visitors are welcome at most times but it is probably best to telephone before setting off.

For golf courses Manchester, rather like London, gets top marks for quantity but is a little shaky on the quality score. Certainly it compares unfavourably with Liverpool and Leeds. It is a shame because historically Manchester was the scene of some of the earliest golf outside Scotland. The **Old Manchester** Club was founded back in **1818**. Its current status is "temporarily without a course" – one can only hope that its Members have found somewhere else to play....**North Manchester** perhaps? Only 4 1/2 miles from the city centre this Club welcomes visitors on Mondays, Wednesdays and Fridays, the green fees for 1986 being £7. Societies are also welcome on the above days and in 1986 for parties of eleven or more a package comprising a light lunch, green fees and three-course meal could be obtained for £13.

A close neighbour of North Manchester is the **Manchester Golf Club**. Visitors are similarly welcome with green fees moderately priced. Elsewhere in Manchester, **Stand** (Whitefield) and **Worsley** (Eccles) are fine courses while to the north the area around Bolton boasts a number of courses of which **Bolton Old Links** is probably the best. It is a tough and interesting moorland course at which visitors are always made welcome. As the for the title "Links" your guess is as good as mine – but there again, what are we to make of Wigan Pier?

Bolton Old Links	(0204) 42307
Bramhall G.C.	(061) 439 4057
Bramhall Park G.C.	(061) 485 3119
Chapel-en-le-Frith G.C.	(0298) 812118
Delamere Forest G.C.	(0606) 882807
Dunham Forest G. & C.C.	(061) 928 2605
Eaton G.C.	(0244) 674385
Manchester G.C.	(061) 643 2718
Mere G. & C.C.	(0565) 830155
North Manchester G.C.	(061) 643 3568
Prestbury G.C.	(0625) 829388
Sandiway G.C.	(0606) 883247
Stand G.C.	(061) 766 3197
Stockport G.C.	(061) 427 4425
Wilmslow G.C.	(056) 587 2148
Worsley G.C.	(061) 789 4202

For the travelling businessman or the hard-working Manchester golfer there must be no greater relief than to adjourn from one's deliberations early, to break away and rejoice in a successful contract on the courses of Mere, Sandiway, Delamere or Prestbury. What may be an even better idea is to forget the meeting – well, not exactly forget it – but have it on the course. It's not for this pen to explain the tactics, but I suppose if you want the contract you really ought to lose – but do it subtly, for goodness' sake. Naturally, howlers can be made – tragedy – you do a Tway – sink it on the eighteeenth – the chairman putts long, you've won – a disaster. Now, how should you placate the fellow?

In a nutshell, the hotels of Cheshire are superior to those in Greater Manchester although there are a number in the city that can be considered, especially if you have business to attend to that can't be settled on the greens of Dunham Forest. You ought to be able to find a room in **The Britannia Hotel (061) 228 2288** for there are 365 (one for every day of the year?). An alternative is the **Hotel Piccadilly 061-236 8414**, which is massive and especially convenient for the city centre. Outside the conurbation, there are several other options to the North in Egerton, **The Egerton House (0204) 57171** is better value especially at weekends and a far better country setting can be enjoyed, the well respected restaurant adds appeal. Another thought is the **Last Drop Village Hotel (0204) 591131** which has many leisure facilities and may act as an ideal placebo to the still fussy chairman. Perhaps the best idea is to let the chap get even with you. To this end, the **Bramhall Moat House 061-439 8116** is convenient and ideal for businessmen. Altrincham also has a trio to consider: **The Cresta Court 061-928 8017** is modern but well equipped, **The Bowdon, 061-928 7121** is Victorian and comfortable, while the former coaching inn, the **George and Dragon, 061-928 9983** has most appeal.

If it's not inconvenient, however, it may be a better idea to sample the Cheshire establishments. The **Chester Grosvenor (0244) 24024** is good value for its quality and stands out, its restaurant and bars add to its appeal. The **Abbots Well Hotel (0244) 332121** is another popular businessman's haunt – this word would be more applicable to **Blossoms Hotel (0244) 23186** for they organise Ghost Hunting and Murder Weekends – on second thoughts this may be a little risky if you've just beaten the boss at golf. Outside the county town the **Stanneylands Hotel** has outstandingly beautiful gardens and is most comfortable. Its first-rate restaurant is also worth taking advantage of – this may be a place to charm the chairman's wife. But don't go too far – a birdie's acceptable but a dickie bird is out of the question! Other hotels to note are the **White House** at Prestbury – a pleasantly converted series of cottages make up the premises and once again the menus are imaginative. Meanwhile, **Mottram Hall (0625) 828135** at Mottram St Andrews has beautifully landscaped gardens and is again most comfortable. Heading west in the county one should consider the **Hartford Hall Hotel (0606) 75711**, on the A556 three miles from Northwich. In Willington near Tarporley, (convenient for Delamere, Sandiway and Eaton Golf Club) **The Willington Hall Hotel (0829) 52321** is both comfortable and good value and has tremendous views of the Welsh mountains. For sheer contrast the new hotel wing of **The Swan Inn (0565) 830295** at Bucklow Hill is worth noting (week-end rates here are excellent value). However, if one is really endeavouring to impress after that near fatal Bunker shot, travel south to Worleston and visit **Rookery Hall (0270) 626866**, a simply wonderful hotel and what is more the restaurant is the finest in the area – if this doesn't do the trick, I'm afraid you've lost your job.

One need not merely rely on the delights of Rookery Hall for a good restaurant. In Acton Bridge, **The Rheingold Riverside Inn (0606) 852310** provides good set lunches and stylish evening dining. In Prestbury the **Galley restaurant (0625) 829466** offers good value and well prepared fish, while in Heald Green, the **Bonne Auberge 061-437 5701** is stylish and excellent French cooking is well served. In Manchester, lovers of Indian and Chinese restaurants have no trouble in providing for themselves. The two recommended establishments are **Truffles 061-832 9393** in Bridge Street, handy for the splendid opera. Away from the dulcet tones to the noise of the aircraft, **Moss Nook 061-437 4778**, a first-rate European menu. Another tremendous establishment is the wonderfully named **Le Bon Viveur**, excellent sauces add to the spice of life. The **Waterside (0794) 517353** in Romiley is another idea for dinner after a day's golf.

It may not be exactly opportune to invite the M.D. out to a pub for lunch, having made a clanger on the course, but if that is what he goes for the **Bells of Peover (05658) 2269** at Little Peover is excellent. Other good suggestions are the Church at Uppermill, The Romper at Marple, and the Ring of Bells at Overton – splendid bar food is available. This can also be said of the Swan with Two Nicks at Little Bollington.

There are other ways, I suppose, of getting back in the good books of the boss, a picnic in Tatton Park could be magnificent and well worthwhile, but hardly appropriate. In Manchester, a wealth of shopping is offered while the **Royal Exchange Theatre, 061-833 9333**, may appeal for an evening's entertainment. Chester is also an excellent place to go shopping. Note The Rows, where galleries and streets of double-tiered shops abound. The Gateway Theatre, Roman ruins and Chester Cathedral are splendid features of the city. Clearly the answer to any blunders on the golfcourse can be rectified by the delights of Cheshire and Manchester – but perhaps the best solution is to play safe. Up in the Bunker or on the Green, why not sink the ball – who likes a loser and if the only way back into the good books is dinner at Rookery Hall that's no bad thing.

The Bears Head Hotel
Brereton, Sandbach,
Tel: (0477) 35251
This charming old coaching inn is situated 2 miles from the M6 motorway and within easy reach of (Cheshire's Golf Courses). Offers excellent cuisine served in an oak beamed candle lit dining room under the direct supervision of Mr Roberto Tanquini, 21 letting bedrooms all bath en suite, 2 delightful bars and also an Italian Pasta restaurant, patio and barbeque.

The Chester Grosvenor Hotel
Eastgate Street,
Chester, CH1 1LT
Tel: (0244) 24024
Even among luxury hotels, the Chester Grosvenor offers something extra, guests never have to ask for the best because to offer something less would be unthinkable. Superb bedrooms, excellent service in elegant surroundings make the Grosvenor a supreme place to stay.

THE CHESTER GROSVENOR

WHERE ANYTHING LESS THAN
THE BEST IS UNTHINKABLE

Even amongst luxury hotels, the Grosvenor has the reputation of being somewhat special, having been dedicated to the creation of the highest standards since 1865.

And, of course, like all great hotels, it has a rather special setting. While offering all the internationally accepted standards of city-centre sophistication, it is placed in one of England's most charming historic cities, surrounded by beautiful countryside.

Part of recorded history since AD79, and the country's best preserved walled city, Chester is a living treasure house of archaeology, architecture and atmosphere with splendid shopping in the unique 'Rows,' which are 14th century galleried walkways.

Indeed, a stay at the Grosvenor is the ideal way to experience all that is best in England – not least, the hotel itself!

THE CHESTER
GROSVENOR
CHESTER ENGLAND

Eastgate Street, Chester CH1 1LT.
Tel: 0244 24024 Telex: 61240

On passing through the impressive Elizabethan styled entrance to the **Mere Golf and Country Club** one is entering historic grounds – not of the St Andrews nature but Mere itself and the Manor are mentioned in the Domesday Book when a gentleman by the name of **Gilbert Venables**, Baron of Kinderton, held the land. Golf alas didn't come to Mere until 1934.

A more modern gentleman by the name of **Mr Edgar W. Hart** founded the Club and obtained the impressive services of **George Duncan** as the first golf professional. Duncan, the Open Champion of **1920** and the Ryder Cup Captain of **1929** was along with **James Braid** responsible for the design of the new course. Nine holes were ready for play on New Years Day in **1935** with an official opening of the full eighteen holes taking place on **May 11th**. A challenge match was arranged for that day and the participants were **Duncan** and **Braid, Henry Cotton** and **J.J. Busson**. Mere quickly acquired a considerable reputation and today is regarded as one of, if not the finest inland course in the north west of England.

The present Golf Secretary at Mere is **Mr Alf Turner**, he may be contacted at **The Mere Golf and Country Club, Mere, Knutsford, Cheshire WA16 6LJ**, telephone (0565) 830155. The Managing Director of the Country Club is **Mr Max Brown** who may also be contacted via the above telephone number.

Subject to making prior arrangements, **visitors** possessing an official handicap are welcome to play the course on Mondays, Tuesdays and Thursdays. Golfing Societies are equally welcome and tees can be reserved for numbers of up to 150. The **green fees** for a day's golf in 1986 were set at **£16** with no increase anticipated for 1987. The Club's professional is **Eddie Goodwin**, a former assistant to George Duncan, he has been the professional at Mere for more than 20 years.

Although set amidst extremely peaceful surroundings Mere is easily accessible from all directions and lies only a few minutes from two motorway junctions: the **M6** exit **19** and the **M56** exit **7**. For those approaching from Manchester motorways can be avoided if the **A56** is picked up – it runs from the city centre directly past the Club entrance (by which time though it has become the **A556**). The Club in fact lies adjacent to both the **A556** and the **A537** Warrington to Knutsford roads. The **M56** is likely to be most helpful for those motoring from the Chester and Wirral areas, while the **M6** should assist the northbound traveller and persons coming from north of Manchester.

The peaceful location referred to is the edge of the Cheshire sand belt. However, the course is more of a parkland nature than heathland (unlike the other outstanding sand belt courses of **Delamere** and **Sandiway**). Adding to the attractive setting are two lakes, "The Mere" and "The Little Mere", neither really comes into play (or at least shouldn't!) although a new green for the 18th has been recently built beside the lake's edge and when in play will turn the final hole into a spectacular par five. The closing stretch at Mere already contains some superb holes and those from the **15th** to the **18th** are known as the 'Famous Last Four'. A brook crosses the middle of the **15th** fairway; the **16th** is a sharp dog-leg left with trees lining oneside of the fairway and an out of bounds the other, while the **17th** is a fairly short par four but the second must be played to a well guarded plateau green.

From its back tees the course measures **6744** yards (par **70** S.S.S. **72**), the tees of the day shorten the length to **6367** yards, and the ladies play over **5811** yards, par **74**.

In addition to Braid, Cotton and of course Duncan many of the games 'greats' have visited Mere, they have included **Harry Vardon, Gene Sarazen, Bobby Locke, Peter Thomson, Bernhard Langer** and **Gary Player**. The latter competed in the **Seniors Championship** held at Mere in the summer of 1986, an event won by **Neil Coles**.

Mere Hall serves as an impressive nineteenth, and although it suffered much damage in 1973 when a terrible fire swept through the entire building, recovery has been remarkable. The catering facilities offered are first class and hot meals are available from 11am to 10pm. Many golfers will be keen to note that there are no fewer than five bars (there is also a bar beside the 11th green – clearly a well organised Club!)

A novel development at Mere has been the recent construction of a driving range where floating golf balls are struck into the Lake. It sounds great fun, but I can't for the life of me imagine quite what Gilbert Venables would mave made of it all.

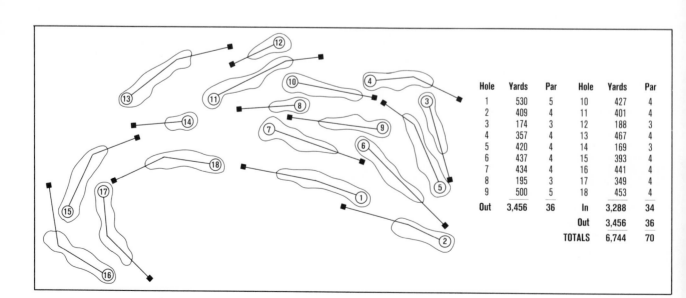

Hole	Yards	Par	Hole	Yards	Par
1	530	5	10	427	4
2	409	4	11	401	4
3	174	3	12	188	3
4	357	4	13	467	4
5	420	4	14	169	3
6	437	4	15	393	4
7	434	4	16	441	4
8	195	3	17	349	4
9	500	5	18	453	4
Out	3,456	36	In	3,288	34
			Out	3,456	36
			TOTALS	6,744	70

CHESHIRE
Alderley Edge G.C. (9)
Alderley Edge
(0625) 585583

Altrincham G.C. (18)
Altrincham (061) 928 0761

Ashton on Mersey G.C. (9)
Sale (061) 973 3220

Astbury G.C. (18)
Congleton (02602) 72772

Birchwood G.C. (18)
Warrington (0925) 818819

Bramhall G.C. (18)
Bramhall (061) 439 4057

Bramhall Park G.C. (18)
Bramhall (061) 485 3119

Chapel-en-le-Frith G.C. (18)
Chapel-en-le-Frith
(0928) 813943

Cheadle G.C. (18)
Chester (0244) 677760

Congleton G.C. (18)
Congleton (02602) 71083

Crewe G.C. (18)
Crewe (0270) 584099

Davenport G.C. (18)
Stockport (0625) 877319

Delamere Forest G.C. (18)
Delamere, Northwich
(0606) 882807

Disley G.C. (18)
Disley, Stockport
(Disley) 2071

Duckinfield G.C. (18)
Duckinfield (061) 338 2340

Dunham Forst G.C. (18)
Altrincham (061) 928 2605

Eaton G.C. (18)
Chester (0244); 674385

Gatley G.C. (9)
Gatley

Hale G.C. (9)
Hale

Hazel Grove G.C. (18)

Hazel Grove, Stockport
(061) 483 3217

Heaton Moor G.C. (18)
Heaton Mersey, Stockport
(061) 432 6458

Helsby G.C. (18)
Helsby, Warrington
(09282) 2021

Knutsford G.C. (9)
Knutsford (0565) 4610

Leigh G.C. (18)
Culcheth, nr Warrington
(092576) 2943

Lymm G.C. (18)
Lymm (092575) 5020

Macclesfield G.C. (18)
Macclesfield (0625); 23227

Malkins Bank G.C. (18)
Sandbach (09367) 5931

Marple G.C. (18)
Marple, Stockpor
(061) 427 2311

Mellor & Townscliffe G.C. (18)
Tardon Mellor, Stockport
(061) 427 2208

Mere G & C.C. (18)
Mere, Knutsford (0565) 830155

Mirrlees G.C. (9)
Hazel Grove, Stockport
(061) 449 9513

New Mills G.C. (9)
New Mills, Stockport
(0663) 43485

Pulton Park G.C. (18)
Grinamon Brow, Warrington
(0925) 812034

Prestbury G.C. (18)
Prestbury (0625) 828241

Reddish Vale G.C. (18)
Stockport (061) 431 3613

Ringway G.C. (18)
Hale Burns
(061) 9802630

Romiley G.C.
Stockport (061) 4307257

Runcorn G.C. (18)
Runcorn (09285) 72909

Sale G.C. (18)
Sale (061) 980 6240

Sandiway G.C. (18)
Sandiway (0606) 883247

Stamford G.C. (18)
Stalybridge (Mossley) 2904

Upton-by-Chester G.C. (18)
Chester (0244) 381183

Vicars Cross G.C. (18)
Chester (0244) 335174

Walton Hall G.C. (18)
Warrington (0925) 66775

Warrington G.C. (18)
Warrington (0925) 61775

Werneth Low G.C. (9)
Hyde (061) 368 2503

Widnes G.C. (18)
Widnes (051) 424 2995

Wilmslow G.C. (18)
Mobberley (056587) 2148

GREATER MANCHESTER
Ashton-under-Lyne G.C. (18)
Ashton-under-Lyne
(061) 330 1537

Blackley G.C. (18)
Blackley (061) 643 2980

Bolton G.C. (18)
Bolton (0204) 43067

Brackley G.C. (18)
Worsley (061) 790 6076

Breightmet G.C. (9)
Bolton (0204) 27381

Brookdale G.C. (18)
Gailsworth (061) 681 4534

Bury G.C. (18)
Bury (061) 7664897

Castle Hawk G.C. (18)
Rochdale (0706) 40841

Chorlton-cum-Hardy G.C. (18)
Manchester (061) 881 5830

Crompton and
Royton G.C. (18)
Oldham (061) 624 2154

Davyhulme Park G.C. (18)
Davyhulme (061) 748 2856

Denton G.C. (18)
Denton (061) 336 3218

Didsbury G.C. (18)
Northenden, Manchester
(061) 998 9278

Dunscar G.C. (18)
Bolton (0204) 53321

Ellesmere G.C. (18)
Worsley, Manchester
(061) 790 2122

Fairfield G.C. (18)
Audenshaw (061) 370 2292

Flixton G.C. (9)
Urmston (061) 748 2116

Gathurst G.C. (9)
Wigan (02575) 2861

Great Lever &
Farnworth G.C. (18)
Bolton

Haigh Hall G.C. (18)
Haigh, Wigan
(0942) 833107

Heaton Park G.C. (18)
Preststwick (061) 798 0925

Hindley Hall G.C. (18)
Wigan (0942) 55131

Horwich G.C. (18)
Bolton (0204) 696980

Holdsworth G.C. (18)
Levenshulme
(061) 224 5055

Lobden G.C. (9)
Rochdale (0786) 343228

Lowes Park G.C. (9)
Bury (061) 764 1231

Manchester G.C. (18)
Middleton (061) 643 3202

Northenden G.C. (18)
Northenden, Manchester
(061) 945 3386

North Manchester G.C. (18)
Oldham (061) 624 4986

Old Links G.C. (18)
Bolton (0204) 43089

Prestwich G.C. (18)
Prestwich (061) 773 4578

Rochdale G.C. (18)
Rochdale
(Rochdale) 46024

Saddleworth G.C. (18)
Oldham (04577) 2059

Springfield Park G.C. (18)
Rochdale
(Rochdale) 49801

Stand G.C. (18)
Whitefield (061) 2388

Switon Park G.C. (18)
Swinton (061) 794 1785

Turton G.C. (9)
Bolton (0204) 43721

Walmersley G.C.
Bury (061) 776 0018

Werneth G.C. (18)
Oldham (061) 6241190

Westhoughton G.C. (9)
Whitefield G.C. (18)
Whitefield
(061) 766 2904

William Wroe G.C. (18)
Flixton (061) 748 8680

Withington G.C. (18)
Didsbury (061) 445 9544

Worsley G.C. (18)
Eccles (061) 789 4202

GWYNEDD AND CLWYD

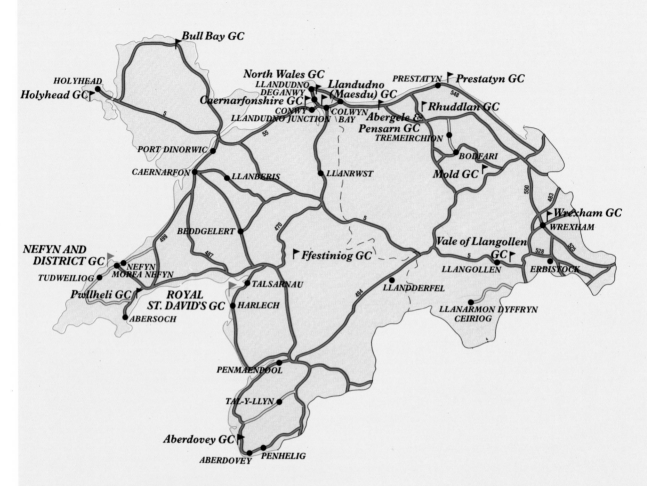

Bull Bay GC

North Wales GC
LLANDUDNO
DEGANWY
Caernarfonshire GC
CONWY
LLANDUDNO JUNCTION

Llandudno
(Maesdu) GC

PRESTATYN ▶ Prestatyn GC
548

COLWYN
BAY

Abergele &
Pensarn GC
TREMEIRCHION

▶ Rhuddlan GC

HOLYHEAD
Holyhead GC

PORT DINORWIC

BODFARI

CAERNARFON

LLANBERIS

LLANRWST

Mold GC

550

483

▶ Wrexham GC
WREXHAM

NEFYN AND
DISTRICT GC

BEDDGELERT

470

Ffestiniog GC

Vale of Llangollen
GC

5

528
525

NEFYN
MORFA NEFYN

487

LLANGOLLEN

ERBISTOCK

TUDWEILIOG

Pwllheli GC

ROYAL
ST. DAVID'S GC

TALSARNAU

HARLECH

LLANDDERFEL

494

LLANARMON DYFFRYN
CEIRIOG

ABERSOCH

PENMAENPOOL

TAL-Y-LLYN

Aberdovey GC

ABERDOVEY   PENHELIG

C.E. BROCK   "The Bunker"   SOTHEBY'S

BODYSGALLEN
—HALL—

Llandudno, Gwynedd
North Wales LL30 1RS
Telephone (0492) 84466
Telex 617163 H.H.H.G.

**OWNED AND RESTORED BY
HISTORIC HOUSE HOTELS LIMITED**

AA 3 Red Stars

One of Britain's Prestige Hotels

First thoughts of North Wales are often of lakes, great castles and even greater mountains, or as a fine fellow by the name of **Hywell ap Owain**, 12th century **Prince of Gwynedd** put it, (I offer it in translation).

"I love its sea-marsh and its mountains,
And its fortress by its forest and its bright lands,
And its meadows and its water and its valleys,
And its white seagulls and its lovely women".

A man who had obviously seen much of the world!

Of course in the 12th century the Welsh didn't play golf, or at least if they did they kept it pretty quiet and in any case you can be confident that **Hywel ap Owain** would have told us about it. Well, what about the golf in North Wales? In a word, "marvellous". Inland it tends to get hilly to put it mildly and should you wish to venture up into 'them thar hills' as well as the climbing gear don't forget to bring the waterproofs! But there again leave room for the camera (hope you've got a large golf bag).

In the main though, it is to the coast the travelling golfer will wish to head. Between Flint to the east of Clwyd and Aberdovey in southern Gwynedd are the Championship links of **Prestatyn, Maesdu, North Wales, Conwy, Royal St. Davids** and of course **Aberdovey** itself. In addition there are several with spectacular locations, **Nevyn**, and **Bull Bay** on Anglesey being two outstanding examples.

Before journeying around the coast though, a mention for some of the inland courses. **Wrexham** on the A53 is the best of these and a regular venue for the major Welsh Championships. Views here are across the Cheshire Plain. In 1986 a day's golf could be enjoyed for £7 during the week, £9 at weekends.

The unfortunately named town of **Mold** has a pleasantly situated parkland course at which green fees in 1986 were £6 midweek, £7.50 at weekends, while deeper in Clwyd the famous festival town of Llangollen has a particularly splendid course, the **Vale of Llangollen**. Set out along the banks of the River Dee you may just sight the landing of one of the famous Dee Salmon. Finally, deep in the Snowdonia National Park there is **Ffestiniog** with its famous Mountain Railway and less famous nine hole golf course. A moorland type this time (as one might expect) short but sweet.

Returning to the coast, **Prestatyn** warrants first attention. Close to Pontin's holiday camp (or is it village nowadays) a genuine links which when the prevailing westerly blows can play very long (the Championship tees stretch the course to 6714 yards). Visitors are welcome at Prestatyn though Tuesdays and weekends can be busy. Fees in 1986 were £6 during the week, £8 at weekends.

Having begun a tour of the coast at this point a slight detour is recommended (didn't take long did it!). Instead of taking the A548 to Rhyl if the A547 is followed the town of Rhuddlan is soon reached. **Rhuddlan Golf Club** enjoys a peaceful setting in the grounds of Bodrhyddan estate with views over the Vale of Clwyd and towards the mountains of Snowdonia. Visitors should have little difficulty arranging a game, a day's golf in 1986 was priced at **£6.50** Mondays to Saturdays and **£8** on Sundays.

Back to the coast via the **A55**, Abergele is the next stopping point. West of the town lies the **Abergele and Pensarn Golf Club**, a fairly new parkland layout (the bulldozer removing the former) lying beneath the walls of Gwrych Castle. Again, visitors are welcome, fees in 1986 being £7 midweek, £9 at weekends.

Golfers in Llandudno are more fortunate than most having two fine courses to choose from – **North Wales** and **Llandudno (Maesdu)**. The latter is perhaps the better known of the two, but both are of a Championship standard and furthermore both offer superb views across the Conway estuary towards Anglesey. Fees are around the £8 mark.

Caernarvonshire Golf Club lies the other side of the Conway Estuary at Conwy. It is another course where the wind can blow very fiercely. The venue of the Welsh Amateur Championship in 1986, it has everything that makes links golf so challenging – gorse, rushes, sandhills and more gorse, rushes and sandhills – very tough. Fees are similar to those at the Llandudno courses and again whilst no general restrictions apply, weekdays are the best times for a visit.

Crossing the Menai Straits and on to **Anglesey**, perhaps the best two here are to the north of the island, **Bull Bay** (near Amlwch) and Holyhead, in fact on Holy Island. Both enjoy magnificent settings and are fairly inexpensive.

Sweeping down the Lleyn Peninsula **Nevyn Golf Club** at Morfa Nevyn (**B4417**) is strongly recommended (see feature page) while **Pwllheli** too has many admirers, (£7 midweek, £8 weekends). **Royal St. David's** at Harlech (also featured on a later page) is the leading course in North Wales and where many will wish to head for, however, though it may look a little remote on the map, continuing on to **Aberdovey** is well worth the journey. The favourite of **Bernard Darwin** it has an interesting layout sandwiched between sand dunes on the one side and a railway line on the other. There is also a fine spirit at the Club and I understand some peculiar things have been taking place recently involving flower pots and periscopes – I shall say no more other than that visitors are most welcome to come and investigate!

GWYNEDD & CLWYD

In the composition of 'Following the Fairways' we have followed the thoughts of golfers living in the locality. No greater contribution has been made than by the simply superb folk of North Wales – many thanks. This makes my job less difficult. It also emphasises the friendly thoughtfulness of the people and it further indicates the splendid hotels and restaurants and golf to be found in the area. The region of Snowdonia is quite breaktaking: to the east of Clwyd and the borders of England the Dee carves its way through some gorgeous ground, including the Duke of Westminster's. On our trip round Wales Edward I is our guide – he was so frightened of the wretched folk of the West territories he built more castles than Sevvie's birdies at Wentworth. His monuments remain at Caernarfon, Conwy and Harlech to name but three! This is Edward, not Mr Ballesteros, you understand. As good a place as any to start our tour is Anglesey. **The Trecasfell**, at Bull Bay is good, while **The Bulkeley Arms at Beaumaris (0248) 810415**, is tremendous in every way. It was near here that Edward started his last castle but sadly Teddy never finished it. The impressive **Trearddur Bay Hotel (0407) 860301**, at a town of the same name lies adjacent to Holyhead Golf Club.

Returning to the mainland the golfer is ready to enjoy a veritable feast as golfer and gourmet. In Llandudno **The Empire (0492) 79955** and the **St George's (0492) 77544** stand out. Meanwhile, slightly inland at Deganwy is the renowned **Bodysgallen Hall (0492) 84466**. Set amid quite idyllic grounds, the hotel offers great style as well as sumptuous cuisine. Less expensive accommodation can be found in the nearby **Deganwy Castle Hotel (0492) 83358**. Returning to town **The Floral (0492) 75735** has a gregarious atmosphere and is most pleasing, while the King's Head in the town serves good food and beer. Nearby in Conwy **The Castle Bank Hotel** and its restaurant **(049 263) 3888** are well thought of – quiet comfort as opposed to style. If you have a minute between golf and golf, have a liquid round at the Liverpool Arms on the Quay. South of Llandudno, at its Junction in fact, is the Queens Head, another pub that merits a visit. There are many attractions in the area: the castle, the town walls, even the smallest house in Great Britain. Colwyn Bay's **Norfolk Arms Hotel** and **Hotel Seventy Degrees** are both good value and the latter also houses a very good restaurant. In Prestatyn, **The Sands Hotel** is fairly comfortable and visiting golfers should try and find the time to drive over the hill to the village of Gwaenysgor and the Eagle and Child pub, where good food and beer are the order of the day. For people who have no time to reach the Welsh coast, fear not. For in Bodfari, **The Dinorben Arms** is an excellent pub, while the Salisbury Arms in Tremeirchion also boasts a good reputation. In Wrexham, the **Wynnstay (0691) 655261** is the hotel of merit. South of Wrexham, the **Boat Inn (0978) 780143** at Erbistock is superb and an ideal gateway to or from Wales. Elsewhere in the area, Llangollen with its splendid Deeside setting hosts the International Eisteddfod. There's no shortage of good hotels in the town, the **Hand (0978) 860303** and **The Royal (0978) 860202** amongst them. Elsewhere in Llangollen, Gale's Wine Bar is relaxed and good value while **Caesar's (0978) 860133** offers some enterprising food.

It would be a pity, however, not to take full advantage of the Welsh mountains if at all possible, as they are quite awesome. Isolated but outstandingly spectacular is **Pale Hall (06783) 285** where excellent use is made of local produce to make dining as well as resting a delight. Another secluded setting is found for the charming **Meadowsweet Hotel** and its fine restaurant **(0492) 640732** is good value.

Having explored inner North Wales, it may be an idea to return to the coast. In Aberdovey **The Trefeddian Hotel (065472) 213** is comfortable and convenient for the golf course while the **Plas Penhelig** in nearby Penhelig is also recommended. Less convenient is the restaurant at Tal-y-Llyn, the **Tyn-y-Cornel** and the **George III Hotel** at Penmaenpool (good snacks). The latter, however, sets us on our way to Harlech and Royal St. Davids. The **Warpool Court Hotel (0437) 720300** is an ideal stopping place for a visiting golfer. Two restaurants, **The Castle Cottage (0766) 780479**, some accommodation and **The Cemlyn (0766) 78425** – excellent fresh food, are to be recommended. Following a round at Royal St Davids, Nefyn might be your port of call and if this is the case the **Maes-y-Neuadd (0766) 780200** is quite excellent and set in the heart of the most beautiful countryside in Britain. Other handy places for Nefyn include **The Linksway (0758) 720258** and **Woodland Hall (0758) 720425**. There are numerous pubs, including the Ty Coch Inn – on the course itself, and the Sportsman. Another inn situated near the cliffs is the provocatively named **Dive Inn (075887) 246** at Tudweiliog – an excellent sea food restaurant. A livelier but equally pleasant establishment is the busy **Bryncynan Inn, Morfa Nefyn (0758) 720879**. Heading back towards our Island of Anglesey, Caernarfon with its splendid castle awaits. South of the town on the A499 **The Stables Hotel (0286) 830711**, is as cosy a place as any in which to stay. East of Caernarfon near Llanberis is for those who have not had enough mountaineering on the golfcourse, the Pen-y-Gwyd is the watering hole to find. To conclude one's journey, come down from the dizzy heights to Port Dinorwic, where you will find a restaurant which keeps a consistently high standard, **The Seahorse (0248) 670546**. A mere fifteen miles from Snowdonia the restaurant illustrates the close proximity that all the above mentioned locations have to simply strikingly beautiful scenery. And a further strong recommendation is the Bodnant Gardens in the Conwy Valley – marvellous!

Two secretaries who help particularly commented that the area in general was ideal for lovers of the good life: boating, fishing, safe swimming, climbing, walking, and bird-watching. Another stated that there were so many places of interest that I should call himself to check them out – I have not been rude in not asking him. I have left it to you to check for yourself. Do visit North Wales, for you are bound to have a splendid time. It is understandable now why Edward I did not want to lose such beautiful lands.

Norfolk House Hotel
Princes Drive, Colwyn Bay,
Tel: (0492) 31757
Ideally situated, close to the sea and in its own beautiful grounds, this three star establishment successfully combines the comforts of the modern day with more traditional virtues. One of North Wales' most welcoming hotels.

St George's Hotel
St Georges's Place
Llandudno
Tel: (0492) 77544
Close to many golf courses on the North Wales coast, this seafront Victorian hotel is ideally situated. Shops and theatre are close by and the hotel itself has many excellent amenities.

'The weather might change —my game doesn't'

Seve Ballesteros (signature)

THE NEW

ballesteros

RAINSUIT

 **Hi-tec Fabric Made in England by Levison Textiles Limited**

The Sunderland Sportswear symbol tells you that you're looking at supreme quality but only the player wearing it knows how good the Ballesteros rain suit really is. YOU can't change the weather but the weather needn't change YOUR scorecard.

With a smart, short zip pullover top this ultra lightweight suit is the ultimate in freedom of movement. The top is cleverly ventilated to reduce condensation and the trousers are superbly cut with waterproof hip pocket.

This exciting new concept in rainwear design is available in a full range of ladies' and men's sizes.

The Sunderland range includes the CLASSIC SUIT in GORE TEX® fabric, the DOLPHIN SUIT in CYCLONE® fabric, the high performance SHARKSKIN SUIT favoured by tournament players, the DOUBLETEX watertight nylon suit, the popular WARM UP JACKET and the budget price range of windproof NYLONTEX PULLOVERS.

On sale where good golf equipment is sold.

MADE IN SCOTLAND BY

S Sunderland Sportswear

WEATHERBEATERS FOR WORLDBEATERS
P.O. BOX 14, GLASGOW G2 1ER
Telephone: 041-552 3261/4
Telex: 779553 (Sunspo)

PALE HALL

Built in 1870 for a weathy Scottish railway engineer, Pale Hall has recently been converted to a luxurious and exquisite hotel. It has however, retained all its finest original Victorian features.

The most interesting of all these must surely be the original barn and adjoining bedroom used by Queen Victoria during her stay at Pale Hall for a short time after Prince Albert's death. Then there is the 'boudoir', a beautiful interior boasts a magnificent hand painted dome ceiling and the Corwen Bar where one can see the unusual bar made from the marble fireplaces that have been removed from the bedrooms.

Each of the seventeen bedrooms are individually designed and finished to compliment their own particular features. It is this fine attention to detail that makes Pale Hall so interestingly unique. Despite its strong historical identity, however, it still provides all the home comforts of the present day subtly blended into this fine regal setting.

The restaurant and its cuisine is also of an exceptionally high standard. Interestingly, breakfast and morning coffee is served in the Bala Kitchen which is still enhanced by its original cooking range from the late nineteenth century.

From the building and its grounds spectacular views can be enjoyed. Here you can walk in solitude, sail serene waters, shoot, fish or enjoy a round of golf. Whatever your interests the Welsh hospitality will ensure a relaxing visit.

PALE HALL
Llandderfel,
Nr. Bala,
Gwynedd.
Tel: (06783) 285

We golfers in Britain are doubly fortunate – not only do we have an infinite variety of courses to play upon (contrast for instance the Surrey heathland with the Scottish links), but we also possess a wealth of outstandingly scenic courses. Perhaps one of our lesser known treasures is perched on the cliffs of North Wales' western tip. Nefyn, or more precisely **Nefyn and District**, was founded in 1907, although the course really came into its own in 1920 when an extension was opened by **James Braid and John H. Taylor** (where was Harry you ask!)

I suppose Nefyn could be described as a 'classic holiday course'; there is a very pleasant drive to the Club (which is probably just as well as it is quite a way off the beaten track); the course is always well maintained with particularly pleasing fairways; whilst the golf is by no means easy it is never too severe or unfair (indeed unless the wind blows fiercely good scores should definitely appear on the cards); the views as mentioned are quite stupendous and Good Lord to cap it all there is even a pub two thirds of the way round! Well, what more could a golfer ask for?

Visitors to Nefyn must be prepared to produce a handicap certificate and be a member of a recognised Club. Should there be a wish to contact the Club before setting off then the **Secretary, Lt. Col. R.W. Parry** can be contacted via **The Nefyn & District Golf Club, MorfaNefyn, Pwllheli, N. Wales, tel. (0785) 720966** and the **professional, John Pilkington on (0785) 720218. Green fees** for **1986** were very reasonably priced at £7 for **weekdays** with £8.50 payable at **weekends** and **Bank Holidays**. Those holidaying close by may well be interested in a **weekly or fortnightly** ticket. In **1986** they cost £35 and £50 respectively – the latter would appear particularly attractive to the serious connoisseur who has a little time on his hands. Keen competitors may well wish to note that the Club stages **open events** annually during the first fortnight in **August**. Societies are welcome at Nefyn although prior arrangement with the secretary is necessary.

A glance at the map tells you that this part of the world is not particularly well served with major roads (although this doubtless contributes to the area's natural beauty). Visitors from afar are more than likely to have planned some kind of golfing holiday and so it is to be assumed that the traveller is already in North Wales. Coming from the Colwyn Bay, Llandudno area one should take the **A55** towards Bangor. Then from Bangor head for Caernarfon on the **A487** and just beyond Caernarfon take the **A499** and the **B4417** roads through Nefyn to Morfa Nefyn. From the South the **A497** connects Pwllheli with Nefyn. From the back markers Nefyn stretches to **6,335 yards** and has a **par of 72. Ian Woosnam**, the Welsh Ryder Cup player, holds the professional course record of **67**. I am reliably informed that another model of Welsh consistency, **Lloyd-George**, was a frequent visitor to Nefyn and that this trend was in turn followed up by **Clement Attlee** – who doubtless found the golf at Nefyn a welcome diversion from the pressures of No. 10.

During the high season it is possible to acquire the services of a caddy. The course is hardly an endurance test, but perhaps this is the place to spoil yourself and let some healthy young lad take the weight off your shoulders as you delight in the splendid surroundings.

After a lengthy opener which certainly invites a hearty belt from the tee (sorry, controlled power) the course moves out along by the cliff edges for a number of spectacular holes. It then turns back on itself before heading in a different direction out on to a headland where holes 11 to 18 are found. There is no real place on the course where you lose sight of the sea and you may just encounter the occasional sunbather who has lost his or her way. If the holiday mood really takes you then down in a cove by the **12th green** is the **Ty Coch Inn**. Yes, it is accessible from the course and on a really hot summer's day can doubtless be mistaken for a heavenly mirage. One cannot help wondering how many steady score cards have suddenly taken on erratic proportions from the 13th hole in!

Returning to the Clubhouse you will find that full catering facilities are offered. There is a snooker room and a genuinely pleasant atmosphere in which to relax and reflect on your day. Well, if you have not enjoyed your golf at Nefyn then I must venture to suggest that you are a very difficult person to please!

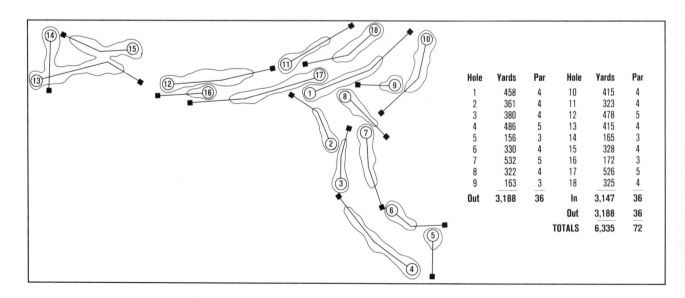

Hole	Yards	Par	Hole	Yards	Par
1	458	4	10	415	4
2	361	4	11	323	4
3	380	4	12	478	5
4	486	5	13	415	4
5	156	3	14	165	3
6	330	4	15	328	4
7	532	5	16	172	3
8	322	4	17	526	5
9	163	3	18	325	4
Out	3,188	36	In	3,147	36
			Out	3,188	36
			TOTALS	6,335	72

ROYAL ST DAVID'S

With a **St Andrews** in Scotland and a **St Georges** in England, it seems only right that there should be a **St David's** in Wales. Along with Royal Porthcawl in the South, the **Royal St David's Golf Club** at **Harlech** is one of the Principality's two greatest Championship links.

The Club was founded in **1894** by **the Hon. Harold Finch-Hatton** together with **Mr W H More** who for twenty years acted as Honorary Secretary. The course itself was open for play at the end of 1894 and the opening competition was fittingly won by the greatest golfer of the day, and the reigning Amateur Champion, **John Ball**. St David's became 'Royal' St David's early this century and in 1935 **The Duke of Windsor** (then Prince of Wales), became the Club's captain.

Of its many attributes St David's is perhaps best known for its glorious setting: on the one side stretch the blue waters of Tremedog Bay, on the other the imperious Snowdon and the other great mountains of Snowdonia National Park; while surveying all from its lofty perch is the almost forbidding presence of Harlech Castle. The massive fortress built by Edward I has known a particularly turbulent past. It played a prominent role in the War of the Roses when a great seige took place eventually ending in surrender. The seige is commemorated in the song 'Men of Harlech'.

The present 'Men of Harlech' to whom I should introduce you are the Secretary, **Mr Harry Fairbrother** and the Club's professional **John Barnett**. Both may be contacted by telephone on (0766) 780361. The Club has the simple address of **Royal St David's Golf Club, Harlech, Gwynedd** (very simple by Welsh standards!)

St David's has a reputation for being one of Britain's friendliest Clubs; subject to being Members of Golf Clubs **visitors** and Golfing Societies are welcome at all times although those wishing to make party bookings must do so by written application to the Secretary. The cost of a day's golf in 1986 was priced at **£8** during the week with **£11** payable at the weekend and on Bank Holidays.

The setting is indeed superb but the journey to get there can be a lengthy one – Harlech alas isn't like the proverbial Rome and there is one road that travellers must join, namely the **A496**.

From the North this road approaches from **Blaenau Ffestiniog** via **Maentwrog (east of Porthmadog)** and from the South via **Dolgellau** and **Barmouth**. Those coming from further afield may find **Bala** (if travelling from the north) and **Welshpool** (if motoring from the south) useful towns to head for. Bala links with Maentwrog by way of the **A4212** and the **A487**, while the **A458** and **A470** link Welshpool to Barmouth. Finally, for those without horsepower the train station at Harlech may prove of assistance.

Measuring **6495** yards from the Championship tees (**6427** yards from the medal tees) St David's may not at first glance seem overly testing. However the general consensus is that the course, to adopt golfers' terminology, plays long. Par is a very tight **69** and there are only two par fives on the card. Furthermore the rough can be very punishing (not to mention frustrating) and it is very rare for there not to be a stiff wind. It is interesting to note that despite countless Championships the course record stands at only three under par.

Perhaps the most difficult holes on the course are the **10th**, a long par four into the prevailing wind, and the **15th** which requires quite a lengthy carry. The round finishes with, to adopt another curious golfing expression, 'a nasty long short hole.'

As one might imagine each of the major Welsh Championships is staged regularly at St David's, in addition the **Ladies British Open Amateur Championship** and both Mens and Ladies **Home International Matches** have also been played at Harlech.

The nineteenth at St David's matches the high standards set by the previous eighteen. There is an excellent bar (for celebration or recuperation) and light snacks, lunches and dinners are all offered. With prior warning a full English (or should one say Welsh?) breakfast can also be arranged.

The friendliness of the Club has already been mentioned; unfortunately there are some English who consider the Welsh a little insular – a visit to Royal St David's can make one realise that the Welsh Golf Clubs, at any rate, could teach many of their English counterparts a thing or two...and on that controversial note, I wish you good golfing!

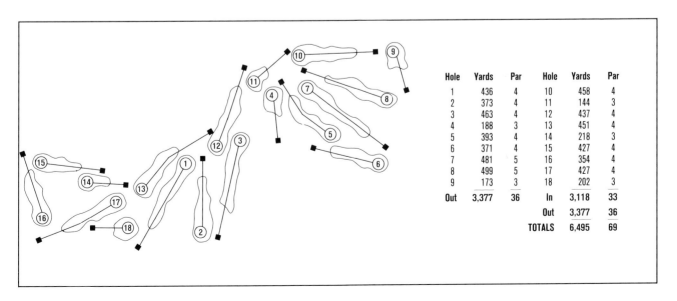

Hole	Yards	Par	Hole	Yards	Par
1	436	4	10	458	4
2	373	4	11	144	3
3	463	4	12	437	4
4	188	3	13	451	4
5	393	4	14	218	3
6	371	4	15	427	4
7	481	5	16	354	4
8	499	5	17	427	4
9	173	3	18	202	3
Out	3,377	36	In	3,118	33
			Out	3,377	36
			TOTALS	6,495	69

LANCASHIRE

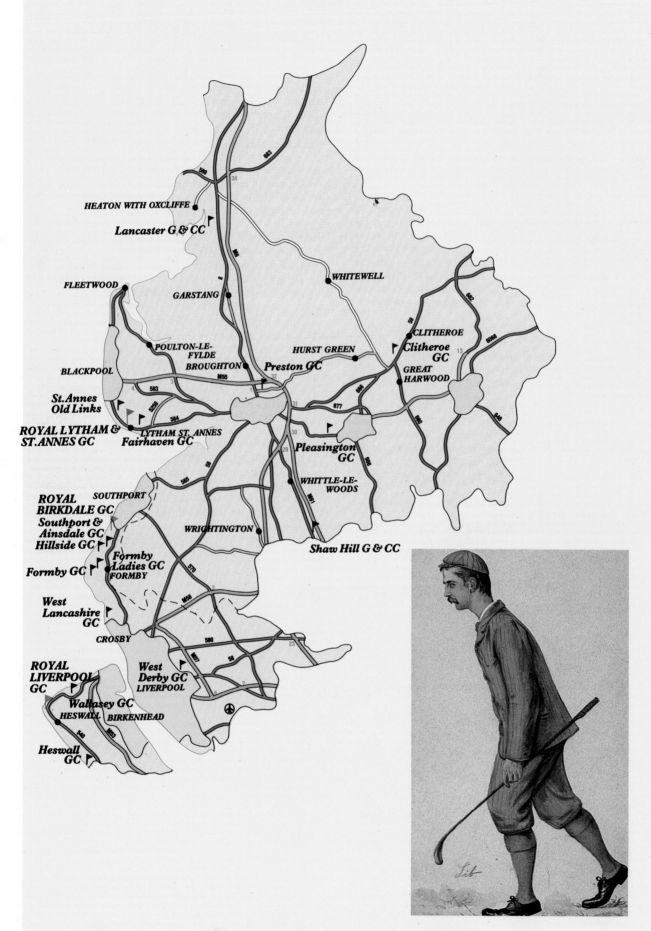

HEATON WITH OXCLIFFE

Lancaster G & CC

FLEETWOOD

WHITEWELL

GARSTANG

POULTON-LE-FYLDE

HURST GREEN

CLITHEROE

Clitheroe GC

BROUGHTON

Preston GC

BLACKPOOL

GREAT HARWOOD

St.Annes Old Links

ROYAL LYTHAM & ST.ANNES GC

LYTHAM ST. ANNES

Fairhaven GC

Pleasington GC

WHITTLE-LE-WOODS

ROYAL BIRKDALE GC

SOUTHPORT

Southport & Ainsdale GC

Hillside GC

WRIGHTINGTON

Formby Ladies GC

Formby GC

FORMBY

Shaw Hill G & CC

West Lancashire GC

CROSBY

ROYAL LIVERPOOL GC

West Derby GC

LIVERPOOL

Wallasey GC

HESWALL

BIRKENHEAD

Heswall GC

LIB   *"John Ball"*   BURLINGTON GALLERY

SHAWHILL

Hotel, Golf and Country Club

WHITTLE·LE·WOODS, CHORLEY

LANCASHIRE

"Caddies are not allowed on the greens when wearing clogs" – recorded in the Minutes of a Lancashire Golf Club, 1894.

I don't suppose they appreciate it in the slightest but the many horses that race across the sands near Southport early each morning (and the donkeys that do their best to race across the same sands) are performing within a few yards of one of the greatest stretches of golfing country in the world. On the Lancashire coast between Liverpool and Blackpool lie a magnificent collection of natural golfing links. Being more particular, between **Hoylake** on the Wirral Peninsula and **Royal Lytham** (a distance of less than 40 miles) are to be found the golf links of **Wallasey, West Lancashire, Formby, Formby Ladies, Southport and Ainsdale, Royal Birkdale, Hillside, Fairhaven** and **St Annes Old Links**. A truly formidable list. Hoylake, Birkdale and Lytham have, of course, each staged the Open Championship on a number of occasions, while the Amateur Championship has been played at both Hillside and Formby and Southport and Ainsdale has twice hosted the Ryder Cup. When the wind hammers across from the Irish Sea any of the eleven links mentioned can become treacherously difficult and the famous Lancashire sandhills rarely provide shelter from the elements.

The green fee for a day's golf in this part of the world tends to range between £10 at the quieter Clubs and £18 at the bigger Clubs. Visitors are welcome to play at any although weekdays are naturally the best times to try and arrange a visit. Telephoning in advance is normally preferred. Hoylake, Birkdale and Lytham are each featured on later pages but a visit to any of the above will certainly not meet with disappointment (though it may result in a little damaged pride!).

Should one not wish to do battle with the pines at Formby or Gumbley's bunker at 'S and A', Lancashire (which for our purposes includes Merseyside) has a wealth of inland courses, generally less testing but often equally enjoyable.

For such a relatively small area the Wirral Peninsula is fairly thick with Clubs. In addition to the links at Hoylake and Wallasey, **Heswall** offers a quite outstanding parkland challenge. Situated alongside the River Dee off the **A540** (via junction **4, M53**) it is a medium length course, beautifully maintained with views towards the distant Welsh hills. Visitors are welcome at all times although a quick telephone call is advisable. The green fees in 1986 were £10 per day midweek, £13.50 at weekends.

Those staying 'across the Mersey' in Liverpool might care for a game at **West Derby**, also a parkland course, very centrally located (off the **A57**) and always good for a game during the week. (Also by arrangement at weekends.) The green fees in 1986 were £7 per round. The nearest of the great links courses is **West Lancashire** at Blundellsands although Formby too is within easy reach, the **A565** being the road to take out of Liverpool.

More centrally in Lancashire, **Shaw Hill Golf and Country Club** is most definitely one to note if travelling along the **M6**. Located just north of Chorley it enjoys a very peaceful setting and is a particular favourite of Golfing Societies. Visitors are welcome seven days a week, the fees in 1986 being £8 per day. The other side of the **M6 Pleasington Golf Club** enjoys similarly secluded surroundings (and very scenic ones too). The course is situated 3 miles west of Blackburn along the **A59**. Visitors are welcome at most times though prior arrangement with the Secretary is essential. The cost of a day's golf in 1986 was priced at £10 during the week, £12 at weekends.

Still moving 'up' the country, **Preston** welcomes visitors throughout the week, a pleasantly undulating course, just north of the town, it can easily be reached from the **M6** (junction **32**).

Clitheroe Golf Club lies on the edge of the Forest of Bowland amidst superb countryside. The course lies approximately 2 miles south of the town with views across to Pendle Hill. Visitors are welcome during the week and on Sundays. The fees in 1986 were £8 midweek, £10 on Sundays.

Lancashire wouldn't be complete without mentioning its county town. There are a number of Clubs at hand, perhaps the best being the **Lancaster Golf and Country Club** located 3 miles south of the city on the **A588** at Stodday. An attractive parkland course close to the River Lune estuary (can be breezy!) visitors are welcome between Mondays and Fridays, the cost of a day's golf in 1986 being £10.

"Golfers on foot have no standing on the course" – notice outside a clubhouse, California 1974.

Clitheroe G.C.	(0220) 22292
Fairhaven G.C.	(0256) 736741
Formby G.C.	(07048) 72164
Formby Ladies G.C.	(07048) 73493
Heswall G.C.	(0704) 67169
Lancaster G. & C.C.	(0524) 751247
Pleasington G.C.	(0254) 22177
Preston G.C.	(0772) 794234
Royal Birkdale G.C.	(0704) 67920
Royal Liverpool G.C.	(051) 632 3101
Royal Lytham and St Annes G.C.	(0253) 724206
St Annes Old Links	(0253) 723597
Shaw Hill G. & C.C.	(02572) 69221
Southport and Ainsdale G.C.	(0704) 78000
Wallasey G.C.	(051) 639 3700
West Derby G.C.	(051) 228 3420
West Lancashire G.C.	(051) 924 1076

LANCASHIRE

As I write this last piece about hotels, restaurants and other delights to be found in the counties of Britain one is left with two clear thoughts. On the one hand, this book is written with the non-golfing partner or friend in mind. The best hotels are included so that some form of bribery can be offered to induce a long week-end's golf. While suggestions are made of alternative relaxations that might also be of interest, on the other hand it may be that Lancashire and Merseyside hardly inspire the non-golfer to any great delights, Liverpool and Southport not perhaps quite capturing the imagination. Well this is not the case – what a perfect place for golfer and non-golfer. From Morecambe Bay – where the spectacular coastal scenery reveals the most striking sunsets to the dunes of Birkdale – there are many places to woo your non-golfing partner. This in short is a golfer's paradise and a fine place also to take the loved one.

The city of Lancaster lies west of some gorgeous moorland scenery. The M6 carves its way through and near to junction 34. **The Post House Hotel** (0524) 65999 is ideal for travellers. A little further north in Heaton with Oxcliffe a pub with a splendid riverside setting is **The Golden Ball** – well worth a visit when visiting these parts. Resist the temptation to travel further north and tie the knot in Gretna Green and instead travel to Morecambe where as well as some excellent shops **The Midland Hotel (0524) 417180** is welcoming.

If you have time, do try and make tracks to Whitewell. Now here amid the delightful Forest of Bowland lies the charming **Inn at Whitewell** (02008) 222. Excellent bar snacks, a splendid restaurant and some charming bedrooms – ideal for hunting, shooting and fishing in between golf. People remaining on the A6 or M6 may select another pub – on this occasion **Th' Owd Tithebarn**. Or further south and near Junction 32 and Broughton, this pub is entitled **The Plough at Eaves**.

If one has decided to play at Preston or Clitheroe a few thoughts for you. In Hurst Green, **The Shireburn Arms Hotel (025486) 518** is well worth a visit. Not only can you enjoy the splendid Ribblesdale countryside but some fine cooking is also to be found. An alternative eating establishment, a restaurant on this occasion is **Tiffany (0254) 889528** at Great Harwood – a fine standard of cuisine where the fish is particularly good. In Clitheroe itself **The Swan and Royal Hotel (0200) 23130** is recommended while people wishing to have a quick tipple before hitting the tees then the **Hodder Bridge Hotel** at Higher Hodder Bridge has a pleasant position.

One place that really should be high on golfers' lists to visit is the **Shaw Hill Hotel (02572) 69221** near Chorley – an excellent golf course and an elegant mansion house in which to hang up one's clubs before ordering dinner. Splendid. Another tremendous place to settle down to first class fodder is **The High Moor (02575) 2364** at Wrightington. A pleasant atmosphere and some first rate cuisine. Ideal if your golf wasn't perhaps as wonderful as you had hoped.

Heading for the coastal delights of Lancashire some thoughts emerge. The fishing of Fleetwood is well known, not grand but a fish restaurant to note is **The Trafalgar (03917) 2266.**

Alternatively try some excellent cooking in the cottage restaurant that calls itself **The Stocks (0253) 882294**. The Stocks opposite may be considered if the mother-in-law or some other unwanted creature is tagging along. And so to Blackpool, the Tower is well known. The town is a doorway to paradise for children who may not be as interested in golf as their mother and fathers. There are obviously many hotels to be found but perhaps the best is **The Pembroke (0253) 23434** on the North Promenade. In Lytham St Annes, a pleasant town, there are a number of ideas – if you like fish and you are not seeking the finest luxury dining room, then **Bennett's Bistro** is certain to appeal. For people wishing to stay nearby then there are two hotels that should be noted. Firstly, **The Chadwick (0253) 720061** on the seafront and secondly, **The Clifton Arms Hotel (0253) 739898**.

The abundance of superb golf in this area is well known although it is fair to say the same brilliance is not reflected in the region's hotels. However, this is not to say that none exist. In Southport there are a number of ideas. **The Prince of Wales (0704) 36688** is excellent and ideal for the nearby golf courses. More golfers exhausted after playing some of the most outstanding holes in golf will be eager to catch a few hours sleep before another bracing day on the fairways. In Formby, **The Tree Tops Motel (07048) 74649** is also welcoming and a good centre point. Following the coastline southwards perhaps to play Royal Liverpool then Crosby may be of appeal, here the **Blundellsands Hotel 051 924 6515** is quiet and fairly good value.

Near to the coastal corner of Merseyside one may wish to visit Heswall, here a fine restaurant can be found, **Les Bougies 051 342 6673**– essentially French and well thought of. In Birkenhead is the particularly popular but rather extraordinarily named **Bowler Hat Hotel 051 652 493** – a small but splendid hotel ideal for golfers playing the courses of the Wirral Peninsula. A pub that could be especially handy if your bank manager or ex-partner is in the Clubhouse bar is the **Green Lodge**. It conveniently lies adjacent to the golf course. It may well be that many people will have some business in Liverpool that has to be dealt with before one can put one's plus fours on and stride out onto the fairways. If you are staying in this Liver city then the **Britannia Adelphi 051 709 7200** and the **Atlantic Tower Thistle 051 227 4444** are both good while excellent leisure facilities can be found in **The Holiday Inn 051 709 0181**. The city has a reputation for splendid Indian and Chinese food but two European establishments are our recommendations. On the one hand **The Armadillo 051 236 4123** and on the other **La Grande Bouffe 051 236 3375**. The city itself with its two cathedrals and its Beatles history is by and large a friendly area but, as so often is the case the city is a pale shadow when compared with the country around it. In this particular area with the Dales to the East, the Wirral to the South, the lakes and hills to the North and to the West, well not only are there charmed sunsets to sweet talk your partner but also and far more importantly there are golf courses, some of the very finest in the world.

Liverpool Playhouse
Williamson Square,
Liverpool L1 1EL
Tel: 051 709 8478
The Playhouse presents a regular programme of new work and classics in its Main House (758) and its Studio (100), as well as performances by visiting companies, dance artists, musicians and others. It is the country's longest established repertory theatre and is a five minute walk down Hood Street from Lime Street station.

Britannia Adelphi Hotel
Ranelagh Place
Liverpool
L3 5UL
Tel: 051 709 7200
The hotel has been recently refurbished to add splendid bedrooms, sporting and leisure facilities and two new restaurants to the host of other more traditional comforts. Situated in central Liverpool, the hotel makes an ideal base when visiting the golf courses on the Lancashire coast.

ROYAL LIVERPOOL (HOYLAKE)

The **Royal Hotel** at Hoylake (alas no longer with us) played a starring role in the early history of the **Royal Liverpool Golf Club**. In **1869** a meeting was held there which led to the famous Club's formation. Perhaps of great significance that day, with no disrespect whatsoever to those founding Members, was the presence in the Hotel of a seven year old boy. **John Ball** whose father was the Hotel proprietor grew to become not only Hoylake's favourite son, but also the finest amateur golfer Britain has ever produced.

In the early days golf at Hoylake must have been at times a trifle frustrating, for the Club shared the links with a racecourse and hoof prints on the fairways were a fairly common hazard. However, by 1876 the horses (doubtless equally frustrated) had found elsewhere to gallop and the golf course quickly developed into England's premier Championship test. The 1869 birthdate in fact makes Hoylake England's second oldest links course, just four years younger than Westward Ho!

Ten Open Championships and sixteen Amateur Championships later the Secretary at Royal Liverpool is **Mr J.R. Davidson**. Mr Davidson can be contacted by telephone on **(051) 632 3101**. **Visitors** are welcome to play at Hoylake, subject to proof of handicap or letter of introduction from their home Club, between Mondays and Fridays and at certain restricted times at weekends.

The **green fees** as set in April 1986 were **£16** during the week (**£14** for ladies) and **£18.40** at weekends (**£16** for ladies). For juniors aged between 15 and 17 the green fee was priced at **£9.50** with **£4** being charged for the under 15's. Golfing Societies are equally welcome at Hoylake, those organising should address written applications to the Secretary, care of **Royal Liverpool Golf Club, Meols Drive, Hoylake, Wirral, Merseyside. John Heggarty** is the Club's professional and sets of golf clubs can be hired from him. It may also be possible to arrange for the services of a caddy. Mr Heggarty can be reached on **(051) 632 5868**.

Hoylake is located at the tip of the Wirral peninsula, approximately ten miles west of Liverpool and fifteen miles north of Chester. The north west of England is particularly well-served by motorway connections and finding the course shouldn't be a problem. Approaching from either the north or south the **M6** is likely to be of assistance, it passes midway between Manchester and Liverpool and should be left at junction **19A**. Thereafter the **M56** can be followed towards Chester joining the **M53** at junction **15**. The **M53** will then take you to the far end of the Wirral where the **A553** Hoylake road should be picked up. (In a nutshell: **M6 – M56 – M53 – A553**).

The course occupies fairly flat ground and is very exposed to elements. It is unusual for the wind not to blow. (You have been warned!) It was his mastery of the wind, a skill acquired playing at Hoylake that enabled John Ball to win many of his record eight Amateur Championships. His victories were achieved between **1888** and **1912**. Ball's great rival during those years both ironically and remarkably, was a fellow Hoylake man **Harold Hilton**. Hilton himself won four Amateur Championships. In addition both Hilton and Ball won the Open Championship, Ball in **1890** and Hilton twice in **1892** and **1897**. The immortal Bobby Jones is the only other Amateur golfer to have won the Open title.

Even on those very rare occasions when all is calm, Hoylake is still a exceptionally difficult test. From the medal tees the course measures **6,780** yards, par **72**, (extended to nearly 7,000 yards during Championships), and it can play every inch of its length. It is helpful to strike the ball, in the words of the Club's motto, 'far and sure'. Rather like Carnoustie, Hoylake is renowned for its exacting final stretch. It contains two par fives and three par fours any of which is capable of wrecking a potentially good score. The 16th in particular can be cruelly punishing with its out of bounds to the right of the fairway.

The ten Opens held at Hoylake have produced ten different Champions including **Harold Hilton, John H. Taylor, Walter Hagen** and **Bobby Jones**. The latter's victory in **1930** was the second leg of the historic **grand slam**. The sole reason for the course being presently off the 'Open rota' (the last staging was in 1967) is that the course cannot accommodate the vast crowds that the event now attracts. Ironically it is the same enthusiastic public who suffer most for there are many who maintain that Hoylake remains the greatest of all England's Championship links.

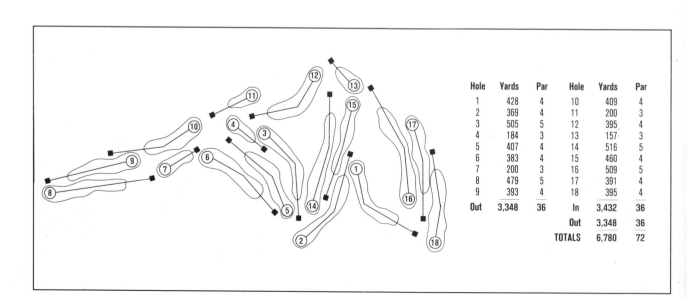

Hole	Yards	Par	Hole	Yards	Par
1	428	4	10	409	4
2	369	4	11	200	3
3	505	5	12	395	4
4	184	3	13	157	3
5	407	4	14	516	5
6	383	4	15	460	4
7	200	3	16	509	5
8	479	5	17	391	4
9	393	4	18	395	4
Out	**3,348**	**36**	**In**	**3,432**	**36**
			Out	**3,348**	**36**
			TOTALS	**6,780**	**72**

Back in 1889 your average J.P. was probably not the most popular man in town, however, in a certain **Mr. J.C. Barrett,** Birkdale possessed a man of rare insight and one clearly cognisant of the finer things in life. Mr. Barrett was a golfer. On the 30th July, 1889, he invited eight fellow addicts to his home and together they resolved to form a Golf Club. One can imagine their enthusiasm as they formulated their plans, perhaps over a brandy and cigars, I know not; but very quickly a clubhouse was secured – a single room in a private residence at a four shilling per week rental! Land (at £5 per year rental) was acquired and soon a 9 hole course was laid out. It all sounds rather unsophisticated, but compared with todays problems of first finding a suitable site and then obtaining planning permission, I suppose it was relatively straightforward.

Whilst no one could question its present day status as one of the country's leading Championship courses, historically **Birkdale** set off rather like the proverbial tortoise. Forced eviction in 1897 led to the Club's rerooting in its present position where a full **18 holes** were available. During the '30's a modern style Clubhouse was built and **John H. Taylor** and **Fred Hawtree** were commissioned to redesign the course. As one would expect they made a splendid job of it and it was only a question of time (and the small matter of a world war) that prevented Birkdale from staging an Open Championship.

Since the war our golfing tortoise has left many of the hares behind. No fewer than six Open Championships have now been held at Birkdale in addition to numerous other major events.

Golfers wishing to play at Birkdale must be able to provide a letter of introduction from their home club and possess a handicap. Before setting off such persons are advised to contact the **Secretary, Mr. M.R. Tapsell.** This would seem to apply to individual visitors as well as those hoping to organise a Society game. Mr. Tapsell can be contacted at **The Royal Birkdale Golf Club, Waterloo Road, Southport, Merseyside. Tel. (0704) 67920.** Golf clubs may be hired from the professional, **Mr. R.N. Bradbeer, (0704) 68857** and it may also be possible to obtain the services of a caddy.

The Club is situated approximately **two miles** from the centre of **Southport** close to the main **A565** road. From the **North** this road can be reached via the **A59**, leaving the **M6** at Preston and from the **South** via the **M62** and **M57** or alternatively, as when travelling from Manchester and the **East**, by taking the **A580** and then following the **A570** into Southport.

Mention has been made of Birkdale's strikingly modern looking **Clubhouse.** Within, the catering has a high reputation and there are three bars. However, hungry golfers should note that dinner is only available to parties of 21 and over. A jacket and tie must be worn inthe lounge.

Whenever the great Championship courses are discussed it is often stated that Birkdale (together with Muirfield) represents the fairest test of skill. Whilst the course possesses many of the towering sandhills so familiar with links golf, the holes tend to wind their way between and beneath the dunes along fairly flat and narrow valleys. From the lush fairways the awkward stance and blind shot are the product of poor golf not poor fortune. Fair it may be, but easy it certainly is not. From the **medal tees** the course measures **6,711 yards** and is a stiff **par 72.** Anyone playing from the **Championship tees (6,968 yards)** can be forgiven for scratching his head and wondering how on earth **Craig Stadler** managed a score of **64.** From the **red tees,** the ladies course is **5,777 yards** and has a **par of 75.**

With its three par 5's the back nine is probably the easier half – at least to the longer hitter – although with the menacingly thick, rough and narrow strategically bunkered fairways the wild long hitter will be severely penalised. A journey into the rough on the 16th, however, is recommended, although only to visit **Arnold Palmer's** plaque – placed in memory of the great man's miraculous 6 iron shot with which he somehow contrived to find the green.

Birkdale may have a relatively short history as an 'Open course', but its list of Champions is as impressive a list as can be found anywhere: **Thomson (twice), Palmer, Trevino, Miller** and most recently **Tom Watson,** who claimed his fifth title in nine years when winning in 1983. The course has also thrown up more than its fair share of drama. Perhaps most notably in **1969** when **Jack Nicklaus,** ever the sportsman, conceded **Tony Jacklin's** very missable putt on the 18th green, so tying the **Ryder Cup.** In **1961,** Palmer's Open, an almighty gale threatened to blow the tented village and all inside far out into the sea. In stark contrast was the **1976** Open when fire engines were close at hand as Birkdale (and all of Britain come to that) suffered in the drought. That 1976 Championship saw the mercurial **Johnny Miller** at his brilliant best as he shook off first the challenge of Jack Nicklaus and then of an inexperienced and unknown 19 year old who had a name no one at the time could pronounce ...... **Severiano Ballesteros.**

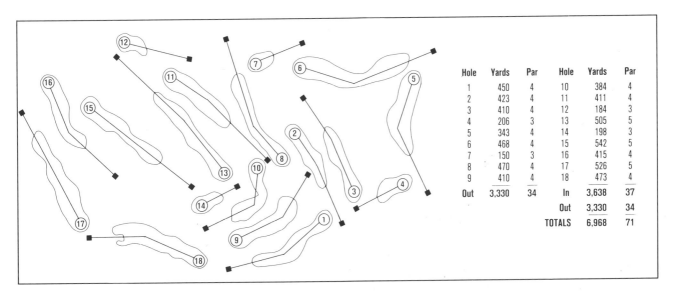

Hole	Yards	Par	Hole	Yards	Par
1	450	4	10	384	4
2	423	4	11	411	4
3	410	4	12	184	3
4	206	3	13	505	5
5	343	4	14	198	3
6	468	4	15	542	5
7	150	3	16	415	4
8	470	4	17	526	5
9	410	4	18	473	4
Out	3,330	34	In	3,638	37
			Out	3,330	34
			TOTALS	6,968	71

"There goes a hundred thousand bucks....." the immortal words of **Al Waltrous** after having witnessed the most magnificently outrageous stroke in golfing history. Imagine yourself in his shoes, striding down the 17th fairway sharing the lead in the Open Championship; you have played two strokes and are safely on the edge of the green, your partner (and effectively opponent) has driven wildly into the rough and has found a small bunker– he faces a terrifying shot over sandhills, scrub and goodness-knows-what else, – a blind shot of fully 170 yards....seconds later the impossible happens and the ball is lying a few yards from the hole, well inside your second. Minutes later you walk from the green having taken five to your opponent's four.

The occasion was, of course, the **1926 Open Championship** at **Royal Lytham** and 'your opponent', the incomparable **Bobby Jones**.

In February 1986 Royal Lytham St Annes celebrated its one hundredth birthday; few Golf Clubs in the world can have enjoyed such a rich and colourful history. Presently in charge of all administrative matters at Lytham is the Club's secretary, **Colonel Hutchison**, he may be contacted by telephone on **(0253) 724206**. **Mr M B Chesters** is the Club's professional and he may be reached on **(0253) 720094**. Visitors wishing to tread the famous fairways are asked to provide a letter of introduction from their home Club but subject to this requirement they are welcome on any day between Mondays and Fridays, restrictions applying at the weekend. Whilst advance booking is not essential it is clearly advisable and those wishing to write to the Club should address correspondence to the Secretary at **Royal Lytham and St Annes Golf Club, Links Gate, Lytham St Annes, Lancashire FY8 3LQ**. In 1986 the cost of a day's golf at Lytham was priced at **£19** per day with a green fee of **£14** securing a single round.

Motoring to the course is assisted greatly by the **M6** and the **M61**. Southbound travellers should leave the **M6** at junction **32**; here the **M55** can be picked up. The **M55** runs out of steam at junction **4** but a left turn will take you to Lytham St Annes. Those travelling northwards along the M6 have a number of choices perhaps the best being to leave at exit **29** and thereafter following a combination of the **A582**, **A583** and **A584** towards Lytham St Annes. The **M61** links the Greater Manchester area to the outskirts of Preston. From Preston the **A583** can be joined and followed as above. The course is situated only a mile from the centre of the town close to the railway line.

The railway line is in fact a major feature of the opening holes at Lytham, forming a continuous boundary to the right. From the back markers the course measures **6673** yards par **71** (sss73) with the ladies playing over **5814** yards par **75** (sss75). Rather unusually Lytham opens with a par three, which at over 200 yards is quite a testing opener. The real threat of the railway, however, looms on the **2nd** and **3rd**. Of the other par three holes at Lytham perhaps the **12th** stands out – normally played into a prevailing wind it calls for a searching tee shot towards a raised and heavily guarded green. The back nine is generally felt to be the more difficult of the two halves although the determining factor at Lytham, as on most links courses, will nearly always be the wind. The **17th** has been mentioned and a plaque marks the spot from where the Jones miracle recovery shot was played. As for the **18th** it of course invokes so many 'Open memories': **Tony Jacklin's** arrow-straight drive en-route to winning the **1969** Championship; **Gary Player** putting left handed from up against the Clubhouse wall in 1974 and then the most recent Championship in **1979** – the 22 year old Ballesteros storming to victory in cavalier fashion.

The nineteenth at Royal Lytham is a marvellous Victorian building, and the golfer can enjoy a full and excellent catering service which is offered throughout the day.

As for the future, Lytham can look forward to the staging of its eighth Open Championship in 1988 – with Lytham's record it should prove a momentous occasion.

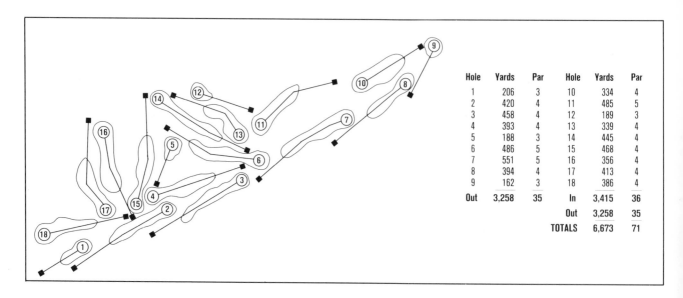

Hole	Yards	Par	Hole	Yards	Par
1	206	3	10	334	4
2	420	4	11	485	5
3	458	4	12	189	3
4	393	4	13	339	4
5	188	3	14	445	4
6	486	5	15	468	4
7	551	5	16	356	4
8	394	4	17	413	4
9	162	3	18	386	4
Out	3,258	35	In	3,415	36
			Out	3,258	35
			TOTALS	6,673	71

THE 11TH: GREASBY TO FOUL MOSS

LANCASHIRE

Accrington & District G.C. (18)
Accrington (0254) 32734

Acre Gate G.C. (18+6)
Manchester (061) 748 1226

Allerton Park G.C. (18)
Liverpool (051) 428 1046

Alt G.C. (18)
Southport (0704) 30435

Ashton & Lea G.C. (18)
Preston (0772) 726480

Ashton-in-Makerfield G.C. (18)
Ashton-in-Makerfield
(0942) 7272678

Ashton-under-Lyne G.C. (18)
Manchester (061) 330 1537

Bacup G.C. (9)
Bacup (0706) 873170

Baxenden & District G.C. (9)
Accrington (0254) 34555

Beacon Park G.C. (18)
Upholland (0695) 622700

Bentham G.C. (9)
Bentham (Bentham) 61081

Blackburn G.C. (18)
Blackburn (0254) 51122

Blackley G.C. (18)
Manchester (061) 643 2980

Blackpool North Shore G.C. (18)
Blackpool (0253) 51017

Blackpool Park G.C. (18)
Blackpool (0253) 33960

Bolton G.C. (18)
Bolton (0204) 43278

Bolton Old Links G.C. (18)
Bolton (0204) 40050

Bolton Municipal G.C. (18)
Bolton (0204) 42336 ·

Bootle G.C. (18)
Liverpool (051) 928 6196

Bawning G.C. (9)
Liverpool (051) 489 1901

Brackley Municipal G.C. (9)
Manchester (061) 790 6076

Breightmet G.C. (9)
Bolton (0204) 27381

Brookdale G.C. (18)
Manchester (061) 681 4534

Burnley G.C. (18)
Burnley (0282) 21045

Bury G.C. (18)
Manchester (061) 766 2213

Castle Hawk G.C. (18)
Rochdale (0706) 40841

Childwall G.C. (18)
Liverpool (051) 487 0654

Chorley G.C. (18)
Adlington (0257) 480263

Clitheroe G.C. (18)
Clitheroe (0200) 22618

Colne G.C. (9)
Colne (0282) 863391

Crompton & Royton G.C. (18)
Manchester (061) 624 2154

Darwen G.C. (18)
Darwen (0254) 71287

Davyhulme Park G.C. (18)
Manchester (061) 748 2856

Dean Wood G.C. (18)
Up Holland (0695) 622980

Deane G.C. (18)
Bolton (0204) 61944

Denton G.C. (18)
Manchester (061) 336 3218

Dunscar G.C. (18)
Bolton (0204) 53321

Duxbury Park G.C. (18)
Chorley (02572) 77049

Ellesmere G.C. (18)
Manchester (061) 790 2122

Fairfield G. & C.C. (18)
Manchester (061) 370 1641

Fairhaven G.C. (18)
Lytham (0256) 736741

Fishwick Hall G.C. (18)
Preston (0772) 798300

Fleetwood G.C. (18+18)
Fleetwood (03917) 3114

Flixton G.C. (9)
Manchester (061) 748 2116

Formby G.C. (18)
Formby (07048) 74273

Formby Ladies G.C. (18)
Formby (07048) 74127

Gathurst G.C. (9)
Appley Bridge (02575) 2861

Grange Park G.C. (18)
St. Helens (0744) 22980

Great Harwood G.C. (9)
Gt. Harwood (0254) 884391

Great Lever &
Farnworth G.C. (18)
Bolton (0204) 62582

Green Haworth G.C. (9)
Accrington (0254) 37580

Greenmount G.C. (9)
Tottington (020488) 3712

Harwood G.C. (9)
Bolton (0204) 22878

Haydock Park G.C. (18)
Newton-Le-Willows
(09252) 4389

Heaton Park G.C. (18)
Manchester (061) 798 0295

Hesketh G.C. (18)
Southport (0704) 30226

Heysham G.C. (18)
Heysham (0524) 51011

Hillside G.C. (18)
Southport (0704) 69902

Hindley Hall G.C. (18)
Wigan (0942) 55131

Horwich G.C. (9)
Horwich (0204) 96980

Huyton & Prescot G.C. (18)
Liverpool (051) 489 1138

Ingol Golf & Squash
Club G.C. (18)
Preston (0772) 734556

Knott End G.C. (18)
Knott End (0253) 810254

Lancaster G. & C.C. (18)
Galgate (0524) 752090

Lansil G.C. (9)
Lancaster (0524) 65252

Lee Park G.C. (18)
Liverpool (051) 487 9861

Leigh G.C. (18)
Culcheth (092576) 3130

Leyland G.C. (18)
Leyland (0772) 421359

Liverpool Municipal G.C. (18)
Liverpool (051) 546 5435

Lobden G.C. (9)
Whitworth (070685) 3228

Longridge G.C. (18)
Longridge, Preston
(077478) 3291

Lewes Park G.C. (9)
Manchester (061) 764 1231

Lytham (Green Drive) G.C. (18)
Lytham (0253) 34782

Manchester G.C. (18)
Manchester (061) 643 2718

Marsden Park G.C. (18)
Nelson (0282) 67525

Morecambe G.C. (18)
Morecambe (0524) 418050

Nelson G.C. (18)
Nelson (0282) 64583

North Manchester G.C. (18)
Manchester (061) 643 2941

Ormskirk G.C. (18)
Ormskirk (0695) 72112

Park (Play over Southport and
Municipal Links
Southport (0704) 30133

Pennington G.C. (9)
Wigan (0942) 672823

Penwortham G.C. (18)
Preston (0772) 743207

Pike Ford G.C. (9)
Manchester (061) 740 1136

Pleasington G.C. (18)
Blackburn (0254) 22177

Poulton-le-Fylde G.C. (9)
Poulton (0253) 892444

Preston G.C. (18)
Preston (0772) 794235/700436

Prestwick G.C. (18)
Manchester (061) 773 2544

Regent Park (Play over Bolton
Municipal Course)
Bolton (0204) 44170

Rishton G.C. (9)
Gt. .Harwood (0254) 884442

Rochdale G.C. (18)
Rochdale (0706) 46024

Rossendale G.C. (18)
Rossendale (0706) 213056

Royal Birkdale G.C. (18)
Southport (0704) 69903/69928

Royal Lytham & St.
Annes G.C. (18)
St. Annes on Sea (0253) 724206/7

Saddleworth G.C. (18)
Saddleworth (04577) 2059

St. Annes Old Links G.C. (18)
St. Annes (0253) 723597/721826

St. Michael Jubilee (Play over
Widnes Municipal)
Liverpool (051) 424 0989

Shaw Hill G. & C.C. (18)
Chorley (02572) 69221

Sherley Park G.C. (9)
St. Helens (0744) 813149

Southport & Ainsdale G.C. (18)
Southport (0704) 78092

Southport Municipal
Links G.C. (18)
Southport (0704) 35286

Southport Old Links G.C. (9)
Southport (0704) 28207

Springfield Park G.C. (18)
Rochdale (0706) 49801

Stand G.C. (18)
Manchester (061) 766 2388

Swinton Park G.C. (18)
Manchester (061) 794 1785

Todmorden G.C. (9)
Todmorden (070681) 2986

Tawneley G.C. (18)
Burnley (0282) 38473

Tunshill G.C. (9)
Rochdale (0706) 342095

Turton G.C. (9)
Bolton (0204) 852235

Walmersley G.C. (9)
Manchester (061) 764 1429

Werneth G.C. (18)
Manchester (061) 624 1190

West Derby G.C. (18)
Liverpool (051) 228 1540

The West Lancashire G.C. (18)
Liverpool (051) 924 4115

West Laughton G.C. (9)
West Laughton (0942) 811085

Whalley G.C. (9)
Whalley (0254482) 2236

Whitefield G.C. (18+18)
Manchester (061) 766 2728

Whittaker G.C. (9)
Littleborough (0706) 78310

Widnes G.C. (18)
Widnes, Liverpool
(051) 424 2440

Widnes Municipal G.C. (9)
Liverpool (051) 424 6230

Wigan G.C. (9)
Standish, Wigan (0257) 421360

Wigan Metropolitan G.C. (18)
Wigan (0257) 42050

William Wroe G.C. (18)
Manchester (061) 748 8680

Wilpshire G.C. (18)
Blackburn (0254) 48260

Woolton G.C. (18)
Liverpool (051) 486 1601

Worsley G.C. (18)
Manchester (061) 789 4202

SOUTH AND WEST YORKSHIRE

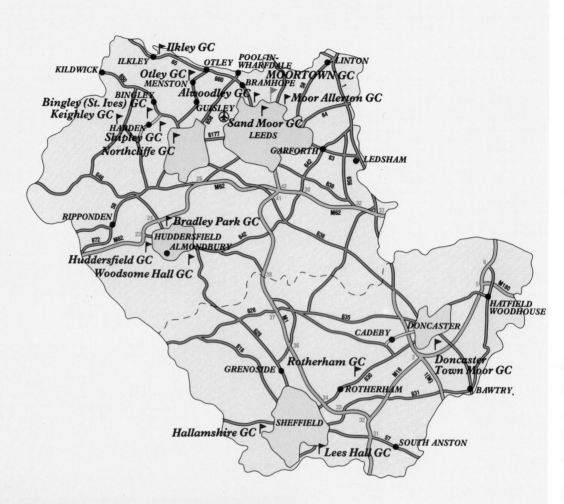

A.B. FROST "Hooked" ROSENSTIELS

KILDWICK HALL
KILDWICK, NR KEIGHLEY
WEST YORKSHIRE
0535 32244

To some people Southern Yorkshire is the pits – mining country; for many it means the Bronte Sisters; the start of the Pennines and Ilkley Moor and then again for others it is about Sand Moor, Alwoodley and Moortown.

A glance at the map tells you that the two counties of South and West Yorkshire are fairly littered with golf courses; the major towns of Leeds and Sheffield are exceptionally well served while Bradford, Huddersfield and Rotherham all have much to offer. In fact wherever you happen to be in Southern Yorkshire there is always a golf course around the corner (well almost).

Perhaps the pick of the courses in the Sheffield area are the moorland course at **Hallamshire**, 3 miles west of the city off the **A57** and **Lees Hall** with its extensive views over the city, the course being situated some 5 miles south of Sheffield off the **A61**. Visitors are welcome at Hallamshire on weekdays (**£10** per day in 1986) and at Lees Hall throughout the week although tees are reserved before 3pm on Wednesdays and before 10.30am at weekends, fees being **£8** midweek, **£9** weekends. It should also be remembered that **Lindrick** in Nottinghamshire is just a short drive from Sheffield.

Rotherham's course is at Thrybergh Park, 2 miles north of the town on the **A630**. It can be visited most days of the week although prior arrangement with the secretary is essential. The other side of the **A1** at Doncaster, **The Doncaster Town Moor** course is situated very close to the famous St Leger racetrack on the **A638**. A parkland course, visitors are welcome at all times excepting Sunday mornings.

West Yorkshire has the greater number of courses with the area just to the north of Leeds being particularly outstanding. Within a short distance of one another are **Moortown**, (featured on a later page), **Alwoodley, Sand Moor** and **Moor Allerton** all of which are of Championship standard and indeed all enjoy the most superb settings.

Whilst Alwoodley and Sand Moor are predominantly moorland in character, Moor Allerton, where there are 27 holes, is more strictly parkland. When travelling to any of the four clubs, the **A61** should be taken out of Leeds. Prior telephoning at each

is strongly recommended. Moor Allerton is widely known for its being attached to the Club. Green fees tend to range between **£12** to **£15**.

To the south of Leeds, the parkland course at **Howley Hall** is worth noting. Located off the **B6123** near Morley visitors can normally play during the week and on Sundays.

There are three notable courses close to Huddersfield: **Bradley Park** to the north of the town fairly close to the **M62**, **Woodsome Hall** with its historic Clubhouse and the **Huddersfield Club**. It was over this latter course that **Sandy Herd** learnt his game. The Open Champion of 1902, Herd finished in the first five in the Championship on no fewer than twelve occasions, he would have doubtless won on several of those but for a fellow from Ganton across the way. The Huddersfield Club is situated to the west of the town, the cost of a day's golf in 1986 being **£11** midweek, **£13** at the weekend.

There is some fine golfing country towards the north west of Bradford. **Bingley (St Ives) Golf Club** has staged several professional tournaments – a wooded moorland course on the **B6429**, visitors are welcome on weekdays, while **Northcliffe, Keighly** and **Shipley** Golf Clubs are fairly close to one another.

Ilkley is a popular area for golfers as well as ducks. **Ilkley Golf Club** has one of the most scenic courses in Yorkshire. The River Wharfe winds its way through much of the course and is a major hazard on several of the early holes. Visitors are welcome at Ilkley seven days a week although prior arrangement with the Club is essential at weekends. Fees in 1986 were **£10.50** per day during the week with **£13** payable on Saturdays and Sundays.

Otley is another very picturesque course that nestles in the Wharfe Valley. Situated a mile from Otley on the Bradford Road a game can usually be enjoyed Mondays to Fridays and on Sundays, although there are restrictions on Tuesday mornings. Fees at Otley are approximately **£10** per day.

Finally for those heading north along the **A1, Wetherby** is most convenient. A fine parkland course it offers extensive views. Visitors are welcome at all times, green fees in 1986 were **£10** midweek, **£15** at weekends.

Alwoodley G.C.	(0532) 681680
Bingley (St Ives) G.C.	(0274) 562506
Bradley Park G.C.	(0484) 39988
Doncaster Town Moor G.C.	(0302) 868316
Hallamshire G.C.	(0742) 302153
Howley Hall G.C.	(0924) 478417
Huddersfield G.C.	(0484) 26203
Ilkley G.C.	(0535) 600214
Keighley G.C.	(0535) 604778
Moor Allerton G.C.	(0532) 661154
Moortown G.C.	(0532) 686521
Northcliffe G.C.	(0274) 596731
Otley G.C.	(0943) 465329
Rotherham G.C.	(0709) 850480
Sand Moor G.C.	(0532) 692718
Shipley G.C.	(0274) 568652
Wetherby G.C.	(0937) 62527
Woodsome Hall G.C.	(0484) 602971

While many consider the delights of Yorkshire to be exclusive to its northernmost area this is totally wrong. The small villages that nestle amid the wild Pennines or the Moors are delightful. The river Wharfe carves its way through the area revealing extraordinary beauty along its trail. From the haunting howls of Haworth and the Bronte country to the jovial singing in a pub on Ilkley Moor there is a rich tradition of comment – reserve your best golf for the eighteenth fairway.

These Yorkshiremen like winners unless of course they lose. This is the ideal position – "Grand golf lad, a little more practice and you'll be giving me a hard game". In case you are equally proud and decide to beat your Yorkshire friend by sinking a 16 footer in front of the Clubhouse (this could be fatal) you had better have some ideas how to quieten the fellow down.

Perhaps the best area to make this blunder is in Ilkely for here there are some really excellent establishments. Your success may have been in part due to your breakfast – "The Edwardian Breakfast" served to you on Sunday morning during your stay at **Rombald's (0943) 603201**. The breakfast is legendary in Yorkshire – really excellent but the hotel itself and the restaurant are both thoroughly recommended. Elsewhere in Ilkley, a town where delightful antique shops clutter the streets one finds **The Craiglands Hotel (0943) 607676** – this has a setting adjoining that famous moor, the hotel is most comfortable. Another good value establishment is **The Cow and Calf (0943) 607335**. The ideal placebo for any Yorkshireman should, however, be booked well in advance, it is of course **The Box Tree (0943) 608484** – one of the county's finest restaurants. Continuing in the tradition of quality in class one need go no further than Kildwick, for here **Kildwick Hall (0535) 32244** is a gorgeous Jacobean manor house which provides an outstanding place to stay and an excellent restaurant. Bingley, Otley, all this area is riddled with enthusiastic cricket and rugby sides as well as golfers – popular pubs for one and all are **The Fox** at Menston and **The Malt Shovel** at Horden – good bar food in both establishments. Another hotel which is comfortable without being lavish is **The Bankfield Hotel, Bingley (0274) 567123**. Before one leaves the area mention should be made of that particular popular Yorkshire pastime – the eating of fish and chips. You may well have heard of **Harry Ramsden's** in Guisley – if you have not and you have a passion for this type of fayre this is the place to go.

Following the Wharfe into the east of West Yorkshire – if you see what I mean, one finds some superb countryside. This is the land of the Brontes – quite delightful. In Bramhope there is an hotel a far cry from the romance of the Brontes but a particularly popular hotel for businessmen visiting Leeds, it is the **Leeds Wharfedale Post House (0532) 842911**. In contrast, the delightful Harewood House is well worth visiting between Easter and October. The gem in this area is however a restaurant with rooms – **The Pool Court** Pool-in-Wharfedale (0532) 842288. Delightfully pleasant rooms are complemented by some of the most excellent cooking in the country – really excellent (delightfully helpful people as well). Another fine restaurant is the **Linton Spring**, Sicklinghall, less well known but thoroughly

recommended **(0937) 65353**. In the village of Linton close by **The Windmill** is a quiet country pub – ideal for a bar snack and a pint or whatever happens to be your tipple.

Leeds itself is an obvious stopping off point for business folk visiting Yorkshire. As one would expect there are a number of hotels in the city. **The Queen's Hotel (0532) 431323** is the better of the older school while the Ladbroke **Dragonara (0532) 442000** is a more modern but extremely comfortable place to stay. Eating in Yorkshire's largest city can be somewhat tricky. **La Grillarde (0532) 459707** is an interesting establishment without being grand. Yorkshire is renowned for its supping and some splendid pubs can be located in Ledsham, **The Chequers** is well worth a visit – while some miles across the county the **Old Bridge**, Ripponden is a pleasant pub to have lunch. Perhaps the focal point of the village is the bridge which crosses the flowing waters of the Ryburn; the aptly named **Over the Bridge (0422) 823722** is particularly good.

Another splendid restaurant lies hidden in the tranquil Pennine village of Golcar, **The Weavers Shed (0484) 654284** superb English menus backed up by a super setting (an 18th century weaving mill). In Huddersfield itself **The George (0484) 25444** is comfortable enough for people frequenting the area. Before we leave this area for South Yorkshire one mention of Holdsworth, near Halifax – also by the **Holdsworth House (0422) 244270**. South Yorkshire does not have the same appeal as the North and West Ridings but this is not to say that there is no attraction to the place. Trekking down the A1 two establishments stand out. To the east in Monk Fryston, **The Monk Fryston Hall (0977) 682369** has a great charm while further south and west of the Great North Road lies Wentbridge. Here the **Wentbridge House Hotel** is an excellent place to stay (0977) 620444. In Doncaster aside from a classic racecourse **The Danum (0302) 62261** and **The Grand St Leger (0302) 64111** are the recommended establishments. In the countryside surrounding the busy railway town Cadeby offers a pleasant establishment in **The Cadeby Inn** while in Hatfield Woodhouse **The Green Tree** offers a warm welcome and some good snacks. The hotel with the most character in the area is **The Crown** at Bawtry **(0302) 710341** – a pleasant High Street inn. In contrast people seeking what are commonly known as leisure facilities i.e. gym, sauna, etc will find Rotherham's modern **Carlton Park Hotel (0709) 364902** to their liking. Golfers playing the Sheffield courses should note another modern hotel with a similarly distinguished name – on this occasion **The Grosvenor House (0742) 20041**: a first rate Indian restaurant can also be found **Nirmal's Tandoori (0742) 24054**. The landmark not to miss while in these parts is **The Crucible Theatre (0742) 79922** – one of Britain's leading repertory companies producing shows of the highest quality as well as snooker!

We leave the area in South Anston amid conversation about winning and losing – we are supping a pint of that Yorkshire institution Tetley's bitter. As the conversation repeats itself several times a thought comes to mind – whoever said the game was about taking part and not winning and losing was not a Yorkshireman!

The Brown Cow Inn
Ireland Bridge
Bingley BD16 2QX
Tel: (0274) 569482
The Brown Cow Inn, a public house dating back to Cromwellian days, can boast 9 golf courses within a 4 mile radius. Weekend breaks can be arranged by the Inn for golf parties, provided they have vacancies. Being a family concern, takes every care to ensure the visitor's stay in the hotel is both happy and memorable.

Pool Court
Pool-in-Wharfdale,
Otley,
LS21 1EH
Tel: (0532) 842288/842414
The Pool Court Restaurant is situated in a fine Georgian Mansion. Endless enthusiasm has secured the highest standards of cuisine as well as elegant surroundings. Only fresh in-season produce is used to create a tempting menu based on both classical and innovative cuisine.

The fact that the new range of Subaru four-wheel drive automatics adapt to changes in the weather is just one of their claims to fame.

They can also adapt to the way you drive. And adapt to the environment you are driving in.

The key to this remarkable adaptability is a little button on the dashboard marked 'auto-select'.

This allows you to pre-set the car to virtually double its traction the moment conditions demand it.

When it rains, for example. Switch on the wipers and the car will switch to four-wheel drive.

Automatically. Instantaneously. On the move.

And exactly the same happens when you put your foot down hard. On the throttle, or on the brake.

Once the need has passed, of course, you revert to front-wheel drive again.

Ingenious don't you think? And unique.

Mind you, we're specialists in the unique a ingenious at Subaru.

Most of our turbo models, for example, ha an electro-pneumatic self-levelling suspension system that's just as clever and just as specific to

Not only does it stop the rear end dipping when there's a heavy load in the back, it also allo you to raise the car's ground clearance when t going gets rough.

Our hill-holder clutch is another excellent case in point.

It holds you still on even a 1:4 gradient wi out the handbrake.

THE FIRST CARS IN THE WORLD TO AUTOMATICALLY CHANGE WIT THE WEATHER.

And our manual four-wheel drive cars are the
y vehicles in the world to have it.

They also have a five-speed dual range
rbox as standard to keep you going on the most
pery of slopes.

But then, when it comes to keeping you going
cars are in a class of their own.

Our record for reliability is truly
narkable. The latest statistics from the Touring
ıb of Switzerland show that no make is more
endable.

And as you would expect, you can enjoy our
sheer engineering excellence in luxury-car comfort.

Would you like to put yourself in the driving
seat?

Your local Subaru dealer will be delighted to
arrange a test-drive for you.

You won't meet a more adaptable range of cars.

And adaptability can be the key to survival.
Ask any dinosaur.

SUBARU
THE WORLD'S FAVOURITE FOUR-WHEEL DRIVES.

THE MOST INTELLIGENT USE OF FOUR WHEELS.

ARU (UK) LIMITED. A SUBSIDIARY OF INTERNATIONAL MOTORS LIMITED. RYDER STREET, WEST BROMWICH, WEST MIDLANDS B70 0EJ. TELEPHONE: 021-557 6200.

Moortown enjoys an enviable situation. It lies within minutes of the town centre of Leeds, yet it also lies within minutes of the Pennines and the beauty of the Yorkshire Moors. The Club was founded in the autumn of **1909** with the course being laid out by **Alister Mackenzie**. Less than twenty years after its formation Moortown was selected to host the first ever **Ryder Cup** to be played on British soil. It proved a momentous occasion. The American side was virtually identical to the one that had crushed the British team 9-2 in the inaugural staging at Worcester Massachusetts two years previously. It included the likes of **Walter Hagen**, then reigning British Open Champion, **Gene Sarazen, Johnny Farrel** the US Open Champion, **Leo Diegel** the U.S.P.G.A. Champion and **Al** (there goes a hundred thousand bucks) **Waltrous**. To cut a long story short the British side won by six matches to four. On the final day **George Duncan** defeated Walter Hagen by 10 and 8 and **Archie Compston** defeated Gene Sarazen 6 and 4. Well whatever it may have done to American pride, and I note that Wall Street collapsed later that summer, it certainly put Moortown on the map!

Stepping forward nearly sixty years, **Keith Symons** is the Secretary at Moortown he may be contacted by telephone on **(0532) 686521**, while the Club's professional **Bryan Hutchinson** can be reached on **(0532) 683636**.

Visitors are welcome at Moortown between Mondays and Fridays. Golfing Societies are also welcome during the week although prior arrangement with the secretary is essential. All written correspondence should be addressed to Mr Symons at **The Moortown Golf Club, Harrogate Road, Leeds LS17 7DB**. In 1986 the green fees were **£15** for a single round with **£17** payable for a full day's golf.

Moortown's aforementioned enviable situation is a product of the **A61** – the Leeds to Harrogate Road which runs from the heart of the city to within yards of Moortown's front door. For those travelling from the city centre if you reach Eccup Reservoir you'll have gone too far! Leeds itself is well served by motorway connections, the **M62** linking Leeds to **Greater Manchester** and the **M1** joining **Sheffield** to Leeds. Some roads which may prove helpful include the **A64** (York to Leeds) and the **A65** (Skipton to Leeds). Our friend the **A61** approaches from the north via **Ripon, Ripley** and **Harrogate**.

With its spread of heather and gorse Moortown can properly be described as heathland, although occasionally it is classed as a moorland type course. Either way, it is always beautifully maintained and has the fine combination of being sufficiently testing yet not too severe.

From its back ties, the course measures **6503** yards, par **69** (S.S.S. **72**). The forward tees reduce the length to **6,200** yards while for the ladies Moortown measures **5743** yards par **74** (S.S.S. **74**). The generally held view is that the front nine is the easier of the two halves, this may have something to do with the fact that it begins with what golfers usually term a 'birdiable hole', being a short par five to a fairly open green. Perhaps Moortown's finest hole is the **8th**, a par three hole named **Gibraltar**, measuring **176** yards it calls for a shot to a plateau green built on a foundation of rock. The **10th** is an excellent par five, aptly titled "The Long" for it stretches to **559** yards. **Archie Compston** once holed out here in two strokes.

Over the years Moortown has been the venue for several major events, both amateur and professional. Three **English Amateur Championships** have been held at Moortown, so also the English **Ladies Amateur** and the **Ladies British Amateur**. Recently the Car Care professional tournament has found a home at Moortown, **Mark Mouland** winning the event in 1986.

Being situated directly behind the 18th green, Moortown's Club house is very much a nineteenth hole. Lunches are served daily (excepting Mondays) and both breakfasts and dinners can be arranged with prior notice.

In concluding it seems appropriate to return to the course. The 18th hole at Moortown seems to have an alarming affect on certain people. Countless numbers, including Severiano Ballesteros, have been known to overclub and fire the ball over the green into the Clubhouse area. In the 1929 Ryder Cup during one of the foursomes matches, Joe Turnesa hooked his second behind the marquee adjoining the Clubhouse whereupon his partner promptly sailed it back over the marquee to within a yard of the hole. In the 1974 English Amateur Stroke Play tournament one player put his second actually into the Men's Bar. Opening the Clubhouse windows he played his third out onto the green. The Clubhouse certainly has a particularly friendly atmosphere but this would seem to be taking things a little too far!

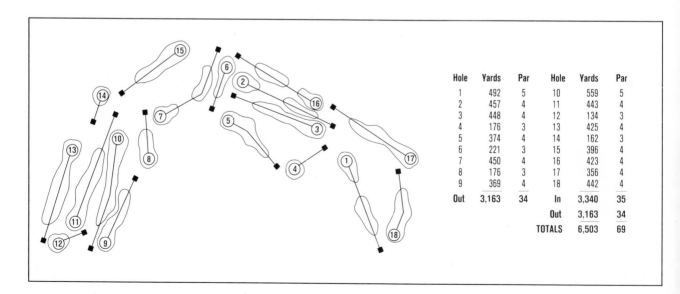

Hole	Yards	Par	Hole	Yards	Par
1	492	5	10	559	5
2	457	4	11	443	4
3	448	4	12	134	3
4	176	3	13	425	4
5	374	4	14	162	3
6	221	3	15	396	4
7	450	4	16	423	4
8	176	3	17	356	4
9	369	4	18	442	4
Out	3,163	34	In	3,340	35
			Out	3,163	34
			TOTALS	6,503	69

THE 12TH: NEW DELIGHT TO LUCY CROSS

YORKSHIRE

Abbeydale G.C. (18)
Dore, Nr Sheffield (0742) 360763

Aldwark Manor G.C. (9 + 18)
Alne, York (03473) 251

Alwoodley G.C. (18)
Leeds (0532) 681680

Ampleforth College G.C. (10)
York (0439) 70678

Austerfield Park G.C. (18)
Bawtry, Nr Doncaster
(0302) 710841

Baildon G.C. (18)
Baildon, Shipley (0274) 584266

Barnsley G.C. (18)
Staincross, Nr Barnsley
(0226) 382856

Beauchief Municipal G.C. (18)
Sheffield (0742) 360648

Bedale G.C. (18)
Bedale (0677) 22568

Ben Rhydding G.C. (9)
Ben Rhydding, Ilkley
(0943) 608759

Beverley & East Riding G.C. (18)
Beverley (0482) 8671900

Bingley St Ives G.C. (18)
Bingley (0274) 562506

Birley Wood G.C. (18)
Sheffield (0742) 390099

Boothferry G.C. (18)
Spaldington, Goole (0430) 30364

Bradford G.C. (18)
Guiseley, Leeds (0943) 75570

Bradford Moor G.C. (9)
Bradford (0274) 638313

Bradley Park G.C. (18)
Huddersfield (0484) 39988

Branshaw G.C. (18)
Oakworth, Nr Keighley
(0535) 43235

Bridlington G.C.
Bridlington (0262) 672092

Brough G.C. (18)
Brough (0482) 667374

Catterick Garrison G.C. (18)
Richmond (0748) 833268

City of Wakefield G.C. (18)
Wakefield (0924) 374316

Clayton G.C. (9)
Clayton, Bradford (0274) 880047

Cleckheaton and District G.C. (18)
Cleckheaton
(0274) 874118/877851

Concord Park C.C. (18)
Sheffield (0742) 613605

Crimple Valley G.C. (8)
Harrogate (0423) 883485

Crookhill Park G.C. (18)
Conisborough, Nr Doncaster
(0709) 862979

Crosland Heath G.C. (18)
Crosland Heath, Huddersfield
(0484) 653216

Dewsbury District G.C. (18)
Mirfield (0924) 492399/496033

Doncaster G.C. (18)
Bessacarr, nr Doncaster
(0302) 868316

Doncaster Town Moor G.C. (18)
Bellevue, Doncaster (0302) 535286

Dore & Totley G.C. (18)
Bradway, Nr Sheffield
(0742) 360492

Driffield G.C. (9)
Sunderlandwick, Driffield
(0377) 43116

Easingwold G.C. (18)
Easingwold, York (0347) 21486

East Bierley G.C. (9)
Bradford (0274) 681023

Elland G.C. (9)
Elland (0422) 72505

Filey G.C. (18)
Filey (0723) 513293

Flamborough Head G.C. (18)
Flamborough, Bridlington
(0262) 850333

Fulford G.C. (18)
York (0904) 412882

Fulneck G.C. (9)
Pudsey (0532) 565191

Ganstead Park G.C. (9)
Coniston, Hull (0482) 811280

Ganton, G.C. (18)
Ganton, Scarborough (0944) 70329

Garforth G.C. (18)
Garforth, Leeds
(0532) 862021/863308

Ghyll G.C. (9)
Tornton-in-Craven,
Barnoldswick (0282) 842466)

Gotts Park G.C. (18)
Armley, Leeds (0532) 638232

Grange Park G.C. (18)
Rotherham (0709) 559497

Grimsby G.C. (18)
Grimsby (0472) 42630

Hainsworth Park G.C. (9)
Brandesburton, Driffield

Halifax G.C. (18)
Ogden, Halifax (0422) 244171

Halifax Bradley Hall G.C. (18)
Halifax (0422) 74108

Halifax West End G.C. (18)
Halifax (0422) 53608

Hallamshire G.C. (18)
Sheffield (0742) 302153

Hallowes G.C. (18)
Dronfield, Sheffield
(0246) 413149/413734

Hanging Heaton G.C. (9)
Dewsbury (0924) 461606

Harrogate G.C. (18)
Starbeck, Harrogate
(0423) 863158/862999

Headingley G.C. (18)
Adel, Leeds (0532) 679573/673052

Headley G.C. (9)
Thornton, Bradford (0274) 833348

Hessle, G.C. (18)
Cottingham, Hull (0482) 650171

Heworth G.C. (11)
York (0904) 424618

Hickleton G.C. (18)
Hickleton, Doncaster
(0709) 892496

Hillsborough G.C. (18)
Sheffield (0742) 343608

Hornsea G.C. (18)
Hornsea (04012) 2020

Horsforth G.C. (18)
Horsforth, Leeds
(0532) 586819/585200

Howley Hall G.C. (18)
Howley, Leeds (0924) 472432

Huddersield G.C. (18)
Huddersield (0484) 267203/20110

Hull G.C. (18)
Kirk Ella, Hull (0482) 658919

Ilkley G.C. (18)
Myddleton, Ilkley (0943) 600214

Keighley G.C. (18)
Utley, Keighley
(0535) 604778/603179

Kingsway G.C. (9)
Kingsway, Scunthorpe
(0724) 840945

Kirkbymoorside G.C. (18)
Kirkbymoorside (0751) 31525

Knaresborogh G.C. (18)
Knaresborough (0423) 863219

Leeds G.C. (18)
Leeds (0532) 658775

Lees Hall G.C. (18)
Norton, Sheffield (0742) 554402

Lightcliffe G.C. (9)
Lightcliffe, Halifax (0422) 202459

Lindrick G.C. (18)
Lindrick, nr Worksop
(0909) 472120

Longley Park G.C. (9)
Huddersfield (0484) 22304

Low Laithes G.C. (18)
Flushdyke, Ossett (0924) 273275

Malton & Norton G.C. (18)
Norton, Malton (0653) 2959

Marsden G.C. (9)
Marsden, Huddersfield
(0484) 844253

Masham G.C. (9)
Masham, Ripon (0765) 89379

Meltham G.C. (18)
Meltham, Huddersfield
(0484) 850227

Middleton Park G.C. (18)
Middleton, Leeds (0532) 700449

Moor Allerton G.C. (18)
Leeds (0532) 661154/5

Moortown G.C. (18)
Leeds (0532) 686521/681682

Mount Skip G.C. (9)
Wodsworth, Hebden Bridge

(0422) 842896

Normanton G.C. (9)
Normanton, Wakefield
(0924) 892943

Northcliffe G.C. (18)
Moorhead, Shipley (0274) 584085

Oakdale G.C. (18)
Oakdale, Harrogate
(0423) 502806/67162

Otley G.C. (18)
Otley (0943) 461015/465329

Outlane G.C. (18)
Outlane, Huddersfield
(0422) 74762

Painthorpe House G.C. (9)
Criggleston, Wakefield
(0924) 255083

Pannal G.C. (18)
Pannal, Harrogate (0423) 871641

Phoenix G.C. (18)
Brimsworth, Rotherham
(0709) 363864

Phoenix Park G.C. (9)
Thornbury Bradford
(0274) 667178

Pike Hills G.C. (18)
Copmanthorpe, York
(0904) 706566

Pontefract & District G.C. (18)
Pontefract (0977) 692241

Pontefract Park G.C. (18)
Pontefract (0977) 702799

Queensbury G.C. (9)
Queensbury, Bradford
(0274) 882155

Rawdon G.C. (9)
Rawdon, Leeds (0532) 506040

Richmond G.C. (18)
Bend Hagg, Richmond
(0748) 2457

Riddlesden G.C. (18)
Riddlesden, Keighley
(0535) 602148

Ripon City G.C. (9)
Ripon (0765) 3640

Rotherham G.C. (18)
Thrybergh, Rotherham
(0709) 850480/850466

Roundhay G.C. (9)
Leeds (0532) 662695

Ryburn G.C. (9)
Sowerby Bridge, Halifax
(0422) 31355

Sand Moor G.C. (18)
Leeds (0532) 681685

Scarborough North
Cliff G.C. (18)
Scarborough (0723) 360786

Scarborough South
Cliff G.C. (18)
Scarborough
(0723) 360522/374737

Scarcroft G.C. (18)
Leeds (0532) 892263

Selby G.C. (18)
Brayton Barff, Selby (075 782) 622

Selby Park G.C. (9)
Selby, Doncaster (0777) 818268

Settle G.C. (9)
Giggleswick, Settle (072 92) 2617

Sheffield Transport
Dept. G.C. (18)
Sheffield (0742) 373216

Shipley G.C. (18)
Cottingley Bridge, Bingley
(0274) 568652

Sicklehome G.C. (18)
Bamford, Sheffield (0433) 51306

Silkstone G.C. (18)
Silkstone, Barnsley
(0226) 790328

Silsden G.C. (18)
Silsden, nr Keighley (0535) 52998

Sitwell Park G.C. (18)
Rotherham (0709) 541046

Skipton G.C. (18)
Skipton (0756) 3922/3257

South Bradford G.C. (9)
Odsal, Bradford (0274) 679195

South Leeds G.C. (18)
Leeds (0532) 700479

Springhead Park G.C. (18)
Hull (0482) 656309

Stocksbridge & District G.C. (18)
Deepcar, Sheffield (0742) 882003

Sutton Park G.C. (18)
Hull (0482) 74242

Tankersley Park G.C. (18)
Sheffield (0742) 468247

Temple Newsam G.C. (18+18)
Leeds (0532) 645624

The Lady Dorothy
Wood G.C. (18)
Halton, Leeds (0532) 645624

The Lord Irwin G.C. (18)
Halton Leeds (0532) 645624

Thirsk & Northallerton G.C. (9)
Thornton-le-Street, Thirsk
(0845) 22170

Tinsley Park G.C. (18)
Darnall, Sheffield (0742) 442237

Wakefield G.C. (18)
Woodthorpe, Wakefield
(0924) 2355104

Wath-upon-Dearne G.C. (9)
Rotherham (0709) 878677

West Bowling G.C. (18)
Bradford (0274) 72449

West Bradford G.C. (18)
Bradford (0274) 4276715

West End G.C. (18)
Halifax (0422) 53608

Wetherby G.C. (18)
Wetherby (0937) 62527

Wheatley G.C. (18)
Doncaster (0302) 831655/831203

Whitby G.C. (18)
Low Straggleton, Whitby
(0947) 602768

Withernsea G.C. (9)
Withernsea (09642) 2258

NORTH YORKSHIRE

WILL HENDERSON   *"Teeing Up"*   *BURLINGTON GALLERY*

MIDDLETHORPE HALL

Bishopthorpe Road, York YO2 1QP
Telephone (0904) 641241
Telex 57802 MIDDLE G

**OWNED AND RESTORED BY
HISTORIC HOUSE HOTELS LIMITED**

AA 3 Red Stars & 1 Rosette

One of Britain's Prestige Hotels

To the south and west the Yorkshire Dales; to the north and east the Yorkshire Moors: England's largest county and quite possibly England's most beautiful.

The Dales and the Moors may not sound like great golfing country and indeed by far the greater number of Yorkshire's golf courses lies in the more populated and industrial regions of South and West Yorkshire. However, visitors to North Yorkshire will not be disappointed: not only does the county boast the likes of **Ganton** and **Fulford**, two of England's greatest inland courses, but there are twenty five or so others, the majority of which are set in quite glorious surroundings and welcome visitors throughout the week.

York, they say, is a city everyone should visit at least once. I would recommend at least twice for there are two outstanding golf courses within 3 miles of York Minster: **Fulford** to the south and **York Golf Club** at Strensall to the north. Fulford (see feature page) is perhaps the better known, but **York** is also a Championship course and has many admirers. Visitors are welcome to play at York on any day of the week although as it is a popular course it is essential to telephone the Club in advance. Green fees in 1986 were priced at **£10** midweek, **£12** at weekends.

As for Harrogate one can only presume that there are many people walking around with misspent youths – not a particularly large town but there are three excellent courses to choose from: **Pannal, Oakdale** and the **Harrogate Club**. **Pannal** lies south of the town off the **A61**. It is the largest of the three, a Championship course in fact, of moorland character and well wooded. The fees in 1986 were **£14** per day. **Oakdale** is situated to the north west of Harrogate off the **A59** and is more of a parkland course (fees approximately **£10**) while Harrogate off the **A59** is more of a parkland course (fees approximately **£10**) while **Harrogate Golf Club** occupies some very pleasant surroundings at Starbeck near Knaresborough – a day's golf here is priced at around the **£14** mark. At each of the Harrogate courses there are no specific restrictions on visiting golfers but again it is probably advisable to make a quick telephone call to the particular Club to check for any tee reservations.

Before heading towards the Dales and Moors it is worth noting **Selby** in the south of the county. Laid out over fairly sandy sub-soil the course could be described as part links, part parkland. The Club welcomes visitors throughout the week, with prior telephoning required at weekends. Green fees at Selby in 1986 were **£9** midweek, **£11** at weekends.

The beautiful City of **Ripon** is often known as the "Gateway to the Dales". There is only a nine hole course (just to the north of the City off the **A6108**) though it can be quite testing with its many hills. There are no restrictions on visitors.

Over to the south west of the county is Skipton, (not to be confused with "Old Mother Shipton" who in any event wandered around somewhat). Skipton is a moorland type course, being on the edge of the Dales, although it is also situated fairly close to the town centre. Weekdays are usually the best times for a visit.

Looking even further west, the Golf Club at **Bentham**, close to the Lancashire border, is another with only nine holes, (two sets of tees) but the surrounding scenery is quite magnificent, with views towards the Lake District hills and across to Ingleborough. In 1986 the cost of a day's golf was a mere **£4** during the week and **£5** at weekends. Bentham can be reached via the **B6480** Settle road.

Catterick was once a Roman Station and is now a 20th century garrison. some of the holes on the **Catterick Garrison** golf course seem to have war-like tendencies – one wonders what to make of an opening hole named "**Stalag**"! Anyway the setting is all very peaceful with views towards the Pennine range and 18 holes can be enjoyed for **£7** midweek, **£10** at weekends.

Two of North Yorkshire's most beautiful courses are situated fairly close to one another in the centre of the county: **Thirsk & Northallerton** and **Bedale**. The former lies very close to Thirsk racetrack. The views here are towards the Cleveland Hills on one side and the Hambleton Hills on another. **Bedale Golf Club** can be found off the **A684** and is known for its beautiful spread of trees. At each course visitors are welcome between Mondays and Saturdays, fees being approximately **£7** per day.

Richmond is another that enjoys glorious surroundings, the golf course lying just north of the town while both **Easingwold** and **Malton and Norton** shouldn't be overlooked, the latter being particularly convenient for those heading towards **Ganton** on the **A64**. Ganton, thought by many to be the finest inland course in the North of England, boasts a superb setting on the edge of the Vale of Pickering, and along with Fulford is featured on a later page.

Yorkshire's coast contrasts greatly with that of Lancashire; with spectacular cliffs rather than dunes dominating the coastline. Not surprisingly there are no links courses to be found here, however, visitors to the resorts of **Filey** and **Scarborough** will be able to enjoy a game with views over sea and sand (hopefully avoiding both!).

I cannot leave North Yorkshire without quoting one of the Secretaries who kindly sent us information. It's probably best that he remains anonymous for when asked if anything of particular note had occurred in his Club's long history he duly replied: "Nothing really other than Births, Deaths, Marriages and a few holes in one"!

Bedale G.C.	(0677) 22568
Bentham G.C.	(0468) 61411
Catterick Garrison G.C.	(0748) 833268
Easingwold G.C.	(0347) 21486
Filey G.C.	(0723) 513293
Fulford G.C.	(0904) 413579
Ganton G.C.	(0944) 70329
Harrogate G.C.	(0423) 863158
Malton and Norton G.C.	(0653) 7912
Oakdale G.C.	(0423) 502806
Pannal G.C.	(0423) 872628
Richmond G.C.	(0748) 2457
Ripon City G.C.	(0765) 3640
Scarborough North Cliff G.C.	(0723) 360786
Selby G.C.	(075 782) 622
Skipton G.C.	(0756) 3922
Thirsk & Northallerton G.C.	(0845) 22170
York G.C.	(0904) 490304

Fulford – a day's golf over – inspired play, I might add, the perfect round. Though these words will never, I fear, be applicable to my game they may be suitable to yours. In order to achieve the best play possible one must be relaxed, confident of one's own ability, contented in one's spirit and enthusiastic for success. Where better place to find these feelings than North Yorkshire? From the dales to the moors, the valleys to the streams, the wild country is an expanse of great delight. Amid these perfect surroundings lie cities and towns as beautiful as any in England. York, Harrogate, Richmond and Scarborough, all have much to offer.

In terms of real variety there is no part of England to match this splendid county. To recommend the places to visit is something of a task. Here are some which we hope will add something to your peace of mind if not necessarily to your game.

Scarborough is as good a place as any to start a trip around Yorkshire. The delightful coast which stretches north and south taking in such delights as Robin Hood's Bay (note the Laurel pub amid the fishermen's cottages and the cobbled streets). **The Royal Hotel in Scarborough**(0723) 364353 caters for all tastes for tourist and businessman alike. For fine views the **Hotel St. Nicholas (0723) 364101** obliges while the **Holbeck Hall (0723) 374374** is most convenient for the South Cliff Golf Club. A little way north in Harkness, **The Harkness Grange (0723) 369966** a pitch and putt course is offered – ideal for knocking up before breakfast. Heading inland to the stunning moorland scenery one travels through the land so beautifully described by James Herriott. The pubs we have to miss are tragic but it is for a good cause. For we are dining in Harom at the **Star Inn's (0439) 70397** splendid restaurant. Another pleasant inn which offers some accommodation is **The Malt Shovel (04393) 461** – Oswaldkirk. In nearby Helmsley – two hotels to note are **The Black Swan (0439) 70466** overlooking the delightful Market Square and **Feversham Arms (0439) 70766** beside the church. Another worthwhile find amidst the Hambleton Hills is Coxwold and the Fauconberg Arms – a delightful pub with excellent bar food. Another hotel surrounded by a superbly tranquil setting – which in turn yields fine golfcourses – is located in Whitwell on the Hill – **The Whitwell Hall Country House (065381) 551**– extremely comfortable.

The solitude of the moors is broken by the busy city of York. Here a wealth of attractions – Shambles has some gorgeous shops, the Minster itself is sensational, museums galore and some delightful hotels. The star of the show is **Middlethorpe Hall (0904) 641241**, a beautiful mansion house and an exquisite restaurant, a delight to visit. **The Mount Royal (0904) 28856** is another well run hotel and is certainly less expensive, while closer to the centre of the town **The Judges Lodging (0904) 38733** is particularly elegant. The town centre has many tea shops and small restaurants as well as some pleasant pubs, note **The Olde Starr** in Stonegate. (The **Ten Green Bottles** is also good fun.) A fine pub outside the city can be found in Wighill – **The White Swan** – good value bar snacks.

If one is heading south and leaving these gorgeous parts then a game of golf at Selby should be followed by a visit to Monk Fryston and its hotel, **The Monk Fryston Hall (0977) 682369**, (another quiet yet convenient country retreat).

A far better idea is to remain in Yorkshire and visit more delightful shops this time in Harrogate. The streets are also home of many fine restaurants, **The Drum and Monkey (0423) 502650** – (superb seafood) or **Number Six (0423) 502908** to name a fine duo. The restaurants in the hotels are also particularly good notably **The Hotel Majestic (0423) 68972, The Russell Hotel (0423) 509866** and **The Studley (0423) 60425**. Having bathed in the delights of this superb spa town we visit some beautiful monuments. The Abbeys of Rievaulx, Jervaulx and Byland are quite stunning. The riverside setting of Fountains Abbey is also a true delight. Spellbound we return to crack the ball around the fairways feeling, as ever in North Yorkshire, inspired. In Knaresborough **The Dower House Hotel (0423) 863302** awaits us– excellent. Also in town a delightful Swiss restaurant should be visited, **Schwallers (0423) 863899**. A little further north and Boroughbridge another pleasant Yorkshire town. Two tips for golfers heading that way. Firstly, **The Crown (09012) 2328** a comfortable old inn. Secondly, **The Fountain House (09012) 2241** – supremely fresh food. Another duo this time in Ripon – (watch the man with the horn), they are **The Ripon Spa Hotel (0765) 2172** and **The Old Deanery (0765) 3518** (relaxed atmosphere for dinner after a grim round). Relentlessly trekking north other jewels lie in store. In the delightfully named Masham – lovers of Theakston's should make a pilgrimage to the **White Bear**. While in Jervaulx, **Jervaulx Hall (0677) 60235** is the ideal place to start one trip – the tranquillity is almost tangible. Other places handy for the A1, well we've got an outstanding combination at Northallerton where **Romanby Court (0609) 774918** has a splendid Italian menu, while nearby in Staddle Bridge **McCoy's** restaurant is quite marvellous **(060982) 671** (you can also stay at the inn **McCoy's at the Tontine**) – marvellous. Up te' road – the **Kirkby Fleetham (0609) 748226** – there a quite excellent hotel with a restaurant to match can be found **(0609) 748226**. In Moulton one cannot fail to find delight in the seafood at **The Black Bull (032 577) 289**. (A similar wonderful problem occurs in Stapleton at the delightful **Bridge Inn (0325) 50106**. In Richmond one finds a queer mixture of medieval, Georgian and Victorian – the castle is dominant and the Swale setting – tremendous (excellent place to discuss the day's golf). Returning south through the wild scenery of the North Yorkshire Dales we arrive at Hetton, where a welcome pint and lunch is enjoyed at **The Angel**. Here we make an easy decision – to play golf at the wildly remote course at Bentham and return for dinner and a night at the outstanding **Devonshire Arms** in Bolton Abbey **(075671) 441**.

We end our venture in style and comfort – Castle Howard, as we wander through the grounds thinking what a perfect fairway the grounds could make and such a clubhouse. We have become enamoured with Yorkshire – we remain inspired suitably so we contemplate our return to Fulford.

Royal Hotel
St Nicholas Street, Scarborough   Tel: (0723) 364333
Close to the Championship course at Ganton, the 4 star Royal Hotel at Scarborough has everything to offer the travelling golfer, not least the special 3 day golf packages it has recently introduced. The hotel's seafront position and its extra luxuries make it a must for the visitor to this beautiful part of the country.

The Tritton Inn
Sledmere
Tel: (0377) 86644
Situated in the shadow of the famous Sledmere House, the Inn is a famous stopping off point for travellers along the scenic route between Bridlington and York. Sledmere is situated on the B1252, 8 miles from Driffield. Good food, fine wine and traditional Scotch bitters.

THE DIFFERENCE BETWEEN GOING FOR THE GREEN AND GOING FOR THE PIN.

When you're playing a ball th[at] offers you the ultimate in distance and control, you'll feel confident w[ith] these difficult shots. It's what mak[es] all the difference between going f[or] the green and going for the pin. I[t's] the kind of difference you get fr[om] playing a Titleist 384 PTS.

You'll have the same confiden[ce] as the majority of the world's top professionals in the UK, Europe a[nd] USA.* They all use a Titleist with t[he] same proven dimple pattern as t[he] 384 PTS. You'll have the same un[-] beatable distance down the fairw[ay]

The high energy windings under the cut-proof Surlyn cov[er] give you a much higher spin rate f[or] optimum trajectory and contro[l] around the greens.

Finally, 32 quality checks o[n] every ball throughout the man[u-] facturing process ensure the sa[me] all round performance you hav[e] come to expect from a Titleist.

Play a Titleist 384 PTS this weekend.

Available in 90 or 100 compres[s...]

Golf Foun[...]
JUNIOR GOLF S[...]

Titleist 384 PTS

THE FIRST CHOICE IN GOLF

Acushnet Ltd., Orchard Road, Great She[l...]
Cambridge CB2 5AB. Tel: (0223) 8427[...]

* Source: Darrell Survey Company/Sports Marketing Sur[vey...]

JERVAULX HALL HOTEL

Set amidst the beautiful scenery of the Yorkshire dales and standing adjacent to one of England's most resplendant ruins, Jervaulx Abbey, there could be no better or more unique place from which to tour the surrounding countryside than this friendly and well run hotel.

Bought in 1979 the idea was to create a splendid hotel from this imposing country house. Eight acres of delightful gardens and mature woodlands, surround the house which lies midway between the quaint market towns of Masham and Middleton.

It is essentially a quiet and peaceful hotel in which to relax and enjoy beautiful surroundings. The gardens are a delight and can be explored. Over 120 species of wild flowers have been recorded in a single season in the grounds of Jervaulx. The Abbey, founded in 1156 by the monks who gave Wensleydale Cheese its name, is also well worth visiting – its walls are a spectacular riot of marjoram and wall flowers.

Despite having been brought up to date, the original character of the house inside has been preserved. The hotel has eight double bedrooms, bathrooms en suite. One bedroom is situated on the ground floor with its own doorway opening on to the garden, making it particularly suitable for the elderly or disabled, or guests with dogs.

The hotel also offers a residential and table licence. Fresh vegetables and soft fruits, local lamb and game are offered on the menu when in season. The hotel's balanced menu and good wines will thus add to the enjoyment of one's stay at Jervaulx.

Having pondered a while in the superb setting of Jervaulx it might be as well to get out and about to sample the rest of Yorkshire's many delights. **Middleham Castle, Fountains Abbey, Castle Howard and Harewood House** are all within easy reach. While further afield, **York, Harrogate, Richmond and Ripon** are all places that should not be missed.

With all of Yorkshire's eleven racecourses conveniently close and the A1 only 20 minutes away, this haven of peace and tranquility is a splendid place to ponder after a days racing or golf.

JERVAULX HALL HOTEL
Jervaulx,
Nr. Masham,
Ripon,
North Yorkshire.
Tel: (0677) 60235

These days golf is not only played in every foreign field but it is also played in the most unlikely of places. In 1971 American Astronaut **Captain Alan Shepherd** struck two golf shots from the surface of the moon, becoming in the process the only man able to shank a ball 200 yards. Not to be outdone, as ever, **Arnold Palmer** in 1977 hit three golf balls from off the second stage of the Eiffel Tower, while in 1981 at Fulford, York, **Bernhard Langer** decided to take golf into further alien territory by shinning up a rather large tree and playing his chip shot to the 17th green from amidst its spreading branches.

The **Fulford Golf** Club was founded soon after the turn of the century, but it was only as recently as 1985 that the club celebrated fifty years of playing over the present course. The televised **Benson and Hedges International** open tournament has undoubtedly turned the North Yorkshire Club into a 'golfing household name', but in golf's more discerning circles it has for a long time possessed the reputation of having one of the country's finest inland courses.

Golfers wishing to visit Fulford must make prior arrangements with the Club's Secretary, **John Gledhill**. Individuals and Society Members alike are required to belong to recognised Golf Clubs and be able to provide proof of handicap. Mr Gledhill can be contacted by writing to the club, the full address being, **Fulford Golf Club, Heslington Lane, Fulford, York,** or by telephoning on **(0904) 413579.**

Fulford is situated about a mile to the South of **York,** just off the **A19.** For persons travelling from the South of England, the **A1** and **M1** can assist as far as the Leeds area from where the **A64** runs straight through to Fulford. Perhaps a more direct route through, is to join the **A19** near **Doncaster.** Those ap proaching York from the North should find their route a little more scenic, the most helpful roads again probably being the **A19** (via **Thirsk**) and the **A64** (via **Malton** – which incidentally passes **Ganton** further to the North East). Those journeying from easterly directions should either use the **A1099** or the **A166** before joining the **A64** East of York. The famous City is well served by rail connections and finally the Leeds/Bradford Airport is located approximately 30 miles to the West of York.

On arriving at the Club a green fee of **£15** entitles the visitor to either a single round or a full day's golf during the week. At weekends and Bank Holidays the same can be purchased for **£17** (figures are for 1987). It is normally possible to hire sets of golf clubs from the professional shop, though some prewarning is probably a good idea. **Brian Hessay** is the resident professional at Fulford, he can be reached by telephone on **(0904) 412882.**

Fulford's homely looking Clubhouse is quite spacious inside with a comfortable Lounge and Dining Room. A full catering service is provided throughout the week with the exception of Mondays. Jackets and ties should be worn at all times.

Measuring just a little under **6,800** yards from the back tees, (par **72**, S.S.S. **72**) Fulford provides quite a stern test for the club golfer, but it is no more than a medium length course for the professionals. Much of the prodigiously low scoring achieved at Fulford during the Benson and Hedges tournament has, however, precious little to do with the length of the course. As the Members will quickly tell you it simply reflects the superb condition in which the fairways and the putting surfaces are maintained. Fulford is renowned for its fast and very true greens. Certainly Welsh Ryder Cup player **Ian Woosnam** found them much to his liking as he holed putt after putt during an extraordinary sequence of eight successive birdies during his final round in the 1985 Championship. Woosnam's score of **62** that day set a new course record but unfortunately it wasn't quite good enough to prevent **Sandy Lyle** from adding the Benson and Hedges title to the British Open Championship he had won a month earlier. The Scotsman, (or Anglo-Scot as many south of the border prefer to call him) joined an already impressive list of winners at Fulford, including four Open Champions **Tony Jacklin** (1971) **Lee Trevino** (1978) **Tom Weiskopf** (1981) and **Greg Norman** (1982).

The more mortal golfer probably won't be leaving Fulford with a 62 under his belt – nor one presumes will he have been shinning up the trees – but he ought to be heading home a contented soul having spent a day on what is unquestionably one of the country's most pleasurable golf courses.

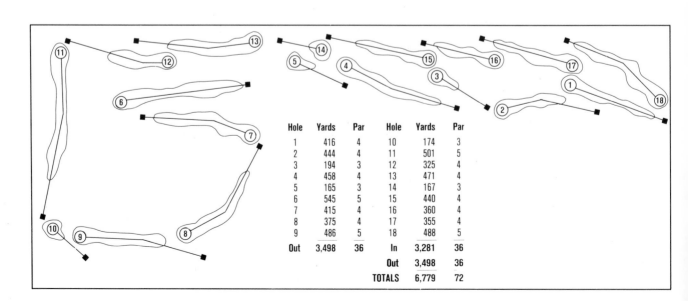

Hole	Yards	Par	Hole	Yards	Par
1	416	4	10	174	3
2	444	4	11	501	5
3	194	3	12	325	4
4	458	4	13	471	4
5	165	3	14	167	3
6	545	5	15	440	4
7	415	4	16	360	4
8	375	4	17	355	4
9	486	5	18	488	5
Out	3,498	36	In	3,281	36
			Out	3,498	36
			TOTALS	6,779	72

They used to say at **Ganton** that when **Harry Vardon** played the course twice in the same day, in his afternoon round he'd often hit his tee shots into the very divots he'd created in the morning. The chances are that this was a little bit of Yorkshire bluff but then the Members at Ganton were fortunate to witness what were probably the very finest years of Britain's greatest ever golfer.

Vardon came to Ganton in **1896**, just five years after the Club's formation. Within a few weeks of his appointment he won his first **Open Championship** at Muirfield defeating the then hat-trick-seeking John H Taylor in a play-off. In **1910** Vardon returned from America with the **U.S. Open** trophy, by which time he'd added two more Open Championships and was half way towards his record number of **six** victories in that event. By the time that Vardon left in 1903 the name of Ganton had been firmly put on the golfing map.

Located approximately nine miles from the sea, Ganton could hardly be called a 'golf links' in the strict sense but it is often said that it has many of the features of links golf with crisp seaside turf and sandy sub-soil. Indeed whenever new bunkers are cut sea-shells are often discovered lying beneath the surface – it appears that the whole of the surrounding area was once an arm of the sea.

Although Ganton may have been 'put on the map' by Vardon, international recognition didn't really arrive until **1949** and the staging of the **Ryder Cup**, the first to be played in Britain after the War. Since 1949 Ganton has played host to numerous major Championships, both amateur and professional and its reputation as one of Britain's finest inland courses is unquestioned.

Golfers wishing to play at Ganton must make prior arrangements with the Club's Secretary, **Air Vice Marshal Price** who may be contacted via the **Ganton Golf Club, Ganton, Scarborough, North Yorkshire YO12 4PA**, telephone (0944) 70329. The Club's professional, **Ian Bamborough**, can be reached on **(0944) 70260**. Subject to proof of handicap visitors are made most welcome and it is possible to pre-book starting times. The **green fees** for 1986 were set at £15 for a day's golf during the week with £20 payable at the weekend. Reductions are available for those teeing off after 4pm. Golfing Societies are equally welcome although those organising should note that no societies are received at weekends.

Although in a non-golfing sense Ganton is a fairly small dot on the map travelling to the Course is made fairly straightforward by the **A64**. This road links the village directly with **Scarborough** to the north east (12 miles) and to both **York** (30 miles) and **Leeds** (60 miles) to the south west. If approaching from the Humberside region a combination of the **A164** to Great Driffield and the **B1249** will take you to within 2 miles of the course, while travellers from further north can avoid the city of York by heading for **Thirsk** and thereafter heading for **Malton** by way of the **A170** and the **B1257**. Malton lies on the **A64** road and like Scarborough is approximately 12 miles from Ganton.

Ganton enjoys a beautifully peaceful setting nestling on the edge of the **Vale of Pickering** and the **Yorkshire Moors**. While the golf course is indeed beautiful, particularly when the gorse is in full bloom, it is very rarely 'peaceful' and when the winds sweep across it can become fearsomely difficult and there are few inland courses with such cavernous bunkers – 105 of them in all. In addition to the many bunkers and the great spread of gorse, there are numerous fir trees and pines which can come into play following the wayward shot, the dog-leg 18th being a notable example and one that provides a very testing finishing hole. The finest hole on the course is thought by many to be the 4th where the second has to be played across a plunging valley towards a plateau green that is heavily bunkered to the right. In total the course measures **6693** yards, par **72**, from the medal tees, with the club tees reducing the length to **6371** yards, par **71**. The ladies play over **6052** yards, par **75**.

The nineteenth at Ganton has a most welcoming atmosphere and offers an extensive range of catering. Lunches are served daily between 12pm and 2.30pm and both breakfast and dinner can be arranged with some warning. Dress is informal in the men's bar until 6pm Mondays to Saturdays, though a jacket and tie should be worn in all other public rooms.

Inevitably Ganton's name will always be linked with Vardon's. But another great player also developed his talents on the Yorkshire course – **Ted Ray** the famed long hitter who found fortune in America winning their Open in **1920**, in so doing ironically held off the challenge of a 50 year old Vardon. The greatest event in Ganton's distinguished history was undoubtedly the great **Ryder Cup** match of **1949** when the home team led by three matches to one at the end of the first day only eventually to lose by seven to five. **Ben Hogan**, convalescing from his near fatal accident led the American side as non-playing captain.

Twice since the War the **Amateur Championship** has been staged at Ganton, in **1964** and **1977**, the only inland course to have done so. In addition to the Amateur Championship, the **English Amateur**, the **Youths Amateur** and the **British Ladies Championship** have each been held at Ganton while the professionals have also visited in recent years with the **Dunlop Masters** of **1975**, won by **Bernard Gallacher** and in **1981** the **P.G.A. Championship**, resulting in a third victory in four years for **Nick Faldo**.

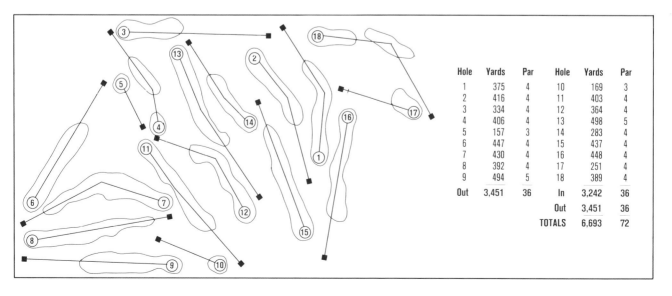

Hole	Yards	Par	Hole	Yards	Par
1	375	4	10	169	3
2	416	4	11	403	4
3	334	4	12	364	4
4	406	4	13	498	5
5	157	3	14	283	4
6	447	4	15	437	4
7	430	4	16	448	4
8	392	4	17	251	4
9	494	5	18	389	4
Out	3,451	36	In	3,242	36
			Out	3,451	36
			TOTALS	6,693	72

CUMBRIA

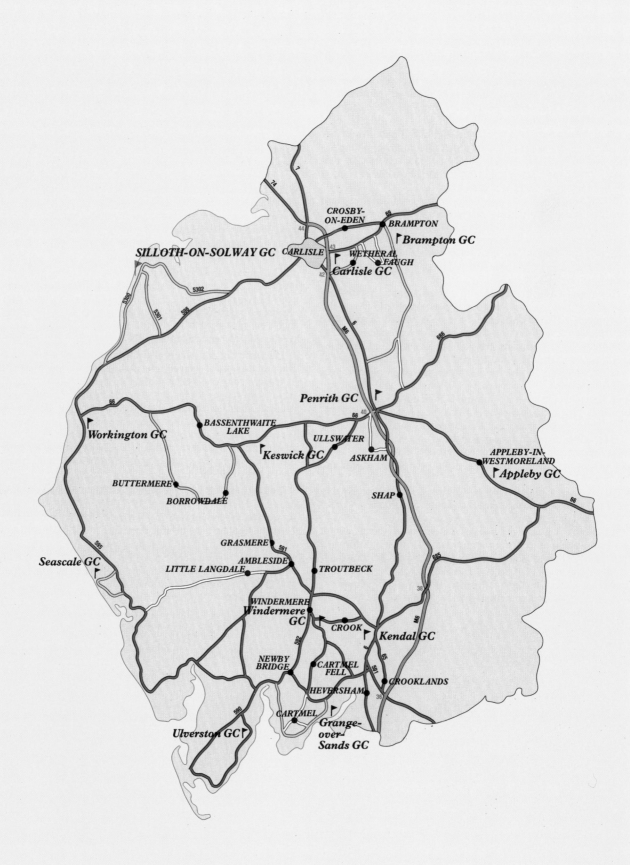

MICHAELS NOOK

a secluded position overlooking the
asmere Valley and surrounded by well-
pt lawns and beautiful trees, Michaels
ook is an unusually fine example of a
ne-built Lakeland home, with a wealth
elegant mahogany woodwork. Built in
59 as a summer residence for the family
a Lancashire cotton industrialist, the
use was named to commemorate the
ore humble dwelling of the shepherd
mortalised by William Wordsworth in his
em "Michael". Its conversion to an hotel
1969 by present owner, Reg Gifford,
as achieved without detriment to the
llowness derived from long years of use
a private residence, and despite its now
ng-established reputation as one of
itain's leading country house hotels, it
mains a home, with a hint of eccentricity,
her than a showpiece.

ough now principally a dedicated
telier, Reg Gifford is also a respected
tique dealer, and furnishings, enhanced
an abundance of flowers and plants,
lect his personal taste and knowledge.
en fires blaze hospitably in the cosy bar,
orned with sets of prints and early
son's porcelain, and the elegant drawing
om, where fine English furniture is offset
delicate plaster mouldings. A beautiful
ite Persian cat and a sleek Russian Blue
sport themselves in the warm glow—an
ormous Great Dane wanders in from
e to time to keep himself informed. It is
e essence of informal, relaxed and
mfortable country living at its choicest.
ere are nine double bedrooms and two
xury suites, all charmingly decorated,
ch with a character of its own, and all
th private bathroom, telephone and
lour television. The Oak Room, with its
ne fireplace, handsome panelling and
t furnishings, is available for executive
etings or private dinner parties.

e Restaurant, its gleaming polished
les set with fine crystal and porcelain,
rfectly complements the hotel, and the
est fresh produce is used to prepare
hes that combine lightness of touch with
licacy of flavour and artistry of
esentation. The wines are chosen by Reg
fford for their quality and value, and
metimes for their great distinction.
rvice throughout is thoughtful, friendly
d efficient.

A number of magnificent walks start from
the doorstep of this delightful house and
there are some spectacular drives in all
directions through some of Britain's most
impressive scenery.

Michaels Nook,
Grasmere, Nr. Ambleside,
English Lakeland.
Telephone: (09665) 496

Let's not beat about the bush – anyone who takes his golf clubs to the **Lake District** must have lost his marbles. But then who said golfers were a sane bunch anyway?

Whilst the poets and the ramblers find solitude and peace of mind in the fells we find it on the Fairways of Life. The splendour of the sweetly struck six iron, the deft chip-shot that rolls to within twelve inches and the long curling putt that slides in the back door.

At Keswick the golfer can meet the poet. **Keswick Golf Club** lies 4 miles east of the Lakeland town via the **A66**. Whilst the course now measures well over 6,000 yards it once held a rather dubious claim to being the shortest course in Britain – in 1976 they had a splendid Clubhouse but only five holes – no doubt some remarkable scores were returned! These days scoring is a little more difficult with several streams and some dense woodland to be avoided. As one might imagine the views are quite breathtaking and a visit is strongly recommended. A full day's golf in 1986 was priced at **£7**.

Still in the Lakes, **Kendal** has a fine parkland course located just three quarters of a mile from the town centre (and only 2 miles from the **M6** linkroad). Although a fair bit shorter than Keswick its first hole is often considered to be the toughest opener in Britain – 231 yards, uphill all the way, out of bounds to the left and woods to the right! Should one make it to the second the holes do get much easier; however there is an infamous quarry on the right of the 15th fairway which has been known to receive more than golf balls – one frustrated chap after firing ball after ball into its depths decided to throw in his bag for good measure. Fortunately he didn't throw himself in as well but word is he never played golf again. (Who said it was only a game!) A proper day's golf in 1986 could be enjoyed for **£6** midweek, **£7** at weekends.

Others to note within the Lake District include **Windermere Golf Club** (1 1/2 miles east of Bowness-on-Windermere) and **Penrith (off the A6)**, the latter being particularly worth a visit with several challenging holes.

What of life beyond the Lakes? Cumbria is of course one of the largest counties in England but being quite sparsely populated there isn't a great demand for golf courses. **Silloth-on-Silway** in the far north west of Cumbria is unquestionably one of the greatest Championship links in Britain, yet there are no restrictions on times visitors can play and arranging a game is never difficult.

Apart from Silloth (featured on a later page) in the north of the county there are two good courses in the Carlisle area, **Brampton** (or Talkin-Tarn as it is sometimes known) and **Carlisle Golf Club**. **Brampton** is located off the **B6413** and is a beautifully-kept course, laid out some four hundred feet above sea-level offering extensive views towards the nearby hills. It is probably best described as a moorland course whereas Carlisle, equally well-maintained, is more of a parkland type. Both courses welcome visitors throughout the week, fees ranging from **£7** to **£8**.

From Silloth dropping down the county, **Cockermouth** is perhaps best famed for being the birthplace of Wordsworth, there is an 18 hole course just to the east of the town. The town of **Workington** is situated close to the coast though its course is meadowland not links – visitors are again welcome at all times (**£7** per round, **£9** per day).

Those who are in search of links golf might try the 10-holer (?!) at **Dunnerholme** or alternatively the tough 18-holer at **Seascale**. One shouldn't be put off by the thought of being close to the Seascale nuclear installations (and jokes about the balls glowing in the dark are uncalled for); it's an excellent test of golf. There are also some tremendous views towards the Wasdale Screes and the Scafell Range. Visitors are welcome at most times though prior telephoning is usually preferred.

The views at **Ulverston** (3 miles from the town on the **B508**) are of a somewhat different nature to those mentioned above – Blackpool Tower can be sighted on a clear day! **Grange-Over-Sands** is another worth noting and a final mention for the **Furness Golf Club**, founded in 1872; it is the oldest in the county and where, it need hardly be said, visitors are guaranteed a friendly welcome.

There are many natural hazards one finds on a golfcourse – bunkers, the rough, water traps and there are less predictable invaders – the weather and of course one's golf itself. Well, the Lake District offers an abundance of water, a phenomenal amount of rough country and some delightful sands on its western boundaries. However, the county does not house an abundance of golf courses despite these delightful features. However, what it lacks in golfcourses it more than makes up for in hotels, restaurants, pubs and other places of interest. It would be wrong to describe this classic shire as barren of golf courses, indeed it leaves the visiting golfer with the happy predicament of being able to play many of the superior courses. While doing so he or she may wish to enjoy at least one of the following finds, especially if play has been a little wayward.

The ideal place to placate one's partner or one's palate is found in Grasmere, the outstanding **Michael's Nook (09665) 496.** The hotel offers some excellent golf packages – do phone and ask. Other delights to be found in this Wordsworth's country include the great poet's former residence, **White Moss House (09605) 295** – once again a superb restaurant. Yet another grand hotel and restaurant in this charmed area is understandably **The Wordsworth (0965) 592.** Other places to note when visiting Keswick and its various delights include **Armathwaite Hall (059681) 551** in Bassenthwaite and **The Pheasant Inn (059681) 234** in Bassenthwaite Lake nearby. Moving on through the beautiful countryside an infinite variety of gems reveal themselves. In Buttermere, **The Bridge Hotel (059685) 252** delights in its outstanding situation while **The Lodore Swiss** in Borrowdale has an excellent reputation **(059684) 285.** In Little Longdale, **The Three Pines Inn (09667) 215** small, comfortable – good value. There is an enormous selection of good hotels in Ambleside perhaps the best is the charming **Rothay Manor** and its excellent restaurant **(0966) 33605.**

Windermere is the largest of the Lakes, the town of the same name has a wealth of good hotels. **The Miller Howe (09662) 2536** has an excellent view over Lake Windermere and the hills. The comfort, the welcome and food all carry the strongest recommendation. Certainly if your game needs a little muscle, breakfast and a stroll in the hills may be as good an answer as any. Other good establishments to consider are **Rogers (09662) 4954** an extremely pleasant restaurant in the High Street. Another hotel that merits particular attention is the **Langdale Chase (0966) 3201** another fine setting. Naturally, the lakes themselves offer a variety of attractions that will act as the perfect contrast to a round of golf. In the surrounding towns and villages a wealth of antique and craft shops can be found, ideal for browsing.

More inspired scenery and Troutbeck where **The Mortal Man (0966) 33193** stands out not merely for its glorious settings, its fine restaurant but also for overall value – thoroughly worthwhile. In **Crook**, another homely hotel even if the name sounds unwelcoming is **The Wild Boar** – another friendly inn. If you're playing a day's golf at Kendal then dinner at the **Castle Dairy (0539) 21170** is an excellent idea – must book. Further south still and into the Fells where the countryside continues its

extraordinary beauty – Cartmel Fell and the **Masons Arms** – a really popular pub – where both bar snacks and beers are excellent. In Newby Bridge, particularly convenient for **Holder Hall**, which is well worth visiting lies **The Seven Hotel (0448) 31681** – another first rate establishment, but once again by no means cheap, a similar appraisal can be made of the **Whitewater Hotel (0448) 31133** also in Newby Bridge. The town itself is where Arthur Ransome wrote his 'Swallows and Amazons' – more inspired literature – perhaps the author of this 'ere piece should pack up the bags and seek a little of the air! Other suitable places to find this pleasant atmosphere include **The Blue Bell Hotel** at Heversham (04482) 3159. In Cartmel which offers some superb Bank Holiday racing amongst its other attractions the **Aynsome Manor (04454) 276** which is cosy and a refreshing visit is guaranteed. While in Crooklands, **The Crooklands Hotel (04487) 432** itself another old coaching inn makes for a pleasant place to hang up one's clubs for the evening, particularly handy for the Club.

While the hotels of real merit tend to gather in the Lakes some of the noted golf courses are located on the shores of Cumbria – this is not to say that there are no hotels to be found. In Workington **The Westland (0900) 4544** springs to mind. What we are aiming to do here though is to drag you back to the Lakes. Failing this then what about Carlisle – the Cathedral is particularly striking. In the town itself **The Crown and Mitre (0228) 25491** is the obvious answer while outside the town in Brampton **The Farlam Hall Hotel (06976) 234** is an excellent place to stay or have dinner after a round at the nearby course. People travelling on a smaller budget should try **The Hare and Hounds Inn (06977) 3456** – good value. One last thought for Brampton (apart from the antiques is the **Tarn End (06977) 2340**, an excellent restaurant which offers some pleasant accommodation. Returning to a water setting this time Crosby-on-Eden where the **Crosby Lodge (022873) 618** is recommended. Another excellent hotel is to be found in Faugh – **The String of Horses (022870) 297.** Final thoughts for the area are to be found in Wetheral, **The Brown Hotel (0228) 61888** and a simply splendid restaurant **Fantails (0228) 60239.**

Returning to the Lakes a few further ideas include Ullswater, where **The Sharrow Bay Hotel (085 36) 301** is another must for lovers of style and charm where the restaurant is outstanding. In Askham nearby further delights include **The Queens Head** – a pub on this occasion – but a fine place to stay just the same. Another ideal retreat is **The Shap Wells Hotel, Shap (09316) 628.** (While visitors to Appleby in Westmorland should note **The Appleby Manor Hotel (0930) 51571.** We conclude our trip in Keswick where you may have visited **The Rembrandt (0596) 72008** a pleasant restaurant or stayed at **The Woolpack (0596) 72775** or **The Underscar Country House (0596) 72469** and by and large you will have been spoilt. The ideal trip will have given you inspiration in abundance, golf may have taken a back seat – probably not – but this is no bad thing for while the Lakes and the delights of Scafell Pike are to be seen golfers will admit that there are other things in life off the golfcourse (well they might not but if they did it would be after visiting Cumbria – give it a try!)

Fantails Restaurant
The Green, Wetheral, Nr Carlisle
Tel: (0228) 60239
Beautifully converted barn and hayloft with oak floors, ancient beams, open fire and good food. A family run establishment of 10 years standing, serving freshly prepared food cooked to order as the customer requests. The restaurant goes to great pains to give good friendly service always

Miller Howe Hotel
Rayrigg Road,
Windermere
Tel: (09662) 2536
The Miller Howe has superb views of Lake Windermere and excellent bedrooms with many extras. Five course menus are imaginative and make the best use of fresh local produce while breakfasts are a delight. Ideal for golfing in the Lake District.

Enough of the endless meetings. The looming deadlines. The shrill, naggi, telephones...it's time for a wild weekeno

As the wipers flicked the last drops of an impetuous shower from the windscreen, a sudden break in the conifers gave us our first glimpse of the vast water, called, without hint of overstatement, Loch Awe.

I glanced down at the tripmeter. Four hundred and eighty-five miles?

Surely by now I should feel as if I'd had a jab of local anaesthetic, slept in a draught and done an honest hour's hoeing.

But no.

This was our first long distance trip since we'd bought the Range Rover and the comforts that stopped me cursing urban driving hadn't diminished one jot.

The coil sprung suspension smoothed bumps to a mere ripple.

The seats, with head and arm rests, managed to stay firm yet sumptuous.

The sound insulation hushed the wearing drone of road and traffic.

As a touch on the wheel eased us into the long lochside bend

I asked myself, yet again, how could such a big, imposing vehicle handle so effortlessly.

How had they engineered the power steering to be both light and positive?

Suddenly Katie spotted the sign for Dalmally. I turned right towards a more pressing question.

How was the fishing?

Next morning with a p hamper and the tackle sto safely in the huge, obliging boo

took the single track road a Glen Orchy.

From the high panorama o Range Rover's driving positi could see, over the jasmine ti

m bushes, the falls and torrents
e enticing river.

wing down to pass an on-
ng BMW, I realised, as we
gingerly past each other,
much of this view he was
ing.

found a likely spot. I cast an
Dun out into the river. Katie
ed a bottle of white wine into
all plunge pool and wandered
ith Norman Mailer.

was watching a pair of oyster
ers heckle overhead when the
suddenly jumped in my hand,
pool surface exploded and a
brown trout came out fighting.
her. Another. Then, as the sun
temperature climbed, nothing.
ck on the road heading for
I flicked on the air condition-
and settled down to a long
drive.

Five miles on, curiosity pulled
me up at the foot of an old forestry
track.

I engaged diff. lock and with
the relentless traction of four wheel
drive, powered up the forty five
degree slope.

"Nice change", laughed Katie
"you're making a molehill of a
mountain".

As we crested the summit, there
below us, browsing through the
heather, was a herd of red deer.

The electric windows hummed
open. We focused our binoculars.
Watched spellbound for a good

hour, then slipped quietly
into reverse and whispered
back towards the road.

Sunday and a brisk walk
along the West Highland Way
from Tyndrum to the Bridge
of Orchy (an even brisker bus

back) and with Katie at the
wheel we headed for lunch
at the Falls of Dochart.

Over the mighty
peak of ,Ben
Lawers. Then
east
along glorious Glen Lyon, where for
a few fleeting seconds we watched a
golden eagle glide across the valley,
wheel westwards, and disappear
into the distant mountains.

Our last day. I dragged myself
out of bed an hour before dawn to
prove Samuel Johnson's point that
a fishing rod is an instrument
with a hook on one end and a fool
on the other.

Katie collected me at ten and
soon the West Highlands were
falling away as the familiar blue
signs loomed up, pointing us back
to the motorway.

I eased into the traffic (curious
how many motorists are deferen-
tial to a Range Rover) slipped
Beethoven into the stereo and with
the Pastoral Symphony pouring
from four speakers, headed back
towards the jungle.

Now you know what people see in a Range Rover.

SILLOTH-ON-SOLWAY

One of the greatest ever lady golfers, **Miss Cecil Leitch** once said: "If you can play Silloth you can play anywhere". The four times British Ladies Champion and the great rival of Joyce Wethered knew better than most for she grew up in Silloth and it was on Silloth's Championship links that she and her four golfing sisters learnt to play.

Silloth-on-Solway Golf Club has a mischievous date of foundation somewhere between **1892** when the first holes were laid out and **1903** when the Club together with its 'new' Clubhouse was formally opened by the Speaker of the House of Commons, **The Rt. Hon. Edward Gully**.

Today Silloth is perhaps one of Britain's lesser known Championship links, this doubtless is a result of its somewhat remote situation lying 23 miles north west of Carlisle. Remote it may be but it is a journey decidedly worth making for not only is this one of Britain's greatest tests of golf but the Silloth Club is just about the most friendly one is likely to come across.

Most responsible for the welcoming atmosphere is the Club's **Secretary, Mr John Todd**, a Silloth man needless to say. Mr Todd may be contacted by telephone on **(0965) 31179**. There are no restrictions on visiting golfers and they may play at all times. Prior telephoning is however advisable during the summer as Silloth is becoming increasingly popular with Societies. Indeed the Secretary informs me that in 1986 at least three separate parties made bookings from Kuala Lumpur!

The cost of a day's golf at Silloth in 1986 was priced at **£8** during the week and **£10** at weekends. The fees for juniors were half the above rates. In 1986 a **weekly** ticket (Monday to Friday) could also be purchased for the sum of **£30**. Golfing Societies must book starting times either by telephoning the Club or by writing to the Secretary at **The Silloth-on-Solway Golf Club, Silloth-on-Solway, Carlisle, Cumbria CA5 4AT**. Should the need arise, sets of clubs may be hired from the professional David Forsythe **(0965) 31304**.

With the **M6** running to Carlisle, Silloth isn't actually quite as remote as it may appear on the map. Those travelling from the south should leave the **M6** at junction **41** and thereafter take the B5302 to **Wigton**. At Wigton the **B5302** should be picked up and followed to Silloth. Those who have been sensible enough to take their golf clubs to the **Lake District** may find the **B5300** road helpful, it runs along the coast from **Maryport** to Silloth. Finally those approaching from Scotland should head for Carlisle and thereafter follow a combination of the **B5307** and the **B5302** to Silloth.

Measuring **6343** yards, par 72 (5780 yards, par 75 for Ladies) Silloth may not sound particularly frightening, and you may just be wondering what all the fuss is about. Standing on the 1st tee with the wind hammering into your face you'll know exactly what all the fuss is about. Humbling is perhaps the best way to describe the sensation. Two shots later (hopefully!) you'll also discover why the large greens at Silloth have acquired such a reputation. Of the many great holes perhaps the par five 13th stands out. Appropriately named "Hogs Back" it has an exceptionally narrow fairway that is heather lined on either side and a plateau green – miss it and you're in trouble!

The Clubhouse at Silloth offers full catering until 9pm after which light snacks may be obtained from the Bar. The lunchtime menu is quite outstanding and provided some warning is given, a full Cumberland breakfast can be arranged (sounds like an excellent idea).

The Club is understandably proud of the fact that twice in the last ten years it has been selected to host the British Ladies Open Championship. However, it can also be proud of the courage some of its members displayed back in 1912; for this information I am indebted to the Secretary: on behalf of all the Clubs in the British Isles Silloth appealed against the assessment of income tax on green fees. Unfortunately for the Golf Clubs the learned judge found in favour of the Inland Revenue; this left Silloth with the task of finding £433. 12s. 9d for legal expenses. Eighty-one Clubs promised subscriptions to help towards the debt and they eventually raised £140. 11s. 0d leaving a deficiency of almost £300. One very famous Club I am told subscribed one shilling!

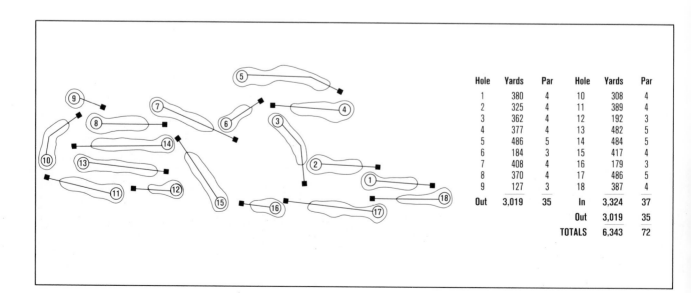

Hole	Yards	Par	Hole	Yards	Par
1	380	4	10	308	4
2	325	4	11	389	4
3	362	4	12	192	3
4	377	4	13	482	5
5	486	5	14	484	5
6	184	3	15	417	4
7	408	4	16	179	3
8	370	4	17	486	5
9	127	3	18	387	4
Out	3,019	35	In	3,324	37
			Out	3,019	35
			TOTALS	6,343	72

DURHAM, CLEVELAND,
TYNE & WEAR AND NORTHUMBERLAND

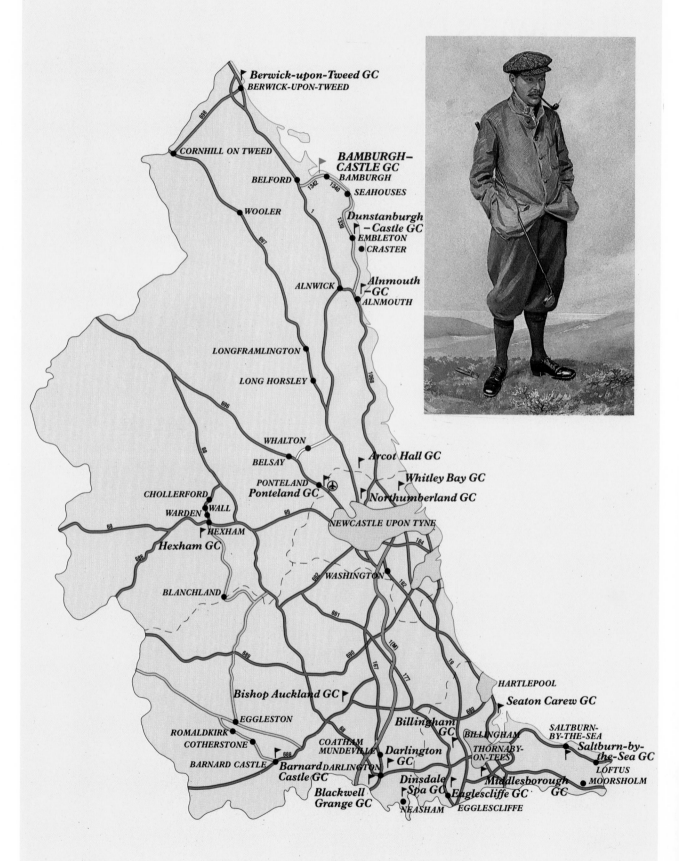

Berwick-upon-Tweed GC
BERWICK-UPON-TWEED

CORNHILL ON TWEED

BAMBURGH–
CASTLE GC
BELFORD
BAMBURGH

SEAHOUSES

WOOLER

Dunstanburgh
–Castle GC
EMBLETON
CRASTER

Alnmouth
–GC
ALNWICK
ALNMOUTH

LONGFRAMLINGTON

LONG HORSLEY

WHALTON

BELSAY
Arcot Hall GC

PONTELAND
Ponteland GC
Whitley Bay GC

CHOLLERFORD
WARDEN   WALL
HEXHAM
Hexham GC
Northumberland GC

NEWCASTLE UPON TYNE

WASHINGTON

BLANCHLAND

HARTLEPOOL

Bishop Auckland GC
Seaton Carew GC

EGGLESTON
Billingham
GC
SALTBURN-
BY-THE-SEA

ROMALDKIRK
COTHERSTONE
COATHAM
MUNDEVILLE
Darlington
GC
BILLINGHAM
Saltburn-by-
the-Sea GC

BARNARD CASTLE
Barnard
Castle GC
DARLINGTON
THORNABY-
ON-TEES
LOFTUS
MOORSHOLM

Dinsdale
Spa GC
Middlesborough
GC

Blackwell
Grange GC
Eaglescliffe GC

NEASHAM
EGGLESCLIFFE

SPY   "Pensive"   BURLINGTON GALLERY

LINDEN HALL HOTEL

Linden Hall, a magnificent Georgian Country House, is situated in 300 acres of splendid park and woodland, in mid-Northumberland. Despite its tranquil setting the hotel is a mere thirty minutes from central Newcastle and only twenty five from the Airport. The house captures feelings of grandness and elegance, but a happy air of informality makes relaxation inevitable.

The facilities include some 45 bedrooms with many different styles and varied form designed to accommodate a range of tastes and requirements, twin and double bedded rooms, family rooms and four poster suites are all available.

The Monck Cocktail Bar is a pleasantly stylish venue for a pre-dinner drink or to meet friends, whilst the inner hall has numerous fine antiques and a sweeping staircase. The Drawing Room is the ideal place to relax while the hotel's Dobson Restaurant offers a delightful menu. While you chat stunning views east over the Croquet Lawn and beyond to the ragged Northumberland coastline and south over gardens to the parkland beyond can be enjoyed.

The hotel offers a variety of While Away weekends which give the opportunity to enjoy the gorgeous countryside of Northumberland. A variety of sporting facilities are also available at the hotel as well as the excellent golf courses and racecourses that can be found conveniently nearby.

LINDEN HALL HOTEL
Longhorsley,
Morpeth,
Northumberland.
Tel: (0670) 56611

DURHAM, CLEVELAND, TYNE & WEAR AND NORTHUMBERLAND

The North East of England encompasses Tyneside, Teesside and Wearside; it also includes the Cleveland Hills, the Cheviots and the wild spectacular coast of ancient Northumbria. The four modern-day counties stretch from the far end of the Yorkshire Pennines and intrude into the Scottish Borders, the greater part of Northumberland lying north of Hadrian's Wall.

The appeal of any golf course can naturally be affected greatly by its surroundings; nowhere in Britain does the accompanying landscape seem to dictate the enjoyment of a game as much as in this part of the world. The contrast between the industrial and rural north east is dramatic, to put it mildly. The golf courses in the former tend towards the uninspiring – **Seaton Carew** being one great exception – whilst the likes of **Bamburgh** and **Hexham** offer such breathtaking scenery that the quality of the golf can often be relegated to a secondary consideration.

Beginning in the south of the region, Cleveland is one of the smallest counties in England and not surprisingly has very few courses. **Seaton Carew** has already been mentioned; along with Silloth on the West Coast it represents England's finest test of linksland golf north of Lytham. Seaton Carew is situated approximately 3 miles south of Hartlepool with a skyline dominated by far-off chimneys, which at night appear like giant torches. Golf here is played amidst the dunes with gorse and thick rough lining the fairways. In recent years the Club has staged several important Championships including the **Boys Amateur** in **1978** and **1986**. Visitors are received at most times though prior telephoning is probably wise.

South of the Tees, despite its name, the golf course at **Saltburn-by-the-Sea** isn't by the sea, it's about a mile west of the town on the **B1268** and is a well-wooded meadowland course, a trifle easier than Seaton Carew, but certainly worth a visit. Around Teesside itself there is an interesting parkland course at **Middlesbrough** but perhaps the best two in the area are at **Billingham**, a fairly tough course with superb greens, and at **Eaglescliffe,** an undulating course with fine views of the Cleveland Hills. Visitors should be able to get a game at both during the week for a fairly modest fee.

Crossing into Durham, people often talk of (some even whistle about) "Old Durham Town", but of course it is very much a city with a cathedral that was recently adjudged the most beautiful building in the world. Golfwise in the county Darlington, the largest town, perhaps has more to offer. It has two excellent courses – one to the north at **Haughton Grange** (**Darlington Golf Club**) and another south of the town, **Blackwell Grange**. Both are parkland courses, well-wooded and always beautifully kept. Darlington is renowned for its many McKenzie greens, Blackwell Grange for its unusual tree-planting programme. A visit to each is strongly recommended.

Elsewhere in the county, **Dinsdale Spa Golf Club** has a

magnificent setting and practically straddles three counties. Visitors can play here on weekdays. Equally tranquil is **Barnard Castle**, a fairly flat moorland course which has a stream that must be crossed seventeen times during a round! **Bishop Auckland** in the middle of the county is also worth noting if in the area.

Between them, Newcastle and Sunderland have a number of courses of which **Northumberland Golf Club** and **Ponteland** are probably the pick. The former is situated alongside Gosforth Park racecourse and like Seaton Carew has staged several national championships. However, it may be easier to get a game (at least during the week) at Ponteland, a very well run Club close to Newcastle Airport. The course is always immaculately kept. **Whitley Bay** is another that welcomes visitors in midweek (fairly inexpensive) too. It is quite a long windswept course with very large greens and a wide stream that can make scoring pretty difficult.

Those seeking a game at the weekend might do well to travel north of Tyne and Wear into Northumberland. Courses here tend to be much less crowded and far more beautiful. First on the way up, as it were, is **Arcot Hall**, 6 miles north of Newcastle. The course is heathland in nature and was designed by James Braid. Its many trees and lake make for a very pleasant game, the 9th being a particularly outstanding hole. Fees in 1986 were **8** midweek, **10** at weekends. The facilities in the Clubhouse are quite excellent – but beware of The Grey Lady who ghosts in and out from time to time!

Further north and along the coast are the superb 'Castle courses' of **Dunstanburgh** (at Embleton) and **Bamburgh**. Dunstanburgh Castle, the ruins of which were immortalised in water colour by Turner, occupies a wondrously remote setting. The golf course is a genuine links, hugging close to the shore and staring out across miles of deserted beach. Visitors are welcome to play at all times. The golf course overlooked by Bamburgh Castle (see feature page) is considered by many to be the most beautiful in England.

For centuries the town of Berwick-on-Tweed didn't know whether it was 'coming or going'. It was passed between England and Scotland like the proverbial shuttlecock. However disorientated, it has a fine golf course at **Goswick**, 3 miles south of the town. It is another outstanding links where visitors are made most welcome. In 1986 a game here was priced at £5 during the week, £8 at weekends. Having sent the golfer north of Newcastle, I am aware of having neglected **Hexham**. It is in fact only a short drive west of Newcastle, along either the **A69** or the **A695**. It is a journey well worth making for the course has the most delightful of settings and the cost of a game is decidely inexpensive.

Arcot Hall G.C.	091 236 2794
Bamburgh Castle G.C.	(06684) 378
Barnard Castle G.C.	(0833) 38355
Berwick-upon-Tweed G.C. (Goswick)	(0289) 87256
Billingham G.C.	(0642) 533 816
Bishop Auckland G.C.	(0388) 602198
Blackwell Grange G.C.	(0325) 464464
Darlington G.C.	(0328) 463936
Dinsdale Spa G.C.	(0325) 332297
Dunstanburgh Castle G.C.	(0665) 76 562
Eaglescliffe G.C.	(0642) 780238
Hexham G.C.	(0434) 603072
Middlesbrough G.C.	(0642) 315533
Northumberland G.C.	(0632) 362009
Ponteland G.C.	(0661) 22689
Saltburn-by-the-Sea G.C.	(0287) 22812
Seaton Carew G.C.	(0429) 66249
Whitley Bay G.C.	091 252 0180

DURHAM, CLEVELAND, TYNE & WEAR AND NORTHUMBERLAND

To compare the Eldon Shopping Centre with the castles of Bamburgh, Alnwick, Dunstanburgh and Holy Island and one finds about as little in common as a city centre hotel and a quiet country inn. However, one similarity that they do share is they can all be found in the North East of Great Britain. The pleasantness of the Geordie people is well known – the striking contrast of the industrial area of Tyneside with the beauty of the Cheviots, the Cleveland Hills and the Northumberland coastline is dramatic to say the least. If you cannot be persuaded to abandon the south of England altogether or indeed you already live in the north east a visit to the following may prove to be good fun.

Holy Island, cut off from the mainland by the tide – a pub – a beer for every putt missed – as the night draws on and the tide draws back. You may be able to leave the island you may not, it depends on your putting. Assuming the best, we find our way back to the Northumberland coast. After a round at the delightful Bamburgh and a walk down the seashore, glancing at the castle a drink is in order. The **Lord Crewe Arms (06684) 243** provides the solution (liquid) . It also provides some accommodation and food. In Seahouses an extremely popular pub, **The Olde Ship (0665) 720200**. Other good value accommodation can be found in Belford, **The Blue Bell Hotel (06683) 3543** – handy for the A1 and a good spot for a drink and bar snack (also a bed if needs be). In Wooler, **The Tankerville Arms (0668) 81581** is also good and recommended. Another golfcourse and castle this time in Dunstanburgh – a good base here is in Embleton and **The Dunstanburgh Castle Hotel. (066576) 203**. Craster, a pleasant fishing village, has an aptly named pub – **The Jolly Fisherman**, worth a visit. Further down the superb coastline and Alnmouth here the **Marine House Hotel (0665) 830349** is a pleasant place to stay in nearby Alnwick. Inland and further south – some excellent establishments. **The Cinder Hall Hotel (0670) 56611** is the most stylish place and well worth a visit. More casual delight can be enjoyed in the **Linden** pub or alternatively at **The Granby**. Longframlington is close by and here **The Besom Barn (066570) 627** is a relaxed place to have a drink and enjoy some splendid English cooking. Before we head on down to Newcastle a word or two about Berwick. Two places to stay in this historic border town which stands at the mouth of the Tweed – firstly, **The Kings Arms Hotel (0289) 307454** and secondly **The Turret Hotel (0289) 307344** which also houses a well thought of restaurant. Trekking inland up the Tweed we arrive in Cornhill and a really outstanding hotel **The Tillmouth Park (0890) 2255**.

From the rural setting of the Tweed to the contrasting industrial location of Tyneside, here some outstanding restaurants to track down. In **Jesmond, Francesca's (0632) 281586** is superb value while more pricey but excellent cooking is found in either **The Fisherman's Lodge (091) 2813281** or **The Fishermans Wharf (0632) 321052**. In Chinatown the **Ming Dynasty (0632) 615787** also has a good reputation. Elsewhere in Newcastle, shopping in the Eldon centre is first class while **The Playhouse (0632) 323431** is a fine theatre. The best hotels to stay in town are **The Gosforth Park Thistle (0632) 364111** and **The Holiday Inn (0632) 365432** both offer all the mod cons and some first class leisure facilities. More character and better prices can be found predictably outside town.

In Cholleford, **The George Hotel (043481) 611** is comfortable while in the appropriately named Wall you have the equally suitable title for the inn – **The Hadrian (04348) 232** ideal for exploring the Roman monument as well as a relaxed location for a bar snack. Other places to visit near the delightful market town of Hexham are the **Dipton** a pub just west of the town, **The Boat** in nearby Warden is also an excellent watering hole.

East of Hexham and Ponteland here the **Waggon Inn** is popular – ideal for a visit en route to the Highlands and equally fitting is Belsay, **The Highlander** (excellent bar snacks and a very popular restaurant). Another popular meeting point is **The Rendezvous** in Ponteland.

As we once again return south the **George Washington Hotel, Washington (091) 4172626** should be considered for people seeking a hotel with many leisure facilities. Cleveland is jam packed with good golfcourses but the same cannot be said of its hotels, modern characterless establishments seem alas to be the norm. An exception to this is the **Crathorne Hall Hotel (0642) 700398**, in Crathorne near Yarm. Other hotels to consider when visiting the area include **The Grand (0429) 66345** in Hartlepool. Another member of a large group is **The Post House, Thornaby-on-Tees (0642) 591213** – modern but a useful place to stop for a break. To conclude on a less contemporary line **The Grinkle Park (0287) 21698**, in Easington – stylish bedrooms but also a good place for a bar snack or dinner. Pubs to note in the county include **The Blue Bell** at Egglescliffe offering good bar snacks and views of the River Tees. Further splendid sights this time over the sea can be enjoyed from **The Ship** at Saltburn. Finally, a little inland in Moorsholm stands **The Jolly Sailor** – more good food.

Durham and its excellent cathedral offer much for someone with time on their hands – places to stay in the area include **The Royal County (0385) 66821** in Durham itself. Just outside the delightful town of Barnard Castle, **The Jersey Farm Hotel (0833) 38223**, is excellent value. For style, Coatham Mundeville is the place to visit – more specifically, **Hallgarth (0325) 313333**, excellent. Another really first rate establishment can be found in Neasham, **The Newbus Arms (0325) 721071**. However, the place that many golfers will earmark as their first port of call will be the **Blackwell Grange Moat House (0325) 460111** ideal for the golfcourse and excellent leisure facilities. If hunger hits them there is no shortage of good restaurants. Two pubs offering fine cooking include **The Bridge (0325) 50106** at Stapleton and the excellent **Three Tuns (0833) 50289** in Eggleston. In Darlington, **Bishops House (0325) 286666** offers a good French menu. People who are merely searching for a bar snack and drink might consider **The Kings Head** in Darlington, **The Rose and Crown**, Romaldkirk or **The Fox and Hounds**, Cotherstone. Here ends one lesson.

Blackwell Grange Moat House
Blackwell Grange,
Darlington DL3 8QH
Tel: (0325) 460111
A beautiful 17th century mansion set in 15 acres of wooded parkland. Blackwell Grange enjoys a superb location between the North Yorkshire Moors and Dales. It is close to the Market Towns of Darlington and Richmond and within easy reach of York.

Gosforth Park Thistle Hotel
High Gosforth Park,
Newcastle
Tel: (0632) 364111
Gosforth Park offers outstanding facilities in a modern hotel living up to its reputation as "the Pride of Northumbria". Standing in wooded parkland a few miles north of the city centre, Gosforth Park is within easy reach of all the North East's premier golf clubs.

After the great outdoors: the great indoors.

Shooting, fishing or playing golf, you'll enjoy a plenitude of pleasures at Turnberry.

You can shoot pheasant and grouse in 30 fine estates. Fish for salmon and trout. And play two of the world's best golf courses, one of which is the site of the 1986 British Open.

Indoors, you can swim or relax in the sauna. Play snooker, or work out in the mini-gymnasium. You can dine on superb French or Scottish cuisine. Admire spectacular sunsets and seascapes from the comfort of your room.

And if you arrive at Glasgow or Prestwick airpo we'll be delighted to meet you and bring you here.

As a civilised base to enjoy good sport there's no hotel to compare with Turnberry.

Not by a long shot.

Rates for shooting £10-£12 per bird. Average cost per day £125.
For reservations contact: Turnberry Hotel and Golf Courses,
Ayrshire, Scotland KA26 9LT.
Tel: Turnberry 202.
Telex 777779.

Turnberry

THE TURNBERRY HOTEL AND GOLF COURSES SCOTT

BAMBURGH CASTLE

In an earlier piece I quoted one of Henry Longhurst's most celebrated comments, namely "What a lovely place to die" (referring to the 18th hole at Killarney). The golf course at Bamburgh merits another from the great man, "Golf takes you to such beautiful places."

The setting is quite stunning. A number of Britain's golf courses are gazed over by castles; Royal St David's and Harlech Castle is perhaps the best known, Cruden Bay and Dunstanburgh are others, but none is quite dominated the way that Bamburgh is. Standing 150 feet high on a rocky crag and covering eight acres, Bamburgh is one of Britain's most majestic castles, it towers over both the village and of course the adjoining 18 hole golf links. Apparently we have to thank the Normans for the splendid keep, it was they who built it having acquired the original castle from Matilda, Countess of Northumberland, after threatening to take out the eyes of her captive husband (charming times!)

Turning to less gory subjects, **Mr T C Osborne** is the Secretary of Bamburgh Golf Club; he may be contacted by telephone on **(06684) 321**. The Club has no golf professional but should you turn up without any balls, fear not, a supply can be purchased from behind the bar.

Visitors are made extremely welcome at Bamburgh, the only times they are restricted is on major Club competition days and on Public Holidays when visitors must be accompanied by a Member.

In 1986 the green fees at Bamburgh varied according to the season. The summer fees, applicable between the 28th March and the 30th September, were as follows: £5 per day for a round during the week (£4 for juniors) and £6 per round, £9 per day at weekends (£7 and £5 respectively for juniors). Those teeing off after 4 p.m. (NB.the longer hours of daylight in these parts) the cost of a game was priced at £3 midweek and £4.50 at weekends. For Autumn and Winter visitors the fees in 1986 were £4 during the week and £6 at weekends. Finally, seven day 'temporary Membership' could be purchased for £25 during the Summer (£20 for juniors) and for £20 (£12 for juniors) during Autumn and Winter. Golfing Societies are equally welcome at Bamburgh, though pre-booking with the Secretary is essential. All written enquiries should be addressed to Mr Osborne at **The Bamburgh Castle Golf Club, The Club House, Bamburgh,**

Northumberland.

Bamburgh has what might be described as an 'invigorating climate'. Situated on the north eastern coast of Northumberland, only Berwick-upon-Tweed lies further north in England and Bamburgh is a shade closer to the North Pole than either Prestwick, Turnberry or Troon. Despite its remoteness the journey is a fairly straightforward one and furthermore it is one that is decidedly worth making. Both northbound and southbound travellers should pick up the **A1** which runs between **Berwick and Alnwick**, passing Bamburgh midway. It doesn't, however, pass through Bamburgh. Those approaching from the north should exit left on the **B3142** at **Belford**, while those approaching from the south are best leaving the **A1** just north of **Warenford** and following the **B3141** to Bamburgh. Anyone motoring across the glorious Northumberland countryside may find **Wooler** a useful place to head for: the **B6348** joins Wooler to the A1 just north of the **B1341** turn off.

By any standards Bamburgh is a short course, measuring **5465** yards (par **68**) from the men's tees and **5064** yards from the ladies tees (par **70**). Short it may be but it isn't without its tests, there are many whin bushes, several of the fairways are flanked with much tangling heather and as with every seaside course the moods of the wind must always be considered. In any event the golfer will not have come to Bamburgh to seek golf's toughest challenge, it is the splendour of the unique setting that is to be enjoyed. The Castle isn't the only sight that demands attention: there are magnificent views across to nearby Holy Island and Lindisfarne Castle and the Cheviot Hills provide a glorious backdrop. As for the course itself, in addition to the great spread of heather a number of fairways are lined with rare wild orchids. It is hardly surprising that Bamburgh is often described as Britain's most beautiful course.

What about the 19th? In short, exceptionally friendly (as one comes to expect in this part of England). There are no formal dress requirements and lunches and dinners are offered daily in addition to light snacks.

There is a saying used in many sports that 'a good big 'un is always better than a good little 'un', the golf course at Bamburgh provides the clearest possible evidence that the phrase has no meaning in golf.

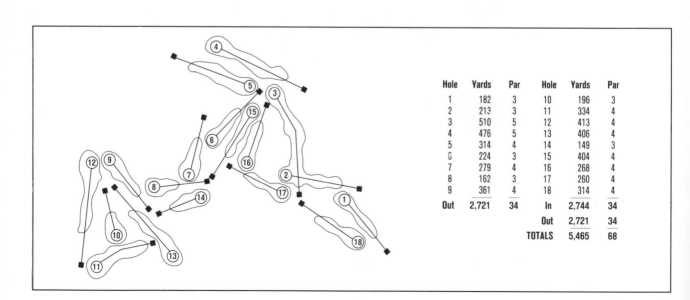

Hole	Yards	Par	Hole	Yards	Par
1	182	3	10	196	3
2	213	3	11	334	4
3	510	5	12	413	4
4	476	5	13	406	4
5	314	4	14	149	3
6	224	3	15	404	4
7	279	4	16	268	4
8	162	3	17	260	4
9	361	4	18	314	4
Out	2,721	34	In	2,744	34
			Out	2,721	34
			TOTALS	5,465	68

THE 13TH: SCARGILL TO WINDY GYLE

CLEVELAND
Cleveland G.C. (18)
Redcar (0642)

Middlesbrough G.C. (18)
Middlesbrough (0642) 315533

Saltburn-by-Sea G.C. (18)
Hobhill, Saltburn-by-Sea
(02878) 22812

Seaton Carew G.C. (18)
Seaton Carew, Hartlepool
(0429) 66249

Teeside G.C. (18)
Thornaby (0642) 676249

Wilton G.C. (18)
Redcar (0642) 454626

CUMBRIA
Alston Moor G.C. (9)
Alston (0498 81675)

Appleby G.C. (18)
Blackenber Moor, Appleby
(0930) 51432

Barrow G.C. (18)
Hawcoat, Barrow-in-Furness
(0229 25444)

Carlisle G.C. (18)
Aglionby, Carlisle (022872) 303

Cockermouth G.C. (18)
Embleton, Cockermouth
(059681) 223

Dunnerholme G.C. (10)
Askam in Furness (0229) 62675

Furness G.C. (18)
Walney Island, Barrow-in-
Furness (0229) 41232

Grange Fell G.C. (9)
Grange-over-Sands (04484) 2536

Grange-over-Sands G.C. (18)
Grange-over-Sands (04484) 3180

Kendal G.C. (18)
Kendal (0539) 24079

Keswick G.C. (18)
Keswick (0596) 83324/72147

Kirkby Lonsdale G.C. (18)
Kirkby Lonsdale (0468) 71483

Maryport G.C. (18)
Maryport (0900) 812605

Penrith G.C. (18)
Penrith (0768) 62217

St. Bees School G.C. (9)
St. Bees (0946) 822694

Seascale G.C. (18)
Seascale (0940) 28202

Sedburgh G.C. (9)
Millthrop, Sedburgh
(0587) 20993

Silecroft G.C. (9)
Silecroft, Milom (0657) 4250

Silloth on Solway G.C. (18)
Silloth on Solway, Carlisle
(0965) 31179

Silverdale G.C. (9)
Silverdale (0524) 300

Stoneyholme Municipal G.C. (18)
Carlisle (0228) 34856

Ulverston G.C. (18)
Ulverston (0229)52824

Windermere G.C. (18)
Cleabarrow, Windermere
(09662) 3123

Workington G.C. (18)
Workington (0900) 3460

DURHAM
Barnard Castle G.C. (18)
Barnard Castle (0833) 38355

Billingham G.C. (18)
Billingham (0642) 533816

Birltey (Portobello) G.C. (9)
Birtley (091) 4102207

Bishop Auckland G.C. (18)
Bishop Auckland (0388) 602198

Blackwell Grange G.C. (18)
Blackwell, Darlington
(0325) 464464

Brancepath Castle G.C. (18)
Brancepath Village, Durham
(0385) 780075

Castle Eden & Peterlee G.C. (18)
Castle Eden, Hartlepool
(0429) 836510/836220

Chester-le-Street G.C. (18)
Lumley Park, Chester-le-Street
(0385) 883218

Consett & District G.C. (18)
Consett (0207) 502186

Crook G.C. (18)
Crook (0388) 762429

Darlington G.C. (18)
Haughton Grange, Darlington
(0325) 463936

Dinsdale Spa G.C. (18)
Middleton St George
(0325) 332297

Dunnerhome G.C. (10)
Askam in Furness (0229) 62675

Dunstanburgh G.C. (18)
Embleton, Alnwick (066576) 672

Durham City G.C. (18)
Littleburn, Langley Moor
(0385) 780069

Eaglescliffe G.C. (18)
Eaglescliffe, Stockon-on-Tees
(0642) 780238

Garesfield G.C. (18)
Chopwell (0207) 561278/861309

Hartlepool G.C. (18)
Hartlepool (0429) 67473

Houghton-le-Spring G.C. (18)
Houghton-le-Spring
(0783) 841198

Mount Oswald G.C. (18)
Durham (0385) 67527

Seaham G.C. (18)
Dawden, Seaham (0783) 812354

South Moor G.C. (18)
Craghead, Stanley (0207) 232848

Stressholme G.C. (18)
Darlington (0325) 461002

NORTHUMBERLAND
Allendale G.C. (9)
Allendale, Hexham (043483) 412

Alnmouth G.C. (18)
Alnmouth, Alnwick (0665)
830231/830368

Alnmouth Village G.C. (9)
Alnmouth (0665) 830370

Alnwick G.C. (9)
Alnwick (0605) 60232

Arcot Hall G.C. (18)
Dudley, Cramlington
(0632) 36274

Bamburgh Castle G.C. (18)
Bamburgh (06684) 378

Bellingham G.C. (9)
Bellingham, Hexham
(0660) 20530

Berwick-upon-Tweed G.C. (18)
Beal, Berwick-upon-Tweed
(0289) 87256

Blyth G.C. (18)
New Delaval, Blyth
(0670) 367728

Dunstanburgh Castle G.C. (18)
Embleton (066576) 672

Hexham G.C. (18)
Hexham (0434) 603072

Magdalene Fields G.C. (18)
Berwick-upon-Tweed
(0289) 306384

Morpeth G.C. (18)
Morpeth (0670) 519980/512065

Newbiggin-by-the-Sea G.C. (18)
Newbiggin-by-the-Sea
(0670) 817344

Prudhoe G.C. (18)
Prudhoe (0661) 32466

Rothbury G.C. (19)
Rothbury, Morpeth (0669) 20718

Seahouses G.C. (18)
Seahouses (0661) 720794

Tynedale G.C. (9)
Tyne Green (0434) 605701

Wallsend G.C. (18)
Wallsend-on-Tyne (091) 2621973

Warkworth G.C. (9)
Warkworth (0670) 760270

TYNE & WEAR
Backworth G.C. (9)
Shiremoor, Newcastle-upon-
Tyne(091) 2681048

City of Newcastle G.C. (18)
Gosforth, Newcastle
(091) 2851775

Gosforth G.C. (18)
Gosforth, Newcastle-upon-Tyne
(091) 2853495

Gosforth Park Golf Centre
Gosforth Park, Newcastle
(0632) 364480/364867

Heworth G.C. (18)
Heworth, Gateshead
(026785) 692137

Hobson Municipal G.C. (18)
Hobson, Burnopfield
(0207) 70941

Newcastle United G.C. (18)
Cowgate, Newcastle-upon-Tyne
(0632) 864693

Northumberland G.C. (18)
Newcastle-upon-Tyne
(0632) 362009

Ponteland G.C. (18)
Ponteland, Newcastle-upon-Tyne
(0661) 22689

Ravensworth G.C. (18)
Wrekenton, Gateshead
(091) 4876014

Ryton G.C. (18)
Ryton (091) 4133737

South Shields G.C. (18)
South Shields (0632) 560475

Stocksfield G.C. (18)
New Ridley, Stocksfield
(0661) 843041

Tynemouth G.C. (18)
Tynemouth, North Shields
(0632) 573381

Tyneside G.C. (18)
Ryton (091) 4132177

Waslington G.C. (18)
Waslington (091) 4172626

Wearside G.C. (18)

Westerhope G.C. (18)

Westerhope, Newcastle-upon-
Tyne (0632) 869125

Whickham G.C. (18)
Whickham, Newcastle-upon-
Tyne (091) 4887309

Whitburn G.C. (18)
South Shields (0783) 292144

Whitley Bay G.C. (18)
Whitley Bay (091) 2520180

DUMFRIES & GALLOWAY AND BORDERS

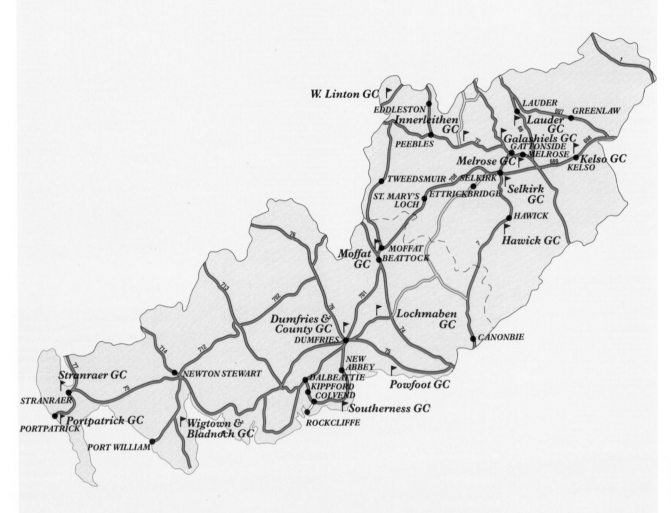

SAM GARRATT *"Peebles"* *BURLINGTON GALLERY*

KNOCKINAAM
LODGE
HOTEL

...ockinaam was built as a holiday house ... Lady Hunter Blair in 1869 and ...larged in 1901. The house stands in a ...cluded enclave at the foot of a deep and ...ckly wooded glen, surrounded on three ...es by sheltering cliffs and looking out to ...a. A beautiful garden with wide lawns ...ns down to a private sandy beach, and ...ests can enjoy magnificent views of the ...stant Irish coastline, the changing moods ...sea and sky, and stupendous sunsets. ...deed such is the timelessness and ...nquillity of this extra-ordinary place that ...· Winston Churchill chose it during the ...cond World War for a secret meeting ...th General Eisenhower and their Chiefs ...Staff.

...1971 the house was bought by a French ...ef who converted it into a 'restaurant ...ec chambres' and quickly established a ...putation for the finest cooking in the ...uth of Scotland. This reputation has ...en assiduously maintained and today ...u can sit in the attractive dining-room ...th the sea breaking over the rocks at the ...d of the lawn and dine on tender ...alloway beef—surely the best in the ...orld?—fresh lobsters, scallops, scampi ...d many other locally-produced delicacies ...cluding home-grown vegetables. In ...oler weather log fires burn in the public ...oms and there is full central heating ...roughout the house. Small business ...eetings can be accommodated during the ...e autumn.

...ockinaam is an ideal base for exploring ...s little-known and unspoiled corner of ...otland. Quaint villages, early Christian ...es, ruined and still inhabited castles, ...nding stones dot an undulating green ...ndscape dissected by rough dry stone ...lls and twisting single-track roads. The ...usually mild climate, engendered by the ...ulf Stream, can support almost every ...ecies of tropical plant, and there are ...any famous gardens within easy reach. ...ere are two excellent golf courses close ...the hotel and world famous Turnberry is ...s than an hour's drive. Farther inland ...ests of spruce and larch lead into vast ...cts of wild country, easily accessible by ...r or on foot, where a wonderful variety ...wild game abounds among lochs, rivers ...d tawny hills.

...ockinaam offers its visitors the chance to ...cape from the pressures of the outside

world, to shed cares and restore neglected values. The passage of time has left the holiday house atmosphere intact, and those romantic qualities that Sir Winston Churchill appreciated remain unchanged.

The resident owners, Simon and Caroline Pilkington, and their attentive young staff, look forward to welcoming you to this unique and unforgettable place.

Knockinaam Lodge Hotel,
Portpatrick, Wigtownshire,
Scotland DG9 9AD
Telephone: (077681) 471

Two of Britain's greatest (and least explored) links courses stare at one another across the Solway Firth – one is on the 'English side' at Silloth and the other lies north of the border at Southerness. As close as they appear on the map, the only way of travelling from one to the other is by a fairly lengthy drive around the coast via Gretna Green. Before the War, a bridge crossed the Solway, but before the War Southerness didn't have a golf course.

Situated 16 miles south of Dumfries off the **A710 Souther-ness** is the only Championship links in Great Britain to have been built since 1945. Not only is it the finest course in the far South of Scotland, but it has also quickly acquired a reputation that is the envy of many of the country's more famous Championship courses. Very much a natural links, designed by Mackenzie Ross (architect of Turnberry) it stretches to **6,548** yards from the medal tees making it a very tough par **69**. Visitors are always welcome (societies also by arrangement with the Secretary) the greens fees in 1986 being **£8** per day during the week, **£10** at weekends and **£30** for a full week's golf.

The two modern counties of Dumfries and Galloway and Borders (bit of a mouthful? – try the old Dumfriesshire, Kirkudbrightshire, Wigtownshire, Berwickshire, Peeblesshire, Roxburghshire and Selkirkshire) encompass most of the Scottish Lowlands. A beautiful area of Britain – as of course is much of Scotland – but not one terribly renowned for its golf. However, even excluding Southerness there are a number of superb courses, many are outstandingly scenic and because the great hordes head for Turnberry, Gleneagles and St Andrews, wonderfully uncrowded. **Powfoot** is a fairly close neighbour of Southerness (though again not by road) the course lying 5 miles west of Annan off the **B724**. A 'semi-links', measuring **6,283** yards, the course is quite undulating and provides extensive views towards the Cumberland Hills to the south and the Galloway Hills to the West. Visitors should be able to get a game here most days, the only general restriction being at weekends before 10.30 am and between 12.30 pm and 2.45 pm. Fees at Powfoot in 1986 were **£8** per round, **£10** per day in summer, £4 per round, £5 per day in Winter with reduced rates for juniors.

Nearby there are two eighteen hole courses at Dumfries, **Dumfries and County** to the north of the town perhaps being the pick of the two, but golfers travelling north would do well to pay **Lochmaben** a visit. It is a very friendly Club with an interesting 9 hole course designed by James Braid. The setting around the Kirk Loch is most picturesque, and the course is famed for its many beautiful old trees and 12th century mott. In 1986 a days golf at Lochmaben could be enjoyed for £6. Between Mondays and Fridays the tees are reserved after 5 pm for Members – if you do have trouble getting a game though, it is perhaps worth noting that the Club hires out fishing rods for £1 a day!

Lochmaben is situated 4 miles west of Lockerbie off the **A709**. Further north in the county and well and truly up in the hills is **Moffat**. The golf course overlooks the town in spectacular style. Visitors are subject to various restrictions and it might be best to telephone the Club before setting off.

Towards the western corner of Dumfries and Galloway the town of Wigtown lies at the mouth of a rather marshy estuary. Less than 200 yards from its attractive square is the **Wigtown and Bladnoch Golf Club**. Another 9 holer, quite short, but good value at only **£3** midweek, **£4.50** at weekends. **Stranraer**, the ferry terminal for Larne, has a fine parkland course north of the town which looks out over Loch Ryan. But the clifftop course at Portpatrick is rated by many to be one of the most beautiful courses in Britain. Gretna Green was mentioned in the opening paragraph, apparently Portpatrick was for many years in the last century Ireland's Gretna Green – couples sailing across the Irish Sea to get 'hitched' in Portpatrick's tiny church. The golf course provides some breathtaking scenery, particularly outstanding is the view from the 13th fairway. It can often get quite breezy and although only 5,644 yards in length, the course is certainly no pushover. Visitors are always welcome, green fees in 1986 being **£6.50** weekdays, **£7.50** at weekends.

The Borders is the land of Sir Walter Scott, delightful country, though it has known a stormy past. Golfwise, no course here could claim to be of Championship proportions, many being rather short 9 hole affairs, the majority though can boast spectacular settings. Visitors are always welcome and the green fees in these parts are just about the cheapest in Britain – a full days golf normally being possible for around the £4 mark.

A cluster of courses are to be found in the centre of the County. The town of **Melrose** is famed for its ruined Abbey where the heart of Robert The Bruce is said to have been buried (gruesome stuff!) It has a fine 9 hole course and there are others equally pleasant at **Selkirk**, **Hawick**, **Lauder** and **Innerliethan**. The 18 hole course at **Kelso** has an interesting layout being inside Kelso racecourse. Finally well worth noting are **Peebles** and **Galashiels** – both are public courses, very well maintained and true to form set amidst some magnificent countryside.

Dumfries & County G.C.	(0387) 53585
Galashiels G.C.	(0986) 3724
Hawick G.C.	(0450) 72293
Innerleithen G.C.	(0896) 830951
Kelso G.C.	(0573) 23009
Lauder G.C.	(05783) 381
Lochmaben G.C.	(038781) 552
Melrose G.C.	(089682) 2855
Moffat G.C.	(0683) 20020
Peebles G.C.	(0721) 20197
Portpatrick G.C.	(0776) 83215
Powfoot G.C.	(04612) 2866
Selkirk G.C.	(0750) 20621
Southerness G.C.	(0387) 53588
Stranraer G.C.	(0776) 87245
Wigtown & Bladnoch G.C.	(09844) 3354

From the Trossachs to the trout streams and the golfcourses to the parks the appeal of Scotland is undoubted. While the wildness of the Highlands is well known it certainly does not have this appeal alone. Indeed from the very border country as one enters this bonny land the sheer wildness and solitude is striking. The calm and beauty of the rolling hills of the lowlands and the mountains of Galloway are the perfect place to visit. It is little wonder that these fitting surroundings play home to some of the world's best loved golfcourses. The lands of Dumfries and Galloway as well as the Border lands are no exception to this fine standard and what is equally important – these are a good deal closer for us southerners. Given that your golf has been good, how can it not be in these splendid conditions, then the following suggestions may be of some interest.

We start our trip having entered the Borders at that most romantic place Gretna Green, with the temptation of an early marriage well behind us and head straight for Newton Stewart and **Kirroughtree Hotel (0671) 2141** – a splendid country house which is doubly appealing to golfers on account of some excellent golfing packages. Apart from golf, all manner of outdoor pursuits can be enjoyed – swimming – yes, I said swimming, no wimping out a bracing swim is just what's needed before an excursion to the fairways. Dinner at Kirroughtree is recommended to round off the day. Another hotel to consider is **The Bruce (0671) 2294**, more modest but particularly welcoming. In Fort William another mansion makes for an ideal base, on this occasion the **Corsemalzie House Hotel (09886) 254**. Another port – can be sampled in the restaurants of Portpatrick – gorgeous. The **Knockinaam Lodge Hotel (077681) 471** is the place to go – quite strikingly beautiful and a really tremendous restaurant. (Galloway beef, fresh lobster – outstanding.) Another good hotel and restaurant can be found at **The Fernhill (077681) 220** while **The Crown** is the place for a pint. Although one may think of chilly winds and rain the area is actually noted for its mild climate, and hillwalking, fishing as well as golf are available. In Stranraer, the **North West Castle (0776) 4413** offers a whole range of leisure options in addition to the more natural splendours.

A buzzard may follow you as you journey to Dumfries where a number of options await (probably not the buzzard though) **The Cairndale Hotel (0387) 5411** is charming in Dumfries itself. Other recommended establishments include **The Dryfesdale in Lockerbie (0427) 2121** and the **The Rockhale Hotel** in Collin, **(038775) 355** – the restaurant here is also particularly good. As with many parts of Scotland some of the best places to have a drink are the hotel bars themselves. Any golfer fortunate to play at Southerness may like antique shops as well as the golf. St Mary's Loch offers the well recommended **Tiblie Meils Inn (0750) 42231** while the **Crook Inn, Tweedsmuir (03997) 272** is a happy place in which to pass time, superb for the delights of the Tweed. Another really good all round hotel is the **Ettrickshaws (0750) 52229** in Ettrickbridge – excellent service and restaurant. Historic Selkirk is one of those particularly heady stop off points. The **Philipburn House Hotel (0750) 20747** is a popular place to stay when travelling in Scotland. Further up the Tweed and Melrose with its splendid Abbey and Abbotsford House. **Burts Hotel (089682) 2285** in Melrose is an excellent small hotel. Another super establishment where food is the order of the day is **The Hoebridge Inn,** Gattonside. Elsewhere in the Borders Kelso is also delightful, where **The Sunlaws House Hotel (057 35) 331** is strongly recommended – lovely grounds on the banks of the Teviot. Another river setting this time the Tweed and the **Ednam House Hotel (0573) 24168** is popular (more so for anglers than golfers but excellent value just the same). In Rockcliffe, **The Baron's Craig Hotel (055663) 225** is a delightful spot while a little closer in Colvend, **Clonyard House (055663) 372** is ideally situated. Places in which to eat include **The Abbey Arms** nearby and **The Griffel Inn** both in New Abbey. **The Pheasant**, in Dalbeattie is another good establishment which one may chance upon. Not so close but a splendid place to visit all the same is Canonbie, here the restaurant at the **Hoebridge Inn (05415) 512** is exceptional and some reasonable bedrooms are also available.

Having sampled the delights of the coast of Southern Scotland one may head inland to the delights of the Border towns. En route, Moffat is an excellent golfcourse which has a gorgeous setting in the valley of Allandale and **The Black Bull** is well worth a visit. People wishing to stay in the area may wish to consider **The Auchen Castle Hotel (068 33) 407** in Beatlock (good value and a pleasant setting). The Border towns offer castles aplenty, some superb woollens and some excellent rugby. **The Waggon Inn** has very good bar snacks. Further east and Greenlaw here Purves Hall **(089084) 558** is a grand place in which to curl up while in Lauder another **Black Bull** should be visited – birdwatchers may prefer a bird of prey – not our friendly buzzard but **The Eagle** (good bar food).

In the northern reaches of the Borders Peebles has two hotels to note. The **Peebles Hotel Hydro (0921) 20602** offers a splendid range of recreational facilities as well as comfortable bedrooms while simpler accommodation can be found in the **Tontine (0921) 20892**. Golfers who like a spot of fishing should also note the **Tweed Valley Hotel (089687) 220** in nearby Walkerburn.

We end our visit to these beautiful border counties with a visit to Hawick. The welcoming people of this region are some of the most amusing characters to be found. With outstanding golf as well as other country pursuits as you return to England you will wear a smile, if not you only blame one thing – your golf.

Cringletie House Hotel
Peebles, Tel: (0721) 3233
Conveniently close to Peebles Golf Club and only 20 miles from Edinburgh, yet within easy access of the surrounding Border country, there could be no better place to stay than the Cringletie House Hotel. From the quality of the food to the spacious, tastefully decorated bedrooms enjoying magnificent views, this ideally situated mansion house has so much to offer the visitor to this beautiful part of Scotland.

Fernhill Hotel
Portpatrick Nr Stranraer,
Wigtownshire DG9 8TD
Tel: (077681) 220
Sitting high above the village and harbour of Portpatrick, and conveniently close to the golf club, the Hotel makes the ideal holiday base. Its magnificent cuisine is doubtless seldom bettered in this part of Scotland. One of the Fernhill's short break holiday packages includes free golf on weekdays.

LOTHIAN

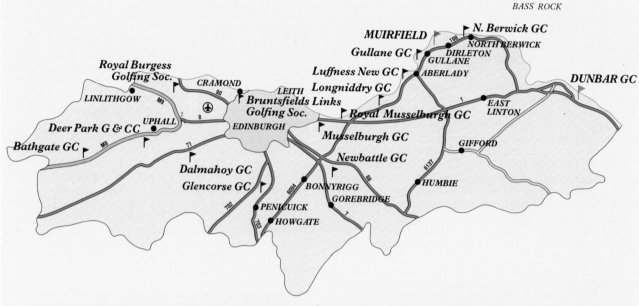

SCOTTISH SCHOOL *"Leith Links"* ***BURLINGTON GALLERY***

GREYWALLS GULLANE

reywalls is a Country House Hotel close
Edinburgh but it is a hotel with a
fference—originally it was designed as an
dwardian home. The Weaver family, who
sed to live in the house, have since
onverted it to an hotel and still live there
oday.

lthough Greywalls was opened as an
otel in 1948 it retains the look and feel of
e house that was designed in 1901 by
e renowned Edwardian architect Sir
dwin Lutyens. The gardens were laid out
y his imaginative partner, Gertrude Jekyll,
the complete arrangement of house and
arden fulfills the Edwardian aspirations of
"Lutyens house with a Jekyll garden"

ing Edward VII used to stay at Greywalls
nd admire the views across the Firth and
outh to the Lammermuir Hills,
nmortalised by Sir Walter Scott. Today
ost bedrooms are still furnished with
eriod pieces and all have their own
athroom. The panelled library, perhaps
e most inviting room in Greywalls, offers
e guests the warmth and comfort of real
res and discreet first-class service. The
uisine, now served in a dining room that
as once a courtyard, is of the highest
andard, using the finest fresh ingredients
or both traditional menus and house
pecialities. Greywalls offers the
tmosphere of home but with the amenities
nd service of one of the country's leading
otels.

For the sportsman, Greywalls and the
Lothians offer a wealth of activity. The
house itself looks out over the immaculate
9th and 18th greens of Muirfield golf
course where the Open Championship is
played regularly. Accordingly the guests at
such times reflect the proximity of such a
course—Nicklaus, Watson, Trevino and
Palmer are just a few of the famous
visitors. There are 10 golf courses within
5 miles and a hard tennis court and a
croquet lawn within the grounds while
there is also fine shooting and fishing
nearby.

For the sightseer Edinburgh is only
40 minutes drive away and the Scottish
Border country is less than an hour away.
Closer to hand are ancient castles such as
Tantallon and the famous bird sanctuary
on the Bass Rock. The Lammermuirs offer
delightful walks as do the endless sandy
beaches along the coast. Even for the
businessman Greywalls can offer the
prospect of countryside comfort, peace and
quiet and the promise of good food at the
end of a hard day's work in the city.

Greywalls provides, for the golfer or
gourmet, businessman or holidaymaker,
the highest standards of comfort and
cooking in an Edwardian house that has
been both home and hotel for the same
family for over 35 years.

Greywalls Hotel,
Muirfield, Gullane,
East Lothian EH31 2EG
Telephone: (0620) 842144

"Hard by in the fields called the links, the citizens of Edinburgh divert themselves at a game called golf, in which they use a curious kind of bat tipt with horn and a small elastic ball of leather stuffed with feathers rather less than tennis balls, but out of a much harder consistency and this they strike with such force and dexterity that it will fly to an incredible distance."

When a gentleman by the name of **Tobias Smollett** wrote these words in **1771** golf had already been played in the 'fields' around Edinburgh for at least three hundred years. The seemingly harmless pastime wasn't always popular with the authorities. In 1593 the Town Council of Edinburgh deplored the fact that a great number of its inhabitants chose to spend the Sabbath in the town of Leith where "in tyme of sermons" many were "sene in the streets, drynking in taverns, or otherwise at Golf." Shame on them!

Today the east coast of Scotland is famous the world over, not only because it was here that it 'all began', but also because its many courses remain among the very finest the game has to offer. The County of Lothian, with Edinburgh of course at its heart, has a staggering number of outstanding golfing attractions all no more than a short drive from one another. In a 30 mile coastal stretch between the courses of Royal Burgess and Dunbar lie the likes of Muirfield, Gullane, North Berwick, Luffness New and Longniddry – truly a 'magnificent seven' and there are many others.

Visitors to the beautiful City of Edinburgh, the so called 'Athens of the North', should have little trouble getting a game on one of the many nearby courses. Quite in contrast it must be said to the problems the stranger is likely to encounter when turning up in Glasgow. To the west of the City lie a particularly historic pair – **Bruntsfield Links** and **Royal Burgess**: between them they have witnessed nearly 500 years of golfing history. Both receive visitors although prior telephoning is essential as a number of restrictions apply. Weekday afternoons are likely to be the best times for arranging a game.

The **Dalmahoy Country Club** situated to the west of the City nestles at the base of the Pentland Hills and has two excellent 18 hole courses. The East Course which measures close to 6,700 yards has been the venue for many important Championships. Visitors are welcome here on any day of the week, green fees for 1986 being £10 midweek, £12 at weekends.

Newbattle Golf Club is another well worth visiting if staying in the Edinburgh region. It is a shorter challenge measuring just over 6,000 yards but its undulating nature and the surrounding woodland can make scoring pretty difficult. Visitors should arrange their schedule so that they tee off before 4 p.m. Fees for 1986 were set at £5.50 per round, £7.50 for a full day's golf.

Still in Midlothian but a little further south of Edinburgh, **Glencorse** is worth noting if a less demanding test is sought. It measures just over 5,200 and at £5 a round is very good value.

The courses of West Lothian are not as well known as their 'Eastern Counterparts', however two are particularly worth considering, **Bathgate** and the **Deer Park Golf and Country Club** at Livingston. Both lie within easy access of Edinburgh and welcome visitors seven days of the week. The Bathgate Club which recently celebrated its centenary can lay claim to having produced two Ryder Cup players – Eric Brown and Bernard Gallacher, both of whom were members of the 1969 and 1971 sides. A moorland type course measuring some 6,300 yards the green fees for 1986 were priced at £5 during the week and £7 at weekends. The Deer Park Golf and Country Club has recently come under new ownership, it was formerly known as the Livingston Golf Club. Set in beautiful countryside a day's golf here in 1986 could be enjoyed for £8 during the week, and for £12 at weekends.

Travellers wishing to explore the delights of the East Coast should aim to pick up the **A198** at Prestonpans near Musselburgh. Before it reaches Longniddry the road passes through Seton, whereabouts **Mary Queen of Scots** is known to have sharpened up her golf swing more than 400 years ago. 13 miles East of Edinburgh, **Longniddry** ought not to be considered as merely a stopping place en route to Muirfield. It is a superb course, part links part parkland with every hole having a view of the sea. A former venue of the P.G.A. Seniors Championship it is regularly used as a qualifying course for the British Open. Starting times can be booked (Tel **0875 52228**) but generally visitors are welcome on any day of the week. Fees in 1986 were £14 per day midweek with £16 at weekends.

Luffness New and the three neighbouring courses of **Gullane**, lie only a short distance further along the coast. Each outstanding in its way though if you only have time to play two then Luffness New and Gullane Number One are probably the pick. The panoramic view from the top of Gullane Hill on the latter's 7th hole is one of the most famous in golf. Visitors are welcome at both Gullane and Luffness though prior telephoning is again essential.

Muirfield and Dunbar are covered on later pages but **North Berwick** is another that shouldn't be missed. Situated within the town itself and laid out alongside the Forth estuary, the West Links at North Berwick is very much a 'natural links', being on ground that links' the land to the sea. The layout is a classic one too – 9 holes out and 9 holes back and there are some spectacular views towards Bass Rock. Two of its holes, the 14th "Perfection" and the 15th "Redan" have been imitated all over the world. Visitors are welcome at North Berwick at all times, the price of a single round in 1986 being £7 during the week and £12 at weekends.

Bathgate G.C.	(0506) 630505
Bruntsfield Links Golfing Society	(031) 336 1479
Dalmahoy Country Club	(031) 333 2055
Deer Park Golf & C.C.	(0506) 38843
Dunbar G.C.	(0368) 62317
Glencorse G.C.	(0968) 77177
Gullane G.C.	(0620) 842255
Longniddry G.C.	(0875) 52141
Luffness New G.C.	(0620) 843336
Muirfield	(0620) 842123
Musselburgh G.C.	(031665) 20005
Newbattle G.C.	(031) 445 3546
North Berwick G.C.	(0620) 2135
Royal Burgess Golfing Society	(031) 339 2075

Central Africa – drought, starvation – disease, death – plague, fatigue– not so much of a life really. I certainly hope you have never known any of these tragic human circumstances. But we all have our problems– heart attack, pressure at work, matrimonial hassle – the list is often as long as the day. The difference in the end between the two – third world and the world we so happily or unhappily enjoy is that often our disasters are of our own making. As we lie pensive one place really to get away from it all is the golf course – quietness and quality are the order of the day. In Lothian there are simply splendid golfcourses coupled with the Scottish air – there are few better places to really experience the magnitude of one's fortune and this we hope is reflected in our golf. If not there is always another day and in Lothian there is certainly another course.

We start our trip to the area in the country's capital Edinburgh. The solemn castle looks down but one is forced to admire this outstanding fortress – home of the Military Tattoo. The city is a splendid place to visit: the National Gallery, Holyrood Palace, the bustle of Princes Street and its excellent shopping and in summer the Edinburgh Festival, the whole city seems to become a theatre – contrasting with the morning of a rugby international at Murrayfield, theatricals of another kind but no less marvellous to be a part of. The city's most outstanding hotel is **The Caledonian 031-225 2433** situated at the west end of Princes Street. The hotel's **Pompadour Restaurant** is quite superb. Although the hotel is most distinguished it does organise week-end breaks– excellent value. Among the many other excellent hotels **The Sheraton 031-229 9131** is superbly relaxing albeit modern while **The George 031-225 1251** is another most impressive edifice. The city is as well blessed with restaurants as it is with hotels. These are some of the many to consider **Aye 031-226 5467** is an outstanding Japanese restaurant (visiting golfers from the Orient who have become a touch homesick please note); **Le Caveau 031-556 5707** and **L'Auberge 031-556 5888** will delight lovers of French food while those who prefer pasta should sample **Cosmo's 031-226 6743**. If Swiss cooking is your preference then do try **The Alp Horn 031-229 4787**, it's excellent. At the risk of not commending the many gorgeous Edinburgh bars – I decline to recommend – suffice it to say that if one wants to play at Gullane with a headache Edinburgh will suit you down to a tee!

Outside Edinburgh in Linlithgow **The Champany Inn (050683) 4532** is outstanding, the steaks here are renowned throughout the land, while in Cramond village **The Cramond Inn 031-336 2035** is also quite delightful – excellent food. Two other restaurants can be located in Leith – their names giving guidance to their interiors, on the one hand **Oysters 031 553 6363** on the other **Skippers 031 554 1018** clearly fish is the order of the day.

Outside the city extremities of Edinburgh some superb golf can be found not least on the North and West Coasts. In Longniddry, the Longniddry Inn is pleasant for a drink or two. There are a number of good hotels and the alphabetical preference is for Aberlady – here the **Kilspindie House Hotel** is most welcoming as is **The Waggon (08757) 319**. Another obviously welcoming establishment is **The Open Arms (062085) 241** in Dirleton. The restaurant is splendid and some bedrooms enjoy excellent views over the 13th century castle. There are numerous other hotels and restaurants to be found in the area but the star of the show is without doubt **Greywalls, Gullane (0620) 842144** – quite splendid. Less grand but no less welcoming is the **Mallard Hotel (0620) 843288** a restaurant to savour while in these parts is **La Potiniere (0620) 843214** – do book well in advance to ensure a table at this tremendous establishment. Other thoughts while playing any one of the splendid golfcourses includes **The Marine (0620) 2406** North Berwick, other well priced alternatives include **The Point Garry Hotel (0620) 2380** and **The Royal (0620) 2401**; for suggested restaurants **The Folly (0620) 3622** and **El Vagabonda** come out best.

It is without question that Dunbar is a superb course but the hotels in the immediate vicinity are not of this class. Fear not, however, at East Linton **The Harvesters Hotel (0620) 860395** is an ideal base before a round. While in Gifford, **The Tweeddale Arms (062081) 240** is also charming and blessed with delightful Scottish hospitality. Another hotel with a less close but quite superb setting is the **Johnstounburn House (087533) 696**, fabulous gardens surround the 17th century house which is refreshingly luxurious. Travelling back westwards and still further through the ages we arrive at Gorebridge, more specifically **The Borthwick Castle (0875) 20514** a 15th century castle and a fine hotel as well. This is probably the place to take a first time American who believes that all castles are twentieth century.

Two establishments which lie in close proximity to each other are firstly the **Old Howgate Inn** in Howgate (ideal for snacks and a drink before trekking north to the greens of Gullane) and secondly **Habbies Howe (0986) 76969** in Penicuik another friendly bar – but also more formal food in the restaurant; ideal to build up one's swing before the challenging demands of that simply wonderful course are undertaken – Muirfield.

One idea that might not be such a particularly brilliant thought is to tackle several of Edinburgh's delightful pubs to be found on and off The Royal Mile. One fine Scotsman did this to this 'ere Sassenach and my hand shakes to this day – what an evening. However, if there's one thing to settle any hangovers or if the world is even more taxing than a sore head then the golfcourses of Lothian might not put the world to rights but they certainly should give you a little peace of mind – (unless of course you miss that short putt on the eighteenth!

Caledonian Hotel
Princes Street, Edinburgh EH1 2AB
Tel: (031) 225 2433
The hotel has an excellent location overlooking Edinburgh Castle and Princes Street Gardens, conveniently positioned for rail stations. An extensive refurbishment programme has restored the Caledonian into one of Scotland's finest hotels. An outstandingly elegant restaurant.

The Cramond Inn
Cramond
Tel: (031) 336 2035
Cramond Inn has long been part of the very character of this historic village by the river. The Inn has a reputation for exquisite food and fine wines and intimate bars. An ideal meeting place for friends and family. Situated close to several of Scotland's superb golf courses.

LEE TREVINO

Born Dallas, Texas, 1.11.39. Ht: 5'7".
Wt: 12st 12lb. Turned Pro: 1960. There are few
American golfers who enjoy competing in Europe
more than Lee or, for that matter, few who are
more popular with the spectators. Yet Lee must
have had bitter-sweet feelings about his trips to
Britain last season. In June he was all smiles as he
won the inaugural Dunhill Masters but in
September he was, understandably, not the
happiest man at The Belfry as he became the first
American captain to lose the Ryder Cup since
1957.

Trevino's quite astonishing career prospered
from the moment he captured the US Open in
1968. He won that title again in 1971 and 1972.
The US Masters has escaped his grasp but he did
win the US PGA Championship in 1974 and
when he took that title for the second time in
1984 it represented his 27th victory on the US
Tour. He has also enjoyed previous successes in
Europe having won the Benson and Hedges
International and the Lancome Trophy in 1978.

MUIRFIELD

Muirfield is of course much more than one of the world's greatest golf links, it is the home of the world's oldest Golf Club. **The Honourable Company of Edinburgh Golfers** are the direct descendants of the 'Gentlemen Golfers' who played at **Leith Links** from at least as early as the fifteenth century. On **7th March 1744** "several Gentlemen of Honour skilful in the ancient and healthful exercise of Golf" petitioned the city fathers of Edinburgh to provide a silver club to be played for annually on the links at Leith. The winner of this competition became 'Captain of Golf' and the club was paraded through the city.

In 1744 the Edinburgh Golfers formulated the game's first code of rules, The Thirteen Articles, which were adopted almost word for word ten years later by the Royal and Ancient Club at St Andrews when it formed its first rules.

The Company played over the five holes at Leith for almost a hundred years before overcrowding forced the decision to move to the nine hole course at **Musselburgh**, to the east of the city. Long before they had left Leith the Members had begun to dine and play in the famous red uniform, failure to wear usually resulting in a fine. A minute from the 1830's records how one member was fined 'two tappit hens' for playing golf without his red coat. The **Open Championship** first came to Musselburgh in **1874** and was held there every third year until 1889. Meanwhile Musselburgh, like Leith, had become terribly crowded and the Company decided that the time had come for a second move. Again they looked to the east and almost twenty miles from Edinburgh, under the lee of Gullane Hill, they discovered Muirfield. The course was designed by **Old Tom Morris** and opened for play on **3rd May 1891**. In its early years the course received much criticism, one professional described it as "nothing but an auld watter meddie" but it appears that this had more to do with the fact that when the Honourable Company left Musselburgh they took the Open Championship with them. It was held at Muirfield in **1892** (the first 72 hole tournament) and it never again returned to Musselburgh. Following the success of the 1892 Championship Muirfield's reputation grew rapidly and today it is widely considered to be the fairest, if not the finest test in golf.

Visitors wishing to play at Muirfield must make prior arrangements with the Secretary, **Major J. G. Vanreenen**, who may be contacted by telephone on **(0620) 842123**. For **gentlemen** golfers there is a requirement that they belong to a recognised Golf Club and carry a handicap of 18 or less, while for **lady golfers** (who may only play if accompanied by a gentleman player) the handicap limit is 24. A letter of introduction from the visitor's home Club is helpful. The days on which visitors are welcome are Tuesdays, Thursdays and on Friday mornings. It should also be noted that by tradition foursome matches are strongly favoured at Muirfield and four ball games will only be permitted in the mornings. Golfing Societies (limited to 40 players) are also received on the usual visiting days and arrangements may be made with Major Vanreenen. All written correspondence should be addressed to **The Secretary, The Honourable Company of Edinburgh Golfers, Muirfield, Gullane, East Lothian, EH31 2EG**.

The **green fees** for 1986 were set at £20 for a single round with £30 entitling a full day's golf. All fees should be paid to the cashier in the Clubhouse Dining Room.

There is no professional shop at Muirfield but the services of a caddie may be arranged if requested in advance (via the above telephone number) and golf trolleys can be hired from the Caddie Master. In the Clubhouse a jacket and tie should be worn in all public rooms, lunches being served between 12.30pm and 2pm and afternoon tea until 5.30pm.

Travelling to Muirfield (or Gullane) will often be by way of **Edinburgh**. Gullane is connected to the capital city by the **A198**. Northbound travellers can avoid Edinburgh by approaching on the **A1** which runs to **Dunbar** to the east of Gullane. From Dunbar the **A198** can be picked up. Those coming from the north and west of Scotland will need to travel via Edinburgh. The **M8** links Glasgow to Edinburgh, the **M9** should be taken from **Stirling** and the **M90** will assist from **Perth**.

One of the unique features of Muirfield (or at least unique in terms of Scottish Championship links) is its layout of two separate loops, an outer and an inner. This ensures that the golfer will not have to play several successive holes into or against the same wind direction. Although quite undulating the course doesn't (or at least shouldn't) require blind shots as at St Andrews, St Georges and Prestwick and this contributes much to Muirfield's "fairness tag". From the Championship tees the course stretches to **6941** yards, with the often prodigiously thick rough it can be a very severe test of golf. From the Medal tees Muirfield still measures a fairly lengthy **6601** yards, par **70**.

Since 1892 the **Open Championship** has been played at Muirfield on **11** occasions. Before the last War winners included **Harry Vardon, James Braid** and **Walter Hagen**. The first Open to be held at Muirfield after the War was in 1948, when **Henry Cotton** won his third title. Cotton's second round of 66 was achieved in front of the watching **King George VI. Gary Player** won in **1959** and **Jack Nicklaus** in **1966**. Perhaps the most dramatic Open in Muirfield's history came in **1972** when **Lee Trevino** holed his famous chip shot from the edge of the 17th green and in the process 'stole' the title from **Tony Jacklin**. The Open was last played at Muirfield in **1980, Tom Watson** gaining his third victory. The championship returns to Muirfield in **1987** – the golfing world eagerly awaits.

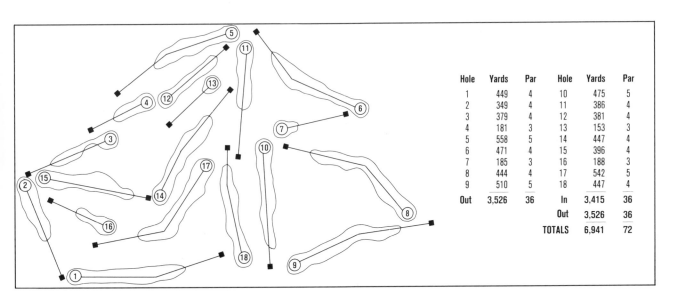

Hole	Yards	Par	Hole	Yards	Par
1	449	4	10	475	5
2	349	4	11	386	4
3	379	4	12	381	4
4	181	3	13	153	3
5	558	5	14	447	4
6	471	4	15	396	4
7	185	3	16	188	3
8	444	4	17	542	5
9	510	5	18	447	4
Out	3,526	36	In	3,415	36
			Out	3,526	36
			TOTALS	6,941	72

In common with much of Eastern Scotland it isn't entirely clear when golf was first played at Dunbar. Whilst the **Dunbar Golf Club** was founded in **1856** following a meeting in the Town Hall, **The Dunbar Golfing Society** had been instituted in **1794**. Furthermore, records suggest that some cruder form of golf had been played at least as early as the beginning of the 17th century. In **1616** two men of the parish of Tyninghame were censured by the Kirk Session for "playing at ye nyneholis" on the Lord's Day and in **1640** an Assistant Minister of Dunbar was disgraced "for playing at gouff".

Times, as they say, change and three hundred years later 'gouff' is still played at Dunbar, though none are likely to be censured or disgraced for doing so and there are now eighteen splendid holes.

Presently 'in charge' of the famous links is the Club's Secretary **Mr Arnold Poole**. He may be contacted on **(0368) 62317**. One of the friendliest Golf Clubs in Britain, Dunbar welcomes visitors at all times. Societies are equally welcome although pre-booking is not surprisingly required. Those organising Societies should write to Mr Poole at **The Dunbar Golf Club, East Links, Dunbar, East Lothian**. In 1986 the **green fees** for a full day's golf were very reasonably priced at **£8.50** during the week and **£11** at weekends. One final introduction; **Derek Small** is the Club's Professional, he may be reached on **(0368) 62086**.

Having spent countless hours poring over maps trying to work out the best routes to a particular Golf Club it is with great pleasure that I turn to Dunbar: from the west, approach via the **A1**; from the south east approach via the **A1**! Less flippantly, the A1 runs from **Berwick upon-Tweed** to **Edinburgh** and passes through Dunbar. Those travelling from the Borders region of **Melrose** and **Galashiels** may find helpful a combination of the **A68** and the **A6137 to Haddington**, thereafter picking up the A1 to Dunbar.

Dunbar is very much a natural links, laid out on a fairly narrow tract of land closely following the contours of the shoreline. It is bounded by a stone wall which runs the full length of the course. Whilst Dunbar is by no means the longest of Scottish links, when the winds blow it can prove to be one of the most difficult – this may have something to do with the fact that there is an 'out of bounds' on the 3rd, 4th, 5th, 6th, 7th, 8th, 9th, 16th 17th and 18th holes, and the beach can come in to play on the 4th, 5th, 6th, 7th, 12th, 14th, 15th, 16th and 17th! (straight hitting would appear to be called for).

Dunbar is without doubt one of the East Coast's most attractive links with some splendid views out across the sea towards **Bass Rock**. The first three holes are played fairly close to the Clubhouse, the opening two being relatively tame par fives and the third a spectacular short hole played from an elevated tee. The fourth then takes you alongside the beach as the course begins to move away from the Clubhouse. Perhaps the most testing holes on the course occur around the turn, the ninth to the twelfth, and there is no let-up either on the closing stretch with the beach readily receiving the mildest of slices. The eighteenth can also be a card-wrecker with the stone wall out of bounds running the length of the fairway to the right.

All the major Scottish Championships have been played at Dunbar, including the **Scottish Amateur** and **Scottish Professional Championships**. The Club has also staged the **British Boys** Championship and has become something of a home in recent years for the Scottish Boys title. The course record stands at an impressive **65**.

Dunbar's 19th is a comfortable building with views from the lounge across much of the course. Lunches and snacks are available seven days a week and with prior arrangement both breakfasts and dinners are also offered. A jacket and tie should be worn after 7.30 p.m. One final thought as you relax in the Clubhouse – one of the Regulations of the Dunbar Golfing Society dated 1794 read as follows: "When the expense of each member for dinner amounts to two shillings and sixpence, the Club shall be dissolved" – times, as they say, change!

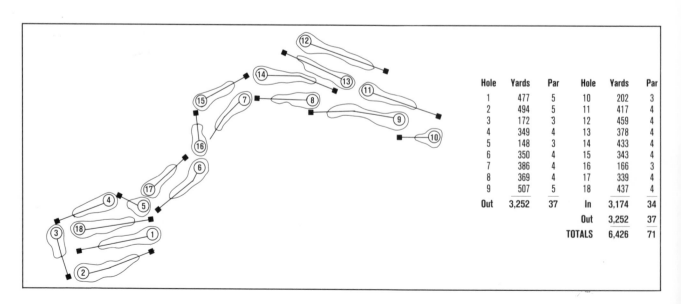

Hole	Yards	Par	Hole	Yards	Par
1	477	5	10	202	3
2	494	5	11	417	4
3	172	3	12	459	4
4	349	4	13	378	4
5	148	3	14	433	4
6	350	4	15	343	4
7	386	4	16	166	3
8	369	4	17	339	4
9	507	5	18	437	4
Out	**3,252**	**37**	**In**	**3,174**	**34**
			Out	**3,252**	**37**
			TOTALS	**6,426**	**71**

THE 14TH: BLACK HEAD TO SPOTT

BORDERS
Eyemouth G.C. (9)
Eyemouth (0390) 50551

Lauder G.C. (9)
Lauder (Lauder) 381

Melrose G.C. (9)
Melrose (089682) 281

Minto G.C. (18)
Hawick (0450) 72267

Peebles G.C. (18)
Pebbles (0721) 20153

St. Boswells G.C. (9)
St Boswells (0835) 22359

Selkirk G.C. (9)
Selkirk (0750) 20621

Torwoodlee G.C. (9)
Galashiels (0896) 266

West Linton G.C. (18)
West Linton (0968) 60256

DUMFRIES & GALLOWAY
Castle Douglas G.C. (9)
Castle Douglas (0556) 2801

Colvent G.C. (9)
Sandyhill, nr Dalbeattie (055663) 398

Dalbeattie G.C. 9)
Dalbeattie (0556) 611421

Dumfries & County G.C.Dumfries
(0387) 53585

Dumfries & Galloway G.C. (18)
Maxwelltown (02387) 3582

Duns G.C. (9)
Duns (03612) 83377

Gatehouse G.C. (9)
Gatehouse-of-Fleet (05574) 654

Hawick G.C. (18)
Hawick (0450) 72293

Hirsel G.C. (9)
Coldstream (0890) 2678

Innerleithen G.C. (9)
Leithen Water (0896) 830951

Jedburgh G.C. (9)
Jedburgh (0835) 63587

Kelso G.C. (18)
Kelso (0573) 23009

Kirkcudbright G.C.
Kirkcudbright (0557) 30547

Lochmaben G.C. (9)
Lochmaben (038781) 552

Lockerbie G.C. (9)
Lockerbie (05762) 3363

Moffat G.C. (18)
Moffat (06833) 20020

New Galloway G.C. (9)
Castle Douglas (06442) 239

Portpatrick G.C. (18+9)
Portpatrick (0776) 81273

Powfoot G.C. (18)
Cummertrees Annan 227

St Medan G.C. (9)
Monreith (09887) 358

Sanquar G.C. (9)
Sanquar (06592) 577

Southerness G.C. (18)
Southerness (038788) 677

Stranraer G.C. (18)
Stranraer (0776) 87245

Thornhill G.C. (18)
(038795) 30546

Wigtown & Bladnoch G.C. (9)
Wigtown (09884) 3354

Wigtonshire County G.C. (9)
Newton Stewart (05813) 420

LOTHIAN
Baberton G.C. (18)
Edinburgh (031) 453 4991

Bathgate G.C. (18)
Bathgate (0506) 630505

Braidhills United G.C. (18+18)
Edinburgh (031) 447 6666

Broomieknowe G.C. (18)
Bonnyrigg, Edinburgh (031) 6639317

Bruntsfield Links (18)
Davidsons Mains (031) 336 1479

Carrick Knowe G.C. (18)
Edinburgh (031) 337 1096

Carrickvale G.C. (18)
Edinburgh (031) 337 1932

Graigmillar Park G.C. (18)
Edinburgh

Dunbar G.C. (18)
East Links, Dunbar (0368) 62317

Dalmahoy C.C. (18)
Kirknewton (031333) 2055

Deer Park G. & C.C. (18)
Livingston (0506) 842585

Dundas Park G.C. (9)
South Queensferry (031) 331 3090

Gifford G.C. (9)
Gifford (062081) 267

Glen G.C. (18)
North Berwick (0620) 2221

Glencorse G.C. (18)
Milton Bridge, Penicuick (0968) 77177

Greenburn G.C. (18)
Fauldhouse (0501) 70292

Gullane G.C. (18+18+18)
Gullane (0620) 842255

Haddington G.C. (18)
Haddington (Haddington 3627)

Harburn G.C. (18)
West Calder (West Calder) 871256

Honourable Company of Edinburgh
Golfers G.C. (18)
Muirfield, Gullane (0620) 842123

Kilspindie G.C. (18)
Aberlady (0875) 358/216

Kingsknowe G.C. (18)
Edinburgh (031) 441 1144

Liberton G.C. (18)
Edinburgh (031) 664 8580

Linlithgow G.C. (18)
Linlithgow (0506) 842585

Longniddry G.C. (18)
Longniddry (0875) 52141

Lothianburn G.C. (18)
Edinburgh (031) 445 2288

Luffness New G.C. (18)
Gullane (0620) 843336

Merchants of Edinburgh G.C. (18)
Edinburgh (031) 447 1219

Mortonhall G.C. (18)
Edinburgh (031) 447 2411

Murrayfield G.C. (18)
Edinburgh (031) 337 3478

Musselburgh G.C. (18)
Musselburgh (031) 665 2005

Newbattle G.C. (18)
Dalkeith (031) 667 2123

North Berwick G.C. (18)
North Berwick (0620) 2135

Portobello G.C. (9)
Edinburgh (031) 669 4361

Prestonfield G.C. (18)
Edinburgh (031) 667 12373

Pumpherstone G.C. (9)
Livingston (0506) 32869

Ratho Park G.C. (18)
Newbridge (031) 3331752

Ravelstone G.C. (9)
Edinburgh (031) 332 32486

Royal Burgess G.C. (18)
Edinburgh (03) 339 2075

Royal Musselburgh G.C. (18)
Prestonpans (0875) 810276

Silverknowes G.C. (18)
Edinburgh (031) 336 5359

Swanston G.C. (18)
Edinburgh (031) 445 2239

Torphin Hill G.C. (18)
Edinburgh (031) 441 1100

Turnhouse G.C. (18)
Edinburgh (031) 339 1014

Uphall G.C. (18)
Uphall (0506) 856404

West Lothian G.C. (18)
Linlithgow (0506) 826030

Winterfield G.C. (18)
Dunbar (0368) 62280

STRATHCLYDE

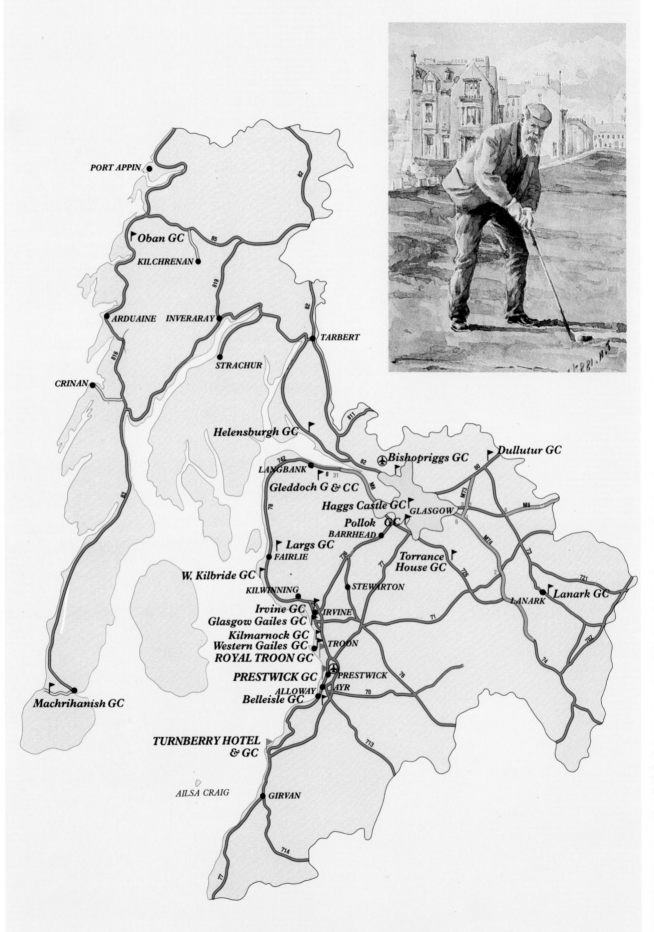

PORT APPIN

Oban GC
KILCHRENAN

ARDUAINE   INVERARAY
STRACHUR
CRINAN

TARBERT

Helensburgh GC

Bishopriggs GC   Dullutur GC
LANGBANK
Gleddoch G & CC
Haggs Castle GC   GLASGOW
Pollok GC
BARRHEAD
Largs GC   Torrance
FAIRLIE   House GC
W. Kilbride GC   Lanark GC
KILWINNING   STEWARTON   LANARK
Irvine GC   IRVINE
Glasgow Gailes GC
Kilmarnock GC
Western Gailes GC   TROON
ROYAL TROON GC
PRESTWICK GC   PRESTWICK
ALLOWAY   AYR
Belleisle GC

Machrihanish GC

TURNBERRY HOTEL
& GC

AILSA CRAIG
GIRVAN

T. HODGE   *"Tom Morris"*   SOTHEBY'S

CHAPELTOUN HOUSE

Chapeltoun is set in the heart of the countryside in a perfect peaceful setting surrounded in all directions by gardens, woodlands and the green pastures of North Ayrshire.

The house was built in 1900 by a wealthy industrialist as a retreat from the bustling city of Glasgow and was converted in 1976 by its present owners into one of Scotland's finest small country house hotels, offering guests a touch of real Scottish hospitality and a most comfortable base from which to see this lovely part of Scotland.

Chapeltoun is indeed a small and traditional country house where the original character and warm friendly atmosphere have been carefully preserved and where guests are afforded every personal attention by Alan and Elizabeth Russell and caring staff.

The rosetted restaurant is recognised as being one of the best in Scotland and makes full use throughout the year of the best of Scottish produce in thoughtful and interesting menus, offering a wide range of international and 'Taste of Scotland' dishes, complemented by an excellent choice of fine wines. Coffee is served in the comfortable lounge or drawing room beside open log fires, surely creating the right atmosphere to sample some of Scotland's finest malt whiskies and liquers.

Although Chapeltoun is in a quiet secluded setting, the excellent road systems make motoring a real pleasure in this part of Scotland. Glasgow is only half an hour's drive away with its historic buildings and fine shops, and the newly created fabulous Burrell Museum which houses the personal collection of international arts and treasures of the late Sir William Burrell, gifted to the city of Glasgow.

There are so many places of interest within an easy drive including such famous landmarks as the Bonnie Banks of Loch Lomond, the picturesque Trossachs, the romantic Robert Burns country, steeped in tale and history, and many National Trust properties including Culzean Castle with its famous Eisenhower Room, Brodick Castle on the majestic Island of Arran and the nearby 14th century Dean Castle.

Dotted all along Ayrshire's holiday coastline are some of the most famous golf courses in the world, including Royal Troon.

Two of Scotland's major airports, Glasgow and Prestwick are equidistant from the hotel, being about half an hour away.

In the Mid-West of Scotland, Chapeltoun offers an ideal holiday or business base in an unique setting.

We hope to welcome you on your visit to Scotland.

Chapeltoun House,
Stewarton, Ayrshire KA3 3ED
Telephone: (0560) 82696

STRATHCLYDE

A golfing rhyme from the land of Burns runs:
"Troon and Prestwick, old and classy,
Bogside, Dundonald, Glasgow Gailes, Barassie,
Prestwick, St. Nicholas, Western Gailes,
St. Cuthbert, Portland – memory fails.
Troon Municipal, Irvine, Ayr.
They faced the list with delighted smiles –
sixteen courses within ten miles."

Even without **Turnberry**, some 15 miles south of Ayr, an extraordinarily impressive list, and little wonder that this small region of Scotland's coast has become something of a Mecca for golfers the world over.

Prestwick, Troon and **Turnberry** have of course, each staged the Open Championship. Prestwick was the birthplace of the Open back in **1860** and Turnberry its most recent venue. Understandably the golfer on a pilgrimage to the Ayrshire coast will try and fit a game in on one or more of the three, however, if time isn't, as they say, of the essence it would be nothing short of a disgrace not to play as many of the nearby delights as possible. Ayr, the town itself, has an outstanding course in **Belleisle**. Often said to be the finest public course outside of St. Andrews and Carnoustie, visitors should have little trouble arranging a game, a day ticket in 1986 was priced at **5.70** during the week and **8.60** at weekends with a single round priced at **4.30** and **5.30** at similar times.

A very short distance to the north of Ayr is to be found a series of outstanding links courses, all within a mile or two of one another: **Barassie** (or **Kilmarnock Golf Club**) **Western Gailes, Glasgow (Gailes)** and **Irvine** (also known, somewhat unfortunately as **Bogside**). Two of these Clubs reach great landmarks in 1987 – **Barassie** celebrates its centenary and **Glasgow** can look back on two hunderd years, making it one of the ten oldest clubs in the world. Each warmly welcomes visitors and they tend to be less busy than Prestwick, Turnberry and Troon, however prior telephoning at each is advisable, especially during the summer months. Weekdays are invariably the best times for a visit and the feēs tend to range around the **£10 to £15** mark.

For those venturing a little further north along the coast the links at **West Kilbride** is well worth noting. Perhaps not as testing as the likes of Western Gailes, but a fine challenge nonetheless. The golf club at **Largs** offers an alternative to the windswept sandhills. Although it is situated very close to the coast, Largs is a parkland course with tree lined fairways. As with West Kilbride, there are spectacular views of the Isle of Arran and Argyle. Visitors are welcome during the week, a day's golf being priced at approximately £12.

Glasgow is Britain's third largest city after London and Birmingham and not surprisingly it is fairly inundated with Golf Clubs. Indeed some wag once said of Glasgow that there was a pub on every street with a golf club around each corner. Unfortunately, the problem for the golfing stranger to Glasgow is that the majority of the city's leading clubs only permit visitors to play if accompanied by a member – **Haggs Castle** and **Killermont** are perhaps two outstanding examples, the former being the current home of a European professional tournament. However, **Pol!ok** is without doubt one of the city's finest parkland courses and gentlemen visitors are welcome on Mondays, Wednesdays, Thurdays and Fridays, fees being **£12** per round, **£15** per day. The course is situated towards the south west of the town centre on the **A736**. There are a number of public courses in Glasgow so the golfer need not get too depressed – the pick of these are probably **Lethamhill** and **Little Hill** a game on either is remarkably inexpensive.

Not too far from Glasgow there is some marvellous golf to be enjoyed at **Gleddoch Golf and Country Club** at Langbank, close to the Clyde Estuary (**M8** from Glasgow). There are some superb views from the course towards the Lomond Hills. Visitors are welcome at Gleddoch throughout the week, although a quick telephone call is advisable at weekends. The fees in 1986 were **£11.50** midweek (£8 for a single round) and **£15** at weekends.

Escaping from Glasgow to the south, **Torrance House** (fortunately named) is a recommended port of call if travelling along the Strathaven road (**A726**), while Strathaven itself has a wonderfully situated course on the outskirts of the town. Surrounded by farms and lying 700 feet above sea level it boasts a gloriously tranquil setting. Visitors are welcome at Strathaven between Mondays and Fridays although they should arrange to tee off before 4.30 pm.

Even further south, and in fact nearer to the Borders country than Glasgow is the moorland course at **Lanark**. An excellent test of golf, Lanark has staged several important Championships and has been used as a qualifying course for the Open Championship. Visitors are welcome during the week.

To the east of Glasgow the outstanding course is **Dullatur** at Cumbernauld – venue for the 1986 West of Scotland Professional Championship. The course is parkland in nature and weekdays are again the best times for a visit, although golfers should make prior arrangements with the Club's Secretary. Cumbernauld can be approached from Glasgow along the **A80**.

Inspecting the map one immediately notices that a certian **Machrihanish** is somewhat isolated. While you can fly to this distant spot another mode of transportation is recommended – take your car or bike or whatever, but do inspect the beautiful scenery to be found here – a drive here is as satisfactory as the finest with any No. 1 wood, and at Machrihanish to get S.S.S. a number of these shots will be required. The very first hole has the golfer teeing off across the waters of the Atlantic – death or glory. Before you leave the area a mellow tune comes to mind that actually sold more copies than any other– Mull of Kintyre by one Paul Macartney – the music inspired millions– the golf course and its surrounds will almost certainly give you equal satisfaction.

"Och aye the Noo, Jimmy" is one of the most misunderstood pieces of gibberish to become tragically involved in the English language, I emphasise English and not Scottish for the Scottish understand exactly what this means. Let me explain. Translated 'och' means 'oh gosh, well done old chap' in Scottish. 'Aye' of course is not aye, but 'I' or 'one', (hole in one). 'The Noo' you should understand is a particularly taxing short hole in one of Scotland's lesser known golf courses situated in the gorgeous scenery of Strathclyde. 'Jimmy' is none other than the great Scotsman himself 'James Braid'. Therefore, we have 'Oh gosh, well done Mr Braid, a hole in one at The Noo'! While the Scottish are a misunderstood race by many, one thing that is patently clear is that their golf courses are the best in the world – Strathclyde is a fine example.

The first ever purpose built Hotel and Golf Course is located in Turnberry. This excellent establishment is none other than **The Turnberry (06553) 202** itself. Both hotel and restaurant are outstandingly luxurious in every way. People who stay there enjoy special green fees and perhaps more importantly have priority on the golf courses; what an excellent place to start one's trip. Mark my words though, this area is magnificent. From **The Kings Arms**, Girvan to the majestic **Old Ferry Inn and The Airds Hotel (063173) 236** in Port Appin the coast exudes a wealth of glorious golf. From Turnberry, Alloway and the birth of Scotland's best known poet, one Burns, the countryside around is known as Burns Country – a visit there will enable you to see why. In Alloway, **The Balgarth Hotel (0292) 42441** is good, while in nearby Ayr, a busy market town overlooking the Firth of Clyde, numerous hotels can be enjoyed. The two best known are **The Caledonian (0292) 269331** and **The Pickwick (0292) 260111**, both are good value and welcoming. One thing you ought to do while in the area is to visit **Culzean Castle** (open between April and October). More delights await a little up the coast – in fact if you really dislike someone who in turn dislikes golf – take them there – they'll hate every minute – marvellous. Prestwick has an airport, no excuses for being late to the tees, it also boasts a splendid hotel, **The Carlton (0292) 76811** – particularly popular with golfers. In Troon another grand welcome can be expected at **The Sun Court (0292) 312727** while **The Marine (0292) 314444** proudly overlooks Royal Troon and the sea beyond, the hotel is one of the most popular in the area, deservedly so. Kilmarnock is a busy industrial centre which doubles as a market town. It also has historic significance – Robbie Burns' first collection of poems was published here. Another busy business area, Irvine, here **The Hospitality Inn (0294) 74272** is modern but certainly worth noting – its restaurant is particularly good.

A little off the beaten track but certainly worth a visit is **The Montgreenan Mansion House (0294) 57733**, at Kilwinning, superbly comfortable. If you are a little seasick then a trip inland is recommended, to Stewarton and another excellent hotel, **The Chapeltoun House (0560) 82696**, do also note the restaurant.

Despite what one hears about Glasgow it really is an ever improving city. **The Burrell Collection** in Pollock Park was Scotland's most visited Art Museum in 1986 and is outstanding. Hotels in the city are sadly not as prolific as the golf courses but this is not to say that none can be found. Essentially, as with many cities the business traveller is dependent on a modern style of hotel. In Glasgow, **The Holiday Inn 041 226 5577** and **The Hospitality Inn 041 332 3311** are two striking examples, while the exteriors lack character, the luxury to be found within more than compensates for someone with a tight schedule, leisure facilities are also good. **The Stakis Grosvenor Hotel 041 339 8811** – a more classic exterior here and an interior to match. An ever increasingly popular restaurant is **Poachers 041 339 0932, Regano's 041 221 5677** in Exchange Square is an old fish restaurant to note and another restored old building in Argyle Street houses **The Buttery 041 221 8188** – good French cuisine here. For people wishing to round the day off with style, **The Theatre Royal 041 331 1234** offers distinguished ballet, opera and drama.

A far cry from Glasgow's city centre and Langbank, home of **Gleddoch House Hotel (047554) 711** and its splendid restaurant – a delightful edifice proudly positioned above the Clyde, not a bad golf course to match!

Continuing ever further northwards, one traverses those bonny banks of **Loch Lomond** and eventually if one is fortunate enough one arrives at Tarbert where **The Stonefield Castle (09902) 207** enjoys a pleasant situation on **Loch Fyne**. Another delight is **The West Loch Hotel (08802) 283** where more modest accommodation is complemented by some superb cuisine. The area as a whole is bleak of golf courses – which is just as well when the bell ringers of Inverary are in full swing.

Although Oban's golf course is a far cry from the delights of the courses of the Ayrshire coast, an absolutely majestic hotel for people wishing to escape from golf – albeit briefly – is **The Ardanaiseig (08663) 333** in Kilchrenan – outstandingly relaxing and super menus. On the long hard slog to that excellent course at Machrihannish do take time to visit Crinan. Here **The Crinan Hotel (054683) 235 and The Loch 16 Restaurant** – outstanding. There is so much character here and to self indulge, one of my fondest memories.

As one drives down the **M74** remorselessly heading back – desperately seeking that hole where our 'Jimmy' sank that legendary putt. You cannot believe your golfing holiday is over – what a time was had by one and all. In fact as you head towards Lanark and book into **The Cartland Bridge Hotel (0555) 4426** you have changed your plans, another week won't go amiss, you are returning to Turnberry – splendid.

The Turnberry Hotel and Golf Courses
Turnberry, KA26 9LT
Tel: (06553) 202
The Turnberry Hotel in southwest Scotland has a world-famous reputation for great comfort, personal attention, excellent cuisine, and unrivalled facilities. The venue for "last year's" Open Golf Championship, Turnberry is an ideal resort and within easy reach of Ayr.

The Marine Hotel
Crosbie Road, Troon
Tel: (0292) 314444
This fine old Scottish sandstone building stands overlooking Royal Troon championship golf course, Isle of Arran and the Firth of Clyde. The hotel has 70 bedrooms all with private bathrooms, colour TV and video systems, three restaurants, hairdressing salon and boutique.

PRESTWICK

One could be forgiven for thinking that they take their golf a little too seriously at Prestwick – at least when one hears of such stories as the monk from a nearby monastery who once played a match against the Lord of Culzean to settle a deadly feud: at stake was the monk's nose!

The truth more likely is that Prestwick folk are a competitive breed. Only nine years after the formation of their Club in **1851** the Members got together and decided to stage an annual Open competition. The winner of the event was to receive an elegant red belt subscribed for by the Members. Whilst there may have been only eight entrants, **the 1860 Open** marks the birth of the world's most prestigious Championship.

Willie Park of Musselburgh (a "foreigner from the east coast") won the 1860 Open and it was decided that if anyone won the event three years in succession they would win the Belt outright. **Young Tom Morris** (somehow Tom Morris Junior doesn't seem quite appropriate) was the greatest player of his day and fittingly enough in 1870 won his third title in as many years. Whereas Tom may have kept the Belt, Prestwick didn't keep the Open, or at least not the sole rights, as St. Andrews and Muirfield now joined Prestwick in the dawning of a new era.

In those early days the combatants played over a twelve hole course, today there are eighteen holes though the distinctive flavour remains (in fact seven of the original greens are in the same place). The modern day golfer must still play over the humps and hillocks, face blind shots and tackle the numerous deep sleeper-faced bunkers. Prestwick more than any other course epitomises natural Scottish links golf.

Visitors wishing to play the historic course are advised to approach **Mr J.A.Reid**, the Club's Secretary, in order to book a starting time. Mr Reid can be contacted at **The Prestwick Golf Club, 2 Links Road, Prestwick, Ayrshire. Tel. (0292) 77404.** Visitors should note that they will not be permitted to play on Saturdays and that the first tee will usually be reserved for Members between the hours of 9am-10am and 12.30pm and 2.30pm. Furthermore prior to 9am three ball and four ball matches are not generally allowed.

In **1986** the summer **green fee** was set at £22 per day, however, for those arriving after 3pm the green fee was reduced to **£13**. Sets of golf clubs and caddies can be hired through the professional, **Frank Rennie, Tel. (0292) 79483.**

I suppose like most things at Prestwick, the Clubhouse could be described as having a traditional atmosphere. Ladies are not permitted in the Dining and Smoking Rooms where jackets and ties must be worn at all times, but all may enter the Cardinal Room where some fine light lunches are offered. Dinners can also be arranged though some prior warning is necessary.

At one time Prestwick was a fairly remote place, however, the opening of an **International Airport** has caused the area to become very accessible from all directions (including overseas). More immediately the **A77** runs directly from Glasgow in the North and along the coast from Stranraer in the South. Those travelling from Edinburgh should use the **A71**, joining the A77 at Kilmarnock. Prestwick Golf Club is actually no more than a mile from the airport, its precise location being adjacent to the Prestwick Railway Station.

From the back markers Prestwick measures **6544 yards** and has a par of 71. Perhaps not overly long by modern Championship standards it is nonetheless extremely challenging and local knowledge (not to mention rub of the green) can make a considerable difference. At 346 yards the opening hole represents small beer when compared to the first on the original twelve hole layout – that one measured a lengthy 578 yards and in an age of hickory shafts and gutty balls no doubt proved a stiff bogey six. One can only wonder as to how in the 1870 Open, en route to his aforementioned hatrick, Young Tom Morris managed to hole out in three strokes! Another of Tom's notable achievements at Prestwick occurred in the 1868 Open when he recorded the first known hole in one. The first ace and first albatross?

The 3rd hole at Prestwick is probably the most famous; here the golfer must carry the vast **Cardinal Bunker** which stretches the width of the fairway. Later on in his round he must also confront the legendary "**Himalayas**" (5th) and the "**Alps**" (17th). The course is not actually quite so mountainous as some of the names suggest and the American who arrived at the Airport saying he was going to take thirteen clubs and a pick-axe was himself going a little 'over the top'. If the golfer does find himself getting frustrated with his game he should at least enjoy the views of Ailsa Craig and Arran.

Prestwick last staged a major Championship in 1952 and the decision to play the **1987 Amateur Championship** over the famous links has been a popular one. The golfing ghosts will doubtless be stirred and though none of the local folk were around to witness, many will talk of the feats of the Strath's, the Park's and the Morris's and Prestwick's halcyon days.

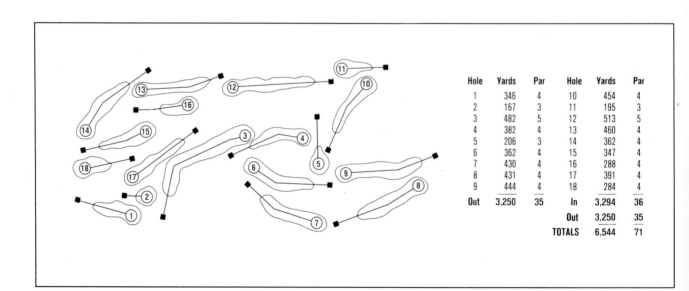

Hole	Yards	Par	Hole	Yards	Par
1	346	4	10	454	4
2	167	3	11	195	3
3	482	5	12	513	5
4	382	4	13	460	4
5	206	3	14	362	4
6	362	4	15	347	4
7	430	4	16	288	4
8	431	4	17	391	4
9	444	4	18	284	4
Out	3,250	35	In	3,294	36
			Out	3,250	35
			TOTALS	6,544	71

Golf Club - Region 15
STRATHCLYDE
Airdrie G.C. (18)
Rocksoles, Airdrie (02364) 62195

Alexandra G.C. (9)
Glasgow (041) 556 3711

Annanhill G.C. (18)
Kilmarnock (0563) 21644

Ardeer G.C. (18)
Greenhead, Stevenston
(0294) 64542

Ayr Beleisle G.C. (18)
Ayr (0292) 41258

Ayr Dalmilling G.C. (18)
Ayr (0292) 263893

Ayr Seafield G.C. (18)
Ayr (0292) 41258

Ballochmyle G.C. (18)
Balochmyle, Mauchline
(0290) 50469

Balmore G.C. (18)
Balmore, Torrance (0360) 21240

Barshaw G.C. (18)
Paisley (041) 89892908

Bearsden G.C. (9)
Bearsden, Glasgow
(041) 942 2351

Beith G.C. (9)
Bigholm, Beith (05055) 3166

Biggar G.C. (18)
Biggar (0899) (20319

Bishopbriggs G.C. (18)
Bishopbriggs, Glasgow
(041) 772 1810

Blairbeth G.C. (18)
Rutherglen, Glasgow
(041) 634 3355

Blairmore & Strone G.C. (9)
Blairmore, Argyll (036 984) 676

Bonnyton G.C. (18)
Eaglesham, Glasgow
Eaglesham 2781

Bothwell Castle G.C. (18)
Bothwell, Glasgow
(0698) 853177

Brodick G.C. (18)
Brodick, Isle of Arran
(0770) 2349

Kingarth, Kitchattan Bay
(0700) 83242

Calderbraes G.C. (9)
Uddingston (0698) 813425

Caldwell G.C. (18)
Uplawmoor (050585) 329

Cambuslang G.C. (9)
Cambuslang, Glasgow,
(041) 641 3130

Campsie G.C. (18)
Lennoxtown, Glasgow
(0360) 310244

Caprington G.C. (18)
Kilmarnock (0563) 23702

Cardross G.C. (18)
Cardross (0389) 841213

Carluke G.C. (18)
Carluke (0555) 71070

Carnwath G.C. (18)
Carnwath (0555) 840251

Carradale G.C. (9)
Campbeltown, Argyll
(05833) 624

Cathcart Castle G.C. (18)
Clarkston, Glasgow
(041) 638 0082

Cathkin Braes G.C. (18)
Rutherglen, Glasgow
(041) 634 4007

Cawder G.C. (18+18)
Bishopbriggs, Glasgow
(041) 772 7101

Clober G.C. (18)
Milngavie (041) 956 1685

Cochrane Castle G.C. (18)
Johnstone (0505) 20146

Colville Park G.C. (18)
Motherwell, Strathyclyde
(0698) 63017

Corrie G.C. (9)
Sannox, Isle of Arran
(077081) 223

Colonsay G.C. (18)
Isle of Colonsay (09512) 316

Cowal G.C. (18)
Dunoon, Argyll (0396) 5673

Cowglen G.C. (18)
Glasgow (041) 632 0556

Craignure G.C. (9)
Isle of Mull (06802) 370

Crow Wood G.C. (18)
Chryston, Glasgow
(041) 779 1943

Dougalston G.C. (18)
Milngavie, Glasgow
(041) 956 5750

Douglas Park G.C. (18)
Bearsden, Glasgow
(041) 942 2220

Douglas Water G.C. (9)
Douglas Water

Drumpellier G.C. (18)
Coatbridge (0236) 24139

Dullatur G.C. (18)
Dullatur, Glasgow (02367) 23230

Dumbarton G.C. (18)
Broadmeadow, Dumbarton
(0389) 32830

Dunaverty G.C. (18)
Campbeltown, Argyll.

Easter Moffat G.C. (18)
Plains, Airdrie
Caldercruix 289

East Kilbride G.C. (18)
Nerston, East Kilbride
(0352) 20913

East Renfrewshire G.C. (18)
Newton Mearns, Glasgow
(03555) 206

Eastwood G.C. (18)
Newton Mearns, Glasgow
03555) 261

Elderslie G.C. (18)
Elderslie (0505) 22835

Erskine G.C. (18)
Bishopton (0505) 863327

Fereneze G.C. (18)
Barrhead, Glasgow
(041) 881 1519

Girvan G.C. (18)
Girvan (0465) 4272

Glasgow (Ayr) G.C. (18)
Gailes, Irvine (041) 942 2011

Glasgow G.C. (18)
Bearsden, Glasgow
(041) 942 2011

Gleddoch G. & C.C. (18)
Langbank (0475) 54304

Glencruitten G.C. (18)
Oban (0631) 62868

Gourock G.C. (18)
Gourock (0475) 31001

Greenock G.C. (27)
Greenock (0475) 20793

Greenock Winhill G.C. (18)
Greenock (0475) 24694

Haggs Castle G.C. (18)
Glasgow (041) 427 0480

Hamilton G.C. (18)
Ferniegair, Hamilton
(0698) 282872

Hayston G.C. (18)
Kirkintilloch, Glasgow
(041) 776 1244

Helensburgh G.C. (18)
Helensburgh (0436) 4173

Hilton Park G.C. (18)
Milngavie, Glasgow
(041) 956 4657

Hollandbush G.C. (18)
Acretophead, Lesmahagow
(0555) 893484

Innellan G.C. (9)
Innellan, Argyll (036983) 242

Irvine G.C. (18)
Bogside, Irvine (0294) 75979

Irvine Ravenspark G.C. (18)
Kidsneuk, Irvine (0294) 79550

Istan G.C. (18)
Kidalton, Isle of Islay
(0496) 2310

Kilbirnie Place G.C. (18)
Kilbirnie (050582) 683398

Kilmacolm G.C. (18)
Kilmalcolm (050587) 2978

Kilmarnock (Barassie) G.C. (18)
Barassie, Troon (0292) 313920

Kilsyth Lennox G.C. (9)
Kilsyth, Glasgow (0236) 822190

Kirkhill G.C. (18)
Cambuslang, Glasgow
(041) 641 3083

Kirkintilloch G.C. (18)
Kirkintilloch, Glasgow
(041) 776 1256

Knightswood G.C. (18)
Knightswood, Glasgow
(041) 959 2131

Kyles of Bute G.C. (9)
Tighnabruaich, Argyll
(0700) 811355

Lamlash G.C. (18)
Lamlash (07706) 296

Lanark G.C. (18)
Lanark (0555) 3219

Largs G.C. (18)
Largs (0475) 672497

Larkhall G.C. (9)
Larkhall (0698) 881113

Leadhills G.C. (9)
Leadhills, Biggar (06594) 222

Lenzie G.C. (18)
Lenzie, Glasgow (041) 776 1535

Lethamhill G.C. (18)
Glasgow (041) 770 6220

Linn Park G.C. (18)
Glasgow (041) 637 5871

Littlehill G.C. (18)
Bishopbriggs, Glasgow
(041) 772 1916

Lochgilphead G.C. (9)
Lochgilphead (0546) 3517

Lochranza G.C. (9)
Brodick, Isle of Arran
(077083) 273

Lochwinnoch G.C. (18)
Lochwinnoch (0505) 842153

Loudoun G.C. (18)
Galston (0563) 821993

Machrie G.C. (18)
Port Ellen, Isle of Islay
(0496) 2310

Machrie Bay G.C. (9)
Machrie, Isle of Arran
(077084) 267

Machrihanish G.C. (18)
Campbeltown, Argyll
(0586) 81213

Millport G.C. (18)
Millport, Isle of Cubrae
(0475) 530485

Milngavie G.C. (18)
Milngavie, Glasgow
(041) 956 1619

Mount Ellen G.C. (18)
Gartcosh, Glasgow (0236) 872277

Old Ranfurly G.C. (18)
Bridge of Weir (0505) 613612

Paisley G.C. (18)
Braehead, Paisley (041) 884 2292

Palacerigg G.C. (18)
Cumbernauld (02367) 34969

Pollok G.C. (18)
Glasgow (041) 632 4351

Port Bannatyne G.C. (13)
Port Bannatyne, Isle of Bute
(0700) 2009

Port Glasgow G.C. (18)
Port Glasgow (0475) 704181

Prestwick G.C. (18)
Prestwick (0292) 77404

Prestwick St. Cuthbert G.C. (18)
Prestwick (0292) 77101

Prestwick St. Nicholas G.C. (18)
Prestwick (0292) 77608

Ralston G.C. (18)
Ralston, Paisley (041) 882 1349

Ranfurly Castle G.C. (18)
Bridge of Weir (0505) 612609

Renfrew G.C. (18)
Renfrew (041) 886 6692

Rothesay G.C. (18)
Rothesay, Isle of Bute
(0700) 3554

Routenburn G.C. (18)
Largs (0475) 673230

Royal Troon G.C. (18+18)
Troon (0292) 311555

Sandyhills G.C. (18)
Glasgow (041) 778 1179

Shiskine G.C. (12)
Blackwaterfoot, Isle of Arran
(077086) 226

Shotts G.C. (18)
Blairhead, Shotts (0501) 20431

Skelmorlie G.C. (13)
Skelmorlie (0475) 520152

Strathaven G.C. (18)
Strathaven (0357) 20421

Tarbert G.C. (9)
Tarbert, Argyll (08802) 565

Torrance House G.C. (18)
E. Kilbride, Glasgow
(03552) 33451

Troon Municipal G.C.
(18+18+18)
Troon (0292) 312464

Turnberry Hotel G.C. (18+18)
Turnberry (06553) 202

Vale of Leven G.C. (18)
Bonfield, Alexandria
(0389) 52351

Vaul G.C. (9)
Scarinish, Isle of Tiree
(08792) 566

Western Gailes G.C. (18)
Gailes, Irvine (0294) 311354

West Kilbride G.C. (18)
Seamill, West Kilbride
(0294) 823123

Whitecraigs G.C. (18)
Giffnock, Glasgow
(041) 639 4530

Whiting Bay G.C.
Whiting Bay, Isle of Arran
(02707) 487

Williamwood G.C. (18)
Netherlee, Glasgow
(041) 637 1783

Windyhill G.C. (18)
Bearsden, Glasgow
(041) 942 2349

Wishaw G.C. (18)
Wishaw (0698) 372869

When the golfing mind focuses on Troon it invariably thinks of the **Postage Stamp,** the Par 3 8th on the Old Course, un-questionably the world's most celebrated short hole. During the 1973 Open Championship **Gene Sarazen**, then at the mature age of 71, holed out with his punched five iron shot in front of the watching television cameras. Sarazen declared that he would take with him to heaven a copy of the film to show to Walter Hagen and Co. Legend has it that on hearing of Sarazen's feat an American flew to Britain and travelled to Troon. He strode to the 8th tee and proceeded to strike 500 balls in succession towards the green. Not suprisingly he failed to equal Sarazen's achievement whereupon he left the course and duly flew home to America. Who said it was only mad dogs and Englishmen?

Anyone contemplating the above ought at least to consult the **Secretary** first, **Mr. J.A. Sword** being the gentleman in question. he can be contacted at the **Royal Troon Golf Club, Craigend Road, Troon, Strathclyde. Tel. (0292) 311555.**

The **Royal Troon** Club possesses two **18 hole** courses, "**The Old**" and "**The Portland**". **Gentlemen** visitors are welcome to play both courses **between Mondays and Fridays** provided prior arrangement is made with the Secretary. **Lady** golfers are also welcome although on **Tuesdays and Thursdays** they are limited to playing on the **Portland Course**. All visitors must be members of a recognised club and be able to produce a certificate of handicap. Society games may be arranged, but organisers should note that their numbers must not exceed forty. In **1987** a **green fee** of **£23** will entitle the visitor to a round on **each** course. Alternatively a fee of **£18** will be payable for a full days golf on the **Portland Course**. There are no concessionary rates for junior golfers who in any event must have attained the age of eighteen before they will be permitted to play over the Old Course. Sets of clubs and trolleys may be hired from the Club's **professional, Brian Anderson (tel. 0292 313281)** and a caddy can also be obtained – provided you can speak the local dialect, something to be seriously considered.

The town of Troon lies just to the north of Prestwick and Ayr. Apparently, its name derives from the Old Welsh word 'trwyn'

meaning nose, describing the rocky promontory that forms part of the coastline around Troon. The town can be reached from Glasgow and the north via the **A77**, which also runs from near Stranraer in the south. The **A78** is the coastal road, running from Largs through Irvine to Loans, just east of Troon. Travelling from Edinburgh, the **A71** should be taken, whilst from the North of England the best route is probably via the **A74** and the **A71**. Finally, **Prestwick Airport** is no more than **two miles** away. Located as it is, bordering the Firth of Clyde, the wind often blows very fiercely across the links and Troon is hardly a place for the faint-hearted golfer.

The Club is proud of its great history. When it was founded in 1878 by twenty-four local enthusiasts there were originally only five holes – by 1923 it staged its first Open Championship. Since then the Club has held four further Opens, in 1950, 1962 (when a rampant Palmer stormed to a six stroke victory), 1973 and most recently in 1982 when Tom Watson won the fourth of his five titles to date. In addition, Troon has played host to four Amateur Championships as well as being the venue for several other important events.

The **Old Course** at Troon has both the **longest** hole of any Open Championship course – the **6th at 577 yards** and the **shortest** – the Postage Stamp which measures a mere **126 yards**. In the **11th** it also possesses one of the **toughest**, with its railway out-of-bounds, thick gorse and painfully narrow fair-way. The great **Jack Nicklaus** once took a 10 at this hole (there's hope for us all yet!). At **6,274 yards** the **Portland Course** represents a more modest test, but it is none the less a very fine course and it has all the challenges of traditional links golf.

If you have played all 36 holes at Troon and waged a successful war against the elements you will have earned your drink at the 19th. The Clubhouse provides all the usual facilities and the catering has a very good reputation. When you leave you will probably not have a film to take to heaven, but you will at least know that you have visited one of the earth's greatest golfing shrines.

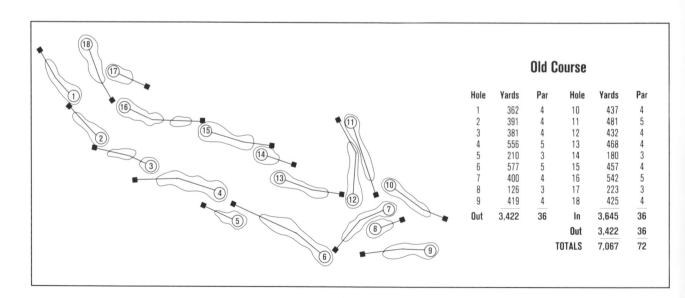

Old Course

Hole	Yards	Par	Hole	Yards	Par
1	362	4	10	437	4
2	391	4	11	481	5
3	381	4	12	432	4
4	556	5	13	468	4
5	210	3	14	180	3
6	577	5	15	457	4
7	400	4	16	542	5
8	126	3	17	223	3
9	419	4	18	425	4
Out	3,422	36	In	3,645	36
			Out	3,422	36
			TOTALS	7,067	72

Ten years ago and more it used to be said that the golfing visitor to Scotland journeyed to **St Andrews** for the history and to **Turnberry** for the beauty. Incomparable is a word often used to describe Turnberry's setting, magnificent and majestic are two others. Quite what causes **Ailsa Craig** to be so mesmerising is a mystery, but mesmerising it is and the views towards the distant **Isle of Arran** and the **Mull of Kintyre** can be equally captivating and enchanting. Since 1977 Turnberry has possessed history as well as beauty.

The Open Championship of **1977**, Turnberry's first, is generally considered to have been the greatest of all Championships. **Nicklaus** and **Watson** the two finest golfers of the day turned the tournament into a titanic, head-to-head confrontation. On the final day both having pulled a long way clear of the field Nicklaus held a two stroke advantage as they left the 12th green. "Who in the world can give Jack Nicklaus two shots over six holes and beat him?" asked Peter Alliss – the rest, as they say, is indeed history.

There are two Championship courses at Turnberry; the better known **Ailsa Course** and the **Arran Course**. Both are owned and run by the **Turnberry Hotel. Visitors** are welcome to play on either course although prior arrangements must be made with the **Golf Club Manager Mr R Hamblett.** Mr Hamblett can be contacted via **The Turnberry Hotel, Turnberry, Strathclyde, KA26 9LT**, telephone (06553) 202.

In 1986 the **green fees** were £25 for a day's golf consisting of one round on each course, or alternatively £20 for two rounds on the Arran. A single round on the Arran was priced at £15. Reduced rates are available to Hotel residents. Turnberry's professional **Bob Jamieson** can also be contacted on (06553) 202. Caddys and hire of clubs are best arranged by telephone.

The Clubhouse facilities are first class at Turnberry with a Golf Club restaurant that is open from 8am to 8pm. The bar is open daily from 11am and there are no specific dress requirements.

The Hotel and golf courses lie approximately 13 miles south of the town of **Ayr** off the **A77**. For those travelling from the **Glasgow** region the **A77** runs direct from Glasgow to Turnberry and is dual carriageway for much of the journey. Motoring from **Edinburgh** the **A71** is the best route, picking up the **A77** at **Kilmarnock** and following it as above, skirting around Ayr. Approaching from England, **Carlisle** is likely to be a starting point (**M6** to Carlisle). The distance from Carlisle to Turnberry is one of just under 120 miles, and although there are two choices, the quickest route is to head north on the **A74** leaving (in what appears to be no man's land) and joining the **A70** towards Ayr. Finally Prestwick Airport is situated just to the north of Ayr.

From its elevated perch the red-roofed Turnberry Hotel enjoys a commanding view over both courses. It will have witnessed much of Turnberry's rather turbulent past. During the War the rolling expanse of links had been used as an air base and a vast runway had been constructed. Much levelling of the ground had also taken place and in 1945 the last thing Turnberry must have looked was the setting for two Championship courses. **Mackenzie Ross** is the architect we all have to thank, for he transformed the concrete clad fairways into the Ailsa and Arran courses we now know. Within ten years of the Ailsa reopening in **1951** the **Amateur Championship** had been staged.

From its **medal tees** the **Ailsa** course isn't a great deal longer than the **Arran**, their respective distances being **6408** yards, par **70**, and **6276** yards, par 69. The same from the ladies tees are **5836** yards, par 75 **and 5732 yards**, par 73. When the Open Championship returned to Turnberry in **1986** the Ailsa course weighed in at 6950 yards, par **70** and the fairways had been narrowed to alarming proportions. **Greg Norman's** second round 63 achieved in far from perfect weather conditions was a remarkable feat. The weather can, of course, be Turnberry's devil and for many the outstanding memory of the 1986 Championship is of the torrential storm that struck at the end of the third day capturing Norman and a handful of others as they struggled to complete their rounds.

After three holes 'inland' as it were, the Ailsa course hugs the shore tightly for a series of dramatic holes between the 4th and the 11th. The **6th**, named **"Tappie Toorie"** is possibly the most difficult par three on the course (although the **15th** can be pretty treacherous) the shot is to a heavily guarded green across a valley. The 9th and the 10th though are the holes most likely to be remembered. The **9th "Bruce's Castle"**, is played alongside the famous Turnberry lighthouse built over the remains of Turnberry Castle, birthplace of Robert the Bruce, the King of the Scots. The Championship tee for this hole is one of the most spectacularly sited in the world perched on a pinnacle of rock with the sea crashing below. The **10th "Dinna Fouter"** calls for a daring drive across the bay, parallels have often been drawn here with the famous 18th at **Pebble Beach**. Following the par three 11th the holes turn inland and if the scenery is a little less spectacular the challenge in no way diminishes. The closing holes will invariably invoke thoughts of the Nicklaus-Watson battle. To complete 'the history' Nicklaus played the final six holes in one under par yet was still beaten. The end of an era cried many – they should have known better!

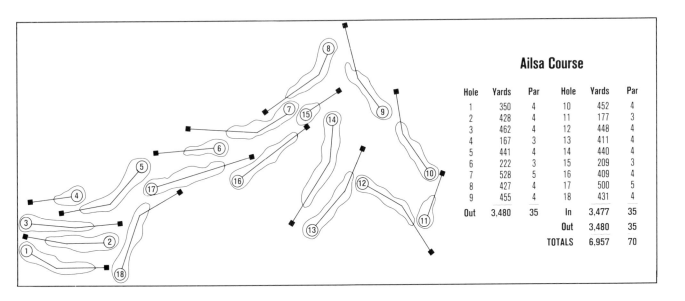

Ailsa Course					
Hole	Yards	Par	Hole	Yards	Par
1	350	4	10	452	4
2	428	4	11	177	3
3	462	4	12	448	4
4	167	3	13	411	4
5	441	4	14	440	4
6	222	3	15	209	3
7	528	5	16	409	4
8	427	4	17	500	5
9	455	4	18	431	4
Out	3,480	35	In	3,477	35
			Out	3,480	35
			TOTALS	6,957	70

FIFE

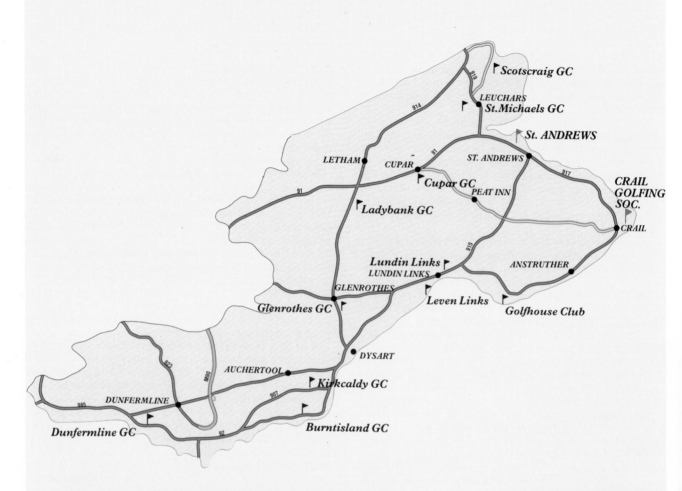

CHARLES WAGSTAFF *"The Golfers"* ROSENSTIELS

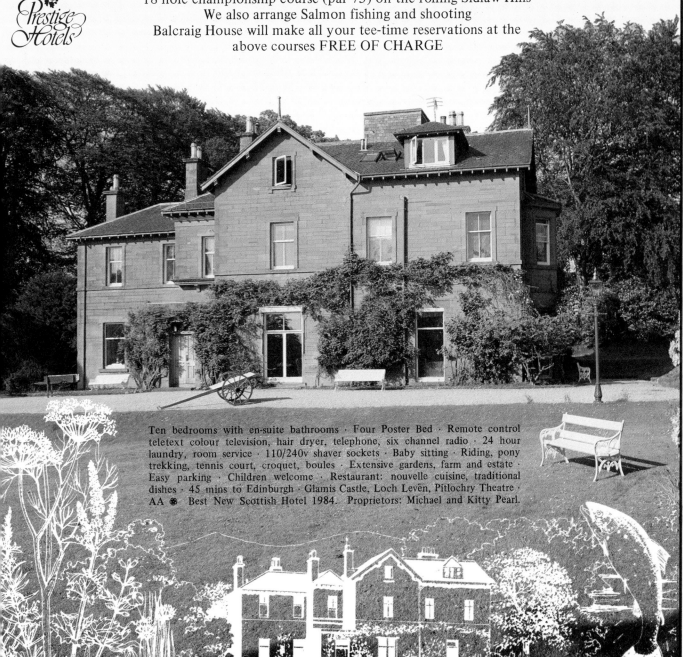

Many years ago watching an England versus Scotland soccer game at Wembley I remember being amused by one of the banners carried by a group of Scottish supporters which boldly declared, "Remember Bannockburn". Being a pig-headed Englishman I thought to myself they ought to remember it – it was just about the only battle they won in centuries. Of course, all is now abundantly clear – the Scots were far too busy priming their golfing skills to bother themselves fighting the Sassenachs.

As long ago as **1457** the Scottish Parliament, unimpressed at the performance of their sharp shooters, felt that too much golf and football were to blame for their lack-lustre performances on the battlefields. An Act was passed stating that because of their interference with the practice of archery "the fute-ball and golf be utterly cryit down and nocht usit". History would seem to suggest that the Scots didn't take a blind bit of notice and golf steadily grew in popularity. Juggle the figures that make up 1457 and we have **1754**, perhaps the most significant date in golf's history – the year the Society of St Andrews golfers drew up the first written rules of golf.

Today St Andrews, deep in the 'Kingdom of Fife', is the place every golfer in the world wants to visit. Even if he's only swung a club at the local municipal he'll be itching to do the same at St Andrews. However, for those contemplating a pilgrimage to the centre of the golfing world it should be said that St Andrews has several near neighbours that warrant the most discerning attention of any intrepid traveller. Between Dunfermline, to the west of Fife, and St Andrews, lie what are undoubtedly some of the finest courses in Scotland.

For six hundred years Dunfermline was the country's capital and the body of its most famous king, Robert the Bruce, lies buried in Dunfermline Abbey (minus his heart which is in Melrose Abbey). The town has two courses, **Dunfermline** and **Pitreavie**, both are parkland courses at which visitors are welcome provided some prior arrangement is made. Neither is unduly hard on the pocket.

East of Dunfermline there is a testing links at **Burntisland** with fine views over the Firth of Forth and there are again two courses in **Kirkcaldy**, the **Dunnikier Park** and **Kircaldy** Golf Clubs, the latter welcoming visitors during the week (Tuesdays excluded) and on Sundays.

Beyond Kirkcaldy along a glorious stretch of spectacular coast lie Fife's famous five – **Leven Links** and **Lundin Links, Elie, Balcomie** and of course **St Andrews**. The first two are often considered as a pair probably on account of there being very little land in between. Two clubs share the 6,433 yards links at Leven, the **Leven Golfing Society** and **Leven Thistle**. Visitors looking for a game should book in advance and whilst there is no similar requirement at **Lundin**, (6,377 yards) being equally popular prior telephoning would seem advisable, especially during the summer. Fees at both are approximately £10.

Elie, or the **Golf House Club**, lies a short distance from the two across Largo Bay, the **A917** linking the town with Leven. Elie is famed for its unique periscope by the first tee and for the fact that it was here that **James Braid** fashioned many of the skills that won him five Open Championships. A charming and very natural links measuring 6,253 yards several of the holes are laid out right alongside a rocky shoreline. A ballot system operates at Elie during the months of July and August but otherwise there are no general restrictions on times visitors can play. The cost of a day's golf in 1986 was £10 during the week, £15 at weekends.

Following the **A917** eastwards from Elie the town of Crail is soon reached. Just beyond the town at Fife Ness is the magnificent **Balcomie** links, the home of the two hundred year old **Crail Golfing Society**. Together with St Andrews it is featured a few pages on. Beyond St Andrews the **A917** joins the **A91** and heads off towards Dundee.

Just as the leading courses of Surrey aren't all heathland and heather neither are those of Fife all seaviews and sandhills: **Ladybank** and **Glenrothes** both in the heart of Fife are two of Scotland's greatest inland courses. **Ladybank** is situated only a few miles north of Leven but is completely different in character with heathland fairways and much pine and heather – a very beautiful course. Golf can be enjoyed at Ladybank for around the £8 to £12 mark, weekend mornings are best avoided.

In an area steeped in history **Glenrothes** is a relative newcomer to the scene being founded less than twenty years ago. Young, perhaps, but an excellent course nonetheless. Situated to the west of the town it is a fairly hilly parkland type offereing many superb views. Visitors are always made welcome though pre-booking (one day before intended play) is advisable. The green fees here are outstandingly good value – in 1986, £2.40 for a day's golf midweek, £3.40 at weekends. The names of two of the holes, however, worry me a little – the 11th, titled "Satan's Gateway" and the 18th, "Hell's End"!

Burntisland G.C.	(0592) 873247
Crail Golfing Society	(0333) 50278
Cupar G.C.	(0334) 53549
Dunfermline G.C.	(0383) 723534
Glenrothes G.C.	(0592) 754561
Golf House Club (Elie)	(0333) 330301)
Kirkcaldy G.C.	(0592) 266597
Ladybank G.C.	(0337) 30814
Leven Golfing Society	(0592) 263455
Lundin G.C.	(0333) 320202
Pitreavie G.C.	(0383) 722591
Royal and Ancient (St Andrews)	(0334) 75757

"Oh to be in England, now that April's there" so wrote Browning – a wise chap to say the least. However, many golfers would take issue with the poetic sage when the good old game is considered. I don't think they would quibble with the timing – April's as good a time as any. No, it's the location that's slightly adrift. Japanese, Americans, Australians and yes the English will consider that where to be is Scotland – and Fife in the spring time air. Narrowing down the country is one thing– the county another but Fife would surely be the answer and to go one stage further St. Andrews the beloved Mecca for the world's golfers.

Although it is the golf that captures the imagination there are a wealth of other pursuits to be enjoyed if one wishes. We will discover them as we race through the area. One point that is worth noting is that relative to the vastness of Scotland Fife is not a large area. We do not start our venture in St. Andrews, but in Crail a delightful fishing village renowned for its outstanding golf. There are a number of friendly little hotels each of whom will welcome you with open arms. Perhaps the best are the predictably named **Golf Hotel (0333) 50206** one of Scotland's oldest licensed Inns, and the **Caiphie Guest House (0333) 50564** – outstandingly good value.

A short drive from Crail (forgive the puny pun) lies St. Andrews. There's not really a great deal one can say that hasn't been said before, but that never stopped a great author – it does however preclude comment from this pen. But what of this "Ye man gan faur an' fare waur" (what we have to offer is as good as you will find anywhere).

The greatness and tradition of St. Andrews gives the hotels nearby a necessity to cater for the many golfers who come to play. Many of the hotels therefore have a very obvious association with the course. The **Old Course Hotel (0334) 74371** stands alongside the 17th fairway and its combination of leisure pursuits headed, of course, by the golf itself makes for a really tremendous time. **The Eden Restaurant** has an excellent reputation and what a place to celebrate a birdie at the seventeenth. St. Andrews does have several other hotels of note they are also less expensive than the Old Course. **Rufflets Hotel (0334) 72594** just outside the town is an excellent base while another room with a view can be booked at the **Rusacks Marine Hotel (0334) 74321**, this time the spectacle is the 18th fairway. Another hotel with something of a golfing interest is the **Links Hotel (0334) 72059** formerly the Golf Inn, the restaurant is also good and rather appropriately named **The Niblick**. The other hotels which might just hint at a round of the good old game include the **St. Andrew's Golf Hotel (0334) 72611** and the **Scores Hotel (0334) 72451** both good value and pleasant. While golf clearly takes centre stage one should not forget the pleasant coastline nearby, the twelth century Cathedral or Scotland's oldest University. If you wish to eat outside your hotel then **Pepitas (0334) 74084** is recommended. One final thought is the popular **Grange Inn (0334) 72670** in Grange village – another excellent place to eat, a varied menu includes both french and local specialities making particularly good use of fish and game.

When it comes to excellence and cuisine one really must point out the delights to be found at the **Peat Inn (033484) 206** one of the very finest restaurants in the country – booking well in advance is quite essential. Another restaurant to note this time in Cupar is **Ostlers Close (0334) 55574** – excellent. If by chance you are not eager to stay in St. Andrews there is a worthy alternative located in Anstruther, **The Craw's Nest Hotel (0333) 310691**, well recommended and good value. If one is seeking a restaurant to visit then **The Cellar (0333) 310378** is another really tremendous fish restaurant. Indeed the fish in the area is renowned – one little gem that may be overlooked is the fish and chip shop in Pitton Wear – remarkably excellent. Fish is also good for the brain – particularly handy if you're unsure on which of Fife's fine golfcourses to play. Jumping somewhat blindly to the North of Fife we land in Leuchars where **The Pinewoods Hotel (033483) 385** greets us – most welcoming on visiting this area. Another 'L' on this occasion **Letham** where the **Fernie Castle (033781) 381** is the place to stay, perfectly comfortable and a good base for enjoying other active pursuits, shooting, riding and fishing spring to mind. Passing another 'L' Ladybank one arrives at four more – Lundin Links and Leven Links (least you devil worshipers believe that I mean the eternal furnace when I say 'L' – let me assure you that these establishments are far from lush, quite the opposite actually). In Lundin Links **The Old Manor (0333) 320368** is a fine hotel. Particularly handy for the golfcourses and pleasant ocean views. The area is somewhat isolated but do not fear the hotel's restaurant is particularly good, there are some interesting week-end breaks on offer in winter – excellent if you wish to gamble with the elements.

Glenrothes, where two hotels can be recommended, although numerous others can be found if needs be. The **Balgeddie House (0592) 742511** is a secluded country house set in six acres of gardens overlooking Glenrothes. While the **Rothes Arms (0592) 753701** is also well though of a good place to visit. Now, on our way to Kirkcaldy two options emerge on the one hand in Dysart one finds the **Old Rectory Inn (0592) 51211**. A restaurant cum pub which provides at the very least two good reasons for stopping by. In Auchertool, another possibility can be found; on this occasion a hotel with a name more akin to Sloane Square than Haskerry, Fife – **The Camilla (0592) 780590** (the hotel may not lack the grace and elegance of our pearl clad darling from London's SW1, but can't be beaten for a good night and an excellent breakfast – Can this be said of many so called Sloane young ladies?)

While many may suggest that a night in Dunfermline is not the best plan– there are those who would recommend at least a short snooze at the **King Malcolm Thistle Hotel (0383) 722611**.

The problem that this hotel must clearly face where golfers are concerned is that on the one hand – St. Andrews lies ahead and on the other the delights of Lothian before …"Oh to be in Scotland now that spring is there" contemplates the golfer who rests many miles away. He begins to reminise of those great delights of man and nature – Golf in the Kingdom of Fife.

The Scores Hotel

St Andrews, Fife   Tel: (0334) 72451

A comfortable traditional hotel only a hundred yards from the first tee of the Old Course, and enjoying superb views over St Andrews Bay. The hotel is within easy walking distance of the city's shops, university, castle and harbour, offering high standards of food and hospitality. A Best Western Hotel.

Old Course Hotel

St Andrews, Fife

Tel: (0334) 74371

There are 150 luxurious and well equipped bedrooms in the hotel, which holds pride of place overlooking the 17th fairway of the marvellous Old Course. As well as golf, the hotel's gardens, sauna, pool, keep fit, solarium and other facilities are renowned.

THE 16TH: SLYMABACK TO WORMIT

CENTRAL

Aberfoyle G.C. (18)
Braeval, Aberfoyle (08772) 493

Alloa G.C. (18)
Schawpark, Sauchie (0259) 50100

Alva G.C. (9)
Alva (0259) 60431

Bonnybridge G.C. (9)
Bonnybridge (0324) 812645

Braehead G.C. (18)
Cambus, by Aloa (0259) 722078

Bridge of Allan G.C. (9)
Sunnlaw, Bridge of Allan
(0786) 832332

Buchanan Castle G.C. (18)
Drymen, Glasgow (0360) 60307

Callander G.C. (18)
Callander (0877) 30090

Dollar G.C. (18)
Dollar (0259) 2400

Dunblane New G.C. (18)
Dunblane (0786) 823711

Falkirk G.C. (18)
Falkirk (0324) 23457

Falkirk Tryst G.C. (18)
Larbert (032456) 2415

Glenbervie G.C. (18)
Larbert (0234) 562605

Grangemouth
Municipal G.C. (18)
Polmont, Falkirk (0324) 711500

Muckhart G.C. (18)
Muckhart, Dollar (25981) 423

Polmont G.C. (9)
Maddiston, by Falkirk
(0324) 71277

Stirling G.C. (18)
Stirling (0786) 64098

Tillicoultry G.C. (9)
Tillicoultry (0259) 50741

Tullialtan G.C. (18)
Kincardine on Forth, by Alloa
(0259) 30396

FIFE

Aberdour G.C. (18)
Aberdour (0383) 860256

Anstruther G.C. (9)
Anstruther (0333) 310224

Auchterderran G.C. (9)
Cardenden 721547

Ballingry G.C. (9)
Crosshill, Lochgelly
(0592) 860086

Burntisland
G.C.Dodhead, Burntistand
(0592) 874093

Canmore G.C. (18)
Dunfermline (0383) 724969

Crail G.S. (18)
Fifeness, Crail (0333) 50278

Cupar G.C. (9)
Hilltarvit, Cupar (0334) 53549

Dunfermline G.C. (18)
Crossford, Dunfermline
(0383) 723534

Dunnikier Park G.C. (18)
Kirkcaldy (0592) 261599

Earlsferry Thistle G.C. (18+9)
Elie (0333) 310053

Elie G.C. (18)
Elie, Leven (0333) 330301

Glenrothes G.C. (18)
Glenrothes (0592) 758686

Golf House Club (Elie) (18)
Elie (0333) 330301

Kinghorn G.C. (18)
Kinghorn (0592) 890345

Kirkcaldy G.C. (18)
Kirkcaldy (0592) 266597

Ladybank G.C. (18)
Annsmuir, Ladybank
(0337) 30814

Leslie G.C. (9)
Balsillie, Leslie 741449

Leven Golfing
Society G.C. (18)
Leven (0592) 263455

Lochgeln G.C. (18)
Lochgelln (0592) 780174

Lundin G.C. (18)
Lundin Links (0333) 320202

Lundin Ladies G.C. (9)
Lundin Links (0333) 320022

Pitreavie
(Dunfermline) G.C. (18)
Dunfermline (0383) 722591

St. Andrews Balgrove Course (9)
St. Andrews (0334) 75757

St. Andrews Eden Course (18)
St. Andrews (0334) 75757

St. Andrews Jubilee Course (18)
St. Andrews (0334) 75757

St. Andrews New Course (18)
St. Andrews (0334) 75757

St. Andrews Old Course (18)
St. Andrews (0334) 75757

St. Michaels G.C. (9)
Leuchars, St. Andrews
(033483) 365

Saline G.C. (9)
Saline (0383) 852591

Scoonie G.C. (18)
Leven 24866

Scotscraig G.C. (18)
Tayport (0382) 552515

Thornton G.C. (18)
Thornton (0592) 77111

TAYSIDE

Aberfeldy G.C. (9)
Aberfeldy (0887) 20535

Alyth G.C. (18)
Pitcrocknie, Alyth (08283) 2268

Abroath G.C. (18)
Elliott, Airbroath Arbroath 72272

Auchterarder G.C. (18)
Auchterarder (07646) 2804

Bishopshive G.C. (9)
Kinnesswood 860379

Blair Atholl G.C. (9)
Blair Atholl (0796) 81407

Blairgowrie G.C. (18+18+9)
Rosemount, Blairgowrie
(0250) 2622

Brechin G.C. (18)
Trinity by Brechin (03562) 2383

Caird Park G.C. (18)
Mains Loan, Dundee
(0382) 453606

Camperdown
(Municipal) G.C. (18)
Dundee (0382) 645450

Carnoustie G.C. (18+18+18)
Carnoustie (0241) 53789

Comrie G.C. (9)
Polinard, Comrie 70544

Craigie Hill G.C. (18)
Cherrybank, Perth (0738) 22644

Crieff G.C. (18+9)
Crieff (0764) 2546

Dalmunzie G.C. (9)
Spittal O'Glenshee, Blairgowrie
(025085) 226

Downfield G.C. (18+18)
Dundee (0382) 825595

Dunkeld & Birnam G.C. (9)
Fungarth, Dunkeld (03502) 524

Dunning G.C. (9)
Dunning, Perth (076484) 398

Edzell G.C. (18)
Edzell, by Brechin (03564) 7283

Forfar G.C. (18)
Cunninghill, by Forfar
(0307) 62120

Glenalmond G.C. (9)
Glenalmond 270

Gleneagles Hotel Golf Courses
(18+18+18+18)
Auchterarder (07646) 3543

Green Hotel G.C. (18)
Kinross (0577) 63467

Killin G.C. (9)
Killin (05672) 234

King James VI G.C. (18)
Moncrieffe Island, Perth
(0738) 32460

Kirriemuir G.C. (18)
Kirriemuir (0575) 72144

Letham Grange G. & C.C.
(18+18)
Colliston, by Arbroath
(0241) 89373

Milnathort G.C. (9)
Milnathort (0577) 64069

Monifieth G.C. (18+18)
Monfieth (0382) 532767

Montrose Links Trust (18+18)
Montrose (0674) 72634

Murrayshall G.C. (18)
Murrayshall, by Scone
(0738) 52784

Muthill G.C. (9)
Muthill, Crieff (0764) 3319

Panmore G.C. (18)B
Barry (0241) 53120

Pitlochry G.C. (18)
Pitlochry (0796) 2792

Royal Perth Golfing
Society G.C. (18)
Perth 22265

St. Fillans G.C. (9)
St. Fillans (076485) 312

Strathtay G.C. (9)
Strathtay (08874) 367

Taymouth Castle G.C. (18)
Kenmore, by Aberfeldy
(08873) 228

THE **BUDGET LEAGUE**

"**FORE!**"

"**OUT OF THE WAY, MY LORD !**"

CRAIL GOLFING SOCIETY, BALCOMIE

On **23rd February 1986** the seventh oldest Golf Club in the world celebrated its bicentenary. Some three years before the Bastille was stormed a group of eleven gentlemen met at the **Golf Inn** in Crail and together formed the **Crail Golfing Society**. The records of that historic day are still preserved, indeed remarkably the Society possesses a complete set of minutes from the date of its inception. In those early days the Society members wore scarlet jackets with yellow buttons and dined at the Golf Inn after a day on the links. The local punch flowed and a good time was doubtless had by all – now those were the days!

Since 1895 the Club has played over the **Balcomie Links** which is located approximately two miles north east of Crail at Fifeness. Earlier the Society had used a narrow strip of land at **Sauchope**, slightly closer to Crail (and of course to the Golf Inn).

The atmosphere is still jovial and visitors are made most welcome. With the exception of a few competition days there are no general restrictions on times of play. However, individual visitors are advised to telephone the Starter one day before playing. The Starter can be contacted on **(0333) 50278**. Societies, or golfing parties, are equally welcome and advance bookings can be made at all times excepting the very peak summer period. Written enquiries should be addressed to the **Secretary, Crail Golfing Society, Balcomie Clubhouse, Crail Fife**. The Secretary, **Mr G.B.Thomson M.B.E.**, can be reached by telephone on **(0333) 50686**.

The **green fees for 1986** were pitched at **£6** per round, **£9** per day during weekdays and **£8** per round, **£11.50** per day at weekends. Juniors could obtain a weekday round for **£3** though at other times full fees were charged. In addition short Temporary Membership is offered: examples from 1986 included, **£18** for 3 consecutive weekdays, **£30** for a weekly ticket (excluding Sunday) and **£48** for a fortnightly ticket (again excluding Sundays).

The Balcomie Links in in fact ideal for 'holiday golf'. Without being overly long (**5,720** yards, **par 69**) – though the wind can affect greatly – it offers some exceptionally spectacular scenery and similar to Cruden Bay, further North, a nearby Castle casts a watchful eye. **Balcomie Castle**, where Mary of Guies, mother-to-be of Mary Queen of Scots, spent her first few days in Scotland, comes complete with ghost. The course is always well maintained and the holes have been so laid out that each provides a view of the sea. They possess some rather interesting names too: "Fluke Dub" (**4th**) "Hell's Hole" (**5th**) "Castle Yetts" (**9th**) and "Lang Wang" (**11th**) – the latter fuelling the belief that Scotland and Taiwan once had closer ties.

From all points south travelling to Crail will be by way of the Forth Road Bridge and thereafter following a combination of 'A roads'. The M90 may also be used though if St. Andrews is to be taken in en route. The **A915/A917** approaches Crail from along the coast via Lundin Links and Elie, while from Cupar and St Andrews the **A91/A917** should be taken. As stated the course is situated two miles from Crail in the direction of Fifeness and is well-signposted.

The 19th at Crail is as it should be, right next to the 18th green and provides commanding views over much of the course. Smart casual dress is acceptable in the Clubhouse, though presumably today if you strolled in wearing a bright scarlet jacket you might raise a few eyebrows. A full complement of catering is offered at all times but for those wishing to make advanced arrangements a quick telephone call to the Steward is never a bad idea. Mr New is the Steward, he can be contacted on **(0333) 50278**.

The temptation for many on crossing the Forth Road Bridge is of course to head straight for the Royal and Ancient. Whereas St Andrews may be the undisputed sovereign in the so-called "Kingdom of Fife" so there are also a number of handsome Princes. Balcomie stands comparison with the best and is a course of which the two hundred year old Society can justifiably be proud.

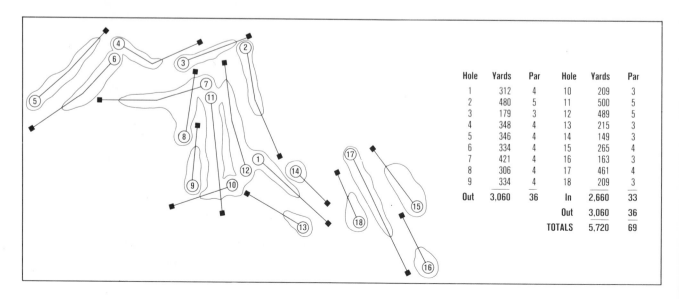

Hole	Yards	Par	Hole	Yards	Par
1	312	4	10	209	3
2	480	5	11	500	5
3	179	3	12	489	5
4	348	4	13	215	3
5	346	4	14	149	3
6	334	4	15	265	4
7	421	4	16	163	3
8	306	4	17	461	4
9	334	4	18	209	3
Out	3,060	36	In	2,660	33
			Out	3,060	36
			TOTALS	5,720	69

ST. ANDREWS

If there is such a thing as a truly global sport then it has to be golf. From its parochial beginnings on the east coast of Scotland it is now played on every continent, in every conceivable corner. Not only are there golf courses on the exotic islands of Tahiti and Bali but there is one in the Himalayas and there is one in the Arctic, golf has even been played on the moon. For all this there remains but one home – St Andrews.

Whilst we will never be able to put an exact date on the time golf was first played on the famous links several documents refer to a crude form of the game being played at least as early as the mid 1400s. Whether it was called gowf, goff or gouffe matters not, it was played on land close to the sea with a club and a small ball which was struck towards a distant hole cut in the ground, the object being to 'hole out' in as few strokes as possible. As for the right to play at St Andrews, which of course, the whole world enjoys, the origins are embodied in a licence dated **1552** drawn up by the **Archbishop of St Andrews**. It permitted the community to breed rabbits on the links and to "play at golf futeball, schueting, at all gamis with all uther, as ever they pleis and in ony time". Furthermore the proprieter was bound "not to plough up any part of said golf links in all time coming."

Organised golf came to St Andrews in **1754** when twenty-two "Noblemen and Gentlemen" formed the **St Andrews Society of Golfers**. In **1834** the Society became the **Royal and Ancient Golf Club**. Today with the exception of the United States the Royal and Ancient is the supreme authority in all matters relating to the government of the game. It is also responsible for the organisation of the Open Championship.

Not only can all the world play at St Andrews but all the world wants to and arranging a game on the Old Course can be a little difficult. The **St Andrews Links Management Committee** handles all matters relating to times of play and they should be contacted well in advance. The summer months are naturally the busiest period and it is best to write to the Committee two to three months prior to intended play, offering if possible a number of alternative dates. The address to write to is **The St Andrews Links Management Committee, Golf Place, St Andrews, Fife KY16 9JA**. The Secretary, **Mr Alex Beveridge** and his staff can be contacted by telephone on **(0334) 75757**. There are no handicap limits to play over the Old Course. However a handicap certificate or letter of introduction is required. It should also be noted that there is no Sunday golf on the Old Course. The green fee for a full day's golf is **£17**.

In addition to the Old Course there are four other links at St Andrews, the **New Course**, which dates from 1896, **the Jubilee** (1897), **the Eden** (1914) and **the Balgove** (1972), the latter being a 9 hole course. No handicap certificate is required to play over any of the above four and the green fees for 1987 on each are **£8, £6, £7** and **£2** respectively.

St Andrews is situated **57** miles north east of **Edinburgh**. For northbound travellers the most direct route is to take the **M90** after crossing the Forth Road Bridge. The **A91** should be joined at junction **8**. This road can be followed to St Andrews. Southbound travellers should head for **Perth** which is linked in turn to **Dundee** by the **A85** and to the north of Scotland by the **A9**. From Perth a combination of the **A90** and the **A913** takes one to **Cupar** where the **A91** can be picked up. Finally, the nearest train station is at **Leuchars**, approximately six miles from the centre of the town..

It was nature that fashioned St Andrews and over the centuries the Old Course has seen little change. Its myriad of tiny pot bunkers remain both a fascination and a frustration – providing just enough room as **Bernard Darwin** put it "for an angry man and his niblick". Laid out on a narrow strip of land ranging from 50 to 100 yards in width St Andrews is famed for its enormous double greens. There are seven in all and some are more than an acre in size. With little definition between the fairways there tends to be no standard way of playing a particular hole and as a rule the wind direction will determine the preferred line. Individual holes are not likely to be easily remembered the first time of playing, especially as one will probably be walking the course in a semi-trance. History is everywhere and on the first hole as you cross the bridge over the **Swilcan Burn** a voice from somewhere says "they've all walked this bridge" – and of course, they have. Just as they've all passed through the **Elysian Fields**, tackled **Hell's Bunker**, **the Beardies** and the **Principal's Nose**. And then of course they've all faced the **Road Hole** with its desperate drive and even more desperate approach and then finally strolled the great expanse of the **18th** fairway towards the **Valley of Sin**.

It isn't always love at first sight with St Andrews and **Bobby Jones** tore up his card on the 11th when he first played. Jones went on to meet great triumph at St Andrews and it is perhaps fitting to end with a few words from the great man, "the more I studied the Old Course the more I loved it and the more I loved it the more I studied it so that I came to feel that it was for me the most favourable meeting ground possible for an important contest."

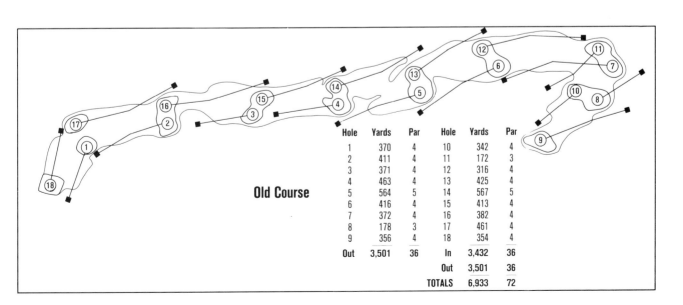

Old Course

Hole	Yards	Par	Hole	Yards	Par
1	370	4	10	342	4
2	411	4	11	172	3
3	371	4	12	316	4
4	463	4	13	425	4
5	564	5	14	567	5
6	416	4	15	413	4
7	372	4	16	382	4
8	178	3	17	461	4
9	356	4	18	354	4
Out	3,501	36	In	3,432	36
			Out	3,501	36
			TOTALS	6,933	72

TAYSIDE AND CENTRAL

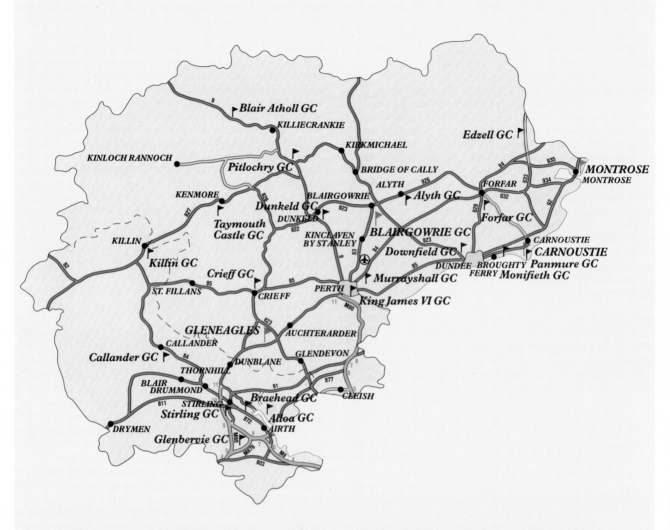

JULIAN BARROW   "Gleneagles"   BURLINGTON GALLERY

CROMLIX House

omlix, a Scottish country house of great gance, is situated on the outskirts of the all village of Kinbuck. It was converted m the Eden family home in 1980. Set in own 5,000 acre estate, which has been ned by the same family for over 400 ars, it offers the peace and comforts of a gone age. The present house was built in 80, and many distinguished visitors have en entertained here, including King ward VII.

ere are fourteen bedrooms, all with vate bathrooms; seven have private ing rooms. Bedrooms and reception oms contain original furnishings dating m 1880, enhanced by exquisite rcelain, silver and glass. Public rooms lude a panelled reception hall, a large awing room, and a dining room, all with en fires. Our library makes a perfect om for top-level business entertaining d exclusive conferences, or just a aceful retreat.

hing for brown or rainbow trout is ailable on four private lochs. Shooting n also be arranged—sport at Cromlix can ige from grouse on the moor to mixed nter shooting on the low ground or ven pheasants. In addition, there is a rd tennis court and riding can be

arranged on the Estate. The celebrated golf courses at Gleneagles are twenty minutes away by car.

Scotland is justifiably renowned for the quality of its beef and lamb; in addition the game from our Estate, and locally caught salmon enable our Master Chef to work with the finest ingredients available. In keeping with a country house which retains the unique traditions of a family home, each evening in the Dining Room we offer a set menu, where you will find traditional country house recipes, mixed with new tastes and unusual presentations. Our Chef's artistically created dishes are complemented by our magnificent cellar, which includes some fine vintage claret.

The central geographical position of Cromlix means that many areas are easily accessible for touring, especially the Highlands and Lowlands. Other destinations, like St. Andrews are less than two hours away, whilst the cities of Edinburgh and Glasgow are within one hour's car journey. In the winter months, we offer mid-week breaks at reduced terms.

Our aim is to provide, in a mood of peace and relaxation, old fashioned comforts, quiet hospitality, and personal service.

Cromlix House,
Kinbuck, Dunblane,
Perthshire FK15 9JT
Telephone: (0786) 822125

If, as the song says, the streams of the mountains please you more than the sea then it is to the likes of **Gleneagles, Pitlochry** and **Callander** you will head; if you are one of the diehards who think there is but one form of the gowf then you will probably set course for **Carnoustie, Monifieth** and **Montrose**, but then again if it is felt that variety is the spice of golf a nice combination of the two can be devised. The heart of Scotland has much to offer of everything.

While there is an inevitable temptation to head for the 'bigger Clubs', the Gleneagles and the Carnousties, the region boasts a staggering number of smaller Clubs where golf can be equally enjoyable. **Taymouth Castle** and **Callander** are perhaps two of Scotland's lesser known courses (at least to many south of the border) yet they are two of the most outstandingly scenic courses one is likely to find anywhere. At Callander in early spring the deer come down from the Perthshire hills to forage, a glorious sight, while the course at Taymouth Castle is situated in a conservation area surrounded by woods. A day's golf at either is priced at around the £7 to £10 mark. There are no general restrictions on visitors at either course although bookings must be made at Taymouth Castle. Callander can be reached via the **A84**, while Taymouth Castle lies 6 miles west of Aberfeldy.

Before **Gleneagles** is reached some excellent golf is to be found at **Glenbervie**, (off the **A9** at Larbert) **Braehead**, and **Alloa** while over to the west of the Central region **Buchanan Castle** is well worth the drive. The town of Stirling is known as the "Gateway to the Highlands" and **Stirling's** golf course (just to the west of the town) has a beautiful setting beneath the Ochil Hills.

While Taymouth Castle is located at the northern end of Loch Tay, **Killin** stands on the other side. Although only a short 9 hole course it is excellent value at only £4 for a full day's golf.

After **Gleneagles, Blairgowrie** is probably the best known course in the centre of Scotland and both are featured on later pages, however, the golfer should undoubtedly pay a visit to the 'fair city of Perth'. **The King James VI** club on Moncrieffe Island is steeped in history while nearby at Scone, Murrayshall is one of Scotland's newest courses but already one with an excellent reputation and one which again offers superb views of the Perthshire countryside. Fees in 1986 at the King James VI Club were **£7.50** during the week and **£9.50** at weekends. The cost of a game at Murrayshall was set at **£6.50** midweek and **£8.50** Saturdays and Sundays. A little to the west of Perth the 27 holes at **Crieff** are also well worth a visit. Fees in 1986 were £6 midweek, £8 at weekends.

If a game cannot be arranged at Blairgowrie the heathland course at **Alyth** is only a short distance away and will certainly not disappoint, while towards the north of Tayside **Pitlochry** is strongly recommended for anyone travelling along the **A9**, fees are approximately **£8 to £10**.

Some of Scotland's greatest links courses are to be found between **Dundee** and **Montrose** on the Tayside coast. However, to the north west of Dundee lies **Downfield**, one of the country's finest inland courses. It is said that Downfield is very popular with American visitors because it reminds them of some of their courses 'back home'. No one though would have found it particularly popular in 1938 when a whirlwind struck the course tossing a wooden shelter fifty feet in the air and causing untold damage! Today things are a little quieter and golf can be enjoyed for £10 per day midweek and for £15 per day at weekends (prior telephoning is preferred.)

East of Dundee **Monifieth** staged the **Scottish Amateur Championship** in 1986. While **Panmure** at Barry has in the past staged the **Seniors Championship**. Both are outstanding links courses and fairly inexpensive to play over. **Carnoustie** is of course one of Scotland's greatest golfing shrines and along with Montrose further north along the coast is featured on a later page.

Still over towards the east of Tayside but away from the coast, **Edzell**, just north of Brechin is a very fine heathland course. Close to the start of the Grampian range there are some marvellous mountain views. Visitors are welcome at Edzell during the week and in the afternoon at weekends. Fees in 1986 were **£36** per round midweek, **£10** per round at weekends.

Finally, less testing golf can be found at **Forfar Golf Club**, located east of Forfar off the **A932**. Tuesdays and Sundays are best avoided but visitors are welcome at all other times, the cost of a game being approximately **£10**.

Alloa G.C.	(0259) 50100
Blairgowrie G.C.	(0250) 2622
Callander G.C.	(0877) 30090
Carnoustie	(0241) 53789
Crieff G.C.	(0764) 2546
Downfield G.C.	(0382) 825595
Edzell G.C.	(03564) 7283
Forfar G.C.	(0307) 63773
Glenbervie G.C.	(0324) 562605
Gleneagles	(07646) 3543
Killin G.C.	(056 72) 234
King James VI (Moncrieffe Island) G.C.	(0738) 32460
Monifieth G.C.	(0382) 532767
Montrose Links	(0674) 72634
Murrayshall G.C.	(0738) 52784
Panmure G.C.	(0241) 53120
Pitlochry G.C.	(0796) 2792
Taymouth Castle G.C.	(08873) 228

"But Doctor it can't be true" Harold comments incredulously. "I'm afraid it is. You have two weeks to live." So heard Charles Doubleday Wigglesworth on the 16th May 1986. As Wiggles, as he was affectionately known, considered his tragic positon and the cancer that grabbed him – he decided to go down fighting. As he looked back on his life – he thought of the pleasures he had enjoyed. He was going to relive them if he could. Golf was his first love, fishing his next, good food, good wine and the country air he adored. He also had a wife. They would go off together to the place where true satisfaction of all the above could surely be found – Perthshire (except arguably Mildred his wife).

Wiggles' first port of call was hardly surprisingly Auchterarder. This delightful area includes some outstanding country house hotels. **Gleneagles (07646) 2231** is the best known and here service and hospitality as well as the golf are quite superb. Another outstanding mansion three miles from Gleneagles is **The Auchterarder House Hotel (07646) 2939**. A stroll through the beautiful gardens before the dinner is one of life's hard-earned treats.

One of the problems with this area is that one is spoilt for choice. What a place to spend a fortnight even if it happens to be your last. The range of tremendous golf is totally reflected in some superb hotels. Perth, with its Tayside setting is a bustling market town and although no longer capital it is still a centre point for people who delight in country sports. Outside its extremities near the delightful Scone Palace (note magnificent porcelain collection) lies **Balcraig House (0738) 51123**. This splendid Victorian house is filled with flowers and antiques – remarkably relaxing. The restaurant is also to be highly praised, it is here that Wiggles enjoys one of his favourites – wild boar. Nearby **The Murrayshall Hotel (0738) 51171** is in an ideal situation as one would expect for the golf course. In Perth itself the **Royal George Hotel (0738) 24455** enjoys a Tayside setting and is comfortable. For lunch or dinner do try the **Coach House (0738) 27950**.

One of Scotland's most superb golfcourses is Blairgowrie. Before a game here Wiggles travelled through Kinclave by Stanley and reminisced on the quiet days spent in **Ballathie House (0294) 57733** – such a calm situation. Racing against time and Alyth – more precisely **The Lands of Loyal Hotel (08283) 3151** – not visited previously but a grand reputation just the same – excellent value as well. Although there are numerous hotels in Blairgowrie, Pitlochry and the surrounding towns– our battling hero despite his eagerness would be unable to visit them. He would especially miss the charm of Pitlochry the convenience of Blairgowrie – ideal for all his favourite pastimes. Memories of fine cooking in **The Kinlock House (025084) 237** and some splendid drinking in **The Meiklour Hotel. The Bridge of Cally Hotel (025086) 231** – no splendour but the food and welcome are truly delightful.

The memories flood back to Kirkmichael and some further splendid cooking on this occasion the delightfully remote **Log Cabin Hotel (025081) 288** – such value and after the great outdoors Wiggles sighs and thinks on. Killiecrankie, a name that always amused him as a child and the **Killiecrankie Hotel (0796) 3220** – peaceful and so handy for the A9. A game at Pitlochry lies ahead, now the memories really hit hard – this is where Wiggles first hit a golf ball. The Theatre in the Hills – how charming – sadly he would miss this year's superb summer presentation.

With a new found zest after seeing these delightful towns Wiggles sets sail for the coast and perhaps his favourite of all golfcourses, Carnoustie. Here **The Links Hotel** is both comfortable and convenient. Montrose to the North and Dundee to the south, in the former **The Park Hotel (0674) 73415** is favoured while in the latter **The Angus Thistle Hotel (0382) 26874** is the best answer. One thought in Broughty Ferry before we move back inland and that's a restaurant – **L'Auberge (0382) 730890**.

The countryside around is a delight, the glens of Angus, Royal Deeside, the Ochill Hills, the Cairngorms, quite superb – face it if you have to keel over what a place to go.

One centre point is the historic Glamis Castle – a real must if you have a little time. This tragically was not the case with Wiggles. Forfar (not one for you boys or girls with a stutter) offers **The Royal Hotel (0307) 62691** it is quiet and convenient and good for a night's kip while visiting. But our hero has other plans valiently shrugging off the desire to have a go at windsurfing – one of the only sports yet to be conquered by this player extraordinaire, he is heading for Dunblane to stay at one of those gems – **Cromlix House**, a large hotel which hides within it a restaurant of quite excellent quality. Back in the heart of Perthshire – having sampled a little fishing another beautiful place, this time Callander, more precisely **The Roman Camp Hotel (0877) 30003**. More outstanding establishments – well, **The Airth Castle** at Airth **(032483) 411** and at Auchterhouse **The Old Mansion House (082626) 366** are outstanding – do try the latter's restaurant. Stirling and its castle – splendid and if you wish to stay, well, perhaps **The Park Lodge (0786) 74862** should be tried. An alternative location in this area can be found in Drymen, situated in a pleasant village **The Buchanan Arms (0360) 60588** – good food, all round good value.

Our final trip takes us through the lochs, streams and burns of this gorgeous area. We start in Cleish at the excellent **Nivingston House (05775) 216** (handy for exit 5 of the M90). From Cleish to Crieff and the **Crieff Hydro (0764) 2401** good sporting facilities and accommodation. Wiggles overlooks a loch he is staying at the charming **Four Seasons, (076 485) 333** St. Fillans, cogitating – looking forward to dinner. Tomorrow, well, Killin and **The Clachaig Hotel** appeal, or possibly Kenmore and **The Kenmore Hotel (08873) 205**. Yes, that's a good idea – some fishing on the Tay as well or why not just get right away from it all and visit Kinloch Rannoch and **The Loch Rannoch Hotel (08822) 201**, – perhaps not – better for the younger families – Wiggles is getting on.

As Wiggles prepared to see his Doctor again he thought of the superb time spent in Scotland. The time had come, but he had had a good innings or shall we say round. An hour later and the smile was for all to see. Wiggles was to live – it does not happen often, but given the right peace of mind cancer can lose its killing bite.

Wiggles was returning to Scotland: **Cancer Research 01-930 8972.**

Crieff Hydro
Crieff, Perthshire
Tel: (0764) 2401
The hotel's splendid position in 650 acres of farmland, woodland and gardens is ideal for those who just want to relax. For the more active, the hotel offers every possible amenity. These include a nine hole golf course, five tennis courts and a riding stable.

Old Mansion House
Auchterhouse,
Nr Dundee, Tayside
Tel: (082626) 366
An exceedingly friendly atmosphere pervades at this comfortable mansion house. Six fully equipped rooms and an excellent restaurant where local produce is put to good use. Ideal for lunch or dinner. Do book in advance.

With so many outstanding courses to choose from, all within fairly close proximity of one another, even the most blinkered of diehard Englishmen would be forced to concede that Scotland is the finest place on earth for a week's golfing holiday. Given seven precious days a large number of would-be travellers on opening their maps of Scotland are likely to plan a trip thus: three days on the west coast playing Prestwick, Turnberry and Troon; a day 'in the middle' visiting Gleneagles, finishing with three on the east coast taking in Carnoustie, St Andrews and Muirfield. Marvellous stuff of course, but many of the golfing sages hold the opinion that such an itinerary misses out the greatest of them all – the **Rosemount** course at **Blairgowrie**.

There are in fact two 18 hole courses at Blairgowrie, the older and more celebrated **Rosemount**, designed by **James Braid** and the **Lansdowne** course, a fairly recent addition, the work of **Peter Alliss** and **Dave Thomas**. On each, golf is played over beautiful moorland fairways, lined by forests of pine and silver birch. A liberal sprinkling of purple heather and gorse add considerable colour to an already majestic setting – as one observer put it, "somebody seems to have gone mad with a paint brush!"

Persons wishing to sample the delights of either course are advised to book starting times through the Club's Professional, **Gordon Kinnock**, tel **(0250) 3116**. Visitors are welcome at Blairgowrie on Mondays, Tuesdays, Thursdays and, to a limited extent, on Fridays. Fourball matches, it should be noted, are not normally allowed before 10 a.m. on the Rosemount course. Furthermore all visitors must be able to provide proof of handicap. Golfing parties are also welcome on the above days though teeing off will not be permitted between 12 p.m. and 2 p.m. nor after 4 p.m. Those wishing to organise golfing parties should address written applications to the Club's Secretary, **Mr Kirkland**, the Club's full address being, **Blairgowrie Golf Club, Rosemount, Blairgowrie, Perthshire**. Mr Kirkland can be contacted by telephone on **(0250) 2622**. In **1986** the **green fee** for

a single round on either course was priced at **£12**, while for the sum of **£18** a full day's golf could be enjoyed.

Having metaphorically chastised the golfer who doesn't make Blairgowrie a 'must' on any golfing tour I had better detail the best routes to reach it. Hopefully the following will prove of assistance: approaching from the south the **A93** Braemar road runs directly from Perth, Perth being linked to Edinburgh by the **A90/M90**. From easterly directions Blairgowrie (Rosemount is just south of the town) is connected to Dundee by the **A923** and to Forfar by the **A926**. Anyone motoring down from the north will probably travel either on the **A9** (via Aviemore and Pitlochry) or on the **A93** passing through Ballater and Braemar. Blairgowrie is 15 miles from Perth and 18 miles from Dundee. Gleneagles (via Perth) and Carnoustie and St Andrews (both via Dundee) are all approximately 30 miles away.

Measuring around the **6600** yard mark, the Rosemount course could be described as having the classic formula: both the front nine and the back nine comprise five par 4's, two par 3's and two par 5's – 36 out and 36 back, making the par a traditional 'level fours'. The official course record at Rosemount stands at 66, though in 1973, during a practice round for the Sumrie Better-Ball tournament, Professional **Lionel Platts** achieved a world record ten consecutive birdies between the 8th and 17th – quite obscene don't you think?!

The Lansdowne course is slightly longer than its older brother, and many would say a much sterner test – either way a game on each is strongly recommended.

It need hardly be added that Blairgowrie with its two courses – three if one includes the aptly named Wee Course, a short nine-holer – has a more than adequate 19th. Lunches, high teas, dinners and light snacks are all offered. There are also two Bars, comfortable places where many will choose to go and celebrate a magnificent day's golfing in one of the most glorious settings the game has to offer.

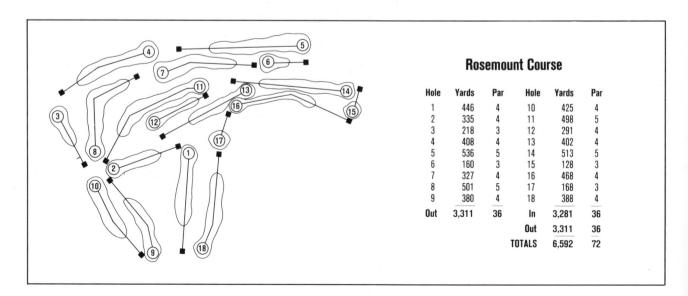

Rosemount Course

Hole	Yards	Par	Hole	Yards	Par
1	446	4	10	425	4
2	335	4	11	498	5
3	218	3	12	291	4
4	408	4	13	402	4
5	536	5	14	513	5
6	160	3	15	128	3
7	327	4	16	468	4
8	501	5	17	168	3
9	380	4	18	388	4
Out	**3,311**	**36**	**In**	**3,281**	**36**
			Out	**3,311**	**36**
			TOTALS	**6,592**	**72**

There is a vast oil painting that hangs in the Tate Gallery in London, the artist is David Martin and the painting is titled **"The Plains Of Heaven"**. Some may know it well others will wonder what on earth I'm jibbering on about – suffice it to say that it depicts in the most vivid colours imaginable the artist's impression of paradise. I suspect that David Martin wasn't a golfer. Blasphemy isn't intended but for many of us who stalk the fairways of the world, Gleneagles is just about our best idea of how heaven might look – give or take a couple of angels.

Gleneagles is set in the heart of some of the most glorious Perthshire countryside. Surrounded by the foothills of the Grampian Mountain range everywhere one turns there is a shock of colour. The mountains themselves often appear wrapped in purples and blues. Heather, silver birch and rowan cover the crisp moorland turf. Gleneagles is also alive with wildlife – deer, squirrels, hares, even weasels and stoats. With so much around one could be forgiven for losing a little concentration, yet the golf too is glorious and there are now four eighteen hole courses – there really is nothing quite like Gleneagles.

The land was first surveyed with a view to designing one or more golf courses before the first World War and **James Braid** was called in to direct affairs. By **1919** the **Kings** and **Queens** courses were both open for play. Braid's work met with instant acclaim and in **1921** the forerunner of the Ryder Cup was staged at Gleneagles, when a team of British Professionals played a team from America. The **Princes** and **Glendevon** courses are fairly recent additions being opened in **1974** and **1980** respectively.

The four courses are efficiently managed and maintained by the **Gleneagles Hotel. Visitors** are welcome to play on any seven days a week and they need not possess a certificate of handicap. However, Gleneagles is understandably extremely popular and prior arrangements must be made in advance. The gentleman to contact is the **Sports Manager, Mr I Bulleid,** either by telephoning on **(07646) 3543 (telex 76105)** or by writing to **The Sports Office, Gleneagles Hotel, Auchterarder, Perthshire PH3 1NF**. The only specific restrictions on teeing times apply to the Kings and Queens courses where before 10.30am and between 1.30pm and 2.30pm the tees are reserved for hotel residents and members.

In 1986 the **green fees** for non-residents at Gleneagles were **£17** for a single round on either the **Kings** or **Queens** and **£11** for a game on the **Princes** or **Glendevon** courses. For hotel residents a day ticket for the **Kings and Queens** courses was priced at **£16** with a day's golf on the **Princes** and **Glendevon**

courses costing **£10**. Golfers wishing to hire sets of clubs and trolleys can do so through the professional **Ian Marchbank** who can be reached on **(07646) 2231**.

Located approximately midway between **Perth** and **Stirling**, Gleneagles is easily reached by road. The **A9** which in fact links Perth to Stirling is likely to prove of most assistance. Travelling from the **Glasgow** region a combination of the **A80** and the **M80** should be taken to Stirling. Those approaching from further South can avoid Glasgow by following the **A74** and the **M74/M73** joining the **A80** below Stirling. Motoring from **Edinburgh** the best route is to cross the Forth Road Bridge via the **A90** heading for **Dunfermline** and thereafter taking the **A823** road to Auchterarder. Southbound travellers will find the **A9** helpful if coming from the Highlands via **Blair Atholl** and **Pitlochry**. Motoring from **Aberdeen** and the North East of Scotland, the **A92** links Aberdeen to Dundee and Dundee is in turn linked to Perth by the **A85** (dual carriageway all the way). Gleneagles can also be reached by rail, with a bus meeting trains from Gleneagles Station.

Measuring **6452** yards, par 71,the **Kings Course** is the longest of the four, the distance of the others being the **Queens, 5964** yards, par **69**, the **Princes, 4664** yards, par **64**, and the **Glendevon, 5719** yards, par **68**. Perhaps the best known hole at Gleneagles is **Braid's Brawest**, the **13th** on the Kings Course – a tough par four which requires a long straight drive to carry a ridge and a second to a raised and heavily guarded sloping green. Each of the 72 holes at Gleneagles is named, and someone has obviously enjoyed themselves: on the Glendevon Course we have, **Muckle Skelp, Wimplin Wyne, Pass O'Pinkie** and **Dinkie Slap**.

The **Gleneagles Dormy House** is the golfers 19th. It provides superb catering and is open throughout the day. The Player's Bar serves bar snacks and basket suppers which are available between 6pm and 9pm. A luncheon buffet is served in the main restaurant between 11.30 and 3.00pm and an à la carte menu is offered between 7.45pm and 10pm.

Many will have viewed the glories of Gleneagles through the media of television – the BBC Pro-Celebrity Series being staged on several occasions over a combination of the Kings and Queens Course. The most warming though of all is that each one of us is welcome to view its glories first hand. We all have different notion of paradise – a perfect morning, a spirited partner, a Scottish breeze and the fairways of Gleneagles might not be paradise itself but for many golfers it's pretty close.

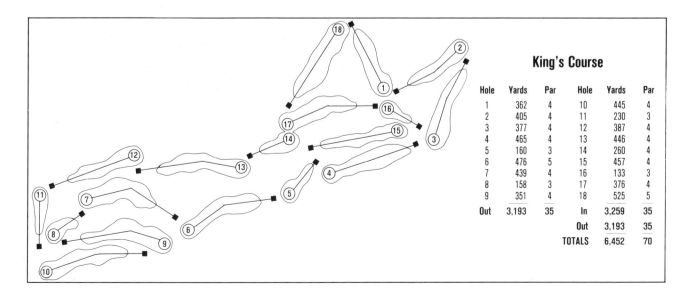

King's Course

Hole	Yards	Par	Hole	Yards	Par
1	362	4	10	445	4
2	405	4	11	230	3
3	377	4	12	387	4
4	465	4	13	446	4
5	160	3	14	260	4
6	476	5	15	457	4
7	439	4	16	133	3
8	158	3	17	376	4
9	351	4	18	525	5
Out	3,193	35	In	3,259	35
			Out	3,193	35
			TOTALS	6,452	70

Perhaps there are two things that strike you most when you arrive at one of the famous golfing links on the east coast of Scotland: the first will almost certainly be the thought 'so this is where it all started' – a feeling that can often leave one slightly numb; the second and equally numb-creating (if there is such a word) is likely to be the thought 'will this wretched wind ever die down?' The famous links at Montrose is just such a place.

Golf has been played on Montrose links since the 16th century and according to the best records it is the fifth oldest course in the world. By 'course' is meant the **Medal Course**, for there are two 18 hole links at Montrose, the Medal and the shorter **Broomfield Course**, the former having altered very little since it was first laid out (by whoever and whenever). In common with St Andrews and Carnoustie Montrose is a public links and although four Golf Clubs play over the two courses, namely, the **Royal Albert, Victoria, Caledonia** and **Mercantile** Clubs, both are run by the Montrose Links Trust who handle all administrative matters. Any written correspondence should be addressed to this body care of **The Secretrary, The Starters Box, Traill Drive, Montrose, Angus D10 8SW**. **Mrs Margaret Stewart** is in fact the Secretary and she may be contacted by telephone on **(0674) 72634**. Also most helpful is the professional **Gary Donovan**, he can be reached on the same telephone number.

Being a public links there are very few restrictions on the times **visitors** can play. Indeed the only one as such is that visitors cannot tee off before 10.30 a.m. on Saturdays and Sundays. The **green fees** are remarkably good value. In 1986 a day ticket to play on the **Medal Course** was priced at £8 during the week and £8.50 at weekends with a single round costing £5.75 midweek and £6 at weekends. To play over the **Broomfield Course** at similar times as above the fees were £4.50 and £5 respectively. Those staying in the area might consider a weekly ticket, in 1986 these were priced at £22 for the **Medal** course and £16.50 for the **Broomfield** Course. Reductions of up to fifty per cent are usually available to junior golfers.

Apart from their length, the **Medal** course measures **6451** yards (par **71**) and the **Broomfield's 4815** yards (par **66**), the two courses differ in other respects. The Broomfield is in fact laid out on the landward side of the Medal and is considerably flatter. With its many undulations the Medal is by far the more testing and it is not surprisingly over this links that the major Championships are held (these have included the **Scottish Amateur Championship**). For twelve of its eighteen holes it follows closely the line of the dunes, though some of its best holes appear at the end of the round: the **16th** ("Gully") being a particularly long par 3 and the **17th** ("Rashes") with its raised green is one of those par fours requiring, as a caddy once put it, "three damned good shots to get up in two"!

As the crow flies Montrose lies approximately midway between St Andrews and Aberdeen. For those of us without wings the **A92** is likely to be of most assistance. Those travelling from the St Andrews region, or indeed from all points south, should head for **Dundee**. The **A92** runs from Dundee to Aberdeen passing though the centre of Montrose. Montrose links lies to the north of the town, east off the **A92** and is well signposted. Anyone approaching from the west (including **Blairgowrie**) can avoid Dundee by heading for **Brechin** and thereafter following the **A935** into Montrose passing Montrose Basin (where in winter you may sight a few pink-footed Arctic geese – quite possibly the only birdies you'll see all day).

As for its 19th hole the catering requirements of visitors are more than adequately met by the Golf Clubs earlier mentioned, each being adjacent to the links.

There are no airs and graces about Montrose, it is what might be described as a 'good honest links'. But if you've come to Scotland to admire the golf Montrose is clearly one that shouldn't be missed.

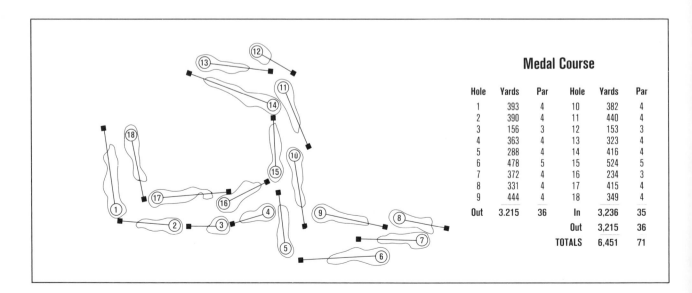

Medal Course

Hole	Yards	Par	Hole	Yards	Par
1	393	4	10	382	4
2	390	4	11	440	4
3	156	3	12	153	3
4	363	4	13	323	4
5	288	4	14	416	4
6	478	5	15	524	5
7	372	4	16	234	3
8	331	4	17	415	4
9	444	4	18	349	4
Out	3.215	36	In	3,236	35
			Out	3,215	36
			TOTALS	6,451	71

CARNOUSTIE

Walter Hagen – a shrewd judge you might think – once described **Carnoustie** as "the greatest course in the British Isles". There are many who would agree with the great man, though doubtless the disciples of **St Andrews** and several honourable gentlemen at **Muirfield** would take leave to differ. Greatest or not, very few would dispute that when the winds blow – as they invariably do in these parts – Carnoustie is the toughest of all our Championship links.

In the days when the Cambells and the Macdonalds were busy slaughtering each other up in the Highlands, down at Carnoustie more civilised pursuits were taking place. Records suggest that golf (or gowf) was being played on the adjoining Barry Links, as early as the **16th** century. The first "official Club" at Carnoustie – today there are six – was founded in 1842 and golf was played over a ten hole course laid out by **Allan Robertson**. **'Old' Tom Morris** came on the scene and extended the links to a full 18 holes, but the present Championship course didn't really begin to take shape until **James Braid** made several alterations in 1926. By 1931 Carnoustie was ready to stage its first **Open Championship**.

As previously mentioned there are presently six Clubs at Carnoustie and play is now over three courses, all of which are publicly owned. Administrative matters are in the hands of the **Carnoustie Golf Links Management Committee** and persons wishing to visit Carnoustie should direct correspondence to the Committee's Secretary, **Mr Richardson**. The full address to write to is The **Carnoustie Golf Links Management Committee, Links Parade, Carnoustie, Tayside**. Contact by telephone can be made on **(0241) 53789**. Starting times must be booked in advance and the above telephone number should also be used to acquire the services of a caddy.

In **1986** the **green fees** to play over the Championship Links were fixed as follows: from Mondays to Fridays £12 for a single round with £14 payable for a full day's golf, while at weekends, £16 for the one round and £18 for the day. A weekly ticket is also available – in 1986 this was priced at £45.

The cluster of Clubs that go to make up Carnoustie's permanent golfing village provide all the ususal amenities for the visiting golfer – golf shops for clothing, equipment and club hire and of course a more than adequate 19th hole.

Travelling to Carnoustie shouldn't present too many problems. For large numbers it will simply be a case of getting over the Firth of Tay and turning right. The Forth Road Bridge and the **M90** link the Edinburgh region with Perth; Perth in turn is linked to Dundee by the **A85** (dual carriageway all the way) and Dundee to Carnoustie by the **A390**. Those on golfing tours will quite likely be coming via St Andrews: the **A91 (A919)** runs from St Andrews towards Dundee, it picks up the **A92** just before the Tay Road Bridge and on crossing the Bridge the **A930** should immediately be joined.

Approaching from northerly directions, the **A92** runs from Aberdeen (and beyond) to within a couple of miles of Carnoustie at Muirdrum, while the **A958** links the town with Forfar. Carnoustie can also be reached by train with connections from Perth, Dundee and Aberdeen.

It isn't only the wind of course that makes Carnoustie such a difficult test. When the Championship tees are in use – or the **Ben Hogan tees** as they are sometimes known – the course stretches close to **7200** yards making it the longest of the 'Open Courses'. From the Club medal tees, **6931** yards is still a formidable proposition. Many courses in America are of similar proportions but anyone expecting the ball to fly through the air as sweetly as it does at Palm Springs or Augusta is in for quite a shock!

Scotland is the land of Burns. It is also the land of 'burns' – streams or rivers anywhere else in the English-speaking world – and Carnoustie is famous for them. The ubiquitous **Barry Burn** and its wee brother **Jocky's Burn** traverse the fairways in the most unfriendly of places, often in front of greens and across the spot you'd ideally like to drive to. More than anything else though, Carnoustie is renowned for its incredibly tough finishing stretch. The **16th**, an exceptionally long 'short hole', and where **Jack Nicklaus** is said to have once needed a driver followed by an 8 iron to get up! The **17th** has the Barry Burn meandering across its fairway making it a particularly difficult driving hole and the **18th** where the Burn crosses in front of the green necessitating one of the most exciting (or nerve-racking) closing shots in golf.

Each of the five Opens held at Carnoustie has produced great Champions – **Tommy Armour** (1931), **Henry Cotton** (1937), **Ben Hogan** (1953), **Gary Player** (1968) and **Tom Watson** (1975). Many consider Hogan's victory in 1953 – he won by four strokes with rounds of 73-71-70-68 – to be the greatest ever performance in a major Championship. There are also those who feel that his final round of 68 represents the true course record. The wind blew that day and Carnoustie's teeth were gnashing. Twenty two years later when Jack Newton scored his 65 Carnoustie was smiling. It was the only Open Hogan ever played in.

Hand on their hearts, no one could describe Carnoustie as picturesque – in fact it's pretty bleak in parts, but on stepping out on to the first tee the sense of history is quite awe-inspiring. Those yet to do battle over the famous links have so far missed out on a unique experience, and, if Walter Hagen was right, the greatest course in the British Isles.

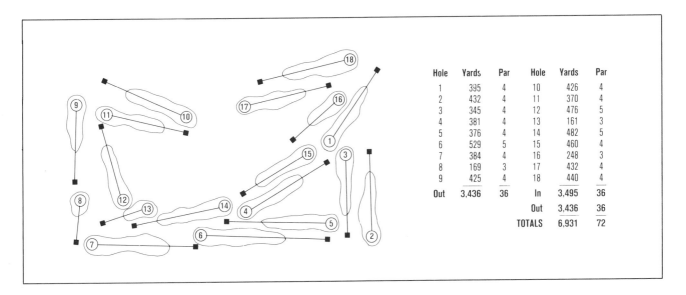

Hole	Yards	Par	Hole	Yards	Par
1	395	4	10	426	4
2	432	4	11	370	4
3	345	4	12	476	5
4	381	4	13	161	3
5	376	4	14	482	5
6	529	5	15	460	4
7	384	4	16	248	3
8	169	3	17	432	4
9	425	4	18	440	4
Out	3,436	36	In	3,495	36
			Out	3,436	36
			TOTALS	6,931	72

GRAMPIAN

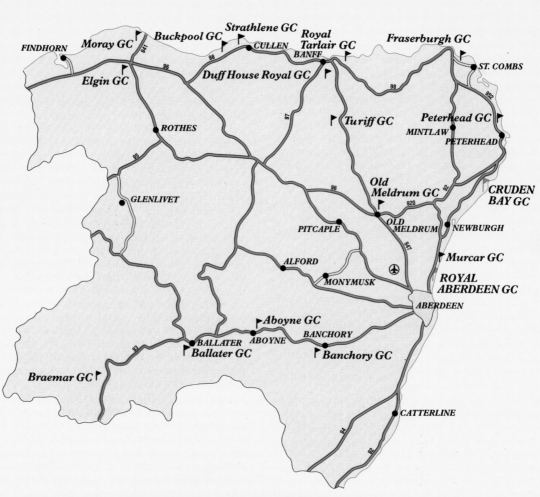

FINDHORN · Moray GC · Buckpool GC · Strathlene GC · CULLEN · Royal Tarlair GC · BANFF · Fraserburgh GC · ST. COMBS

Elgin GC · Duff House Royal GC

ROTHES · Turiff GC · Peterhead GC · MINTLAW · PETERHEAD

GLENLIVET · Old Meldrum GC · CRUDEN BAY GC

PITCAPLE · OLD MELDRUM · NEWBURGH

ALFORD · MONYMUSK · Murcar GC · ROYAL ABERDEEN GC

ABERDEEN

Aboyne GC · ABOYNE · BANCHORY

BALLATER · Ballater GC · Banchory GC

Braemar GC

CATTERLINE

"Maghie"   BURLINGTON GALLERY

Aberdeenshire has contributed more than a few threads to the historical tapestry of Scotland.

In 1562 on the Hill o' Fare, Mary, Queen of Scots, defeated the Earl of Huntly at the Battle of Corrichie. Her finest portrait hangs to this day at Blair's College on the banks of the Dee.

About 300 years later, Prince Albert brought Queen Victoria to their recently acquired estate in the Highlands—Balmoral. Deeside sprang to prominence. The Royal Family still spend summer here. Tullich Lodge, the residence of a gentleman, is a product of this era.

Begun in 1897 by an Aberdeen advocate, the lodge was later enlarged by another Scot who made a comfortable fortune in India. Solidly built of pink-hued granite from a local quarry, in the Scottish Baronial style, it is all crenellations, crowsteps, turret and tower.

Bedrooms, though not large, are finely furnished and very comfortable. All have open views. The sitting-room and the elegant drawing-room, furnished in keeping with the period of the house, overlook the woodland garden towards the Dee or the tree-covered hills of Muick to Lochnagar, immortalized by Byron. Once a volcano, its crater is now a deep loch.

The dining-room is handsomely panelled in mahogany and in perfect proportion to the house. Sparkling silver, crisp linen and fine glass complement the proprietor's cooking. In 1968 Hector Macdonald and Neil Bannister were almost alone in Scotland when they offered a menu without choice for dinner. Classical casseroles and traditional roasts alternate with fresh fish and local game. Vegetables are picked in the garden. The seasons still provide the variety. To appreciate the well-balanced menus and careful cooking guests should stay for more than just a night as do so many regular visitors. Diets or special dishes are a pleasure to prepare—with a little warning!

The friendly little bar with its peat fire is a popular meeting place before and after dinner. Light lunches are served here.

In its dramatic setting of mountain, moor, forest and glen, Tullich Lodge has become not so much an hotel but more a way of life.

Tullich Lodge,
by Ballater,
Aberdeenshire,
Scotland AB3 5SB
Telephone: (0338) 55406

The North East of Scotland was at one time covered by a dense forest of pine broken only by the soaring granite peaks of the Grampian mountain range. It was the home of the savage Caledonian tribe, a land where wolves hunted in packs. Nowadays very little of the forest remains. As for the wolves, most of them were killed by the Caledonians, but then unfortunately most of the Caledonians were killed by the Romans. No wonder they called life "nasty, brutish and short"!

Switch scenes – forget the wolves, the savages and the Romans – we are in Aberdeen, having just spent several months on an oil rig being battered by mighty waves and even mightier winds and we are desperate for a game of golf. Where should we go?

Aberdeen is an excellent base to commence a golfing tour of the region. **Balgownie** and **Murcar** lie right on the town's doorstep and they are unquestionably two of the finest courses in Scotland. Balgownie links is the home of the 200 year old **Royal Aberdeen Golf Club** and is featured a few pages on. Murcar is situated some 2 miles north of Aberdeen along the **A92**. Although not particularly long, measuring 6240 yards, the often strong winds can cause it to be a very difficult test. It should be possible to arrange a game at Murcar on any day of the week although the tees are normally reserved for Members on Wednesday mornings, before 10 a.m. on Sundays and between 4.30 p.m. and 6.30 p.m. daily during the summer. Being a popular course it is probably a good idea to telephone the Club before setting off. Green fees in 1986 were £12 weekdays, £14 at weekends.

Looking to travel beyond Aberdeen, the golfer is faced with two equally appealing choices – he can either head north along the coast towards Cruden Bay, or alternatively head inland along the A93. The latter choice broadly involves following the path of the River Dee and will take the traveller through some truly magnificent scenery. The 18 hole courses at **Banchory, Aboyne, Ballater** and **Braemar** all lie along this road and not surprisingly boast spectacular settings. Each welcomes visitors seven days a week at green fees representing excellent value, a day's golf costing around the £5-£8 mark.

Should one choose to journey northwards, **Cruden Bay** is clearly the first stopping point. However, not for us though, we will carry on simply because it too is featured on a later page. The fishing ports of **Peterhead** and **Fraserburgh** both have interesting seaside courses at which getting a game shouldn't be too difficult (nor expensive) once again though, the sea winds can make scoring tricky.

From fishing ports to Georgian elegance – the **Duff House Royal Golf Club** at Macduff is looked over by an impressive baroque-style Georgian mansion. The course too has a touch of class, being designed by the McKenzie brothers immediately prior to their constructing the famous Augusta National course in America. Duff House's many two-tiered greens clearly bear the McKenzie hallmark. Visitors are always made welcome but as the Club often uses a booking sheet system, telephoning in advance is to be recommended. The fees for a full day's golf in 1986 were **£6.50** midweek, **£7.50** at weekends with a reduced rate of **£4.50** in winter. Also worth noting in the area is **Royal Tarlair** at Banff. A fairly short seaside course but like Duff House it is always very well kept and similarly not too hard on the pocket. There is also an excellent 18 holes to be had at **Turriff**, set in scenic surroundings approximately 10 miles south of Banff along the A947. Green fees in 1986 at Turriff were £6 per day during the week, £7 at weekends.

Reverting to the windswept coast, there are two fine courses situated either side of Buckie – **Strathlene** to the east and **Buckpool** to the west. Both lie pretty open to the elements and both provide superb views of the Moray Firth. Again visitors should be able to secure a game most days of the week.

Crossing the salmon-filled River Spey at Fochabers the City of **Elgin** is soon reached. There aren't too many cathedrals in this part of the world but Elgin, the capital of Morayshire, has a beautiful one that dates from the 13th century. It also possesses one of the finest inland golf courses in the north of Scotland. A mile or so south of the city and some distance away from the often fierce coastal winds, the course is sheltered by many pines and silver birch trees. Inevitably, it occupies a glorious setting with distant purple hills forming a spectacular horizon. A day's golf at Elgin in 1986 was priced at £7.50 during the week (£4.50 for a single round) and £8.50 at weekends. Visitors should note that the tees are usually reserved between 1 p.m. and 2.30 p.m. during the week and between 5 p.m. and 7 p.m. on Saturdays and Sundays.

Returning one final time to the coast and Lossiemouth, **the Moray Golf Club** has two outstanding links courses, the 'Old Course' which is approaching its centenary, and the 'New Course', less than 10 years old. Whilst the fighter aircraft from nearby RAF Lossiemouth may occasionally irritate, it would be difficult to find a finer combination of superb natural golf and scenic splendour. The visitor is always welcome, the fees in 1986 to play over the Old Course were **£7** per day during the week, **£10** at weekends with **£5** and **£7** respectively the cost of a day's golf on the New.

Aboyne G.C.	(0339) 2328
Ballater G.C.	(0338) 55567
Banchory G.C.	(03302) 2365
Braemar G.C.	(03383) 618
Buckpool G.C.	(0542) 32236
Cruden Bay G.C.	(0779) 812285
Duff House Royal G.C.	(026 12) 2062
Elgin G.C.	(0343) 2338
Fraserburgh G.C.	(0346) 28287
Moray G.C.	(034381) 2018
Murcar G.C.	(0224) 704354
Old Meldrum G.C.	(06512) 2212
Peterhead G.C.	(0779) 72149
Royal Aberdeen G.C.	(0224) 702571
Royal Tarlair G.C.	(0261) 32897
Turriff G.C.	(0888) 68789

There are said to be over sixty golf courses listed in Aberdeen's Yellow Pages. With this in mind one may assume a game of golf is high on the list of priorities of most Aberdonians. However, one fact that may be overlooked is that there are some pretty keen players invariably itching for a round located on the oil rigs that lie off-shore. Now I would imagine that the rig isn't the best place to keep in the swing – so to speak – unless of course one takes to diving into the North Sea aiming somewhat tirelessly at the frothy fairways beneath. As winds and waves clutch the rigs – what better place from which to look forward to a visit to the mainland with a day on one of the delightful Grampian golf courses?

As with many boom industries – there are certain implications for the community. While Aberdeen has seen tremendous growth of late the prices charged in hotels and restaurants are fairly steep. It may therefore be an idea to stay outside the city. If business commitments do not allow this possibility then the best hotels to consider include **The Bucksburn Moat House (0224) 713911** (I cannot say whether the name is supposed to emphasise a waste of money – but it certainly isn't cheap!) Two other quality if modern hotels are **The Holdiday Inn (0224) 770011** and **The Shean Dhu Hotel (0224) 725252**. The restaurants and facilities of all these hotels are good, especially the Holiday Inn. If you prefer to eat outside your hotel then try some of the excellent seafood offered at **Atlantis (0224) 591403**. Two other hotels to note include **The Atholl (0224) 323505** in Kings Gate and **The New Marcliffe (0224) 321371** in Queens Road – both strongly recommended by the golfing fraternity.

Seeemingly miles from the busy Aberdeen Airport but actually most convenient for it lies Newburgh. Here the **Udny Arms (03586) 444** is ideally situated and a total contrast to the modern hotels of Aberdeen. Views over The Ythan Estuary and traditional comfort make the spot ideal for golfers endeavouring to play at Cruden Bay. In Old Meldrum, also convenient for golfing at Cruden Bay as well as its own more locally situated course is the splendid Meldrum House Hotel **(06512) 2294** – a perfect place to stay. Further up the coast one reaches the charming fishing port – Peterhead. Here **The Waterside Inn** may not have the quality of Berkshire's cuisine, but in its own way this establishment is thoroughly good. **Jade Gardens** is another answer for golfers wishing to eat out after playing a game. In Mintlaw another hotel restaurant is worth noting on this occasion that of the **Saplinbrae House (0771) 23515**. While sneaking around the golf courses of this area one or two bars to visit. On the way to Cruden Bay from Aberdeen try **The Viking** or alternatively if you are heading towards the north coast of this gorgeous region then **The Tufted Bank (0346) 52481** is an excellent place to have a drink or a bar snack, come to think of it, you may as well stay there – it's particularly good!

There are a number of outstanding golf courses on this stretch of coast and some places to inhabit while playing them may include **The Country Hotel (02612) 5353** in the High Street of Banff, offering some golfing packages, or alternatively **The Seafield Arms Hotel (0542) 40791** in Cullen. Following the fairways around the coast one arrives in the busy market town of Elgin. Here there are a number of hotels, **The Eight Acres Hotel (0343) 3077** is worth trying while south, away from the coast in Rothes, **The Rothes Glen (03403) 254** is particularly relaxing. In Findhorn, another establishment that one should have a peep at is **The Crown and Anchor** – ideal for a post round beverage.

This region is well known for its castles as well as its oil and fish. One can visit the beautiful grounds of Balmoral while you know who is not in town, while the castles of Brodie, Spynie and Cawdor are all romantically historic edifices. Another castle to see is Crathes – beware of the Green Lady. Another attribute of this area is of course whisky – visit Glenlivet, **The Blairfindy Lodge Hotel (08073) 376** here is most comfortable and has a fine restaurant.

Returning south having played some splendid golf on the Highland courses the greedy golfer is anxious to enjoy still more of his passioned sport. Stopping in Pitcaple to catch the breath in **The Pittodrie House Hotel (04676) 202** – more charming countryside and an excellent restaurant. Another striking location is found at Kildrummy by Alford. Here the **Kildrummy Castle (03365) 288** is simply delightful – superb views over the thirteenth century castle. One further thought here – **The Pine Lodge (0339) 2253** is another tranquil base from which to attack the surrounding courses.

Heading relentlessly south – more splendid golf and in **The Grant Arms**, Monymusk, a fine establishment in which to celebrate an eagle (this may of course be a Golden Eagle seen in the skies nearby – but an eagle just the same!).

Ballater, and the really splendid **Tullich Lodge (0338) 55406** a splendid mansion at which to stay – no golfer should play badly after staying and equally significantly dining at this residence. Less expensive but another sumptuous setting this time overlooking the golf course and The Dee, **The Darrock Learg Hotel (0338) 55443**. Another restaurant to sample in this superb seaside village is found in **The Green Inn (0338) 55701** – a good value bistro. Incidentally Royal Deeside is the home of The Royal Highland Gathering which takes place in Braemar.

In Aboyne more golf and the **Pine Lodge (0339) 2253** should suit anyone wishing to stay nearby. Alternative accommodation is found in and around Banchory. In Raemoir, **The Raemoir House (03302) 4884** stands out – most welcoming. While the Tor-na-Coille **(03302) 2242** has excellent facilities and is also charming.

With head low almost distraught golfers realise their two weeks' golf have simply flown by – **The Crill Inn**, Catterline and further thoughts of golf in Grampian. But as the helicopter returns to the rig more strokes into the frothy fairways that lie below seem inevitable.

Pittodrie House Hotel
Pitcaple, Inverurie, Tel: (04676) 202
Standing in its own grounds Pittodrie House is personally run by Theo Smith whose family have owned the estate since 1900. All rooms have private bath/shower, TV, tea and coffee making facilities. Other facilities include squash, tennis, croquet, snooker, clay pigeon shooting and golf. Fishing and shooting can be arranged.

Atlantis Restaurant
145 Crown Street,
Aberdeen
Tel: (0224) 591403
An excellent seafood restaurant in the centre of Aberdeen. Lobster is the speciality here, prepared fresh from the tank. Its very good reputation is thoroughly deserved by this particularly popular place. Please book in advance.

THE 17TH: COLONEL'S BED TO JOHN O'GROATS

GRAMPIAN

Aboyne G.C. (9)
Aboyne (0339) 2328

Auchenblae G.C. (9)
Auchenblae, Laurencekirk
(05612) 407

Auchmill G.C. (9)
Auchmill

Ballater G.C. (18)
Ballater (0338) 55567

Balnagask G.C. (18)
Aberdeen (0224) 516407

Banchory G.C. (18)
Kinneski, Banchory (03302) 2365

Braemar G.C. (18)
Braemar (03383) 618

Buckpool G.C. (18)
Buckie (0542) 32236

Cruden Bay G.C. (9+18)
Cruden Bay, Peterhead
(0779) 812285

Cullen G.C. (18)
Cullen, Buckie (0542) 40685

Duff House Royal G.C. (18)
Banff (02612) 2062

Dufftown G.C. (9)
Dufftown (0340) 20325

Fraserburgh G.C. (18)
Philarth, Fraserburgh
(0346) 28287

Haglehead G.C. (18+18)
Aberdeen (0224) 317336

Huntly G.C. (18)
Huntly (0466) 2643

Inverallochy G.C. (18)
Inverallochy (03465) 2324

Inverurie G.C. (18)
Inverurie (0467) 24080

Keith G.C. (18)
Keith (05422) 2469

Kings Links G.C. (18)
Aberdeen (0224) 632269

Kintore G.C. (9)
Kintore, Inverurie (0467) 32631

McDonald G.C. (18)
Ellon (0358) 20576

Murcar G.C. (18)
Bridge of Don, Aberdeen
(0224) 704354

Newburgh-on-Ythan G.C. (9)
Newburgh (03586) 389

Nigg Bay G.C. (18)
Balnagask (0224) 871286

Peterhead G.C. (9+18)
Peterhead (0779) 72149

Royal Aberdeen G.C. (18+18)
Bridge of Don, Aberdeen
(0224) 702571

Royal Tarlair G.C. (18)
Macduff (0251) 32897

Spey Bay G.C. (18)
Spey Bay, Fochabers
(0343) 820424

Stonehaven G.C. (18)
Cowie, Stonehaven (0569) 62124

Strathlene G.C. (18)
Buckie (0542) 31798

Tarland G.C. (9)
Tarland, Aboyne (033981) 413

Torphins G.C. (9)
Torphins, Bauchory
(033982) 493

Turriff G.C. (18)
Rosehall, Turriff (0888) 62745

Westhill G.C. (18)
Westhill, Skene (0224) 740159

HIGHLAND

Abernethy G.C. (9)
Nethybridge (047982) 305

Alness G.C. (9)
Alness (0349) 883877

Askernish G.C. (9)
Askernish, South Dist

Boat of Garten G.C. (18)
Boat of Garten (047983) 351

Brora G.C. (18)
Brora (048) 21417

Carrbridge G.C. (9)
Carrbridge (047986) 674

Elgin G.C. (18)
Hardhillock, Elgin (0343) 2338

Forres G.C. (18)
Muiryshade, Forres (0309) 72949

Fort Augustus G.C. (9)
Fort Augustus

Fortrose & Rosemarkie G.C. (18)
Fortrose (0381) 20529
Fort William G.C. (18)
Torlundy, Fort William
(0397) 4464

Gairoch G.C. (9)
Gairloch (0445) 2407

Garmouth & Kingston G.C. (18)
Garmouth, Fochabers
(034387) 388

Golspie G.C. (18)
Golspie (040830) 3266

Grantown-on-Spey G.C. (18)
Grantown-on-Spey (0479) 2079

Hopeman G.C. (18)
Hopeman (0343) 830578

Invergordon G.C. (9)
Invergordon (0349) 852116

Inverness G.C. (18)
Inverness (0463) 239882

Kingussie G.C. (18)
Kingussie (05402) 374

Lybster G.C. (9)
Lybster (05932) 359

Moray G.C. (18+18)
Lossiemouth, Moray
(034381) 2338

Muir of Ord G.C. (18)
Muir of Ord (0463) 870825

Nairn G.C. (18)
Nairn (0667) 53208

Nairn Dunbar G.C. (18)
Nairn (0667) 52741

Newtonmore G.C. (18)
Newtonmore (05403) 328

Orkney G.C. (18)
Kirkwall, Orkney (0856) 2457

Reay G.C. (18)
by Thurso (084781) 288

Royal Dornoch G.C. (18)
Dornoch (0862) 810219

Sconser G.C. (9)
Sconser, Isle of skye (0478) 2277

Shetland G.C. (18)
Dale, Shetland (059584) 369

Stornoway G.C. (18)
Stornoway, Isle of Lewis
(0851) 2240

Strathpeffer Spa G.C. (18)
Strathpeffer (0997) 21219

Stromness G.C. (18)
Stromness, Orkney
(0856) 850772

Tain G.C. (18)
Tain (0862) 2314

Tarbat G.C. (9)
Portmahomack (086287) 519

Thurso G.C. (18)
Newlands of Geise, Thurso
(0847) 63807

Torrean G.C. (18)
Inverness (0463) 237543

Western Isle G.C. (9)
Tobermory, Isle of Mull
(0688) 2020

Wick G.C. (18)
Reiss, Wick (0955) 2726

RAEMOIR HOUSE HOTEL

The Raemoir House Hotel located sixteen and a half miles South West of Aberdeen, is delightfully situated in spacious grounds, liberally wooded and sheltered from the northerly winds by the Hill of Fare which rises some 1,500 feet behind the house.

The main mansion was built in the 18th century and extended at later dates. Immediately, to the rear of the Mansion is the Ha' Hoose adjudged to be the finest example of this type of building in existence, and which has now been officially included in the list of buildings of special architectural and historic interest. There are 24 principal bedrooms and suites with private bathrooms. A great many of these rooms face South, with fine views of the surrounding countryside. The furnishings are in a style in keeping with the house, many of the rooms having valuable tapestried walls. The hotel is centrally heated throughout, fully licensed amd open all the year round. There is spacious parking around the hotel and a private Helipad is also available.

3,500 acres of low ground shooting adjoins the hotel and fishing, shooting and stalking are available by arrangement. Many beautiful walks may be taken in the wooded grounds of the hotel. An 18 hole golf course is situated nearby at Banchory. The Raemoir Hotel offers ideal conditions for a restful holiday in the luxurious surroundings of a country house with good food, perfect service and the personal attention of the resident Director.

RAEMOIR HOUSE HOTEL
Banchory,
Kincardineshire.
Tel: (03302) 2622

One often reads of famous Golf Clubs having been founded in local hostelries – **Deal** (The Black Horse), **Crail** (The Golf Inn) and **Hoylake** (The Royal) to name but three, well the birth of **Cruden Bay** apparently took place during a meeting in the North of Scotland Bank – one presumes a much more sober affair! The precise date of the meeting was **16th June 1898** and in March the following year the Cruden Bay Hotel and Golf Course were opened.

The Hotel (alas long since demolished) and the 18 hole golf course were originally both owned by the Great North of Scotland Railway Company. Within a month of their opening the company staged a professional tournament which attracted many of the day's leading players including **Harry Vardon** (then Open Champion), **James Braid** and **Ben Sayers**. The event proved an outstanding success with Vardon taking the first prize of **£30**. Cruden Bay was firmly on the golfing map.

Since 1961 the Club's full title has been the **Cruden Bay Golf and Country Club** with its full address being **Aulton Road, Cruden Bay, Peterhead, Aberdeenshire.** In addition to the 18 hole Championship Course there is also a well-kept 9 hole short course, the **St Olaf**, opened in 1968.

The present Secretary (or Golf Manager) is **Mr Ian McPherson**. He may be contacted via the above address and by telephone on **(0779) 812285**. The Club's professional, **Harry Bannerman**, can be reached on **(0779) 812414**. Casual **visitors** are welcome at Cruden Bay, although not surprisingly certain restrictions apply during Saturdays and Sundays. It is generally advisable to telephone the Club at weekends to check whether the tees have been reserved for any competition or, as may be the case during holiday periods, a starting sheet system is being operated. Visitors should also note that they are not permitted to play the 18 hole course between 4.30 pm and 6.30 pm on Wednesdays and that at weekends, unless accompanied by a Member, handicap certificates must be provided. No specific restrictions relate to the St Olaf course.

In **1986** the **green fee** to play on the Championship course was priced at **£8** for a weekday ticket, with **£10** payable at weekends. A week's golf could be purchased for **£35** and a full fortnight for **£45**. For juniors (under 18) the respective rates were **£3, £4, £15** and **£20**. A day's golf on the St Olaf course could be obtained for **£4** during the week and **£5** at weekends (£2.50 and £3 for juniors). Further reductions were also available to juniors aged under 14.

Cruden Bay is situated on Scotland's Buchan Coast, some 23 miles north east of Aberdeen and seven miles south of the old whaling port of Peterhead. The Golf Course itself has a dramatic setting with nearby **Slains Castle** providing a rather eerie backdrop. **Bram Stoker** who spent some time in these parts is reputed to have been inspired by the castle when writing his **Dracula** stories.

Fortunately the rest of the surrounding countryside bears little resemblance to Transylvania (wherever it may be) and strangers should find travelling in the area a pleasant experience. The best route when journeying from the south is probably by way of the **A92** coastal road which runs from **Dundee** via **Montrose** and through **Aberdeen**. One should leave the **A92** near **Newburgh** and follow the **A975** direct to Cruden Bay. The **A92** approaches from the North via **Fraserburgh** and **Peterhead**.

Originally laid out by **Thomas Simpson**, Cruden Bay is very much a traditional Scottish links of fairly medium length, being around the **6400** yards mark (or as the score card will tell you, a little over **5800 metres**). Par is a fairly tight **70** (s.s.s. 71) with the amateur course record standing at 67. From the ladies tees the course measures **5761** yards (par being **74**). A good old Scottish Burn is a predominant feature of the course affecting several of the holes while the beach too (if one is a little wayward) can come into play around the 14th and 15th. The two par fives on the course are genuine fives and as a rule accurate approach play as opposed to sheer length is likely to determine the quality of scoring. As one might expect given its geography the wind is often a major factor and the golfer that can master the low run-up shot to the subtly-contoured greens will be on to a winner. The magnificent views over the Bay of Cruden naturally add to the pleasure of the round.

The Clubhouse at Cruden Bay has the kind of atmosphere one comes to expect in this part of the world – friendly, and casual dress may be worn at all times. Meals are served throughout the day with lunches, high teas, dinners and some delightful steak suppers being offered in addition to bar snacks.

South of Hadrian's Wall Cruden Bay is probably not as well known as it ought to be. The legions who arrange their golfing trips around the more traditional favourites often miss out on some of Scotland's finest courses. Cruden Bay should be included in anyone's itinerary – it is a magnificent course and perhaps of equal importance, a place where the warmest of welcomes can be guaranteed.

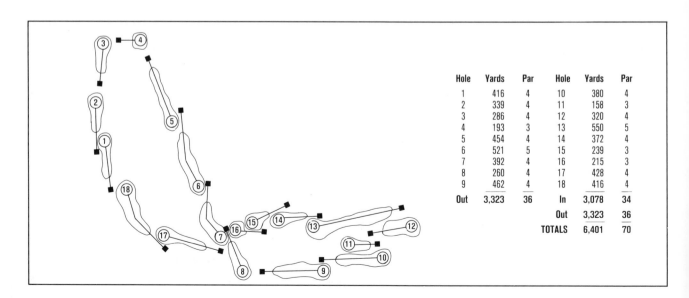

Hole	Yards	Par	Hole	Yards	Par
1	416	4	10	380	4
2	339	4	11	158	3
3	286	4	12	320	4
4	193	3	13	550	5
5	454	4	14	372	4
6	521	5	15	239	3
7	392	4	16	215	3
8	260	4	17	428	4
9	462	4	18	416	4
Out	3,323	36	In	3,078	34
			Out	3,323	36
			TOTALS	6,401	70

ROYAL ABERDEEN

Founded in **1780, Royal Aberdeen** is the sixth oldest Golf Club in the world. For the first thirty five years of its existence the Club was known as **The Society of Golfers at Aberdeen** with membership of the Society being determined by ballot. They were clearly a meticulous group of gentlemen, for in **1783** they became the first to introduce the five minute limit on searching for golf balls. A sensible idea you may think, but one that has caused the modern day Aberdeen Golfer much distress – a subject to which I shall return in due course.

In **1815** on the eve of the Battle of Waterloo the Society changed its name to the Aberdeen Golf Club and in 1903 the 'Royal' prefix was bestowed on the Club. Originally the members played over a strip of common land between the Rivers Don and Dee but in the second half of the 19th century the Club acquired its own course at **Balgownie** on the northern side of the River. Today Balgownie Links is regarded as one of Scotland's greatest Championship courses.

Mr. A.W. Baird is the Secretary at Royal Aberdeen, he may be contacted by telephone on **(0224) 648797**. All written correspondence should be addressed to the Secretary at **Royal Aberdeen Golf Club, Bridge of Don, Aberdeen. Mr R.A. MacAskill** is the Club's professional and he may be reached on **(0224) 702221**.

Visitors are made extremely welcome at Royal Aberdeen and they may play at Balgownie on any day of the week with the exception of most Saturday and Sunday mornings. The **green fees** for 1986 were set at **£15** per day during the week with **£11** for a single round. A flat rate of **£15** was applied at weekends.

Travelling to Aberdeen is made fairly straightforward by the **A92**. From the south this road passes along the coast from **Dundee** via **Arbroath, Montrose** and **Stonehaven** to Aberdeen. It also connects the town to **Fraserburgh** in the North. Those approaching from the north west should find the **A96** helpful (it in fact runs directly from **Inverness**). Other roads which may prove of assistance are the **A947** from **Oldmeldrum** and the **A93** which links Aberdeen to **Perth** and passes through **Blairgowrie**. The links itself is situated 2 miles north of Aberdeen and can be sighted immediately to the right after crossing the River Don.

From its medal tees Balgownie measures **6372** yards par **70** with the forward tees reducing the length to **6104** yards, par **69**. Although perhaps not overly long the course is fairly open to the elements and the wind can often make a mockery of some of the distances. There is also a considerable spread of gorse and the rough can be very punishing. It should be added that there are no fewer than ninety-two bunkers – ten of which appear on the par three 8th! Balgownie has the traditional 'out and back' links layout, the front nine hugging the shore and the back nine returning on the landside towards the Clubhouse.

The outward nine is perhaps the more interesting of the two halves, the eminent golf writer **Sam McKinlay** was moved to say: "There are few courses in these islands with a better, more testing, more picturesque outward nine than Balgownie." However, the most difficult hole on the course is possibly the last hole, a lengthy par four, well bunkered and usually played into the teeth of the prevailing wind.

Royal Aberdeen has played host to a number of major events. Both the **Scottish Amateur** and the **Northern Open Championship** are regularly played over Balgownie Links. Numerous exhibition matches have also taken place, participants have included Tom Morris Junior, Harold Vardon, James Braid, John H Taylor, Walter Hagen and Henry Cotton.

I now return to the matter of the five minute rule. In the opening paragraph, I mentioned how in 1783 the Aberdeen Golfers had introduced the five minute limit on searching for lost balls. Well somebody somewhere it seems didn't approve and 200 years later a plague of crows was sent to deliver retribution. Throughout the long summers of 1983 and 1984 the crows determined that no one should search for his ball. They descended on the links stealing Titleists and Top-Flites, Pinnacles and Penfolds. Several Members had more than one ball stolen in a round. Use of the larger American ball was encouraged but alas to no avail. Even a crow trap was built but still they plundered. Then just as suddenly as they came, they left, never it is presumed to return. Sanity restored, Balgownie became once more one of Britain's friendliest links.

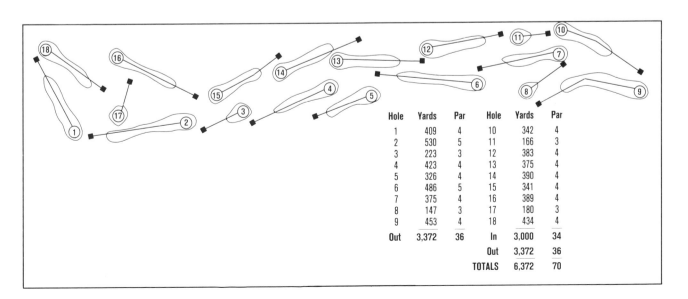

Hole	Yards	Par	Hole	Yards	Par
1	409	4	10	342	4
2	530	5	11	166	3
3	223	3	12	383	4
4	423	4	13	375	4
5	326	4	14	390	4
6	486	5	15	341	4
7	375	4	16	389	4
8	147	3	17	180	3
9	453	4	18	434	4
Out	**3,372**	**36**	**In**	**3,000**	**34**
			Out	**3,372**	**36**
			TOTALS	**6,372**	**70**

HIGHLAND

KINLOCHBERVIE

Thurso GC

Wick GC

LYBSTER

GOLSPIE
Brora GC
Golspie GC
ROYAL DORNOCH GC
DORNOCH
Tain GC

AULTBEA
DUNDONNELL
Strathpeffer Spa GC
Fortrose and Rosemarkie GC
NAIRN GC
Nairn Dunbar GC
Gairloch GC
GAIRLOCH
ACHNASSEN
NAIRN
MUIR OF ORD
Inverness GC
INVERNESS
ADVIE
GRANTOWN-ON-SPEY
Fort Augustus GC
BOAT OF GARTEN
Boat-of-Garten GC
AVIEMORE
Kingussie GC
KINGUSSIE
Newtonmore GC
ARISAIG
FORT WILLIAM
Fort William GC
BALLACHULLISH

W. HAY *"The Caddy"* **BURLINGTON GALLERY**

TULCHAN LODGE

Tulchan Lodge commands impressive views over the Spey Valley and was built in 1906 as the fishing and shooting lodge for the 22,000 acre Tulchan Estate.

The Lodge has recently been entirely refurbished to a standard of comfort and luxury that would meet the demands of any of the famous and discerning Edwardians, including King Edward VII himself, who used to visit Tulchan to shoot and fish. Now the Lodge is open from April through January not only for sportsmen but also for today's discerning traveller, to live the atmosphere of a bygone age. The beautiful scenery of sparkling mountain rivers, pine forests and open moorland provide a wonderful setting in which to spend a relaxing holiday.

Tulchan is the ideal centre for visiting north-east Scotland, an area steeped in history, with a profusion of ancient castles and stately homes; nearby is Cawdor Castle—immortalised by Shakespeare's "Macbeth", and Culloden Moor—the site of the battle in which Bonnie Prince Charlie was defeated in 1746. To the north lies the Moray Firth coastline with its dramatic cliffs, quaint fishing villages and a scattering of excellent golf courses. To the east are country parks and gardens set amidst undulating countryside. To the south is Deeside with Balmoral and all its royal connections. To the west are the rugged mountains and lochs which characterise the Scottish Highlands, and all round throughout the summer months kilted competitors perform their ritual sports of tossing the caber and throwing the hammer at the traditional Highland Gatherings.

The Lodge is in the midst of the Highland malt whisky distilling country where the unique whisky heritage trail provides the opportunity for visitors to inspect the working distilleries and sample their potent brew.

You are unlikely to find anywhere in Scotland more comfortable to stay than Tulchan Lodge, with its magnificent collection of paintings and sporting firearms; the splendid panelled hall and library, elegant drawing room and a billiards room with full size table.

The eleven bedrooms are each individual in size and character, one is a garden cottage suite in the grounds ideal as a retreat, and all have en-suite bathrooms with showers.

Two attractive dining rooms have tables gleaming with silver candelabra and crystal glass. Home cooking provides Scottish and International set menus with an emphasis

on prime Scottish beef and lamb, game from the Estate, fresh local seafoods, lobster and langoustine, as well as vegetables fresh from the garden. All this is complemented by one of the finest wine cellars in Scotland.

The young staff at Tulchan provide the highly personalised service which can only be possible in a country house of this style and character.

Tulchan Lodge,
Advie, Grantown-on-Spey,
Morayshire PH26 3PW
Telephone:(08075) 200 & 261
Telex: 75405 (TULCAN G)

Mist-covered mountains and bottomless lochs, bagpipes, whisky and haggis. I doubt whether there is a more romantic place in the world than the Highlands of Scotland. I doubt also that there is a place quite so shatteringly beautiful.

For administrative purposes, and for our purposes come to that, the **Highland** Region, as opposed to the 'Highlands', extends from the Cairngorms northwards, encompassing the Great Glen and the Western Isles. Of course, where there is land in Scotland there is golf and though this be a wild and somewhat remote part of the country it nonetheless has its share of golfing gems – and more than that, in the minds of many, it has in **Royal Dornoch** the finest of them all.

As well as its gems, the region has a number of golf's genuine outposts, no more so than the **Gairloch Golf Club** situated in the far west of Scotland with views across to the Isle of Skye. There are 9 holes at Gairloch, each wonderfully named. The 6th, however, baffles me – "Westward Ho!" is its title?! The 9th though has more of a Celtic ring to it, "Mo Dhachaidh". There is no Sunday golf at Gairloch though visitors can play at all other times, £35 being the cost of a day's golf in 1986. Others in the 'lonely category' include the 9 holer at **Fort Augustus** on the edge of Loch Ness and the 18 holes at **Fort William**, a moorland course, laid out in the shadows of Ben Nevis. Both can be reached from Inverness via the **A82**.

In the south of Highland, the area around Aviemore has become an increasingly popular holiday retreat, particularly for winter sports enthusiasts. However, whilst the skis must go on the roof, the golf clubs can fit in the boot, and there are five or six courses at hand each of which possesses a truly glorious setting. Picking two of them, the **Kingussie** and **Boat of Garten** Golf Clubs lie either side of Aviemore close to the **A9** (the road that links Perth with Inverness). Both have spectacular 18 hole courses at which visitors are always welcome, the green fees being around the £5 mark. Neither course is particularly long, though the hills at Kingussie and the narrow fairways and small greens at Boat of Garten can make scoring extremely difficult and you are more likely to see eagles than score one. At Boat of Garten you may also catch a glimpse of one of the famous ospreys.

Inverness as the so-called "Capital of the Highlands" is where many may choose to spend a day or two – the Loch Ness monster lives nearby and the famous 'fields of destruction' at Culloden Moor are only a few miles to the east. Golfers may wish to note the town's 18 hole course situated just south of the town centre, fees here in 1986 being £8 midweek, £10 at weekends. **Nairn's** Championship links (see feature page) lies 16 miles from Inverness and shouldn't be missed (nor for that matter should the town's other course, **Nairn Dunbar**, good value at around £6 a game), while to the north, or the other side of the Moray Firth, lie a series of attractive propositions.

On the Chanonry Peninsula linked to Inverness by way of the Kessock Bridge, the **A9** and the **A832**, is the flattish links course of **Fortrose and Rosemarkie** – well worth a visit, although lunchtime and early evenings are best avoided. **Strathpeffer Spa**, a moorland course, is the prettiest of stepping stones for those heading north of Inverness along the A9. A day's golf at **Strathpeffer Spa** (try saying it when you've had one too many!) was priced at £4.50 in 1986. Still heading northwards the **A9** passes through the peaceful town of **Tain** and its 18-hole golf course at which a game can be enjoyed for around £6, but by now most will be itching to reach Dornoch.

Having played **Royal Dornoch** (also featured a few pages on), many, Tom Watson included, find it difficult to tear themselves away, but there are two excellent courses a short distance to the north, **Golspie** and **Brora** that are decidedly worth visiting. Both are testing links courses set in the most majestic surroundings with views to distant hills and along a spectacular coast. Brora in fact stretches out right alongside 3 miles of deserted sandy beach. Being so far north golf can be played at absurdly late hours and at both, the fees in 1986 were a mere £5.

Beyond Brora we really are getting remote! However, the **A9** makes it all the way to John O'Groats. There is an 18 hole course at **Wick** measuring close to 6000 yards, where the fees are only £4 per day. But the furthest north is **Thurso**, not too far from the Dounreay Power Station. I should imagine it gets pretty cold up there, but if you do make it, and are looking for fresh challenges then there is always the golf club in the Arctic – fittingly called the '**Polar Bear Club**' – and which, I suppose it goes without saying, was founded by Scotsmen!

For centuries whisky was made by Highlanders for Highlanders; about a hundred years ago it crossed the Border to capture the flavour of Londoners. Today its appeal is worldwide. And like whisky, golf is now enjoyed worldwide – what better place to play the game and sample the malt, ideally at one and the same time. Remember well the words of William Lithgow: "He that eateth well, drinketh well; he that drinketh well, sleepeth well; he that sleepeth well, sinneth not; he that sinneth not goes straight through Purgatory to Paradise." This sounds ideal and no doubt the place in question is Dornoch upon the first tee – with, one presumes, a bottle in one's bag.

The Scottish Highlands are renowned for their beauty. Golden eagles grace the air and ospreys soar over the lochs; trout and salmon abound; shooting and stalking are common. The tradition of suspicion also hangs in the air. Cawdor Castle in all its mediaeval beauty was scene of Shakespeare's Macbeth and the murder of the natural order in King Duncan; Glencoe where the hosting McDonalds were murdered in their sleep and Culloden where the Duke of Cumberland viciously concluded the efforts of the '45 and the aspirations of Bonnie Prince Charlie. But instead of this unhappy talk, consider these thoughts: Cawdor's grounds hid the most beautiful wild gardens as well as a pitch and putt course. In the skiing centre of Aviemore the best place to start one's trip is likely to be in the **Dalfaber Golf and Country Club (0479) 811244** – the restaurants all complement the free spirit (not whisky) one finds in Scotland. South West of Aviemore and the Newtonmore and Kingussie Golf Club – two thoughts here: in Newtonmore, **The Highlander (05403) 341** is modern but has colourful entertainment, some Highland evenings – pipers, haggis et al. In Kingussie a restaurant stands out – **The Cross (05402) 762**, excellent starters and some fine wines. Continuing our trip westward, along the A86 Fort William finally arrives; the scenery we saw was breathtaking – Ben Nevis, the pinnacle of this splendid range. In Fort William lies one of the country's most superb hotels and restaurants – **The Inverlochy Castle (0397) 21777**. Less expensive accommodation can be found at Onich, at **The Lodge on the Loch (08553) 238** which enjoys a splendid setting and offers good bar facilities and comfortable rooms. In Ballachulish, **The Ballachulish Hotel (08552) 239** is another Lochside hotel standing as it does at the meeting point of Lochs Linnhe and Leven. Before one leaves these parts and I have a little tip: if you've had an argument with your partner, golfing or otherwise, and want to get away from it all – golf I mean – then visit **Ardanaiseig (08663) 333** in Kilchrenan, unsurpassed civility and excellent dining. One other gem in the area is centred in Arisaig – **Arisaig House (06875) 622** and its splendid restaurant is thoroughly recommended.

Returning to the west coast the **Tulchan Lodge (08075) 200** is another isolated but extremely gracious former residence where once again dining is recommended. In Granton-on-Spey yet more beautiful scenery and Britain's fastest flowing river – the Spey. The **Grant Arms Hotel (0479) 2526** is comfortable and an excellent value place to stay while in these parts. **The Boat (047 983) 258** at Boat of Garten, overlooks the golf course and its doors are particularly welcoming to golfers who are offered special golf weeks.

Trekking up the road, so to speak, (the A9) one arrives at the capital of the Highlands, Inverness itself. Here the theatre at Eden Court is very good and among other things one can delight one's eye in the craft of handloom weaving and tweed spinning. The superior hotels in Inverness include **The Duncan Park Hotel (0463) 230512** and its fine restaurant and the 18th century **Kingsmills (0463) 237166** nearby. Near to the ill-fated Culloden battlefield itself stands in its majesty **The Culloden House Hotel (0463) 790461** where a portrait of the Bonnie Prince among others awaits to welcome you. North of Inverness lies Muir of Ord where **The Ord House Hotel (0463) 870492** is another charming country house hotel, ideal for Strathpeffer Spa as is the **Coal House Hotel (0997) 21487**, while **The Holly Lodge (0997) 21254** is a mere three hundred yards from the hotel is also good. Gairloch **The Gairloch Hotel (0445) 2001** an excellent setting for a hotel and golf to boot; the **Old Inn** is grand for a pint and lunch; while some three miles south the **Shieldaig Lodge (044583) 250** is another to consider – (note also the self-catering in the cottage of former gamekeepers).

Without further ado we arrive in Nairn – a golfer's paradise. **The Clifton (0667) 53119** offers Victorian grandeur and a splendid restaurant while the **Golf View (0662) 52301** is right beside Nairn's superb golf course. The **Newton, (0662) 53144** a mansion, is another to consider – it is comfortable and probably the best value. And so to Dornoch, Purgatory or Paradise it depends on your golf. **The Dornoch Castle (0862) 810216** is genuinely splendid, while Dornoch itself with its ruined Castle and Cathedral is a delight to the eye. Another hotel to try is **The Burghfield House (0862) 6102112** – ideal for the golfcourse.

Further north in Brora, **The Royal Marine (0408) 21252** and **The Links (0408) 21225 Hotels** are both strategically placed on the aptly named Golf Road, while another well titled hotel can be found at Golspie, **The Golf Links Hotel (04083) 3408**, all three are recommended and the latter puts together some splendid golfing packages. Unless one wishes to make a detour to the fishing village of Kinlochbervie and its well loved hotel and restaurant **(097182) 275**, one is duty bound to make for Wick which Robert Louis Stephenson described as "the bleakest of God's towns on the baldest of God's bays". This, one should point out, is totally unjustified. I understand if you decide to stay in the area **The Ladbroke (0955) 3344** is comfortable, while the **Bayview Hotel (05932) 346** at Lybster offers cosy accommodation and good food. The neighbouring areas are also blessed with castles to catch the imagination and without doubt the imagination leds to inspiration to aid which a bottle in one's bag is a bonnie idea; but note well Shakespeare's words "drink provokes and unprovokes: it provokes the desire, but it takes away the performance" – was he talking of golf or something else? Golf, I should say.

Dornoch Castle
Castle Street, Dornoch,
Tel: (0862) 810216
5 minutes walk from the world famous Royal Dornoch Championship Golf Course and renowned for its excellent cuisine ("Taste of Scotland") and friendly old world atmosphere. Taxi from Inverness Airport and tee-times can be arranged. Dinner, Bed and Breakfast from £30 per person.

Dunain Park Hotel
Inverness
Tel: (0463) 230512
Dunain Park is a beautiful and secluded small country house hotel within easy reach of golf clubs at **Inverness** and, a little further afield, **Nairn** and **Dornoch**. The hotel is only a mile from Inverness yet stands in six acres of garden and woodland and offers a high standard of cuisine and comfort.